Barnet & Stubbs's Practical Guide to Writing

Barnet & Stubbs's Practical Guide to Writing

with Readings

Seventh Edition

Sylvan Barnet
Tufts University

Marcia Stubbs
Wellesley College

HarperCollins*CollegePublishers*

Acquisitions Editor/Executive Editor: Lisa Moore
Project Coordination, Text and Cover Design: York Production Services
Art Coordination: York Production Services
Photo Researcher: Nina Page
Electronic Production Manager: Christine Pearson
Electronic Page Makeup: Interactive Composition Corporation
Printer and Binder: R.R. Donnelley & Sons Company
Cover Printer: The Lehigh Press, Inc.

For permission to use copyrighted material, grateful
acknowledgment is made to the copyright holders on pp. 632–634,
which are hereby made part of this copyright page.

Barnet & Stubbs's Practical Guide to Writing with Readings, 7/e

Copyright © 1995 by Sylvan Barnet and Marcia Stubbs

Library of Congress Cataloging-in-Publication Data

Barnet, Sylvan.
    Practical guide to writing : with readings / Sylvan Barnet, Marcia
Stubbs. — 7th ed.
        p.   cm.
    Rev. ed. of: Barnet & Stubb's practical guide to writing. 6th ed.
1980.
    Includes bibliographical references and index.
    ISBN 0-673-52493-0
    1. English language—Rhetoric.   2. College readers.   I. Stubbs.
Marcia.   II. Barnet, Sylvan.   Barnet & Stubbs's practical guide to
writing.   III. Title.
PE1408.B4314 1995
808'.042—dc20   94-13863
                                                           CIP

95 96 97 9 8 7 6 5 4 3 2

Contents

Chapter 2

Revising Drafts   27

Part Two

Explaining Ideas: The Writer's Materials and Strategies

Chapter 9

Analytical Thinking   164

Chapter 13

Persuading 264

Part Three

Special Assignments, Special Forms

Chapter 14

Outlining and Summarizing 298

Chapter 17

Reviewing   427

Chapter 18

Interviewing   433

Chapter 22

Chapter 23

Part Five

Additional Readings

Preface

*Where there is too much,
something is missing.*

We have tried to keep this proverb in mind; we hope we have written a compact book rather than an undiscriminating one.

The book is designed for college courses in which students write essays, instructors read them, and students and instructors together discuss them. We hope we offer a practical guide to all three activities. The student, looking for information about choosing a topic, writing an analysis, constructing a paragraph, using a semicolon, can use the text as a guide to the week's writing assignment. The instructor can suggest chapters or passages the student should consult in revising a draft or in starting the next assignment. Students and instructors together can discuss the exercises, the techniques used in the reprinted essays, the assumptions we make, and the suggestions we offer.

Although we include discussions and examples of description and narration, we emphasize analysis, exposition, and argument because those are the chief activities, usually rolled into one, that we all engage in, both in school and later. When students write papers, or professors write articles, or social workers write case studies, most of what they write explains ideas and how the writers arrived at them. Because they want to be believed they present their ideas and evidence persuasively.

In addition to including many examples from the writing of our students, we have included more than fifty short essays, as well as numerous paragraphs from books and essays, the work for the most part of first-rate contemporary writers. There are also a sample book review, a sample record review, a summary, two essays based on interviews, and two research papers. We include all these readings both to illustrate ways of writing and to provide students with something to write about. The suggested topics for writing often require the students to write about something outside of themselves. The Polonian advice, offered to Laertes—"This above all, to thine own self be true"—seems to us as useless to most people of college age as it is to Laertes. As Erik Erikson has helped us to see, most young people are engaged in a "search for something and somebody to be true to." They experiment with roles in a search for "the rock-bottom of some truth."[1] Asked to write about how they spent last summer, they may feel a profound uneasiness; however necessary last summer was, they are not sure what it added up to, and they are not yet distant enough from their experience to be articulate about it. Some writing topics do present opportunities for introspection, and all of them in fact require it, but we think that much of a student's writing should be directed outward, not solely a look into the heart but a look around—at people, at places, and especially at ideas.

We have tried therefore to balance the advice "Trust your feelings," "Ask yourself questions," with prescriptions: "Avoid clichés," "Keep your reader in mind." We have tried to increase the student's awareness that writing is both an exploration of self ("Choose a topic you can write about honestly") and a communication with others ("Revise for clarity").

Chapter 1 includes three essays by students, a brief article by Philip Roth, and some informal exercises. Chapter 2 focuses on revising drafts; it includes an example of peer review and a case history of a student paper from assignment through several revisions. Instructors may find these chapters useful for the first few class meetings. During the first week of the semester, we commonly suggest that students browse through the book from beginning to end, reading what interests them, skimming the rest, and generally familiarizing themselves with the book's contents and organization. But because each chapter can stand by itself, the instructor can assign chapters for study in whatever seems a suitable order. Similarly the student can consult whatever passages seem most relevant to writing a draft, revising, or editing a particular essay.

A Note to the Seventh Edition

Overall, our objective in preparing the seventh edition was to make the contents of the book clearer and more accessible to both students and instructors. Users of earlier editions will find some additions, some highlighting of what was already in place, much updating and pruning, and a fair amount of restructuring. The chapter on Analytical Thinking and Writing, for example, comes later in the text. In the chapter, the discussion of comparing has been pruned, but a discussion of analyzing cause and effect has been added. Acquiring Style comes earlier and has been completely rethought and rewritten. It now, we believe, explains more clearly what we mean by the writer's voice; at the same time it also discusses the variety of disciplinary styles that students will be learning (but

[1] Identity: Youth and Crisis (New York: W. W. Norton, 1968) 235–36.

may well be puzzled by) in courses across the curriculum. Totally new to this edition is a chapter on Writing about Literature, which includes four brief stories, five poems, and samples of students' notes, journal entries, drafts, and essays.

In making these changes we have responded to requests from many loyal users of our book and are indebted to many colleagues, students, editors, and other friends. These include Lois Avery, Houston Community College; Judith Barisonzi, University of Wisconsin, Fond du Lac; David Cavitch, Tufts University; Don Richard Cox, University of Tennessee; Carol A. David, Iowa State University; Janet Ellerby, University of North Carolina, Wilmington; Cinthia Gannett, University of New Hampshire; Brenda Gotthelf, Houston Community College; Christopher Gould, University of North Carolina-Wilmington; Maggie Griffith, Chadron State College; Stephen Hahn, William Patterson College; Viki Hull, Southern Methodist University; Lisa J. McClure, Southern Illinois University, Carbondale; Charles Nash, Cottey College; Julie Owen-Streit, Trinidad State Junior College; Maureen Potts, University of Texas; Hope Rajala; Alice Robertson, Arizona State University; Hephzibah Roskelly, University of North Carolina, Greensboro; John Rusciewicz, University of Texas; Charles Schuster, University of Wisconsin, Milwaukee; Suzanne Sheppard, Broome Community College; Sally Bishop Shigley, Weber State University; Judith Stanford, Rivier College; John Swan, Bennington College; Ruth Thomas, Boston University; Alison Warriner, Sacred Heart University; Barbara Weaver, Ball State University; Lance Wilcox, University of Minnesota; Mary Ann Wilson, University of Southwestern Louisiana; Winifred Wood, Wellesley College; Strohn Woodard, University of Maine.

We also remain indebted to: John Ambrose, Jeannine Atkins, Richard Audet, Barbara Balfour, Hannah Barrett, Tim Barretto, James Beaton, Pat Bellanca, Kay Berenson, Helle Bering-Fensen, Barbara Jane Berk, Morton Berman, Phyllis Braumlich, Gary Brienzo, Daniel V. Brislane, Lillian Broderick, James Brothers, Pearl L. Brown, Peter Brunette, Carroll Burcham, Pat Burnes, William Burto, A. Butrym, Terry P. Caesar, Joan Carberg, Susan Carlisle, Thomas Carnicelli, Sally Carson, Cynthia Chapin, Charles H. Christensen, Sandra Christianson, Sarah Clark, Michael Cleary, John M. Clum, James Cobb, Phyllis Cole, William F. Coles, S. Cooney, Shirley Corvo, John Covell, Claire Crabtree, Leslie Crabtree, Mary Ann Creadon, Mary Bryan H. Curd, Leopold Damrosch, Marlene Baldwin Davis, Robert Dees, Tom De Palma, Imogene De Smet, Aviva Diamond, T. Di Paolo, Pat Dorazio, Nicholas Durso, James Early, Nathaniel Elliott, Doris Eyges, Marina Femmer, Denise Ferguson, Cathy Fiore, Nancy E. Fischer, Terry Flaherty, Thomas F. Flynn, Jan Fontein, C. Dennyy Freese, John Fugate, Krin Gabbard, Cynthia Galivan, Thomas J. Gasque, Walker Gibson, David Giele, James Gifford, Walker Gilmer, David Goldfaden, Margaret Gooch, John Grass, Jack Guillon, Steve Hamelman, Nigel Hampton, James Hauser, Owen Hawley, Mark Heidmann, Thomas W. Herzing, Gervase Hittle, Robert Hosmer, Susan Jamison, Owen Jenkins, Peter M. Johnson, Ronna C. Johnson, Mary D. Jones, George Kearns, Joseph Keefe, Robert Keefe, Kathryn Keller, Dr. Frank Kelly, Nancy Kneeland, Judith Kohl,

Molly Moore Kohler, Roberta Kramer, George Kugler, Richard L. Lane, Andrea La Sane, Jonathan Lawson, Elsie Leach, Helen M. Lewis, Peter Lindblom, E. Darlene Lister, Marget Livesay, Jane Lump, Kathryn Lynch, Ian C. Mackenzie, D'Ann Madewell, Teruko Maki, George Marcopoulos, Sr. Lynda Martin-Boyle, H.O.O.M., Victoria McCabe, Leo McCauley, Joan McCoy, Patricia McGowan, Ken McLaurin, Celeste A. Meister, Michael Meyer, George Miller, Eva Mills, Melodie Monahan, Joan Moon, Betty Morgan, Denise Muller, Margaret A. Murphy, Richard Muth, Robert A. Myers, Barbara Nelson, Thomas Newkirk, J. Stephan Newmann, Donald Nontelle, Jo Anna Norris, Richard D. Olson, John O'Neill, Mary O'Sullivan, Joan Patrie, Donald Pattow, Mary Mocsary Pauli, Douglas Peterson, Russell O. Peterson, Bill Pierce, Elaine Plasberg, Carolyn Potts, Charles Quagliata, S. Quiroz, John Rath, Martha Reid and her colleagues at William and Mary, Stephen Reid, Gerald Richman, Leo Rockas, Judith Root, Zelda Rouillard, Melissa Ruchhoeft, Scott Ruescher, Richard Sandler, Stephen Sapious, Frances W. Sauers, Carl Schaffr, Gerald Schiffhorst, Sybil Schlesinger, Carmen Schmersahl, William Scott, Patrick W. Shaw, James M. Siddens, Earl Sigmund, Joyce Monroe Simmons, Martha Simonsen, Edward Sims, Mark Slater, James Slattery, Audrey Smith, John Smolens, James Sodon, Jay Soldner, David Solheim, Dr. Harold Spicer, Robert Stein, Ann Steinmetz, Frances M. Stowe, Kay Sturdivant, Elaine Supowitz, Ann M. Tarbell, Luther T. Tyler, Larry Uffelman, Kathy Valdespino, Renita Weems, Adrienne Weiss, Melinda Westbrook, Dorothy Widmayer, Lisa Wien, Anita C. Wilson, Howard Winn, Donald Winters, Elizabeth Wood, Arthur P. Wooley, Hae Yong Yi, Mallory Young, and all our students.

Sylvan Barnet
Marcia Stubbs

Part One

An Overview of the Writing Process

The Balloon of the Mind

Hands, do what you're bid:
Bring the balloon of the mind
That bellies and drags in the wind
Into its narrow shed.

—William Butler Yeats

Chapter 1

Discovering Ideas

Starting

How to Write: Writing as a Physical Act

"One takes a piece of paper," William Carlos Williams wrote, "anything, the flat of a shingle, slate, cardboard and with anything handy to the purpose begins to put down the words after the desired expression in mind." Good advice, from a writer who produced novels, plays, articles, book reviews, an autobiography, a voluminous correspondence, and more than twenty-five books of poetry, while raising a family, enjoying a wide circle of friends, and practicing medicine in Rutherford, New Jersey. Not the last word on writing (we have approximately 85,000 of our own to add), but where we would like to begin: "One takes a piece of paper . . . and . . . begins to put down the words. . . ."

Writing is a physical act, like swimming, and like most physical acts, to be performed skillfully, to bring pleasure to both performer and audience, it requires practice. Talent helps. But few of us are born to become great writers, just as few of us are born to become great swimmers. Nevertheless, we can learn to write, as we can learn to swim, for all practical purposes, including pleasure.

In this book we offer some suggestions, definitions, rules, and examples to help you learn not simply to write, but to write well. We hope that they will help you to avoid some of the trials and errors—and the fear of drowning—that sometimes accompany uninstructed practice.

Why Write? Writing as Thinking

Born writers often describe their need to write as a compulsion, an inner drive to explore their feelings and ideas through words; they also regularly complain that writing is hard work. ("Hard labor for life" was Joseph Conrad's summary of his own career.) For the rest of us, writing may be easier, because it is *not* our vocation and perhaps we may demand less than perfection from ourselves. But it's still hard work, and we usually need something to motivate us to take it on. In real life (as opposed to school) people are motivated by their jobs and other interests to put their ideas in writing. Scientists and social scientists write proposals for research and they report the results of their work in journals. Parents and other citizens petition school boards and lawmakers; through prepared talks and newsletters, volunteers reach the communities they serve. In short, anyone who is engaged with ideas or who wants to influence the course of events finds it necessary to convert what Williams called "the desired expression in mind" into words on paper.

As a student, you may not always see a connection between the assignment you are given today and the need you will have several years from now to put your ideas in writing. The rewards of seeing your proposal accepted or of serving your community are probably a bit distant to motivate you to write five hundred words on an assigned topic this week. There is, though, a closer reward. "To be learning something new," said Aristotle, "is ever the chief pleasure of humankind." We believe that. We also believe that writing is not simply a way to express ideas, but a way to acquire them. Whenever you put your thoughts into words on a page, whether you scribble a few words on a scrap of paper while you eat lunch, or edit your final draft of an essay on a computer, you are not simply recording what you already know. You are discovering ideas and refining them. When you have them on paper or disk you are also inscribing them in your own memory. To quote Aristotle again, "What is expressed is impressed."

We emphasize ideas because we are making some assumptions about you: that you are an adult, that you're acquiring an education, either in school or on your own, and that the writing skill you need most help with is not grammar or spelling—though you may need help with them too—but with learning to express ideas clearly and interestingly. We begin, then, with some ideas about ideas.

Some Ideas About Ideas: Invention

Would-be writers have one of two complaints: either "I have the ideas but I don't know how to express them," or "I have nothing to say." When we are faced with a blank page, ideas and even words may seem to elude us. We must actively seek them out. Since classical times the term "invention" has been used to describe the active search for ideas. ("Invention" comes from the Latin word *invenire,* "to come upon," or "to find.") Invention includes activities with which you may already be familiar, such as free writing, brainstorming, listing, and clustering. A related activity is the practice of keeping a journal. In the following pages we'll briefly describe several invention strategies and provide guidelines for keeping a journal. All of these activities have one step in common: starting to write by writing.

Starting to Write by Writing

Suppose your assignment is to choose and respond to a recent editorial. You have chosen an editorial, read it several times, underlined a few key sentences, made a few notes. You have some ideas, but they don't seem connected; you don't know how to start. Here are five suggestions for getting started.

1. **Sit down and start writing.** Many writers find that they need a period to incubate ideas, to let ideas develop at their own pace, undisturbed by conscious thought. Some writers also find that they must go through certain rituals—sharpening pencils, rearranging things on the desk, and so on—before they can put words on paper. But at some point you have to sit down at the word processor or before a blank piece of paper and start writing. Don't be surprised if you must actively resist the temptation to do something else. Watch yourself think of other things to do, but take control. Resist the temptation to sharpen another pencil, to make a cup of soup, to call your mother. Now is *not* the time to do your laundry or to make your bed. Sit down and start. Following the next suggestion may help you to start.

2. **Give yourself a time limit.** If procrastination is a chronic problem (as it is for many writers), try limiting the amount of time you will spend in your first session. Tell yourself that you'll work without interruption for half an hour (or twenty minutes or fifteen minutes—you may need to experiment). We all want to delay starting tasks we're anxious about. If at the start you limit each writing session to fifteen or twenty minutes, you accomplish two things. You reduce or even eliminate anxiety—the thought of working at your desk for fifteen minutes is not nearly as daunting as the thought of writing four or five pages. And after fifteen or twenty minutes you will have *something* down on paper, something you can start with and can even look forward to working on during your next session. Then in your next session, if you find that after fifteen or twenty minutes you want to continue, you can allow yourself to add another fifteen minutes or so, but take a break after that. You will have accomplished your immediate goal: to get started. Gradually you can build up to working on your essay for an hour at a time, or whatever is reasonable, given the assignment and your schedule. Of course, you can follow this advice only if you have started to work on an assignment reasonably soon after you have received it. Setting a time limit for the initial stages of writing will help you to get an early start. So will the next suggestion.

3. **Start with something easy.** Start anywhere. Start with what comes to mind first. You might, for example, start by summarizing the article you are responding to or by sketching any one of your ideas about it. *Don't think you must start with an introductory paragraph;* you can write an introduction later, once your ideas have become better defined. The point is, it doesn't matter where you begin, only that you do begin. Simply start putting one word after another, and keep going.

4. **Write freely.** It may help to put out of your mind some rules about writing you may have learned. Forget about the five paragraph essay, along with the opening paragraph. Don't worry about grammar or spelling or punctuation. No one but you is going to read what you write. If you can't think of the right word, write something close to it, or leave a blank space for the word, and move on. If you find yourself going in the "wrong" direction, that is, a direction you hadn't anticipated, keep writing anyway. Maybe there's something down the road worth thinking about; you won't know until you get there. If, for example, you are writing about why you disagree with one argument in the editorial, a

point on which you agree with the author may occur to you. Fine. Write it down now, while you're thinking of it. You can organize your points of agreement and disagreement later. If, however, you reach what appears to be a dead end, simply move on, or start again someplace else. You are writing to discover what you think, and it's a good idea to work at the quickest pace you can. (Take Satchel Paige's advice: Don't look back; something might be gaining on you.

5. **Plan to revise later.** Don't worry about making false starts. After a few false starts (and probably more than one session), your ideas will begin to take visible form on the page. But don't expect them to appear at this early stage in final form, beautifully organized and in polished sentences. Ideas rarely exist that what in one's mind. In fact, until we put them in words, ideas are usually only rough ideas or images, not clear thoughts at all. But if you start to write by writing, quickly and without looking back, you will have the satisfaction of seeing your ideas begin to take form on paper, and it's much easier to improve ideas once you see them in front of you than it is to do the job in your head. You can always delete or discard, add or improve. In fact, as we will suggest many times in this book, the secret of good writing is *re*writing. Once you learn to control your urge to procrastinate, to wait until you're better prepared, or are more inspired, or have thought of the perfect way to begin, you will find that in starting to write by writing, you have mined some ideas on your topic and have come close to expressing them. (As E. M. Forster wrote, "How do I know what I think until I see what I say?") You may even have come close to producing a first draft. You can determine if you are near a first draft by looking back over what you've written and saved. Whether or not you like what you read (your response probably depends more on your temperament than on your actual accomplishment) take a rest from it. Do something else: make your bed, or if you like, just climb into it.

Listing

Listing is another way to discover ideas or to pin them down by writing. The process is something like making a shopping list. You write down "soap" and are immediately reminded that you also must pick up some laundry.

Similarly, if you plan to argue for a course of action, listing one reason for it may bring others to mind. Listing is also often a good way to make a decision. You list (perhaps in a journal, which we discuss later in this chapter) the reasons for dropping a course or for taking a job, and then the reasons against. Listing is often especially useful when you are making a comparison—of two figures in a photograph, for example, or two characters in a story, or two positions on an issue. Start writing by listing the similarities, and then list the differences. Or, start writing both lists at once, making brief entries, as they occur to you, in parallel columns.

In the above examples, listing was used to develop ideas. Listing can also help you to find a topic to write about. Suppose, for example, you have been assigned to write an essay on a form of popular culture that interests you. You can begin simply by listing some of the possibilities that occur to you as you think about the subject:

Popular Culture

```
movies, sci-fi, sci-fi movies?
TV movies, detective serials
soap operas (why are they called operas? Why soap
   operas?)
music videos
mysteries—Murder She Wrote
male/female detectives
the blues
```

But having written "the blues" above, you begin to think of the words to a song:

> When a woman takes the blues
> She tucks her head and cries
> But when a man catches the blues
> He catches a freight and rides

By the time you have written these lyrics out from memory, you have pretty much decided that you'll write on the blues. You're interested in the blues and already know something about them; you have some CDs and tapes at hand; and an idea for an essay is beginning to form:

"He catches a freight and rides . . . "

Why all this talk of traveling? (It's worth remembering that an unanswered question is an essay topic in disguise.) You begin to search your memory, perhaps you play some tapes, maybe take some notes. The blues are full of travel, you find, but of different kinds. You begin, once again, to make a list, to jot down words or phrases:

disappointed lover	back to the South
travel to a job	life is a trip
from the South	jail
fantasy travel	

Your new list provides more than a topic; you are now several steps closer to a draft of an essay that you think maybe you can write, on the reason for (or meaning of?) travel in the blues.

Clustering

Clustering (or **mapping**) is similar to listing, though it takes a different visual form. Sometimes ideas don't seem to line up vertically, one after another. Instead, they seem to form a cluster, with one idea or word related to a group of several others. It may be useful then to start by putting a key word or phrase (let's stay with TRAVEL IN THE BLUES) in a circle in the center of a page, and then to jot down other words as they occur, encircling them and connecting them appropriately. A map or cluster might look like the diagram shown here.

If you start writing by putting down words that occur to you in a schematic way—in a map or cluster—it may help you to visualize the relationship between ideas. The visualization may also prompt still other ideas and the connections between them.

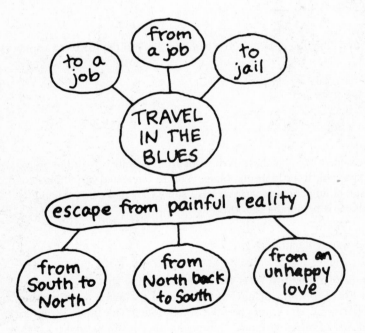

Asking Questions (and Answering Them)

Almost the first thing a journalist learns to do in getting a story is to ask six questions:

- Who?
- What?
- When?
- Where?
- Why?
- How?

If you borrow this approach, asking yourself questions and answering them, you will often find that you can get a start on a writing project. The questions that journalists ask are appropriate to their task: to report what happened, who made it happen, how it happened, and so on. Learning to write academic essays is largely learning to ask—and to answer—questions appropriate to academic disciplines.

In analyzing a painting or a sculpture, for example, an art historian might answer certain basic questions:

When, where, and by whom was the work made?

Where would the work originally have been seen?

What purpose did the work serve?

In what condition has the work survived?

and then, depending on the work, more detailed questions. If, for example, the work is a landscape painting, the following questions might be appropriate:

What is the relation between human beings and nature?

What does the medium (oil paint or watercolor, for instance) contribute?

What is the effect of light in the picture?

What is the focus of the composition?

How does the artist convey depth?

Similarly, a social scientist writing a review of research on a topic might ask about each study under review:

What major question is posed in this study?

What is its chief method of investigation?

What mode of observation was employed?

How is the sample of observations defined?

Students in all sorts of courses—art history and social science courses are given here only as examples—learn what the useful questions are by listening to lectures, participating in class discussions, and reading assigned books and articles. But the learning is passive and largely subconscious. When writing a paper, however, students must actively learn and practice the forms of critical inquiry at the heart of each discipline.

An Exercise in Invention: Philip Roth, Reflections on the Death of a Library

In a writing course, the subject is writing—not art history, sociology, or anything else. Commonly, however, writing assignments, like the assignments in other disciplines, are designed to give students practice in critical reading, that is, practice in such skills as summarizing, analyzing, and evaluating written texts. We explain these skills in some detail in many places in this text. Here by way of introduction, we take you through a brief exercise in invention:

discovering ideas by *asking questions and answering* them.

First read the following article from *The New York Times.* The author, Philip Roth, was born in Newark, New Jersey, in 1933. Although Roth is primarily known as a novelist, he also writes occasional essays. (We have numbered the paragraphs to facilitate reference to them.)

Philip Roth[1]

Reflections on the Death of a Library

---

1   What will the readers of Newark do if the City Council goes ahead with its money-saving plan to shut down the public library system on April 1? Will they loot the stacks as Newarkers looted furniture and appliance stores in the riot of 1967? Will police be called in to Mace down thieves racing off with the *Encyclopaedia Britannica?* Will scholars take up sniping positions at reference room windows and school children "seize" the main Washington Street building in order to complete their term papers? If the City Council locks up the books, will library card holders band together to "liberate" them?

2   I suppose one should hope not. Apparently there must be respect for Law and Order, even where there is none for aspiration and curiosity and quiet pleasure, for language, learning, scholarship, intelligence, reason, wit, beauty, and knowledge.

3   When I was growing up in Newark in the forties we assumed that the books in the public library belonged to the public. Since my family did not own many books, or have much money for a child to buy them, it was good to know that solely by virtue of my municipal citizenship I had access to any book I wanted from that grandly austere building downtown on Washington Street, or from the branch library I could walk to in my neighborhood. No less satisfying was the idea of communal ownership, property held in common for the common good. Why I had to care for the books I borrowed, return them unscarred and on time,

[1]In February 1969, after riots had already destroyed much of Newark's black slum neighborhoods, the Newark City Council voted to strike from the city budget the $2.8 million required to finance the Newark Museum and the Newark Public Library. Hundreds of Newark residents vehemently opposed this move, which would have shut down two exceptional civic institutions. In the face of the protest, the Council eventually rescinded their decision. This article appeared on the editorial page of *The New York Times,* March 1, 1969, about two weeks after the Council had announced the budget cutback [Roth's note].

was because they weren't mine alone, they were everybody's. That idea had as much to do with civilizing me as any I was ever to come upon in the books themselves.

4   If the idea of a *public* library was civilizing so was the place, with its comforting quiet, its tidy shelves, its knowledgeable, dutiful employees who weren't teachers. The library wasn't simply where one had to go to get the books, it was a kind of exacting haven to which a city youngster willingly went for his lesson in restraint and his training in self-control. And then there was the lesson in order, the enormous institution itself serving as instructor. What trust it inspired— in both oneself and in systems—first to decode the catalogue card, then to make it through the corridors and stairwells into the open stacks, and there to discover, exactly where it was supposed to be, the desired book. For a ten-year-old to find he actually can steer himself through tens of thousands of volumes to the very one he wants is not without its satisfactions. Nor did it count for nothing to carry a library card in one's pocket; to pay a fine if need be; to sit in a strange place, beyond the reach of parent and school, and read whatever one chose, in anonymity and peace; finally, to carry home across the city and even into bed at night a book with a local lineage of its own, a family-tree of Newark readers to which one's name had now been added.

5   In the forties, when Newark was mostly white and I was being raised there, it was simply an unassailable fact of life that the books were "ours" and that the public library had much to teach us about the rules of civilized life, as well as civilized pleasures to offer. It is strange, to put it politely, that now when Newark is mostly black, the City Council (for fiscal reasons, we are told) has reached a decision that suggests that the books don't really belong to the public after all, and that the lessons and pleasures a library provides for the young are no longer essential to an education. In a city seething with social grievances there is, in fact, probably little that could be *more* essential to the development and sanity of the thoughtful and ambitious young than access to those libraries and books. For the moment the Newark City Council may, to be sure, have solved a fiscal problem: it is too bad, however, that they are unable to calculate the frustration, cynicism, and rage that such an insult must inevitably generate, or to imagine what shutting down the libraries may cost the community in the end.

Questions

Now answer the following questions.

1. a. What was the occasion for this article?
   b. What was Roth's response?

2. a. How does Roth support his position in paragraph 3? Why does he mention his childhood?
   b. What are the two main reasons he gives in paragraph 3 in support of his position?
3. What does Roth mean by "civilizing" in paragraphs 3 and 4?
4. In paragraph 5, what new reasons does he state or imply in support of his position?
5. How does he engage our interest in his first two paragraphs?

   How does he enlist our support for his point of view?
6. How successful is he?

If you were to write out your answers and then to review and revise them a bit, you would probably have a draft of an essay something like the student's essay that follows. (Numbers in parentheses refer to the questions.)

On Philip Roth's *Reflections*

The City Council of Newark introduced a plan to shut down the public library system in order to save money. (1a) Philip Roth in his article (*The New York Times*, March 1, 1969), argues that the closing of the libraries will be a costly mistake, and that the action will be an insult to the citizens of Newark. (1b)

He supports his position by telling how the library helped him when he was young. (2a) He says that the public library gave him a chance to use books that his family couldn't afford, but more important, the very idea of a public library, of the communal ownership of books, played a part in civilizing him. (2b) By civilizing Roth means socializing. The quiet and orderly fashion in which the library was arranged and run taught him restraint, and taught him to value solitude, privacy, and self-control. Looking for books was itself a lesson in order: he learned, for example,

that he could find, through the card catalog, one book
among the many thousands there. (3)

Roth suggests that since Newark has become
predominantly black, the City Council's attitude
toward the library's functions and importance has
changed. He implies that the Council's plan is
irresponsible and discriminatory. He points out that
in a city with as many social problems as Newark's the
lessons and pleasures given to the young by the
library are more, not less, essential to their
education. He says that although the Council's move
may solve an immediate fiscal problem, it will in the
end create greater social problems because of the
frustration and rage it will generate. (4)

To develop ideas about a text, then, become a critical reader of it. Approach it, especially on rereading it, asking such questions as:

- Who wrote this?
- When was it written?
- Why and for what audience was it written?
- What point or argument does the author make?
- How does the author make it?
- How successful (believable, interesting, persuasive) do I find it?

As you study various disciplines, in the courses you take, try to become aware of what questions are being asked or implied by the textbooks you use, the lectures you attend, the outside reading you do. When you write essays in those disciplines, use those questions as your guide.

Keeping a Journal

Writing in a journal is for many professional writers a way to both stimulate ideas and to keep a record of those ideas for future use. A journal is an ideal place to store some of the thoughts that you may have scribbled on little scraps of paper during the day, especially those that are not yet usable for a current writing project. Rereading journal entries is often a good way to get started on a new project. Writing daily in a journal, also helps writers to remain fluent. As we said at the start, writing is a physical act, and to keep in trim, you should practice daily. (Or, to be honest, as close to daily as you can manage.) Keeping a journal, then, is practical; for many writers it is, from the start enjoyable.

Because they have so many uses, journals are often assigned in writing courses. If keeping a journal is required of you, you may be asked to write in a loose-leaf notebook—so that pages may be turned in occasionally, and your instructor won't have to stagger home with twenty or thirty notebooks. If you keep a journal strictly for your own use, write with whatever materials feel comfortable: pen, pencil, computer; loose sheets, bound notebook, or whatever. (Dr. William Carlos Williams often wrote poems on prescription blanks.)

Guidelines

1. **When to write?** Any time; ten to fifteen minutes a day if possible. Some people find it helpful to establish a regular time of day for writing, just before they go to sleep, for example. Habits can be helpful; but not all of us can or should lead well-regulated lives. Writing for a minute or two several times a day may work best for you.

2. **How long is an entry?** An entry may be a few words, a line or two, a few pages. There's no special length, but keep writing for the length of time it takes to complete a useful entry.

Dr. William Carlos Williams jotted down his ideas for poems on prescription blanks.

3. **Form.** Date each entry but then write freely. Don't correct or revise. Don't worry about spelling, vocabulary, punctuation. Use whatever language, idiom, voice you wish. It's a good way to keep in touch with yourself, and the friends and family you've temporarily left. (You *can* go home again.)

4. **As for content,** write about anything that comes to mind. But don't confuse a journal with a diary. A diary mentions things that have happened ("Concert at 8, with J. and R."); a journal reflects on the happenings. A diary lists appointments; a journal records events, but gives some sense of why they were meaningful. Think of your journal as a record of your life now, which you might read with pleasure some years from now when many of the rich details of your daily experience would otherwise be buried in your memory. Still, it's probably better to write "Had a peanut butter sandwich for lunch" than to write nothing.

Write down your thoughts, feelings, impressions, responses, dreams, memories. May Sarton once said, "The senses are the keys to the past." If you have a strong sensory memory of something—the mixed smell of saltwater, sand, and machinery oil, for example—try to describe it in words, and then to track it down. You may find a buried scene from your childhood that you can rescue from your memory by a train of associations. If you keep tracking, and writing, you may discover why that scene is important.

Here, to prime the pump, are some examples of journal entries.

Examples: Journal Entries by Students

1. It is difficult to believe that not understanding a physics problem isn't the worst problem in the world.

2. Old people have been following me all my life. . . . And at times scaring me out of my wits. When I was a very young child, one of my mother's best friends was an old crone named Bettina. . . . A witch-like figure dressed (always) in black with a pointed nose and chin. She had startling blue eyes that pierced one's being and a voice that cackled and shrieked in Italian. She filled the air with ethnic gossip and snide attacks on the marital behavior of her daughter, deriding her treatment of her son-in-law of whom she was extremely fond. My mother would smile and nod, all the while cooking, a major occupation of her life.

SUBJECT—ECHOES FROM MY CHILDHOOD

TOPIC—KITCHEN MEMORIES

3. "Teruko-san! How come you don't understand what I am saying to you!! How come you are repeating these errors so many times!! One! Two! Three! Go!!" My arms, hands, fingers and even my brain are frozen. Tears are running down my cheek. My both hands are sitting on the keyboard frighteningly. Silence. I hear my heart, beating thump thump thump. With a deep sigh, Mrs. Ikebuchi closes the page of a score which is blackened with fingering numbers, circles and crosses. Without saying any words, she leaves the room, and goes to

the kitchen. The lesson is over. I sigh and wipe off my tears with the back of my hands, pick up the scores, go to the living room and sit on the tatami-floor stiffly. "By the way Teruko-san, did you see my gardenia? It is so beautiful! Come! come and see it!" She comes out from the kitchen with a big round black lacquer tray with tea and cookies on it. She puts the tray on the table and walks out to the garden to the gardenia bush. "Isn't this pretty?" "Yes." "Isn't this a nice smell?" "Yes." Mrs. Ikebuchi walks back to the living room and I follow her three steps behind and sit on the tatami-floor stiffly again. Mrs. Ikebuchi pours tea and asks me merrily, "How much sugar do you want? how much cream do you want? which cookie do you want? rabbit? elephant? or duck?" I answer politely, "two sugars, please? (it is cube sugar), that's enough, thank you (for cream). May I have a rabbit?" "Oh you like the rabbit! Good! By the way do you know the story about the rabbit? Ah—what was it? Ah, Peter Rabbit!" Her story is going on and on and on. Meanwhile I finish my tea and cookie. "Well, Teruko-san, see you next Monday." I stand up, my legs are numb from sitting on the tatami-floor, and start to walk slowly, my toes are tickling. I pick up my scores and bow and say "Thank you very much." Walk out the sliding door. Release! I skip home.

4. 9/20 Lab was a trip today. Right before my eyes, I observed an egg cell being invaded by an army of sperm cells. Think of it. That's how I began. I used to be a nothing, and now I'm something, an "I." (I was only looking at a sea urchin's egg, but that sure beats not looking at a sea urchin's egg.)

5. A belief I had when I was small: For some reason I thought every person was allowed only a certain number of words per life time. Of course, at that time in my life I was quiet, except when I was mad and all reason left me.

6. Political scientists are masters of Instant Prose who like to stuff sentences as full of multisyllabic words as possible so that it takes 10 minutes to decipher a paragraph. For example:

> "Mann's survey leads us to believe that alongside consensual processes of voluntary deference, nationalism, and rational support of the govern-ment (the mobilization of bias, deference to political symbols, or indoc-trination in hegemonoic ideology—according to various viewpoints) there also exists a vast reservoir of dissensus."

7. Anticipating something is like falling off a cliff and never reaching the bottom.

8. Intro to Women's Studies upset me today. We talked about the role of women in religion. We discussed how feminist theologians (the*a*logians?) believe that God is not necessarily a man but could be a woman. Their argument is that the Bible was translated and interpreted by men for their own purposes. They wanted to utilize the Bible to give women a subordinate role to men. I do believe

that, or at least I think all this is worth questioning. But it's hard for me—no, sad—to think of God as a woman when I have grown to love him as a man, a father.

Focusing

What to Write About: Subject, Topic, Thesis

If you're taking a course in composition, you will probably receive assignments to write on something you are reading or on something out of your personal experience, which may include your experience of books. In other courses, it's usually up to you to choose a *subject* from those covered in the course, to focus on a *topic* within the subject, and to narrow the topic by formulating a *thesis.* Any assignment requires you to narrow the subject so that you can treat it thoroughly in the allotted space and time. Therefore you write not on *Time* magazine, but on the political bias of *Time,* or on a comparison of *Time* and *Newsweek,* based on one or two issues of each, arguing for the superiority of one over the other; not on political primaries (a subject), but on a specific proposal to abolish them (a topic); not on penguins (a subject), but on the male penguin's role in hatching (a topic). A good general rule in finding a topic is to follow your inclinations: focus on something about the subject that interests you.

Suppose your assignment is to read the Book of Ruth in the Hebrew Bible and to write an essay of 500 to 1000 words on it. If you start with a topic like "The Book of Ruth. A Charming Tale" you're in trouble. The topic is much too vague. In writing about it you'll find yourself hopping around from one place in the book to another, and in desperation saying insincere things like "The Book of Ruth is probably one of the most charming tales in all literature," when you haven't read all literature, and couldn't define *charm* precisely, if your life depended on it.

What to do? Focus on something that interested you about the book. (If you read the book with pencil in hand, taking some notes, underlining some passages, putting question marks at others, you'll have some good clues to start with.) The book is named after Ruth, but perhaps you find Naomi the more interesting character. If so, you might jot down: "Although the Book of Ruth is named after Ruth, I find the character of Naomi more interesting."

Stuck again? Ask yourself some questions. *Why* do you find her more interesting? To answer that question, reread the book, focusing your attention on all the passages in which Naomi acts or speaks or is spoken of by others. Ruth's actions, you may find, are always clearly motivated by her love for Naomi. But Naomi's actions are more complex, more puzzling. If you're puzzled, trust your feeling—*there is something puzzling there. What* motivated Naomi? Convert your question to "Naomi's Motivation" and you have a *topic.*

With this topic in mind, if you explore Naomi's actions one by one you may conclude that "Although Naomi shows in many of her actions her concern for her daughter-in-law, her actions also reveal self-interest." Now you have a *thesis,* that is, a brief statement of your main point. It's a bit awkwardly worded but you can work on a smoother, more natural expression later.

"Naomi's Motivation" is a topic in literary criticism, but if your special interest is, for example, economics, or sociology, or law, your topic might be one of these:

Economic Motivation in the Book of Ruth

Attitudes toward Intermarriage in the Book of Ruth.

The Status of Women in the Book of Ruth

Any one of these topics can be managed in 500 to 1000 words. But remember, you were assigned to write on the Book of Ruth. Formulate a thesis with evidence from that book. Suppress the impulse to put everything you know about economics or intermarriage or the-status-of-women-through-the-ages in between two thin slices, an opening sentence and a concluding sentence, on the Book of Ruth.

Let's take another example. Suppose that in a course on Modern Revolutionary Movements you're assigned a term paper on any subject covered by the readings or lectures. A term paper is usually about three thousand words and requires research. You're interested in Mexican history, and after a preliminary search you decide to focus on the Revolution of 1910 or some events leading up to it. Depending on what is available in your library, you might narrow your topic to one of these:

Mexican Bandits—The First Twentieth Century Revolutionists

The Exploits of Joaquin Murieta and Tiburcio Vasquez—Romantic Legend and Fact.

In short, it is not enough to have a subject (the Book of Ruth, revolutions); you must concentrate your vision on a topic, a significant part of the field, just as a landscape painter or photographer selects a portion of the landscape and then focuses on it. Your interests are your most trustworthy guides to the portion of the landscape on which to focus.

As you think about your topic and information relating to it, try to formulate a *tentative* or working thesis. Think of your tentative sentence—which may not appear in your final paper—as a working hypothesis, a proposition to be proved, disproved, or revised in light of information you discover.

Naomi's character is more interesting than Ruth's.

Murieta and Vasquez were in the vanguard of a revolution.

Closing the Newark Public Library will incur enormous social costs.

Your "working thesis" will help you to maintain your focus, to keep in mind the points that you must support with evidence, such as quotations, facts, statistics, reasons, descriptions, and illustrative anecdotes. But be prepared to modify your working thesis, perhaps more than once, and perhaps substantially. Once you begin amassing evidence and arguments, you may find that they support a different thesis. Your best ideas on your topic may turn out to be radically different from the ideas with which you began. As we pointed out earlier, writing is not simply a way to express ideas you already have, it is also a way to acquire them.

Although essays based on substantial research almost always include an explicit thesis sentence in the finished essay, short essays based on personal experience often do not. An essay recounting a writer's experience of racism, for example, or conveying the particular atmosphere of a neighborhood, is likely to have a central idea or focus, a *thesis idea,* rather than a *thesis sentence.* But whether stated or implied, the thesis idea must be developed (explained, supported, or proved) by evidence presented in the body of the essay. The kind of evidence will vary, of course, not only with your topic but also with your audience and purpose.

Developing Ideas

Materials that writers use to develop ideas, to explain and support a thesis, are largely byproducts of the writer's thinking about a topic and formulating a thesis. The materials, for the most part, are already at hand from the reading, notetaking, freewriting, questioning, and remembering that are part of the writing process from beginning to end. Materials for developing an essay on Naomi's motivation will be primarily brief quotations from the Book of Ruth, quotations that the essay writer introduces and explains. Similarly, materials for an essay on the blues will be quotations from a thoughtful selection of lyrics. An essay on a memorable experience, one that led to an interesting idea, will rely on the writer's memory of that experience, examined with a reader in mind. In all of these instances, in fact, imagining a reader is an important means of developing ideas.

Thinking About Audience and Purpose

Thinking about the audience for whom a piece of writing is intended and thinking about what you want that audience to understand and to believe are always important at the final stages of writing. You read over a draft you have written to see if it will be clear and interesting to someone else, to someone who is not you, who does not know what you know, and does not necessarily share your beliefs. If you use a technical term, will a likely reader understand it? Should you define the term, or can you substitute a more familiar word? Have you identified the source of a quotation? And is it clear why you are using the quotation at this point in your essay? Are the paragraphs arranged in a clear sequence? Have you provided effective transitions? And so on. Reading your draft (preferably aloud), imagining an audience, you can often spot unclear patches, and then revise them. Reading your draft to an actual audience, a friend or classmate, is even better.

But thinking about audience and purpose can be helpful at earlier stages of writing too, when you are trying to develop an idea and to work up evidence to support it. If you are uncertain how to begin, or if, on the other hand, you are overwhelmed by the materials you have unearthed and don't know how to sort them out, try asking yourself these questions:

- Who are my readers?
- What do they need to know?
- What do I want them to believe?

When you ask, "Who is my reader?" the obvious answer might seem to be the teacher who assigned the essay. But that answer, when you think about it, is likely to be the least helpful. Why bother to write for someone who presumably knows all the answers? Moreover "writing for the teacher" might inspire inappropriate responses, ranging from stilted or inflated writing to half-hearted attempts to guess "the right answer." Try to remember writing that you have felt comfortable about and enjoyed. Think of letters that you have written to friends, or an article you wrote for the school paper, or a business brochure you prepared. In those (or similar) instances, you knew both who your readers were and what you wanted them to know and to believe. In writing an essay, try to put yourself in a similar frame of mind. The writing assignment may have included instructions about the audience your essay should address. If not, imagine a reader who is in many ways your counterpart—that is someone intelligent and reasonably well informed—but who does not happen to be you and who therefore can't know your thoughts unless you explain them clearly and thoroughly.

In other words, we suggest that you begin thinking of yourself not as a student but as a writer. Like writers out in the real world, *when you write you are the teacher*. If you have a topic but are uncertain how to develop it, ask yourself what a reader who knows less than you do about your topic needs to know and what you want that reader to believe. Write for that reader.

Writing from Experience: Two Essays by Students

Let's look at two essays, each written by a student during the first week of the semester in a composition course. The students were invited as an introductory exercise to write about an idea provided by their own experience, something they knew or understood well that they could describe or explain to others who were unfamiliar with it. Perhaps you are familiar with such an assignment. You try to think of something interesting you've done, but you've led a most unremarkable life. Your classmates, all strangers, seem to know more than you do about almost everything. They've all been to Europe or Mexico or South

America—well, some of them. All you did last summer was file cards and run errands in an office full of boring people. Here is the first student's essays, on, as it happens, a boring job.

Example 1

A Lesson

As I look back at it, my first thought is that my job was a waste of time. It consisted of compiling information from the files of the Water and Assessor's Department in a form suitable for putting on the city's computer. Supposedly this would bring the water billing and property taxing to an efficient level. If the job sounds interesting, don't be deceived. After the first week of work, I seriously doubted that I would survive through the summer.

But I was able to salvage a lesson in the self-discipline of coping with people. Of course we all know how to succeed with friends, family, acquaintances, and employers. But try it in a situation where you have a distinct disadvantage, where you are the seller and they are the customers. And remember, the customer is always right.

By observing the situation, though I was not a participant. I learned that patience, kindness, and understanding can remove the difficulties you cross at the time.

Not a bad topic, really. One can learn something valuable from a boring, menial, frustrating job. Or if not, one can examine boredom (what exactly is it? is it the same as impatience? how does it come about? how does it feel?) and write about it without boring the reader. But this essay doesn't teach us anything about boredom. It doesn't allow us through concrete, specific details to feel with the writer that we too would have doubted we could survive the summer. Instead, it offers generalizations such as "compiling information from our files" and "a form suitable for putting on the city's computer." These words give us no sense of the tedium of daily transferring numbers from 500 manila index cards to 500 gray index cards. In fact, the essay gives us almost no sense of the job. The second paragraph ends with the words "the customer is always right," but nothing in the essay suggests that the writer (whose work "consisted of compiling information from the files") had any contact with customers. We really don't know what she did. Nor does the essay present any evidence that the experience was redeemed by a lesson in "patience, kindness, and understanding."

As it turns out, there was no such lesson. In class discussion, the student frankly admitted that the job was a waste of time. She had, out of habit, tried to come up with some pious thought to please the instructor. The habit had short-circuited the connection between the student's feelings and the words she was writing. The class discussion led to some genuinely interesting questions. Why, for example, are we reluctant to admit that something we've done was a waste of time? "The job was a waste of time" would have been, for most of us, a more productive thesis than "I was able to salvage a lesson." What experiences lead to the conclusions: I must write what the instructor expects; the instructor expects a pious thought? (We'd like to hear from a student willing to explore that topic in 500 to 1000 words.)

The class discussion, as we said, revealed the student's real attitude toward her job. The questions that, as readers, the class asked also provided a focus for the writer, which helped her to formulate a more productive thesis. It's helpful to imagine such a discussion with real readers in the early stages of writing as you grope for what you have to say. For although it would be tidy if writers could simply, and in the following order, (1) choose a subject, (2) focus on a topic, (3) formulate a thesis, (4) support the thesis in the body of the essay, things don't often work out that way. More commonly, writers discover their topic, formulate their thesis and develop support for their thesis in the act of writing and revising, in asking questions and in answering them, in discarding the answers, or even the questions, and starting again.

Example 2

Now look at the second essay, again on a common experience. Ask yourself as you read it, or reread it, what makes it uncommonly interesting.

```
        Dedication Doth Not a Good Teacher Make
        The worst teacher I ever had was a brilliant and
charming man. Fergy (it was short for Mr. Ferguson)
had written the textbook we used for Chemistry. He had
designed his house and built it himself, getting
professional help only for the electricity and
plumbing. He could remember the scores of all the
```

football games he'd seen, and the names of the players on each team. He never kept lists—"Lists rot the memory," he said—so he memorized which type of lab implement he kept in which of fifty drawers, and he could tell you instantly, without pause. Sometimes we would ask him where a certain type of obscure bottle could be found just to test him, but he never failed. "Middle left-hand drawer in Lab Station Six," would say old Fergy, and in that middle left-hand drawer it would be. I never knew him to forget a name, a face, or a formula, either.

That, I think, was his failing as a teacher. Because he had no trouble grasping or recalling a concept, he had trouble in understanding how we could. The one thing his extraordinary mind seemed unable to comprehend was that it was extraordinary, that not everyone could think as completely and as easily as he. If the class had questions he would try to answer them, but he tended to complicate and expand on ideas, rather than to simplify them. He could not believe that we needed not expansion but explanation, with the result that we soon learned not to ask too many questions for fear of extra material to learn. And it did become a fear of learning, because, try as we would, we somehow never managed to pin down concepts like electron shells and the wave theory of gravitation, but we would still have to answer for them on tests—and, ultimately, at home. (I never decided which was worse, knowing that once again I had made a complete fool of myself by taking a chem test, or having to listen to my parents sigh and claim that

I could have done better if I'd tried.)

　　Fergy would have been horrified to know that he had this discouraging effect on us. He loved us and he loved teaching and he loved chemistry. He was always available for outside help, not only for chemistry, but for any problem, whether in English or your social life. He tried to make class interesting by telling little anecdotes and playing with the chemicals. Actually, he was funny, and interesting, and charming, and he kept us hoping that we'd understand chem so that he would approve of us and so we could relax and enjoy him. But although he is one of the best people it has been my good fortune to have known, he never did manage to teach me a lick of chemistry.

As you study this book, you'll frequently find questions following examples of writing. Critical reading and writing are closely intertwined. If you practice asking and answering questions as you read, as well as when you write, the skills you develop will reinforce each other. Try answering the following questions on "Dedication Doth Not a Good Teacher Make":

What is the writer's thesis?
How does she support the thesis?
If you found the essay interesting, what makes it interesting?
If you found it convincing, what makes it convincing?

The Groucho Marx Complex

Clearly—examining these essays should make it clear—there is no such thing as an uninteresting life, or moment in life. There are only uninteresting ways to talk about them. It's also clear that some people are more interested in introspection and in talking and writing about their personal experiences than others. The others may be suffering from the Groucho Marx Complex: as Groucho put it, "I don't want to belong to any club that would have me as a member." Students who freeze at the notion of writing about themselves often feel that everything they have done is so ordinary, no one else could possibly be interested in it; anything they know is so obvious, everyone else must know it already. If this is your problem, remember that no one else knows exactly what you know; no one else can know what it feels like to live inside your skin. If you work at summoning up from your memory concrete and specific details, you can turn the most ordinary experience into a first-rate essay.

Remember too that writing from your own experience does not necessarily mean writing about private experience. We all have areas of experience we'd rather keep private, and we have a right to remain private about them. The important thing in writing about experience is, as Marianne Moore said, that "we must be as clear as our natural reticence allows us to be." Think, then, of experiences that you are willing to share and to be clear about. If, for example, you have just learned in a psychology course what "operant conditioning" means, define it for someone unfamiliar with the term. You might find yourself narrating an experience of your own to exemplify it; to be clear, you will have to provide an example. Or if an object in a local museum or craft exhibit or store interests you, ask yourself a question—why do I like it?—and you'll probably be able to turn an object into an experience. You'll also be turning an experience into an object—an essay—that will interest your readers.

Writing academic papers usually requires examining and evaluating texts and other evidence beyond your personal experience or previous knowledge. Nevertheless, you still must trust your own ideas. Trusting your own ideas does not, of course, mean being satisfied with the first thought that pops into your head. Rather, it means respecting your ideas enough to examine them thoughtfully; it means testing, refining, and sometimes changing them. But it is always your reading of a text, your conduct of an experiment, your understanding of an issue that your essay attempts to communicate.

Starting to write by writing will help you to discover ideas interesting enough to develop. Along the way, trying out various means to engage a reader's interest as well, you will clarify your ideas and understand them more deeply than you could have imagined had you not put them into words on paper.

Exercises

1. Make two lists of reasons, one for taking an action, and the other against. Examples: dropping a course, changing jobs, making an expensive purchase, calling someone you don't know but would like to know, majoring in . . . (whatever you're now thinking of), becoming a vegetarian.

2. Quickly scan several editorials or op-ed pieces in *The New York Times* (or another newspaper or newsmagazine) until you find one that you really want to *read*. Read it. Then for each paragraph, or group of paragraphs, write one or two questions that call for a summary of the paragraph's content or an explanation of the paragraph's purpose. Overall, your questions should explore why the editorial is particularly interesting or effective.

3. Write journal entries on two or three assignments (of writing, reading, lab work, or problem sets) made in your courses in the first two weeks of classes.

4. Write a journal entry recalling, in as much detail as you can, your earliest memory.

5. Narrow the following subjects to a topic. Then for each find a more specific focus for a 500-word essay.

Example:

Mental Retardation

    Housing for the mentally retarded

        A controversial proposal to house mentally retarded adults in my neighborhood

    Homelessness

    Athletic scholarships

    Welfare reform

    The Olympics

    Gun control

    Animal rights

    AIDS

    The writing requirement

6. Formulate a thesis sentence for two topics derived from Exercise 5.

Suggestions for Writing

1. Write a piece somewhat like Roth's (pages 10–11) in which you respond to a current proposal in your community. (Suggested length: 500 words.) Or, respond to Roth's article. (Perhaps something he says reminds you of something you have read or experienced; or maybe you agree or disagree strongly with some point he makes.)

2. Explain something clearly—a process, a concept, a place, an experience— that you know well but that others in your class may not know about or may understand less well than you. (Suggested length: 500 words.)

Chapter 2

Revising Drafts

I have never thought of myself as a good writer. Anyone who wants reassurance of that should read one of my first drafts. But I'm one of the world's great revisers.

—*James Michener*

Reading Drafts

In Chapter 1, we focused on how to have ideas and how to get them down on paper. We suggested that from the start of a project the writer is almost simultaneously both inventing ideas and refining them. But we also advised that, particularly at the start, it's often best to suspend critical judgment, if you can, until you have begun to capture your thoughts, however roughly expressed, on paper. In this chapter, we will focus on ways to improve and refine rough drafts. And, first, we want to make what may seem like an obvious point: *to improve the draft you have written, you must first read it.* Moreover, you must try to read it objectively and critically.

Asking Questions

To read your draft objectively, to make sure that you have said what you intended to say, first put it aside for a day, or at least for a couple of hours. Then read it through thoughtfully, as if you were not the writer, but someone reading if for the first time. As you read, try to imagine the questions such a reader might want or need to ask you to understand what you meant. Then, read your draft again, asking yourself the following questions:

1. Does the draft present an idea? Does it have a focus or make a unified point?

2. Is the idea or are the ideas clearly supported? Is there convincing evidence? Are there sufficient specific details?

3. Is the material effectively organized?

There are, of course, many other questions you might ask, and we'll suggest some before we're done. But let's start with these.

1. **Does the draft present an idea? Does it have a focus or make a unified point?** If, on reading your draft objectively, you find that it doesn't have an idea, a point to develop, then there's probably no reason to tinker with it (or to hand it in). It may be best to start again, using the invention techniques we discussed earlier. (Rereading the assignment is probably a good idea too.)

Let's suppose, however, that you do find some interesting material in your draft but that you're not yet sure what it adds up to. The chances are that some extraneous material is getting in your way—some false starts, needless repetition, or interesting but irrelevant information. Some pruning is probably in order.

Picasso said that in painting a picture he advanced by a series of destructions. A story about a sculptor makes a similar point. When asked how he had made such a lifelike image of an elephant from a block of wood, the sculptor answered, "Well, I just knocked off everything that didn't look like elephant." Often, revising a draft begins with similar "destruction." Having identified the main point that you want to pursue, don't be afraid to hack away competing material until you can see that point clearly in its bold outline. Of course you must have a lot of stuff on paper to begin with (at the start, nothing succeeds like excess). But often you must remove some of it before you can see that you have in fact roughly formulated the main point you want to make, and even produced some evidence to support it.

2. **Is the idea (or are the ideas) clearly supported? Is there convincing evidence? Are there sufficient specific details?** Writers are always reluctant to delete. Students with an assignment to write 500 or 1000 words by a deadline are, understandably, among the most reluctant. But, almost certainly, once you have settled on the focus of your essay, you will be adding material as well as deleting it. It isn't enough simply to state a point; you must also prove or demonstrate it.

If you argue, for example, that smoking should be banned in all public places, including professors' offices, you must offer reasons for your position and also meet possible objections with counterarguments; perhaps you will cite some statistics. If you are arguing that in Plato's *Apology* Socrates' definition of truth goes beyond mere correspondence to fact, you will need to summarize relevant passages of the *Apology* and introduce quotations illuminating Socrates' definition. Almost always a draft needs the addition of specific details and examples to support and clarify its generalizations.

3. **Is the material effectively organized?** As you prune away the irrelevancies and add the specific details and examples that will clarify and strengthen your point, as your draft begins more and more to "look like elephant," ask yourself if the parts of your draft are arranged in the best order. If you have given two examples, or stated three reasons, with which one is it best to begin? Ask yourself if paragraphs are in a reasonable sequence. Will the relationship of one point to the next be clear to your reader? Does the evidence in each paragraph support the point of that paragraph? (The same evidence may

be more appropriate to a different paragraph.) Does your opening paragraph provide the reader with a focus? Or, if it performs some other important function, such as getting the reader's attention, does the essay provide the reader with a focus soon enough?

In general, in working on the organization of drafts, follow two rules:

- Put together what belongs together.
- Put yourself in the position of your reader to make it as easy as possible for the reader to follow you.

Peer Review

Occasionally a writing assignment will specify the reader you should address. For example: "Write a letter to the editor of your hometown newspaper arguing that. . . ." More often, your reader must be imagined. We usually suggest imagining someone in your class who has not thought about your topic or considered the specific evidence you intend to examine.

In many writing classes students routinely break up into small groups to read and discuss each other's work. Peer review (as this practice is commonly called) is useful in several ways.

First, peer review gives the writer a real audience, readers who can point to what puzzles or pleases them, who ask questions and make suggestions, who may often disagree (with the writer or with each other) and who frequently, though not willfully, misread. Though writers don't necessarily like everything they hear (they seldom hear, "This is perfect. Don't change a word!"), reading and discussing their work with others almost always gives them a fresh perspective on their work, and a fresh perspective may stimulate thoughtful revision. (Having your intentions misread, because your writing isn't clear enough, can be particularly stimulating.)

Moreover, when students write drafts that will be commented on, they are doing what writers in "the real world" do. Like journalists, scholars, engineers, lawyers—anyone whose work is ordinarily reviewed many times, by friends and spouses, by colleagues, and by editors, before the work is published—students who write drafts for peer review know they will have a chance to discuss their writing with their colleagues (other students) before submitting a final version for evaluation. Writers accustomed to writing for a real audience are able, to some extent, to internalize the demands of a real audience. Even as they work on early drafts, they are sensitive to what needs to be added, or deleted, or clarified. Students who discuss their work with other students derive similar benefits. They are likely to write and revise with more confidence, and more energy.

The writer whose work is being reviewed is not the sole beneficiary. When students regularly serve as readers for each other, they become better readers of their own work, and consequently better revisers. Learning to write is in large measure learning to read.

Peer review in the classroom takes many forms; we'll look in a moment at an example as we trace a student's essay that is revised largely as a result of peer review. But even if peer review is not part of your writing class, you may want to work with a friend or another student in the class, reading each other's drafts. (One caution: be sure to acknowledge in a footnote or an endnote any substantial contribution, in idea or wording, a reader has made to your essay).

From Assignment to Essay: A Case History

On September 12, Suki Hudson was given the following assignment: Write an essay (roughly 500 words) defining racism or narrating an experience in which you were either the victim or the perpetrator of a racist incident. Bring a first draft with two copies to class on September 16 for peer review. Revised essay due September 26.

Suki kept no record of her first thoughts and jottings on the topic, but what follows is an early attempt to get something down on paper. Because it was far from the finished essay she would write, not yet even a first draft, we label it a Zero Draft:

```
Zero Draft. Sept. 13

It was a warm sunny day in the playground. My
three-year-old brother and other children were playing
gaily until one of the boys' mothers interrupted. She
called her son, whispered something, and when he went
back to the playground he excluded my brother from
playing together. I didn't know what to call the
incident, but my heart ached as I watched my little
brother enviously looked at the other kids. I
immediately left the playground with him, and the
playground has never been the same since that day.
```

At that point, having reached the end of the anecdote, Suki stopped. What she had written was not yet an essay, and it was far short of the suggested 500 words, but it was a start, which is all she had hoped to accomplish on this first try.

Later she read what she had written, and asked a friend to read it and see if he had any suggestions. It was a frustrating conversation. The friend didn't understand why Suki thought this was a "racist incident." Why did Suki leave the playground? Why hadn't she just asked the boy's mother for an explanation? The questions took her by surprise; she felt annoyed, then miserable. So she changed the subject.

But "the subject" didn't go away. Still later, she wrote the following account of the conversation in her journal:

```
Sept. 13:
```

```
    I asked J to read my paper and he thought I was
being paranoid. Why didn't I just ask the boy's mother
what was the matter? But I could not have even thought
of going up to the woman to question her motives. It
was beyond my control if she wanted to be ignorant and
cruel to a different race. (Or was it really my
ignorance to walk away from a simple explanation?)
```

The following day, looking over what she had written, it occurred to her to try adding the journal entry to the anecdote. Maybe in a concluding paragraph she could explain why what happened in the playground was obviously a racist incident.

Here is the conclusion:

```
Sept. 14
```

```
    Most people in modern society don't recognize the
more subtle cases of racism. People feel if they are
not assaulting physically they are not violating the
law, and as long as they are living according to the
law, racism is not committed. However, the law or the
constitution does not protect the human heart from
getting hurt, and without a doubt the most critical
racist action could be committed by close friends or
their loved ones.
```

But having written that last line Suki was struck by something odd about it. The woman in the playground was not a loved one, nor was she a close friend. Still, it was true that racist acts can be committed by friends, and even if the acts are undramatic, they should be recognized as racist acts. At this point, she thought that she had a thesis for her essay, but she also realized that she had begun to recall a different experience. Starting again, she wrote the following account:

```
    In Korea, I had a very close friend whose father
was Chinese. Although her mother was a Korean woman,
they were treated as foreign people in town, and they
```

were singled out on many occasions. Her father died when she was little but everyone in town knew she was a half Chinese. Her mother ran a Chinese restaurant, and they lived very quietly. My family knew her mother well and I was close friends with the girl and for many years I was the only friend she ever had. However, as I entered junior high school my new group of friends didn't approve of her background, and I drifted away from her. She was a very quiet, shy person and although I stopped calling or visiting her, she always remembered me on holidays to send presents. After graduating from junior high school she went to Taiwan to live with her grandparents, whom she had never met. I gathered she could not stand the isolation any longer at her age. Many years later I realized how cruel I had been to her, and I tried to locate her without success.

The following day Suki combined the two drafts (hoping to come closer to the 500 words), added a new concluding paragraph, and (rather disgusted with the whole assignment), typed up her first draft to hand in the next day. She photocopied it, as instructed, for peer review in class.

As we said earlier, peer review in the classroom takes many forms. Ordinarily, the instructor distributes some questions to be answered by both the writer and the readers. Typically the writer is asked to speak first, explaining how far along he or she is in writing the essay, and what help readers might give. The writer might also be asked "What are you most pleased with in your writing so far?"

Readers are then asked to respond. Instructions may vary, depending upon the particular assignment, but the questions distributed in Suki's class, shown here, are fairly typical.

First Draft

What follows is first the draft Suki gave the two members of her group, and then a summary of the group's discussion. Before reading her draft aloud (the procedure the instructor recommended for this session), Suki explained how she had happened to narrate two experiences and asked which narrative she should keep, or if she could keep both.

First Draft

S. Hudson

Questions for
Peer Review   Writing 125R

Read each draft once, quickly. Then read it again,
with the following questions in mind:

1. What is the essay's topic? Is it one of the
assigned topics, or a variation from it? Does the
draft show promise of fulfilling the assignment?

2. Looking at the essay as a whole, what thesis
(main idea) is stated or implied? If stated, where
is it stated? If implied, try to state it in your
own words.

3. Looking at each paragraph separately:

What is the basic point (the topic sentence or idea)?
How does the paragraph relate to the essay's main
idea or to the previous paragraph?

Is each sentence clearly related to the previous
sentence?

Is the paragraph adequately developed? Are there
sufficient specific details or examples?

Is the transition from one paragraph to the next
clear?

4. Look again at the introductory paragraph. Does
it focus your attention on the main point of the
essay? If not, does it effectively serve some
other purpose? Does the opening sentence interest
you in the essay? Do you want to keep reading?

5. Is the conclusion clear? Is the last sentence
satisfying?

6. Does the essay have a title? Is it interesting?
Informative?

Sept. 16

It was a warm sunny day in the playground. My
three-year-old brother and other children were playing
gaily until one of the boys' mothers interrupted. She

called her son to whisper something and when he went back to the playground he excluded my brother from playing together. I didn't know what to call the incident, but my heart ached as I watched my little brother enviously looked at other kids. I immediately left the playground with him, and the playground has never been the same since that day.

A friend of mine said I was being paranoid. It would have been appropriate to ask the boy's mother what was the matter, or if she had anything to do with the kids excluding my brother from playing. But I could not have even thought of going up to the woman to question her motives. It was beyond my control if she wanted to be ignorant and cruel to a different race, or perhaps my ignorance to walk away from a simple explanation.

Most people in modern society recognize only the dramatic instances of racism, and on a daily basis people don't recognize the more subtle cases of racism. People feel if they are not assaulting physically they are not violating the law, and as long as they are living according to the law, the racism is not committed. However, the law or the constitution does not protect the human heart from getting hurt, and without a doubt the most critical racist action could be committed by close friends or their loved ones.

In Korea, I had a very close friend whose father was Chinese. Although her mother was a Korean woman they were treated as foreign people in town, and they were singled out on many occasions. Her father died when she was little, but everyone in town knew she was a half Chinese. Her mother ran a Chinese restaurant, and they lived very quietly. My family knew her mother well and I was close friends with the girl and for many years I was the only friend she ever had. However, as I entered junior high school my new group of friends didn't approve of her background and I drifted away from her. She was a very quiet, shy person, and although I stopped calling or visiting her, she always remembered me on holidays to send presents. After graduating from junior high school she went to Taiwan to live with her grandparents whom she had never met. I gathered she could not stand the isolation any longer at her age. Many years later, I realized how cruel I have been to her, and I tried to locate her without success.

She was a victim in a homogeneous society, and had to experience the pain she did not deserve. It is part of human nature to resent the unknown, and sometimes people become racist to cover their fears or ignorance.

Summary of Peer Group Discussion

1. The group immediately understood why the friend (in the second paragraph) had difficulty understanding that the first incident was racist. It might well have been racist, but, they pointed out, Suki had said nothing about the racial mix at the playground. It does become clear by the fourth paragraph that the writer and her brother are Korean, but we don't get this information early enough, and we know nothing of the race of the woman who whispers to her son. Suki had neglected to say—because it was so perfectly obvious to her—that she and her brother were Korean; the mother, the other child, in fact all others in the playground, were white.

2. Suki's readers confirmed her uneasiness about the third paragraph. They found it confusing. (a) Suki had written "people don't recognize the more subtle cases of racism." Did she mean that the mother didn't recognize her action as

racist, or that Suki didn't? (b) In the first paragraph Suki had written "I didn't know what to call the incident." But then the second paragraph is contradictory. There she seems to accuse the mother of being "cruel to a different race." (c) And the last sentence of the third paragraph, they agreed, in which Suki writes of racist acts "committed by close friends," did not tie in at all with the first part of the essay, although it did serve to introduce the second anecdote.

3. Her group was enthusiastic, though, about Suki's telling of the two stories and advised her to keep both. Both were accounts of more or less subtle acts of racism. One student thought that they should appear in chronological order: first the Korean story and then the more recent story, set in the playground. But both readers were sure that she could find some way to put them together.

4. They were less sure what the essay's thesis was, or whether it even had one. One student proposed:

> Subtle racist acts can be as destructive as dramatic instances (implied in paragraph 3).

The other proposed combining:

> It is part of human nature to resent the unknown

and

> . . . sometimes people become racist to cover their fears or ignorance (from the final paragraph).

All three members of Suki's group (Suki included) thought that the ideas in the essay were supported by the narratives. But the draft didn't yet hang together: Suki would have to work on the way the separate parts connected.

5. One member of the group then pointed out that the second paragraph could be deleted. The friend mentioned in it (who called Suki "paranoid") had been important to Suki's thinking about her first draft, but served no useful purpose in the draft they were looking at, and other details in that paragraph were murky.

6. On the other hand, the first paragraph probably needed additional details about the setting, the people involved, what each did. How does a three-year-old know he's been excluded from a play group? What happened? What did the other children do? What did he do? And, as the group had seen at once, some details were needed to establish the racist nature of the incident. They also reminded Suki that her essay needed a title.

7. Finally, some small details of grammar. Suki's English is excellent, although English is her second language (her third actually). But the other two in her group, being native speakers of English, were able to catch the slightly odd diction in

> she always remembered me on holidays to send presents

and the error in

> my heart ached as I watched my little brother enviously looked at other kids.

Suki asked if the past tense was right in

> I realized how cruel I have been to her

and the others supplied:

> I realized how cruel I had been to her

(though they could not explain the difference).

Several days later Suki consulted her notes and resumed work on her draft, and by September 25, the night before it was due, she was able to print the final version, which now included a title.

Suki Hudson

Writing 125R

Two Sides of a Story

It was a warm sunny day in the playground. My three-year-old brother and two other small boys were playing together in the sandbox. My brother was very happy, digging in the sand with a shovel one of the other boys had brought, when one of the mothers sitting on a bench across from me called to her son. She bent over and whispered something to him, and he went right over to my brother and pulled the shovel out of his hand. He pushed my brother aside and moved to the other side of the sandbox. The other boy followed him, and they continued to play. My heart ached as I watched my little brother enviously looking at the other kids. I didn't fully understand what had happened. I looked across at the mother, but she turned her head away. Then I picked up my brother and immediately left the playground with him.

I thought the woman was extremely rude and cruel, but I didn't think then that she was behaving in a racist way. We had only recently come here from Korea, and although I had been told that there was much racism in America, I thought that meant that it was hard for some people, like blacks, to find jobs or go to good schools. In some places there were street gangs and violence. But I didn't understand that there could be subtle acts of racism too. I was aware, though, in the playground that my brother and I were the only Koreans, the only nonwhites. When the woman turned her face away from me it felt like a sharp slap, but I was ignorant about her motives. I only guessed that she told her child not to play with my brother, and I knew that the playground was never the same since that day.

That incident was several months ago. When I started to think about it again recently, I thought also of another time when I was ignorant of racism.

In Korea, I had a very close friend whose father was Chinese. Although her mother was a Korean woman they were treated as foreign people in town, and they were singled out on many occasions. Her father died when she was little, but everyone in town knew she was half Chinese. Her mother ran a Chinese restaurant, and they lived very quietly. My family knew her mother well and I was close friends with the girl, and for many years I was the only friend she ever had. However, as I entered junior high school my new group of friends didn't approve of her background and I drifted away from her. She was a very quiet, shy person, and although I stopped calling or visiting her, she always remembered to send me presents on holidays. After graduating from junior high school, she went to Taiwan to live with her grandparents, whom she had never met. I gathered she could not stand the isolation any longer at her age. Many years later, I realized how cruel I had been to her, and I tried to locate her without success.

She was a victim in a homogeneous society, and had to experience pain she did not deserve. There was no law to protect her from that, just as there was no law to protect my little brother. Perhaps the woman in the playground did not realize how cruel she was being. She probably didn't think of herself as a racist, and maybe she acted the way I did in Korea, without thinking why. It isn't only the dramatic acts that are racist, and maybe it isn't only cruel people who commit racist acts. It is part of human nature to fear the unknown, and sometimes people become racist to cover their fears, or ignorance.

An Overview: From Subject to Essay

We each must work out our own procedures and rituals (John C. Calhoun liked to plow his farm before writing); but the following suggestions may help. The rest of the book will give you more detailed advice.

1. If a topic is assigned, write on it; if a topic is not assigned, turn a subject into a topic. Get an early start. The day the assignment is given, try to settle on a topic that interests you. Do this by employing any and all of the strategies—free-writing, listing, clustering, asking questions, keeping a journal—that we have discussed. When you look over your jottings, take note of what especially interests you, and try to decide what topic you can sensibly discuss in the assigned length. Unfortunately, few of us can in a few pages write anything of interest on a large subject. We simply cannot in 500 words say anything readable (that is, true and interesting to others) on subjects as broad as music, sports, ourselves. Given such subjects, we have nothing to say, probably because we are desperately trying to remember what we have heard other people say. Trying to remember blocks our efforts to look hard and to think. To get going, we must narrow such subjects down to specific topics: from music to country music, from sports to commercialization of athletics, from ourselves to a term with a roommate.

2. Get a focus. Once you have turned a subject into a topic, you need to shape the topic by seeing it in a particular focus, by having a thesis, an attitude, a point: Country music is popular because . . . ; College athletes are exploited . . . ; Problems between roommates can be avoided if. . . . Probably you won't find your exact focus or thesis immediately, but you will be able to jot down a few things, including some questions to yourself that come to mind on the topic you have carved out of the broad subject. For example: Why is country music popular? What kind of people like it? Why are some performers more successful than others?

If you ask yourself questions now, you'll probably be able to answer them a day or two later. It doesn't matter whether you make each jotting on a separate card or group them on a sheet of paper as a list or in a few roughly sketched paragraphs; the important thing is to write something, perhaps a few generalizations, perhaps a few striking details, perhaps some of each. If you compose on a word processor, make a print-out after a page or two. You'll probably find that reading what you have jotted down leads to something else— something you probably would not have thought of if you hadn't jotted down the first thing. Few of us have good ideas about anything at the start, but as we put our ideas into words we find better ideas coming to mind.

Remember, too, that keeping your audience and your purpose in mind will help you to produce ideas. If, for example, you assume that you are writing about country music to interest a reader who is unfamiliar with it, you will begin to find things that you must say.

3. Turn your reveries into notes. Put your jottings aside for a day or two (assuming you have a week to do the essay), but be prepared to add to them at any moment. Useful thoughts—not only ideas, but details—may come to you while you are at lunch, while you read a newspaper or magazine, while your mind wanders in class. Write down these thoughts. Do not assume that you will remember them when you come to draft your essay.

4. Sort things out. About two days before the essay is due, look over your jottings and see if you can discover a workable thesis in them. This might be a good moment to practice free writing on your topic, or to arrange your notes into what looks like a reasonable sequence.

Perhaps now is the time to give your essay a provisional title. A title will help you to keep your thesis in focus. Don't be afraid to be obvious. If you look back at some of the titles of sections in this book, you will see such things as "Why Write?" "Starting to Write by Writing," and "Developing Ideas." Such titles help the writer to keep to the point, while letting readers know what the topic will be. Sometimes wordplay produces an attractive but still informative title—for example, a student's "If You Have *Time,* read *Newsweek.*"

In any case, whether or not you choose a title at this point, you should now have a focus. Next, look again at your jottings and add what comes to mind. Keep asking yourself questions, and try to jot down the answers. Draw arrows to indicate the sequence you think the phrases should be in.

5. Write. Even if you are not sure that you have a thesis and an organization, start writing. Don't delay; you have some jottings, and you have a mind that, however casually, has already been thinking. Don't worry about writing an effective opening paragraph (your opening paragraph will almost surely have to be revised later anyway); just try to state and develop your point, based on the phrases or sentences you have accumulated, adding all of the new details that flow to mind as you write. If you are stuck, ask yourself questions. Have I supported my assertions with examples? Will a comparison help to clarify the point? Which quotation best illustrates this point? If you are not using a word processor, leave lots of space between the lines, leave wide margins, and write on one side of the page only. Later you'll fill the spaces with additional details, additional generalizations, and revisions of sentences. Keep going until you have nothing left to say.

6. Save what you can. Immediately after writing the draft, or a few hours later, look it over to see how much you can salvage. Don't worry about getting the exact word here or there; just see whether or not you have a thesis, whether or not you keep the thesis in view, and whether or not the points flow reasonably. Delete irrelevant paragraphs, however interesting; shift paragraphs that are relevant but that should be somewhere else. You can do this best by scissoring the sheets and gluing the pieces onto another paper in the right order. (If you use a word processor, you can move paragraphs just by hitting some keys on the keyboard.) Don't assume that tomorrow you will be able to remember that the paragraph near the bottom of page 3 will go into the middle of page 2. Scissor and glue it, or move the block, now, so that when you next read the essay you will easily be able to tell whether in fact the paragraph does belong in the middle of page 2. Finally, settle on a title. Probably you can't do much more with your manuscript at this moment. Put it aside until tomorrow.

7. Revise. Reread your draft, first with an eye toward large matters. Revise your opening paragraph or write one to provide the reader with a focus; make sure each paragraph grows out of the previous one, and make sure you keep the thesis in view. Remember, *when you write, you are the teacher.* As you revise, make sure that assertions are supported by evidence; try to imagine that you are the reader, and let this imagined reader tell you where you get off the point, where you are illogical, where you need an example—in short, where you are in any way confusing.

Next, after making the necessary large revisions, read the draft with an eye toward smaller matters: make sure that each sentence is clear and readable. (You can do this only by reading slowly—preferably aloud, unless you have developed the ability to hear each sentence, each word, in the mind's ear.) Let's say that in telling a reader how to handle disks for a word processor, you have written, "When you write the label for the disk, use a felt pen." You notice, in revising, that the reader may wonder *why* a pencil or a ballpoint pen should not be used, and so you'll alter the sentence to "Because the pressure of a pencil or a ballpoint pen can damage the surface of the disk, label the disk with a felt pen."

Cross out extra words; recast unclear sentences. Keep pushing the words, the sentences, the paragraphs into shape until they say what you want them to say from the title onward. (This contest between writers and their words is part of what Muhammad Ali had in mind when he said, referring to his work on his autobiography, "Writing is fighting.") Correct anything that disturbs you—for instance, awkward repetitions that grate.

8. Edit. When your draft is as good as you can make it, take care of the mechanical matters: if you have any doubt about the spelling of a word, check it in a dictionary; if you are unsure about a matter of punctuation, check it in this book. You will also find instructions about manuscript form (for example, where to put the title, what margins to leave) in this book. And be sure to acknowledge the source not only of quotations but also of any ideas that you borrowed, even though you summarized or paraphrased them in your own words. (On plagiarism, see pages 323–326.)

9. Prepare the final copy. Now write or type the final copy; if you are on the schedule, you will be doing this a day before the essay is due. (If you take our advice and use a word processor, you already have a final copy on a disk and now need only to instruct the machine to print it.) After writing, typing, or printing it, you will probably want to proofread it; there is no harm in doing so, but even if you do it now, you will have to proofread again later because at the moment you are too close to your essay. If you put the essay aside for a few hours and then reread it, again aloud, you will be more likely to catch omitted words, transposed letters, inconsistent spelling of names, and so forth. Change these neatly (see pages 160–161).

10. Hand the essay in on time. In short, the whole business of moving from a subject to a finished essay on a focused topic adds up to Mrs. Beeton's famous recipe: "First catch your hare, then cook it."

Writing from Experience

Celia E. Rothenberg

Child of Divorce

Celia E. Rothenberg graduated from Wellesley College in 1991. A history major with a special interest in the lives of Middle Eastern women, she was awarded a Marshall fellowship to study modern Middle Eastern history at Oxford and is now enrolled in a Ph.D. program in social anthropology at the University of Toronto. She has served as an intern in an Israeli-Palestinian women's peace group in Jerusalem, and she plans to continue working for understanding between these two groups.

Rothenberg wrote the following essay while she was an undergraduate.

1   Over this past winter vacation my parents, brother, and I spent a few days together—a rare event now that the four of us live in four different states. As I watched my parents and brother engage in our usual laughter and reminiscing, accompanied by an occasional tear at a past both bitter and sweet, I listened more closely than ever before to what is a frequent topic of discussion, our relationship as a family.

2   Perhaps because my parents divorced when I was a small child, it seems to surprise my friends that my family's recollections of those years are filled with many pleasant memories. After all, those who don't know my family have reason to assume that the memories of growing up with divorced parents in some tough economic times might be rather dreary. In fact, however, my memories center on the results of the thoughtfulness and conscious effort exerted by both my parents to create a sense of love and protection for my brother and me. I have always felt that my family was a team, a team that sometimes fumbled, and sometimes seemed to have two, three, or even four captains, and a team that underwent a change in plan mid-game, but a team nevertheless. It is only recently, however, that I have realized how much patience and understanding went into achieving that sense of belonging and love, and how achieving it was part of the long and often painful process for us of divorce and healing.

3   My parents divorced, after fifteen years of marriage, when I was six. I have nearly no memories of living in a two-parent household. From the time of my earliest memories, my mother has always studied or worked full time. Immediately after the divorce, she, like many women who find themselves single after many years as a "housewife," went back to school. My brother at the time was twelve. Although I remember my Cinderella-shaped cake for my seventh birthday, a few of my favorite pets, and a well-loved school teacher, I remember very little of my mom's return to school, or my own or brother's adjustment to our new surroundings. Perhaps the gaps in my memory serve as some kind of mental defense mechanism to protect me from the reality of the harder times; no matter the reason for my memory voids, however, my brother's recollections are so vivid, and my mom and dad so open about those years, that my scattered memories have been augmented by their storytelling—to the point that I often confuse my memories with theirs.

4   It is only recently, in fact, that I have realized how difficult the initial years following the divorce were for my mother, brother and father. Over this past winter vacation, my mom told me for the first time how taxing even the simplest tasks seemed to be. For example, locking the doors to our new, small house conjured up all the difficulties and sadnesses of this new beginning. Because my dad had customarily locked up, she had rarely been the one to lock each lock and turn off each light. Doing these tasks in a new house in a new city was a constant reminder of her changed circumstances. Late in the evening she would carefully plot the order in which to turn off the lights, so as not to be alone in the dark. She would lock a door, and then a window, pausing in between the locks

to distract her mind from the task at hand—and the frightening and lonely feelings these new responsibilities brought with them.

5   My family now openly recalls that those years were a difficult time of adjustment to new schools, a new city, and a new life. We had moved from a small suburb of St. Louis to Champaign-Urbana, a community largely centered on the life of the University of Illinois. Our first house in Champaign and my mom's tuition for the Master's degree in Library and Information Science were largely financed by the sale of the lovely Steinway baby grand piano that had graced my parents' living room since before I was born. Before the divorce, my father was an attorney until he found himself in legal difficulties, which ultimately led him to give up the practice of law. His reduced income and my mom's tuition bills placed us under a great financial strain.

6   My brother, who was twelve at the time of the divorce, particularly recalls how difficult communication was between the three of us and my father, and at times even among the three of us. To help ease the tension of my dad's monthly visits and maintain a relationship which included some fun, my brother and dad played checkers through the mail. They carefully conceived of a plan of multiple paper copies of the checker board and colored pencils for their game. One of my few early memories of those years focusses on the checker board we set up on the dining room table to represent the game my brother and dad played on paper. One evening, the cat we brought with us from (as my mother often said) our "other life," jumped on the board, knocking the pieces all over the table. Steve was inconsolable, and only a prolonged long-distance phone call to figure out where each piece belonged resolved the situation.

7   That first year my brother escaped into a world of books, often reading fiction and plays when he should have been doing homework, a coping behavior he practiced until he was nearly through high school.

8   But even the deepest hurts can heal over time. With encouragement and support from both my parents, Steve channeled his considerable energy and anger into planning for an early graduation from high school and a year in Israel between high school and college. The only conditions set were that he had to earn enough money to buy his own plane ticket and he had to have a college acceptance letter in hand before he left. These goals gave him something to work for at a time when he felt that he had lost friends and status in coming to a new, very different, and less comfortable environment than had been part of his early days.

9   As for me, perhaps because I was six years younger, I appeared to go blithely along, oblivious to most of the tensions and strains that Steve seemed to feel. With my mother studying for her classes and Steve spending almost all his time reading, I became an avid reader myself, almost in self-defense. I found new friends and reveled in my new elementary school, a magnet school where we studied French every day. I wrote long, detailed stories of a young girl who

lived on a farm with both parents and a dozen brothers and sisters and a beautiful horse. Perhaps I, too, was seeking some consolation in an imaginary life far removed from our little house.

10   It can take years for wounds to heal, and I am happy to say that my family healed more quickly than most. Perhaps we got past that initial phase early on because my parents did not make too many mistakes. They avoided some common pitfalls of divorcing families. The divorce was quick—the process was completed a few months after my parents sold their house and moved to their new homes—there were no court battles, no screaming fights, no wrenching decisions that we children were required to make. Steve and I were never asked—or allowed—to choose sides or express a preference for one parent over the other. Although my own memories are blurry, the few recollections I have of those first five years focus on my dad's regular monthly visits (he lived a few hours away by car). By the time I was ten, he was spending nearly every weekend with us at the house, a pattern which continued for the next decade, until I was out of high school and off to Wellesley.

11   Nothing worthwhile, my mother has always told me, is ever easy. It could not have always been easy for either of my parents to spend so much of their free time together when they had chosen to create separate lives, but at the time Steve and I rarely saw anything but civility and fondness. As parents they were determined not to let their children suffer for mistakes they may have made in their marriage. It is one of their greatest gifts to Steve and me, for it was the ultimate lesson in learning about the commitment and cost of love and the lifelong responsibilities of family.

12   The stories we have accumulated over the years have become more hilarious as I have grown older. My dad, determined not to be a "Disneyland daddy," showing up on the weekends for shopping and dinners out, was not uncomfortable in our new home. In fact, he helped us figure out how to do various home improvement projects. Under his direction, we rewired our house (and nearly electrocuted Steve in the process), insulated our attic (the family story lingers that we nearly blew off the roof), and painted the house (and, of course, ourselves). Our projects probably didn't save us very much money, since we seemed to spend as much money on fixing the mistakes we made as on the project itself, yet we were not merely building the house, or growing gardens, or mowing the lawn. We were rebuilding our lives, making memories, and creating a sense of togetherness.

13   My own clear and more complete memories begin at the age of eleven, when my mother, brother, and I began a new lifestyle, which reflected a newly achieved flexibility and confidence in our ability to manage our lives. When my brother entered the University of Illinois, we moved into a big old house and I began high school. The house was what a real estate broker fondly calls a "fixer-upper," and was perfect for my mom's income (she worked for the University af-

ter she finished her Master's degree) and our need for space for friends of mine and Steve's. Steve, in particular, brought home countless Jewish college students whom he knew from his involvement in the campus Jewish student organization. They often needed a good meal, a shoulder to lean on, an opinion on a paper, or a good night's sleep.

14   I remember our dining room on Shabbos, furnished with a dining room set probably beautiful in my grandmother's day but battered after three generations of use, packed with college students eating dinner. I remember vividly the talk and the laughter, the jesting and the endless debates. My mom was not only an intellectual support for those students but also an inspiration, someone who had experienced a marriage gone bad, the trials and tribulations of parenting alone (at least during the week), and the tough economics of a single-parent household. Conversations stretched from the abstract to the concrete, from the politics of the Eastern bloc to the intricacies of love and sex.

15   Over the years it has become clear that the divorce, although traumatic, opened our minds, enriched our relationships with each other, and loosened restraints we did not know we were subject to. I vividly remember my high school years as a busy time full of my friends and my brothers' who simply enjoyed being around the house. The slightly chaotic, easy-going atmosphere of the house was fostered in large part by our mom; she had disliked the isolated feeling of life in suburbia when she was married. She wanted to create a different atmosphere for Steve and me, a place where young people were comfortable to come and go.

16   My friends in high school were fascinated by my home, and I enjoyed it as much as they did. My dad was able to watch us grow and change from weekend to weekend, his place secure and comfortable at the head of the Shabbos table surrounded by students. He helped us with science projects, participated in countless car-pools, and, most of all, was there when we needed him. Although from the point of view of the Census Bureau we were a "single parent household," in actuality we were a *family* that happened to have divorced parents. Perhaps our experience was not typical of some families in which there has been a divorce, but the labels obscure our understanding of the needs and hopes of all families, which I think are probably the same, divorced or not. My parent's expectations for Steve and me were not altered by their marital status, nor do I think that Steve and I let them get away with very much on the excuse that they were divorced!

17   I have always loved my family, but I find that I admire each of them increasingly as time goes on. Now, when we gather from different corners of the country and world during vacations a few times a year, we admit that the best and the worst, but always the most precious times, were when we were together on the weekends in that big old house, sometimes with the students and sometimes with only each other. On special occasions, we have a (very patient) long-

distance operator connect the four of us on the same phone line, and we talk as if there is no tomorrow. We are fiercely proud of one another; I often have to restrain myself from blurting out the merits of my exceptional family to my unsuspecting friends.

18   At times I wonder how different we would be if we had not gone through the divorce, but for that question I can conjure up no really meaningful speculation. I know that we immensely value our time together, freely share our money (or, I should say, our student loans, as my brother is now in law school, my mom is a full-time doctoral student and my father shoulders the Wellesley burden), and exorbitantly rejoice in each other's company. What more could any of us want from family? So often, it seems to me, I see families that do not realize they possess a great wealth—time. They are together all the time. They don't miss the moments of their mother/father/brother/sister's lives that are irreplacable.

19   There is no question that it is often difficult to be a family. My own family's life took a path with an unexpected curve. We weathered times of tough adjustments, economic difficulties, and typical adolescent rebellion. Through it all, though, there was a guiding (if unspoken until many years later) principle of life: family is family forever, and there is no escaping either the trials or the rewards. My parents expect my brother and me to extend ourselves and do work that in some way will bring more light into the world. I have parents who, on modest incomes and budgets, have endowed me with dreams and a sense that the impossible is possible. I have parents for whom I am extremely grateful.

20   When I told my family that Wellesley asked me to write an article on growing up in a single parent household, they responded in their typical chaotic fashion. My brother forced each of us to sit and write a page about the "Single-Parent Thing" before he let us eat dinner. My mother began plotting a book made up of chapters written from the different perspectives of mother, father, son, and daughter in the single-parent household. My dad insisted we discuss it over dinner (and promised to write his page immediately after dessert). In the end, I took their contributions with me back to Wellesley and wrote down my own feelings, late at night in Munger Hall.

Topics for Discussion and Writing

1. What are your earliest memories of your family? How would you account for the fact that Rothenberg has "nearly no memories of living in a two-parent household"?

2. Rothenberg calls her family "exceptional." What do you find to be her strongest evidence for this claim?

3. In paragraph 2 Rothenberg refers to assumptions that her friends make about a child who grew up with divorced parents. What are or were your assumptions? On what are (or were) they based?

4. A highly personal essay runs the risk of being of little interest to persons other than the author. If you found this essay interesting, try to account for its appeal.

Henry Louis Gates Jr.

Malcolm, the Aardvark and Me

Henry Louis Gates Jr., born in West Virginia in 1950, did his undergraduate work at Yale University (summa cum laude) *and his graduate work (M.A. and Ph.D.) at Cambridge University. He has taught at Yale, Cornell, and Duke, and now at Harvard, where he is the director of the Afro-American Studies program. Gates is the author of several books, including* Black Literature and Literary Theory *and* The Signifying Monkey: A Theory of African-American Literary Criticism. *The essay that we reprint originally appeared in* The New York Times Book Review.

1   One of the most gratifying effects of Spike Lee's film *Malcolm X* is that its success has prompted the restoration of Malcolm's autobiography to the best-seller lists. The country is *reading* the 1965 book once again, as avidly, it seems, as it is seeing Mr. Lee's movie. For 17 weeks *The Autobiography of Malcolm X,* written with the assistance of Alex Haley, has been on the *New York Times* paperback best-seller list, and for 10 of those weeks it was No. 1. Today, on the 28th anniversary of his assassination, Malcolm's story has become as American—to borrow H. Rap Brown's famous aphorism—as violence and cherry pie.

2   Malcolm first came into my life some three decades ago, when I was 9 years old and Mike Wallace and CBS broadcast a documentary about the Nation of Islam. It was called *The Hate That Hate Produced,* and it showed just about the scariest black people I had ever seen: black people who talked right into the faces of white people, telling them off without even blinking. While I sat in our living room, I happened to glance over at my mother. A certain radiance was slowly transforming her soft brown face, as she listened to Malcolm naming the white man as the devil. "Amen," she said, quietly at first. "All right now," she continued, much more emphatically. All this time and I had not known just how deeply my mother despised white people. The revelation was terrifying but thrilling.

3   The book came into my life much later.

4   I was almost 17, a junior in high school, and I was slowly and pleasurably devouring *Ebony* magazine. More precisely, I was reading a profile of the Roman Catholic basketball player Lew Alcindor, who was then a star at U.C.L.A. and who later became a legend with the Los Angeles Lakers as the Muslim basketball player Kareem Abdul-Jabbar. In the profile he said that *The Autobiography of Malcolm X* had meant more to him than any other book, and that *all* black Americans should read it—*today.*

5   Today was not possible for me, since I lived in a village in the hills of West Virginia where nobody carried such things. I had to go down to Red Bowl's newsstand, make a deposit and wait while they sent away for it. But when the book arrived, I read it straight through the night, as struck by its sepia-colored photograph of a dangerous-looking, gesticulating Malcolm as I was by the contents, the riveting saga of a man on the run, from whites (as the son of a Garveyite father) and blacks (his former mentors and colleagues at the Nation of Islam, after his falling-out with Elijah Muhammad).

6   I loved the hilarious scene in which Malcolm is having his hair "conked," or "processed" ("relaxed" remains the euphemism); unable to rinse out the burning lye because the pipes in his home are frozen, he has no recourse but to dunk his head in a toilet bowl. A few months before, the benignly parochial principal of our high school had "paddled" my schoolmate Arthur Galloway when Arthur told him that his processed hairstyle was produced by a mixture of eggs, mashed potatoes and lye. "Don't lie to me, boy," the principal was heard saying above Arthur's protests.

7   What I remember most, though, is Malcolm's discussion of the word "aardvark."

8   "I saw that the best thing I could do was get hold of a dictionary—to study. . . . I spent two days just riffling uncertainly through the dictionary's pages. I'd never realized so many words existed! . . . Funny thing, from the dictionary's first page right now, that 'aardvark' springs to my mind. The dictionary had a picture of it, a long-tailed, long-eared, burrowing African mammal, which lives off termites caught by sticking out its tongue as an anteater does for ants."

9   Years later, near the end of his life, Malcolm found himself heading to the American Museum of Natural History in New York to learn more about that exotic creature, even while trying to figure out how to avoid an almost certain Muslim death sentence. "Boy! I never will forget that old aardvark!" he had mused to Alex Haley. What manner of politician was this, I wondered, in this the year that Stokely Carmichael and Rap Brown, Eldridge Cleaver and Huey P. Newton, Ron Karenga and Amiri Baraka, simultaneously declared themselves to be the legitimate sons of Malcolm the father, to linger with aardvarks when his world was collapsing around him?

10   Although Malcolm proudly avowed that he read no fiction (he says he read only one novel "since I started serious reading," and that was *Uncle Tom's*

Cabin), he still loved fiction—"fiction" defined as a making, a creating, with words. His speeches—such as the oft-repeated "Ballot or the Bullet" or "Bandung Conference"—are masterpieces of the rhetorical arts. More than Martin Luther King Jr., more than any of the black nationalists or the neo-Marxists, Malcolm X was a *writer,* a wordsmith.

11   In 1968, my English teacher told me that in years to come, long after the civil rights struggle was a footnote in history, this man would be remembered—like St. Augustine, like Benjamin Franklin, like Henry Adams—because of his gift with words. High praise: and yet the teacher's observation, I must confess, didn't go down well with me at the time. Imagining the book stretched on the autopsy slab of purely literary analysis, I somehow felt that the overriding immediacy of Malcolm's experience—and my special relation to it—had been diminished. Despite Malcolm's cautious if heartfelt moves toward universalism, I felt that part of him would always belong to African mammals like aardvarks, like me.

Topics for Discussion and Writing

1. What was the occasion for Gate's article, and where does Gates refer to it?

2. Read the last sentence of the first paragraph. How would you describe its tone? (H. Rap Brown, a militant black power leader, said—we are quoting from memory, assisted by Gates—that "violence is as American as cherry pie.")

3. The third paragraph is only one sentence long. Why do you suppose Gates isolated the sentence, instead of beginning the next paragraph with it? What effect does he create?

4. What magazine, if any, was especially important to you in high school (Gates remembers "slowly and pleasurably devouring *Ebony*")? Why was it important?

5. If you have a "special relation" (Gates's words, in his final paragraph) with any book (or film) write an essay of 500 words, giving the reader some idea of what this relation may be. (Notice how Gates uses examples—of the "sepia-colored photographs," of an "hilarious scene," of the surprising discussion of "aardvark." Try to be just as specific in your discussion.)

Suggestion for Writing

Think about how you usually respond to a writing assignment. Try to trace, step by step, your thoughts, actions, and feelings from the moment that you receive an assignment to the moment that you turn in a finished essay.

Looking back, what experiences have you had as a writer, in class or out, that have lead to your current practice and attitude toward writing? Do you find writing under some circumstances (writing letters, for example, or writing for a school newspaper) easier than others?

Turn your reflections into an essay of about 500 words.

Chapter 3

Shaping Paragraphs

Paragraph Form and Substance

It is commonly said that a good paragraph has *unity* (it makes one point, or it indicates where one unit of a topic begins and ends); it has *organization* (the point or unit is developed according to some pattern); and it has *coherence* (the pattern of development, sentence by sentence, is clear to the reader). We will say these things too. Moreover, we will attempt to demonstrate that, generally speaking, they are true. Along the way we also hope to show you how to shape your ideas into effective paragraphs. But first we feel obliged to issue this warning: you can learn to write a unified, organized, coherent paragraph that no one in his or her right mind would choose to read. Here is an example:

Charles Darwin's great accomplishments in the field of natural science resulted from many factors. While innate qualities and characteristics played a large part in leading him to his discoveries, various environmental circumstances and events were decisive factors as well. Darwin, himself considered his voyage on the *Beagle* the most decisive event of his life, precisely because this was to him an educational experience similar to if not more valuable than that of college, in that it determined his whole career and taught him of the world as well.

Notice that the paragraph is unified, organized, and coherent. It has a topic sentence (the first sentence). It uses transitional devices ("while," "as well," "Darwin," "himself") and, as is often helpful, it repeats key words. But notice also that it is wordy, vague, and inflated ("in the field of," "many factors," "qualities and characteristics," "circumstances and events," "precisely because," "educational experience," "similar to if not more valuable than"). It is, in short, thin and boring. To whom does it teach what?

Consider, by contrast, these two paragraphs from the beginning of another essay on Darwin:

> Charles Darwin's youth was unmarked by signs of genius. Born in 1809 into the well-to-do Darwin and Wedgwood clans (his mother was a Wedgwood, and Darwin himself was to marry another), he led a secure and carefree childhood, happy with his family, indifferent to books, responsive to nature. The son and grandson of impressively successful physicians, he eventually tried medical training himself, but found the studies dull and surgery (before anesthesia) too ghastly even to watch. So, for want of anything better, he followed the advice of his awesome father (6'2", 336 pounds, domineering in temperament) and studied for the ministry, taking his B.A. at Christ's College, Cambridge, in 1831.

> Then a remarkable turn of events saved Darwin from a country parsonage. His science teacher at Cambridge, John Stevens Henslow, arranged for Darwin the invitation to be naturalist on H.M.S. *Beagle* during a long voyage of exploration. Despite his father's initial reluctance, Darwin got the position, and at the end of 1831 left England for a five-year voyage around the globe that turned out to be not only a crucial experience for Darwin himself, but a passage of consequence for the whole world.

> —PHILIP APPLEMAN

Notice how full of life these paragraphs are, compared to the paragraph that begins by asserting that "Charles Darwin's great accomplishments in the field of natural science resulted from many factors." These far more interesting paragraphs are filled with specific details, facts, and names that combine to convey ideas. We finish reading them with a sense of having learned something worth knowing, from someone fully engaged not only with the topic, but also with conveying it to someone else.

The one indispensable quality of a good paragraph, the quality that the first paragraph on Darwin lacks, is *substance*. A paragraph may define a term, describe a person or a place, make a comparison, tell an anecdote, summarize an opinion, draw a conclusion; it may do almost anything provided that it holds the readers' attention by telling them something they want or need to know, or are reminded of with pleasure.

But even a substantial paragraph, as we shall soon see, does not guarantee the reader's attention, because readers (like writers) are often lazy and impatient. The important difference is that readers can afford to be. If they find that they must work too hard to understand you, if they are puzzled or confused by what you write, if the effort they must expend is greater than their reward, they can—and will—stop reading. The art of writing is in large part the art of keeping your readers' goodwill while you teach them what you want them to learn. Now, experienced writers can usually tell—not so much while they are writing as while they are revising—what does or does not make a satisfactory unit, and their paragraphs do not always exactly follow the principles we are going to suggest. But we think that by following these principles, more or less as you might practice finger exercises in learning how to play the piano, you will develop a sense of paragraphing. Or, to put it another way, you will improve your sense of how to develop an idea.

Paragraph Unity: Topic Sentences, Topic Ideas

The idea developed in each paragraph often appears, briefly stated, as a topic sentence. Topic sentences are most useful, and are therefore especially common, in paragraphs that offer arguments; they are much less common, because they are less useful, in narrative and descriptive paragraphs.

The topic sentence usually is the first sentence in the paragraph—or the second, following a transitional sentence—because writers usually want their readers to know from the start where the paragraph is going. Sometimes, though, you may not wish to forecast what is to come; you may prefer to put your topic sentence at the end of the paragraph, summarizing the points that earlier sentences have made, or drawing a generalization based on the earlier details. Even if you do not include a topic sentence anywhere in the paragraph, the paragraph should have a topic idea—an idea that holds the sentences together.

Examples of Topic Sentences at Beginning and at End, and of Topic Ideas

1. The following paragraph begins with a topic sentence.

The Marx Brothers' three best films at Paramount—*Monkey Business* (1931), *Horse Feathers* (1932), and *Duck Soup* (1933)—all hurl comic mud at the gleaming marble pillars of the American temple. The target of *Monkey Business* is money and high society, the rich society snobs merely happen to be gangsters who made their money from bootlegging. The target of *Horse Feathers* is the university; knowledge and the pursuit of it are reduced to thievery, bribery, lechery, and foolishness. The target of *Duck Soup* is democracy and government itself; grandiose political ceremonies, governmental bodies, international diplomacy, the law courts, and war are reduced to the absurd. All three films also parody popular "serious" genres—gangster films, college films, and romantic European-kingdom films. The implication of this spoofing is that the sanctified institution is as hollow and dead as the cinematic cliché; the breezy, chaotic, revolutionary activities of the comic anarchists give society's respectable calcifications a much-deserved comeuppance.

—GERALD MAST

The first sentence announces the topic. Everything that follows this topic sentence develops or amplifies it, first by commenting one by one on the three films named at the outset, then by speaking of the three films as a group, and then by offering a closely related generalization (the films spoof serious films) and a comment on the implications of this generalization. In short, the writer begins by stating or summarizing his idea, then offers specific evidence to support it, and then offers a related idea. The development is from the general to the particular and then again to the general.

2. The next paragraph has its topic sentence at the end:

If we try to recall Boris Karloff's face as the monster in the film of *Frankenstein* (1931), most of us probably think of the seams holding the pieces together, and if we cannot recall other details we assume that the face evokes horror. But when we actually look at a picture of the face rather than recall a memory of it, we are perhaps chiefly impressed by the high, steep forehead (a feature often associated with intelligence), by the darkness surrounding the eyes (often associated with physical or spiritual weariness), and by the gaunt cheeks and the thin lips slightly turned down at the corners (associated with deprivation or restraint). The monster's face is of course in some ways shocking, but probably our chief impression as we look at it is that this is not the face of one who causes suffering but of one who himself is heroically undergoing suffering.

—LESLIE RODRIGUEZ

What is the difference between putting the topic sentence at the beginning and putting it at the end? A paragraph that begins with the topic sentence offers readers the satisfaction of receiving, as they move through the paragraph, what was promised at the outset. On the other hand a paragraph with the topic sentence at the end, such as this one on the monster, usually offers readers the pleasure of mild suspense during most of the paragraph and finally, in the topic sentence, offers the clarification that they had half anticipated.

When the topic sentence is at the end, the paragraph usually develops from the particular to the general, the topic sentence serving to generalize or summarize the information that precedes it. Such a topic sentence can be especially effective in presenting an argument: the reader hears, considers, and accepts the evidence before the argument is explicitly stated, and if the evidence has been effectively presented the reader willingly accepts the conclusion.

3. The next paragraph has no topic sentence:

A few years ago when you mentioned Walt Disney at a respectable party—or anyway this is how it was in California, where I was then—the standard response was a headshake and a groan. Intellectuals spoke of how he butchered the classics—from *Pinocchio* to *Winnie the Pooh,* how his wildlife pictures were sadistic and coy, how the World's Fair sculptures of hippopotamuses were a national if not international disgrace. A few crazies disagreed, and since crazies are always the people to watch, it began to be admitted that the early Pluto movies had a considerable measure of *je ne sais quoi,* that the background animation in *Snow White* was "quite extraordinary," that *Fantasia* did indeed have *one* great sequence (then it became two; now everyone says three, though there's fierce disagreement on exactly which three).

—JOHN GARDNER

The topic here is, roughly, "Intellectuals used to scorn Disney, but recently they have been praising him." Such a sentence could easily begin the paragraph, but it is not necessary because even without it the reader has no difficulty following the discussion. The first two sentences talk about Disney's earlier reputation; then the sentence about the "crazies" introduces the contrary view and the rest of the paragraph illustrates the growing popularity of this contrary view. The paragraph develops its point so clearly and consistently (it is essentially a narrative, in chronological order) that the reader, unlike the reader of a complex analytic paragraph, does not need the help of a topic sentence either at the beginning, to prepare for what follows, or at the end, to pull the whole together.

Unifying Ideas into Paragraphs

Although we emphasize unity in paragraphs, don't assume that every development or refinement or alteration of your thought requires a new paragraph. Such an assumption would lead to an essay consisting entirely of one-sentence paragraphs. A good paragraph may, for instance, both ask a question and answer it, or describe an effect and then explain the cause, or set forth details and then offer a generalization. Indeed, if the question or the effect or the details can be set forth in a sentence or two, and the answer or the cause or the generalization can be set forth in a sentence or two, the two halves of the topic should be pulled together into a single paragraph. Only if the question (for example) is long and complex and the answer equally long or longer, will you need two or more paragraphs—or, to put it more precisely, will your reader need two or more paragraphs.

Let's consider three paragraphs from an essay on ballooning. In the essay from which the following paragraphs are taken, the writer has already explained that ballooning was born in late eighteenth-century France and that almost from its start there were two types of balloons, gas and hot air. Notice that in the paragraphs printed below the first is on gas, the second is chiefly on hot air (but it helpfully makes comparisons with gas), and the third is on the length of flights of both gas and hot-air balloons. In other words, each paragraph is about one thing—gas balloons, hot-air balloons, length of flight—but each paragraph also builds on what the reader has learned in the previous paragraphs. That the third paragraph is about the flights of gas *and* of hot-air balloons does not mean that it lacks unity; it is a unified discussion of flight lengths.

> Gas balloons swim around in air like a sleeping fish in water, because they weigh about the same as the fluid they're in. A good, big, trans-Atlantic balloon will have 2,000 pounds of vehicle, including gas bag and pilot, taking up about 30 cubic feet (as big as a refrigerator), plus 300 pounds of a "nothing" stuff called helium, which fills 30,000 cubic feet (as big as three houses). Air to fill this 30,000 cubic feet would also weigh 2,300 pounds, so the balloon system averages the same as air, floating in it as part of the wind.
>
> Hot-air balloons use the same size bag filled with hot air instead of helium, kept hot by a boot-sized blowtorch riding just over the pilot's head. Hot air is light, but not as light as helium, so you can't carry as much equipment in a hot-air balloon. You also can't fly as long or as far. Helium will carry a balloon for days (three and a half days is the record), until a lot of gas has leaked out. But a hot-air balloon cools down in minutes, like a house as soon as its heat source runs out of fuel; and today's best fuel (heat for-weight), propane, lasts only several hours.
>
> A good hot-air flight goes a hundred miles, yet the gas record is 1,897 miles, set by a German in 1914 with the junk (by today's standards) they had then. Unmanned scientific gas balloons have flown half a million miles, staying up more than a year. Japan bombed Oregon in World War II with balloons. Two hot-air balloonists, Tracy Barnes and Malcolm Forbes, have made what they called transcontinental flights, but each was the sum of dozens of end-to-end hops, trailed by pick-up trucks, like throwing a frisbee from Hollywood to Atlantic City.
>
> —DAVID ROYCE

Now contrast the unity of any of the previous three paragraphs on ballooning with the lack of focus in this paragraph from a book on athletic coaching.

> Leadership qualities are a prerequisite for achievement in coaching. A leader is one who is respected for what he says and does, and who is admired by his team. The coach gains respect by giving respect, and by possessing knowledge and skills associated with the sport. There are many "successful" coaches who are domineering, forceful leaders, gaining power more through fear and even hate than through respect. These military-type men are primarily from the old school of thought, and many younger coaches are achieving their goals through more humanistic approaches.

Something is wrong here. The first half of the paragraph tells us that "a leader is one who is respected for what he says and does," but the second half of the paragraph contradicts that assertion, telling us that "many" leaders hold their position "more through fear and even hate than through respect." The trouble is *not* that the writer is talking about two kinds of leaders; a moment ago we saw that a writer can in one paragraph talk about two kinds of balloons. The trouble here is that we need a unifying idea if these two points are to be given in one paragraph. The idea might be: There are two kinds of leaders, those who are respected and those who are feared. This idea might be developed along these lines:

> Leadership qualities are a prerequisite for achievement in coaching, but these qualities can be of two radically different kinds. One kind of leader is respected and admired by his team for what he says and does. The coach gains respect by giving respect, and by possessing knowledge and skills associated with the sport. The other kind of coach is a domineering, forceful leader, gaining power more through fear than through respect. These military-type men are primarily from the old school of thought, whereas most of the younger coaches achieve their goals through the more humane approaches of the first type.

Organization in Paragraphs

A paragraph needs more than a unified point; it needs a reasonable organization or sequence. After all, a box containing all of the materials for a model airplane has unity (all the parts of the plane are there), but not until the parts are joined in the proper relationship do we get a plane. In the following paragraph, a sentence is out of place.

> Leonardo da Vinci's *Mona Lisa* has attracted and puzzled viewers for almost five hundred years, and I don't suffer from the delusion that I can fully account for the spell the picture casts. Still, I think it is easy enough to account for at least part of the mystery. The most expressive features of a face are the mouth and the eyes, and we notice that Leonardo slightly blurred or shaded the corners of the mouth so that its exact expression cannot be characterized, or, if we characterize it, we change our mind when we look again. Lisa herself is something of a mystery, for history tells us nothing about her personality or about her relationship to Leonardo. The corners of her eyes, like the corners of her mouth, are slightly obscured, contributing to her elusive expression.

Which sentence is out of place in the paragraph you have just read? How might you work it into its proper place?

Exactly how the parts of a paragraph will fit together depends, of course, on what the paragraph is doing.

1. If it is *describing* a place, it may move from (for example) a general view to the significant details—or from immediately striking details to some less obvious but perhaps more important ones. It may move from near to far, or from far to near, or from the past to the present.

2. If it is *explaining,* it may move from (for example) cause to effect, or from effect to cause, or from past to present; or it may offer an example.

3. If it is *arguing,* it may move (for example) from evidence to conclusion, or from a conclusion to supporting evidence; or it may offer one piece of evidence, for instance an anecdote (a short narrative), that illustrates the argument.

In the following paragraph, written by a student, we move *chronologically*—from waking at 7:00 A.M., to washing and combing, to readiness for the day's work, and then to a glance at the rest of the day that will undo the 7:00 A.M. cleanup.

> I can remember waking at seven to Ma's call. I'd bound out of bed because Ma just didn't allow people to be lazy. She'd grab me and we'd rush to the bathroom for the morning ritual. Bathing, tooth-brushing, lotioning, all overseen by her watchful eyes. She didn't let anything go by. No missing behind the ears, no splashing around and pretending to bathe. I bathed and scrubbed and put that lotion on till my

```
whole body was like butter on a warm pan. After
inspection it was back to my room and the day's
clothes were selected. A bit of tugging and I was
dressed. Then she'd sit me down and pull out the big
black comb. That comb would glide through my hair and
then the braiding would begin. My head would jerk but
I never yelled, never even whimpered. Finally I was
ready. Ready to start the day and get dirty and spoil
all of Ma's work. But she didn't care. She knew you
couldn't keep a child from getting dirty but you could
teach it to be respectable.
```

If a paragraph is classifying (dividing a subject into its parts) it may begin by enumerating the parts and go on to study each, perhaps in climactic order. Here is an example.

The chief reasons people wear masks are these: to have fun, to protect themselves, to disguise themselves, and to achieve a new identity. At Halloween, children wear masks for fun; they may, of course, also think they are disguising themselves, but chiefly their motive is to experience the joy of saying "boo" to someone. Soldiers wore masks for protection, in ancient times against swords and battle-axes, in more recent times against poison gas. Bank robbers wear masks to disguise themselves, and though of course this disguise is a sort of protection, a robber's reason for wearing a mask is fairly distinct from a soldier's. All of these reasons so far are easily understood, but we may have more trouble grasping the reason that primitive people use masks in religious rituals. Some ritual masks seem merely to be attempts to frighten away evil spirits, and some seem merely to be disguises so that the evil spirits will not know who the wearer is. But most religious masks are worn with the idea that the wearer achieves a new identity, a union with supernatural powers, and thus in effect the wearer becomes—really becomes, not merely pretends to be—a new person.

Notice that the first sentence offers four reasons for wearing masks. The rest of the paragraph amplifies these reasons, one by one, and in the order indicated in the first sentence. Since the writer regards the last reason as the most interesting and the most difficult to grasp, he discusses it at the greatest length, giving it about as much space as he gives to the first three reasons altogether.

The way in which a paragraph is organized, then, will depend on what the writer is trying to do—what the writer's purpose is. Almost always one of the writer's purposes is to make something clear to a reader. Among the common methods of organizing a paragraph, and keeping things clear, are the following:

1. General to particular (topic sentence usually at the beginning)
2. Particular to general (topic sentence usually at the end)
3. Enumeration of parts or details or reasons (probably in climactic order)
4. Question and answer
5. Cause and effect
6. Comparison and contrast
7. Analogy
8. Chronology
9. Spatial order (e.g., near to far, or right to left)

The only rule that can cover all paragraphs is this: readers must never feel that they are stumbling as they try to follow the writer to the end of the paragraph.

Vladimir Koziakin. *Spaghetti.*

They should not have to go back and read the paragraph again to figure out what the writer had in mind. It is the writer's job, not the reader's, to give the paragraph its unity and organization. A paragraph is not a maze; it should be organized so that the reader can glide through it in seconds, not minutes.

Coherence in Paragraphs

In addition to having a unified point and a reasonable organization, a good paragraph is coherent: A reader can unhesitatingly follow its train of thought. Coherence can often be achieved, in revising a paragraph, by inserting the right transitional words or by taking care to repeat key words.

Transitions

Richard Wagner, commenting on his work as a composer of operas, once said "The art of composition is the art of transition," for his art moved from note to note, measure to measure, scene to scene. Because transitions establish connections between points, they contribute to coherence. Here are some of the most common transitional words and phrases. In effect, they are cues that alert the reader to what will follow.

1. **amplification or likeness:**

similarly, likewise, and, also, again, second, third, in addition, furthermore, moreover, finally

2. **emphasis:**

chiefly, equally, indeed, even more important

3. **contrast or concession:**

but, on the contrary, on the other hand, by contrast, of course, however, still, doubtless, no doubt, nevertheless, granted that, conversely, although, admittedly

4. **example:**

for example, for instance, as an example, specifically, consider as an illustration, that is, such as, like

5. **consequence or cause and effect:**

thus, so, then, it follows, as a result, therefore, hence

6. **restatement:**

in short, that is, in effect, in other words

7. **place:**

in the foreground, further back, in the distance

8. **time:**

afterward, next, then, as soon as, later, until, when, finally, last, at last

9. **conclusion:**

finally, therefore, thus, to sum up

Consider the following paragraph:

> Folklorists are just beginning to look at Africa. A great quantity of folk-lore materials has been gathered from African countries in the past century and published by missionaries, travelers, administrators, linguists, and anthropologists incidentally to their main pursuits. No fieldworker has devoted himself exclusively or even largely to the recording and analysis of folklore materials, according to a committee of the African Studies Association reporting in 1966 on the state of research in the African arts. Yet Africa is the continent supreme for traditional cultures that nurture folklore. Why this neglect?
>
> —RICHARD M. DORSON

The reader gets the point, but the second sentence seems to contradict the first: the first sentence tells us that folklorists are just beginning to look at Africa, but the next tells us that lots of folklore has been collected. An "although" between these sentences would clarify the author's point, especially if the third sentence were hooked on to the second, thus:

> Folklorists are just beginning to look at Africa. Although a great quantity of folklore materials has been gathered from African countries in the past century by missionaries, travelers, administrators, linguists, and anthropologists incidentally to their main pursuits, no fieldworker has devoted himself . . .

But this revision gives us an uncomfortably long second sentence. Further revision would help. The real point of the original passage, though it is smothered, is that although many people have incidentally collected folklore materials in Africa, professional folklorists have not been active there. The contrast ought to be sharpened:

> Folklorists are just beginning to look at Africa. True, missionaries, travelers, administrators, linguists, and anthropologists have collected a quantity of folklore materials incidentally to their main pursuits, but folklorists have lagged behind. No fieldworker . . .

In this revision the words that clarify are, of course, the small but important words "true" and "but." The original paragraph is a jigsaw puzzle, missing some tiny but necessary pieces.

When you are writing a first draft, of course, you need not stop and worry about whether or not the transitions in your thoughts will be clear to a reader. For most writers, saying something and saying it clearly are two different processes, and if you are like most writers it is best to attend to one thing at a time. The first thing is to get something down on paper. But after you have a rough draft, reread it with a reader in mind. Check each paragraph, sentence by sentence, to see if each sentence is clearly related to the preceding one. Ask yourself if a transitional word or phrase ("first," "in addition," "nevertheless," "by contrast") would make the relationship clearer to your reader. If you find that the relationship is unclear, you may have to do more than provide a transition; you may have to rethink the point or extensively revise the sentence. In any case, your goal is to allow your imagined reader, furnished with proper clues, to move effortlessly through your essay.

Repetition

Coherence is also achieved through the repetition of key words. When you repeat words or phrases, or when you provide clear substitutes (such as pronouns and demonstrative adjectives), you are helping the reader to keep step with your developing thoughts. Grammatical constructions too can be repeated, the repetitions or parallels linking the sentences or ideas.

In the following example, notice how the repetitions provide continuity.

> Sir Kenneth Clark's *The Nude* is an important book; and, luckily, it is also most readable; but it is not a bedside book. Each sentence needs attention because each sentence is relevant to the whole, and the incorrigible skipper will sometimes find himself obliged to turn back several pages, chapters even in order to pick up the thread of the argument. Does this sound stiff? The book is not stiff because it is delightfully written. Let the student have no fears; he is not going to be bored for a moment while he reads these 400 pages; he is going to be excited, amused, instructed, provoked, charmed, irritated, and surprised.

Notice not only the exact repetitions ("each sentence," "stiff") but also the slight variations, such as "an important book," "not a bedside book"; "he is not going," "he is going"; and the emphatic list of participles ("excited, amused, instructed," and so on) at the conclusion.

Here is another example of a paragraph that unobtrusively uses repetition.

> The main skill is to keep from getting lost. Since the roads are used only by local people who know them by sight nobody complains if the junctions aren't posted. And often they aren't. When they are it's usually a small sign hiding unobtrusively in the weeds and that's all. Country-road-sign makers seldom tell you twice. If you miss that sign in the weeds that's *your* problem, not theirs. Moreover, you discover that the highway maps are often inaccurate about country roads. And from time to time you find your "county road" takes you onto a two-rutter and then a single rutter and then into a pasture and stops, or else it takes you into some farmer's backyard.

—ROBERT M. PIRSIG

What repetitions do you note? (For additional comments on repetition and variation as transitions, see page 128.)

Transitions Between Paragraphs

As you move from one paragraph to the next—from one step in the development of your thesis to the next—you probably can keep the reader with you if you make the first sentence of each new paragraph a transition, or perhaps a transition and a topic sentence. The first sentence of a paragraph that could follow the paragraph quoted a moment ago on Kenneth Clark's *The Nude* might run thus:

> Among the chief delights of these 400 pages are the illustrations.

Clearly "Among the chief delights of these 400 pages" is a transition, picking up the reference to "400 pages" near the end of the previous paragraph, and the rest of the sentence introduces the topic—the illustrations—of the new paragraph. Often a single transitional word or phrase (such as those listed on page 62) will suffice.

Paragraph Length

Of course, hard-and-fast rules cannot be made about the lengths of paragraphs, but more often than not a good paragraph is between 100 and 200 words, consisting of more than one or two but fewer than eight or ten sentences. It is not a matter, however, of counting words or sentences; paragraphs are coherent blocks, substantial units of your essay, and the spaces between them are brief resting places allowing the reader to take in what you have said. One page of typing (approximately 250 words) is about as much as the reader can take before requiring a slight break. On the other hand, one page of typing with half a dozen paragraphs is probably faulty because the reader is too often interrupted with needless pauses and because the page has too few *developed* ideas: an assertion is made, and then another, and another. They are unconvincing because they are not supported with detail. To put it another way, a paragraph is a room in the house you are building. If your essay is some five hundred words long (about two double-spaced typewritten pages) you probably will not break it down into more than four or five rooms or paragraphs; if you break it down into a dozen paragraphs, readers will feel they are touring a rabbit warren rather than a house.

The Use and Abuse of Short Paragraphs

A short paragraph can be effective when it summarizes a highly detailed previous paragraph or group of paragraphs, or when it serves as a transition between two complicated paragraphs, but unless you are sure that the reader needs a break, avoid thin paragraphs. A paragraph that is nothing but a transition can usually be altered into a transitional phrase or clause or sentence that starts the next paragraph. But of course there are times when a short paragraph is exactly right. Notice the effect of the two-sentence paragraph between two longer paragraphs:

> After I returned to prison, I took a long look at myself and, for the first time in my life, admitted that I was wrong, that I had gone astray—astray not so much from the white man's law as from being human, civilized—for I could not approve the act of rape. Even though I had some insight into my own motivations, I did not feel justified. I lost my self-respect. My pride as a man dissolved and my whole fragile moral structure seemed to collapse, completely shattered.
>
> That is why I started to write. To save myself.
>
> I realized that no one could save me but myself. The prison authorities were both uninterested and unable to help me. I had to seek out the truth and unravel the snarled web of my motivations. I had to find out who I am and what I want to be, what type of man I should be, and what I could do to become the best of which I was capable. I understood that what had happened to me had also happened to countless other blacks and it would happen to many, many more.

> —ELDRIDGE CLEAVER

If the content of the second paragraph were less momentous, it would hardly merit a paragraph. Here the brevity helps to contribute to the enormous impact; those two simple sentences, set off by themselves, are meant to be equal in weight, so to speak, to the longer paragraphs that precede and follow. They are the hinge on which the door turns.

Now read the following horrible example, a newspaper account—chiefly in paragraphs of one sentence each—of an unfortunate happening.

Reuters

Fish Eat Brazilian Fisherman

1   MANAUS, BRAZIL—Man-eating piranha fish devoured fisherman Zeca Vicente when he tumbled into the water during a battle with 300 farmers for possession of an Amazon jungle lake.

2   Vicente, a leader of a group of 30 fishermen, was eaten alive in minutes by shoals of the ferocious fish lurking in Lake Januaca.

3   He died when the farmers—packed in an armanda of small boats—attacked the fishermen with hunting rifles, knives, and bows and arrows after they refused to leave.

4   The farmers, who claimed the fishermen were depleting the lake's fish stocks, one of their main sources of food, boarded the fishing vessels and destroyed cold storage installations.

5   Last to give way was Vicente, who tried to cut down the farmers' leader with a knife. But farmers shot him and he fell wounded into the water, and into the jaws of the piranhas.

6   Fifteen persons have been charged with the attack which caused Vicente's death and the injury of several other fishermen.

7   Lake Januaca, about four hours from this Amazon River town by launch, is famous for its pirarucu and tucunare fish which are regarded as table delicacies.

Most marvelously wrong is the final paragraph, with its cool—and therefore utterly inappropriate—guidebook voice, but what concerns us at the moment is the journalist's common practice of writing one-sentence paragraphs. Probably all six paragraphs (the seventh, final paragraph is irrelevant) can be effectively combined into one paragraph. Better, perhaps, the material can be divided into two paragraphs, one describing the event and another describing the cause or background. At the most, there is the stuff of three paragraphs, one on the background, one on the event itself, and one on the consequences (fifteen people are charged with the attack). Imagine how it could be reorganized into one paragraph, into two paragraphs, and into three. Which do you think would be most effective? Even the present final paragraph can be worked in. How?

If you spend a few minutes revising the newspaper account of the Brazilian fisherman's death, you will notice that sometimes you can make at least a small improvement merely by joining one paragraph to the next, such as the second to the third. But unsatisfactory short paragraphs usually cannot be repaired to simply; most are unsatisfactory not because sentences have been needlessly separated from each other, but because sentences with generalizations have not been supported by details. Consider these two consecutive paragraphs from a draft of a student's essay on Leonardo's *Mona Lisa.*

Leonardo's "Mona Lisa," painted about 1502, has caused many people to wonder about the lady's expression. Different viewers see different things

The explanation of the puzzle is chiefly in the mysterious expression that Leonardo conveys. The mouth and the eyes are especially important.

Here is the student's revised version, strengthening the two thin paragraphs of the draft.

Leonardo's "Mona Lisa," painted about 1502, has caused many people to wonder about the lady's expression. Doubtless she is remarkably life-like but exactly what experience of life, what mood, does she reveal? Is she sad, or gently mocking, or uncertain or self-satisfied, or lost in daydreams? Why are we never satisfied when we try to name her emotion?

Part of the uncertainty may of course be due to the subject as a whole. What can we make out of the combination of this smiling lady and that utterly unpopulated landscape? But surely a large part of the explanation lies in the way that Leonardo painted the face's two most expressive features, the eyes and the mouth. He slightly obscured the corners of these, so that we cannot precisely characterize them: and although on one viewing we may see them one way, on another viewing we may see them slightly differently. If today we think she looks detached, tomorrow we may think she looks slightly threatening.

This revision is not simply a padded version of the earlier paragraphs; it is a necessary clarification of them, for without the details the generalizations mean almost nothing to a reader.

Introductory Paragraphs

As the poet Byron said, at the beginning of a long part of a long poem, "Nothing so difficult as a beginning." Woody Allen thinks so too. In an interview he said that the toughest part of writing is "to go from nothing to the first draft."

We can give two pieces of advice. Unfortunately, they are apparently contradictory.

1. *The opening paragraph is unimportant.* It's great if you can write a paragraph that will engage your readers and let them know where the essay will be taking them, but if you can't come up with such a paragraph, just put down anything in order to prime the pump.

2. *The opening paragraph is extremely important.* It must engage your readers, and, probably by means of a thesis sentence it should let the readers know where the essay will be taking them.

The contradiction is, as we said, only apparent, not real. The first point is relevant to the opening paragraph of a *draft;* the second point is relevant to the opening paragraph of the *final version.* Almost all writers—professionals as well as amateurs—find that the first paragraphs in their drafts are false starts. Don't worry too much about the opening paragraphs of your draft; you'll almost surely want to revise your opening later anyway. (Surprisingly often your first paragraph may simply be deleted; your second, you may find, is where your essay truly begins.)

When writing a first draft you merely need something—almost anything may do—to break the ice. But in your finished paper the opening cannot be mere throat-clearing. The opening should be interesting. Among the commonest *un*interesting openings are:

1. A dictionary definition ("Webster says. . . .")

2. A restatement of your title. The title is (let's assume) "Anarchism and the Marx Brothers," and the first sentence says, "This essay will study the anarchic acts of the Marx Brothers." True, there is a thesis statement here, but there is no information about the topic beyond what has already been given in the title, and there is no information about you either—that is, no sense of your response to the topic, such as might be present in, say, "The Marx Brothers are funny, but one often has the feeling that under the fun the violence has serious implications."

3. A broad generalization, such as "Ever since the beginning of time, human beings have been violent." Again, such a sentence may be fine if it helps you to start drafting, but because it sounds canned and because it is insufficiently interesting it should not remain in your final version.

What is left? What *is* a good way for a final version to begin? Your introductory paragraph will be at least moderately interesting if it gives information, and it will be pleasing if the information provides focus: that is, if it lets the reader know exactly what your topic is, and where you will be going. Remember, when you write, *you* are the teacher; it won't do to begin,

```
George Orwell says he shot the elephant because
. . .
```

We need some information, identifying the text you are writing about.

```
George Orwell, in "Shooting an Elephant," says he
shot the elephant because . . .
```

Even better is,

```
In "Shooting an Elephant," George Orwell sets
forth his reflections on his service as a policeman in
Burma. He suggests that he once shot an elephant
because . . . but his final paragraph suggests that we
must look for additional reasons.
```

Compare, for example, the opening sentences from three essays written by students on Anne Moody's *Coming of Age in Mississippi*. The book is the autobiography of an African-American woman, covering her early years with her sharecropper parents, her schooling, and finally her work in the civil rights movement.

> The environment that surrounds a person from an early age tends to be a major factor in determining their character.

This is what we call a **zonker** (see page 84), an all-purpose sentence that serves no specific purpose well. Notice also the faulty reference of the pronoun (the plural "their" refers to the singular "a person"), the weaseling of "tends to be a major factor," and the vagueness of "early age" and "environment" and "character." These all warn us that the writer will waste our time.

> It is unfortunate but true that racial or color prejudice shows itself early in the life of a child.

Less pretentious than the first example, but it labors the obvious, and sounds annoyingly preachy:

> Anne Moody's autobiography, *Coming of Age in Mississippi*, vividly illustrates how she discovered her identity as an African-American.

Surely this is the best of the three openings. Informative and focused, it identifies the book's theme and method, and it offers an evaluation. The essayist has been considerate of her readers: if we are interested in women's autobiographies or life in the South, we will read on. If we aren't, we are grateful to her for letting us off the bus at the first stop.

Let's look now not simply at an opening sentence but at an entire opening paragraph. Here is an example from a relatively personal essay, an essay entitled "Interviewing for Oral History." As a reader can guess from the title, and from the paragraph, the student's focus is on how to conduct an interview. She begins by briefly telling the reader how she acquired her experience, but she also provides a focus; by the end of the paragraph the reader knows that the essay will give information about how to conduct an interview.

> Waltham will celebrate its 250th birthday this year with a six hundred page hardcover book containing more than four hundred photographs. This document,

which took over two years to complete, details
Waltham's ethnic history with taped, personal
interviews of first and second generation residents.
As a volunteer for the Interviewing Project, I not
only had the pleasure of hearing about historical
events firsthand from the people who experienced them,
but I also learned something else: I learned how to
interview for oral histories.

Here is a second example, this one from a less personal and more analytic
essay. Notice how the student provides the reader with the necessary
information about the book he is discussing (the diary of a man whose son is
brain-damaged) and also focuses the reader's attention on the topic that he will
discuss (the quality that distinguishes this diary from others).

Josh Greenfeld's diary, *A Place for Noah*, records
the attempts of a smart, thoughtful man to reconcile
himself to his son's autism, a severe mental and
physical disorder. Most diaries function as havens for
secret thoughts. And Greenfeld's diary does frequently
supply a voice to Greenfeld's darkest fears about who
will ultimately care for Noah. It provides, too, an
intimate glimpse of a family striving to remain a
coherent unit despite their tragedy. But beyond
affording such urgent and personal revelations. *A
Place for Noah,* in chronicling the isolation of the
Greenfelds, reveals how inadequate and ineffectual our
medical and educational systems are in responding to
families victimized by catastrophic illness.

Again, these two examples are from final versions, not from drafts. They
are both fairly direct, but of course you can provide interest and focus by other,
more indirect means, among them the following:

- A quotation
- An anecdote or other short narrative
- An interesting fact (a statistic, for instance, showing the reader that you know something about your topic)
- A definition of an important term—but not merely one derived from a desk dictionary
- An assertion (in an essay offering a proposal) that a problem exists
- A glance at the opposition (disposing of it)
- A question—but an interesting one, such as "Why do we call some words obscene?"

Many excellent opening paragraphs do not use any of these devices, and you need not use any of them if they seem unnatural to you. But observe in your reading how widely and successfully these devices are used. Here is an example of the second device, an anecdote that makes an effective, indeed an unnerving, introduction to an essay on aging.

> There is an old American folk tale about a wooden bowl. It seems that Grandmother, with her trembling hands, was guilty of occasionally breaking a dish. Her daughter angrily gave her a wooden bowl, and told her that she must eat out of it from now on. The young granddaughter, observing this, asked her mother why Grandmother must eat from a wooden bowl when the rest of the family was given china plates. "Because she is old!" answered her mother. The child thought for a moment and then told her mother, "You must save the wooden bowl when Grandma dies." Her mother asked why, and the child replied, "For when you are old."
>
> —Sharon R. Curtin

The following paragraph—the first in a student's essay comparing two portraits by the American painter John Singleton Copley—also begins with a story, this one a bit of autobiography.

> Several Sundays ago while I was wandering through the Museum of Fine Arts, a professorial bellow shook me. Around the corner strode a well-dressed mustachioed member of the art historical elite, a gaggle of note-taking students following in his wake. "And here," he said, "we have John Singleton Copley." He marshalled his group about the rotunda, explaining that, "as one can easily see from these paintings, Copley never really learned to paint until he went to England."

The third strategy, an interesting detail, shows the reader that you know something about your topic and that you are worth reading. We have already seen (page 53) a rather quiet example of this device, in a paragraph about

Charles Darwin, which began "Charles Darwin's youth was unmarked by signs of genius." Here is a more obvious example, from an essay on blue jeans:

> That blue jeans or denims are not found only in Texas is not surprising if we recall that jeans are named for Genoa (Gene), where the cloth was first made, and that denim is cloth *de Nimes,* that is, from Nimes, a city in France.

Interesting information about the origins of a word can easily be found by consulting a college dictionary.

The fourth strategy, a definition, is fairly common in analytic essays; the essayist first clears the ground by specifying what the topic really is, or at least what the topic in the speaker's mind is. Here is the beginning of an essay on bilingual education.

> Let's begin by defining "bilingual education." As commonly used today, the term does *not* mean teaching students a language other than English (almost everyone would agree that foreign-language instruction should be available, and that it is desirable for Americans to be fluent not only in English but also in some other language); nor does "bilingual education" mean offering courses in English as a second language to students whose native language is, for example, Chinese, or Spanish or Navajo or Aleut. (Again, almost everyone would agree that such instruction should be offered where economically possible.) Rather, it means offering instruction in such courses as mathematics, history, and science *in the student's native language,* while also offering courses in English as a second language. Programs vary in details, but the idea is that the non-native speaker should be spared the trauma of total immersion in English until he or she has completed several years of studying English as a second language. During this period, instruction in other subjects is given in the student's native language.

> —TINA BAKKA

Here is yet another example of an opening definition, this one a bit less formal. It comes from a review of a book called *Snow White, Blood Red.*

> When something is classified as an "adult book," you don't know whether to look for it among the classics or on the pornography shelf. *Snow White, Blood Red* is described by one of its editors as an anthology of "adult" fairy tales, and this time the word carries both meanings. What makes this book adult is a sophistication that reaches beyond the scope of children, as well as a dose of sexually graphic content. The result is a strange hybrid that is at times puzzling and at other times as disturbing as some of the characters found in these retold tales.

> —MEG WOLITZER

The fifth strategy, the assertion that a problem exists, is common in essays that make proposals. The following example is the first paragraph of an essay that offers suggestions to employers on how to deal with discontented employees. Notice that the paragraph does not in fact offer the author's proposal; it simply points out that there really is an unsolved problem, and the reader infers that the essay will provide the solution.

> For over four decades, management has been jumping on and off a suc-
> cession of behavioral-science bandwagons searching for *the* answer to
> harmonious and productive industrial relations:
> —Human relations in the 1930's and 1940's
>
> —Participative management in the 1950's
>
> —T-groups in the 1960's
>
> —Job enrichment in the 1970's
> Despite considerable enthusiasm and a few well-publicized successes,
> these and other potentially effective behavioral-science tools have had a
> discouragingly high failure rate in the corporate sector. Moreover, in
> the current climate of employee alienation and mounting grievances
> about nonfinancial matters, management is increasingly turning to the
> behavioral theorists for help—with similarly disappointing results.
>
> —DAVID SIROTA AND ALAN D. WOLFSON

The sixth strategy, a glance at the opposition, is especially effective if the opposing view is well-established, but while you state it, you should manage to convey your distrust of it. We have already seen one example, in the paragraph about Copley's paintings. How does the writer convey her distrust of the opinion quoted in the paragraph? She tells us that she heard a "bellow" and she saw "a well-dressed mustachioed member of the art historical elite" leading "a gaggle of note-taking students." She then quotes the man's condescending remark about Copley: "One can easily see from these paintings, Copley never really learned to paint until he went to England." Surely it's not hard to sense that the essay will argue against this smug evaluation. Her next paragraph explicitly states her thesis.

Here is another example of a paragraph that glances at the opposition:

> One often hears, correctly, that there is a world food crisis, and one al-
> most as often hears that not enough food is produced to feed the
> world's entire population. The wealthier countries, it is said, jeopardize
> their own chances for survival when they attempt to subsidize all of the
> poorer countries in which the masses are starving. Often the life-boat
> analogy is offered: There is room in the boat for only X people, and to
> take in $X + 1$ is to overload the boat and to invite the destruction of all.
> But is it true that the world cannot and does not produce enough food to
> save the whole population from starving?
>
> —V. NAGARAJAN

The seventh strategy, a question, is briefly but adequately illustrated by a paragraph from an essay in which a student discussed the connection between Frankenstein and the ancient Greek myth of Prometheus:

> Mary Shelley did not simply call her book *Frankenstein;* she called it *Frankenstein or, The Modern Prometheus.* But who was Prometheus, and why did Mary Shelley include him in the title?

Obviously the writer will go on to summarize the myths of Prometheus (there are more than one), and will demonstrate the correspondence of the relevant myth.

Here is another opening paragraph, about this one from an essay whether it is sometimes permissible for doctors to lie to their patients.

> Should doctors ever lie to benefit their patients—to speed recovery or to conceal the approach of death? In medicine as in law, government, and other lines of work, the requirements of honesty often seem dwarfed by greater needs: the need to shelter from brutal news or to uphold a promise of secrecy; to expose corruption or to promote the public interest.

—Sissela Bok

We have said enough to indicate that there is no one way that must be used for an opening paragraph, but we want to add that you cannot go wrong in suggesting your thesis. Often such a paragraph moves from a rather broad view to a narrower one. This kind of introductory paragraph can be conceived as a funnel, wide at the top and narrowing into what will be the body of the essay. A common version of this kind of paragraph offers some background and concludes with the subject at hand.

> In *Frankenstein,* Mary Shelley frames the novel with narratives of two similar characters who meet markedly different fates. Frankenstein, the medical researcher, and Walton, the explorer, are both passionately determined to push forward the boundaries of human knowledge. But while Walton's ambition to explore unknown regions of the earth is directed by reason and purpose, Frankenstein's ambition to create life is unfocussed and misguided. This difference in the nature of their ambitions determines their fates. Walton's controlled ambition leads him to abandon his goal in order to save the lives of his crew members. When we last see him, he is heading toward home and safety. Frankenstein's unchecked ambition leads to his own death and the self-destruction of his creature.

But bear in mind that although the first sentence of an introductory paragraph may be broader, more general than the last, it must nevertheless have substance. It is obvious, when you think about it, that sentences beginning "Ever since the beginning of time . . . " are too broad. They cannot be substantiated. Less obvious, perhaps, so you must watch out for them, are sentences like the one on Darwin that we quoted at the beginning of this chapter (p. 52). "Charles Darwin's great accomplishments in the field of natural science resulted from many factors" is so broad, so general, so lacking in substance, that it teaches us nothing either about Darwin or about the writer of the essay. If your opening sentence lacks substance, it will not matter what you say next. No one will bother to read more.

Concluding Paragraphs

Concluding paragraphs, like opening paragraphs, are especially difficult if only because they are so conspicuous. Fortunately, you are not always obliged to write one. Descriptive essays, for example, may end merely with a final paragraph, not with a paragraph that draws a conclusion. In an expository essay explaining a process or mechanism you may simply stop when you have finished. Just check to see that the last sentence is a good one, clear and vigorous, and stop. In such essays there is usually no need for a crescendo signaling your farewell to the reader. Persuasive essays are more likely to need concluding paragraphs, not merely final paragraphs. But even persuasive essays, if they are short enough, may end without a formal conclusion; if the last paragraph sets forth the last step of the argument, that may be conclusion enough.

Let's assume, however, that you do feel the need to write a concluding paragraph. With conclusions, as with introductions, try to say something interesting. It is not of the slightest interest to say "Thus we see . . . " and then echo your title and first paragraph. There is some justification for a summary at the end of a long paper because the reader may have half forgotten some of the ideas presented thirty pages earlier, but a paper that can easily be held in the mind needs something different. A good concluding paragraph does more than provide an echo of what the writer has already said. It rounds out the previous discussion, normally with a few sentences that summarize (without the obviousness of "We may now summarize"), but it also may draw an inference that has not previously been expressed. To draw such an inference is not to introduce a new idea—a concluding paragraph is hardly the place for a new idea—but is to see the previous material in a fresh perspective. A good concluding paragraph closes the issue while enriching it. For example, an essay on being assaulted and robbed ends with these two paragraphs:

> What do they take when they rob you? Maybe a thousand dollars' worth of stuff. A car. A jar of pennies and small change—the jar, which they would probably end up breaking, worth more than the change in-

side. A portable radio bought years before at an Army PX. Little things that it takes days to discover are missing.

And what else? The ability to easily enter a darkened apartment or to freely open the door after going out. The worst loss is the sense of private space, whether it's in your head or your home, and you can never be certain it will not be invaded again.

—CHARLES T. POWERS

Powers moves from the theft of material objects to the psychological implications of the theft—that is, to a more profound kind of robbery. This is not a new topic because the idea is implicit throughout a discussion of assault and robbery and so it enlarges rather than abandons the topic. It is just that Powers is explicitly stating the idea for the first time.

In the first two chapters of this book we tried to make the point that what you write depends partly on your audience. It depends also, of course, on you—on your purpose in writing and on your attitude toward your subject and toward your audience. And what you write in your concluding paragraph will depend on everything that precedes it. For instance, if you have been writing an argument and have been bombarding your reader with statistics, you may feel that now is the time to ease up, to end in a more conversational, relaxed manner. Or, conversely, if you have been making your point rather genially, you may feel that in your last paragraph you want to hammer the point home, unforgettably.

Because all writers have to find out what they think about any given topic, and have to find the strategies appropriate for presenting these thoughts to a particular audience, we hesitate to offer a do-it-yourself kit for final paragraphs, but the following simple devices often work:

- End with a quotation, especially a quotation that amplifies or varies a quotation used in the opening paragraph.

- End with some idea or detail from the beginning of the essay and thus bring it full circle.

- End with an allusion, say to a historical or mythological figure or event, putting your topic in a larger framework.

- End with a glance at the readers—not with a demand that they mount the barricades, but with a suggestion that the next move is theirs.

If you adopt any of these devices, do so quietly; the aim is not to write a grand finale, but to complete or round out a discussion.

Here are two concluding paragraphs; notice how they wrap things up and at the same time open out by suggesting a larger frame of reference. The first example, from a student's essay on Anthony Burgess's *A Clockwork Orange*, includes quotations from the book and an allusion to a common expression.

Both worlds, youthful anarchy and repressive
government are undesirable. For while "you can't run a
country with every chelloveck comporting himself in
Alex's manner of the night," there should never be a
government with the power to "turn you into something
other than a human being . . . with no power of choice
any longer." What is frightening is that there is no
apparent solution to this futuristic society's
dilemma. In fact, with the friendly alliance of Alex
and the Minister of the Interior at the end of the
book come hints that society may soon enjoy the worst
of both worlds.

The second is a concluding paragraph from a student's essay on *Black Elk Speaks,* the life story of an Oglala Sioux holy man. The paragraph includes quotations, and then goes on to suggest that the rest is up to the reader.

"Truth comes into this world with two faces. One
is sad with suffering and the other laughs; but it is
the same face." The terrible tragedy of the Indian
people can never fully be undone. Their "hoop is
broken, and there is no center anymore." But perhaps
the rising circulation of Black Elk's story will
inspire people to look more closely into person-to-
person and person-to-nature relationships. Black Elk's
message "was given to him for all men and it is true
and it is beautiful," but it must be listened to,
understood, and acted on.

All essayists will have to find their own ways of ending each essay; the four strategies we have suggested are common but they are not for you if you don't find them comfortable. And so, rather than ending this section with rules about how to end essays, we suggest how not to end them: don't merely summarize, don't say "in conclusion," don't introduce a totally new point, and don't apologize.

A Checklist for Revising Paragraphs

1. Does the paragraph *say* anything? Does it have substance?

2. Does the paragraph have a topic sentence? If so, is it in the best place? If the paragraph doesn't have a topic sentence, might one improve the paragraph? Or does it have a clear topic idea?

3. If the paragraph is an opening paragraph, is it interesting enough to attract and to hold a reader's attention? If it is a later paragraph, does it easily evolve out of the previous paragraph, and lead into the next paragraph?

4. Does the paragraph contain some principle of development, for instance from cause to effect, or from general to particular?

5. Does each sentence clearly follow from the preceding sentence? Have you provided transitional words or cues to guide your reader? Would it be useful to repeat certain key words, for clarity?

6. What is the purpose of the paragraph? Do you want to summarize, or tell a story, or give an illustration, or concede a point, or what? Is your purpose clear to you, and does the paragraph fulfill your purpose?

7. Is the closing paragraph effective, and not an unnecessary restatement of the obvious?

Exercises

1. Reread the paragraph on page 54, in which a topic sentence (about three films by the Marx Brothers) begins the paragraph. Then write a paragraph with a similar construction, clarifying the topic sentence with details. You might, for example, begin thus: "When facing a right-handed batter, a left-handed pitcher has a distinct advantage over a right-handed pitcher." Another possible beginning: "All three major television networks offer pretty much the same kinds of entertainment during prime time."

2. Reread the paragraph on page 55, discussing the face of Frankenstein's monster, and then write a paragraph on some other widely known face, ending your paragraph with a topic sentence. The cover of a recent issue of *Time* or *Newsweek* may provide you with the face you need.

3. The following paragraph is unified, but incoherent. How could it be reorganized?

   Abortion, the expulsion of a fetus which could not develop and function alone successfully, is an issue which has caused much discussion in the past decade. There exist mainly two opposing groups concerning this subject, but many people's opinions lie somewhere in the middle. Some believe that abortions should be legalized unconditionally throughout the United States, while others believe that abortions should be illegal in all cases.

4. The following paragraph is both unified and fairly well organized, but it is still lacking in coherence. What would you do to improve it?

> The cyclist must also master prerace tactics. Not only what to wear and what food to bring are important, but how to strip the bike of unnecessary weight. Cycling shoes are specially designed for bike racing. They have a metal sole that puts the energy directly to the pedal, thus efficiently using one's power. The food that one brings is important in a long-distance race. It must not only be useful in refueling the body, but it must be easily eaten while pedaling. Candy bars and fruit, such as bananas, satisfy both requirements. The bike must be stripped of all unnecessary weight, including saddlebags and reflectors. Some cyclists drill holes in parts of the frame, saddle post, and handlebars to lessen the weight of the bike.

5. On page 57 we printed a paragraph on athletic coaches and we also printed a more unified revision of the paragraph. But the revision is still weak, for it lacks supporting details. Revise the revision, giving it life.

6. Here is the opening paragraph of an essay (about 750 words) on the manufacture of paper in the fifteenth century, the days of the earliest printed books. On the whole it is very good, but the unity and the organization can be improved. Revise the paragraph.

> We take paper for granted, but old as it is it did not always exist. In fact, it was invented long after writing was invented, for the earliest writing is painted or scratched on cave walls, shells, rocks, and other natural objects. Paper was not even the first manufactured surface for writing; sheets made from papyrus, a reed-like plant, were produced about 2500 B.C., long before the invention of paper. Although the Chinese may have invented paper as early as the time of Christ, the oldest surviving paper is from early fifth-century China. The Arabs learned the secret of paper-making from the Chinese in the eighth century, but the knowledge traveled slowly to Europe. The oldest European paper, made by the Moors in Spain, is of the twelfth century. Early European paper is of poor quality and so not until the quality improved, around the fourteenth century, did paper become widely used. Most writing was done on parchment, which is the skin of a sheep or goat, and vellum, which is the finer skin of a lamb, kid, or calf. Whatever the animal, the skin was washed, limed, unhaired, scraped, washed again, stretched, and rubbed with pumice until a surface suitable for writing was achieved. Until it was displaced by paper, in the fourteenth century, parchment was the chief writing surface in Europe.

7. Here is the concluding paragraph of a book review. What repetitions do you find? What is their effect?

> Mr. Flexner's book is more than a political argument. He has written so vividly and involved us so deeply that there are moments when we yearn to lean over into the pages, pull Hamilton aside, and beg him to reconsider, to pity, to trust, to wait, or merely to shut up. Yet the book's effect is not melodramatic. It is tragic—a tragedy not of fate but of character, the spectacle of an immensely gifted man who tried to rule a nation and could not rule himself.

> —NAOMI BLIVEN

8. Read the following query. Observe its organization. Then read the answer that follows.

> Q. *My house is centrally air-conditioned and I am thinking of installing either a ceiling fan in my living room or an attic exhaust fan in the hallway leading to the three rear bedrooms. Which would be the best and most energy-efficient?*

> A. This is like comparing apples and oranges. A ceiling fan is used to circulate air inside the house and stir up a breeze; a whole-house attic exhaust fan is used to draw cool air in from outside through several open windows (usually through bedroom windows at night after the outside air has cooled off). The ceiling fan can be used when the air-conditioning system is running, to help create a slight breeze that will enable you to turn the air-conditioner's thermostat to a higher setting. But you would use the attic fan only when the air-conditioner is off, or if you wanted to cool the house before turning the system on in the morning. On a marginal day the ceiling fan might keep you comfortable without air-conditioning; an attic fan at night might eliminate the need for air-conditioning.

Write one paragraph following the organization of the paragraph above as closely as you can. Your paragraph should compare two things that seem to you as unlike as "apples and oranges." Example: running and dieting (to lose weight); golf and tennis (as spectator sports); attending a small college and a large university; alpine and cross country skiing. . . .

Chapter 4

Fine-Tuning Sentences: Revising for Conciseness

Excess is the common substitute for energy.

—MARIANNE MOORE

All writers who want to keep the attention and confidence of their readers revise for conciseness. The general rule is to say everything relevant in as few words as possible. The conclusion of the Supreme Court's decision in *Brown v. the Board of Education of Topeka,* for example—"Separate educational facilities are inherently unequal"—says it all in six words.

The writers of the following sentences talk too much; they bore us because they don't make every word count.

There are two pine trees which grow behind this house.

On his left shoulder is a small figure standing. He is about the size of the doctor's head.

The judge is seated behind the bench and he is wearing a judicial robe.

Compare those three sentences with these revisions:

Two pine trees grow behind this house.

On his left shoulder stands a small figure, about the size of the doctor's head.

The judge, wearing a robe, sits behind the bench.

We will soon discuss in some detail the chief patterns of wordiness, but here it is enough to say that if you prefer the revisions you already have a commendable taste for conciseness. What does your taste tell you to do with the following sentences?

A black streak covers the bottom half. It appears to have been painted with a single stroke of a large brush.

The time to begin revising for conciseness is when you think you have an acceptable draft in hand—something that pretty much covers your topic and comes reasonably close to saying what you believe about it. As you go over it, study each sentence to see what, without loss of meaning or emphasis, can be deleted. Read each paragraph, preferably aloud, to see if each sentence supports the topic sentence or idea and clarifies the point you are making. Leave in the concrete and specific details and examples that support your ideas (you may in fact be adding more) but cut out all the deadwood that chokes them: extra words, empty or pretentious phrases, weak qualifiers, redundancies, negative constructions, wordy uses of the verb *to be,* and other extra verbs and verb phrases. We'll discuss these problems in the next pages, but first we offer some examples of sentences that cannot be improved upon; they're so awful there's nothing to do but delete them and start over. Zonker, in Garry Trudeau's cartoon, is a master of what we call Instant Prose (stuff that sounds like the real thing, but isn't).

Instant Prose (Zonkers)

Here are some examples of Instant Prose from students' essays:

> Frequently a chapter title in a book reveals to the reader the main point that the author desires to bring out during the course of the chapter.

We could try revising this, cutting the twenty-seven words down to seven:

> A chapter's title often reveals its thesis.

But why bother? Unless the title is an exception, is the point worth making?

> The two poems are basically similar in many ways, yet they have their significant differences.

True; all poems are both similar to and different from other poems. Start over with your next sentence, perhaps something like: "The two poems, superficially similar in rough paraphrase, are strikingly different in diction."

> Although the essay is simple in plot, the theme encompasses many vital concepts of emotional makeup.

> Following a transcendental vein, the nostalgia in the poem takes on a spiritual quality.

> Cassell only presents a particular situation concerning the issue, and with clear descriptions and a certain style sets up an interesting article.

Pure zonkers. Not even the writers of these sentences now know what they mean.

Writing Instant Prose is an acquired habit, like smoking cigarettes or watching soap operas; fortunately it's easier to kick. It often begins in high school, sometimes earlier, when the victim is assigned a ten-page paper, or is told that a paragraph *must* contain at least three sentences, or that a thesis is stated in the introduction to an essay, elaborated in the body, and repeated in the conclusion. If the instructions appear arbitrary, and the student is bored or intimidated by them, the response is likely to be, like Zonker's, meaningless and mechanical.

Students like Zonker have forgotten, or have never learned, the true purpose of writing—the discovery and communication of ideas, attitudes, and judgments. They concentrate instead on the word count: stuffing sentences, padding paragraphs, stretching and repeating points, and adding flourishes. Rewarded by a satisfactory grade, they repeat the performance, and in time, through practice, develop some fluency in spilling out words without thought or commitment, and almost without effort. Such students enter, as Zonker would say, the college of their choice, feeling somehow inauthentic, perhaps even aware that they don't really mean what they write: symptoms of habitual use of, or addiction to, Instant Prose.

How to Avoid Instant Prose

1. **Trust yourself.** Writing Instant Prose is not only a habit; it's a form of alienation. If you habitually write zonkers you probably don't think of what you write as your own but as something you produce on demand for someone else. (Clearly Zonker is writing for that unreasonable authority, the teacher, whose mysterious whims and insatiable appetite for words he must somehow satisfy.) Breaking the habit begins with recognizing it, and then acknowledging the possibility that you can take yourself and your work seriously. It means learning to respect your ideas and experiences (unlearning the passive habits that got you through childhood) and determining that when you write you'll write what you mean—nothing more, nothing less. This involves taking some risks, of course; habits offer some security or they would have no grip on us. Moreover, we all have moments when we doubt that our ideas are worth taking seriously. Keep writing honestly anyway. The self-doubts will pass; accomplishing something— writing one clear sentence—can help make them pass.

2. **Learn to recognize Instant Prose Additives** when they crop up in your writing, and in what you read. And you *will* find them in what you read—in textbooks and in academic journals, notoriously.

Here's an example from a recent book on contemporary theater:

> One of the principal and most persistent sources of error that tends to bedevil a considerable proportion of contemporary literary analysis is the assumption that the writer's creative process is a wholly conscious and purposive type of activity.

Notice all the extra stuff in the sentence: "principal and most persistent," "tends to bedevil," "considerable proportion," "type of activity." Cleared of deadwood the sentence might read:

> The assumption that the writer's creative process is wholly conscious bedevils much contemporary criticism.

3. **Acquire two things: a new habit, Revising for Conciseness; and what Isaac Singer calls "the writer's best friend," a wastebasket.**

Extra Words and Empty Words

Extra words should, by definition, be eliminated; vague, empty, or pretentious words and phrases may be replaced by specific and direct language.

Wordy

> However, it must be remembered that Ruth's marriage could have positive effects on Naomi's situation.

Concise

> Ruth's marriage, however, will also provide security for Naomi.

In the second version, the unnecessary "it must be remembered that" has been eliminated; for the vague "positive effects" and "situation," specific words communicating a precise point have been substituted. The revision, though briefer, says more.

Wordy

> In high school, where I had the opportunity for three years of working with the student government, I realized how significantly a person's enthusiasm could be destroyed merely by the attitudes of his superiors.

Concise

> In high school, during three years on the student council, I saw students' enthusiasm destroyed by insecure teachers and cynical administrators.

Again, the revised sentence gives more information in fewer words. How?

Wordy

> The economic situation of Miss Moody was also a crucial factor in the formation of her character.

Concise

> Anne Moody's poverty also helped to form her character.

"Economic situation" is evasive for poverty; "crucial factor" is pretentious. Both are Instant Prose.

Wordy

> It creates a better motivation of learning when students can design their own programs involving education. This way students' interests can be focused on.

Concise

> Motivation improves when students design their own programs, focused on their own interests.

Now revise the following wordy sentences:

1. Perhaps they basically distrusted our capacity to judge correctly.
2. The use of setting is also a major factor in conveying a terrifying type atmosphere.

Notice how, in the examples provided, the following words crop up: "basically," "significant," "situation," "factor," "involving," "effect," "type." These words have legitimate uses, but are often no more than Instant Prose Additives. Cross them out whenever you can. Similar words to watch out for: *aspect, facet, fundamental, manner, nature, ultimate, utilization, viable, virtually, vital.* If they make your writing sound good, don't hesitate—cross them out at once.

Weak Intensifiers and Qualifiers

Words like *very, quite, rather, completely, definitely,* and *so* can usually be struck from a sentence without loss. Paradoxically, sentences are often more emphatic without intensifiers. Try reading the following sentences both with and without the bracketed words:

At that time I was [very] idealistic.

We found the proposal [quite] feasible.

The remark, though unkind, was [entirely] accurate.

It was a [rather] fatuous statement.

The scene was [extremely] typical.

Both films deal with disasters [virtually] beyond our control.

The death scene is [truly] grotesque.

What she did next was [completely] inexcusable.

The first line [definitely] establishes that the father had been drinking.

Always avoid using intensifiers with *unique.* Either something is unique—the only one of its kind—or it is not. It can't be very, quite, so, pretty, or fairly unique.

Circumlocutions

Roundabout ways of saying things enervate your prose and tire your reader. Notice now each circumlocution in the first column is matched by a concise expression in the second.

I came to the realization that	I realized that
She is of the opinion that	She thinks that
The quotation is supportive of	The quotation supports
Concerning the matter of	About
During the course of	During
For the period of a week	For a week
In the event that	If
In the process of	During, while
Regardless of the fact that	Although
Due to the fact that	Because
For the simple reason that	Because
The fact that	That
Inasmuch as	Since
If the case was such that	If
It is often the case that	Often
In all cases	Always
I made contact with	I called, saw, phoned, wrote
At that point in time	Then
At this point in time	Now

Now revise this sentence:

> These movies have a large degree of popularity for the simple reason that they give the viewers insight in many cases.

Wordy Beginnings

Vague, empty words and phrases clog the beginnings of some sentences. They're like elaborate windups before the pitch.

Wordy

> By analyzing carefully the last lines in this stanza, you find the connections between the loose ends of the poem.

Concise

> The last lines of the stanza connect the loose ends of the poem.

Wordy

> What the cartoonist is illustrating and trying to get across is the greed of the oil producers.

Concise

The cartoon illustrates the greed of the oil producers.

Wordy

Dealing with the crucial issue of the year, the editorial is expressing ironical disbelief in any of the possible solutions to the Middle East crisis.

Concise

The editorial ironically expresses disbelief in the proposed solutions to the Middle East crisis.

Wordy

In the last stanza is the conclusion (as usual) and it tells of the termination of the dance.

Concise

The last stanza concludes with the end of the dance.

Wordy

In opposition to the situation of the younger son is that of the elder who remained in his father's house, working hard and handling his inheritance wisely.

Concise

The elder son, by contrast, remained in his father's house, worked hard, and handled his inheritance wisely.

Notice in the above examples that when the deadwood is cleared from the beginning of the sentence, the subject appears early, and the main verb appears close to it:

The last lines . . . connect . . .
The cartoon illustrates . . .
The editorial . . . expresses . . .
The last stanza concludes . . .
The elder son . . . remained. . .

Locating the right noun for the subject, and the right verb for the predicate, is the key to revising sentences with wordy beginnings. Try revising the wordy beginnings in the following sentences:

1. The way that Mabel reacts toward her brother is a fine representation of her nature.
2. In Langston Hughes's case he was "saved from sin" when he was going on thirteen.

Empty Conclusions

Often a sentence that begins well has an empty conclusion. The words go on but the sentence seems to stand still; if it's not revised, it requires another sentence to explain it.

Empty

> "Those Winter Sundays" is composed so that a reader can feel what the poet was saying. (How is it composed? What is he saying?)

Concise

> "Those Winter Sundays" describes the speaker's anger as a child, and his remorse as an adult.

Empty

> In both Orwell's and Baldwin's essays the feeling of white supremacy is very important. (Why is white supremacy important?)

Concise

> Both Orwell and Baldwin trace the insidious consequences of white supremacy.

Empty

> Being the only white girl among about ten black girls was quite a learning experience. (What did she learn?)

Concise

> As the only white girl among about ten black girls, I began to understand the experiences of isolation, helplessness, and rage regularly reported by minority students.

Wordy Uses of the Verbs to Be, to Have, *and* to Make

Notice that in the preceding unrevised sentences a form of the verb *to be* introduces the empty conclusion: *"was* saying," *"is* very important," *"was* quite a learning experience." In each revision, the right verb added and generated substance. In the following sentences, substitutions for the verb *to be* both invigorate and shorten otherwise substantial sentences. (The wordy expressions are italicized, and so are the revisions.)

Wordy

The scene *is taking place* at night, in front of the capitol building.

Concise

The scene *takes place* at night, in front of the capitol building.

Wordy

In this shoeshining and early rising *there are indications* of church attendance.

Concise

The early rising and shoeshining *indicate* church attendance.

Wordy

The words "flashing," "rushing," "plunging," and "tossing" *are suggestive of* excitement.

Concise

The words "flashing," "rushing," "plunging," and "tossing" *suggest* excitement.

The rule is, whenever you can, replace a form of the verb *to be* with a stronger verb.

To Be	*Strong Verb*
• and a participle ("is taking")	• takes
• and a noun ("are indications")	• indicate
• and an adjective ("are suggestive")	• suggest

Try revising the following sentence:

The rising price of oil is reflective of the spiraling cost of all goods.

Sentences with the verbs *to have* and *to make* can similarly be reduced:

Wordy

The Friar *has knowledge* that Juliet is alive.

Concise

The Friar *knows* that Juliet is alive.

Wordy

The stanzas *make a vivid contrast* between Heaven and Hell.

Concise

The stanzas *vividly contrast* Heaven and Hell.

Like all rules, this one has exceptions. We don't list them here; you'll discover them by listening to your sentences.

Redundancy

The word *redundancy,* derived from a Latin word meaning "overflowing, overlapping," refers to unnecessary repetition in the expression of ideas. "Future plans," after all, are only plans, and "to glide smoothly" or "to scurry rapidly" is only to glide or to scurry. Unlike repetition, which often provides emphasis or coherence (for example, "government of the people, by the people, for the people"), redundancy can always be eliminated.

Redundant

Any student could randomly sit anywhere. (If the students could sit any-where, the seating was random.)

Concise

Students could sit anywhere.
Students chose their seats at random.

Redundant

I have no justification with which to excuse myself.

Concise

I have no justification for my action.
I can't justify my action.
I have no excuse for my action.
I can't excuse my action.

Redundant

> In the orthodox Cuban culture, the surface of the female role seemed degrading. (Perhaps this sentence means what it says. More probably "surface" and "seemed" are redundant.)

Concise

In the orthodox Cuban culture, the female role seemed degrading.
In the orthodox Cuban culture, the female role was superficially degrading.

Redundant

> In "Araby" the boy feels alienated emotionally from his family.

Concise

> In "Araby" the boy feels alienated from his family.

Try eliminating redundancy from the following sentences:

1. The reason why she hesitates is because she is afraid.
2. Marriage in some form has long existed since prehistoric times.

What words can be crossed out of the following phrases?

a. throughout the entire article
b. her attitude of indifference
c. a conservative type suit
d. all the different tasks besides teaching
e. his own personal opinion
f. elements common to both of them
g. emotions and feelings
h. shared together
i. falsely padded expense accounts
j. alleged suspect

Many phrases in common use are redundant. For example, there is no need to write "blare noisily," since the meaning of the adverb "noisily" is already in the verb "blare." Watch for phrases like these when you revise:

round in shape	resulting effect
purple in color	close proximity
poetic in nature	connected together
tall in stature	prove conclusively
autobiography of her life	must necessarily
basic fundamentals	very unique
true fact	very universal
free gift	the reason why is because

Negative Constructions

Negative constructions are often wordy and sometimes pretentious.

Wordy

Housing for married students is *not unworthy of* consideration.

Concise

Housing for married students is worth considering.

Better

The trustees should earmark funds for married students' housing.
(Probably what the author meant.)

Wordy

After reading the second paragraph *you aren't left with* an immediate reaction as to how the story will end.

Concise

The first two paragraphs create suspense.

The following example from a syndicated column is not untypical:

Although it is not reasonably to be expected that someone who fought his way up to the Presidency is less than a largely political animal and

"See what I mean? You're never sure just where you stand with them."

Drawing by Rossi; © 1971 The New Yorker Magazine, Inc.

sometimes a beast, it is better not to know—really—exactly what his private conversations were composed of.

The Golden Rule of writing is "Write for others as you would have them write for you," not "Write for others in a manner not unreasonably dissimilar to the manner in which you would have them write for you." (But see the discussion of *not . . . un-* in the Glossary p. 506, for effective use of the negative.)

Extra Sentences, Extra Clauses: Subordination

Sentences are sometimes wordy because ideas are given more elaborate grammatical constructions than they need. In revising these constructions often can be reduced. Two sentences, for example, may be reduced to one, or a clause may be reduced to a phrase.

Wordy

The Book of Ruth was probably written in the fifth century B.C. It was a time when women were considered the property of men.

Concise

The Book of Ruth was probably written in the fifth century B.C., when women were considered the property of men.

Wordy

> The first group was the largest. This group was seated in the center the of dining hall.

Concise

> The first group, the largest, was seated in the center of the dining hall.

Wordy

> The colonists were upset over the tax on tea and they took action against it.

Concise

> The colonists, upset over the tax on tea, took action against it.

Who, Which, That

Watch particularly for clauses beginning with *who, which,* and *that.* Often they can be shortened.

Wordy

> George Orwell is the pen name of Eric Blair, *who was* an English writer.

Concise

> George Orwell is the pen name of Eric Blair, an English writer.

Wordy

> They are seated at a table *which* is covered with a patched and tattered cloth.

Concise

> They are seated at a table covered with a patched and tattered cloth.

Wordy

> There is one feature *that is* grossly out of proportion.

Concise

> One feature is grossly out of proportion.

It Is, This Is, There Are

Also watch for sentences and clauses beginning with *it is, this is, there are* (again, wordy uses of the verb *to be*). These expressions often lead to a *which* or a *that,* but even when they don't they may be wordy.

Wordy

> The trail brings us to the timberline. This is the point where the trees become stunted from lack of oxygen.

Concise

> The trail brings us to the timberline, the point where the trees become stunted from lack of oxygen.

Wordy

> This is a quotation from Black Elk's autobiography which discloses his prophetic powers.

Concise

> This quotation from Black Elk's autobiography discloses his prophetic powers.

Wordy

> It is frequently considered that *Hamlet* is Shakespeare's most puzzling play.

Concise

> *Hamlet* is frequently considered Shakespeare's most puzzling play.

Wordy

> In Notman's photograph of Buffalo Bill and Sitting Bull there are definite contrasts between the two figures.

Concise

> Notman's photograph of Buffalo Bill and Sitting Bull contrasts the two figures.

Try revising the following sentences:

1. There are many writers who believe that writing can't be taught.

2. Always take more clothes than you think you will need. This is so that you will be prepared for the weather no matter what it is.

3. This is an indication that the child has a relationship with his teacher which is very respectful.

(For further discussion of subordination see pages 140–43. On *which* clauses, see also page 512.)

Some Concluding Remarks About Conciseness

We spoke earlier about how students learn to write Instant Prose and acquire other wordy habits—by writing what they think the teacher has asked for. We haven't forgotten that instructors assign papers of a certain length in college too. But the length given is not an arbitrary limit that must be reached—the instructor who asks for a five-page or twenty-page paper is probably trying to tell you the degree of elaboration expected on the assignment. Such, apparently, was the intention of William Randolph Hearst, the newspaper publisher, who cabled an astronomer, "Is there life on Mars? Cable reply 1000 words." The astronomer's reply was, "Nobody knows," repeated 500 times.

What do you do when you've been asked to produce a ten-page paper and after diligent writing and revising you find you've said everything relevant to your topic in seven and a half pages? Our advice is, hand it in. We can't remember ever counting the words or pages of a substantial, interesting essay; we assume that our colleagues elsewhere are equally reasonable and equally overworked. If we're wrong, tell us about it—in writing, and in the fewest possible words.

Exercises

1. First identify the fault or faults that make the following sentences wordy, and then revise them for conciseness.

   a. There were quite a number of contrasts that White made between the city school and the country school which was of a casual nature all throughout.

   b. The study of political topics involves a careful researching of the many components of the particular field.

   c. Virtually the most significant feature of any field involving science is the vital nature of the technical facilities, the fundamental factor of all research.

d. Like a large majority of American people, I, too, have seen the popular disaster films.

e. Something which makes this type of film popular (disaster) is the kind of subconscious aspect of "Can man overcome this problem?" Horror films, on the other hand, produce the aspects of whether or not man can make amends for his mistakes.

f. The average American becomes disappointed and downtrodden due to the fact that he can't help himself and is at the mercy of inflation and unemployment.

g. Some relationships have split up because of the simple fear of having an abnormal child, while perhaps there might have been other alternatives for these couples.

h. Reading has always been a fascinating and exciting pastime for me for as long as I can remember.

i. This cartoon appeared in the 17 September 1993 issue of *Newsweek*. This political cartoon was originally taken from the *Tulsa Tribune*. The cartoonist is Simpson.

j. Only once in the first two sentences does the author make reference to the first person.

k. The length of the sentences are similar in moderation and in structural clarity.

l. The magnitude of student satisfaction with the program ranged from total hatred to enthusiastic approval.

m. Taking a look at the facial expressions of the man and the woman in both pictures one can see a difference in mood.

n. One drawing is done in watercolor and the other is done in chalk which is a revision of the watercolor.

o. The dialogue places the role of the two gods on a believable basis.

p. Senseless crimes such as murder and muggings are committed on a daily basis.

q. One must specify that the current heavy metal craze which is so very popular today is not considered to be African-American music.

r. The two major aspects behind the development of a performer are technique and musicianship.

s. I remember my first desire to smoke cigarettes as I watched my father smoke. My father often sat in his favorite easy chair idly smoking cigarettes.

t. Christopher Stone's article "Putting the Outside Inside the Fence of Law" is concerning the legal rights of the environment. He comments on the legal rights of other inanimate entities which seem to be acceptable. Just as these entities are represented, so should the environment be represented.

2. In the following paragraph, circle all forms of the verbs *to be, to have,* and *to make.* Then, wherever possible, eliminate these verbs by reducing clauses or by substituting stronger, more exact, or active verbs.

"Confidential Chat" is a column in the *Boston Globe* that anonymously publishes letters from readers and then publishes subsequent responses. In one letter, submitted by Mrs. Mike, advice is sought on a moral issue. Mrs. Mike, a landlord and mother of teenage children, has a tenant who "has been having her boyfriend sleep over almost every night." Mrs. Mike feels that her tenant's behavior could make an undesirable impression upon her children whom she is trying to "raise with a strong sense of Christian morality" and thus has resolved that eviction would be a solution. Her dilemma being stated as "being basically spiritual in nature" receives several responses which address the moral conflict and make suggestions for handling the situation.

Chapter 5

Fine-Tuning
Sentences: Revising
for Clarity

Here's to plain speaking and clear understanding.

—SIDNEY GREENSTREET, IN THE MALTESE FALCON

Clarity

We have seen new realities created by the advance of physics. But this chain of creation can be traced back far beyond the starting point of physics. One of the most primitive concepts is that of an object. The concepts of a tree, a horse, any material body, are creations gained on the basis of experience, though the impressions from which they arise are primitive in comparison with the world of physical phenomena. A cat teasing a mouse also creates, by thought, its own primitive reality. The fact that the cat reacts in a similar way toward any mouse it meets shows that it forms concepts and theories which are its guide through its own world of sense impressions.

—ALBERT EINSTEIN AND LEOPOLD INFELD

Skills constitute the manipulative techniques of human goal attainment and control in relation to the physical world, so far as artifacts or machines especially designed as tools do not yet supplement them. Truly human skills are guided by organized and codified *knowledge* of both the things to be manipulated and the human capacities that are used to manipulate them. Such knowledge is an aspect of cultural-level symbolic processes, and, like other aspects to be discussed presently, requires the capacities of the human central nervous system, particularly the brain. This organic system is clearly essential to all of the symbolic processes; as we well know, the human brain is far superior to the brain of any other species.

—TALCOTT PARSONS

Why is the first passage easier to understand than the second?

Both passages discuss the relationship between the brain and the physical world it attempts to understand. The first passage, by Einstein and Infeld, is, if anything, more complex both in what it asserts and in what it suggests than the second, by Parsons. Both passages explain that the brain organizes sense impressions. But Einstein and Infeld further explain that the history of physics can be understood as an extension of the simplest sort of organization, such as we all make in distinguishing a tree from a horse, or such as even a cat makes in teasing a mouse. Parsons only promises that "other aspects" will "be discussed presently." How many of us are eager for those next pages?

Good writing is clear, not because it presents simple ideas, but because it presents ideas in the simplest form the subject permits. A clear analysis doesn't falsely reduce a complex problem to a simple one; it breaks it down into its simple, comprehensible parts and discusses them, one by one, in a logical order. A clear paragraph explains one of these parts coherently, thoroughly, and in language as simple and as particular as the reader's understanding requires and the context allows. Where Parsons writes of "organized and codified *knowledge* of . . . the things to be manipulated," Einstein and Infeld write simply of the concept of an object. And even "object," a simple but general word, is further clarified by the specific, familiar examples, "tree" and "horse." Parsons writes of "the manipulative techniques of . . . goal attainment and control in relation to the physical world, so far as artifacts or machines especially designed as tools do not yet supplement them." Einstein and Infeld show us a cat teasing a mouse.

Notice also the clear organization of Einstein and Infeld's paragraph. The first sentence, clearly transitional, refers to the advance of physics traced in the preceding pages. The next sentence, introduced by "But," reverses our direction: we are now going to look not at an advance, but at primitive beginnings. And the following sentences, to the end of the paragraph, fulfill that promise. We move back to primitive human concepts, clarified by examples, and finally to the still more primitive example of the cat. Parson's paragraph is also organized, but the route is much more difficult to follow.

Why do people write obscurely? Surely some students learn to write obscurely by trying to imitate the style of their teachers or textbooks. The imitation may spring from genuine admiration for these authorities. Or students may feel that a string of technical-sounding words is what the teacher expects. If this thought has crossed your mind, we can't say you're entirely wrong. Learning a new discipline often involves acquiring a specialized vocabulary. But we add the following cautions:

- Teachers expect your writing to show thought and make sense. They are likely to be puzzled by the question "Do you want me to use technical terms in this paper?"

- If you try to use technical terms appropriate to one field when you write about another, you are likely to write nonsense. Don't write "the machine was viable" if you mean only that it worked.

- When you do write for specialists in a particular field, use technical terms precisely. Don't write in an art history paper "This print of Van Gogh's *Sunflowers*" if you mean "This reproduction of Van Gogh's *Sunflowers*."

- No matter what you are writing, don't become so enamored of technical words that you can't write a sentence without peppering it with *input, interface, death-symbol, parameter, phallocentric, feedback,* and so on.

But to return to the question, "Why do people write obscurely?" It's difficult to write clearly.[1] Authorities may be obscure not because they want to tax you with unnecessary difficulties, but because they don't know how to avoid such difficulties. If you have ever tried to assemble a mechanical toy or to thread an unfamiliar sewing machine by following the "easy instructions," you know that the simplest kind of expository writing, giving instructions, can foil the writers most eager for your goodwill (that is, those who want you to use their products). Few instructions, unfortunately, are as unambiguous as "Go to jail. Go directly to jail. Do not pass Go. Do not collect $200."

You can, though, learn to write clearly, by learning to recognize common sources of obscurity in writing and by consciously revising your own work. We offer, to begin with, three general rules:

1. Use the simplest, most exact, most specific language your subject allows.

2. Put together what belongs together, in the essay, in the paragraph, and in the sentence.

3. Keep your reader in mind, particularly when you revise.

Now for more specific advice, and examples—the cats and mice of revising for clarity.

Clarity and Exactness: Using the Right Word

Denotation

Be sure the word you choose has the right *denotation* (explicit meaning). Did you mean sarcastic or ironic? Fatalistic or pessimistic? Disinterested or uninterested? Biannual or semiannual? Enforce or reinforce? Use or usage? If you're not sure, check the dictionary. You'll find some of the most commonly misused words discussed in our Glossary (p. 496). Here are examples of a few others.

[1]Our first draft of this sentence read "Writing clearly is difficult." Can you see why we changed it?

1. Daru faces a dilemma between his humane feelings and his conceptions of justice. (Strictly speaking, a dilemma requires a choice between two equally unattractive alternatives. "Conflict" would be a better word here.)

2. However, as time dragged on, exercising seemed to lose its charisma. (What is charisma? Why is it inexact here?)

3. Ms. Wu's research contains many symptoms of depression which became evident during the reading period. (Was Ms. Wu depressed by her research? We hope not. Probably she described or listed the symptoms.)

4. When I run I don't allow myself to stop until I have reached my destiny. (Which word is inexact?)

Connotation

Be sure the word you choose has the right *connotation* (association, implication). As Mark Twain said, the difference between the right word and the almost right word is the difference between lightning and the lightning bug.

1. Boston politics has always upheld the reputation of being especially crooked. ("Upheld" inappropriately suggests that Boston has proudly maintained its reputation. "Has always had" would be appropriate here, but pale. "Deserved" would, in this context, be ironic, implying—accurately—the writer's scorn.)

2. This book, unlike many other novels, lacks tedious descriptive passages. ("Lacks" implies a deficiency. How would you revise the sentence?)

3. New Orleans, notorious for its good jazz and good food. . . . (Is "notorious" the word here? or "famous"?)

4. Sunday, Feb. 9. Another lingering day at Wellesley. (In this entry from a student's journal, "lingering" strikes us as right. What does "lingering" imply about Sundays at Wellesley that "long" would not?)

Because words have connotations, most writing—even when it pretends to be objective—conveys attitudes as well as facts. Consider, for example, this passage by Jessica Mitford, describing part of the procedure used today for embalming:

A long, hollow needle attached to a tube . . . is jabbed into the abdomen, poked around the entrails and chest cavity, the contents of which are pumped out. . . .

Here, as almost always, the writer's *purpose* in large measure determines the choice of words. Probably the sentence accurately describes part of the procedure, but it also, of course, records Mitford's contempt for the procedure. Suppose she wanted to be more respectful—suppose, for example, she were an undertaker writing an explanatory pamphlet. Instead of the needle being "jabbed" it would be "inserted," and instead of being "poked around the entrails" it would be "guided around the viscera," and the contents would not be "pumped out" but would be "drained." Mitford's words would be the wrong words for an undertaker explaining embalming to apprentices or to the general public, but, given her purpose, they are exactly the right ones because they convey her attitude with great clarity.

Notice, too, that many words have social, political, or sexist overtones. We read for example of the *children* of the rich, but the *offspring* of the poor. What is implied by the distinction? Consider the differences in connotation in each of the following series:

1. friend, boyfriend, young man, lover (What age is the speaker?)
2. dine, eat (What was on the menu? Who set the table?)
3. spinster, bachelor (Which term is likely to be considered an insult?)
4. underdeveloped nations, developing nations, emerging nations
5. preference, bias, prejudice
6. upbringing, conditioning, brainwashing
7. message from our sponsor, commercial, ad, plug
8. intelligence gathering, espionage, spying
9. emigrate, defect, seek asylum
10. antiabortion, pro-life; pro-abortion, pro-choice

*"I'm not quite clear on this, Fulton. Are you moaning about
your prerequisites, your requisites, or your perquisites?"*

Drawing by Richter; © 1976 The New Yorker Magazine, Inc.

Quotation Marks as Apologies

When you have used words with exact meanings (denotations) and appropriate associations (connotations) for your purpose, don't apologize for them by putting quotation marks around them. If the words *copped a plea, ripped off,* or *kids* suit your purpose better than *plea-bargained, stolen,* or *children,* use them. If they are inappropriate, don't put them in quotation marks; find the right words.

Being Specific

In writing descriptions, catch the richness, complexity, and uniqueness of things. Suppose, for example, you are describing a scene from your childhood, a setting you loved. There was, in particular, a certain tree . . . and you write: "Near the water there was a big tree that was rather impressive." Most of us would produce something like that sentence. Here is the sentence Ernesto Galarza wrote in *Barrio Boy:*

> On the edge of the pond, at the far side, there was an enormous walnut
> tree, standing like an open umbrella whose ribs extended halfway
> across the still water of the pool.

We probably could not have come up with the metaphor of the umbrella because we wouldn't have seen the similarity. (As Aristotle observed, the gift for making metaphors distinguishes the poet from the rest of us.) But we can all train ourselves to be accurate observers and reporters. For "the water" (general) we can specify "pond"; for "near" we can say how near, "on the edge of the pond," and add the specific location, "at the far side"; for "tree" we can give the species, "walnut tree"; and for "big" we can provide a picture, its branches "extended halfway across" the pond: it was, in fact, "enormous."

Galarza does not need to add limply, as we did, that the tree "was rather impressive." The tree he describes *is* impressive. That he accurately remembered it persuades us that he was impressed, without his having to tell us he was. For writing descriptions, a good general rule is: show, don't tell.

Be as specific as you can be in all forms of exposition too. Take the time, when you revise, to find the exact word to replace vague, woolly phrases or clichés. In the following examples we have to guess or invent what the writer means.

Vague

> The clown's part in *Othello* is very small.

Specific

> The clown appears in only two scenes in *Othello.*

> The clown in *Othello* speaks only thirty lines. (Notice the substitution of the verb "appears" or "speaks" for the frequently debilitating "is." And in place

of the weak intensifier "very" we have specific details to tell us how small the role is.)

Vague

He feels uncomfortable at the whole situation. (Many feelings are uncomfortable. Which one does he feel? What's the situation?)

Specific

He feels guilty for having distrusted his father.

Vague

The passage reveals a somewhat calculating aspect behind Antigone's noble motives. ("A somewhat calculating aspect" is vague—and wordy—for "calculation." Or did the writer mean "shrewdness"? What differences in connotation are there between "shrewd" and "calculating"?)

Vague

She uses simplicity in her style of writing. (Do we know, exactly, what simplicity in style means?)

Specific

She uses familiar words, normal word order, and conversational phrasing.

Vague cliché

Then she criticized students for living in an ivory tower. (Did she criticize them for being detached or for being secluded? For social irresponsibility or studiousness?)

Specific

Then she criticized students for being socially irresponsible.

Using Examples

In addition to exact words and specific details, illustrative examples make for clear writing. Einstein and Infeld, in the passage quoted on page 101, use as an example of a primitive concept a cat teasing not only its first mouse, but "any mouse it meets." Here are two paragraphs which clarify their topic sentences through examples; the first is again from *Barrio Boy*.

> In Jalco people spoke in two languages—Spanish and with gestures.
> These signs were made with the face or hands or a combination of both.
> If you bent one arm and tapped the elbow with the other hand, it meant

"He is stingy." When you sawed one arm across the other you were saying that someone you knew played the fiddle terribly. To say that a man was a tippler you made a set of cow's horns with the little finger and the thumb of one hand, bending the three middle fingers to the palm and pointing the thumb at your mouth. And if you wanted to indicate, without saying so for the sake of politeness, that a mutual acquaintance was daffy, you tapped three times on your forehead with your middle finger.

—ERNESTO GALARZA

In the next paragraph, Northrop Frye, writing about the perception of rhythm, illustrates his point:

Ideally, our literary education should begin, not with prose, but with such things as "this little pig went to market"—with verse rhythm reinforced by physical assault. The infant who gets bounced on somebody's knee to the rhythm of "Ride a cock horse" does not need a footnote telling him that Banbury Cross is twenty miles northeast of Oxford. He does not need the information that "cross" and "horse" make (at least in the pronunciation he is most likely to hear) not a rhyme but an assonance. . . . All he needs is to get bounced.

Frye does not say our literary education should begin with "simple rhymes" or with "verse popular with children." He says "with such things as 'this little pig went to market,' " and then he goes on to add "Ride a cock horse." We know exactly what he means. Notice, too, that we do not need a third example. Be detailed, but know when to stop.

Your reader is likely to be brighter and more demanding than Lady Pliant, who in a seventeenth-century play says to a would-be seducer, "You are very alluring—and say so many fine Things, and nothing is so moving to me as a fine Thing." "Fine Things," of course, are what is wanted, but only exact words and apt illustrations will convince intelligent readers that they are hearing fine things.

Now look at a paragraph from a student's essay whose thesis is that rage can be a useful mechanism for effecting change. Then compare the left-hand paragraph with the same paragraph, revised, at the right. Note the specific ways, sentence by sentence, the student revised for clarity.

In my high school we had little say in the learning processes that were used. The subjects that we were required to take were irrelevant. One had to take them to earn enough points to graduate.	In my high school we had little say about our curriculum. We were required, for example, to choose either American or European History to earn enough points for graduation. We wanted, but were

Some of the teachers were sympathetic to our problem. They would tell us about when they were young, how they tried to oppose their school system. But when they were young it was a long time ago, for most of them. The principal would call assemblies to speak on the subject. They were entitled "The Value of an Education" or "Get a Good Education to Have a Bright Future." The titles were not inviting. They had nothing to do with our plight. Most students never came to any agreements with the principal because most of his thoughts and views seemed old and outdated.

at first refused, the option of Black History. Some of our teachers were sympathetic with us; one told me about her fight opposing the penmanship course required in her school. Nor was the principal totally indifferent— he called assemblies. I remember one talk he gave called "The Value of an Education in Today's World," and another. "Get a Good Education to Have a Bright Future." I don't recall hearing about a Black History course in either talk. Once, he invited a group of us to meet with him in his office, but we didn't reach any agreement. He solemnly showed us an American History text (not the one we used) that had a whole chapter devoted to Black History.

Jargon and Technical Language

Most dictionaries give three meanings for *jargon:* technical language, meaningless language, and inflated or pretentious language.

The members of almost every profession or trade—indeed, almost all people who share any specialized interest—use technical language. Composition teachers talk of conjunctions, misplaced modifiers, and writer's block; baseball fans talk of southpaws, the hit-and-run, and the hat trick; Freudians talk of cathect, libido, and the oral phase; magicians talk of the French drop, double-lifts, and second-dealing.

Properly used, technical language communicates information concisely and clearly, and it can create a comfortable bond between speakers, or between the writer and the reader. But to the outsider it may seem meaningless, hence the second definition of the word, meaningless talk. In fact, *jargon* originally meant (some six hundred years ago) the twittering of birds—and this is what the language of specialists sounds like to the outsider's ear. The third meaning, pretentious language, comes from the outsider's impatience with other people's technical language. We wonder if all of that twittering—all of the mysterious vocabulary—really is necessary, and we suspect that perhaps the speaker is making a big deal out of what can be said much more simply, maybe in an effort to impress us.

Consider, for instance, a twenty-eight-page manual issued in Dallas to parents of children in kindergarten through the third grade. The manual, intended to help parents decipher their children's report cards, is entitled *Terminal Behavioral Objectives for Continuous Progression Modules in Early Childhood Education.* Terminal objectives, it seems, means goals. What does the rest mean? If you were one of the parents, would you expect much help from the manual? It was intended to be helpful, but it sounds like a parody, doesn't it?

"With you, I think I've found a maximization of experience."

Drawing by Donald Reilly; © 1978 The New Yorker Magazine, Inc.

And finally, a deliberate parody. A. P. Herbert in his book *What a Word!* tells us how a social scientist might write a familiar biblical command:

> In connection with my co-citizens, a general standard of mutual good
> will and reciprocal non-aggression is obviously incumbent upon me.

What is the command? (See Leviticus 19.18.)

In general, when you write for nonspecialists, avoid technical terms; if you must use them, define them. If you use a technical term when writing for specialists, be sure you know its precise meaning. But whenever you can, even among specialists, use plain English.

Clichés

Clichés (literally, in French, molds from which type is cast) are trite expressions, mechanically—that is, mindlessly—reproduced. Since they are available without thought they are great Instant Prose Additives (see pages 84–98). Writers who use them are usually surprised to be criticized: They find the phrases attractive, and may even think them exact. (Phrases become clichés precisely because they have wide appeal and therefore wide use.) But clichés, by their very nature, cannot communicate the uniqueness of your thoughts. Furthermore, because they come instantly to mind, they tend to block the specific detail or exact expression that will let the reader know what precisely is in your mind. When, in revising, you strike out a cliché, you force yourself to do the work of writing clearly. The following example is full of clichés:

> Finally, the long awaited day arrived. Up bright and early. . . . She
> peered at me with suspicion; then a faint smile crossed her face.

Other examples:

first and foremost	time honored
the acid test	bustled to and fro
fatal flaw	short but sweet
budding genius	few and far between
slowly but surely	D-day arrived
little did I know	sigh of relief
the big moment	last but not least

In attempting to avoid clichés, however, don't go to the other extreme of wildly original, super-vivid writing—" 'Well then, say something to her,' he roared, his whole countenance gnarled in rage." It's often better to simply say, "he said." (Anyone who intends to write dialogue should memorize Ring Lardner's intentionally funny line, " 'Shut up!' he explained.") Note also that such common expression as "How are you?" "Please pass the salt," and "So long" are not clichés; they make no claim to be colorful.

Metaphors and Mixed Metaphors

Ordinary speech abounds with metaphors. We speak or write of the foot of a mountain, the germ (seed) of an idea, the root of a problem. Metaphors so deeply embedded in the language that they no longer evoke pictures in our minds are called *dead metaphors*. Ordinarily, they offer us, as writers, no problems: we need neither seek them nor avoid them; they are simply there. (Notice, for example, "embedded" two sentences back). Such metaphors become problems, however, when we unwittingly call them back to life. Howard Nemerov observes: "That these metaphors may be not dead but only sleeping, or that they may arise from the grave and walk in our sentences, is something that has troubled everyone who has ever tried to write plain expository prose."

Dead metaphors are most likely to haunt us when they are embodied in clichés. Since we use clichés without attention to what they literally say or point to, we are unlikely to be aware of the dead metaphors buried in them. But when we attach one cliché to another, we may raise the metaphors from the grave. The result is likely to be a mixed metaphor; the effect is almost always absurd.

Water seeks its own level whichever way you want to slice it.

"You're right as rain. It's the dawn of history, and there are no clichés as yet. I'll drink to that."

Drawing by Handelsman; © 1972 The New Yorker Magazine, Inc.

Traditional liberal education has run out of gas and educational soup kitchens are moving into the vacuum.

The low ebb has been reached and hopefully it's turned the corner.

Her energy, drained through a stream of red tape, led only to closed doors.

We no longer ask for whom the bell tolls but simply chalk it up as one less mouth to feed.

As comedian Joe E. Lewis observed, "Show me a man who builds castles in the air and I'll show you a crazy architect."

Fresh metaphors, on the other hand, imaginatively combine accurate observations. They are not prefabricated ideas; they are a means of discovering or inventing new ideas. They enlarge thought and enliven prose. Here are two examples from students' journals:

I have some sort of sporadic restlessness in me, like the pen on a polygraph machine. It moves along in curves, then suddenly shoots up, blowing a bubble in my throat, making my chest taut, forcing me to move around. It becomes almost unbearable and then suddenly it will plunge, leaving something that feels like a smooth orange wave.

Time is like wrapping papers. It wraps memories, decorates them with sentiment. No matter (almost) what's inside, it's remembered as a beautiful piece of past time. That's why I even miss my high school years, which were filled with tiredness, boredom, confusion.

And here is a passage from an essay in which a student analyzes the style of a story he found boring:

Every sentence yawns, stretches, shifts from side to side, and then quietly dozes off.

Experiment with metaphors, let them surface in the early drafts of your essays and in your journals, and by all means, introduce original and accurate comparisons in your essays. But leave the mixed metaphors to politicians and comedians.

Euphemisms

Euphemisms are words substituted for other words thought to be offensive. In deodorant advertisements there are no armpits, only *underarms,* which may *perspire,* but not sweat, and even then they don't smell. A parent reading a report card is likely to learn not that his child got an F in conduct, but that she "experiences difficulty exercising self-control: (a) verbally (b) physically." And where do old people go? To Sun City, "a retirement community for senior citizens."

Euphemisms are used for two reasons: to avoid giving offense, and, sometimes unconsciously, to disguise fear or animosity. We do not advise you to write or speak discourteously; we do advise you, though, to use euphemisms consciously and sparingly, when tact recommends them. It's customary in a condolence letter to avoid the word *death,* and, depending both on your own feelings and those of the bereaved, you may wish to follow that custom. But there's no reason on earth to write "Hamlet passes on." You should be aware, moreover, that some people find euphemisms themselves offensive. Margaret Kuhn, for instance, argues that the word *old* is preferable to *senior.* "Old," she says "is the right word. . . . I think we should wear our gray hair, wrinkles, and crumbling joints as badges of distinction. After all, we worked damn hard to get them." She has organized a militant group called the Gray Panthers to fight agism.

In revising, replace needless euphemisms with plain words. Your writing will be sharper, and you might, in examining and confronting them, free yourself of a mindless habit, an unconscious prejudice, or an irrational fear.

A Digression on Public Lying

There is a kind of lying which, in the words of Walker Gibson, we may call *public lying.* Its rules are to avoid substance, direct answers, and plain words. Its tendency is to subvert the English language. It employs and invents euphemisms, but the public liar intends to protect not his listeners, but himself and his friends, and he misleads and deceives consciously. Public lying was not invented during the Vietnam War (in 1946 George Orwell had already written what some people call the definitive essay on it, "Politics and the English Language"). But the war produced some classic examples, from which we select a few.

The war in Vietnam, of course, was not a war, but a "conflict" or an "era." "Our side" never attacked "the other side," we made "protective reaction raids"; we didn't invade, we "incursed." We didn't bomb villages, we "pacified" them; peasants were not herded into concentration camps, but "relocated." We didn't spray the countryside with poisons, destroying forests, endangering or killing plant, animal, and human life, we "practiced vegetation control." When American intelligence agents drowned a spy, they referred to their action as "termination with extreme prejudice."

Feiffer

There is a Gresham's law in rhetoric as there is in economics: bad language drives out good. Bad language is contagious; learn to detect the symptoms: use of vague words for clear words; use of sentences or phrases where words suffice; evasive use of the passive voice; and outright lying.

Passive or Active Voice?

1. I baked the bread. (active voice)
2. The bread was baked by me. (passive voice)
3. The bread will be baked. (passive voice)

Although it is the verb that is in the active or the passive voice, notice that the words *active* and *passive* describe the subjects of the sentences. That is, in the first sentence the verb "baked" is in the active voice; the subject "I" acts. In the second and third sentences the verbs "was baked" and "will be baked" are in the passive voice; the subject "bread" is acted upon. Notice also the following points:

- The *voice* of the verb is distinct from its *tense.* Don't confuse the passive voice with the past tense. (Sentence 2 above happens to be in the past tense, but 3 is not; both 2 and 3 are in the passive voice.)
- The passive voice uses more words than the active voice. (Compare sentences 1 and 2.)
- A sentence with a verb in the passive voice may leave the doer of the action unidentified. (See sentence 3.)
- Finally, notice that in each of the three sentences the emphasis is different.

In revising, take a good look at each sentence in which you have used the passive voice. If the passive clarifies your meaning, retain it; if it obscures your meaning, change it. More often than not, the passive voice obscures meaning.

Passive voice

The revolver given Daru by the gendarme *is left* in the desk drawer. (Left by whom? The passive voice here obscures the point.)

Active voice

Daru leaves the gendarme's revolver in the desk drawer.

Passive voice

Daru serves tea and the Arab *is offered* some. (Confusing shift from the active voice "serves" to the passive voice "is offered.")

Active voice

Daru serves tea and *offers* the Arab some.

Avoid what has been called the Academic Passive: "In this essay it has been argued that. . . ." This cumbersome form used to be common in academic writing (to convey scientific objectivity) but "I have argued" is usually preferable to such stuffiness.

When is the passive voice appropriate? The passive is appropriate when (1) the doer is obvious ("Clinton was elected president in 1992"), or (2) the doer is unknown ("The picture was stolen between midnight and 1:00 A.M."), or (3) the doer is unimportant ("Unexposed film should be kept in a light-proof container").

The Writer's "I"

It is seldom necessary in writing an essay (even on a personal experience) to repeat "I think that" or "in my opinion." Your reader knows that what you write is your opinion. Nor is it necessary, if you've done your job well, to apologize. "After reading the story over several times I'm not really sure what it is about, but. . . ." Write about something you are reasonably sure of. Occasionally, though, when there is a real problem in the text, for example the probable date of the Book of Ruth, it is not only permissible to disclose doubts and to reveal tentative conclusions; it may be necessary to do so.

Note also that there is no reason to avoid the pronoun *I* when you are in fact writing about yourself. Attempts to avoid *I* ("this writer," "we," expressions in the passive voice such as "it has been said above" and "it was seen") are noticeably awkward and distracting. And sometimes you may want to focus on your subjective response to a topic in order to clarify a point. The following opening paragraph of a movie review provides an example:

> I take the chance of writing about Bergman's *Persona* so long after its showing because this seems to me a movie there's no hurry about. It will be with us a long time, just as it has been on my mind for a long time. Right now, when I am perhaps still under its spell, it seems to me Bergman's masterpiece, but I can't imagine ever thinking it less than one of the great movies. This of course is opinion; what I know for certain is that *Persona* is also one of the most difficult movies I will ever see; and I am afraid that in this case there is a direct connection between difficulty and value. It isn't only that *Persona* is no harder than it has to be; its peculiar haunting power, its spell, and its value come directly from the fact that it's so hard to get a firm grasp on.

> —ROBERT GARIS

Students who have been taught not to begin sentences with *I* often produce sentences that are eerily passive even when the verbs are in the active voice. For example:

1. Two reasons are important to my active participation in dance.
2. The name of the program that I enrolled in is the Health Careers Summer Program.
3. An eager curiosity overcame my previous feeling of fear to make me feel better.

But doesn't it make more sense to say:

1. I dance for two reasons.
2. I enrolled in the Health Careers Summer Program.
3. My curiosity aroused, I was no longer afraid.

A good rule: **Make the agent of the action the subject of the sentence.**

Clarity and Coherence

Writing a coherent essay is hard work; it requires mastery of a subject and skill in presenting it; it always takes a lot of time. Writing a coherent paragraph often takes more fussing and patching than you expect, but once you have the hang of it, it's relatively easy and pleasant. Writing a coherent sentence requires only that you stay awake until you get to the end of it.

We all do nod sometimes, even over our own prose. But if you make it a practice to read your work over several times, at least once aloud, you give yourself a chance to spot the incoherent sentence before your reader does, and to revise it. Once you see that a sentence is incoherent, it's usually easy to recast it.

Cats Are Dogs

Looking at a picture of a woman, a man once said to the painter Henri Matisse, "That woman's arm is too long." "That's not a woman," Matisse replied, "it's a painting."

In some sentences a form of the verb *to be* mistakenly asserts that one thing is in a class with another. Is a picture a woman? Are cats dogs? Students did write the following sentences:

Incoherent

X. J. Kennedy's poem "Nothing in Heaven Functions as It Ought" is a contrast between Heaven and Hell. (As soon as you ask yourself the question "Is a poem a contrast?" you have, by bringing the two words close together, isolated the problem. A poem may be a sonnet, an epic, an ode—but not a contrast. The writer was trying to say what the poem does, not what it is.)

Coherent

X. J. Kennedy's poem "Nothing in Heaven Functions as It Ought" contrasts Heaven and Hell.

Incoherent

Besides, he tells himself, a matchmaker is an old Jewish custom. (Is a matchmaker a custom?)

Coherent

Besides, he tells himself, consulting a matchmaker is an old Jewish custom.

Try revising the following:

The essay is also an insight into imperialism.

In a related problem, one part of the sentence doesn't know what the other is doing:

Incoherent

Ruth's devotion to Naomi is rewarded by marrying Boaz. (Does devotion marry Boaz?)

Coherent

Ruth's marriage to Boaz rewards her devotion to Naomi.

Incoherent

He demonstrates many human frailties, such as the influence of others' opinions upon one's actions. (Is influence a frailty? How might this sentence be revised?)

Items in a Series

If you were given a shopping list that mentioned apples, fruit, and pears, you would be puzzled and possibly irritated by the inclusion of "fruit." Don't puzzle or irritate your reader with a **false series** of this sort. Analyze sentences containing items in a series to be sure that the items are of the same order of generality. For example:

False series

His job exposed him to the "dirty work" of the British and to the evils of imperialism. ("The 'dirty work' of the British" is a *specific* example of the more *general* "evils of imperialism." The false series makes the sentence incoherent.)

Revised

His job, by exposing him to the "dirty work" of the British, brought him to understand the evils of imperialism.

In the following sentence, which item in the series makes the sentence incoherent?

Why should one man, no matter how important, be exempt from investigation, arrest, trial, and law enforcing tactics?

Modifiers

A modifier should appear close to the word it modifies (that is, describes or qualifies). Three kinds of faulty modifiers are common: misplaced, squinting, and dangling.

Misplaced Modifiers

If the modifier seems to modify the wrong word, it is called *misplaced.* Misplaced modifiers are often unintentionally funny. The judo parlor that advertised "For $20 learn basic methods of protecting yourself from an experienced instructor" probably attracted more amused readers than paying customers.

Misplaced

Orwell shot the elephant under pressured circumstances. (Orwell was under pressure, not the elephant. Put the modifier near what it modifies.)

Revised

Orwell, under pressure, shot the elephant.

Misplaced

Orwell lost his individual right to protect the elephant as part of the imperialistic system. (The elephant was not part of the system; Orwell was.)

Revised

As part of the imperialistic system, Orwell lost his right to protect the elephant.

Misplaced

Amos Wilder has been called back to teach at the Divinity School after ten years retirement due to a colleague's illness. (Did Wilder retire for ten years because a colleague was ill? Revise the sentence.)

Revise the following:

1. Sitting Bull and William Cody stand side by side, each supporting a rifle placed between them with one hand.
2. Complete with footnotes the author has provided her readers with some background information.

Sometimes other parts of sentences are misplaced:

Misplaced

We learn from the examples of our parents who we are. (The sentence appears to say we are our parents.)

Revised

We learn who we are from the examples of our parents.

Misplaced

It is up to the students to revise the scheme, not the administrators. (We all know you can't revise administrators. Revise the sentence.)

Squinting Modifiers

If the modifier is ambiguous, that is, if it can be applied equally to more than one term, it is sometimes called a *squinting modifier*: it seems to look forward, and it seems to look backward.

Squinting

Being with Jennifer more and more enrages me. (Is the writer spending more time with Jennifer, or is she more enraged? Probably more enraged.)

Revised

Being with Jennifer enrages me more and more.

Squinting

Writing clearly is difficult. (Is this sentence about "writing" or about "writing clearly"?)

Revised

It is clearly difficult to write.

Revised

It is difficult to write clearly.

Squinting

Students only may use this elevator. (Does "only" modify students? If so, no one else may use the elevator. Or does it modify elevator? If so, students may use no other elevator.)

Revised

Only students may use this elevator.

Students may use only this elevator.

Note: The word *only* often squints, seeming to look in two directions. In general, put *only* immediately before the word or phrase it modifies. Often it appears too early in the sentence. (See Glossary.)

Dangling Modifiers

If the term being modified appears nowhere in the sentence, a modifier is called *dangling*.

Dangling

Being small, his ear scraped against the belt when his father stumbled. (The writer meant that the boy was small, not the ear. But the boy is not in the sentence.)

Revised

Because the boy was small his ear scraped against the belt when his father stumbled.

Being small, the boy scraped his ear against the belt when his father stumbled.

Dangling

> A meticulously organized person, his suitcase could be tucked under an airplane seat. (How would you revise the sentence?)

The general rule: **when you revise sentences, put together what belongs together.**

Reference of Pronouns

A pronoun is used in place of a noun. Because the noun usually precedes the pronoun, the noun to which the pronoun refers is called the antecedent (Latin: "going before"). For example:

>   *antecedent*   *pronoun*
>
> When *Sheriff Johnson* was on a horse, *he* was a big man.

But the pronoun can also precede the noun:

>   *pronoun*   *noun*
>
> When *he* was on a horse, *Sheriff Johnson* was a big man.

The word antecedent can be used here too. In short, the antecedent is the word or group of words referred to by a pronoun.

Whenever possible, make sure that a pronoun has a clear reference. Sometimes it isn't possible: *it* is commonly used with an unspecified reference, as in "It's hot today," and "Hurry up please, it's time"; and there can be no reference for interrogative pronouns: "What's bothering you?" and "Who's on first?" But otherwise always be sure that you've made clear what noun the pronoun is standing for.

Vague Reference of Pronouns

Vague

> Apparently, they fight physically and it can become rather brutal. ("It" doubtless refers to "fight," but "fight" in this sentence is the verb, not an antecedent noun.)

Clear

> Their fights are apparently physical, and sometimes brutal.

Vague

> I was born in Colon, the second largest city in the Republic of Panama. Despite this, Colon is still an undeveloped town. ("This" has no specific antecedent. It appears to refer to the writer's having been born in Colon.)

Clear

> Although Colon, where I was born, is the second largest city in Panama, it remains undeveloped.

> (On *this,* see also Glossary, p. 511.)

Revise the following sentence:

> They're applying to medical school because it's a well-paid profession.

Shift in Pronouns

This common error is easily corrected.

1. In many instances the child was expected to follow the profession of your father. (Expected to follow the profession of whose father, "yours" or "his"?)
2. Having a tutor, you can get constant personal encouragement and advice that will help me budget my time. (If "you" have a tutor will that help "me"?)

Revise the following sentences:

1. Schools bring people of the same age together and teach you how to get along with each other.
2. If asked why you went to the dance, one might say they were simply curious.

Ambiguous Reference of Pronouns

A pronoun normally refers to the first appropriate noun or pronoun preceding it. Same-sex pronouns and nouns, like dogs, often get into scraps.

Ambiguous

> Her mother died when she was eighteen. (Who was eighteen, the mother or the daughter?)

Clear

> Her mother died when Mabel was eighteen.

> Her mother died at the age of eighteen. (Note the absence of ambiguity in "His mother died when he was eighteen.")

Ambiguous

> Daru learns that he must take an Arab to jail against his will. (Both Daru and the Arab are male. The writer of the sentence meant that Daru learns he must act against his will.)

Clear

Daru learns that he must, against his will, take an Arab to jail.

The general rule: put together what belongs together.

Agreement

Noun and Pronoun

Everyone knows that a singular noun requires a singular pronoun, and a plural noun requires a plural pronoun, but writers sometimes slip.

Faulty

    singular   **plural**

A *dog* can easily tell if people are afraid of *them.*

Correct

    singular   **singular**

A *dog* can easily tell if people are afraid of *it.*

Faulty

        singular   **plural**

Every student feels that Wellesley expects *them* to do their best.

Correct

          singular   *singular*

Every student feels that Wellesley expects *her* to do her best.

Each, everybody, nobody, no one, and *none* are especially troublesome. See the entries on these words in the Glossary.

Subject and Verb

A singular subject requires a singular verb, a plural subject a plural verb.

Faulty

        plural   **singular**

Horror *films* bring to light a subconscious fear and *shows* a character who succeeds in coping with it.

Correct

        plural   **plural**

Horror *films* bring to light a subconscious fear and *show* a character who succeeds in coping with it.

The student who wrote "shows" instead of "show" thought that the subject of the verb was "fear," but the subject really is "Horror films," a plural.

Faulty

The manager, as well as the pitcher and the catcher, were fined.

Correct

The manager, as well as the pitcher and the catcher, was fined.

If the sentence had been "The manager and the pitcher. . . ," the subject would have been plural and the required verb would be *were:*

The manager and the pitcher were fined.

But in the sentence as it was given, "as well as" (like *in addition to, with,* and *together with*) does *not* add a subject to a subject and thereby make a plural subject. "As well as" merely indicates that what is said about the manager applies to the pitcher and the catcher.

Revise the following:

About mid-morning during Spanish class the sound of jeeps were heard.

Three Additional Points:

1. A **collective noun**—that is, a noun that is singular in form but that denotes a collection of individuals, such as *mob, audience, jury*—normally takes a *singular* verb:

Correct

The mob is at the gate.

Correct

An audience of children *is* easily bored.

(The subject is "an audience," *not* "children.")

Correct

The jury is seated.

But when the emphasis is on the individuals within the group—for instance when you are calling attention to a division within the group—you can use a plural verb:

The jury disagree.

Still, because this sounds a bit odd, it is probably better to recast the sentence:

The jurors disagree.

2. Sometimes a sentence that is grammatically correct may nevertheless sound awkward:

One of its most noticeable features is the lounges.

Because the subject is "one"—*not* "features"—the verb must be singular, "is," but "is" sounds odd when it precedes the plural "lounges." **The solution: revise the sentence.**

Among the most noticeable features are the lounges.

3. When a singular and a plural subject are joined by or, *either . . . or,* **or** *neither . . . nor,* **use a verb that agrees in number with the subject closest to the verb.** Examples:

Correct

Either the teacher *or the students are* mistaken.

Correct

Either the students *or the teacher is* mistaken.

The first version uses "are" because the verb is nearer to "students" (plural) than to "teacher" (singular); the second uses "is" because the verb is nearer to "teacher" than to "students."

Repetition and Variation

1. Don't be afraid to repeat a word if it is the best word. The following paragraph repeats "interesting," "paradox," "Salinger," "What makes," and "book"; notice also "feel" and "feeling." Repetition, a device necessary continuity and clarity, holds the paragraph together.

> The reception given to *Franny and Zooey* in America has illustrated again the interesting paradox of Salinger's reputation there: great public enthusiasm, of the *Time* magazine and Best Seller List kind, accompanied by a repressive coolness in the critical journals. What makes this a paradox is that the book's themes are among the most ambitiously highbrow, and its craftsmanship most uncompromisingly virtuoso. What makes it an interesting one is that those who are most patronizing about the book are those who most resemble its characters: people whose ideas and language in their best moments resemble Zooey's. But they feel they ought not to enjoy the book. There is a very strong feeling in American literary circles that Salinger and love of Salinger must be discouraged.
>
> —MARTIN GREEN

2. Use pronouns, when their reference is clear, as substitutes for nouns. Notice Green's use of pronouns; notice also his substitution of "the book," for

"*Franny and Zooey*," and then "its" for "the book's." Substitutions that neither confuse nor distract keep a paragraph from sounding like a broken phonograph record.

3. Do not, however, confuse the substitutions we have just spoken of with the fault called Elegant Variation. A groundless fear of repetition sometimes leads students to write first, for example, of "Salinger," then of "the writer," then of "our author." Such variations strike the reader as silly. They can, moreover, be confusing. Does "the writer" mean "Salinger," or the person writing about him? Substitute "he" for "Salinger" if "he" is clear and sounds better. Otherwise, repeat "Salinger."

4. But don't repeat a word if it is being used in two different senses.

Confusing

My theme focuses on the theme of the book. (The first "theme" means "essay"; the second means "underlying idea" or "motif.")

Clear

Green's essay focuses on the theme of the book.

Confusing

Caesar's character is complex. The comic characters, however, are simple. (The first "character" means "personality"; the second means "persons" or "figures in the play.")

Clear

Caesar is complex; the comic characters, however, are simple.

5. Finally, eliminate words repeated unnecessarily. Use of words like *surely, in all probability, it is noteworthy* may become habitual. If they don't help your reader to follow your thoughts, they are Instant Prose Additives. Cross them out.

In general, when you revise, decide if a word should be repeated, varied, or eliminated, by testing sentences and paragraphs for both sound and sense.

Euphony

The word is from the Greek, "sweet voice," and though you need not aim at sweetness, try to avoid cacophony, or "harsh voice." Avoid distracting repetitions of sound, as in "The story is marked by a remarkable mystery," and "This is seen in the scene in which. . . ." Such echoes call attention to themselves, getting in the way of the points you are making. When you revise, tune out irrelevant sound effects.

Not all sound effects are irrelevant; some contribute meaning. James Baldwin, in his essay "Stranger in the Village," argues that the American racial experience has permanently altered black and white relationships throughout the world. His concluding sentence is

> This world is white no longer, and it will never be white again.

As the sentence opens, the repetition of sounds in "*w*orld is *w*hite" binds the two words together, but the idea that they are permanently bound is swiftly denied by the most emphatic repetition of sounds in *no, never, again,* as the sentence closes. Or take another example:

> America, Love It or Leave It.

If it read, "America, Love It or Emigrate," would the bumper sticker still imply, as clearly and menacingly, that there are only two choices, and for the patriot, only one?

Transitions

Repetition holds a paragraph together by providing continuity and clarity. Transitions such as *next, on the other hand,* and *therefore* also provide continuity and clarity. Because we discuss transitions at length on pages 62–64, in our chapter on paragraphs, we here only remind you to make certain that the relation between one sentence and the next, and one paragraph and the next, is clear. Often it will be clear without an explicit transition: "She was desperately unhappy. She quit school."

But do not take too much for granted; relationships between sentences may not be as clear to your readers as they are to you. You know what you are talking about; they don't. After reading the passage readers may see, in retrospect, that you have just given an example, or a piece of contrary evidence, or an amplification, but readers like to know in advance where they are going; brief transitions such as *for example, but, finally* (readers are keenly interested in knowing when they are getting near the end) are enormously helpful.

Clarity and Sentence Structure: Parallelism

Make the structure of your sentence reflect the structure of your thought. This is not as formidable as it sounds. If you keep your reader in mind, remembering that you are explaining something to someone who understands it less well than you, you will almost automatically not only say *what* you think but show *how* you think.

Almost automatically. In revising, read your work as if you were not the writer of it, but your intended reader. If you reach a bump or snag, where the shape or direction of your thought isn't clear, revise your sentence structure. Three general rules help:

- Put main ideas in main (independent) clauses.
- Subordinate the less important elements in the sentence to the more important.
- Put parallel ideas and details in parallel constructions.

The time to consult these rules consciously is not while you write, but while you revise. (The first two rules are amplified in the next chapter, "Revising for Emphasis." Clarity and emphasis are closely related, as the following discussion of parallel construction makes evident.)

Consider the following sentence and the revision:

Awkward

He liked eating and to sleep.

Parallel

He liked to eat and to sleep.

In the first version, "eating" and "to sleep" are not grammatically parallel; the difference in grammatical form blurs the writer's point that there is a similarity. Use parallel constructions to clarify relationships—for instance to emphasize similarities or to define differences.

I divorce myself from my feelings and immerse myself in my obligations.

—FROM A STUDENT JOURNAL

She drew a line between respect, which we were expected to show, and fear, which we were not.

—ERNESTO GALARZA

I will not accept if nominated and will not serve if elected.

—WILLIAM TECUMSEH SHERMAN

Fascist art glorifies surrender; it exalts mindlessness; it glamorizes death.

—SUSAN SONTAG

In the following examples, the parallel construction is printed in italic type.

Awkward

The dormitory rules needed revision, a smoking area was a necessity, and a generally more active role for the school in social affairs were all significant to her.

Parallel

> She recommended that the school *revise* its dormitory rules, *provide* a smoking area, and *organize* more social activities.

Awkward

> Most Chinese parents disapprove of interracial dating or they just do not permit it.

Parallel

> Most Chinese parents *disapprove* of interracial dating, and many *forbid* it.

> Revise the following sentence:

> The rogallo glider is recommended for beginners because it is easy to assemble, to maintain, and it is portable.

In parallel constructions, be sure to check the consistency of articles, prepositions, and conjunctions. For example, "He wrote papers on a play by Shakespeare, a novel by Dickens, and a story by Oates," *not* "He wrote papers on a play by Shakespeare, a novel of Dickens, and a story by Oates." The shift from "by" to "of" and back to "by" serves no purpose and is merely distracting.

Let's study this matter a little more, using a short poem as our text.

Robert Bly

Love Poem

> When we are in love, we love the grass,
> And the barns, and the lightpoles,
> And the small mainstreets abandoned all night.

Suppose we change "Love Poem" by omitting a conjunction or an article here and there:

> When we are in love, we love the grass,
> Barns, and lightpoles,
> And the small mainstreets abandoned all night.

We've changed the rhythm, of course, but we still get the point: the lover loves all the world. In the original poem, however, the syntax of the sentence, the consistent repetition of "and the . . . " "and the . . . " makes us feel, without our thinking about it, that when we are in love we love the world, everything in it, equally. The list could extend infinitely, and everything in it would give us identical pleasure. In our altered version, we sacrifice this unspoken assurance. We bump a little, and stumble. As readers, without consciously being aware of it, we wonder if there's some distinction being made, some qualification we've missed. We still get the point of the poem, but we don't feel it the same way.

To sum up:

A pupil once asked Arthur Schnabel (the noted pianist) whether it was better to play in time or to play as one feels; his characteristic mordant reply was another question: "Why not feel in time?"

—DAVID HAMILTON

Exercises

1. In the following sentences, underline phrases in which you find the passive voice. Recast the sentences, using the active voice:

   a. The phrases in which the passive voice is found should be underlined.

   b. The active voice should be used.

   c. In the letter from Mrs. Mike advice was sought regarding her problem with her tenant.

   d. The egg is guarded, watched over, and even hatched by the male penguin.

   e. After the Industrial Revolution, the workers' daylight hours were spent in factories.

   f. Tyler found that sexual stereotyping was reinforced in the kindergarten: the girls were encouraged to play with dolls and the boys with Mack trucks.

   g. Insufficient evidence was given in the report to prove her hypothesis that reading problems originate in peer relationships.

2. Revise the following sentences to eliminate faults in modifiers:

   a. At the age of ten years, my family moved to Zierenberg, West Germany.

   b. Without knowing the reason, my father's cheeks became red with embarrassment.

   c. Buffalo Bill became friends with Sitting Bull while performing together in the Wild West Show.

   d. During a drought, annual plants will succumb without help.

   e. Looking out from my window, the sky was inky black.

   f. Mr. Karajan conducted the orchestra three times during the weekend before returning to his home in the Alps to the delight of the audience.

3. In the following sentences, locate the errors in agreement and correct them.

   a. Locate the error and correct them.

   b. One must strive hard to reach their goal.

   c. I would recommend the book to anyone who wants to improve their writing.

   d. Her collection of antique toys fill the house.

4. Recast the following sentences, using parallel constructions to express parallel ideas:

   a. Jacoby's aim in writing is to disgrace the passively committed and opposition to feminism.

   b. The boys segregated themselves less, the girls showed broader career interests, and unromantic, cross-sex relationships were achieved.

   c. The study shows parents and educators that it is important to change and it can be done.

   d. I do believe that there should be equality between men and women: equal pay for equal work; everybody should have an equal chance to attain whatever goals they may have set for themselves; and everybody should share the same responsibilities toward society.

5. Identify the specific faults that make the following sentence unclear, then revise each sentence for clarity. (Note that you will often have to invent what the writer thought he or she had said.)

   a. Actually, she was aging, and quite average in other respects.

   b. If technology cannot sort out its plusses and minuses, and work to improve them, man must.

   c. Brooks stresses the farm workers' strenuous way of life and the fact that they have the bare necessities of life.

   d. Instead of movable furniture, built-in ledges extend into the center of the room to be used as tables or to sit on.

   e. The issue has been saved for my final argument because it is controversial.

   f. I am neither indifferent nor fond of children.

   g. When the students heard that their proposal was rejected a meeting was called.

   h. A viable library is the cornerstone of any college campus.

   i. Her main fault was that she was somewhat lacking in decision-making capabilities.

   j. After industrialization a swarm of immigrants came bantering to our shores.

   k. Each group felt there was very personal rapport and thus very candid feedback resulted.

l. He can tolerate crowding and pollution and seems disinterested or ignorant of these dangers.

m. The wooden door occupies the majority of the stone wall.

n. Yale students frequently write to Ann Landers telling her fictional stories of their so-called troubles as a childish prank.

o. At my grandmother's house vegetables were only served because meat was forbidden.

p. My firm stand seemed to melt a little.

q. The conclusion leaves the conflict neatly tied in smooth knots.

r. The paragraph reeks of blandness.

6. The following sentences, published in *AIDE,* a magazine put out by an insurance company, were written to the company by various policyholders. The trouble is that the writers mean one thing but their sentences say another. Make each sentence clearly say what the writer means.

a. The other car collided with mine without giving warning of its intentions.

b. I collided with a stationary truck coming the other way.

c. The guy was all over the road; I had to swerve a number of times before I hit him.

d. I pulled away from the side of the road, glanced at my mother-in-law, and headed over the embankment.

e. In my attempt to kill a fly, I drove into a telephone pole.

f. I had been driving for forty years when I fell asleep at the wheel and had the accident.

g. To avoid hitting the bumper of the car in front, I struck the pedestrian.

h. The pedestrian had no idea which direction to run, so I ran over him.

i. The indirect cause of this accident was a little guy in a small car with a big mouth.

7. In 1983, while conflicting reports were being broadcast about an invasion of Grenada by U.S. troops, Admiral Wesley L. McDonald, in the Pentagon, answered a reporter's question thus: "We were not micromanaging Grenada intelligencewise until about that time frame." Bruce Felknor, director of year-books for the *Encyclopaedia Britannica,* says that he was "inspired" by that answer to translate "a small selection of earlier admirals' heroic prose for the edification, indeed enjoyment, of our young." Below we list Felknor's translations and, in parentheses, the names of the admirals, the battles, and the dates of their heroic prose. What were the original words?

a. "Combatwise, the time frame is upcoming." (John Paul Jones, off the English coast, September 23, 1779)

b. "Area accessed in combat mode; mission finished." (Oliver Hazard Perry, after the Battle of Lake Erie, September 10, 1813)

    c. "Disregard anticipated structural damage. Continue as programmed." (David Farragut, Mobile Bay, August 5, 1864)

    d. "Implementation of aggressive action approved; time frame to be selected by fire control officer." (George Dewey, Manila Bay, May 1, 1898)

8. Translate the following euphemisms into plain English:

    a. revenue enhancement

    b. atmospheric deposition of anthropogenically derived acidic substances

    c. resize our operations to the level of profitable opportunities (spoken by a business executive)

    d. reconcentrate (or redeploy) our forces

Chapter 6

Fine-Tuning Sentences: Revising for Emphasis

In revising for conciseness and clarity we begin to discover what we may have been largely unaware of in the early stages of writing: what in our topic most concerns us and precisely why it interests us. That moment of discovery (or those several discrete moments) yields more pleasure than any other in writing. From there on we work, sometimes as if inspired, to make our special angle of vision seem as inevitable to our readers as it is to us. Now as we tighten sentences or expand them, as we shift the position of a word or a paragraph, or as we subordinate a less important idea to a more important one, we are assigning relative value and weight to each of our statements. The expression of value and weight is what is meant by emphasis.

Inexperienced writers may *try* to achieve emphasis as Queen Victoria did, by a style consisting *almost entirely* of italics and—dashes—and—exclamation marks!!! Or they may spice their prose with clichés ("little did I realize," "believe it or not") or with a liberal sprinkling of intensifiers ("really beautiful," "definitely significant," and so on). But experienced writers abandon these unconvincing devices, preferring to exploit the possibilities of position, of brevity and length, of repetition, and of subordination.

Emphasis by Position

First, let's see how a word or phrase may be emphasized. If it appears in an unusual position it gains emphasis, as in "This course he liked." Because in

English the object of the verb usually comes after the verb as in "He liked this course," if the object appears first, it gains emphasis. But this device is tricky; words in an unusual position often seem ludicrous, the writer fatuous: "A mounted Indian toward the forest raced."

Let's now consider a less strained sort of emphasis by position. The beginning and the end of a sentence or a paragraph are emphatic positions; of these two positions, the end is usually the more emphatic. What comes last is what stays most in the mind. Compare these two sentences:

> The essay is brief but informative.

> The essay is informative but brief.

The first sentence leaves the reader with the impression that the essay, despite its brevity, is worth looking at. The second, however, ends more negatively, leaving the reader with the impression that the essay is so brief that its value is fairly slight. Because the emphasis in each sentence is different, the two sentences say different things.

The rule: it usually makes sense to put the important point near the end, lest the sentence become anticlimactic. Here is a sentence that properly moves to an emphatic end:

> Although I could not read its six hundred pages in one sitting, I never willingly put it down.

If the halves are reversed the sentence trails off:

> I never willingly put it down, although I could not read its six hundred pages in one sitting.

This second version straggles away from the real point—that the book was interesting.

Anticlimactic

> Besides not owning themselves women also could not own property.

Emphatic

> Women could not own property; in fact, they did not own themselves.

The commonest anticlimaxes are caused by weak qualifiers (*in my opinion, it seems to me, in general, etc.*) tacked on to interesting statements. Weak qualifiers usually can be omitted. Even useful ones rarely deserve an emphatic position.

Anticlimactic

Poodles are smart but they are no smarter than pigs, I have read.

Emphatic

Poodles are smart, but I have read that they are no smarter than pigs.

The rule: try to bury dull but necessary qualifiers in the middle of the sentence.

Emphasis by Brevity and Length: Short and Long Sentences

How long should a sentence be? One recalls Lincoln's remark to a heckler who asked him how long a man's legs should be: "Long enough to reach the ground." No rules about length can be given, but be careful not to bore your reader with a succession of short sentences (say, under ten words) and be careful not to tax your reader with a monstrously long sentence. In *Les Misérables* Victor Hugo wrote a sentence containing 823 words and punctuated by ninety-three commas, fifty-one semicolons, and four dashes—not a good model for beginners.

Consider this succession of short sentences:

The purpose of the refrain is twofold. First, it divides the song into stanzas. Second, it reinforces the theme of the song.

These sentences are clear, but since the points are simple, readers may feel they are being addressed as if they were children. There is too much emphasis (too many heavy pauses) on too little. The reader can take all three sentences at once:

The purpose of the refrain is twofold: it divides the song into stanzas and it reinforces the theme.

The three simple sentences have been turned into one compound sentence, allowing the reader to keep going for a while.

Now compare another group of sentences with a revision.

Hockey is by far the fastest-moving team sport in America. The skaters are constantly on the go. They move at high speeds. The action rarely stops.

These four sentences, instead of suggesting motion, needlessly stop us. Here is a revision:

> Hockey is by far the fastest-moving team sport in America. The skaters, constantly on the go, move at high speeds, and the action rarely stops.

By combining the second, third, and fourth sentences, the writer keeps the reader on the go, like the players.

Next, a longer example that would be thoroughly delightful if parts of it were less choppy.

Conceit

At my high school graduation we had two speakers. One was a member of our class, and the other was a faculty member. The student speaker's name was Alva Reed. The faculty speaker's name was Mr. Williams. The following conversation took place after the graduation ceremony. Parents, relatives, faculty, and friends were all outside the gymnasium congratulating the class of 1989. Alva was surrounded by her friends, her parents, and some faculty members who were congratulating her on her speech. Not standing far from her was Mr. Williams with somewhat the same crowd.

"Alva dear, you were wonderful!"

"Thanks Mom. I sure was scared though: I'm glad it's over."

At that moment, walking towards Alva were her grandparents. They both were wearing big smiles on their faces. Her grandfather said rather loudly, "That was a good speech dear. Nicely done, nicely done." Walking past them at that moment was Mr. Williams.

He stuck his head into their circle and replied, "Thank you," and walked away.

The first four sentences of this amusing anecdote seem to be written in spurts. They can easily be combined and improved thus:

> At my high school graduation we had two speakers. One was a member of our class, Alva Reed, and the other was a faculty member, Mr. Williams.

If we think that even this version, two sentences instead of four, is a little choppy, we can rewrite it into a single sentence:

> At my high school graduation we had two speakers, Alva Reed, a member of our class, and Mr. Williams, a faculty member.

or:

> The two speakers at my high school graduation were Alva Reed, a member of our class, and Mr. Williams, a faculty member.

The rest of the piece is less choppy, but reread it and see if you don't discover some other sentences that should be combined.

Sometimes, however, the choppiness of a succession of short sentences is effective. Look at this description of the methods by which George Jackson, in prison, resisted efforts to destroy his spirit:

> He trains himself to sleep only three hours a night. He studies Swahili, Chinese, Arabic and Spanish. He does pushups to control his sexual urge and to train his body. Sometimes he does a thousand a day. He eats only one meal a day. And, always, he is reading and thinking.
>
> —JULIUS LESTER

These six sentences add up to only fifty-one words. The longest sentence—the one about pushups—contains only thirteen words. That the author is at ease also with longer and more complicated sentences is evident in the next paragraph, which begins with a sentence of forty-two words.

> Yet, when his contact with the outside world is extended beyond his family to include Angela Davis, Joan, a woman who works with the Soledad defense committee, and his attorney, he is able to find within himself feelings of love and tenderness.

Can we account for the success of the passage describing Jackson's prison routine? First, the short sentences, with their repeated commonplace form (subject, verb, object) in some degree imitate Jackson's experience: they are almost monotonously disciplined, almost as regular as the pushups the confined Jackson does.

He trains himself. . . .

He studies Swahili. . . .

He does pushups. . . .

Sometimes he does a thousand. . . .

He eats only one meal a day.

Later, when Jackson makes contact with Angela Davis and others, the long sentence (forty-two words) helps to suggest the expansion of his world. Second, the brevity of the sentences suggests their enormous importance, certainly to Jackson and to Julius Lester and, Lester hopes, to the reader.

Keep in mind this principle: **any one sentence in your essay is roughly equal to any other sentence.** If a sentence is short, it must be relatively weighty. A lot is packed into a little. Less is more. (The chief exceptions are transitional sentences such as, "Now for the second point.") Consider the following passage:

> It happened that in September of 1933 Lord Rutherford, at the British Association meeting, made some remark about atomic energy never becoming real. Leo Szilard was the kind of scientist, perhaps just the kind of good-humored, cranky man, who disliked any statement that contained the word "never," particularly when made by a distinguished colleague. So he set his mind to think about the problem.
>
> —JACOB BRONOWSKI

The first two sentences are relatively long (twenty-three words and thirty-one words); the third is relatively short (ten words), and its brevity—its weight or density—emphasizes Szilard's no-nonsense attitude.

Emphasis by Repetition

Don't be afraid to repeat a word if it is important. The repetition will add emphasis. Notice in these lucid sentences by Helen Gardner the effective repetition of "end" and "beginning."

> *Othello* has this in common with the tragedy of fortune, that the end in no way blots out from the imagination the glory of the beginning. But the end here does not merely by its darkness throw up into relief the brightness that was. On the contrary, beginning and end chime against each other. In both the value of life and love is affirmed.

The substitution of "conclusion" or "last scene" for the second "end" would be worse than pointless; it would destroy Miss Gardner's point that there is *identity* or correspondence between beginning and end.

Emphasis by Subordination

Five Kinds of Sentences

Before we can discuss the use of subordination for emphasis, we must first talk about what a sentence is, and about five kinds of sentences.

If there is an adequate definition of a sentence, we haven't found it. Perhaps the best definition is not the old one, "a complete thought," but "a word or group of words that the reader takes to be complete." This definition includes such utterances as "Who?" and "Help!" and "Never?" and "Maybe." Now, in speaking, "While he was walking down the street" may be taken as a complete thought, if it answers the question "When did the car hit him?" In writing, however, it would be a sentence fragment that probably should be altered to, say, "While he was walking down the street he was hit by a car." We will discuss intentional fragments on pages 142–43. But first we should take a closer look at complete sentences.

Usually a sentence names someone or something (this is the subject) and it tells us something about the subject (this is the predicate); that is, it "predicates" something about the subject. Let us look at five kinds of sentences: simple, compound, complex, compound-complex, and sentence fragments.

1. A **simple sentence** has one predicate, here italicized:

Shakespeare *died.*

Shakespeare and Jonson *were contemporaries.*

The subject can be elaborated ("Shakespeare and Jonson, England's chief Renaissance dramatists, were contemporaries"), or the predicate can be elaborated ("Shakespeare and Jonson were contemporaries in the Renaissance England of Queen Elizabeth"); but the sentence remains technically a simple sentence, consisting of only one main (independent) clause with no dependent (subordinate) clause.

2. A **compound sentence** has two or more main clauses, each containing a subject and a predicate. It is then, two or more simple sentences connected by a coordinating conjunction (*and, but, for, nor, or, so, yet*) or by *not only . . . but also,* or by a semicolon or colon or, rarely, by a comma.

Shakespeare died in 1616, and Jonson died in 1637.

Shakespeare not only wrote plays, but he also acted in them.

Shakespeare died in 1616; Jonson died twenty-one years later.

3. A **complex sentence** has one main (independent) clause and one or more subordinate (dependent) clauses. The main clause (here italicized can stand as a sentence by itself.

Although Shakespeare died, *England survived.*

Jonson did not write a commemorative poem when Shakespeare died.

The parts not italicized are subordinate or dependent because they cannot stand as sentences by themselves.

4. A **compound-complex sentence** has two or more main-clauses (here italicized) and one or more subordinate clauses.

> *In 1616 Shakespeare died* and *his wife inherited the second-best bed* because he willed it to her.

Each of the two italicized passages could stand by itself as a sentence, but "because he willed it to her" could not (except as the answer to a question). Each italicized passage, then, is a main (independent) clause, and "because he willed it to her" is a subordinate (dependent) clause.

We will return to subordination, but let us first look at the fifth kind of sentence, the sentence fragment.

5. A **sentence fragment** does not fit the usual definition of a sentence, but when the fragment is intended the thought is often clear and complete enough. Intentional fragments are common in advertisements:

Made of imported walnut. For your pleasure. At finer stores.

More native than the Limbo. More exciting than the beat of a steel drum. Tia Maria. Jamaica's haunting liqueur.

And yet another example, this one not from an advertisement but from an essay on firewood:

> Piles of it. Right off the sidewalk. Split from small logs of oak or ash or maple. Split. Split again.

> —John McPhee

All these examples strike us as pretentious in their obviously studied efforts at understatement. Words are hoarded, as though there is much in little, and as though to talk more fully would demean the speaker and would desecrate the subject. A few words, and then a profound silence. Here less is not more; it is too much. The trouble with these fragmentary sentences is not that they don't convey complete thoughts but that they attract too much attention to themselves; they turn our minds too emphatically to their writers, and conjure up images of unpleasantly self-satisfied oracles.

Here, however, is a passage from a student's essay, where the fragmentary sentences seem satisfactory to us. The passage begins with a simple sentence, and then gives three fragmentary sentences.

The film has been playing to sellout audiences. Even though the acting is inept. Even though the sound is poorly synchronized. Even though the plot is incoherent.

If this passage is successful, it is because the emphasis is controlled. The author is dissatisfied, and by means of parallel fragments (each beginning with the same words) she conveys a moderately engaging weariness and a gentle exasperation.

Then, too, we see that if the first three periods were changed to commas we would have an orthodox complex sentence. In short, because the fragments are effective we find them acceptable.

For ways to correct ineffective or unacceptable fragments, see pages 462–63 in Chapter 21.

Subordination

Having surveyed the kinds of sentences, we can at last talk about using subordination to give appropriate emphasis.

Make sure that the less important element is subordinate to the more important. Consider this sentence, about the painter Vincent van Gogh, who was supported by his brother Theo.

Supported by Theo's money, van Gogh painted at Arles.

The writer puts van Gogh in the independent clause ("Van Gogh painted at Arles"), subordinating the relatively unimportant Theo.

Had the writer wished to give Theo more prominence, the passage might have run:

Theo provided money, and van Gogh painted at Arles.

Here Theo (as well as van Gogh) stands in an independent clause, linked to the next clause by "and." The two clauses, and the two people, are now of approximately equal importance.

If the writer had wanted to emphasize Theo and to deemphasize van Gogh, he might have written:

While van Gogh painted at Arles, Theo provided the money.

Here van Gogh is reduced to the subordinate clause, and Theo is given the dignity of the only independent clause.

In short, though simple sentences and compound sentences have their place, they make everything of equal importance. Since everything is not of equal importance, you must often write complex and compound-complex sentences, subordinating some things to other things.

Exercise

1. Here is one way to test your grasp of the relationship of independent and subordinate elements in a sentence. This *haiku* (a Japanese poetic form) consists of one sentence that can be written as prose: "After weeks of watching the roof leak, I fixed it tonight by moving a single board."

Hitch Haiku
After weeks of watching the roof leak

I fixed it tonight

by moving a single board.

—GARY SNYDER

    a. Identify the independent clause and the subordinate elements in the poem.

    b. The "I" in the poem's sentence does or has done three things. Write three simple sentences, each expressing one of the actions.

    c. Write one sentence in which all three of the poem's actions are expressed, but put in the independent clause one of the two actions that appear in a subordinate element in the poem.

    d. Compare your sentence with the poem's. Both sentences should be clear. How do they vary in emphasis?

    e. Optional: Compare the original sentence written as poetry and written as prose.

2. First identify the fault or faults that make the following sentences unemphatic, and then revise them for emphasis.

    a. He lists some of the rights given to humans and to nonhumans and both admits and accounts for the oddity of his proposal well by citing examples.

    b. Rights for women, African-Americans and the insane were granted though many couldn't see the value in it and so now our environment should be granted rights even though it takes some getting used to the idea.

    c. Thus Creon's pride forces Antigone's death which drives his son to suicide and then his wife.

    d. Stock breeding will give the same result as population evolution, defenders of positive eugenics claim.

    e. The family today lacks the close relationship it had before the industrial age, for example.

    f. The woman's face is distraught, her hair is unkempt, and her dress is rumpled.

    g. There is probably no human being who would enjoy being eaten by a shark.

3. Analyze the ways Theodore Roosevelt achieved emphasis in the following passage on Grand Canyon.

In Grand Canyon Arizona has a natural wonder which, so far as I know, is in kind absolutely unparalleled throughout the rest of the world. . . . Leave it as it is. You cannot improve upon it. The ages have been at work on it, and man can only mar it. What you can do is to keep it for your children, your children's children, and for all those who come after you as one of the great sights which every American, if he can travel at all, should see.

Chapter 7

Acquiring Style

The friends that have it I do wrong
When ever I remake a song,
Should know what issue is at stake:
It is myself that I remake.

—WILLIAM BUTLER YEATS

Defining Style

The Mechanics of Style

The third edition of *The American Heritage Dictionary of the English Language* gives fifteen definitions of *style,* two of which are of special interest to writers. Let's begin with the easier of the two. *Style,* according to the seventh definition, is "a customary manner of presenting printed material, including usage, punctuation, spelling, typography, and arrangement." Thus the American Medical Association issues a publication called *Style Book: Editorial Manual,* which instructs contributors to medical journals such as *Journal of American College Health* to use margins of a certain width and to head their list of books, at the end of an article, "References." (The heading may seem obvious, but authors writing in the humanities are instructed by the style book that guides *their* profession to head the list "Works Cited.") If you consult *The Chicago Manual of Style,* now in its fourteenth edition, will find exhaustive instructions on "Chicago Manual" style—about margins, about whether to write *per cent* or *percent,* about when to spell out numbers and when to use numerals, and so forth.

Manuals of *style* in this sense ("a customary manner of presenting printed material") usually go a bit further, and suggest, for instance, that contractions ("don't," "it's") may (or may not) be used, and they may contain a warning against using the first person singular ("*Unacceptable:* 'I dissected the frog.' *Preferred:* 'The frog was dissected' "). Here, however, in moving from mechanics to something more personal, we are getting into the second definition of interest to writers.

The Writer's Voice

According to the second relevant definition, *style* is "The way in which something is said, done, expressed, or performed." The late Arthur Ashe had his own distinctive style of playing tennis, recognizably different from that of Jimmy Connors or John McEnroe. Indeed we all have *our* ways of doing things, for instance our ways of dressing or of writing our names. If you are telling a friend about an unpleasant conversation, the friend may say, "Why didn't you tell him off?" and you might answer, "That's not my style." That is, anger and perhaps rudeness just aren't part of the way you express yourself.

In this sense, everyone has style, characteristic ways of doing things. The person who keeps saying "Uh, you know what I mean," has a style (an annoying style), and so does the person who talks like a book (also an annoying style). Or think of any cartoonists whose work you are familiar with. The style of drawing of, say, *The Amazing Spider-Man* (by Stan Lee and Larry Lieber) is clearly different from the style of *Doonesbury* (Garry Trudeau), and neither of these styles resembles that of *Garfield* (Jim Davis). In one sense, then, a cartoonist— or a writer—is free to develop a distinctive style (a "way in which something is said, done"), but in another sense of *style* ("a customary manner of presenting printed material") strong constraints operate: the cartoon can extend only a certain number of inches, the number of words it contains is severely limited by the available space, racial slurs will not be tolerated by the publisher, and so on.

All writers know that they must work in accordance with certain principles that are imposed. Take an obvious point: if you write a letter to the editor of your local newspaper, you know that you can't write more than perhaps 300 words—newspapers simply will not publish a letter of a thousand words—and you know that you cannot use obscenities. Further, if the newspaper publishes your letter, they will impose their editorial style (in the first sense) on it, perhaps (for instance) using numerals where you spelled out numbers. But in other matters you are free to develop your individual style or voice, let's say a voice that sounds informal or ironic or objective.

Academic Styles

When you write a paper for a course, you are to some degree learning how people working in that discipline express themselves, and so you must adapt your voice to the conventions of the discipline. Thus some disciplines call for an abstract at the beginning of the paper, and some do not. Some call for an immediate statement of purpose, and some do not. Here, for instance, is the first paragraph of an article in the *Cambridge Journal of Economics* 25:3 (August 1992): 69:

> In this paper I shall develop a framework which may be used to examine several alternative theories of the rate of interest. The four most widely accepted approaches are the Neoclassical Loanable Funds, Keynes's Liquidity Preference, Neoclassical Synthesis ISLM, and Basil Moore's Horizontalist (or endogenous money). I will use the framework developed here to present a fifth: an integration of liquidity preference theory with an endogenous money approach. I first briefly set forth the primary alternative approaches, then develop an analytical framework based on an asset or stock approach and use it to discuss several theories of the interest rate: those advanced by Keynes, by Moore, by neoclassical theory and the monetarists, by Kregel, and by Tobin. Finally, I shall use the framework to reconcile liquidity preference theory with an endogenous money approach.
>
> —L. Randall Wray

When economists talk to each other in journals, that's pretty much the way they talk. It is not at all the way professors of literature talk, most of whom would not conceive of beginning with anything so obvious as "In this paper I shall develop a framework," or of going on to say "I will use . . . I first briefly set forth," and so forth. We are not saying that one style is better than the other, only that different disciplines use different styles—in both senses of the word *style,* the "customary manner of presenting printed material" (very few literary journals require an abstract), and, second, "the way in which something is said" ("In this paper I shall develop . . . ").

Style and Tone

The trick, then, in writing your papers in various courses is to write in the manner appropriate to the discipline—to put yourself into harness, so to speak—and yet *within these restrictions to maintain your own voice,* your own style. A writer's style is in large measure a composite of his or her attitude toward the self, toward the subject, and toward the reader. These attitudes are reflected, or, better, are conveyed, in what is usually called tone.

Let's look at some sentences by a distinguished medical researcher and writer, Lewis Thomas. They come from an essay, "On Natural Death," written for the general reader. Because he is writing for the general reader, Thomas cannot use the sort of technical language ("endogenous money") that Wray used when he was writing for an audience of specialists. If Thomas needs to use a technical term, he will have to define it.

> There are so many new books about dying that there are now special shelves set aside for them in bookstores, along with the health-diet and home-repair paperbacks and the sex manuals.

This sentence could have ended where the comma is placed: the words after "bookstores" are, it might seem, not important. One can scarcely claim that by specifying some kinds of "special shelves" Thomas clarifies an otherwise difficult or obscure concept. What, then, do these additional words do? They tell us nothing about death and almost nothing about bookshops, but they tell us a great deal about Thomas's *attitude toward his subject,* the new books on death. Thomas suggests—without explicitly saying so—that such books are faddish and perhaps (like "the sex manuals") vulgar. After all, if he had merely wanted to call up a fairly concrete image of a well-stocked bookstore he could have said "along with books on politics and the environment," or some such thing. His next sentence runs:

> Some of them are so packed with detailed information and step-by-step instructions for performing the function you'd think this was a new sort of skill which all of us are now required to learn.

Why does Thomas write "you'd think" (a colloquial expression inconceivable in *Cambridge Journal of Economics*) instead of, say, "one might believe"? Thomas uses a colloquial form, and a very simple verb, because he wants to convey to us his common-sense, homely, down-to-earth view that these books are a bit pretentious—a pretentiousness conveyed in his use of the words "performing the function," words that might come from the books themselves. In short, when we read Thomas's paragraph we are hearing a voice, perceiving an attitude, and we want to keep reading, not only because we are interested in death but also because Thomas has managed to make us interested in Thomas, a thoughtful but amusing fellow.

The Writer's Sense of Audience and Purpose

Speakers usually have a good idea of who their audience is—members of the PTA, or classmates, or fellow skiers, or whatever, and because the audience is right in front of them, they can usually establish contact fairly easily, though probably all of us recall some disaster when, as a member of the audience, we were put off by, say, the speaker's monotone or technical language. Writers, unlike speakers, have to imagine their audience. This audience may be fairly unified; readers of *Cambridge Journal of Economics* are likely to be professional economists; readers of *National Review* are not members of any particular profession but by and large they are conservative and thus they share certain values; readers of *The New Republic* by and large are liberal. Writers for

National Review may (like writers for a journal read chiefly by economists) write about the president's economic programs but (unlike writers for a professional journal) they cannot assume their audience is familiar with "endogenous money." They *can* assume, however, that they will get a friendly response by criticizing liberals, and can assume that their readers know who William Buckley is, since Buckley founded the magazine, frequently contributes to it, and is a well-known conservative. The purpose of a conservative writer writing for *National Review* is more or less to reassure the readers that the values they hold are correct, to bring the readers up to date on the latest conservative good sense, and on the latest liberal nonsense. A comparable purpose moves the liberal who writes for *The New Republic,* though here, of course, the aim is to reveal the latest conservative nonsense.

What is a student's purpose in writing an essay? To fulfill the assignment, of course. But surely the purpose often is larger, including a desire to learn about some subject and also (though probably this purpose is only dimly sensed) a desire to *think like* an economist or biologist or art historian or whatever. The student who is writing a laboratory report in a biology course is, for a short period, taking on the role of a biologist, just as the student writing a paper in an economics course is taking on the role of an economist. And therefore the audience is not simply the specific instructor whom the student sees three times a week; rather, the audience is a person like that instructor, but somewhat generalized. You are writing, say, about Alice Walker's novel *The Color Purple,* and you know that your instructor has a detailed knowledge of the book, since she has conducted two class sessions on it, but your imagined audience is a literate person who, though familiar with the language of literary criticism ("symbolism," "point of view") does *not* have in mind all of the details of the book and cannot know what you think about it.

If you keep your imagined audience in mind, you will of course not be entirely free. You will have to remind your reader of some details in the plot, and you will have to quote an occasional passage that even a careful reader of the book would not easily recall. You will find, then, that imagining a fairly particular audience will help you to get into your role, as literary critic or art historian or biologist or economist. And you probably will also find, strange though this sounds, that once you have felt your way into this role, you will be writing (at least when you revise) with a style that is a combination of the demands of the discipline and your distinctive voice.

Tone: Five Examples

1. Here is the opening of an essay ("Parental Leave Is a Myth-take") by a nationally syndicated columnist.

> Let's face it. There's a myth parading as equal rights. That's the myth that a father's attention to a newborn is as important/significant/ necessary, minute by minute as a mother's.

Everyone knows this isn't so. But we've all been encouraged/persuaded/intimidated to pretend that it is.

The myth is what lies behind the proposed government-mandated parental leave bill. We used to talk about maternity leave. Now we talk about "parental" leave, telling employers that if Daddy wants to take off work for twelve weeks after he's "given birth," he's just as entitled to it as the other mommy is. We have to pretend to forget that he's not recovering from carrying extra pounds for nine months, that he hasn't experienced labor pains (no matter how good he was at breathing in the "birthing" room), that his body is not trying to deal with changing (not raging) hormones and the flow of mother's milk.

—SUZANNE FIELDS

a. How would you characterize Fields's attitude toward herself? Her topic? Her audience?

b. In a word or two characterize the writer's style. For instance, is it pretentious or dull or lively or silly or what? Explain your view.

2. The following passage is the first paragraph from an essay entitled "Rape and Modern Sex War." It originally appeared in a newspaper and has been republished in *Sex, Art, and American Culture* (1992), a collection of essays by the author.

Rape is an outrage that cannot be tolerated in civilized society. Yet feminism, which has waged a crusade for rape to be taken more seriously, has put young women in danger by hiding the truth about sex from them.

—CAMILLE PAGLIA

a. The first sentence says something that presumably everyone agrees with. Why, then, did Paglia bother to say it? Would the paragraph be significantly different if it began, "Feminism, which has waged a crusade,. . . "? Explain.

b. If you had read this paragraph in the newspaper, do you think you would have continued to read the essay? Why? (The entire essay is reprinted in this book, beginning on page 593.)

3. The following paragraph, from an essay called "First Amendment Pixillation," was originally published in *National Review*.

Freedom of the press is in mortal peril again, this time out in Kansas, where pseudonymous postal officials tricked New York pornographer Al Goldstein into mailing them his brainchildren, *Screw* and *Smut*. Civil libertarians are swarming to the defense of Goldstein and his former partner, one James Buckley (don't even ask), who are now on trial on federal charges of mailing obscene materials. "*Screw* is a despicable publication," says Harvard's Alan Dershowitz, "but that's what the First Amendment was designed to protect." False. That's what the First Amendment is currently *used* to protect, but . . . well, class, let's have a short review.

—WILLIAM BUCKLEY

a. Buckley begins by saying that "Freedom of the press is in mortal peril again. . . ." Does he mean what he says? Or is he being ironic? (When you use irony, you *say* one thing but *mean* another.) How do you know?

b. In his second sentence Buckley says that civil libertarians "are swarming" to the defense of a pornographer. Why "swarming" rather than, say, "hastening"? What are the connotations of "swarming"?

c. In this paragraph what sort of person does Buckley present himself as? Deeply thoughtful? Cocky? Concessive? Or what? Explain.

4. The following paragraph begins an essay entitled "Connected Education for Women," written by four psychologists and published in the *Journal of Education.*

> Most of the institutions of higher education in this country were de-signed by men, and most continue to be run by men. In recent years feminist teachers and scholars have begun to question the structure, the curriculum, and the pedagogical practices of these institutions, and they have put forth useful proposals for change (e.g., Bowles & Duelli Klein, 1983; Martin, 1984; Nicholson, 1980; Rich, 1979; Spanier, Bloom, & Borovik, 1984). But in order to design an education appro-priate for women we must learn about the academic experiences of or-dinary women, women who are, in most cases, neither teachers nor scholars nor even feminists, but simply students.

> —MARY FIELD BELENKY, BLYTHE MCVICKER CLINCHY, NANCY GOLDBERGER, AND JILL MATTUCK TARULA

a. From this excerpt, how would you characterize the writers' intended audience? What is the writers' purpose? What features of the writing suggest the audience and purpose?

b. This passage strikes us as good academic prose, clear and shapely. Do you agree or disagree? In any case, support your answer by pointing to and commenting on particular words or phrases.

5. We print the opening paragraph of an article that originally appeared in an education supplement published by *The New York Times.* The essay, called "The Key to Basic Skills," argued on behalf of bilingual education.

> If we accept that a child cannot learn unless taught through the lan-guage he speaks and understands; that a child who does not speak or understand English must fall behind when English is the dominant medium of instruction; that one needs to learn English so as to be able to participate in an English-speaking society; that self-esteem and moti-vation are necessary for effective learning; that rejection of a child's native language and culture is detrimental to the learning process: then any necessary effective educational program for limited or no English-speaking ability must incorporate the following:

Language arts and comprehensive reading programs taught in the child's native language

Curriculum content areas taught in the native language to further comprehension and academic achievement

Intensive instruction in English

Use of materials sensitive to and reflecting the culture of children within the program

—ANGELO GONZALEZ AND LUIS O. REYES

a. In what way or ways is the first sentence highly unusual? What effect(s) does it convey?

b. Gonzalez and Reyes were writing chiefly for an audience of schoolteachers and school administrators. If you were to rewrite the passage—i.e., give the ideas but in your own words—in a form that would be suitable for a publication in a newsletter issued to English-speaking junior high school students, what are some of the changes you would have to make?

Chapter 8

Manuscript Form

When your draft at last says what you want to say, you are ready to get it into good physical shape, into an edited manuscript that you will hand in to your instructor.

Basic Manuscript Form

Much of what follows is ordinary academic procedure. Unless your instructor specifies something different, you can adopt these principles as a guide.

1. **Use 8½-by-11-inch paper of good weight.** Do not use paper torn out of a spiral notebook; the ragged edges will distract the reader. If you have written your essay on a computer and have printed it on a continuous roll of paper, remove the perforated strips from each side of the paper and separate the sheets before you hand in the essay.

2. **Write on one side of the paper only.** If you submit a handwritten copy, use lined paper and write, in black or dark blue ink, on every other line if the lines are closely spaced. If you typewrite, double-space, typing with a reasonably fresh ribbon. If you write on a word processor, use a letter-quality printer.

3. **In the upper left-hand corner, one inch from the top, put your name, your instructor's name, the course number, and the date.** Double-space

between lines. It's a good idea to put your last name before the page number (in the upper right-hand corner) of each subsequent page, so the instructor can easily reassemble your essay if somehow a page gets detached and mixed with other papers. (If you write your paper on a word processor, you can instruct it to print your name before each page number.)

4. **Titles.** Use this form for your title: Double-space after the date and then center the title of your essay. Capitalize the first letter of the first and last words of your title, the first word after a semicolon or colon if you use either one, and the first letter of all the other words except articles, conjunctions, and prepositions, thus:

```
Two Kinds of Symbols in To Kill a Mockingbird
```

Notice that your own title is neither underlined nor enclosed in quotation marks. (If, as here, your title includes material that would normally be italicized or in quotation marks, that material continues to be so written.) If the title runs more than one line, double-space between the lines.

5. **Begin the essay by double-spacing below the title.** If your instructor prefers a title page, begin the essay on the next page and number it 1. The title page is not numbered.

6. **Margins.** Except for page numbers, leave a one-inch margin at top, bottom, and sides of text.

7. **Number the pages consecutively,** using arabic numerals in the upper right-hand corner, half an inch from the top. Do not put a period or a hyphen after the numeral, and do not precede the numeral with "page" or "p." (Again, if you give the title on a separate sheet, the page that follows it is page 1. Do not number the title page.)

8. **Paragraphs.** Indent the first word of each paragraph five spaces from the left margin.

9. **Make a copy of your essay** for yourself and keep it until the original has been returned. It is a good idea to keep notes and drafts too. They may prove helpful if you are asked to revise a page, substantiate a point, or supply a source you omitted.

10. **Fasten the pages of your paper with a paper clip in the upper left-hand corner.** Stiff binders are unnecessary; indeed, they are a nuisance to the instructor, adding bulk and making it awkward to write annotations.

Using Quotations (and Punctuating Quotations Correctly)

If you are writing about a text, or about an interview, quotations from your material or subject are indispensable. They not only let your readers know what you are talking about, they give your readers the material you are responding to, thus letting them share your responses. But quote sparingly and quote briefly. Use quotations as evidence, not as padding. If the exact wording of the original is crucial, or especially effective, quote it directly, but if it is not, don't bore the reader with material that can be effectively reduced either by summarizing or by cutting. And make sure, by a comment before or after a quotation, that your reader understands why you find the quotation relevant. Don't count on a quotation to make your point for you.

Here are some additional matters to keep in mind, especially as you revise.

1. **Identify the speaker or writer of the quotation.** Usually this identification precedes the quoted material (e.g., "Smith says, . . . ") in accordance with the principle of letting readers know where they are going. But occasionally it may follow the quotation, especially if the name will provide a meaningful surprise. For example, in a discussion of a proposed tax reform, you might quote a remark hostile to it and then reveal that the author of the proposal was also the author of the remark.

2. **When you introduce a quotation, consider using verbs other than "says."** Depending on the context—that is, on the substance of the quotation and its place in your essay—it might be more accurate to say "Smith argues," "adds," "contends," "points out," "admits," or "comments." Or, again with just the right verb, you might introduce the quotation with a transitional phrase: "In another context Smith had observed that . . . " or "To clarify this point Smith refers to . . . " or "In an apparent contradiction Smith suggests . . . " But avoid such inflated words as "opines," "avers," and "is of the opinion that." The point is not to add "elegant variation" (see page 000) to your introduction of someone else's words, but accuracy and grace. A verb often used *in*accurately is "feels." Ralph Linton does not "feel" that "the term *primitive art* has come to be used with at least three distinct meanings." He "points out," "writes," "observes," or "says" so.

3. **Distinguish between short and long quotations** and treat each appropriately.

Enclose *short quotations,* four (or fewer) lines of typing, within quotation marks:

> Anne Lindbergh calls the harrowing period of the kidnapping and murder of her first child the "hour of lead." "Flying," she wrote, "was freedom and beauty and escape from crowds."

Set off *long quotations* (more than four lines of typing). Do *not* enclose them within quotation marks. To set off a quotation, begin a new line, indent ten spaces from the left margin, and type the quotation double-spaced:

> The last paragraphs of *Five Years of My Life* contain Dreyfus's words when he was finally freed:

The Government of the Republic gives me back my liberty. It is nothing to me without honor. Beginning with today. I shall unremittingly strive for the reparation of the frightful judicial error of which I am still the victim. I want all France to know by a final judgment that I am innocent.

But he was never to receive that judgment.

Note that long quotations are usually introduced by a sentence ending with a colon (as in the above example) or by an introductory phrase, such as "Dreyfus wrote:"

4. **Don't try to introduce a long quotation into the middle of one of your own sentences.** It is too difficult for the reader to come out of the quotation and to pick up your thread. Instead, introduce the quotation, as we did above, set the quotation off, and then begin a new sentence of your own.

5. **An embedded quotation (that is, a quotation embedded into a sentence of your own) must fit grammatically into the sentence of which it is a part.** For example, suppose you want to use Othello's line "I have done the state some service."

Incorrect:

Near the end of the play Othello says that he "have done the state some service."

Correct:

Near the end of the play Othello says that he has "done the state some service."

Correct:

Near the end of the play, Othello says, "I have done the state some service."

6. **Quote exactly.** Check your quotation for accuracy at least twice. If you need to edit a quotation—for example, in order to embed it grammatically, or to inform your reader of a relevant point—observe the following rules:

a. To add or to substitute words, enclose the words in square brackets—not parentheses.

"In the summer of 1816 we [Mary Wollstonecraft and Percy Bysshe Shelley] visited Switzerland and became the neighbors of Lord Byron."

Trotsky became aware that "Stalin would not hesitate a moment to organize an attempt on [his] life."

b. Indicate the omission of material with ellipses (three periods, with a space before and after each period).

The New York Times called it "the most intensive man-hunt . . . in the country's history" (3 March 1932).

If your sentence ends with the omission of the last part of the original sentence, use four periods: one immediately after the last word quoted, and three (spaced) to indicate the omission.

The manual says, "If your sentence ends with the omission of the last part of the original sentence, use four spaced periods. . . ."

Notice that if you begin the quotation with the beginning of a sentence (in the example we have just given "If your" is the beginning of a quoted sentence) you do *not* indicate that material preceded the words you are quoting. Similarly, if you end your quotation with the end of the quoted sentence, you give only a single period, not an ellipsis, although of course the material from which you are quoting may have gone on for many more sentences. But if you begin quoting from the middle of a sentence, or end quoting before you reach the end of a sentence in your source, it is customary to indicate the omissions. But even such omissions need not be indicated when the quoted material is obviously incomplete—when, for instance, it is a word or phrase.

7. **Use punctuation accurately.** There are three important rules to observe:

a. Commas and periods go inside the quotation marks.

"The land," Nick Thompson observes, "looks after us."

b. Semicolons and colons go outside quotation marks.

He turned and said, "Learn the names of all these places"; it sounded like an order.

    c. Question marks, exclamation points, and dashes go inside if they are part of the quotation, outside if they are your own.

Amanda ironically says to her daughter, "How old are you, Laura?"

(The question mark is part of the quotation and therefore goes inside the quotation marks.)

    In the following example, why is the question mark placed outside of the quotation marks?

Is it possible to fail to hear Laura's weariness in her reply, "Mother, you know my age"?

8. Use single quotation marks for a quotation within a quotation.

The student told the interviewer, "I ran back to the dorm and I called my boyfriend and I said, 'Listen, this is just incredible,' and I told him all about it."

    9. **Enclose titles of short works in quotation marks.** Short works include: chapters in books, short stories, essays, short poems, songs, lectures, speeches, and unpublished works (even if long).

    Underline, or use italic type, for titles of long works. (Underlining indicates *italic* type, used in print and available on computers but ordinarily not available on typewriters.) Underline titles of published book-length works: novels, plays, periodicals, collections of essays, anthologies, pamphlets, textbooks, and long poems (such as *Paradise Lost*). Italicize (or underline) also titles of films, record albums, tapes, television programs, ballets, operas, works of art, and the names of planes, ships, and trains.

    Exception: titles of sacred works (for example, the New Testament, the Hebrew Bible, Genesis, Acts, the Gospels, the Koran) are neither underlined nor enclosed within quotation marks. To cite a book of the Bible with chapter and verse, give the name of the book, then a space, then an arabic numeral for the chapter, a period, and an arabic numeral (*not* preceded by a space) for the verse, thus: Exodus 20.14–15. Standard abbreviations for the books of the Bible (for example, Chron.) are permissible in footnotes and in parenthetic citations within the text.

10. **Use quotation marks to identify a word or term to which you wish to call special attention.** (But italics, indicated by underlining, may be used instead of quotation marks.)

By "comedy" I mean not only a funny play, but any play that ends happily.

11. **Do not use quotation marks to enclose slang** or a term that you fear is too casual; use the term or don't use it, but don't apologize by putting it in quotation marks, as in these examples.

Incorrect:

Because of "red tape" it took three years.

Incorrect:

At last I was able to "put in my two cents."

In both of these sentences the writers are signaling their uneasiness; in neither is there any cause for uneasiness.

12. **Do not use quotation marks to convey sarcasm,** as in the following sentence:

These "politicians" are nothing but thieves.

Sarcasm, usually a poor form of argument, is best avoided. But of course there are borderline cases when you may want to convey your dissatisfaction with a word used by others.

African sculpture has a long continuous tradition, but this tradition has been jeopardized by the introduction of "civilization" to Africa.

Perhaps the quotation marks here are acceptable, because the writer's distaste has not yet become a sneer and because she is, in effect, quoting. But it is probably better to change "civilization" to "western culture," omitting the quotation marks.

13. **Do not enclose the title of your own essay in quotation marks,** and do not underline or italicize it.

Corrections in the Final Copy

Extensive revisions should have been made in your drafts, but minor last-minute revisions may be made on the finished copy. Proofreading may catch some typographical errors, and you may notice some small weaknesses. You need not retype the page, or even erase your errors. You can make corrections with the following proofreader's symbols.

If you did not find an error in each triangle, look again.

1. *Changes* in wording may be made by crossing through words and rewriting just above them, either on the typewriter or by hand in pen:

```
When I first moved to the United States at the age of nine, I
         no
had few doubts as to my identity.
```

2. *Additions* should be made above the line, with a caret (') below the line at the appropriate place:

```
                                                   of
When I first moved to the United States at the age nine, I
                                                  ^
had no doubts as to my identity.
```

3. *Transpositions* of letters may be made thus:

```
When I first moved to the United States at the age of nine, I
had no doubts as to my identity.
```

4. *Deletions* are indicated by a horizontal line through the word or words to be deleted. Delete a single letter by drawing a vertical or diagonal line through it.

```
When I first moved to the United States at at the age of nine,
I had no doubts as to my identity.
```

5. *Separation* of words accidentally run together is indicated by a vertical line, *closure* by a curved line connecting the things to be closed up.

```
When I first moved to the United States at the age of nine, I
had no dou bts as to my identity.
```

6. *Paragraphing* may be indicated by the paragraph symbol before the word that is to begin the new paragraph.

```
When I first moved to the United States at the age of nine, I
had no doubts as to my identity. ¶Within a year, however,...
```

Part Two

Explaining Ideas: The Writer's Materials and Strategies

Chapter 9

Analytical Thinking

All there is to writing is having ideas. To learn to write is to learn to have ideas.

—*Robert Frost*

Look at this drawing by Pieter Brueghel the Elder, entitled "The Painter and the Connoisseur" (about 1565), and then jot down your responses to the questions that follow.

Questions

1. One figure is given considerably more space than the other. What is probably implied by this fact?
2. What is the painter doing (beside painting)?
3. What is the connoisseur doing?
4. What does the face of each figure tell you about the character of each figure? The figures are physically close; are they mentally close? How do you know?

Now consider this brief discussion of the picture.

> The painter, standing in front of the connoisseur and given more than two-thirds of the space, dominates this picture. His hand holds the brush with which he creates, while the connoisseur's hand awkwardly fumbles for money in his purse. The connoisseur apparently is pleased with the picture he is looking at, for he is buying it, but his parted lips give him a stupid expression and his eyeglasses imply defective vision. In contrast, the painter looks away from the picture and fixes his eyes on the model (reality) or, more likely, on empty space, his determined expression suggesting that he possesses an imaginative vision beyond his painting and perhaps even beyond earthly reality.

This paragraph is a concise explanation based on analysis. It doesn't simply tell us that the picture shows two people close together; it separates the parts of the picture, pointing out that the two figures form a contrast. It explains why one figure gets much more space than the other, and it explains what the contrasting gestures and facial expressions imply. The writer of the comment has "read" the picture by seeing how the parts function, that is, how they relate to the whole.

Analytical Thinking and Writing

The material that you read in most courses, with the exception of literature courses, is chiefly expository writing, that is, writing that explains; you read of the various causes of a revolution, of the effects of inflation, or of the relative importance of heredity and environment. Similarly, most of your writing in college will be chiefly expository: you will analyze and explain to your reader the characters in a play, the causes and effects of poverty, the strengths and weaknesses of some proposed legislative action.

Classifying and Thinking

Analysis (literally a separating into parts) is not only the source of much writing that seeks to explain, it is a way of thinking, a way of arriving at conclusions (generalizations), or of discovering how conclusions were arrived at. One form of analytical thinking, classifying, is, at its simplest, an adult version of sorting out cards with pictures of baseball players on them. Now, if you have identical items—for instance, one hundred bricks to unload from a truck—you can't sort them; you can only divide them for easier handling into groups of, say, ten, or into armloads. But if the items vary in some way you can sort them out. You can, for example, put socks into one drawer, underwear into another, trousers or dresses in a closet—all in an effort to make life a little more manageable. Similarly, you can sort books by size or by color or by topic or by author; you do this, again, in order to make them manageable, to make easier the job of finding the right one later, and so, ultimately, to learn about what is in the book.

Thinking, if broadly defined, must include intuitions and even idle reveries, but much of what we normally mean by analytical thinking requires classifying into categories and seeing how the categories relate to each other. When you think about choosing courses at school, for example, you classify the courses by subject matter, or by degree of difficulty ("Since I'm taking two hard courses, I ought to look for an easy one"), or by the hour at which they are offered, or by their merit as determined through the grapevine, or by the degree to which they interest you. When you classify, you establish categories by breaking down the curriculum into parts, and by then putting into each category courses that significantly resemble each other but that are not identical. We need categories or classifications; we simply cannot get through life treating every object as unique. Almost everything has an almost infinite number of characteristics and can therefore be placed in any number of categories, but for certain purposes (and we must know our purposes) certain characteristics are significant. It is on these significant characteristics that we fasten.

In classifying, the categories must be established on a single basis of division: you cannot classify dogs into purebreds and small dogs, for some dogs belong in both categories. You must classify them into consistent, coordinate categories, let's say either by breeding or by size. Of course, you can first classify or sort dogs into purebreds and mutts and *then* sort each of these groups into two subordinate categories, dogs under twelve inches at the shoulder and dogs twelve inches or more at the shoulder. The categories, as we shall see in a few minutes, will depend on your purpose. That the categories into which things are sorted should be coordinate is, alas, a principle unknown to the American Kennel Club, which divides dogs into six groups. The first four seem reasonable enough: (1) sporting dogs (for example, retrievers, pointers, spaniels), (2) hounds (bassets, beagles, whippets), (3) working dogs (sheepdogs, Saint Bernards, collies), (4) terriers (airedales, Irish terriers, Scottish terriers). Trouble begins with the fifth classification, toy dogs (Maltese, Chihuahuas, toy poodles), for size has not been a criterion up to now. The sixth category is desperate: non-sporting dogs (chow chow, poodle, dalmatian). Nonsporting! What a category. Why not nonworking or nonhound? And is a poodle really more like a chow chow than like a toy poodle?[1] Still, the classifications are by now established.

---

[1] Equally zany were the labels on the five cells in the jail at Beaufort. Texas, a few decades ago: White Male, White Female, Colored Male, Colored Female, and U.S. Marines.

Every purebred must fit into one and only one, and thus every purebred can be measured against all of the dogs that in significant ways are thought to resemble it.

Examples of Classifying

Suppose you were to turn your mind to thinking about punishment for killers. You would need to distinguish at least between those killers whose actions are premeditated and those killers whose actions are not. And in the first category you might make further distinctions:

1. Professional killers who carefully contrive a death
2. Killers who are irrational except in their ability to contrive a death
3. Robbers who contrive a property crime and who kill only when they believe that killing is necessary in order to commit that crime

You can hardly talk usefully about capital punishment or imprisonment without making some such analysis of killers. You have, then, taken killers and sorted or *classified* them, not for the fun of inventing complications but for the sake of educating yourself and those persons with whom you discuss the topic. Unless your attitude is the mad Queen of Hearts's "Off with their heads," you will be satisfied with your conclusion only after you have tested it by dividing your topic into parts, each clearly distinguished from the others, and then showed how they are related.

A second example: if you think about examinations—especially if you think about them with the aid of pencil and paper—you may find that they can serve several purposes. Examinations may test knowledge, intelligence, or skill in taking examinations; or they may stimulate learning. Therefore, if you wish to discuss what constitutes a good examination, you must decide what purpose an examination *should* serve. Possibly you will decide that in a particular course an examination should chiefly stimulate learning, but that it should also test the ability to reason. To arrive at a reasonable conclusion, a conclusion worth sharing, and if need be, defending, you must first recognize and sort out the several possibilities.

Often the keenest analytical thinking considers not only what parts are in the whole, but what is *not* there—what is missing in relation to a larger context that we can imagine. Here is an example. If we analyze the women in the best-known fairy tales, we will find that most are either sleeping beauties or wicked stepmothers. These categories are general: "sleeping beauties" includes all passive women valued only for their appearance, and "wicked stepmothers" includes Cinderella's cruel older sisters. (Fairy godmothers form another category, but they are not human beings.) Analysis helps us to discover the almost total absence of resourceful, productive women. ("Almost total," rather than "total," because there are a few resourceful women in fairy tales, such as

Gretel.) You might begin a thoughtful essay with a general statement to this effect and then support the statement with an analysis of "Cinderella," "Little Red Riding Hood." and "Snow White."

Cause and Effect

What causes that whistling noise in the car when I turn left?

Why won't she go out with me?

What will my father say when I tell him I'm not going to medical school?

Without much thought, we usually can find momentarily reassuring answers to dispel such questions: the noise probably isn't important; I didn't like her anyway; maybe my father already knows. But analytical reasoning from cause to effect might, in the long run, be more productive. In any case, it is the kind of thinking usually expected in academic discussions, which are much given to questions such as the following:

What part did the Bay of Pigs attack on Cuba play in the Cuban missile crisis of 1962?

What is the effect of labeling on mental patients?

What is the function of Mrs. Linde in Ibsen's *A Doll's House?*

Does pornography lead to violence against women?

How does the death penalty affect jury verdicts?

Why do people enjoy horror movies?

Let's look at the first four paragraphs of a journalist's article on the fear of public speaking, a clear example of moving from cause to effect:

Madeline Drexler

Center Stage

1   What is it about giving a speech that turns the most self-possessed person into a quivering collection of neuroses? What imagined gaffe could merit the thumping heart, arid throat, and intestinal chaos? In a national survey of people's fears, public speaking ranked No. 1; death was seventh. This order of phobias doesn't surprise psychologists who treat stage fright. After all, they say, giving a formal talk to a group of strangers—or even friends—is like publicly revealing one's private demons.

2   Much of the fright in stage fright comes from the messages we send ourselves in anticipation of the dread event. Some people are afraid of

appearing incompetent. Others are convinced they will forget their speech. Still others believe the audience will find them boring, foolish, or physically unattractive. "Whatever your area of vulnerability, that's what you put forward," notes Peter Desberg, a Los Angeles psychologist who specializes in helping people with performance anxiety.

3   Desberg describes a cycle of fear gripping mind and body. It usually begins with a fretful prediction that something will go wrong during the speech—calamities that range from losing one's place to watching the audience snicker. This prediction prompts a burst of adrenalin that speeds up the heart. The rapid pulse in turn reinforces the original fear: Hey, things must really be bad or I wouldn't feel this way. Once the talk is under way, the agitated speaker often scrutinizes the audience for signs of judgment—which only diverts attention from the speech itself and increases the chances of messing up.

4   Other factors also feed stage anxiety. According to William Donohue, professor of communications at Michigan State University, novice speakers have virtually no control over how their audiences perceive them—in contrast to daily interactions, in which we can tailor our image in response to others. Stage fright looms larger if we try to create a flawless performance, an impossible standard set by our culture's media stars. (For professional stage performers, who get the jitters as much as amateurs, perfection is a necessary standard and just as unnerving.)

Now let's analyze the paragraphs. In the first paragraph Drexler introduces the question "What causes us to fear public speaking?" (our paraphrase). She also reveals that, according to a national survey, fear of public speaking ranks first among our fears, thus suggesting that it is worthwhile to understand what causes the fear. In the second paragraph, we find the following causes:

1. Fear of appearing incompetent
2. Fear of forgetting our speech
3. Fear that the audience will find us boring, foolish, or unattractive.

In the third paragraph we learn that the fear is cyclical: fear that *something* will go wrong causes a burst of adrenalin, which speeds up the heart, its rapid beating making us more fearful, which causes us to search the audience for signs of disapproval, thus distracting us from the speech itself. And in the fourth paragraph we learn that our fear is enhanced by two other causes: the lack of control over the audience that novice speakers experience, and the "impossible standards" of perfection that we may set for ourselves.

By using the same form of analytical reasoning (moving from cause to effect), Drexler answers the question "What cures this nearly universal anxiety?" Here are the four paragraphs presenting her solution:

1   What cures this nearly universal anxiety? Three approaches work. One focuses on the volatile emotions preceding the big event. Speakers learn

breathing and relaxation exercises that calm both body and mind before they step up to the microphone. Using a technique called systematic desensitization, Donohue takes this even further. He places his students in a comfortable chair, with soothing music in the background, and then asks them to think about their favorite form of communication—talking with someone they love, for instance. He then turns the subject to speechmaking, drawing parallels between the two forms of expression. By the end of the exercise, the student can contemplate giving a speech without becoming flustered.

2   A second technique dispels worrisome thoughts. A psychologist or coach will refute such irrational beliefs as "I'm going to forget everything" or "People will see that I'm shaking" with statements such as: "Did you ever see a speaker forget everything?" or "When was the last time you noticed someone's heart beating behind the lectern?" As Donohue puts it, "People tremendously overestimate the extent to which audiences see their flaws."

3   The third technique supplies the skills to polish a performance. These include memorizing, outlining, and improving gestures and delivery. "If people believe they have the skills, that's 90 percent of the battle," Donohue says. "If they use all three approaches together, that's the best."

4   Novices might assume that silver-tongued performers are born with the gift—and the guts. Not so, experts say. Just as all of us are more confident in some settings than in others, many stage performers and speechmakers become awkward and self-conscious when their script is gone, such as during interviews. That's why Desberg calls stage fright a state, not a trait. "Everyone gets nervous," he says, "if the state is right."

What effect is Drexler examining here? What three approaches (causes) lead to this effect?

Your writing course may offer you some practice in writing cause and effect analyses; other academic courses, especially in the sciences and social sciences, almost certainly will. You can also practice by noticing patterns as you read assigned academic texts as well as newspapers and magazines. Make it a habit to underline or highlight such phrases as *The three causes everyone agrees on were* . . . , or *Among the most notable effects* . . . , and then number the causes and effects in the margins of the text. When you are studying for a quiz or an exam, make lists of causes and effects; make lists too when your writing calls for an analysis of cause and effect. In the essays at the end of this chapter, see where you can spot this pattern of thinking and writing.

Comparing

We began this chapter with a brief analysis of a Brueghel drawing. The analysis *compared* Brueghel's handling of the two figures: the amount of space each figure occupied, their activities, their facial expressions, the directions of their gaze. We might say that the drawing invites the comparison, and in so doing communicates Brueghel's understanding of the artist's vision, or of the true value of art.

Writers, too, often use comparisons to explain a concept or idea or to arrive at a judgment or conclusion. As in drawing or painting, the point of a comparison in writing is not simply to list similarities or differences, but to explain something, to illuminate what the similarities and differences add up to. What the comparison—or analysis—adds up to is sometimes referred to as a *synthesis*, literally, a combination of separate elements to form a coherent whole.

Notice in the following paragraph, from an essay entitled "England, Your England," written during World War II, how George Orwell clarifies our understanding of one kind of military march, the Nazi goose-step, by calling attention to how it differs from the march used by English soldiers. Notice, too, the point of his comparison, which he makes clear in his second sentence, and which resonates throughout the comparison.

> One rapid but fairly sure guide to the social atmosphere of a country is the parade-step of its army. A military parade is really a kind of ritual dance, something like a ballet, expressing a certain philosophy of life. The goose-step, for instance, is one of the most horrible sights in the world, far more terrifying than a dive-bomber. It is simply an affirmation of naked power; contained in it, quite consciously and intentionally, is the vision of a boot crashing down on a face. Its ugliness is part of its essence, for what it is saying is "Yes, I *am* ugly, and you daren't laugh at me," like the bully who makes faces at his victim. Why is the goose-step not used in England? There are, heaven knows, plenty of army officers who would be only too glad to introduce some such thing. It is not used because the people in the street would laugh. Beyond a certain point, military display is only possible in countries where the common people dare not laugh at the army. The Italians adopted the goose-step at about the time when Italy passed definitely under German control, and, as one would expect, they do it less well than the Germans. The Vichy government, if it survives, is bound to introduce a stiffer parade-ground discipline into what is left of the French army. In the British army the drill is rigid and complicated, full of memories of the eighteenth century, but without definite swagger; the march is merely a formalised walk. It belongs to a society which is ruled by the sword, no doubt, but a sword which must never be taken out of the scabbard.
>
> —GEORGE ORWELL

Organizing Short Comparisons

An essay may be devoted entirely to a comparison, say of two kinds of tribal organization. But such essays are relatively rare. More often, an essay includes only a paragraph or two of comparison—for example, explaining something unfamiliar by comparing it to something familiar. Let's spend a moment discussing how to organize a paragraph that makes a comparison—though the same principles can be applied to entire essays.

The first part may announce the topic, the next part may discuss one of the two items being compared, and the last part may discuss the other. We can call this method *lumping,* because it presents one item in a lump, and then the other in another lump. Thus Orwell says all that he wishes to say about the goose-step in one lump, and then say what he wishes to say about the British parade-step in another lump. But in making a comparison a writer may use a different method, which we'll call *splitting.* The discussion of the two items may run throughout the paragraph, the writer perhaps devoting alternate sentences to each. Because almost all writing is designed to help the reader to see what the writer has in mind, it may be especially useful here to illustrate this second structure, splitting, with a discussion of visible distinctions. The following comparison of a Japanese statue of a Buddha with a Chinese statue of a bodhisattva (a slightly lower spiritual being, dedicated to saving humankind) shows how a comparison can run throughout a paragraph.

Sakyaumi Buddha. Wood, 33½";
Japanese, late tenth century.

Bodhisattva Kuan Yin. Wood, 56½" ;
Chinese, twelfth century.

The Buddha sits erect and austere, in the lotus position (legs crossed,
each foot with the sole upward on the opposing thigh), in full control of
his body. In contrast, the bodhisattva sits in a languid, sensuous posture
known as "royal ease," the head pensively tilted downward, one knee
elevated, one leg hanging down. The carved folds of the Buddha's garments, in keeping with his erect posture, are severe, forming a highly
disciplined pattern, whereas the bodhisattva's garments hang naturalis-
tically. Both figures are spiritual but the Buddha is remote, constrained,
and austere; the bodhisattva is accessible, relaxed, and compassionate.

In effect the structure of the paragraph is this:

the Buddha (posture)

the bodhisattva (posture)

the Buddha (garments)

the bodhisattva (garments)

the Buddha and the bodhisattva (synthesis)

Notice, again, that although this paragraph on two images is chiefly devoted to
offering an analysis, it also offers a *synthesis*. That is, the analytic discussion of

the Buddha calls attention to the posture and garments, but it also brings these elements together, seeing the figure as "remote, constrained, austere." Similarly, the discussion of the bodhisattva calls attention to the posture and garments, and synthesizes these, or brings them together, by characterizing the image as "accessible, relaxed, compassionate." And notice, finally, that the paragraph brings the two images together, characterizing both as "spiritual."

As we have said, the paragraph comparing the two Buddhist sculptures illustrates splitting. An outline of that paragraph might look like this:

The Buddha
   cranial bump
   robe and unadorned head
The bodhisattva
   rich garment
   crown
The Buddha
   color
The bodhisattva
   color
The Buddha
   pose
   carving of garment
The bodhisattva
   pose
   carving of garment
Summary of the two figures

Whether in any given piece of writing you should compare by lumping or by splitting will depend largely on your purpose and on the complexity of the material. We can't even offer the rule that splitting is good for brief, relatively obvious comparisons, lumping for longer, more complex ones, though such a rule usually works. We can, however, give some advice:

1. If you split, in re-reading your draft

imagine your reader, and ask yourself if it is likely that this reader can keep up with the back-and-forth movement. Make sure (perhaps by a summary sentence at the end) that the larger picture is not obscured by the zig-zagging;

don't leave any loose ends. Make sure that if you call attention to points 1, 2, and 3 in *X,* you mention all of them (not just 1 and 2) in *Y.*

2. If you lump, do not simply comment first on *X* and then on *Y.*

Let your reader know where you are going, probably by means of an introductory sentence;

Don't be afraid in the second half to remind your reader of the first half. It is legitimate, and even desirable, to relate the second half of the

comparison to the first half. A comparison organized by lumping will
not break into two separate halves if the second half develops by
reminding the reader how it differs from the first half.

Longer Comparisons

Now let's think about a comparison that extends through two or three
paragraphs. If you are comparing the indoor play (for instance, board games or
play with toys) and the sports of girls with those of boys, you can, for example,
devote one paragraph to the indoor play of girls, a second paragraph to the
sports of girls, a third to the indoor play of boys, and a fourth to the sports of
boys. If you are thinking in terms of comparing girls and boys, such an
organization uses lumps, girls first and then boys (with a transition such as
"Boys on the other hand . . ."). But you might split, writing four paragraphs
along these lines:

> indoor play of girls
>
> indoor play of boys
>
> sports of girls
>
> sports of boys

Or you might organize the material into two paragraphs:

> play and sports of girls
>
> play and sports of boys

There is no rule, except that the organization and the point of the comparison be
clear.

Consider these paragraphs from an essay by Sheila Tobias on the fear of
mathematics. The writer's thesis in the essay is that although this fear is more
commonly found in females than in males, biology seems not to be the cause.
After discussing some findings (for example, that girls compute better than boys
in elementary school, and that many girls tend to lose interest in mathematics in
junior high school), the writer turns her attention away from the schoolhouse.
Notice that whether a paragraph is chiefly about boys or chiefly about girls, the
writer keeps us in mind of the overall point: reasons why more females than
males fear math.

> Not all the skills that are necessary for learning mathematics are
> learned in school. Measuring, computing, and manipulating objects that
> have dimensions and dynamic properties of their own are part of the
> everyday life of children. Children who miss out on these experiences
> may not be well primed for math in school.
>
> Feminists have complained for a long time that playing with dolls
> is one way of convincing impressionable little girls that they may only

be mothers or housewives—or, as in the case of the Barbie doll, "pinup girls"—when they grow up. But doll-playing may have even more serious consequences for little girls than that. Do girls find out about gravity and distance and shapes and sizes playing with dolls? Probably not.

A curious boy, if his parents are tolerant, will have taken apart a number of household and play objects by the time he is ten, and, if his parents are lucky, he may even have put them back together again. In all of this he is learning things that will be useful in physics and math. Taking parts out that have to go back in requires some examination of form. Building something that stays up or at least stays put for some time involves working with structure.

Sports is another source of math-related concepts for children which tends to favor boys. Getting to first base on a not very well hit grounder is a lesson in time, speed, and distance. Intercepting a football thrown through the air requires some rapid intuitive eye calculations based on the ball's direction, speed, and trajectory. Since physics is partly concerned with velocities, trajectories, and collisions of objects, much of the math taught to prepare a student for physics deals with relationships and formulas that can be used to express motion and acceleration.

The first paragraph offers a generalization about "children," that is, about boys and girls. The second paragraph discusses the play of girls with dolls, but discusses it in a context of its relevance, really irrelevance, to mathematics. The third paragraph discusses the household play of boys, again in the context of mathematics. The fourth paragraph discusses the outdoor sports of boys, but notice that girls are not forgotten, for its first sentence is "Sports is another source of math-related concepts for children which tends to favor boys." In short, even when there is a sort of seesaw structure, boys on one end and girls on the other, we never lose sight of the thesis that comprises both halves of the comparison.

Ways of Organizing an Essay Devoted to a Comparison

Let's now talk about organizing a comparison or contrast that runs through an entire essay, say a comparison between two political campaigns, or between the characters in two novels. Remember, first of all, one writes such a comparison not as an exercise, but in order to make a point, let's say to demonstrate the superiority of *X* to *Y*.

Probably your first thoughts, after making some jottings, will be to lump rather than to split, that is, to discuss one half of the comparison and then to go on to the second half. We'll discuss this useful method of organization in a moment, but here we want to point out that many instructors and textbooks disapprove of such an organization, arguing that the essay too often breaks into two parts and that the second part involves a good deal of repetition of categories set up in the first part. They prefer splitting. Let's say you are comparing the narrator of *Huckleberry Finn* with the narrator of *The Catcher in the Rye,* in order to show that despite superficial similarities, they are very different, and that the difference is partly the difference between the nineteenth century and the twentieth. An organization often recommended is something like this:

1. first similarity (the narrator and his quest)
    a. Huck
    b. Holden
2. second similarity (the corrupt world surrounding the narrator)
    a. society in *Huckleberry Finn*
    b. society in *The Catcher in the Rye*
3. first differences (degree to which the narrator fulfills his quest and escapes from society)
    a. Huck's plan to "light out" to the frontier
    b. Holden's breakdown

And so on, for as many additional difference as seem relevant. Here is another way of splitting and organizing a comparison:

1. first point: the narrator and his quest
    a. similarities between Huck and Holden
    b. differences between Huck and Holden
2. second point: the corrupt world
    a. similarities between the worlds in *Huck* and *The Catcher*
    b. differences between the worlds in *Huck* and *The Catcher*
3. third point: degree of success
    a. similarities between Huck and Holden
    b. differences between Huck and Holden

But a comparison need not employ either of these methods of splitting. There is even the danger that an essay employing either of them may not come into focus until the essayist stands back from the seven-layer cake and announces, in the concluding paragraph, that the odd layers taste better. In your preparatory thinking you may want to make comparisons in pairs, but you must come to some conclusions about what these add up to before writing the final version. The final version should not duplicate the thought processes; rather, it should be organized so as to make the point clearly and effectively. The point of the essay is not to list pairs of similarities or differences, but to illuminate a topic by making thoughtful comparisons. Although in a long essay you cannot postpone until page 30 a discussion of the second half of the comparison, in an essay of, say, fewer than ten pages, nothing is wrong with setting forth half of the comparison and then, in the light of what you've already said, discussing the second half. True, an essay that uses lumping will break into two unrelated parts if the second half makes no use of the first or fails to modify it; but the essay will hang together if the second half looks back to the first half and calls attention to differences that the new material reveals.

The danger of organizing the essay into two unrelated lumps can be avoided if in formulating your thesis you remember that the point of a comparison is to call attention to the unique features of something by holding it up against something similar but significantly different. If the differences are great and apparent, a comparison is a waste of effort. ("Blueberries are different from elephants. Blueberries do not have trunks. And elephants do not grow on bushes.") Indeed, a comparison between essentially and evidently unlike things can only obscure, for by making the comparison the writer implies there are significant similarities, and readers can only wonder why they do not see them. The essays that do break into two halves are essays that make *un*instructive comparisons: the first half tells the reader five things about baseball, the second half tells the reader five unrelated things about football.

A Checklist for Revising Comparisons

- Is the point of the comparison—your reason for making it—clear?
- Do you cover all significant similarities and differences?
- Is the passage readable, that is, is it clear and yet not tediously mechanical?
- Is lumping or is splitting (see pages 172, 174–175) the best way to make this comparison?
- If you are offering a value judgment, is it fair? Have you overlooked weaknesses in your preferred subject, and strengths in your less preferred subject?

Analyzing a Process

Explaining a process is a form of writing frequently encountered in both popular and scholarly writing. In the last few weeks we have come across newspaper articles on how to acquire a home aquarium, how to begin weight training, how to "detail" your car to improve its resale value, and how to make a safe exit in an airplane emergency. The requirements for writing such an article, sometimes called *a directive process analysis,* can be simply stated. The writer must:

Know the material thoroughly

Keep his or her audience in mind

Set forth the steps clearly, usually in chronological order

Define unfamiliar terms

In addition, in the introductory paragraph or in the conclusion writers often express their pleasure in the process or their sense of its utility or value. But such comments must be brief, must not interrupt the explanation of the process, and must not gush. Surely everyone has one such article to write, and you may be asked to write one.

Explaining a process is common in academic writing too, though usually the explanation is of how something happens or has happened, and it is thus sometimes called an *informative process analysis*. The writer's purpose is for the reader to understand the process, not to perform it. You may find yourself reading or writing about a successful election strategy or a botched military campaign. In an exam you may be explaining your plan to solve a mathematical problem, or you may be explaining how the imagery works in a Shakesperian sonnet. You might write an essay on the camera techniques Hitchcock used in a sequence, or a term paper based on your research in marine biology. Once again, you will need to keep your reader in mind, to organize your explanation clearly and logically, and, of course, to write with expert knowledge of your subject. Anne Hebald Mandelbaum, in her essay "It's the Portly Penguin That Gets The Girl, French Biologist Claims" (181-83), reports on a lecture which was, from the evidence, an entertaining example of an *informative process analysis*.

Two Essays Analyzing a Process

Susan Pope

Tennis Tips to a Beginning Player

Susan Pope wrote this essay while taking an undergraduate course at Wellesley College.

1   The beginning player needs tennis tips on the two basic skills of tennis: footwork, the way in which you move to prepare to hit the ball, and form, the way in which you hit the ball. The most important coaching command relevant to both skills is "Concentrate and keep your eye on the ball." As soon as you see the opposing player hit the ball, determine where it will land and move quickly to that spot, never taking your eyes from the ball.

2   Moving requires footwork, the most subtle and often overlooked aspect of tennis. In order to hit the ball well, you must first reach it in plenty of time. When receiving a serve you should stand behind the point where you expect to receive the ball; you may then run smoothly forward to receive it rather than tripping

backwards. Stand, facing the net, with your feet shoulder width apart, knees flexed, and holding the neck of your racket lightly in your free hand. This is called the ready position. Bounce up and down on the balls of your feet and prepare to move. The instant the server makes contact with the ball, jump; this enables you to move quickly in any direction. Move laterally by jumping and sliding with your feet parallel; never cross your feet. After completing your swing, return immediately to the center of the back court line, assume the ready position, bounce on the balls of your feet, and prepare to move again. If you can predict where your opponent will return the ball, move to this area instead and assume your ready stance. The objective of footwork is to reach the ball quickly so you can prepare to hit it with good form.

3   Form involves the position and use of the parts of your body as you hit the ball. By the time you have reached the place where you intend to hit the ball, you should have completed your backswing, cocking your racket back until it points behind you. A short backswing resulting from not bringing your racket back soon enough will almost always result in a mistake. On the other hand, by having your racket back, you still may be able to successfully return a ball hit beyond the physical range you can usually reach.

4   As you wait for the ball with your racket held back, plant your feet firmly, shoulder width apart. If you are using forehand, your left shoulder should be pointing approximately in the direction you wish to hit the ball. Concentrate on firmly gripping the racket handle because a loose grip can result in a wobbly shot. As the ball comes toward you, bend your knees and step with your lead foot toward the ball, the left foot when using forehand. The ball often goes in the net if you hit it standing stiffly. Keep your wrist and elbow rigid as you swing at the ball; using either of these joints for the force of your swing will cause inconsistency in your ground strokes and promote tennis elbow. Use your arm and shoulder as a unit and twist your torso, throwing the weight of your body onto your lead foot and into your swing. Make your swing quick, snappy, and parallel to the ground. If your stroke is not level, the ball will either be scooped up into the air by a rising swing or be hit directly into the net by a swing directed toward the ground. Stroke through the ball as if it were not there and then follow through with your swing bringing the racket up over your shoulder close to your ear. You will have good control over the ball if you hit it in the middle of your racket, the sweet spot, when it is slightly in front of you. Deviations from these basic coaching instructions may cause problems with your form and weaken your ground strokes. Try to concentrate on them while you practice until you develop an unconscious, smooth, consistent swing.

5   It requires conscious effort to pinpoint the flaws in your tennis game but often your repeated errors will indicate what you are doing incorrectly. Footwork and form, the basics of the game of tennis may be constantly improved with attention to a few coaching tips. Most important, however, remember to "keep your eye on the ball."

Topics for Discussion and Writing

1. The essay addresses itself to a beginning player. How successful, for a beginner, would you expect these tips to be?

2. An earlier draft of the essay began with the following paragraph:

> Playing tennis requires determined practice and hard work. There are many well-known coaching suggestions which can help improve the consistency of your ground strokes and thereby increase your confidence in your game. With practice, you can integrate these coaching prompts until you execute them automatically. Your concentration may then be focused on game strategy, such as how to capitalize on your opponent's weaknesses, and on more difficult strokes, such as the top spin.

Do you agree with the writer's decision to drop the paragraph from her revised essay? Why, or why not?

Anne Hebald Mandelbaum

Anne Hebald Mandelbaum was born in New York City in 1944, and was educated at Radcliffe College and Yale University. She is a freelance writer.

It's the Portly Penguin That Gets the Girl, French Biologist Claims

1   The penguin is a feathered and flippered bird who looks as if he's on his way to a formal banquet. With this stiff, kneeless strut and natural dinner jacket, he moves like Charlie Chaplin in his heyday dressed like Cary Grant in his.

2   But beneath the surface of his tuxedo is a gallant bird indeed. Not only does he fast for 65 days at a time, sleep standing up, and forsake all others in a lifetime of monogamy, but the male penguin also guards, watches over, and even hatches the egg.

3   We owe much of our current knowledge of the life and loves of the king and emperor penguins to—*bien sûr*—a Frenchman. Twenty-eight-year-old Yvon Le Maho is a biophysiologist from Lyons who visited the University last week to discuss his discoveries and to praise the penguin. He had just returned from 14 months in Antarctica, where he went to measure, to photograph, to weigh, to take blood and urine samples of, to perform autopsies on—in short, to study the penguin.

4   Although his original intent had been to investigate the penguin's long fasts, Monsieur Le Maho was soon fascinated by the amatory aspect of the penguin. Copulating in April, the female produces the egg in May and then

heads out to sea, leaving her mate behind to incubate the egg. The males huddle together, standing upright and protecting the 500-gram (or 1.1-pound) egg with their feet for 65 days. During this time, they neither eat nor stray: each steadfastly stands guard over his egg, protecting it from the temperatures which dip as low as -40 degrees and from the winds which whip the Antarctic wilds with gusts of 200 miles an hour.

5　　For 65 days and 65 nights, the males patiently huddle over the eggs, never lying down, never letting up. Then, every year on July 14th—Bastille Day, the national holiday of France—the eggs hatch and thousands of penguin chicks are born, M. Le Maho told his amused and enthusiastic audience at the Biological Laboratories.

6　　The very day the chicks are born—or, at the latest, the following day—the female penguins return to land from their two-and-a-half month fishing expedition. They clamber out of the water and toboggan along the snow-covered beaches toward the rookery and their mates. At this moment, the males begin to emit the penguin equivalent of wild, welcoming cheers— *"comme le cri de trompette,"* M. Le Maho later told the *Gazette* in an interview—"like the clarion call of the trumpet."

7　　And, amid the clamorous thundering of 12,000 penguins, the female recognizes the individual cry of her mate. When she does, she begins to cry to him. The male then recognizes *her* song, lifts the newborn chick into his feathered arms, and makes a beeline for the female. Each singing, each crying, the males and females rush toward each other, slipping and sliding on the ice as they go, guided all the while by the single voice each instinctively knows.

8　　The excitement soon wears thin for the male, however, who hasn't had a bite to eat in more than two months. He has done his duty and done it unflaggingly, but even penguins cannot live by duty alone. He must have food, and quickly.

9　　Having presented his mate with their newborn, the male abruptly departs, heading out to sea in search of fish. The female, who has just returned from her sea-going sabbatical, has swallowed vast quantities of fish for herself and her chick. Much of what she has eaten she has not digested. Instead, this undigested food becomes penguin baby food. She regurgitates it, all soft and paplike, from her storage throat right into her chick's mouth. The chicks feed in this manner until December, when they first learn to find food on their own.

10　　The penguins' reproductive life begins at age five, and the birds live about 25 years. Their fasting interests M. Le Maho because of its close similarities with fasting in human beings. And although many migratory birds also fast, their small size and indeed their flight make it almost impossible to study them closely. With the less-mobile and non-flying penguin, however, the scientist has a relatively accessible population to study. With no damage to the health of the penguin, M. Le Maho told the *Gazette,* a physiobiologist can extract blood from the flipper and sample the urine.

11   "All fasting problems are the same between man and the penguin," M. Le Maho said. "The penguin uses glucose in the brain, experiences ketosis as does man, and accomplishes gluconeogenesis, too." Ketosis is the build-up of partially burned fatty acids in the blood, usually as a result of starvation; gluconeogenesis is the making of sugar from non-sugar chemicals, such as amino acids. "The penguin can tell as a great deal about how our own bodies react to fasting conditions," M. Le Maho said.

12   He will return to Antarctica, M. Le Maho said, with the French government-sponsored *Expéditions Polaires Françaises* next December. There he will study the growth of the penguin chick, both inside the egg and after birth; will continue to study their mating, and to examine the penguin's blood sugar during fasting.

13   During the question-and-answer period following his talk, M. Le Maho was asked what the female penguin looks for in a mate. Responding, M. Le Maho drew himself up to his full five-foot-nine and said, *"La grandeur."*

Topics for Discussion and Writing

1. In three or four sentences explain the male penguin's role in hatching chicks.
2. Pick out three or four sentences that strike you as especially interesting, and explain what makes them interesting.

Topic for Writing

Addressing an audience pretty much like yourself—say, your classmates—in 300 to 500 words explain a process with which you are familiar but which is likely to be new to them. Examples: how to perform a card trick, win an argument, make Chinese dumplings, housebreak a puppy, refinish a table, prepare for a marathon, develop a photograph. If you choose a topic you are strongly interested in, you will probably find that an interesting voice emerges, and that the process will engage the reader.

Explaining an Analysis

As we have suggested, the writer of an analytical essay arrives at a thesis by asking questions and answering them, by separating the topic into parts and by seeing—often through the use of lists and scratch outlines—how those parts relate. Or, we might say, analytic writing presupposes detective work: the writer looks over the evidence, finds some clues, pursues the trail from one place to the next, and makes the arrest. Elementary? Perhaps. Let's observe a famous detective at work. Dr. Watson give this report.

Arthur Conan Doyle

The Science of Deduction

"I wonder what that fellow is looking for?" I asked, pointing to a stalwart, plainly dressed individual who was walking slowly down the other side of the street, looking anxiously at the numbers. He had a large blue envelope in his hand, and was evidently the bearer of a message.

"You mean the retired sergeant of Marines," said Sherlock Holmes.

"Brag and bounce!" thought I to myself. "He knows that I cannot verify his guess."

The thought had hardly passed through my mind when the man whom we were watching caught sight of the number on our door, and ran rapidly across the roadway. We heard a loud knock, a deep voice below, and heavy steps ascending the stair.

5   "For Mr. Sherlock Holmes," he said, stepping into the room and handing my friend the letter.

Here was an opportunity of taking the conceit out of him. He little thought of this when he made that random shot. "May I ask, my lad," I said, in the blandest voice, "what your trade may be?"

"Commissionaire, sir" he said, gruffly. "Uniform away for repairs."

"And you were?" I asked; with a slightly malicious glance at my companion.

"A sergeant, sir, Royal Marine Light Infantry, sir. No answer? Right, sir."

10   He clicked his heels together, raised his hand in salute, and was gone.

I confess that I was considerably startled by this fresh proof of the practical nature of my companion's theories. My respect for his powers of analysis increased wondrously. There still remained some lurking suspicion in my mind, however, that the whole thing was a prearranged episode, intended to dazzle me, though what earthly object he could have in taking me in was past my comprehension. When I looked at him, he had finished reading the note, and his eyes has assumed the vacant, lack-lustre expression which showed mental abstraction.

"How in the world did you deduce that?" I asked.

"Deduce what?" said he, petulantly.

"Why, that he was a retired sergeant of Marines."

15   "I have no time for trifles," he answered, brusquely; then with a smile, "Excuse my rudeness. You broke the thread of my thoughts; but perhaps it is as

well. So you actually were not able to see that that man was a sergeant of Marines?"

"No, indeed."

"It was easier to know it than to explain why I know it. If you were asked to prove that two and two made four, you might find some difficulty, and yet you are quite sure of the fact. Even across the street I could see a great blue anchor tattooed on the back of the fellow's hand. That smacked of the sea. He had a military carriage, however, and regulation side whiskers. There we have the marine. He was a man with some amount of self-importance and a certain air of command. You must have observed the way in which he held his head and swung his cane. A steady, respectable, middle-aged man, too, on the face of him—all facts which led me to believe that he had been a sergeant."

"Wonderful!" I ejaculated.

"Commonplace," said Holmes, though I thought from his expression that he was pleased at my evident surprise and admiration.

—FROM *A STUDY IN SCARLET*

Even when, as a writer, after preliminary thinking you have solved a problem—that is, focused on a topic and formulated a thesis—you are, as we have said before, not yet done. It is, alas, not enough simply to present the results of your analytical thinking to a reader who, like Dr. Watson, will surely want to know "How in the world did you deduce that?" And like Holmes, writers are often impatient; we long to say with him "I have no time for trifles." But the real reason for our impatience is, as Holmes is quick to acknowledge, that "It was easier to know it than to explain why I know it." But explaining to readers why or how, presenting both the reasoning that led to a thesis and the evidence that supports the reasoning, is the writer's job.

In your preliminary detective work (that is, in reading, taking notes, musing, jotting down some thoughts, and writing rough drafts) some insights (perhaps including your thesis) may come swiftly, apparently spontaneously, and in random order. You may be unaware that you have been thinking analytically at all. In preparing your essay for your reader, however, you become aware, in part because *you must become aware.* You must persuade *your* Dr. Watson that what you say is not "brag and bounce." To replace your reader's natural suspicion with respect for your analysis (and for yourself), you must, we repeat, explain your reasoning in an orderly and interesting fashion and you must present your evidence.

In the hypothetical example on pages 7–8, we showed a writer of an essay musing over the frequency of the motif of travel in the blues. Perhaps, we imagined, those musings were triggered by a few lines he happened to remember, or to hear. The writer then began to ask himself questions, to listen to some tapes, to jot down some notes. His thesis (which turned out to be that themes of travel are a metaphor for the trip through life) might have been formulated only in a late draft. But it might easily have occurred to the writer much earlier. Perhaps the thesis came almost simultaneously with the writer's first musings. But no matter when or how he arrived at a conclusion interesting enough to offer as the thesis of an essay, he still had the job of explaining to his reader (and perhaps to himself) how he had arrived at it. He probably had to examine his own thought processes carefully—replaying them in slow motion to see each part separately. He would certainly have had to marshal some evidence from available books and tapes. And he would have had to arrange the parts of his analysis and the supporting evidence clearly and interestingly to demonstrate the accuracy of his conclusion to a reader who knew less about the blues than he did.

To turn to another example, notice how Jeff Greenfield, on pages 193–195, solves and presents his case, one involving another famous detective. We will never know in what order the thoughts leading to his thesis came to him. But we can observe how Greenfield organized and supported his analysis. How can we do this? Elementary. By asking questions and answering them.

Analysis and Summary: A Cautionary Note

Analysis should be clearly distinguished from summary. The word "summary" is related to "sum," the total something adds up to. (We say "adds *up to*" because the Greeks and Romans counted upward, and wrote the total at the top.)

A summary is a condensation or abridgement; it briefly gives the reader the gist of a longer work. Or, to change the figure, it boils down the longer work, resembling the longer work as a bouillion cube resembles a bowl of soup. A summary of Philip Roth's "Reflections on the Death of a Library" (pages 10-11) will reduce the essay; perhaps to a paragraph or two, perhaps even to a sentence. It will not call attention to Roth's various strategies, and it will not evaluate his argument; it will merely present the gist of what he says.

If, then, you are asked to write an analysis of something you have read, you should not hand in a summary. On the other hand, however, a very brief summary may appropriately appear within an analytic essay. Usually, in fact, the reader needs some information, and the writer of the essay will summarize this information briefly. For example, the student who wrote about Roth's essay is *summarizing* when she writes,

> Roth, in his article . . . argues that the closing of the libraries will be a costly mistake, and that the action will be an insult to the citizens of Newark,

She is summarizing because she is briefly reporting what Roth said. On the other hand, she is *analyzing* when she writes:

> By overdramatizing the possible reactions, Roth gains the interest of the reader.

In this sentence, the writer is not reporting *what* Roth said but is explaining *how* he achieved an effect.

Most of your writing about other writing will be chiefly analytical, but it will probably include (for the benefit of the reader) an occasional sentence or even a paragraph summarizing some of your reading. And part of your preparation for writing your essay may involve writing summaries as you take notes on the reading you are going to analyze. But if the assignment calls for an analysis, do not hand in a summary.

You will find an explanation of how to write a summary on page 324.

Topics for Discussion and Writing

1. In an essay of 750 to 1000 words describe and analyze a family photograph, describing the relationships of the people as they are revealed in the picture. In an introductory paragraph or a sentence or two you may want to explain the circumstances of the photograph, whether it was posed or candid, and the occasion that it captures or celebrates. If the setting contributes to the meaning of the picture, analyze that as well. (You will find an example of a student's essay analyzing a photograph on pages 191-193.)

2. It is often said that television has had a bad effect on sports. If you believe this, write an essay of 500 to 1000 words setting forth these effects.

3. An aunt has offered to buy you a subscription to *Time* or *Newsweek*. Compare in about 750 words the contents of the current issues, the length and depth with which they are treated, and other special features (photographs, essays, layout). Explain which magazine you prefer. (If neither magazine is of interest, try comparing *Sport* and *Sports Illustrated* or *Cosmopolitan* and *Ms.*)

4. Compare baseball with hockey or soccer as a sport suitable for television. Consider the visual appeals of the sports, the pace—including the degree to which the camera operator can predict the action and thus follow it with the camera, the opportunity for replays and for close-ups—and anything else you think relevant.

5. Write a paragraph comparing a magazine advertisement of the 1990s with a counterpart of the 1950s. (You can easily find ads for cars and cigarettes in old copies of *Time* and *Newsweek* in your library.) How are the appeals similar and how are they different? Include copies of the advertisements with your paper.

6. The photograph shown here of Sitting Bull and Buffalo Bill was taken in 1885 by William McFarlane Notman. Reread the discussion of Brueghel's drawing on page 165, and then write two or three paragraphs describing and analyzing this photograph, paying special attention to the contrasting poses, expressions, and costumes. Reading brief biographical accounts of Buffalo Bill (William Frederick Cody) and Sitting Bull will help you to understand the photograph. Append a list of "Works Cited" to your paper, and document where appropriate. (See page 338.)

7. Reread the discussion of Brueghel's drawing on page 165, and of the comparison on page 173, and then write a paragraph comparing the photograph of Picasso's son Paul with the painting that Picasso made from it in 1923. Imagine your audience as visitors to a Picasso exhibition at a museum, reading a label on the wall next to the two works.

8. Study the two drawings (p. 190) by Francisco Goya (1746–1828). They show a woman holding a dying lover, who has fought a duel for her. The first version is a watercolor; the revision is in chalk. Write a brief essay of two or three paragraphs comparing them.

Sitting Bull and Buffalo Bill, 1885.

Pablo Picasso. *Paul, Son of the Artist,*
1923. Gouache, 40 x 52 inches.
S.P.A.D.E.M., Paris/V.A.G.A., New York,
1985.

Photographer unknown. *Picasso's Son
Paul on a Donkey,* c. 1923. S.P.A.D.E.M.,
Paris/V.A.G.A., New York, 1985.

Francisco de Goya y Lucientes.
Spanish, 1746–1828. *Woman Holding
Up Her Dying Lover.* Brush and gray
wash, touched with brown wash. $9\frac{1}{4}$ x
$5\frac{11}{16}$ inches (234 x 145 mm). Gift of
Frederick J. Kennedy Memorial
Foundation. 1973. Courtesy, Museum
of Fine Arts, Boston.

Francisco de Goya y Lucientes, *El
amor y la muerte.* (Love and Death)
197 x 141 mm. Courtesy, Museo del
Prado, Madrid.

Analysis at Work

Cheryl Lee

The Story Behind the Gestures:
A Family Photograph

Cheryl Lee, an undergraduate student, wrote this essay in response to an assignment that called upon the student to "select a family photograph and write a paper in which you both analyze and describe the relationship of the people as they are revealed in the picture."

1   At the close of my graduation ceremony, my entire family gathered together to immortalize the special moment on film. No one escaped the flash of my mother's camera because she was determined to document every minute of the occasion at every possible angle. My mother made sure that she took pictures of me with my hat on, with my hat off, holding the bouquet, sitting, standing, and in countless other positions. By the time this family picture was taken, my smile was intact, frozen on my face. This is not to say that my smile was anything less than genuine, for it truly was a smile of thankfulness and joy. It is just that after posing for so many pictures, what initially began as a spontaneous reaction became a frozen expression.

2   The viewer should, however, consider not so much the frozen expressions of those in the photograph, but rather the fact that the picture is posed. A posed picture supposedly shows only what the people in the picture want the viewer to see—in this case, their happiness. But ironically the photograph reveals much more about its subjects than the viewer first imagines. The photograph speaks of relationships and personalities. It speaks about the more intimate details that first seem invisible but that become undeniable through the study of gestures.

3   In the photograph, the most prominent and symbolic of gestures is the use and position of the arms. Both my father and mother place an arm around me and in turn around each other. Their encircling arms, however, do more than just show affection; they unify the three figures into a close huddle that leads the viewer's eye directly to them as opposed to the background or the periphery. The slightly bended arms that rest at their sides act as arrows that not only reinforce the three figures as the focal point but also exclude the fourth figure, my brother, from sharing the "spotlight." Unlike the other members of the family whose arms and hands are intertwined, Edwin stands with both hands down in front of him, latching onto no one. The lack of physical contact between the huddled figures and Edwin is again emphasized as he positions himself away from the viewer's eye as he stands in the periphery.

4   Edwin's position in the photograph is indicative of him as a person, for he always seems to isolate himself from the spotlight, from being the center of attention. Thus, it is his decision to escape public scrutiny, not the force of my parents' arms that drives him to the side. His quiet, humble nature directs him away from even being the focal point of a picture and leads him towards establishing his own individuality and independence in privacy. His long hair and his "hand-me-down" clothes are all an expression of his simply being himself. The reason behind his physical independence is the emotional independence that he already possesses at the age of sixteen. He stands alone because he can stand alone.

5   While Edwin stands apart from the other three figures, I stand enclosed and protected. The lock of arms as well as the bouquet restrain me; they dissuade me from breaking away in favor of independence. Although my mother wants me to achieve the same kind of independence that Edwin has achieved, she works to delay the time when I actually will move away to the periphery. Perhaps my being the only daughter, the only other female in the family, has something to do with my mother's desire to keep me close and dependent as long as possible. Her arm reaches out with bouquet in hand as if to shield me from the world's unpleasantness. Even though my father also holds onto me with an encircling arm, it is my mother's firm grip that alone persuades me to stay within the boundary of their protective arms.

6   Her grip, which proves more powerful than my father's hold, restrains not only me but also my father. In the picture, he falls victim to the same outstretched hand, the same touch of the bouquet. Yet this time, my mother's

bouquet does more than just restrain; it seems to push my father back "into line" or into his so-called place. The picture illustrates this exertion of influence well, for my mother in real life does indeed assume the role of the dominant figure. Although my father remains the head of the household in title, it is my mother around whom the household revolves; she oversees the insignificant details as well as the major ones. But my father doesn't mind at all. Like me, he also enjoys the protection her restraining arm offers. It is because of our mutual dependence on my mother that my father and I seem to draw closer. This dependence in turn strengthens both of our relationships with my mother.

7   At the time the picture was taken, I seriously doubt that my mother realized the significance of her position in the picture or the import of her gestures. All of us in fact seem too blinded by the festivity of the occasion to realize that this photograph would show more than just a happy family at a daughter's graduation. The family photograph would inevitably become a telling portrait of each member of the family. It would, in a sense, leave us vulnerable to the speculative eyes of the viewer, who in carefully examining the photograph would recognize the secrets hidden in each frozen expression.

Topics for Discussion and Writing

1. Is the essay devoted chiefly to analyzing a picture or is it devoted chiefly to exploring Lee's feelings about the picture?
2. What is the function of Lee's opening paragraph? What is your response to her statement that the family gathered together "to immortalize" her graduation? What is the effect of "with my hat on, with my hat off"? How would you characterize the writer of this paragraph?
3. Do you think that Lee's interpretation is probably sound, or do you think that she reads too much (or too little) into the picture? Support your view.
4. Evaluate the final paragraph as a final paragraph.

Jeff Greenfield

Columbo Knows the Butler Didn't Do It

Jeff Greenfield wrote speeches for Robert F. Kennedy and has exchanged sharp words with William F. Buckley on television. He has published essays on sports and on other popular entertainments, and he can be seen regularly on Nightline.

1   The popularity of *Columbo* is as intense as it is puzzling. Dinner parties are adjourned, trips to movies postponed, and telephone calls hastily concluded ("It's starting now, I gotta go." "Migod, it's 8:40, what did I miss?"), all for a detective show that tells us whodunit, howhedunit, and whyhedunit all before the first commercial.

2   Why? Peter Falk's characterization is part of the answer of course; he plays Lieutenant Columbo with sleepy-eyed, slow-footed, crazy-like-a-fox charm. But shtick—even first-class shtick—goes only so far. Nor is it especially fascinating to watch Columbo piece together clues that are often telegraphed far in advance. No, there is something else which gives *Columbo* a special appeal—something almost never seen on commercial television. That something is a strong, healthy dose of class antagonism. The one constant in *Columbo* is that, with every episode, a working-class hero brings to justice a member of America's social and economic elite.

3   The homicide files in Columbo's office must contain the highest per-capita income group of any criminals outside of antitrust law. We never see a robber shooting a grocery store owner out of panic or savagery; there are no barroom quarrels settled with a Saturday Night Special; no murderous shoot-outs between drug dealers or numbers runners. The killers in Columbo's world are art collectors, surgeons, high-priced lawyers, sports executives, a symphony conductor of Bernsteinian charisma—even a world chess champion. They are rich and white (if Columbo ever does track down a black killer, it will surely be a famous writer or singer or athlete or politician).

4   *Columbo*'s villains are not simply rich; they are privileged. They live the lives that are for most of us hopeless daydreams: houses on top of mountains, with pools, servants, and sliding doors; parties with women in slinky dresses, and endless food and drink; plush, enclosed box seats at professional sports events; the envy and admiration of the Crowd. While we choose between Johnny Carson and *Invasion of the Body-Snatchers,* they are at screenings of movies the rest of us wait in line for on Third Avenue three months later.

5   Into the lives of these privileged rich stumbles Lieutenant Columbo—a dweller in another world. His suspects are Los Angeles paradigms: sleek, shiny, impeccably dressed, tanned by the omnipresent sun. Columbo, on the other hand, appears to have been plucked from Queens Boulevard by helicopter, and set down an instant later in Topanga Canyon. His hair is tousled, not styled and sprayed. His chin is pale and stubbled. He has even forgotten to take off his raincoat, a garment thoroughly out of place in Los Angeles eight months of the year. Columbo is also unabashedly stunned by and envious of the life style of his quarry.

6   "Geez, that is some car," he tells the symphony conductor. "Ya know, I'll bet that car costs more than I make in a year."

7   "Say, can I ask you something personal?" he says to a suspect wearing $50 shoes. "Ya know where I can buy a pair of shoes like that for $8.95?"

8   "Boy, I bet this house musta cost—I dunno, hundred, what, hundred fifty thousand?"

9   His aristocratic adversaries tolerate Columbo at first because they misjudge him. They are amused by him, scornful of his manners, certain that while he possesses the legal authority to demand their cooperation, he has neither the grace nor wit to discover their misdeeds. Only at the end, in a last look of consternation before the final fadeout, do they comprehend that intelligence may indeed find a home in the Robert Hall set. All of them are done in, in some measure, by their contempt for Columbo's background, breeding, and income. Anyone who has worked the wrong side of the counter at Bergdorf's, or who has waited on tables in high-priced restaurants, must feel a wave of satisfaction. ("Yeah, baby, *that's* how dumb we working stiffs are!")

10   Further, Columbo knows about these people what the rest of us suspect: that they are on top not because they are smarter or work harder than we do, but because they are more amoral and devious. Time after time, the motive for murder in *Columbo* stems from the shakiness of the villain's own status in high society. The chess champion knows his challenger is his better; murder is his only chance to stay king. The surgeon fears that a cooperative research project will endanger his status; he must do in his chief to retain sole credit. The conductor owes his position to the status of his mother-in-law; he must silence his mistress lest she spill the beans and strip him of his wealth and position.

11   This is, perhaps, the most thorough-going satisfaction *Columbo* offers us: the assurance that those who dwell in marble and satin, those whose clothes, food, cars, and mates are the very best, *do not deserve it*. They are, instead, driven by fear and compulsion to murder. And they are done in by a man of street wit, who is afraid to fly, who can't stand the sight of blood, and who never uses force to take his prey. They are done in by Mosholu Parkway and P. S. 106, by Fordham U. and a balcony seat at Madison Square Garden, by a man who pulls down $11,800 a year and never ate an anchovy in his life.

12   It is delicious. I wait only for the ultimate episode: Columbo knocks on the door of 1600 Pennsylvania Avenue one day. "Gee, Mr. President, I really hate to bother you again, but there's *just one thing. . . .* "

Topics for Discussion and Writing

1. What is Greenfield's thesis? Where does he state it?

2. Describe what Greenfield is doing in his first paragraph; in his second paragraph.

3. Beginning with the third paragraph, Greenfield looks first at the characteri-

zation of the hero and villains, then at the underlying conflict, and finally at the implicit meaning of the conflict. Why does he present the parts of his analysis in this order?

Howard Gardner

Learning, Chinese-Style

Howard Gardner, a professor of Education at Harvard University, is the author of many books, including Frames of Mind. *We reprint an essay that originally appeared in 1989 in* Psychology Today.

1   For a month in the spring of 1987, my wife Ellen and I lived in the bustling eastern Chinese city of Nanjing with our 1½-year-old son Benjamin while studying arts education in Chinese kindergartens and elementary schools. But one of the most telling lessons Ellen and I got in the difference between Chinese and American ideas of education came not in the classroom but in the lobby of the Jinling Hotel where we stayed in Nanjing.

2   The key to our room was attached to a large plastic block with the room number embossed on it. When leaving the hotel, a guest was encouraged to turn in the key, either by handling it to an attendant or by dropping it through a slot into a receptacle. Because the key slot was narrow and rectangular, the key had to be aligned carefully to fit snugly into the slot.

3   Benjamin loved to carry the key around, shaking it vigorously. He also liked to try to place it into the slot. Because of his tender age, lack of manual dexterity and incomplete understanding of the need to orient the key just so, he would usually fail. Benjamin was not bothered in the least. He probably got as much pleasure out of the sounds the key made as he did those few times when the key actually found its way into the slot.

4   Now both Ellen and I were perfectly happy to allow Benjamin to bang the key near the key slot. His exploratory behavior seemed harmless enough. But I soon observed an intriguing phenomenon. Any Chinese attendant nearby would come over to watch Benjamin and, noting his lack of initial success, attempt to intervene. He or she would hold onto Benjamin's hand and, gently but firmly, guide it directly toward the slot, reorient it as necessary, and help him to insert it. The "teacher" would then smile somewhat expectantly at Ellen or me, as if awaiting a thank you—and on occasion would frown slightly, as if to admonish the negligent parent.

5   I soon realized that this incident was directly relevant to our assigned tasks in China: to investigate the ways of early childhood education (especially in the

arts), and to illuminate Chinese attitudes toward creativity. And so before long I began to incorporate this key-slot anecdote into my talks to Chinese educators.

TWO DIFFERENT WAYS TO LEARN

6   With a few exceptions my Chinese colleagues displayed the same attitude as the attendants at the Jinling Hotel. Since adults know how to place the key in the key slot, which is the ultimate purpose of approaching the slot, and since the toddler is neither old enough nor clever enough to realize the desired action on his own, what possible gain is achieved by having the child flail about? He may well get frustrated and angry—certainly not a desirable outcome. Why not show him what to do? He will be happy, he will learn how to accomplish the task sooner, and then he can proceed to more complex activities, like opening the door or asking for the key—both of which accomplishments can (and should) in due course be modeled for him as well.

7   We listened to such explanations sympathetically and explained that, first of all, we did not much care whether Benjamin succeeded in inserting the key into the slot. He was having a good time and was exploring, two activities that *did* matter to us. But the critical point was that, in the process, we were trying to teach Benjamin that one can solve a problem effectively by oneself. Such self-reliance is a principal value of child rearing in middle-class America. So long as the child is shown exactly how to do something—whether it be placing a key in a key slot, drawing a rooster or making amends for a misdeed—he is less likely to figure out himself how to accomplish such a task. And, more generally, he is less likely to view life—as Americans do—as a series of situations in which one has to learn to think for oneself, to solve problems on one's own and even to discover new problems for which creative solutions are wanted.

TEACHING BY HOLDING HIS HAND

8   In retrospect, it became clear to me that this incident was indeed key—and key in more than one sense. It pointed to important differences in the educational and artistic practices in our two countries.

9   When our well-intentioned Chinese observers came to Benjamin's rescue, they did not simply push his hand down clumsily, hesitantly or abruptly, as I might have done. Instead, they guided him with extreme facility and gentleness in precisely the desired direction. I came to realize that these Chinese were not just molding and shaping Benjamin's performance in any old manner: In the best Chinese tradition, they were *ba zhe shou jiao*—"teaching by holding his hand"—so much so that he would happily come back for more.

10   The idea that learning should take place by continual careful shaping and molding applies equally to the arts. Watching children at work in a classroom setting, we were stunned at their facility. Children as young as 5 or 6 were painting flowers, fish and animals with the dexterity and panache of an adult; calligraphers 9 and 10 years old were producing works that could have been displayed in a museum. In a visit to the homes of two of the young artists, we learned from their parents that they worked on perfecting their craft for several hours a day.

11   Interested as I was in the facility of the young artists, I wondered whether they could draw any object or only something they had been taught to portray. After all, in the practice of calligraphy, the ordinary method involves painstaking tracing of the same characters over and over. Suddenly I had a minor inspiration. I decided to ask three 10-year-olds to draw my face. The assignment at first nonplussed my three guinea pigs, but soon they undertook it with gusto, and each produced a credible job. To be sure, one picture had me looking like one of the Beatles, the second like a Chinese schoolboy, the third as Charlie's aunt is usually portrayed, but each of them bore at least a family resemblance to its subject. I had found out what I wanted: Chinese children are not simply tied to schemata; they can depart to some extent from a formula when so requested.

CREATIVITY: EVOLUTIONARY OR REVOLUTIONARY?

12   If I had to indicate the typical Chinese view of creativity, it would run as follows: In every realm, there are accepted means for achieving competence—prescribed and approved performances. There is really no good reason for attempting to bypass a long-established route, although a modest degree of latitude can be tolerated as the traditional form is acquired. Though the point of acquisition may never be totally reached (Zen Buddhist masters ask their charges to create the same sound or form or movement thousands of times), competent performers are sanctioned to introduce increasing departures from the approved forms. By this distinctly evolutionary path, the products of the master eventually come to be reasonably deviant from the canon. This is "approved creativity." Even so, the relationship to the canon continues to be evident, and critical discussion of an adult master may center on fruitful as opposed to idiosyncratic deviations.

13   While these views of the creative realm are not the modern Western ones, they seem entirely viable to me. We might contrast the Western, more "revolutionary" view, with a more "evolutionary" view espoused by the Chinese. There is a virtual reversal of priorities: the young Westerner making her boldest departures first and then gradually reintegrating herself into the tradition; and the young Chinese being almost inseparable from the tradition,

but, over time, possibly evolving to a point as deviant as the one initially staked out by the innovative Westerner.

14   One way of summarizing the American position is to state that we value originality and independence more than the Chinese do. The contrast between our two cultures can also be conceptualized in terms of the fears we both harbor. Chinese teachers are fearful that if skills are not acquired early, they may never be acquired; there is, on the other hand, no comparable hurry to inculcate creativity. American educators fear that unless creativity has been acquired early, it may never emerge; on the other hand, skills can be picked up later.

15   However, I do not want to overstate my case. There is certainly creativity in China: creativity by groups, by selected individuals in the past and by numerous Chinese living in diverse societies around the world today. Indeed, as a society, China compares favorably with nearly every other in terms of the scientific, technological and aesthetic innovations that have emerged over the centuries.

16   There is also the risk of overdramatizing creative breakthroughs in the West. When any innovation is examined closely, its reliance on previous achievements is all too apparent (the "standing on the shoulder of giants" phenomenon). Perhaps as Claude Levi-Strauss has argued, it is misleading to speak of creativity as though it ever occurs from scratch; every symbolic breakthrough simply represents a certain combination of choices from within a particular symbolic code.

17   But assuming that the antithesis I have developed is valid, and that the fostering of skills and creativity are both worthwhile goals, the important question becomes this: Can we glean, from the Chinese and American extremes, a superior way to approach education, perhaps striking an optimal balance between the poles of creativity and basic skills?

Topics for Discussion and Writing

1. In his first four paragraphs Gardner describes "an intriguing phenomenon"—the Chinese response to his young son Benjamin's attempt to put a key in a slot. Why does he find the incident "intriguing" and "one of the most telling lessons" of their experience in Nanjing?

2. How do you think an American hotel employee would respond to a very young Chinese child attempting to put a key into a slot? Would he or she behave differently from the way the Chinese attendant behaves? Whether or not the key-slot narrative clearly establishes Gardner's point, how successful is it as an introduction to his essay?

3. Gardner does not entirely rely on the narrative of the key-slot anecdote to make his point. In what paragraphs does he explain the chief differences between the Gardners' attitudes toward Benjamin's play and the attitudes of

the Chinese hotel attendants who try to teach Benjamin and colleagues who hear the anecdote? What are those differences?

4. In paragraph 7 Gardner claims that "self-reliance is a principal value of child rearing in middle-class America." Since he is analyzing an *ethnic* difference is there any reason for him to introduce the idea of *class?*

5. From your own experience, do you agree that adults in America encourage self-reliance in children? For example, what tasks did you or your siblings learn to accomplish by figuring them out yourself? Or were you more often guided by an adult "holding [your] hand"?

6. Drawing on your own experience of creativity, are you American or Chinese in style? That is, did you at first boldly depart from the norm and then gradually reintegrate yourself (American, in Gardner's view), or did you, Chinese-style, begin in a traditional fashion and gradually develop an individual style? (We encourage you to interpret this question creatively. You needn't limit yourself to traditional notions of the arts: include in the "creative realm," if you will, learning to throw a basketball, or to roller-blade, or to prepare a dinner, or to decorate your room, or to restyle your hair, your clothes, your person.)

Nicolaus Mills

The Endless Autumn

The following essay was published in The Nation, *a periodical with a reputation for being politically liberal.*

1   The headline for Adelphi University's full-page *New York Times* ad was apologetic: "Why the Most Interesting University in the Country Stoops So Low as to Advertise Itself." The apology was understandable. Colleges and universities aren't supposed to sell themselves. They are supposed to present themselves—at most in user-friendly fashion—so their future students can make an informed choice.

2   What Adelphi was doing with its hard sell was, however, similar to what most colleges do now: offer themselves with a Madison Avenue format and treat their students as customers who need to be won over. The change—and with it the rise of firms specializing in institutional promotion and market research—is hardly surprising. Since the baby-boom days of the 1960s the pool of college-age students has shrunk, while in the past ten years the price of a college education has risen by 118 percent at private universities and 82 percent at public ones.

3   Nonetheless, for most colleges a full-page *New York Times* ad remains too blatant. They prefer a forty- to sixty-page booklet—the viewbook, *a.k.a.* the register or the bulletin. Bigger than a prospectus, smaller than a catalogue, college viewbooks circulate in the millions. For every freshman it accepts, a college often sends out fifty viewbooks. At big schools an annual printing of 100,000 is common.

4   On these grounds alone, the college viewbook is worth taking seriously. We can no more afford to ignore its mix of rhetoric and social motive than we can that of other mass-circulation publications such as *The Official Boy Scout Handbook* or *The Red Cross First Aid Manual*. But circulation alone is not what makes college viewbooks important. Although the immediate audience is college freshmen and their parents (the paying customers), no other publication so represents college culture as colleges wish it to be seen.

5   What this idealized picture means in 1990 begins with the college code word of the 1980s—diversity. "Diversity is the hallmark of the Harvard/Radcliffe experience," the first sentence in the Harvard University register declares. "Diversity is the virtual core of University life," the University of Michigan bulletin announces. "Diversity is rooted deeply in the liberal arts tradition and is key to our educational philosophy," Connecticut College insists. "Duke's 5,800 undergraduates come from regions which are truly diverse," the Duke University bulletin declares. "Stanford values a class that is both ethnically and economically diverse," the Stanford University bulletin notes. Brown University says, "When asked to describe the undergraduate life at The College—and particularly their first strongest impression of Brown as freshmen—students consistently bring up the same topic: the diversity of the student body."

6   What diversity means in this context is that a college is doing its best to abolish the idea that it caters to middle-class whites. By focusing on diversity rather than desegregation or some made-up word like "de-eliting," the college sees itself getting a bargain. It doesn't have to own up to a history of bigotry, and by focusing on the variety that diversity implies, the college avoids the charge of social engineering that it would be subject to if it said it was seeking more minority students.

7   In an era when racial tensions are on the rise and the Supreme Court has put affirmative action beyond the reach of all but the most determined employer, any institution that insists on diversity is noteworthy. In our colleges and universities, faith in diversity is much more than a political stance, however. It is also an expression of faith in their own transforming power, in their ability to create a special world. Connecticut College puts this specialness most extravagantly when it declares that its students are led into "another universe of discourse." Indeed, in 1990 it's impossible for any leading college to imagine

that its students won't, as Oberlin College notes with ten banner headlines in the first five pages of its bulletin, "THRIVE."

8   What thriving means in this context is exemplified by the boxed cameo portraits of superstudents (for example, the Stanford Rhodes scholar who aids battered women and intends to play basketball on the Oxford team) that every viewbook seems to feature. If ever a student undertook a project that failed, it is never mentioned. Nor is there a hint that a project might have caused a student to see humanity less hopefully.

9   Above all, there is never an indication that students don't mature on schedule. While even in the Ivy League there is a difference between a Columbia University, which requires its students to take a core curriculum, and a Brown, which emphasizes that it has no core curriculum, the guiding assumption in all cases is that by their junior year at the latest students will find their academic path. As Princeton University, which emphasizes the independent work its juniors and seniors do, notes in its viewbook, "A first-rate education is not something that happens to you, but rather is something you yourself make happen." Never in any viewbook do we get a senior who confesses he coasted through too many courses, nor does any student ever worry that four years of study may make a 9-to-5 job unbearably dull.

10   What underlies this faith in the college experience is never systematically argued in any viewbook, but it is not hard to find the philosophical source: It is the virtues of a liberal education. "A liberal education must be the thread that weaves a pattern of meaning into the total learning experience," Brown president Vartan Gregorian writes. "By stressing the value of a liberal education we encourage students to seek the infinitely precious affirmation of their most authentic selves," Dartmouth College president James Freedman states. "A liberally educated person is 'liberated' to the extent that education has deepened his or her capacity and inclination for clear thought, analytical reasoning, comprehension and empathy," Wesleyan University's dean of admission declares.

11   The result is that while viewbooks may read differently (less so if copy as well as graphics have been turned over to a Madison Avenue firm), they remain remarkably similar in structure. Almost all contain the following:

12   *The Melting-Pot Ideal.* In addition to their viewbooks, most colleges now have special brochures for minority students. But in the viewbook itself nothing is more important to convey than a picture of students of all races mixing, and doing so in approximately equal numbers of men and women (a problem at single-sex schools that have only marginally turned coed). The result is the ubiquitous posed group photo in which white, black, Asian and Latino students look into the camera and grin like crazy. The photo, if the college can afford it, will be in color, and if not on the cover of its viewbook, within the first few pages. Significantly, candid photos are not used to make the same point.

13   *The Endless Autumn Motif.* Falling yellow leaves at Indiana University. Falling red leaves at Smith College. In the college viewbook autumn never seems to stop. At its simplest the point is that college is a beautiful place. But the real function of the endless autumn motif is to convince students that college is a timeless world where they can forget the day-to-day pressures of ordinary life. Even at Columbia, where campus guards have been attacked by New York City muggers, the viewbook makes the school sound like a utopia. "No traffic rumbles across its paths, no skyscrapers skewer its sunshine, no urban tumult disturbs its placid terraces," the Columbia viewbook declares before going on to conclude that the "Columbia landscape is a classic collegiate stage."

14   *The Small-but-Big Paradox.* Its aim is to convince students they can have the best of two possible worlds without sacrificing anything. Wesleyan declares that it "brings together the best features of the liberal arts college and the large university." Duke, with 5,800 undergraduate students in contrast with Wesleyan's 2,600, describes its size as "midway between that of small liberal arts colleges and larger research universities." The key here is for the viewbook never to pose the kinds of questions that make the difference between bigness and smallness clear: What percentage of their students do teachers see in office hours? Could an unrecruited athlete expect to play on a varsity team? Do teachers give out written student evaluations or only grades?

15   *The Admissions Fudge.* Its intention is to assure prospective students that there is no conflict between selecting a freshman class on merit and opting for a diversity that means, as one admissions dean put it, "We take in more in the groups with weaker credentials and make it harder for those with stronger credentials." There is no attempt to explain why strong board scores will benefit some minorities (blacks) more than other minorities (Asians), or why some minorities (Italian-Americans) are of interest to almost nobody. The result is the kind of admissions statement that, like the following one by Stanford, could mean anything: "The long and labored evaluation process cannot be reduced to a quantifiable formula. . . . While we are focusing on each individual, we also are mindful of putting together a freshman class that cuts across a number of dimensions. Consequently, many factors enter into the process over which individual candidates have no control."

16   For colleges, even the leading ones, there would of course be a price to pay for turning out a candid viewbook. Harvard, which insists that "good teaching and scholarship go hand in hand," would have to explain why the winners of its 1986 and 1987 Levenson Award for Outstanding Teaching were both rejected for tenure. Yale University, which in its bulletin stresses a folksy concern for student life (you can get Cap'n Crunch for breakfast), would have to explain why it forced clerical employees with an average salary of $13,318 to go through a bitter ten-week strike in 1984 just to get union recognition and improved pay. Stanford, which advertises its social concern with a picture of folk singer Joan Baez at a

Stanford antiapartheid rally, would have to explain why so many of its minority students saw its required Western culture courses as racist.

17   The irony is that in college publications sent to alumni, candor on controversial subjects is usual. In the *Princeton Alumni Weekly* one can read a harrowing account of the rape of a student, and the *Dartmouth Alumni Magazine* carried a series of articles on the racial confrontations that have made Dartmouth national news. Indeed, the assumption our leading colleges make is that the only way to keep the support of students and alumni is to come clean about their troubles. Where they draw the line is with prospective freshmen and their parents.

18   The closest any viewbook comes to being candid is at Williams College, where the prospectus in its between-the-pages inserts offers such information about the Williams freshman class as the percentage who admit they cheated on a high school test. But even in the Williams viewbook (yearly cost, $100,000) candor is primarily a tactic, part of an overall antihype strategy. In the final analysis the viewbooks of our leading colleges are a sad performance, made sadder still by the fact that, given what it can cost to visit a far-off school, the viewbook remains the most democratic mechanism a college has for reaching new students.

Topics for Discussion and Writing

1. According to Mills, what has caused colleges to advertise themselves through viewbooks and other means? When you were applying to college, were you aware that colleges were selling themselves to you, and if so, what techniques did you notice?

2. For whom are college viewbooks intended? Does Mills suggest why he is analyzing them? If the answer is yes, what reason does he give? Do you find the reason adequate?

3. In paragraph 5, Mills calls diversity "the college code word of the 1980s." First explain what he means and then what attitude the phrase, particularly "code word," reveals.

4. According to Mills, what information will we *not* find in viewbooks? Is he suggesting that this information should be included? If not, what *is* he suggesting?

5. Mills more or less debunks college viewbooks. Does he seem reasonably impartial, or do you think he has an ax to grind? Explain.

6. If your college or university issues a viewbook, examine it to see to what degree it fits Mills's description of a viewbook and to what extent it fairly represents your institution. Or, if your institution has a videotape, describe and analyze the videotape for someone who has not seen it. (Give credit to Mills's article if it provides you with some ideas for your analysis.)

Rubén Blades

The Politics Behind the Latino's Legacy

Rubén Blades, a composer and performer of Afro-Cuban music, an actor and a graduate of the Harvard Law School, is currently organizing a new political party in his native Panama.

1   During the 1980's, much was anticipated on behalf of Spanish-speaking communities. A phrase was coined, "La décade de los Hispanos," and numerous publications eagerly speculated that Latinos would influence the political, economic, artistic, cultural and social front in the United States.

2   Other than having a distinguished Mexican-American actor, Edward James Olmos, on the cover of *Time* magazine, the 80's came and went without much sign of a Hispanic cultural explosion in this country. In fact, in the wake of that decade's social dislocations, the Latin community provided a substantial percentage of the economically drowned and artistically ignored.

3   Over the years, attitudes and perceptions in the United States toward those south of its border have oscillated from outright ridicule and contempt to appeasement and courtship to rejection and indifference. Today a precarious impasse exists between the two cultures.

4   Since the silent era of films, Latin culture and its character have been grotesquely distorted and misrepresented. Consider the Anglo screenwriter's creation of the Latin lover and the greaser, an amoral character of unspeakable violence who came to personify the Mexican national and, by extension, any person of Spanish-speaking ancestry.

5   The negative portrayal of Latinos continued in films like *Tony the Greaser* (1911), *Rio Grande* (1919) and *Ne'er Do Well,* a film from the early 20's in which a rich Anglo hops a freighter bound for Panama and, inevitably, wins the hand of the lovely Chiquita from her Panamanian boyfriend. Those kinds of portrayals only lessened due to the combined action of the Mexican and Panamanian governments, which threatened in 1922 to boycott Hollywood movies that depicted Latin Americans in a demeaning manner.

6   The actual demise of the infamous greaser character was brought on by a fortuitous combination of political events. In the 1930's, a larger coalition of Latin American countries, headed by President Lézaro Cardenas of Mexico, decided to ban films that depicted their nationals in a negative way. The boycott coincided with the rise of Hitler in Europe; as it turned out, the war was the most important political factor in explaining the sudden change in attitudes toward Latinos.

7   President Franklin D. Roosevelt's Good Neighbor Policy was partly responsible. The United States wanted to counter German influence in Latin American, which could result in Nazi beachheads in the Western Hemisphere. For political expediency, Hollywood, following Washington's agenda, produced sympathetic Latin characters and musical comedies that prominently featured Latin roles: *South of the Border* (1939), *Down Argentine Way* (1940), *That Night in Rio, Down Mexico Way* (both 1941) and *The Three Caballeros,* a 1945 Disney film starring Donald Duck. But whenever a Latin character demonstrated honorable traits, the portrayer invariably turned out to be Anglo: Paul Muni was Benito Pablo Juarez, the President of Mexico, in the 1939 movie *Juarez;* Tyrone Power played Latinos in *The Mark of Zorro* (1940), *Blood and Sand* (1941) and *Captain From Castille* (1947). And in 1952 it fell to Marlon Brando to portray the Mexican rebel leader Emiliano Zapata in *Viva Zapata.*

8   President Roosevelt's desire in the 40's to create a better relationship with Latin American republics also had economic considerations. The war had closed European and Asian markets, leaving the Americas the only guaranteed place to sell movies and phonographic records. As George Hadley-Garcia said in his 1991 book *Hispanic Hollywood:* "After the war the Pan-American market output was considerable; by 1949, 20 Latin Western Hemisphere nations accounted for nearly one-fifth of the foreign market for American films. In other words, less than 10 percent of the world's population supplied about 20 percent of foreign film royalties."

9   But politics giveth, and politics taketh away. The danger of Nazism over, the United States assumed its new and indisputable position as leader of the free world by enforcing American values at home and abroad. The early 1950s saw the political agenda defined in the United States by the containment of the new enemy, Communism. With the closing of the American mind, and the emergence of the Communist blacklist that devastated Hollywood leftists, multidimensional Latin characters disappeared and blond, Caucasian features reappeared at the center of action and story development. Paradoxically, it is precisely during this racist, "all-white" decade that there came the biggest triumph of Latinos in the United States.

10   Music from the tropics became the national rage, with Perez Prado, the original Mambo King, occupying the No. 1 spot in the hit parade with "Cherry Pink and Apple-Blossom White" in 1955. And then there was *I Love Lucy,* which portrayed the adventures of an interracial couple formed by a Cuban-born bandleader, Ricky Ricardo, and a goofy but adorable redheaded Anglo, Lucy. Originally, ABC turned down Desiderio Arnaz as the counterpart to Lucille Ball's antics. But Ball refused to do the show without her real-life husband. *I Love Lucy* became the most popular program in the United States and proved that, given the opportunity, a Latino could become the subject of national adoration and artistic acceptance.

11   But just when a favorable change toward Latin culture seemed at hand, politics intervened, influenced by two unlikely individuals: Fidel Castro and Rosa Parks. When Castro created in Cuba the first Communist regime on the American continent, only 90-odd miles from Eisenhower's shores, any warming toward Latinos was suddenly deemed suspect.

12   The mutually expressed hostility by the two governments resulted in United States action against Cuba, including a failed military invasion, a blockade and an economic embargo. It also reinforced a negative perception toward Latin America, which persists to this day. The Latin paradise of the Busby Berkeley musicals featuring the Brazilian Carmen Miranda was turned into what was perceived to be a war zone, populated with anti-Yankee leftists (who stoned Richard Nixon in Venezuela), Communist-leaning leaders (against whom the United States organized an invasion of the Dominican Republic in 1965) and masses bent on the destruction of the American way of life (as in the bloody 1964 riots in Panama). It wasn't until 1975, 16 years after the Cuban Revolution, that a network took a chance with another lead role for a Latin character: Chico of *Chico and the Man,* starring the Puerto Rican comedian Freddie Prinze.

13   Even before the United States and Cuba began locking horns, a seemingly unimportant incident that would have repercussions worldwide took place in a bus in Montgomery, Ala. Rosa Parks, a black woman going home after a hard day's work, refused to give her seat to a white man because she was too tired and her feet hurt. Thus, the civil-rights movement began its march toward the abolition of the overt Jim Crow policies that perpetuated segregation. With this action, blacks seized the limited attention span of the country's ruling class.

14   American blacks, as a group, began to demonstrate skill and determination in organizing and enforcing a political and economic agenda, a skill yet to be matched by the Latin community. The long struggle by the black community for respect and equal opportunity in the arts has paid off. Almost without exception, movies, television and music feature blacks in multifaceted roles. Television particularly is filled with black characters, with several programs revolving exclusively around the black experience, however inanely conceived some of the shows may seem to critics.

15   Yet there are currently no Latinos in major roles on prime-time television. Both Jimmy Smits (*L.A. Law*) and Mr. Olmos (*Miami Vice*) are no longer on television in their supporting roles. If you happen to find a Latin character in television nowadays, he or she is likely to be a drug dealer, guerrilla, pimp, whore, maid or that perennial favorite, the Latin lover.

16   Despite Latinos' ever-growing numbers in the United States and their cultural wealth, no parts are written for them that take into consideration their contributions to this country's social fabric, or its economic and political development. One reason for this omission can be found in the behavior of the

diverse groups that make up the Latin presence in the United States. Latinos, who come from racially and geographically distinct backgrounds, behave more like warring, independent factions than a group united by similar idiom, culture and idiosyncrasy.

17   Unless Latin groups coalesce—to present a coherent position on access, opportunity and political respect, and to end negative stereotyping—their fortunes in the United States may well fail to flourish.

Topics for Discussion and Writing

1. Blades notes that in the 1930s and 1940s "whenever a Latin character demonstrated honorable traits, the portrayer invariably turned out to be Anglo. . . ." What is he getting at? And why, in your opinion, did Hollywood use Anglo actors in these roles?

2. In the last sentence of paragraph 10 Blades characterizes the 1950s in the United States as "racist," but he later says, in the same sentence, that this was the period of "the biggest triumph of Latinos in the United States." Do you find a contradiction here? Explain.

3. In paragraph 15 Blades, writing in 1992, says that "if you happen to find a Latino character in television nowadays, he or she is likely to be a drug dealer, guerrilla, pimp, whore, maid or that perennial favorite, the Latin lover." Is his comment true today? Explain.

4. In paragraph 16 Blades, noting that Latinos "come from racially and geographically distinct backgrounds," says they "behave more like warring, independent factions than a group united by similar idiom, culture and idiosyncrasy." Exactly what do you think he means by "similar idiom, culture and idiosyncrasy "? Does your experience lead you to agree that Latinos are united by these factors? Explain.

5. In paragraphs 13 and 14 Blades introduces African-Americans into an essay about Latinos. Why does he do this?

6. In the next week or so notice how Latinos, or Asians, or Native Americans, or African-Americans are depicted in television dramas or in films. Concentrate on one group. Do you find realistic portrayals or mostly negative or mostly positive stereotypes? Or is the group represented infrequently, or not at all? Write a paragraph or two setting forth your findings, supporting any generalizations you arrive at with specific examples.

Chapter 10

Narrating

The Uses of Narrative

Usually we think of narrative writing as the art of the novelist or short story writer, but narratives need not be restricted to fiction. Biographies, autobiographies, history books, travel books, and television documentaries are also largely narrative. In *narrative essays* too, a writer may make a point or explain an idea by means of a story, offered as a true account. At the end of this chapter you will find an *autobiographical essay* by Zora Neale Hurston. As you read it, ask yourself what point or idea the author communicates, and perhaps has discovered, by telling the story. You might ask yourself the same questions if you read George Orwell's celebrated narrative essay, "Shooting an Elephant," among the Additional Readings.

Narrative Introductions

Narrative paragraphs also frequently appear in analytical essays, to introduce or illuminate an idea. Here is the way Fan Shen introduces an article in a journal whose audience is primarily teachers of college composition courses. She begins with an incident from her life in China:

> One day in June 1975, when I walked into the aircraft factory where I was working as an electrician, I saw many large-letter posters on the walls and many people parading around the workshops shouting slogans like: Down with the word 'I'!" and "Trust in masses and the Party!" I then remembered that a new political campaign called "Against Individualism" was scheduled to begin that day. Ten years later, I got back my first English composition paper at the University of Nebraska-Lincoln. The professor's first comments were: "Why did you always use 'we' instead of 'I'?" and "Your paper would be stronger if you eliminated some sentences in the passive voice." The clashes between my Chinese background and the requirements of English composition had begun. At the center of this mental struggle, which has lasted several years and is still not completely over, is the prolonged, uphill battle to recapture "myself."

The two brief narratives, the first introduced by "One day in June 1975" and the next by "Ten years later," placed one after the other in the opening paragraph, dramatize Fan Shen's struggle. At the end of the paragraph the word "myself" is in quotation marks; the two incidents described here have prepared us to understand why.

Here is another *narrative introduction* to an essay. Flannery O'Connor begins "The King of the Birds" (an essay on her passion for collecting and raising peacocks) with the following story:

> When I was five, I had an experience that marked me for life. Pathé
> News sent a photographer from New York to Savannah to take a pic-
> ture of a chicken of mine. This chicken, a buff Cochin Bantam, had the
> distinction of being able to walk either forward or backward. Her fame
> had spread through the press, and by the time she reached the attention
> of Pathé News, I suppose there was nowhere left for her to go—for-
> ward or backward. Shortly after that she died, as now seems fitting.

What makes this anecdote arresting? First of all, we can hardly read that an experience marked a person for life without wanting to know what the experience was. We expect to learn something sensational; perhaps, human nature being what it is, we hope to learn something horrifying. But O'Connor cannily does not gratify our wish. Instead she treats us to something like a joke. The chicken, whose fame had "spread through the press," has her picture taken by Pathé News (one of the companies that made the newsreels shown regularly in movie theaters before television became popular) and then dies. If the joke is partly on us, O'Connor takes the sting out of it by turning it around on herself. In her second paragraph she explains:

> If I put this information in the beginning of an article on peacocks, it is
> because I am always being asked why I raise them, and I have no short
> or reasonable answer.

But of course her answer, contained in the first paragraph, *is* short, and about as reasonable an explanation as any of us can offer about our passion for collecting anything. If these opening paragraphs persuade us to keep reading, it is not because they deliver the melodrama they at first hinted at, but because O'Connor's irony persuades us that she is entertaining, and that she is honest about her experience. We want to learn more about her, and we may thereby be seduced into learning what she wants to teach us about peacocks. Moreover, O'Connor's explanation that she tells the story because "I have no short or reasonable answer," reveals a profound truth about the impulse to tell stories. When a writer, even the writer of an essay, tells a story, it is because that story happens to be the best way to make the particular point he or she wants to make.

Narratives in Other Positions in an Essay

Although writers often use narratives in opening paragraphs of essays (just as speakers often begin their speeches with anecdotes) narration can be introduced effectively in almost any position in an essay. If you look back at essays that appear in earlier chapters of this book, you will see that one student, Suki Hudson, introduces her essay "Two Sides of a Story" (page 37), naturally enough, with a story, but she tells another story (which illuminates the first) in the second half of her essay. In several places in Philip Roth's essay describing his opposition to a plan to close the Newark Public Library (page 10), Roth vividly recalls how he used the library and what it meant to him when he was young. By contrast, the brief essay "A Lesson" (page 21), an account of what a student learned from a boring job, would have been invigorated had the writer included a narrative—an account of what happened during one day or one hour on the job. Not only would we have better understood what the "lesson" was, very likely she would have understood it better herself. Recounting an event or experience, *reliving* it, so that someone else can understand it deepens our own understanding of it as well.

Inventing Stories

Some people are more apt to tell stories than others, but we all have stories to tell. We have stories about our childhood, or work, or travel; the beginning of a relationship, the death of a friend. Sometimes a memory is contained in an image, a sense impression, an emotion, even a dream, and we must examine the traces of memory to remember the event and its meaning. Once on the track of a story, you can capture and develop it by writing about it. Try *freewriting,* or *asking yourself questions.* The journalist's questions are specifically designed to elicit stories. They are, you may remember:

- *What* happened?
- *Who* was involved?
- *When* did it happen?
- *Where* did it happen?
- *Why* did it happen?
- *How* did it happen?

Narrative Pace: Scene and Summary

In telling a story, you have some decisions to make: will you present it as a scene or will you summarize it? A **scene** brings the characters and actions before the eyes and often, with dialogue, before the ears of your readers. A **summary** briefly comments on an action, giving them a synopsis. Brent Staples, in his essay "Just Walk On By: A Black Man Ponders His Power to Alter Public Space" (page 217), begins with a scene, his encounter with a white woman on a deserted street in Hyde Park. The scene dramatizes his first experience of "being perceived as dangerous." Later in the essay he summarizes "the standard unpleasantries with police, doormen, bouncers, cab drivers, and others whose business it is to screen out troublesome individuals *before* there is any nastiness." When you are writing an essay, as opposed to a novel, you can't present everything as a scene. When you read Staples's essay, ask yourself why he summarizes the "unpleasantries" instead of presenting them as scenes.

The general rule is to keep the point of the story in mind and to cut any details or incidents that clog the action or blur the point. Flannery O'Connor describes her chicken only enough to convince us of its reality—it was a "buff Cochin Bantam." The point of the anecdote lies not in the unremarkable chicken (who achieves her fame and dies in three sentences) but in the effect on the writer of a brief moment of celebrity. On a deeper level, the point of the anecdote is the writer's wish to secure our attention and goodwill.

Organizing a Narrative

The usual way to organize a narrative is chronologically. As the King tells the White Rabbit in *Alice's Adventures in Wonderland:* "Begin at the beginning, and go on till you come to the end: then stop." Sometimes, though, it's effective to start with the end of the action, or somewhere in the middle, and then tell the story through a *flashback.* If on television you have seen *Sunset Boulevard,* a classic film, you will remember the opening scene: as we look down at a man's corpse in a swimming pool, his voice begins the story of how he got there! Narratives, however they are organized, are almost always told in the past tense; and good storytellers help us to follow the succession of events, the passage of time, by using such transitional words as *first, then, next, at last,* and *finally.*

Finally, we reprint a letter to the editor in which a college student, an assault victim, tells her experience. You may observe that the organization is for the most part chronological, made clear by transitions, and framed by the writer's analysis of her experience and her reasons for revealing it. As readers, we may or may not notice these points; gripped by the story being told, we are largely unaware of the techniques of successful writers. As students of writing, however, we study these techniques.

A Letter To the Editor:

1   I write this letter out of concern for women of the college community. I am one of the two students who were assaulted during the winter recess. I do not feel any shame or embarrassment over what happened. Instead, I want to share some of my experience because in doing so I may help other women to think about rape and rape prevention.

2   First I think it is important for the community to understand what happened to me. At my request, during the vacation a well-intentioned employee let me into my residence hall to collect some things from my room. It was after dark. I was alone in my room when a man appeared at the door with a stocking over his head and a knife in his hand. He said he was going to rape me. I had no

intention of submitting, and I struggled with him for about five minutes. One of the reasons why I chose not to submit but to resist was that as a virgin I did not want my first sexual experience to be the horror of rape. While struggling I tried to get him to talk to me, saying such things as "Why do you want to rape me? Don't you understand I want no part of this? I am a woman, not an object. In God's name, please don't rape me." He finally overpowered me and attempted to rape me, but stopped when he realized I had a tampax in. Then at knife point he asked me a number of questions. He ended by threatening that if I reported and identified him he would kill me. As he was leaving he made me lie on my bed and count to five hundred, which I started to do. Then as I reached one hundred he returned and told me to start over. Thus it was good I did not get up right after he left.

3   It is impossible to say what should be done in all instances of assault. Each incident is different and requires a different response. I think what helped me most was my ability to remain calm, assess the situation, and then act firmly, I did struggle, I did talk, but I also did act in such a way as to ensure my own safety at knife point.

4   I believe there are some reasons why I was able to cope with the situation. One is that I had talked with other women about rape and self-defense. As a result I was more aware of the possibility of rape and had thought some about what I might do if confronted with an attacker. Also my active involvement in the women's movement has helped me develop confidence in myself, especially in my strength, both emotional and physical. I believe such confidence helped me not to panic. Another reason why I was able to cope was that I prayed.

5   I think it is important also to share with you the aftermath of the attack. The first thing I did after leaving my room was to report the incident to security and to the campus police. I did not hesitate to report the attack since I realized that reporting it was vital to protect the safety of the college community. The police were efficient and helpful in taking the report and starting search procedures. (The police also told me they did not think I was in further danger, despite the threats on my life. There seemed to be little reason for him to come back.) Also, two female members of the student services staff stayed with me most of the evening. Their presence and support were very helpful to me, especially while I talked to the police. Since the incident, I have also found support from professional staff and from friends. The residence office, the medical and psychiatric staff, the dean's office, and the chaplaincy staff have all been helpful. All have protected my confidentiality.

6   At first I did not realize that I would want or need to seek out people's help, but now I am glad I did. The rape experience goes beyond the assault itself. I have come to understand the importance of dealing with the complex emotions that follow. Also I now know that there is no reason for women to feel ashamed, embarrassed, or scared about seeking help.

7   I hope you now have a greater concern for your own safety after reading about what happened to me. I think this is the most important point of my

writing. It never occurred to me that entering an unoccupied residence hall was dangerous. We all have been too accustomed to doing things on and off this campus without considering our own safety or vulnerability to attacks. But we ourselves are our own best security, so please protect yourselves and each other.

8   I am aware I will be working through this experience for a long time to come. I am thankful that there are people in this community to help me do that. I in turn want to be helpful in any way I can. So I invite women who are genuinely concerned about rape and assault to join me in sharing experiences and thoughts next Tuesday, February 18 at 7 P.M. in the Women's Center.

Name withheld upon request.

Topics for Discussion and Writing

1. In one or two paragraphs tell a story that illustrates an abstraction, such as anger, courage, endurance, a misunderstanding, a putdown, pride, the generation gap, embarrassment, racism, loneliness. For an example, see "Conceit" (page 138) and the brief discussion following it.

2. In 750 to 1000 words survey your development as a writer and explain your current attitude toward writing. Include a narrative or two contrasting narratives to exemplify what you have learned and how you learned it.

3. For an essay on any topic you choose, write an opening paragraph that includes an anecdote. Don't write the essay, but indicate from the anecdote and, if you wish, an additional sentence or two, the topic of your essay.

4. In 500 to 1000 words narrate an experience in such a way that you communicate not only the experience but the significance of it. For example, you might tell of an interview for a job which gave you some awareness of the attitude of people with jobs toward those without jobs. Or you might narrate an experience at school that seems to you to illuminate the virtues or defects or assumptions of the school. A variation: John Keats in a letter says, "Nothing ever becomes real till it is experienced—Even a proverb is no proverb to you till your life has illustrated it." Recount an experience that has made you feel the truth of a proverb.

Narration at Work

Zora Neale Hurston

A Conflict of Interest

Zora Neale Hurston (1891?–1960) was brought up in Eatonville, Florida, a town said to be the first all-black self-governing town in the United States. Her early years were spent working at odd jobs (domestic servant, manicurist, waitress), but she managed to attend Howard University and then, with the aid of a scholarship, entered Barnard College, where she was the first black student. She graduated from Barnard in 1928. At Barnard, influenced by the anthropologists Franz Boas and Ruth Benedict, she set out to study the folklore of Eatonville. Later she published several volumes of folklore, as well as stories, novels, and an autobiography (the source of our selection) called Dust Tracks on a Road *(1942).*

In the 1950s her writing seemed reactionary, almost embarrassing in an age of black protest, and she herself—working as a domestic, a librarian, and a substitute teacher—was almost forgotten. She died in a county welfare home in Florida and was buried in an unmarked grave. In the 1980s Hurston was, so to speak, rediscovered, partly because of the attention given to her by Alice Walker.

An incident happened that made me realize how theories go by the board when a person's livelihood is threatened. A man, a Negro, came into the shop one afternoon and sank down in Banks's chair. Banks was the manager and had the first chair by the door. It was so surprising that for a minute Banks just looked at him and never said a word. Finally, he found his tongue and asked, "What do you want?"

"Hair-cut and shave," the man said belligerently.

"But you can't get no hair-cut and shave here. Mr. Robinson[1] has a fine shop for Negroes on U Street near Fifteenth," Banks told him.

4   "I know it, but I want one here. The Constitution of the United States—"

But by that time, Banks had him by the arm. Not roughly, but he was helping him out of his chair, nevertheless.

"I don't know how to cut your hair," Banks objected. "I was trained on straight hair. Nobody in here knows how."

"Oh, don't hand me that stuff!" the crusader snarled. "Don't be such an Uncle Tom."

8   "Run on, fellow. You can't get waited on in here."

"I'll stay right here until I do. I know my rights. Things like this have got to be broken up. I'll get waited on all right, or sue the place."

---

[1]**Robinson** George Robinson, an African-American, owned a chain of barber shops. Most of his shops catered to whites in Washington, D.C. (Editors' note)

"Go ahead and sue," Banks retorted. "Go on uptown, and get your hair cut, man. Don't be so hard-headed for nothing."

"I'm getting waited on right here!"

12 "You're next, Mr. Powell," Banks said to a waiting customer. "Sorry, mister, but you better go on uptown."

"But I have a right to be waited on wherever I please," the Negro said, and started towards Updyke's chair which was being emptied. Updyke whirled his chair around so that he could not sit down and stepped in front of it. "Don't you touch *my* chair!" Updyke glared. "Go on about your business."

But instead of going, he made to get into the chair by force.

"Don't argue with him! Throw him out of here!" somebody in the back cried. And in a minute, barbers, customers all lathered and hair half cut, and porters, were all helping to throw the Negro out.

16 The rush carried him way out into the middle of G Street and flung him down. He tried to lie there and be a martyr, but the roar of oncoming cars made him jump up and scurry off. We never heard any more about it. I did not participate in the mêlée, but I wanted him thrown out, too. My business was threatened.

It was only that night in bed that I analyzed the whole thing and realized that I was giving sanction to Jim Crow, which theoretically, I was supposed to resist. But here were ten Negro barbers, three porters and two manicurists all stirred up at the threat of our living through loss of patronage. Nobody thought it out at the moment. It was an instinctive thing. That was the first time it was called to my attention that self-interest rides over all sorts of lines. I have seen the same thing happen hundreds of times since, and now I understand it. One sees it breaking over racial, national, religious and class lines. Anglo-Saxon against Anglo-Saxon, Jew against Jew, Negro against Negro, and all sorts of combinations of the three against other combinations of the three. Offhand, you might say that we fifteen Negroes should have felt the racial thing and served him. He was one of us. Perhaps it would have been a beautiful thing if Banks had turned to the shop crowded with customers and announced that this man was going to be served like everybody else even at the risk of losing their patronage, with all of the other employees lined up in the center of the floor shouting, "So say we all!" It would have been a stirring gesture, and made the headlines for a day. Then we could all have gone home to our unpaid rents and bills and things like that. I could leave school and begin my wanderings again. The "militant" Negro who would have been the cause of it all, would have perched on the smuddled-up wreck of things and crowed. Nobody ever found out who or what he was. Perhaps he did what he did on the spur of the moment, not realizing that serving him would have ruined Mr. Robinson, another Negro who had got what he had the hard way. For not only would the G Street shop have been forced to close, but the F Street shop and all of his other six downtown shops. Wrecking George Robinson like that on a "race" angle would have been ironic tragedy. He always helped out any Negro who was trying to do anything progressive as far as he was able. He had no education himself, but he was for it. He would give any Howard University student a job in his shops if they could qualify, even if it was only a few hours a week.

So I do not know what was the ultimate right in this case. I do know how I felt at the time. There is always something fiendish and loathsome about a person who threatens to deprive you of your way of making a living. That is just human-like, I reckon.

Topics for Discussion and Writing

1. Hurston published this account in 1942, and she was writing about an event that had taken place a couple of decades earlier. Given the period, and given Hurston's analysis of her action, do you find her behavior understandable and excusable, or do you think that she is rationalizing cowardice? Explain.

2. Words like "Outrageous," "ironic," "pathetic," and even "tragic" probably can be appropriately applied to this episode. Would you agree, however, that, as Hurston narrates it, it also has comic elements? If so, explain.

3. Hurston argues that self-interest overrides "racial, national, religious, and class lines." Do you agree? Does she persuade you that at least in this incident it was true, or might there have been other reasons for the employees' actions?

Brent Staples

Just Walk On By: A Black Man Ponders His Power to Alter Public Space

Brent Staples, born in 1951, holds a Ph.D. from the University of Chicago. He is an editor of The New York Times Book Review.
This essay originally appeared in Ms. *magazine.*

1   My first victim was a woman—white, well dressed, probably in her early twenties. I came upon her late one evening on a deserted street in Hyde Park, a relatively affluent neighborhood in an otherwise mean, impoverished section of Chicago. As I swung onto the avenue behind her, there seemed to be a discreet, uninflammatory distance between us. Not so. She cast back a worried glance. To her, the youngish black man—a broad six feet two inches with a beard and billowing hair, both hands shoved into the pockets of a bulky military jacket— seemed menacingly close. After a few more quick glimpses, she picked up her

pace and was soon running in earnest. Within seconds she disappeared into a cross street.

2   That was more than a decade ago. I was 22 years old, a graduate student newly arrived at the University of Chicago. It was in the echo of that terrified woman's footfalls that I first began to know the unwieldy inheritance I'd come into—the ability to alter public space in ugly ways. It was clear that she thought herself the quarry of a mugger, a rapist, or worse. Suffering a bout of insomnia, however, I was stalking sleep, not defenseless wayfarers. As a softy who is scarcely able to take a knife to a raw chicken—let alone hold it to a person's throat—I was surprised, embarrassed, and dismayed all at once. Her flight made me feel like an accomplice in tyranny. It also made it clear that I was indistinguishable from the muggers who occasionally seeped into the area from the surrounding ghetto. That first encounter, and those that followed, signified that a vast, unnerving gulf lay between nighttime pedestrians—particularly women—and me. And I soon gathered that being perceived as dangerous is a hazard in itself. I only needed to turn a corner into a dicey situation, or crowd some frightened, armed person in a foyer somewhere, or make an errant move after being pulled over by a policeman. Where fear and weapons meet—and they often do in urban America—there is always the possibility of death.

3   In that first year, my first away from my hometown, I was to become thoroughly familiar with the language of fear. At dark, shadowy intersections in Chicago, I could cross in front of a car stopped at a traffic light and elicit the *thunk, thunk, thunk, thunk* of the driver—black, white, male, or female— hammering down the door locks. On less traveled streets after dark, I grew accustomed to but never comfortable with people who crossed to the other side of the street rather than pass me. Then there were the standard unpleasantries with police, doormen, bouncers, cab drivers, and others whose business it is to screen out troublesome individuals *before* there is any nastiness.

4   I moved to New York nearly two years ago and I have remained an avid night walker. In central Manhattan, the near-constant crowd cover minimizes tense one-on-one street encounters. Elsewhere—visiting friends in SoHo, where sidewalks are narrow and tightly spaced buildings shut out the sky—things can get very taut indeed.

5   Black men have a firm place in New York mugging literature. Norman Podhoretz in his famed (or infamous) 1963 essay, "My Negro Problem—And Ours," recalls growing up in terror of black males; they "were tougher than we were, more ruthless," he writes—and as an adult on the Upper West Side of Manhattan, he continues, he cannot constrain his nervousness when he meets black men on certain streets. Similarly, a decade later, the essayist and novelist Edward Hoagland extols a New York where once "Negro bitterness bore down mainly on other Negroes." Where some see mere panhandlers, Hoagland sees "a mugger who is clearly screwing up his nerve to do more than just *ask* for money." But Hoagland has "the New Yorker's quick-hunch posture for broken-field maneuvering," and the bad guy swerves away.

6   I often witness that "hunch posture," from women after dark on the warrenlike streets of Brooklyn where I live. They seem to set their faces on neutral and, with their purse straps strung across their chests bandolier style, they forge ahead as though bracing themselves against being tackled. I understand, of course, that the danger they perceive is not a hallucination. Women are particularly vulnerable to street violence, and young black males are drastically overrepresented among the perpetrators of that violence. Yet these truths are no solace against the kind of alienation that comes of being ever the suspect, against being set apart, a fearsome entity with whom pedestrians avoid making eye contact.

7   It is not altogether clear to me how I reached the ripe old age of 22 without being conscious of the lethality nighttime pedestrians attributed to me. Perhaps it was because in Chester, Pennsylvania, the small, angry industrial town where I came of age in the 1960s, I was scarcely noticeable against a backdrop of gang warfare, street knifings, and murders. I grew up one of the good boys, had perhaps a half-dozen fist fights. In retrospect, my shyness of combat has clear sources.

8   Many things go into the making of a young thug. One of those things is the consummation of the male romance with the power to intimidate. An infant discovers that random flailings send the baby bottle flying out of the crib and crashing to the floor. Delighted, the joyful babe repeats those motions again and again, seeking to duplicate the feat. Just so, I recall the points at which some of my boyhood friends were finally seduced by the perception of themselves as tough guys. When a mark cowered and surrendered his money without resistance, myth and reality merged—and paid off. It is, after all, only manly to embrace the power to frighten and intimidate. We, as men, are not supposed to give an inch of our lane on the highway; we are to seize the fighter's edge in work and in play and even in love; we are to be valiant in the face of hostile forces.

9   Unfortunately, poor and powerless young men seem to take all this nonsense literally. As a boy, I saw countless tough guys locked away; I have since buried several, too. They were babies, really—a teenage cousin, a brother of 22, a childhood friend in his mid-twenties—all gone down in episodes of bravado played out in the streets. I came to doubt the virtues of intimidation early on. I chose, perhaps even unconsciously, to remain a shadow—timid, but a survivor.

10   The fearsomeness mistakenly attributed to me in public places often has a perilous flavor. The most frightening of these confusions occurred in the late 1970s and early 1980s when I worked as a journalist in Chicago. One day, rushing into the office of a magazine I was writing for with a deadline story in hand, I was mistaken for a burglar. The office manager called security and, with an ad hoc posse, pursued me through the labyrinthine halls, nearly to my editor's door. I had no way of proving who I was. I could only move briskly toward the company of someone who knew me.

11   Another time I was on assignment for a local paper and killing time before an interview. I entered a jewelry store on the city's affluent Near North Side. The proprietor excused herself and returned with an enormous red Doberman pinscher straining at the end of a leash. She stood, the dog extended toward me, silent to my questions, her eyes bulging nearly out of her head. I took a cursory look around, nodded, and bade her good night. Relatively speaking, however, I never fared as badly as another black male journalist. He went to nearby Waukegan, Illinois, a couple of summers ago to work on a story about a murderer who was born there. Mistaking the reporter for the killer, police hauled him from his car at gunpoint and but for his press credentials would probably have tried to book him. Such episodes are not uncommon. Black men trade tales like this all the time.

12   In "My Negro Problem—And Ours," Podhoretz writes that the hatred he feels for blacks makes itself known to him through a variety of avenues—one being his discomfort with that "special brand of paranoid touchiness" to which he says blacks are prone. No doubt he is speaking here of black men. In time, I learned to smother the rage I felt at so often being taken for a criminal. Not to do so would surely have led to madness—via that special "paranoid touchiness" that so annoyed Podhoretz at the time he wrote the essay.

13   I began to take precautions to make myself less threatening. I move about with care, particularly late in the evening. I give a wide berth to nervous people on subway platforms during the wee hours, particularly when I have exchanged business clothes for jeans. If I happen to be entering a building behind some people who appear skittish, I may walk by, letting them clear the lobby before I return, so as not to seem to be following them. I have been calm and extremely congenial on those rare occasions when I've been pulled over by the police.

14   And on late-evening constitutionals along streets less traveled by, I employ what has proved to be an excellent tension-reducing measure: I whistle melodies from Beethoven and Vivaldi and the more popular classical composers. Even steely New Yorkers hunching toward nighttime destinations seem to relax, and occasionally they even join in the tune. Virtually everybody seems to sense that a mugger wouldn't be warbling bright, sunny selections from Vivaldi's *Four Seasons*. It is my equivalent of the cowbell that hikers wear when they know they are in bear country.

Topics for Discussion and Writing

1. What did Staples learn, from the first experience that he narrates, about other people? What did he learn about himself?
2. In paragraph 3 Staples gives a second example (the response of people in cars) of the effect that he has on others. Why do you suppose he bothered to give a second example, since it illustrates a point already made by the first example?

3. In paragraph 12 Staples quotes Norman Podhoretz's remark about the "special brand of paranoid touchiness" that Podhoretz finds in many blacks. What would you say is Staples's view of Podhoretz's idea?

4. In paragraph 13 Staples discusses the "precautions" he takes to make himself "less threatening." Are these precautions reasonable? Or do they reveal that he is, in Podhoretz's word, "paranoid"? Do you think he ought to be less concerned with taking precautions? Why, or why not?

5. Evaluate Staples's final paragraph as a way of ending the essay.

6. The success of a narrative as a piece of writing often depends on the reader's willingness to identify with the narrator. From an analysis of "Just Walk On By," what explanation can you give for your willingness (or un-willingness) to identify yourself with Staples?

Laura Cunningham

The Girls' Room

Laura Cunningham was born in 1947. Orphaned at the age of eight, she was brought up by two unmarried uncles, both of whom were writers. She says that she became a writer because she didn't know that one could become anything else. Had she known of other possibilities, she says, she would have become a ballerina. The essay that we reprint appeared originally in The New York Times.

1   When I heard she was coming to stay with us I was pleased. At age eight I thought of "grandmother" as a generic brand. My friends had grandmothers who seemed permanently bent over cookie racks. They were a source of constant treats and sweets. They were pinchers of cheeks, huggers and kissers. My own grandmother had always lived in a distant state; I had no memory of her when she decided to join the household recently established for me by my two uncles.

2   But with the example of my friends' grandmothers before me, I could hardly wait to have a grandmother of my own—and the cookies would be nice too. For while my uncles provided a cuisine that ranged from tuna croquettes to Swedish meatballs, they showed no signs of baking anything more elegant than a potato.

3   My main concern on the day of my grandmother's arrival was: How soon would she start the cookies? I remember her arrival, my uncles flanking her as they walked down the apartment corridor. She wore a hat, a tailored navy blue suit, an ermine stole. She held, tucked under her arm, the purple leather folder that contained her work in progress, a manuscript entitled "Philosophy for Women." She was preceded by her custom-made white trunk packed with purses, necklaces, earrings, dresses and more purple-inked pages that stress "the spiritual above the material."

4   She was small—at five feet one inch not much taller than I was—thin and
straight, with a pug nose, one brown eye (the good eye) and one blue eye (the
bad eye, frosted by cataracts). Her name was "Esther in Hebrew, Edna in
English, and Etka in Russian." She preferred the Russian, referring to herself as
"Etka from Minsk." It was not at once apparent that she was deaf in her left ear
(the bad ear) but could hear with the right (the good ear). Because her good ear
happened to be on the opposite side from the good eye, anyone who spoke to
her had to run around her in circles, or sway to and fro, if eye contact and
audibility were to be achieved simultaneously.

5   Etka from Minsk had arrived not directly from Minsk, as the black-eyed
ermine stole seemed to suggest, but after many moves. She entered with the
draft of family scandal at her back, blown out of her daughter's home after
assaults upon her dignity. She held the evidence: an empty-socketed peacock
pin. My cousin, an eleven-year-old boy, had surgically plucked out the
rhinestone eyes. She could not be expected to stay where such acts occurred.
She had to be among "human beings," among "real people" who could
understand. We seemed to understand. We—my two uncles and I—encircled
her, studied her vandalized peacock pin and vowed that such things would never
happen with "us."

6   She patted my head—a good sign—and asked me to sing the Israeli
national anthem. I did, and she handed me a dollar. My uncles went off to their
jobs, leaving me alone with my grandmother for the first time. I looked at her,
expecting her to start rolling out the cookie dough. Instead she suggested: "Now
maybe you could fix me some lunch?"

7   It wasn't supposed to be this way, I thought, as I took her order: "toasted
cheese and a sliced orange." Neither was she supposed to share my pink and
orange bedroom, but she did. The bedroom soon exhibited a dual character—
stuffed animals on one side, a hospital bed on the other. Within the household
this chamber was soon referred to as "the girls' room." The name, given by
Uncle Abe, who saw no incongruity, only the affinity of sex, turned out to be apt,
for what went on in the girls' room could easily have been labeled sibling rivalry
if she had not been eighty and I eight. I soon found that I had acquired not a
traditional grandmother but an aged kid sister.

8   The theft and rivalry began within days. My grandmother had given me her
most cherished possession, a violet beaded bag. In return I gave her my heart-
shaped "ivory" pin and matching earrings. That night she stole back the purse
but insisted on keeping the pin and earrings. I turned to my uncles for mediation
and ran up against unforeseen resistance. They thought my grandmother should
keep the beaded bag; they didn't want to upset her.

9   I burned at the injustice of it and felt the heat of an uncomfortable truth:
where I once had my uncles' undivided indulgence, they were now split as my
grandmother and I vied for their attention. The household, formerly geared to
my little-girl needs, was rearranged to accommodate hers. I suffered serious

affronts—my grandmother, in a fit of frugality, scissored all the household blankets, including what a psychiatrist would have dubbed my "security" blanket, in half. "Now," she said, her good eye gleaming, "we have twice as many." I lay under my narrow slice of blanket and stared hopelessly up at the ceiling. I thought evilly of ways of getting my grandmother out of the apartment.

10   Matters worsened, as more and more of my trinkets disappeared. One afternoon I came home from school to find her squeezed into my unbuttoned favorite blouse. Rouged and beribboned, she insisted that the size 3 blouse was hers. Meanwhile, I was forced to adapt to her idiosyncracies: she covered everything black—from the dog to the telephone—with white doilies. She left saucers balanced on top of glasses. She sang nonstop. She tried to lock my dog out of the apartment.

11   The word that explained her behavior was "arteriosclerosis." She had forgotten so much that sometimes she would greet me with "You look familiar." At other times she'd ask, "What hotel is this?" My answer, shouted in her good ear, was: "We're not in a hotel! This is our apartment!" The response would be a hoot of laughter: "Then why are we in the ballroom?"

12   Finally we fought: arm-to-arm combat. I was shocked at her grip, steely as the bars that locked her into bed at night. Her good eye burned into mine and she said, "I'll tell." And she did. For the first time I was scolded. She had turned their love to disapproval, I thought, and how it chafed. Eventually our rivalry mellowed into conspiracy. Within months we found we had uses for each other. I provided the lunches and secret, forbidden ice cream sundaes. She rewarded me with cold cash. She continued to take my clothes; I charged her competitive prices. I hated school; she paid me not to go. When I came home for lunch I usually stayed.

13   Our household endured the status quo for eight years: my uncles, my grandmother and I. Within the foursome rivalries and alliances shifted. I became my grandmother's friend and she became mine. We were the source of all the family comedy. When she said she wanted a college diploma we gave her one— with tinfoil stars and a "magna magna summa summa cum laude" inscription. We sang and performed skits. We talcum-powdered hair and wearing one of her old dresses, I would appear as her "long-lost friend." We had other themes, including a pen pal, "The Professor."

14   Of course, living with an elderly person had its raw aspects. When she was ill our girls' room took on the stark aura of a geriatrics ward. I imagined, to my shame, that neighbors could stare in through curtainless windows as I tended to my grandmother's most personal needs.

15   Yet, in these times of age segregation, with grandmothers sent off to impersonal places, I wonder if the love and the comedy weren't worth the intermittent difficulties. Certainly I learned what it might be to become old. And I took as much comfort as my grandmother did in a nightly exchange of Russian

endearments—"Ya tebya lyublyu," "Ya tebya tozhe lyublyu—"I love you," "I love you, too."

16   If I sold my grandmother blouses and baubles, maybe she gave me the truth in exchange. Once, when we were alone in the girls' room, she turned to me, suddenly lucid, her good eye as bright as it would ever be—a look I somehow recognized as her "real" gaze—and said, "My life passes like a dream."

Topics for Discussion and Writing

1. In the second sentence, what does Cunningham mean by "a generic brand"?
2. What is the title of Esther's manuscript? What is it about? Do you detect any irony in the way Cunningham conveys this information? Explain.
3. In the second sentence of paragraph 4, what is conveyed by putting the names within quotation marks?
4. Is paragraph 4—about Esther's physical disabilities—in bad taste? Explain.
5. In her last paragraph Cunningham says that perhaps her grandmother gave her "the truth." What does she mean?
6. "I burned at the injustice of it and felt the heat of an uncomfortable truth." Where in the narrative does Cunningham say this? What was the "truth"? If you remember a similar experience, write a narrative that discloses both the experience and the truth on which it was based. Or, write an essay of 500 words on your own most potent experience of living with or near an elderly person.

Wu-tsu Fa-yen

Zen and the Art of Burglary

Wu-tsu Fa-yen (1025–1104) was a Chinese Zen Buddhist priest. More exactly, he was a Ch'an priest; Zen is Japanese for the Chinese Ch'an.

The practitioner of Zen (to use the more common name) seeks satori, "enlightenment" or "awakening." The awakening is from a world of blind strivings (including those of reason and of morality). The awakened being, free from a sense of the self in opposition to all other things, perceives the unity of all things. Wu-tsu belonged to the branch of Zen that uses "shock therapy, the purpose of which is to jolt the student out of his analytical and conceptual way of thinking and lead him back to his natural and spontaneous faculty" (Kenneth Ch'en, Buddhism in China [1964, rptd. 1972], p. 359).

The title of this story, from The Sayings of Goso Hōyen, *is the editors'.*

1   If people ask me what Zen is like, I will say that it is like learning the art of burglary. The son of a burglar saw his father growing older and thought, "If he is unable to carry on his profession, who will be the breadwinner of the family, except myself? I must learn the trade." He intimated the idea to his father, who approved of it.

2   One night the father took the son to a big house, broke through the fence, entered the house, and, opening one of the large chests, told the son to go in and pick out the clothing. As soon as the son got into it, the father dropped the lid and securely applied the lock. The father now came out to the courtyard and loudly knocked at the door, waking up the whole family; then he quietly slipped away by the hole in the fence. The residents got excited and lighted candles, but they found that the burglar had already gone.

3   The son, who remained all the time securely confined in the chest, thought of his cruel father. He was greatly mortified, then a fine idea flashed upon him. He made a noise like the gnawing of a rat. The family told the maid to take a candle and examine the chest. When the lid was unlocked, out came the prisoner, who blew out the light, pushed away the maid, and fled. The people ran after him. Noticing a well by the road, he picked up a large stone and threw it into the water. The pursuers all gathered around the well trying to find the burglar drowning himself in the dark hole.

4   In the meantime he went safely back to his father's house. He blamed his father deeply for his narrow escape. Said the father, "Be not offended, my son. Just tell me how you got out of it." When the son told him about his adventures, the father remarked, "There you are, you have learned the art."

Topics for Discussion and Writing

1. What assumptions about knowledge did the father make? Can you think of any of your own experiences that substantiate these assumptions?

2. Is there anything you have studied or are studying to which Zen pedagogical methods would be applicable? If so, explain by setting forth a sample lesson.

Chapter 11

Describing

Looking is not as simple as it looks.

—AD REINHARDT

Observing Details

Description represents in words our sensory impressions caught in a moment of time. In much descriptive writing visual imagery dominates. Look at the following example, part of a letter Vincent Van Gogh wrote to his brother, Theo.

> Twilight is falling, and the view of the yard from my window is simply wonderful, with that little avenue of poplars—their slender forms and thin branches stand out so delicately against the gray evening sky; and then the old arsenal building in the water—quiet as the "waters of the old pool" in the book of Isaiah—down by the waterside the walls of that arsenal are quite green and weatherbeaten. Farther down is the little garden and the fence around it with the rosebushes, and everywhere in the yard the black figures of the workmen, and also the little dog. Just now Uncle Jan with his long black hair is probably making his rounds. In the distance the masts of the ships in the dock can be seen, in front the Atjeh, quite black, and the gray and red monitors—and just now here and there the lamps are being lit. At this moment the bell is ringing and the whole stream of workmen is pouring towards the gate; at the same time the lamplighter is coming to light the lamp in the yard behind the house.

First, notice that Van Gogh does not attempt to describe the view from the window at all times of day, but only now, when "twilight is falling." Thus, the figures of the workmen, the little dog, the masts in the distance, appear black; the evening sky is gray, and "just now here and there the lamps are being lit."

Second, notice that Vincent tells Theo that he sees not "a row of trees" but a "little avenue of poplars—their slender forms and thin branches stand out so delicately against the gray evening sky." These details, the result of close observation, help the reader to see what Van Gogh saw, and to feel as he felt.

Third, notice that while Van Gogh describes primarily what he *sees* (not surprising in a painter) he also notices and tells Theo what he *hears:* "At this moment the bell is ringing." And through every detail he communicates what he feels about the scene he describes: "the view of the yard from my window is simply wonderful."

Description is often a kind of persuasion. Writers wish to persuade us to share their judgment that what they describe is beautiful or ugly, noble or ignoble, valuable or worthless. If we are persuaded, it is not so much because the writer tells us what to feel (often the judgment is not stated, but implied) as it is because the writer skillfully represents to us what he or she sees, or experiences through other senses.

Organizing a Description

Patient observation of details, and willingness to search for exactly the right words with which to communicate our impressions, are both part of the secret of good descriptive writing. Still another part is organization, the translation of our disorderly, even chaotic, impressions into orderly structures. Limiting the description to what is sensed at a particular moment in time in itself imposes some order. But in addition, our descriptions must have some discernible pattern, such as from left to right, from bottom to top, from general to particular, or, as in Van Gogh's description, from near to far.

Notice this structure, from near to far, as Walt Whitman uses it in his poem "A Farm Picture."

Through the ample open door of the peaceful country barn,
A sunlit pasture field with cattle and horses feeding,
And haze and vista, and the far horizon fading away.

Although the poem is only three lines long, the view is leisurely, beginning where the observer stands, inside the "ample open door," and then stretching slowly out to the "sunlit pasture field," still distinct, because still close up, then to the slightly more general "cattle and horses," and last to the indistinct "far horizon fading away." The leisurely pace persuades us that the scene is indeed "peaceful"; the orderly structure of the poem allows us to feel that it is.

Now look, by contrast, at a description not of a place, but of a phenomenon, a phenomenon not seen but felt, not peaceful, but "uneasy."

There is something uneasy in the Los Angeles air this afternoon, some unnatural stillness, some tension. What it means is that tonight a Santa Ana will begin to blow, a hot wind from the northeast whining down through the Cajon and San Gorgonio Passes, blowing up sandstorms out along Route 66, drying the hills and the nerves to the flash point. For a few days now we will see smoke back in the canyons, and hear sirens in the night. I have neither heard nor read that a Santa Ana is due, but I know it, and almost everyone I have seen today knows it too.

We know it because we feel it. The baby frets. The maid sulks. I rekindle a waning argument with the telephone company, then cut my losses and lie down, given over to whatever it is in the air. To live with the Santa Ana is to accept, consciously or unconsciously, a deeply mechanistic view of human behavior.

—JOAN DIDION

Here the governing pattern of the description is more complex—from the general to the specific, and back to the general. Didion begins with the relatively general statement "There is something uneasy in the Los Angeles air this afternoon." She then moves to the specific details that support the generalization: the visible effects of the unseen wind first on the landscape and then on people (the baby, the maid, Didion herself). In the final sentence, again a relatively general one, she summarizes a further effect of what it is "to live with the Santa Ana." The organization is complex, but the passage is not disorderly. Or, we might say, it is just disorderly enough to make us feel, with the writer, "something uneasy in the Los Angeles air."

Specific details and concrete language help us to imagine what the writer has observed; a suitable organization further assists us in following the writer's representation of impressions and feelings.

Establishing the Observer's Position

In addition to observing closely, finding the right word, and organizing the material, there is yet another technique that helps persuade the reader to accept the writer's observations as true, and his or her judgment as sound. This technique can be discovered by comparing two descriptions of a building on fire. The first is by a student.

The thick, heavy smoke, that could be seen for miles, filled the blue July sky. Firemen frantically battled the blaze that engulfed Hempstead High School, while a crowd of people sadly looked on. Eyes slowly filled up with tears as the reality of having no school to go to started to sink in. Students that had once downed everything that the high school stood for and did, began to realize how much they cared for their school. But it was too late, it was going up in smoke.

This is surely a competent description, and it is well organized. But compare it to the second description by a professional writer, a practiced hand.

We were on the porch only a short time when I heard a lot of hollering coming from toward the field. The hollering and crying got louder and louder. I could hear Mama's voice over all the rest. It seemed like all the people in the field were running to our house. I ran to the edge of the porch to watch them top the hill. Daddy was leading the running crowd and Mama was right behind him.

"Lord have mercy, my children is in that house!" Mama was screaming. "Hurry, Diddly!" she cried to Daddy. I turned around and saw big clouds of smoke booming out of the front door and shooting out of cracks everywhere. "There, Essie Mae is on the porch," Mama said. "Hurry, Diddly! Get Adline outta that house!" I looked back at Adline. I couldn't hardly see her for the smoke.

George Lee was standing in the yard like he didn't know what to do. As Mama got closer, he ran into the house. My first thought was that he would be burned up. I'd often hoped he would get killed, but I guess I didn't really want him to die after all. I ran inside after him but he came running out again, knocking me down as he passed and leaving me lying face down in the burning room. I jumped up quickly and scrambled out after him. He had the water bucket in his hands. I thought he was going to try to put out the fire. Instead he placed the bucket on the edge of the porch and picked up Adline in his arms.

Moments later Daddy was on the porch. He ran straight into the burning house with three other men right behind him. They opened the large wooden windows to let some of the smoke out and began ripping the paper from the walls before the wood caught on fire. Mama and two other women raked it into the fireplace with sticks, broom handles, and anything else available. Everyone was coughing because of all the smoke.

—ANNE MOODY

What can we learn from the professional writer? First notice her patience with detail, the concreteness of the passage. In the first passage we read: "Firemen frantically battled the blaze that engulfed Hempstead High School." Moody, by contrast, shows us individuals and exactly what each does. The first passage generalizes the reaction of the observers—"Eyes slowly filled up with tears" and "Students . . . began to realize how much they cared for their school"—in Moody's passage Mama screams, "Lord have mercy, my children is in that house!"

But equally important, the professional writer captures the reader's attention, and secures the reader's identification with the observer or narrator, by establishing the observer's physical position. At the beginning she is on the porch, looking toward the field. It is only when she hears her mother scream that she turns around and sees the smoke. And notice that she *does have to turn,* and the writer has the patience to tell us "I turned around and saw. . . ." We could, if we wished to, place the position of the observer, exactly, throughout the action, as if we were blocking a scene in a play. By contrast, notice that there is no real observer in the student's description. If there were, she would first have to be miles away from the scene and looking up into the sky to see the smoke. Then, in the second sentence she would be across the street, watching the firemen. By the third sentence she'd be closer still—not close to the fire, but close to the other observers. In fact, she'd have to be inside their heads to know what they were thinking. As readers we sense this lack of focus; we have no one to identify with. Though we may find the passage interesting, it will not engage us and we will soon forget it.

Establishing the Observer's Point of View

In addition to the observer's physical location, a good description also provides a consistent psychological position, or *point of view,* with which we can identify ourselves. In the following passage from *Black Elk Speaks,* Black Elk, an Oglala Sioux holy man, is describing the Battle of Little Bighorn (1876).

> The valley went darker with dust and smoke, and there were only shadows and a big noise of many cries and hoofs and guns. On the left side of where I was I could hear the shod hoofs of the soldiers' horses going back into the brush and there was shooting everywhere. Then the hoofs came out of the brush, and I came out and was in among men and horses weaving in and out and going upstream, and everybody was yelling, "Hurry! Hurry!" The soldiers were running upstream and we were all mixed there in the twilight and the great noise. I did not see much; but once I saw a Lakota charge at a soldier who stayed behind and fought and was a very brave man. The Lakota took the soldier's horse by the bridle, but the soldier killed him with a six-shooter, I was small and could not crowd in to where the soldiers were, so I did not kill anybody. There were so many ahead of me, and it was all dark and mixed up.

Black Elk was an old man when he told this story. How old would you guess he was at the time it happened? How do you know?

Describing an Action

At the beginning of this chapter we defined description as a representation, in words, of sensory impressions caught in a moment of time. Strictly speaking, description is static. The passage from Van Gogh's letter, and Whitman's poem, most nearly conform to this definition: they each describe a scene caught in a single moment, like a snapshot. Didion's paragraph about the Santa Ana is less static; it implies the passage of time. That time passes is, however, somewhat masked because Didion represents almost everything as happening simultaneously: "The baby frets. The maid sulks. I rekindle a waning argument with the telephone company." By contrast, in Moody's description of a house on fire, we not only hear (with Essie Mae) "a lot of hollering," and see "big clouds of smoke booming out of the front door and shooting out of cracks everywhere," we also know that moments have passed between the first sensory impression and the second, and that several more have passed before the passage ends with all the adults raking the burning wallpaper into the fireplace. The description is thoroughly interwoven with narration. Black Elk's account of the Battle of Little Bighorn is similarly a blend of description and narration.

Long passages of pure description are rare. The reason is simple. A description of a place will be much more interesting if the writer shows us something happening there. Similarly, descriptions of people are seldom (except briefly) static. In real life we seldom observe people at dead rest; we see them in action; we form our impressions of them from how they move, what they do. Good descriptions, then, frequently show us a person performing some action, a particularly revealing action, or a characteristic one. If, for example, you want to suggest a person's height and weight, it's much more interesting to show him maneuvering through a subway turnstile, perhaps laden with packages, than to say, "He was only five feet four but weighed 185 pounds" or "he was short and stocky." Here is Maya Angelou describing Mr. Freeman, a man who lived for a while with her mother.

> Mr. Freeman moved gracefully, like a big brown bear, and seldom spoke to us. He simply waited for Mother and put his whole self into the waiting. He never read the paper or patted his foot to the radio. He waited. That was all.
>
> If she came home before we went to bed, we saw the man come alive. He would start out of the big chair, like a man coming out of sleep, smiling. I would remember then that a few seconds before, I had heard a car door slam; then Mother's footsteps would signal from the concrete walk. When her key rattled the door, Mr. Freeman would have already asked his habitual question, "Hey, Bibbi, have a good time?"
>
> His query would hang in the air while she sprang over to peck him on the lips. Then she turned to Bailey and me with the lipstick kisses. "Haven't you finished your homework?" If we had and were just reading—"O.K., say your prayers and go to bed." If we hadn't—"Then go to your room and finish . . . then say your prayers and go to bed."
>
> Mr. Freeman's smile never grew, it stayed at the same intensity. Sometimes Mother would go over and sit on his lap and the grin on his face looked as if it would stay there forever.

Notice how animated this description is, how filled not only with Mr. Freeman's physical presence but also with his mysterious inner life. We have a portrait of Mother, too, reflected in Mr. Freeman's waiting, his concentration on the slam of her car door, her footsteps, her key rattling, and, most of all, in his smile. More subtly and more pervasively, the description is animated by our identification with the observer, the small child watching the man who waits so intently for the woman who is her mother.

Description and Analysis

Descriptive passages are also commonly used in essays to support analysis. In the following brief essay, for example, a writer asks and answers the question "What are the functions of cemeteries for the living?" Doherty's essay is primarily analytical; reading it, we share the writer's thoughts, but these thoughts are not the random and fleeting notions of reverie. The thoughts have been organized for us; the effects of cemeteries on the living have been classified and presented to us in an orderly and coherent account made vivid by passages of description. Through description writer's we share at least imaginatively in the experiences that gave rise to the thinking. And through description, if the communication between writer and reader has been successful, we are persuaded to share the writer's opinions.

Jim Doherty

How Cemeteries Bring Us Back to Earth

Jim Doherty, a writer and editor, served as executive editor for National Wildlife.

1   A while ago, we said goodbye to a beloved aunt in a rural Wisconsin cemetery pulsing with birdsong. It was a splendid morning, gusty and bright. Puffy white clouds went sailing across the deep blue sky and calves were bawling in the distance. Later, we would sing hymns in a pretty church that smelled of coffee and candle wax, but first we stood blinking in the sunlight while a choir of robins, red-winged blackbirds and meadowlarks lustily serenaded the casket.

2   Curiously enough, graveyards often seem more alive than the places where many of us live. To soften the harshness of tombstones and obelisks, we plant trees and bushes, create ponds and manicure vast lawns. Even as developers transform old marshlands and forests into shopping centers and subdivisions, our forebears moulder away in lush new groves that nourish raccoons, woodchucks, rabbits and birds.

3   Cemeteries are good places for living people, too. My oldest daughter attends a Connecticut college where she spends many pleasant afternoons studying in a 17th-century boneyard. I remember a shady marble orchard in Mamaroneck, N.Y., where couples could usually find enough privacy for petting. Out here in southeastern Wisconsin, rabbit hunters patrol secluded country cemeteries that are bounded by overgrown fence rows and cornfields.

4   Tombstones can teach us a little about history but the overall ambience of a cemetery tells us much more.

5   One snowy spring morning near a ghost town in Idaho, my wife and I happened across a cluster of faded wooden markers surrounded by a rusting wrought-iron fence. The wind blew mournfully through the tall evergreens, and off in the distance the peaks of the Rockies glowed like The Promised Land. As

we meandered among the graves, we tried to imagine what kind of lives those pioneers led and gradually we seemed to absorb an impression of it—the loneliness, the uncertainty, the overpowering presence of the mountains.

6   Hiking in Vermont one day, we found a century-old family plot on a hillside where two generations lived and died. Most of those who perished were children—eight of them were buried side-by-side—and there were also a number of small unmarked stones. It was impossible to romanticize the past at the gravesite of a patriarch preceded in death by two wives and so many sons and daughters. We wondered: Was he ready to go when his time came?

7   Cemeteries bring us back to earth in more ways than one.

8   By their very presence, they remind us that the meter is running. In so doing, they admonish us not to love winter less but to appreciate summer more. They reassure us, too, for if the dead can reside in such benign surroundings, then death itself somehow seems less formidable.

9   A man I know works as a caretaker up north. Whenever an old grave caves in, he spades off the sod and throws in enough dirt to fill the hole. Now and then he turns up a bone and simply tamps it down into the soil before replacing the sod. It bothers him not at all.

10   Recently, I took a 90-year-old woman to a hilltop cemetery in Johnson Creek, the small town where she grew up. It was a hot summer day and the air was sweet with the perfume of cedar trees and cut hay. Somewhere, a meadowlark was calling. My companion was looking for the headstone of a distant relative, which she did not find, but she came across many other familiar names: a neighbor, the man who ran the creamery, the banker, several childhood friends, some students from her teaching days. She stopped at each one to remember a story or two and then moved on until she grew tired, and we left.

11   I retain a vivid image of that windblown lady tottering gamely between the rows of mossy tombstones, full of anticipation and absolutely unafraid. It is a brave picture. I shall cherish it until the day I die.

Doherty's essay is primarily analytical; reading it, we share the writer's thoughts, but these thoughts are not the random and fleeting notions of reverie. The thoughts have been organized for us; the effects of cemeteries on the living have been classified and presented to us in an orderly and coherent account made vivid by passages of description. Through description we share at least imaginatively in the experiences that gave rise to the writer's thinking. And through description, if the communication between writer and reader has been successful, we are persuaded to share the writer's opinions.

Topics for Discussion and Writing

1. In one paragraph, describe what you see from your window. Choose a particular time of day and describe only what you see (or might see) or otherwise sense within a moment or two.

2. In one paragraph, describe something that cannot be seen, or cannot be seen except by the effects it creates. (Something hot, or smelly, or loud?)

3. In one paragraph, describe something from the point of view of a child, or an old person, or someone of the opposite sex. (Note *person*. The point of view of a dog, or stone, or carrot is *out*.)

4. In one paragraph, describe a room—for example, a doctor's waiting room or an elementary school classroom—by showing something happening in it. Your description should reveal (without explicitly stating) your attitude toward it. The reader should be able to sense that the room is, for example, comfortable or sterile or pretentious or cozy or menacing, though no such words are used in the description.

5. First read the following two paragraphs from Saul Bellow's novel *The Victim*. Then answer the questions that follow the paragraphs.

> Leventhal's apartment was spacious. In a better neighborhood, or three stories lower, it would have rented for twice the amount he paid. But the staircase was narrow and stifling and full of turns. Though he went up slowly, he was out of breath when he reached the fourth floor, and his heart beat thickly. He rested before unlocking the door. Entering, he threw down his raincoat and flung himself on the tapestry-covered low bed in the front room. Mary had moved some of the chairs into the corners and covered them with sheets. She could not depend on him to keep the windows shut and the shades and curtains drawn during the day. This afternoon the cleaning woman had been in and there was a pervasive odor of soap powder. He got up and opened a window. The curtains waved once and then were as motionless as before. There was a movie house strung with lights across the street; on its roof a water tank sat heavily uneven on its timbers; the cowls of the chimneys, which rattled in the slightest stir of air, were still.
>
> The motor of the refrigerator began to run. The ice trays were empty and rattled. Wilma, the cleaning woman, had defrosted the machine and forgotten to refill them. He looked for a bottle of beer he had noticed yesterday; it was gone. There was nothing inside except a few lemons and some milk. He drank a glass of milk and it refreshed him. He had already taken off his shirt and was sitting on the bed unlacing his shoes when there was a short ring of the bell. Eagerly he pulled open the door and shouted, "Who is it?" The flat was unbearably empty. He hoped someone had remembered that Mary was away and had come to keep him company. There was no response below. He called out again, impatiently. It was very probable that someone had pushed the wrong button, but he heard no other doors opening. Could it be a prank? This was not the season for it. Nothing moved in the stairwell, and it only added to his depression to discover how he longed for a visitor. He stretched out on the bed, pulling a pillow from beneath the spread and doubling it up. He thought he would doze off. But a little later he found himself standing at the window, holding the curtains with both hands. He was under the impression that he had slept. It was only

eight-thirty by the whirring electric clock on the night table, however. Only five minutes had passed.

Questions: How old, approximately, is Leventhal? Of what social or economic class is he? Who is Mary? What do you know of her relationship to Leventhal? What is the weather like? What is Leventhal's mood? How did you know all these things?

6. In one or two paragraphs, describe a person by showing him or her performing some action that takes less than five minutes. From the description we should be able to infer some of the following: the time of day; the weather; and the person's height, weight, age, sex, occupation, economic or educational background, and mood.

7. Describe and analyze an advertisement from a magazine or newspaper, in about 500 words. To do this, you will need a thesis, such as "This advertisement appeals to male chauvinism," or "This advertisement plays on our fear that we may lack sex appeal." Include a copy of the advertisement with your essay.

8. Choose a recent political cartoon to describe and analyze. In your first paragraph identify the cartoon (cartoonist's name, place and date of publication) and describe the drawing (including any words in it) thoroughly enough so that someone who has not seen it can visualize or even draw it fairly accurately. In a second paragraph explain the political message. Don't inject your own opinion; present the cartoonist's point objectively. Submit a copy of the cartoon with your essay. Be sure to choose a cartoon of sufficient complexity to make the analysis worthwhile.

DESCRIPTION AT WORK

Gina Men

Observing Mrs. Taylor

Gina Men wrote the following essay when she was a first-year student.

Every morning, she floats into the classroom with her red-striped bookbag cradled in her arms. Swiftly, she arranges her tools, with the textbook in the upper left corner of her table, the notebook in the center, and a mechanical pencil beside it. Explaining some problems from the previous day's assignment, she knows that no matter how hard she tries, her voice is never quite loud enough. And so she articulates each word by shaping her mouth to make sure that we at least *see* what she is trying to say. Occasionally, she even uses her arms, legs, and torso to construct a graph. For instance, she will uplift her arms to form a parabola (a graph which is symmetrical with respect to the y-axis) with her body acting as the y-axis. Using her stomach as the origin (the center of the graph), she will turn toward us sideways, with one arm uplifted to the left and one leg uplifted to the right in order to represent a tangent graph. (I remember, too, how she demonstrated that the quadratic equation fits perfectly into the melody of "Pop Goes the Weasel.") Although a difficult question from one of us sometimes causes a frown on her face, she always jots the question down immediately and promises to think it over in the evening. Finally, almost buried in the rustle of paper and book-packing, her meek voice rises: *"Girls, you ought to learn this lesson in your heart of hearts."* And she is out the door.

Topics for Discussion and Writing

1. How does Men establish her physical position and point of view? What is the effect of her use of the present tense? How does she organize the description?

2. The description depends largely on visual images. What other sense impressions are evoked?

3. What is Mrs. Taylor's subject? How does Men persuade you that she was an effective teacher?

4. Search your memory for the image of a teacher, religious leader, or coach with a distinctive physical style. Then, in a paragraph, describe your subject at work.

Dolores Hayden

Advertisements, Pornography, and Public Space

Dolores Hayden was born in New York City in 1945. She did her undergraduate work at Mount Holyoke, and she earned a master's degree in architecture at Harvard. Hayden has taught architecture at the University of California (Berkeley) and at Massachusetts Institute of Technology. She is especially concerned with the political and social implications of public spaces.

1   Americans need to look more consciously at the ways in which the public domain is misused for spatial displays of gender stereotypes: These appear in outdoor advertising, and to a lesser extent in commercial displays, architectural decoration, and public sculpture. While the commercial tone and violence of the American city is often criticized, there is little analysis of the routine way that crude stereotypes appear in public, urban spaces as the staple themes of commercial art. Most Americans are accustomed to seeing giant females in various states of undress smiling and carressing products such as whiskey, food, and records. Male models also sell goods, but they are usually active and clothed—recent ad campaigns aimed at gay men seem to be the first major exception. Several geographers have established that men are most often shown doing active things, posed in the great outdoors; women are shown in reflective postures responding to male demands in interior spaces. As the nineteenth-century sexual double standard is preserved by the urban advertising, many twentieth-century urban men behave as if good women are at home while bad ones adorn the billboards and travel on their own in urban space; at the same time, many urban women are encouraged to think of emotionlessness, war-mongering, and sexual inexhaustibility as natural to the Marlboro cowboy, war heroes' statues, and every other male adult.

2   This double standard is the result of advertising practices, graphic design, and urban design. Sanctioned by the zoning laws, billboards are approved by the same urban planning boards who will not permit child care centers or mother-in-law apartments in many residential districts. But the problem with billboards is not only aesthetic degradation. By presenting gender stereotypes in the form of nonverbal body language, fifty feet long and thirty feet high, billboards turn the public space of the city into a stage set for a drama starring enticing women and stern men.

3   Let us observe outdoor advertising and other urban design phenomena with similar effects, as they are experienced by two women on an urban commuting trip along the Sunset Strip in Los Angeles in June 1981. Standing on a street corner, the two women are waiting for a bus to go to work. The bus

arrives, bearing a placard on the side advertising a local night club. It shows strippers doing their act, their headless bodies naked from neck to crotch except for a few blue sequins. The two women get on the bus and find seats for the ride along Sunset Boulevard. They look out the windows. As the bus pulls away, their heads appear incongruously above the voluptuous cardboard female bodies displayed on the side. They ride through a district of record company headquarters and film offices, one of the most prosperous in L.A.

4   Their first views reveal rows of billboards. Silent Marlboro man rides the range; husky, khaki-clad Camel man stares at green hills; gigantic, uniformed professional athletes catch passes and hit home runs on behalf of booze. These are the male images. Then, on a billboard for whiskey, a horizontal blonde in a backless black velvet dress, slit to the thigh, invites men to "Try on a little Black Velvet." Next, a billboard shows a well-known actress, reclining with legs spread, who notes that avocadoes are only sixteen calories a slice. "Would this body lie to you?" she asks coyly, emphasizing that the body language which communicates blatant sexual availability is only meant to bring attention to her thin figure. Bo Derek offers a pastoral contrast garbed in nothing but a few bits of fur and leather, as she swings on a vine of green leaves, promoting *Tarzan, the Ape Man.*

5   Next the bus riders pass a club called the Body Shop that advertises "live, nude girls." Two reclining, realistic nudes, one in blue tones in front of a moonlight cityscape, one in orange sunshine tones, stretch their thirty-foot bodies along the sidewalk. This is the same neighborhood where a billboard advertising a Rolling Stones' record album called "Black and Blue" made news ten years ago. A manacled, spread-legged woman with torn clothes proclaimed "I'm Black and Blue from the Rolling Stones—and I love it!" Members of a group called Women Against Violence Against Women (WAVAW) arrived with cans of spray paint and climbed the scaffolding to make small, uneven letters of protest: "This is a crime against women." Demonstrations and boycotts eventually succeeded in achieving the removal of that image, but not in eliminating the graphic design problem. "Black and Blue" has been replaced by James Bond in a tuxedo, pistol in hand, viewed through the spread legs and buttocks of a giant woman in a bathing suit and improbably high heels, captioned "For Your Eyes Only."

6   When the two women get off the bus in Hollywood, they experience more gender stereotypes as pedestrians. First, they walk past a department store. In the windows mannequins suggest the prevailing ideals of sartorial elegance. The male torsos lean forward, as if they are about to clinch a deal. The female torsos, pin-headed, tip backward and sideways, at odd angles, as if they are about to be pushed over onto a bed. The themes of gender advertisements are trumpeted here in the mannequins' body language as well as on billboards. Next, the women pass an apartment building. Two neoclassical caryatids support the entablature over the front door. Their breasts are bared, their heads

carry the load. They recall the architecture of the Erechtheum on the Acropolis in Athens, dating from the 5th century B.C., where the sculptured stone forms of female slaves were used as support for a porch in place of traditional columns and capitals. This is an ancient image of servitude.

7   After the neo-classical apartment house, the commuters approach a construction site. Here they are subject to an activity traditionally called "running the gauntlet," but referred to as "girl watching" by urban sociologist William H. Whyte. Twelve workers stop whatever they are doing, whistle, and yell: "Hey, baby!" The women put their heads down, and walk faster, tense with anger. The construction workers take delight in causing exactly this response: "You're cute when you're mad!" Whyte regards this type of behavior as charming, pedestrian fun in "Street Life," where he even takes pleasure in tracing its historic antecedents, but he has never been whistled at, hooted at, and had the dimensions of his body parts analyzed out loud on a public street.[1]

8   Finally, these women get to the office building where they work. It has two statues out front of women. Their bronze breasts culminate in erect nipples. After they pass this last erotic public display of women's flesh, sanctioned as fine art, they walk in the door to begin the day's work. Their journey has taken them through an urban landscape filled with images of men as sexual aggressors and women as submissive sexual objects.

9   The transient quality of male and female interaction in public streets makes the behavior provoked by billboards and their public design images particularly difficult to attack. Psychologist Erving Goffman has analyzed both print ads and billboards as *Gender Advertisements* because art directors use exaggerated body language to suggest that consumers buy not products but images of masculinity or femininity.[2] If passers-by are driving at fifty miles per hour, these gender cues cannot be subtle. In *Ways of Seeing,* art historian John Berger describes the cumulative problem that gender stereotypes in advertising create for woman as "split consciousness."[3] While many women guard themselves, some men assume that ogling is part of normal public life. Women are always wary, watching men watch them, and wondering if and when something is going to happen to them.

10   Urban residents also encounter even more explicit sexual images in urban space. Tawdry strip clubs, X-rated films, "adult" bookstores and sex shops are

[1]William H. Whyte, "Street Life," *Urban Open Spaces* (Summer 1980), 2. For a more detailed critique of hassling: Lindsy Van Gelder, "The International Language of Street Hassling," *Ms.* 9 (May 1981), 15–20, and letters about this article, *Ms.* (Sept. 1981); and Cheryl Benard and Edith Schlaffer, "The Man in the Street: Why He Harasses," *Ms.* 9 (May 1981), 18–19.

[2]Erving Goffman, *Gender Advertisements* (New York: Harper Colphon, 1976), 24–27; Nancy Henley, *Body Politics: Power, Sex, and Nonverbal Communication* (Englewood Cliffs, N.J.: Prentice-Hall, 1977), 30, Marianne Wex, *Let's Take Back Our Space* (Berlin: Movimento Druck, 1979).

[3]John Berger, et al., *Ways of Seeing* (Harmondsworth, England: BBC and Penguin, 1972), 45–64.

not uncommon sights. Pornographic video arcades are the next wave to come. Pornography is a bigger, more profitable industry in the United States than all legitimate film and record business combined.[1] It spills over into soft-porn, quasi-porn, and tasteless public imagery everywhere. In the midst of this sex-exploitation, if one sees a real prostitute, there is mild surprise. Yet soliciting is still a crime. Of course, the male customer of an adult prostitute is almost never arrested, but the graphic designer, the urban designer, and the urban planner never come under suspicion for their contributions to a commercial public landscape that preserves the sexual double standard in a brutal and vulgar way.

11   Feminist Laura Shapiro calls our society a "rape culture."[2] Adrienne Rich has written of "a world masculinity made unfit for women or men"[3] But surely most Americans do not consciously, deliberately accept public space given over to commercial exploitation, violence and harassment of women. Indeed, the success of the "Moral Majority" displays how a few activists were able to tap public concern effectively about commercialized sexuality, albeit in a narrow, antihumanist way. In contrast, the example of the Women's Christian Temperance Union under Frances Willard's leadership, and the parks movement under Olmsted's,[4] show religious idealism, love of nature, and concern for female safety can be activated into dynamic urban reform movements that enlarge domestic values into urban values, instead of diminishing them into domestic pieties.

Topics for Discussion and Writing

1. How does Hayden organize her material? Note, in particular, the narrative of two women traveling to work. What does this device add to the essay?

2. How does Hayden suggest that displays of gender stereotypes contribute to violence against women? What evidence supports this assumption?

3. In a paragraph or two, describe and analyze a magazine advertisement that promotes gender stereotypes or one that is aimed at gay men. (See Hayden's first paragraph.)

4. If you are familiar with a sculpture of a female figure in a public space in your neighborhood (perhaps in a plaza or in a public building), in a paragraph set forth what the image "says." Or, compare two sculptures, one of a female and one of a male, and explain what each says.

---

[1]Tom Hayden, *The American Future: New Visions Beyond Old Frontiers* (Boston: South End Press, 1980), 15.
[2]Laura Shapiro, "Violence: The Most Obscene Fantasy," in Freeman, ed., *Women: a Feminist Perspective*, 469–73.
[3]*Ibid.*, 469.
[4]Frederick Law Olmsted (1822–1903) was an American landscape architect. Among his noble works are Central Park in Manhattan and Prospect Park in Brooklyn.

5. In an essay of two or three pages, describe and analyze two billboards, one featuring a man and one featuring a woman. How do they present the "gender stereotypes" that Hayden talks about? Your essay should respond to this question with a clearly formulated thesis sentence (see pages 18-19).

Joan Didion

Los Angeles Notebook

Joan Didion was born in California in 1934 and educated at the University of California, Berkeley. While she was still a senior she wrote a prize-winning essay for a contest sponsored by Vogue, *and soon she became an associate feature editor for* Vogue. *She has written novels, essays, and screenplays.*

1   There is something uneasy in the Los Angeles air this afternoon, some unnatural stillness, some tension. What it means is that tonight a Santa Ana will begin to blow, a hot wind from the northeast whining down through the Cajon and San Gorgonio Passes, blowing up sandstorms out along Route 66, drying the hills and the nerves to the flash point. For a few days now we will see smoke back in the canyons, and hear sirens in the night. I have neither heard nor read that a Santa Ana is due, but I know it, and almost everyone I have seen today knows it too. We know it because we feel it. The baby frets. The maid sulks. I rekindle a waning argument with the telephone company, then cut my losses and lie down, given over to whatever it is in the air. To live with the Santa Ana is to accept, consciously or unconsciously, a deeply mechanistic view of human behavior.

2   I recall being told, when I first moved to Los Angeles and was living on an isolated beach, that the Indians would throw themselves into the sea when the bad wind blew. I could see why. The Pacific turned ominously glossy during a Santa Ana period, and one woke in the night troubled not by the peacocks screaming in the olive trees but by the eerie absence of surf. The heat was surreal. The sky had a yellow cast, the kind of light sometimes called "earthquake weather." My only neighbor would not come out of her house for days, and there were no lights at night, and her husband roamed the place with a machete. One day he would tell me that he had heard a trespasser, the next a rattlesnake.

3   "On nights like that," Raymond Chandler once wrote about the Santa Ana, "every booze party ends in a fight. Meek little wives feel the edge of the carving knife and study their husbands' necks. Anything can happen." That was the kind of wind it was. I did not know then that there was any basis for the effect it had on all of us, but it turns out to be another of these cases in which science bears

out folk wisdom. The Santa Ana, which is named for one of the canyons it rushes through, is a *foehn* wind, like the *foehn* of Austria and Switzerland and the *hamsin* of Israel. There are a number of persistent malevolent winds, perhaps the best known of which are the mistral of France and the Mediterranean sirocco, but a *foehn* wind has distinct characteristics: it occurs on the leeward slope of a mountain range and, although the air begins as a cold mass, it is warmed as it comes down the mountain and appears finally as a hot dry wind. Whenever and wherever a *foehn* blows, doctors hear about headaches and nausea and allergies, about "nervousness," about "depression." In Los Angeles some teachers do not attempt to conduct formal classes during a Santa Ana, because the children become unmanageable. In Switzerland the suicide rate goes up during the *foehn,* and in the courts of some Swiss cantons the wind is considered a mitigating circumstance for crime. Surgeons are said to watch the wind, because blood does not clot normally during a *foehn.* A few years ago an Israeli physicist discovered that not only during such winds, but for the ten or twelve hours which precede them, the air carries an unusually high ratio of positive to negative ions. No one seems to know exactly why that should be; some talk about friction and others suggest solar disturbances. In any case the positive ions are there, and what an excess of positive ions does, in the simplest terms, is make people unhappy. One cannot get much more mechanistic than that.

4   Easterners commonly complain that there is no "weather" at all in Southern California, that the days and the seasons slip by relentlessly, numbingly bland. That is quite misleading. In fact the climate is characterized by infrequent but violent extremes: two periods of torrential subtropical rains which continue for weeks and wash out the hills and send subdivisions sliding toward the sea; about twenty scattered days a year of the Santa Ana, which, with its incendiary dryness, invariably means fire. At the first prediction of a Santa Ana, the Forest Service flies men and equipment from northern California into the southern forests, and the Los Angeles Fire Department cancels its ordinary non-firefighting routines. The Santa Ana caused Malibu to burn the way it did in 1956, and Bel Air in 1961, and Santa Barbara in 1964. In the winter of 1966–67 eleven men were killed fighting a Santa Ana fire that spread through the San Gabriel Mountains.

5   Just to watch the front-page news out of Los Angeles during a Santa Ana is to get very close to what it is about the place. The longest single Santa Ana period in recent years was in 1957, and it lasted not the usual three or four days but fourteen days, from November 21 until December 4. On the first day 25,000 acres of the San Gabriel Mountains were burning, with gusts reaching 100 miles an hour. In town, the wind reached Force 12, or hurricane force, on the Beaufort Scale; oil derricks were toppled and people ordered off the downtown streets to avoid injury from flying objects. On November 22 the fire in the San Gabriels was out of control. On November 24 six people were killed in automobile

accidents, and by the end of the week the Los Angeles *Times* was keeping a box score of traffic deaths. On November 26 a prominent Pasadena attorney, depressed about money, shot and killed his wife, their two sons, and himself. On November 27 a South Gate divorcée, twenty-two, was murdered and thrown from a moving car. On November 30 the San Gabriel fire was still out of control, and the wind in town was blowing eighty miles an hour. On the first day of December four people died violently, and on the third the wind began to break.

6   It is hard for people who have not lived in Los Angeles to realize how radically the Santa Ana figures in the local imagination. The city burning is Los Angeles's deepest image of itself: Nathanael West perceived that, in *The Day of the Locust;* and at the time of the 1965 Watts riots what struck the imagination most indelibly were the fires. For days one could drive the Harbor Freeway and see the city on fire, just as we had always known it would be in the end. Los Angeles weather is the weather of catastrophe, of apocalypse, and, just as the reliably long and bitter winters of New England determine the way life is lived there, so the violence and the unpredictability of the Santa Ana affect the entire quality of life in Los Angeles, accentuate its impermanence, its unreliability. The wind shows us how close to the edge we are.

Topics for Discussion and Writing

1. Paraphrase or explain the last sentence of the first paragraph. What passages in the essay offer the most persuasive evidence supporting the point?
2. Beginning with the third paragraph, Didion defines the Santa Ana. Would the essay have been clearer or more effective if the definition had introduced the essay? Explain.
3. Explain the last sentence, and evaluate it as a conclusion.

E. B. White

Education

E[lwyn] B[rooks] White (1899–1985) wrote poetry and fiction, but he is most widely known as an essayist and as the coauthor (with William Strunk, Jr.) of The Elements of Style. *After a long career at* The New Yorker, *he retired to Maine, but he continued to write until the year before his death at the age of 86.*

1   I have an increasing admiration for the teacher in the country school where we have a third-grade scholar in attendance. She not only undertakes to instruct her charges in all the subjects of the first three grades, but she manages to

function quietly and effectively as a guardian of their health, their clothes, their habits, their mothers, and their snowball engagements. She has been doing this sort of Augean task for twenty years, and is both kind and wise. She cooks for the children on the stove that heats the room, and she can cool their passions or warm their soup with equal competence. She conceives their costumes, cleans up their messes, and shares their confidences. My boy already regards his teacher as his great friend, and I think tells her a great deal more than he tells us.

2   The shift from city school to country school was something we worried about quietly all last summer. I have always rather favored public school over private school, if only because in public school you meet a greater variety of children. This bias of mine, I suspect, is partly an attempt to justify my own past (I never knew anything but public schools) and partly an involuntary defense against getting kicked in the shins by a young ceramist on his way to the kiln. My wife was unacquainted with public schools, never having been exposed (in her early life) to anything more public than the washroom of Miss Winsor's. Regardless of our backgrounds, we both knew that the change in schools was something that concerned not us but the scholar himself. We hoped it would work out all right. In New York our son went to a medium-priced private institution with semi-progressive ideas of education, and modern plumbing. He learned fast, kept well, and we were satisfied. It was an electric, colorful, regimented existence with moments of pleasurable pause and giddy incident. The day the Christmas angel fainted and had to be carried out by one of the Wise Men was educational in the highest sense of the term. Our scholar gave imitations of it around the house for weeks afterward, and I doubt if it ever goes completely out of his mind.

3   His days were rich in formal experience. Wearing overalls and an old sweater (the accepted uniform of the private seminary), he sallied forth at morn accompanied by a nurse or a parent and walked (or was pulled) two blocks to a corner where the school bus made a flag stop. This flashy vehicle was as punctual as death: seeing us waiting at the cold curb, it would sweep to a halt, open its mouth, suck the boy in, and spring away with an angry growl. It was a good deal like a train picking up a bag of mail. At school the scholar was worked on for six or seven hours by half a dozen teachers and a nurse, and was revived on orange juice in mid-morning. In a cinder court he played games supervised by an athletic instructor, and in a cafeteria he ate lunch worked out by a dietitian. He soon learned to read with gratifying facility and discernment and to make Indian weapons of a semi-deadly nature. Whenever one of his classmates fell low of a fever the news was put on the wires and there were breathless phone calls to physicians, discussing periods of incubation and allied magic.

4   In the country all one can say is that the situation is different, and somehow more casual. Dressed in corduroys, sweatshirt, and short rubber boots, and carrying a tin dinner-pail pail, our scholar departs at the crack of dawn for the village school, two and a half miles down the road, next to the cemetery. When

the road is open and the car will start, he makes the journey by motor, courtesy of his old man. When the snow is deep or the motor is dead or both, he makes it on the hoof. In the afternoons he walks or hitches all or part of the way home in fair weather, gets transported in foul. The schoolhouse is a two-room frame building, bungalow type, shingles stained a burnt brown with weather-resistant stain. It has a chemical toilet in the basement and two teachers above the stairs. One takes the first three grades, the other the fourth, fifth, and sixth. They have little or no time for individual instruction, and no time at all for the esoteric. They teach what they know themselves, just as fast and as hard as they can manage. The pupils sit still at their desks in class, and do their milling around outdoors during recess.

5   There is no supervised play. They play cops and robbers (only they call it "Jail") and throw things at one another—snowballs in winter, rose hips in fall. It seems to satisfy them. They also construct darts, pinwheels, and "pick-up sticks" (jackstraws), and the school itself does a brisk trade in penny candy, which is for sale right in the classroom and which contains "surprises." The most highly prized surprise is a fake cigarette, made of cardboard, fiendishly lifelike.

6   The memory of how apprehensive we were at the beginning is still strong. The boy was nervous about the change too. The tension, on that first fair morning in September when we drove him to school, almost blew the windows out of the sedan. And when later we picked him up on the road, wandering along with his little blue lunch-pail, and got his laconic report "All right" in answer to our inquiry about how the day had gone, our relief was vast. Now, after almost a year of it, the only difference we can discover in the two school experiences is that in the country he sleeps better at night—and *that* probably is more the air than the education. When grilled on the subject of school-in-country vs. school-in-city, he replied that the chief difference is that the day seems to go so much quicker in the country. "Just like lightning," he reported.

Topics for Discussion and Writing

1. Which school, public or private, does White prefer? Since White doesn't state his preference outright, from what evidence were you able to infer it?

2. In the first half of paragraph 2 White admits to a bias in favor of public schools, and he speculates, half-seriously, about the origins of his bias. If his intention here is not simply to amuse us, what is it?

3. What is White's strongest argument in favor of the school he prefers? Where in the essay do you find it?

Chapter 12

Defining

The Need for Definition

To explain an idea or to argue a point, writers frequently need to define words. The words may be *specialized* or unfamiliar to the writer's intended audience—for example, the words "venture capitalism" or "enterprise zones." Or, we might define a word that the audience may think it knows but that (in the writer's opinion) the audience may misunderstand. For instance, a writer might argue that the words "guerilla" and "terrorist" are not synonyms, and then go on to define each word, showing the differences between them.

Often, however, providing a *synonym* is a reasonable strategy. Talking about the word "civilizing" in Roth's argument against closing the Newark Public Library (page 10), a student briefly explained a point by saying, "By 'civilizing,' Roth meant 'socializing.'"

In addition to defining a word because it is specialized ("venture capitalism."), or because we want to distinguish it from another word ("guerilla" and "terrorist"), or because we may think that a synonym will clarify it ("civilizing" and "socializing"), we may define a word because the word has many meanings, and we want to make sure that readers take the word in a particular way. A work like "ability," for example, may require defining in a discussion of the Scholastic Aptitude Test. To argue that the SAT does or does not measure "academic ability," the writer and reader need, in a sense, to agree on a specific meaning for "ability." This kind of definition, where the writer specifies or stipulates a meaning, is called a *stipulative definition*.

The word "stipulate," by the way, comes from a Latin word meaning "to bargain." Explaining a word's *etymology*, its *history* or its *origin*, as we have just done, is often an aid in definition.

In short, in defining a word or term, writers have many options and they need to take into account both their own purpose in writing and their reader' needs. Let's look at some examples.

Kinds of Definitions

Inclusive/Exclusive Definitions

Here is a writer defining a *specialized* term for readers of a Central Florida newspaper:

> Enterprise zones are government-designated areas of severe poverty and high unemployment to which businesses are encouraged to relocate through tax breaks and other incentives. Where once there were vacant lots and boarded-up buildings, the theory goes, new companies attracted by the tax breaks would provide badly needed jobs, and the newly employed residents would spend their earnings on other local businesses, creating a ripple effect that revitalizes an entire community.
>
> —MAX FRIEDMAN

Notice how Friedman defines "enterprise zones." In the first sentence, he places "enterprise zones" in a category or class, "government-designated areas." He next shows how they differ from other members of the class: they are areas "of severe poverty and high unemployment to which businesses are encouraged to relocate through tax breaks and other incentives." Such a definition is sometimes called *inclusive/exclusive* because it *includes* the word in a relevant category (government-designated areas) and then *excludes* other members of that category (for example, "disaster zones" or "postal zones" or "war zones"). Notice too that Friedman's definition uses a parallel form, a noun for a noun: "zones" are "areas." (Avoid saying "enterprise zones are when the government designates.")

Notice, also, that Friedman briefly describes "enterprise zones": they contain "vacant lots and boarded-up buildings." In the rest of the sentence he also describes, with a few details, the presumed effects of enterprise zones. (In the words, "the theory goes," what does he imply about the actual effect of these zones?)

A definition of a specialized term can be very brief, for example: "Venture capitalists, *the specialized firms that raise money for new technological inventions. . . .*" Here the definition is accomplished in a phrase (which we have italicized). A term can be defined in a paragraph, as Friedman does above. But a writer might need the space of an essay to define a word. Notice how, in the following short essay—a book review—the writer begins with a whimsical definition of *caricature* as "a portrait with an attitude," but throughout the essay she further defines caricature as "an acerbic and accessible form of social and political criticism" and "a savage mirror that confronts society."

> A caricature is a portrait with an attitude, a likeness meant to provoke recognition by its distortions. Although its purpose is often nothing more than to be a visual prank, caricature at its best has often been an acerbic and accessible form of social and political criticism. In *The Savage Mirror: The art of Contemporary Caricature* (Watson-Guptil, paper, $29.95), Steven Heller, the art director of *The New York Times Book Review,* and Gail Anderson, the deputy art director of *Rolling Stone,* present an overview of contemporary caricature, tracing its evolution from 19th-century France through its powerful resurgence in the United States from the mid-1950's to the mid-1970's. The authors explain the roles that editorial preferences, design fads and technology have played in creating the current scene, which they seem, almost in spite of themselves, to find disappointing. For Ms. Anderson and Mr. Heller, caricaturists have great power—and perhaps even a duty—to address the issues of the day, to use their skills to rouse the public.

Today the subjects of caricature are less likely to be political figures than celebrities, who menace our sensibilities more than our freedom. As the book amply illustrates, in changing from pen to airbrush, caricature has gone from inspired anger to dextrous hipness. Ms. Anderson and Mr. Heller clearly believe that a caricature should communicate an idea; as they survey contemporary caricature, they see "little gems of mild distortion" rather than a savage mirror that confronts society with its sorry reflection. This profusely illustrated book provides an excellent introduction to its subject, and the authors are persuasive in their arguments for the importance of caricature.

—ROSEMARY RANCK

Stipulative Definitions

Now let's look at an example of a *stipulative definition*. In "The Morality and Rationality of Suicide," Richard B. Brandt asks his readers to agree on a *neutral* definition of suicide.

"Suicide" is conveniently defined, for our purposes, as doing something which results in one's death, either from the intention of ending one's life or the intention to bring about some other state of affairs (such as relief from pain) which one thinks it certain or highly probable can be achieved only by means of death or will produce death. It may seem odd to classify an act of heroic self-sacrifice on the part of a soldier as suicide. It is simpler, however, not to try to define "suicide" so that an act of suicide is always irrational or immoral in some way; if we adopt a neutral definition like the above we can still proceed to ask when an act of suicide in that sense is rational, morally justifiable, and so on, so that all evaluations anyone might wish to make can still be made.

Notice that Brandt concedes that there are apparent problems with this definition. It would, for example, include a soldier's self-sacrifice. But, he argues, if we adopt the definition he proposes, we can still evaluate a particular act as "rational, morally justifiable, and so on." In *stipulating* this definition of suicide we can see Brandt striking a bargain with his readers.

Stipulative definitions are often necessary. Although technical words have relatively stable meanings, many of the words that you will be defining—words such as *democracy, identity, family, society*—have so many meanings that your reader won't know what you mean until you explain which definition you are using.

Definition by Origin or History

The passage that follows, from a column called "The Word Watchers," is a *definition by origin and history* of the word "stonewall" used as a verb.

"Stonewall" as a verb originated in the game of cricket, as a term for playing solely on the defensive. Australian political slang picked it up in the late nineteenth-century, and it was adopted quickly by British politicians.

In America, stonewalling was rarely used: the citation in *Webster's New International Unabridged Dictionary* is a James Reston column of the late fifties, "stonewalling for time in order to close the missile gap." But then Henry Kissinger picked up the term: I first heard him use it in late 1969 as, "the North Vietnamese are stonewalling us."

As a needed figure of speech, the word's usage increased; more stones were added as a strategy of silence was adopted by the Watergaters, and when the President's tapes revealed him to have said "I want you to stonewall it," the word was sealed into the language.

Stonewalling has a pejorative connotation today. But long before its scornful use by cricketers, politicians from Down Under and up above, the figure of speech was used in admiration during our Civil War about one of the Confederacy's greatest generals: "There stands Jackson, like a stone wall!"

Might it be possible, someday, for stonewalling to regain an admirable connotation? The word-watchers will be watching.

—WILLIAM SAFIRE

Safire's engaging discussion comes not only from his zeal for "word-watching" but also, we imagine, from the legwork of a staff of researchers, and an office wall of dictionaries and other reference books. But all writers must become word-watchers, to some degree, and it is fascinating as well as useful to learn word origins and histories. With nothing more than a good desk dictionary, we can learn that "yoga" derives from a Sanskrit word for union, or joining or yoking ("join" and yoke" both come from this same root: yoga seeks to join or yoke the individual's consciousness to its spiritual source); that "Islam" is Arabic for "submission to God," and comes ultimately from an Arabic word for safety; that "science" comes from a Latin verb meaning "to know"; and that "holocaust" comes from a Greek word meaning "completely burnt." Here is the word history that accompanies the definition of "holocaust" in the third edition of *The American Heritage Dictionary of the English Language*.

Totality of destruction has been central to the meaning of *holocaust* since it first appeared in Middle English in the 14th century and referred to the biblical sacrifice in which a male animal was wholly burnt on the altar in worship of God. *Holocaust* comes from Greek *holokauston* ("that which is completely burnt"), which was a translation of Hebrew *old* (literally "that which goes up," that is, in smoke). In this sense of "burnt sacrifice," *holocaust* is still used in some versions of the Bible. In the 17th century the meaning of *holocaust* broadened to "something totally consumed by fire," and the word eventually was applied to fires of extreme destructiveness. In the 20th century *holocaust* has taken on a variety of figurative meanings, summarizing the effects of war, rioting, storms, epidemic diseases, and even economic failures. Most of these usages arose after World War II, but it is unclear whether they permitted or resulted from the use of *holocaust* in reference to the mass murder of European Jews and others by the Nazis. This application of the word occurred as early as 1942, but the phrase *the Holocaust* did not become established until the late 1950's. Here it parallels and may have been influenced by another Hebrew word, *sho'ah* ("catastrophe"). In the Bible *sho'ah* has a range of meanings including "personal ruin or devastation" and "a wasteland or desert." *Sho'ah* was first used to refer to the Nazi slaughter of Jews in 1939, but its phrase *hasho'ah* ("the catastrophe") only became established after World War II. *Holocaust* has also been used to translate *hurban* ("destruction"), another Hebrew word used to summarize the genocide of Jews by the Nazis. This sense of *holocaust* has since broadened to include the mass slaughter of other peoples, but when capitalized it refers specifically to the destruction of Jews and other Europeans by the Nazis and may also encompass the Nazi persecution of Jews that preceded the outbreak of the war.

The Limits of Definition by Synonym

A Last Example.

Paralyzed by illness, a professor of anthropology reflects on the meaning of the word "disabled." The passage is from his book, *The Body Silent:*

> I was badly damaged, yet just as alive as ever, and I had to make the best of it with my remaining capabilities. It then occurred to me that this is the universal human condition. We all have to muddle through life within our limitations, and while I had certain physical handicaps, I retained many strengths. My brain was the only part of the central cortex that still worked well, but that also is where I made my living. *Disability* is an amorphous and relativistic term. Some people are unable to do what I do because they lack the mental equipment, and in this sense, they are disabled and I am not. Everybody is disabled in one way or another. And even though my growing paralysis would one day end my active participation in the affairs of the world, I could still sit back and watch them unfold.
>
> —ROBERT F. MURPHY

Without calling attention to it, Murphy takes into account the *origin* of the word disability. "Dis" as a prefix (from Latin) means "not" or "deprived of." What does it mean, he seems to ask, to be deprived of or to not have ability? His discussion acknowledges that "damaged" and "handicapped" are *synonyms* for disabled. But, he argues, "*Disability* is an amorphous and relativistic term." Its meaning, he implies, needs to be *stipulated.* Above all, what his discussion makes clear is that he has a compelling reason to reexamine and explain how he defines the word "disability" and how we all should define it.

A Note on Using a Dictionary

A dictionary is for a writer an invaluable resource. If you do not own a recent hardback college dictionary, we advise you to buy one and to keep it handy as you read and write. You will use it to look up the meaning or several meanings of a word you're not sure of, to check its spelling or pronunciation, to see how its form changes in its various functions, to discover its origin. In some dictionaries, you will find usage notes that will tell you, for example, whether a word is considered slang, or obscene, or whether a usage is now generally accepted. We particularly recommend *The American Heritage Dictionary,* Third Edition, for its extensive list of words and its superb notes on word histories and word usage. Any good bookstore will have several other excellent dictionaries, among them, *Webster's New World Dictionary* (3rd edition*), Merriam-Webster's Collegiate Dictionary* (tenth edition), or *The Random House Dictionary of the English Language: College Edition.* But if you are shopping for a dictionary, be sure to check out the third edition of *The American Heritage Dictionary.*

You should also become acquainted, in the library, with the great multi-volume *Oxford English Dictionary (OED).* In it you will find quotations illustrating the meanings of words over the centuries. It is an unparalleled source for shedding light on texts (especially poetry) written before our times.

The one use to which you ought *not* put a dictionary is this: Do not introduce an essay with the words "Webster says . . . " or "According to the dictionary. . . ." Because the name Webster is no longer copyrighted, it appears on all sorts of dictionaries, bad as well as good. Besides, there is no staler opening.

A Checklist for Revising Definitions

1. Do you give brief definitions, where needed—for example, of a specialized or technical term?

2. Do you give sufficient examples to clarify the definition?

3. Do you distinguish the term from a near synonym—for example communism from socialism, revolution from resistance, terrorism from guerrilla warfare? Will a comparison help to define the term?

4. Would it be helpful to mention the etymology or origin of the word?

5. Do you make clear which meaning of a word you are using (stipulating), and why?

6. Is the need for a definition implied or, in a long definition, do you explain the need?

Topics for Discussion and Writing

1. Define, for an audience unfamiliar with the term, *bebop, rap, hiphop,* or *country music,* in 250 to 500 words.

2. Write one paragraph defining one of the following terms: *security blanket, twilight zone, holding pattern, stalking.* Your paragraph should disclose the origin of the term (if you can't find it, make a reasonable guess) and some examples of current use distinct from its original meaning.

3. Write an opening paragraph for an essay in which you stipulate a meaning for *death,* or *vegetarianism,* excluding one or two other meanings. Don't write the essay, just the opening paragraph.

4. In a paragraph explain the difference between "a reason" (for some action) and "an excuse." Provide a specific example, real or invented. Your audience is someone who expects you to offer an excuse.

5. If you are fluent in a language other than English, or in a dialect other than Standard American, write a paragraph defining for native speakers of Standard American a word that stands for some concept. Examples: Spanish *machismo* or *commoción,* Yiddish *haimish* or *chutzpa,* Japanese *shibui,* or African-American English *bad* or *cool.*

6. Write an essay of approximately 500 words on the word *natural* as it is used to advertise products such as cereals, yogurt, cosmetics, and cigarettes. Your essay should stipulate a definition of natural, and should have a thesis. An example of a thesis: "Yogurt may be a wholesome food, but most commercial yogurts are not as 'natural' as we are led to believe."

7. Write an essay defining sexual harassment. Explain the need for definition, what the term includes and excludes, and the relevance of the etymology of *harass.* Use examples of what is and is not sexual harassment to clarify your point.

8. Write an essay (about 500 words) explaining one of the following terms: *horror film, situation comedy, soap opera, junk food, nostalgia, ethnic joke, yuppie.* Your essay will probably include a definition, reference to several examples, and perhaps an extended discussion of one example, explaining the reasons for its popularity, or arguing its merits or lack of merits.

Definition at Work

Billy Altman

Country Just Ain't What It Used to Be

Billy Altman writes about pop music for Entertainment Weekly. *This essay, however, appeared in* The New York Times, *in 1993.*

1   Time was when listeners tuning into a country radio station had a pretty good idea what kind of music they were likely to find. For decades, country songs meant stories of rabble-rousing, working-class everymen loving, cheating on and/or crawling back to strong, understanding girlfriends, wives or mistresses. Throw in an undercurrent of alcohol-soaked, moralistic ruminations about a fixed set of mandatory topics (prison, religion, mom) and certain basic

sociopolitical tenets (when in doubt, wave the flag), and there, with few exceptions, was the genre in a shot glass.

2   Lately, however, country has been redefining itself, particularly when it comes to the relationship between the sexes, and even its supposedly firmest clichés have been dropping off lyric sheets faster than an unsecured payload falling off the back end of an 18-wheeler on the interstate. Garth Brooks's recent album, *The Chase,* for example, found the singer-songwriter using his megastar pulpit to attack some of country's longest-standing attitudes with the anthemic eye-opener "We Shall Be Free." "When we're free to love anyone we choose," he sings, "When this world's big enough for all different views / When we can all worship from our own kind of pew / Then we shall be free." In so doing, he poses a direct challenge to country's traditionally conservative positions on sexual preference, political affiliation and religious persuasion.

3   "We Shall Be Free" is no isolated statement, either—a fact underscored by other tracks on the album, most notably, "Face to Face," in which a date-rape victim is both supported and encouraged in a courtroom confrontation with her attacker, and "That Summer," in which a young, virginal field hand learns about sex from a widowed farm woman. Put the messages of these songs together and one begins to understand not only why Mr. Brooks is selling millions of albums to country's predominantly female audience, but also why the music is drawing new followers from outside its customary strongholds.

4   Simply put, the old country song just ain't what it used to be. Yes, there are still hurt-pride hunks like Billy Ray Cyrus pining over their achy-breaky hearts; the homefires-burning housewife that Reba McIntyre sings about will continue to look out the window and wonder "Is There Life Out There?" without ever venturing forth on her own. But at both ends of the gender gap, a growing number of artists are displaying raised consciousnesses about the eternal battle of the sexes and helping to, if not erase, then at least recast many of country's male-female stereotypes into more enlightened models.

5   This updated sensibility is a function of a several factors. For one, country music has been appealing of late to a different breed of fan—adults who grew up on rock and have found in country music the kind of listener-friendly melodies and narrative styles that have been elbowed off the airwaves by youth-oriented grunge, metal and hip-hop. But the standard if-it's-too-loud-you're-too-old argument fails to recognize one crucial point: from its very beginnings, country music has been an adult medium, with an adult tone and addressing adult concerns. Yet nobody saw adults running for country cover during the British Invasion of the 60's or when punk exploded in rock's face in the 70's.

6   The last time country music captured the public's attention to an even remotely comparable degree was in the "Urban Cowboy" days of the early 80's. But in retrospect, that revival seems to have been more a fashion-driven fad than anything else, with denim jeans replacing polyester leisure suits and the mechanical bull replacing the mirrored ball for the post-disco crowd. The music

served merely as a background accessory, created no major stars and carried little import. Not exactly a movement.

7   What's going on now, though, definitely is a movement. And its leaders—Mr. Brooks, Clint Black, Rosanne Cash and Mary-Chapin Carpenter—clearly display a different perspective than those of an earlier era. Country's new songs, like its old songs, still focus on the social currents rumbling through American life—remember, this is a genre that prides itself on being real people's music. But the observations being made, and the conclusions being drawn, about such well-traveled terrain as drinking and carousing, loving and losing and familial responsibilities, reflect the influences of contemporary concerns like feminism, the men's movement, the environment and AIDS.

8   For the men, macho swagger is out and ego-secure emotional maturity is in. Mr. Brooks's "Everytime That It Rains," a ballad about a failed attempt at re-creating a chance sexual encounter, ends in (of all things) friendship, Clint Black's 1989 debut hit, "A Better Man," avoids tears-in-your-beer self-pity in describing the breakup of a long-term relationship ("I'm leaving here a better man / Knowing you this way / Things I couldn't do before now I think I can / And I'm leaving here a better man").

9   Speaking of beer, even erstwile honky-tonkers like Alan Jackson now know when to say when. He raised a few eyebrows in 1991 with "Midnight in Montgomery," which invoked the spirit of the legendary Hank Williams Sr., in a demythologized form—"a drunk man in a cowboy hat." And, just in case anybody missed the message, his latest album includes the all-sobered up with somewhere to go "I Don't Need the Booze (to Get a Buzz On)," which finds the singer "hooked on my baby's love / There ain't nothing in a jug this strong."

10   The idea of unquestioned male dominance in the home is also taking it on the chin in songs like Mr. Brooks's "Thunder Rolls." His depiction of a husband's unwarranted attack on his wife is probably the first song by a male country artist to confront spousal abuse. For a genre that once gave us Fiddlin' John Carson singing "It's a Shame to Whip Your Wife on Sunday" ("When you've got Monday, Tuesday, Wednesday . . . "), the empathy Mr. Brooks exhibits says a lot.

11   Country's women, meanwhile, are asserting themselves as never before. The bend-but-don't-break philosophy of Tammy Wynette's late-60's classic, "Stand By Your Man," is becoming a thing of the past. As Ms. Cash proclaimed on "The Real Me" a few years ago, "A woman's her own mystery / Not a shadow of a man."

12   Similarly, Mary-Chapin Carpenter uses songs on her latest album, *Come On Come On,* to address a range of women's issues, from men's need to express their emotions to women's need to have their own emotional space. The album's pivotal track, "He Thinks He'll Keep Her," describes the plight of a 36-year-old mother of three who has been taken so completely for granted by her

husband that she wakes up one morning, packs his bags and tosses him out, without regard for what the future will bring.

13   Even sexy sirens like Lorrie Morgan are trying to define relationships on their own terms. On one of her singles, "Watch Me," a lover tells her cheating man, "If you think I won't go, just watch me." Ms. Morgan's latest song is about an unescorted woman getting hit on by a stranger at a bar. "I'm not interested in romance, or what you have in mind," she says without a trace of country-belle flirtatiousness in her voice. "What part of no don't you understand?"

14   If country music is a gauge of what Middle America thinks and feels, it's probably safe to say that happy hour will never be the same—and that, in country music at least, the "kinder, gentler" America envisioned by George Bush may finally have manifested itself. Country music, nonsexist and politically progressive? Sounds like a cultural elitist's pipe dream.

Topics for Discussion and Writing

1. What is unusual about Altman's first sentence? How do you explain this element?

2. In his first paragraph Altman in effect defines older country music, although he allows for exceptions. If you are familiar with the material, do you think his definition is adequate, or, on the other hand, are the exceptions so numerous or so important that Altman's definition is misleading?

3. In paragraph 2 Altman argues that "country has been redefining itself." In what way or ways does he claim that it has been changing? How (by what methods) does he establish that it has been redefining itself in these ways?

4. *The American Heritage Dictionary of the English Language,* Third Edition, defines country music thus:

   Popular music based on the folkstyle of the southern rural United States or the music of cowboys in the American West. Also called *country and western.*

   Is this a reasonable definition? Why, do you suppose, Altman doesn't quote it or any other dictionary definition?

5. In paragraph 5 Altman mentions "grunge, metal and hip-hop." Define one of these, in a paragraph.

6. Is k. d. lang a country singer? Explain, in a paragraph.

Marie Winn

Television Addiction

Marie Winn, born in Czechoslovakia in 1936, came to New York when she was a small child. She later graduated from Radcliffe College and then did further academic work at Columbia University. We reprint here an excerpt from her chapter entitled "Television Addiction" in The Plug-in Drug.

1   The word "addiction" is often used loosely and wryly in conversation. People will refer to themselves as "mystery book addicts" or "cookie addicts." E. B. White wrote of his annual surge of interest in gardening: "We are hooked and are making an attempt to kick the habit." Yet nobody really believes that reading mysteries or ordering seeds by catalogue is serious enough to be compared with addictions to heroin or alcohol. The word "addiction" is here used jokingly to denote a tendency to overindulge in some pleasurable activity.

2   People often refer to being "hooked on TV." Does this, too, fall into the lighthearted category of cookie eating and other pleasures that people pursue with unusual intensity, or is there a kind of television viewing that falls into the more serious category of destructive addiction?

3   When we think about addiction to drugs or alcohol we frequently focus on negative aspects, ignoring the pleasures that accompany drinking or drug-taking. And yet the essence of any serious addiction is a pursuit of pleasure, a search for a "high" that normal life does not supply. It is only the inability to function without the addictive substance that is dismaying, the dependence of the organism upon a certain experience and an increasing inability to function normally without it. Thus people will take two or three drinks at the end of the day not merely for the pleasure drinking provides, but also because they "don't feel normal" without them.

4   Real addicts do not merely pursue a pleasurable experience one time in order to function normally. They need to *repeat* it again and again. Something about that particular experience makes life without it less than complete. Other potentially pleasurable experiences are no longer possible, for under the spell of the addictive experience, their lives are peculiarly distorted. The addict craves an experience and yet is never really satisfied. The organism may be temporarily sated, but soon it begins to crave again.

5   Finally, a serious addiction is distinguished from a harmless pursuit of pleasure by its distinctly destructive elements. Heroin addicts, for instance, lead a damaged life: their increasing need for heroin in increasing doses prevents them from working, from maintaining relationships, from developing in human ways. Similarly alcoholics' lives are narrowed and dehumanized by their dependence on alcohol.

6   Let us consider television viewing in the light of the conditions that define serious addictions.

7   Not unlike drugs or alcohol, the television experience allows the participant to blot out the real world and enter into a pleasurable and passive mental state. The worries and anxieties of reality are as effectively deferred by becoming absorbed in a television program as by going on a "trip" induced by drugs or alcohol. And just as alcoholics are only vaguely aware of their addiction, feeling that they control their drinking more than they really do ("I can cut it out any time I want—I just like to have three or four drinks before dinner"), people similarly overestimate their control over television watching. Even as they put off other activities to spend hour after hour watching television, they feel they could easily resume living in a different, less passive style. But somehow or other, while the television set is present in their homes, the click doesn't sound. With television pleasures available, those other experiences seem less attractive, more difficult somehow.

8   A heavy viewer (a college English instructor) observes:

9   "I find television almost irresistible. When the set is on, I cannot ignore it. I can't turn it off. I feel sapped, will-less, enervated. As I reach out to turn off the set, the strength goes out of my arms. So I sit there for hours and hours."

10   Self-confessed television addicts often feel they "ought" to do other things—but the fact that they don't read and don't plant their garden or sew or crochet or play games or have conversations means that those activities are no longer as desirable as television viewing. In a way the lives of heavy viewers are as imbalanced by their television "habit" as a drug addict's or an alcoholic's. They are living in a holding pattern, as it were, passing up the activities that lead to growth or development or a sense of accomplishment. This is one reason people talk about their television viewing so ruefully, so apologetically. They are aware that it is an unproductive experience, that almost any other endeavor is more worthwhile by any human measure.

11   Finally it is the adverse effect of television viewing on the lives of so many people that defines it as a serious addiction. The television habit distorts the sense of time. It renders other experiences vague and curiously unreal while taking on a greater reality for itself. It weakens relationships by reducing and sometimes eliminating normal opportunities for talking, for communicating.

12   And yet television does not satisfy, else why would the viewer continue to watch hour after hour, day after day? "The measure of health," writes Lawrence Kubie, "is flexibility . . . and especially the freedom to cease when sated."[1] But heavy television viewers can never be sated with their television experiences— these do not provide the true nourishment that satiation requires—and thus they find that they cannot stop watching.

[1]Lawrence Kubie, *Neurotic Distortion and the Creative Process* (Lawrence: University of Kansas Press, 1958).

Topics for Discussion and Writing

1. So far as developing a definition goes, what is Winn doing in her first two paragraphs? That is, what function do the paragraphs serve? Might these paragraphs appear with equal effectiveness at the end?

2. In which paragraphs does Winn most explicitly define addiction? How many characteristics of addiction does she find? How many paragraphs does she devote to these characteristics? Do you think that the number of paragraphs is appropriate?

3. In paragraph 12 Winn writes, "And yet television does not satisfy, else why would the viewer continue to watch hour after hour?" Drawing on your knowledge of someone—perhaps yourself—who watches television "hour after hour," would you say that such prolonged viewing is proof that television does not satisfy.

Gloria Naylor

A Question of Language

Gloria Naylor, university teacher, essayist, and novelist, holds an M.A. in Afro-American Studies from Yale University. Her first novel, The Women of Brewster Place *(1983), won an American Book Award. This essay originally appeared in* The New York Times.

1   Language is the subject. It is the written form with which I've managed to keep the wolf away from the door and, in diaries, to keep my sanity. In spite of this, I consider the written word inferior to the spoken, and much of the frustration experienced by novelists is the awareness that whatever we manage to capture in even the most transcendent passages falls far short of the richness of life. Dialogue achieves its power in the dynamics of a fleeting moment of sight, sound, smell, and touch.

2   I'm not going to enter the debate here about whether it is language that shapes reality or vice versa. That battle is doomed to be waged whenever we seek intermittent reprieve from the chicken and egg dispute. I will simply take the position that the spoken word, like the written word, amounts to a nonsensical arrangement of sounds or letters without a consensus that assigns "meaning." And building from the meanings of what we hear, we order reality. Words themselves are innocuous; it is the consensus that gives them true power.

3   I remember the first time I heard the word *nigger.* In my third-grade class, our math tests were being passed down the rows, and as I handed the papers to a little boy in back of me, I remarked that once again he had received a much lower mark than I did. He snatched his test from me and spit out that word. Had he called me a nymphomaniac or a necrophiliac, I couldn't have been more puzzled. I didn't know what a nigger was, but I knew that whatever it meant, it was something he shouldn't have called me. This was verified when I raised my hand, and in a loud voice repeated what he had said and watched the teacher scold him for using a "bad" word. I was later to go home and ask the inevitable question that every black parent must face—"Mommy, what does 'nigger' mean?"

4   And what exactly did it mean? Thinking back, I realize that this could not have been the first time the word was used in my presence. I was part of a large extended family that had migrated from the rural South after World War II and formed a close-knit network that gravitated around my maternal grandparents. Their ground-floor apartment in one of the buildings they owned in Harlem was a weekend mecca for my immediate family, along with countless aunts, uncles, and cousins who brought along assorted friends. It was a bustling and open house with assorted neighbors and tenants popping in and out to exchange bits of gossip, pick up an old quarrel or referee the ongoing checkers game in which my grandmother cheated shamelessly. They were all there to let down their hair and put up their feet after a week of labor in the factories, laundries, and shipyards of New York.

5   Amid the clamor, which could reach deafening proportions—two or three conversations going on simultaneously, punctuated by the sound of a baby's crying somewhere in the back rooms or out on the street—there was still a rigid set of rules about what was said and how. Older children were sent out of the living room when it was time to get into the juicy details about "you-know-who" up on the third floor who had gone and gotten herself "p-r-e-g-n-a-n-t!" But my parents, knowing that I could spell well beyond my years, always demanded that I follow the others out to play. Beyond sexual misconduct and death, everything else was considered harmless for our young ears. And so among the anecdotes of the triumphs and disappointments in the various workings of their lives, the word *nigger* was used in my presence, but it was set within contexts and inflections that caused it to register in my mind as something else.

6   In the singular, the word was always applied to a man who had distinguished himself in some situation that brought their approval for his strength, intelligence, or drive:

7   "Did Johnny really do that?"

8   "I'm telling you, that nigger pulled in $6,000 of overtime last year. Said he got enough for a down payment on a house."

9   When used with a possessive adjective by a woman—"my nigger"—it
became a term of endearment for husband or boyfriend. But it could be more
than just a term applied to a man. In their mouths it became the pure essence of
manhood—a disembodied force that channeled their past history of struggle and
present survival against the odds into a victorious statement of being: "Yeah,
that old foreman found out quick enough—you don't mess with a nigger."

10   In the plural, it became a description of some group within the community
that had overstepped the bounds of decency as my family defined it: Parents
who neglected their children, a drunken couple who fought in public, people
who simply refused to look for work, those with excessively dirty mouths or
unkempt households were all "trifling niggers." This particular circle could
forgive hard times, unemployment, the occasional bout of depression—they had
gone through all of that themselves—but the unforgivable sin was lack of self-
respect.

11   A woman could never be a *nigger* in the singular, with its connotation of
confirming worth. The noun *girl* was its closest equivalent in that sense, but only
when used in direct address and regardless of the gender doing the addressing.
Girl was a token of respect for a woman. The one-syllable word was drawn out
to sound like three in recognition of the extra ounce of wit, nerve or daring that
the woman had shown in the situation under discussion.

12   "G-i-r-l, stop. You mean you said that to his face?"

13   But if the word was used in a third-person reference or shortened so
that it almost snapped out of the mouth, it always involved some element
of communal disapproval. And age became an important factor in these
exchanges. It was only between individuals of the same generation, or from an
older person to a younger (but never the other way around), that "girl" would be
considered a compliment.

14   I don't agree with the argument that use of the word *nigger* at this social
stratum of the black community was an internalization of racism. The dynamics
were the exact opposite: the people in my grandmother's living room took a
word that whites used to signify worthlessness or degradation and rendered it
impotent. Gathering there together, they transformed *nigger* to signify the
varied and complex human beings they knew themselves to be. If the word was
to disappear totally from the mouths of even the most liberal of white society,
no one in that room was naïve enough to believe it would disappear from white
minds. Meeting the word head-on, they proved it had absolutely nothing to do
with the way they were determined to live their lives.

15   So there must have been dozens of times that the word *nigger* was spoken
in front of me before I reached the third grade. But I didn't "hear" it until it was
said by a small pair of lips that had already learned it could be a way to
humiliate me. That was the word I went home and asked my mother about. And

since she knew that I had to grow up in America, she took me in her lap and explained.

Topics for Discussion and Writing

1. Why, according to Naylor (in paragraph 1) is written language inferior to spoken language? Can you think of any way or any circumstance in which written language is superior? How does Naylor's essay support her position here? Or does it?

2. In paragraph 2 Naylor says "Words themselves are innocuous; it is the consensus that gives them true power." What does this mean? In the rest of the essay Naylor discusses meanings of the word "*nigger.*" To what extent does her discussion demonstrate that consensus "assigns meaning" and gives words power.

3. If as a child you were the victim of an ethnic slur, explain how you reacted to it and how others (perhaps a parent or teacher) reacted to it. Or, if you ever delivered an ethnic slur, explain how you felt then, and how you feel now, about the incident or incidents.

Barbara Lawrence

Four-Letter Words Can Hurt You

Barbara Lawrence was born in Hanover, New Hampshire, and she was educated at Connecticut College and at New York University. She teaches at the State University of New York at Old Westbury. This essay first appeared in The New York Times.

1   Why should any words be called obscene? Don't they all describe natural human functions? Am I trying to tell them, my students demand, that the "strong, earthy, gut-honest"—or, if they are fans of Norman Mailer, the "rich, liberating, existential"—language they use to describe sexual activity isn't preferable to "phony-sounding, middle-class words like 'intercourse' and 'copulate'?" "Cop You Late!" they say with fancy inflections and gagging grimaces. "Now, what is *that* supposed to mean?"

2   Well, what is it supposed to mean? And why indeed should one group of words describing human functions and human organs be acceptable in ordinary conversation and another, describing presumably the same organs and functions, be tabooed—so much so, in fact, that some of these words still cannot appear in print in many parts of the English-speaking world?

3   The argument that these taboos exist only because of "sexual hangups"
(middle-class, middle-age, feminist), or even that they are a result of class
oppression (the contempt of the Norman conquerors for the language of their
Anglo-Saxon serfs), ignores a much more likely explanation, it seems to me, and
that is the sources and functions of the words themselves.

4   The best known of the tabooed sexual verbs, for example, comes from the
German *ficken,* meaning "to strike"; combined, according to Partridge's
etymological dictionary *Origins,* with the Latin sexual verb *futuere;* associated in
turn with the Latin *fustis,* "a staff or cudgel"; the Celtic *buc,* "a point, hence to
pierce"; the Irish *bot,* "the male member"; the Latin *battuere,* "to beat"; the
Gaelic *batair,* "a cudgeller"; the Early Irish *bualaim,* "I strike"; and so forth. It is
one of what etymologists sometimes call "the sadistic group of words for the
man's part in copulation."

5   The brutality of this word, then, and its equivalents ("screw," "bang," etc.),
is not an illusion of the middle class or a crotchet of Women's Liberation. In their
origins and imagery these words carry undeniably painful, if not sadistic,
implications, the object of which is almost always female. Consider, for example,
what a "screw" actually does to the wood it penetrates; what a painful, even
mutilating, activity this kind of analogy suggests. "Screw" is particularly
interesting in this context, since the noun, according to Partridge, comes from
words meaning "groove," "nut," "ditch," "breeding sow," "scrofula" and
"swelling," while the verb, besides its explicit imagery, has antecedent
associations to "write on," "scratch," "scarify," and so forth—a revealing fusion
of a mechanical or painful action with an obviously denigrated object.

6   Not all obscene words, of course, are as implicitly sadistic or denigrating to
women as these, but all that I know seem to serve a similar purpose: to reduce
the human organism (especially the female organism) and human functions
(especially sexual and procreative) to their least organic, most mechanical
dimension; to substitute a trivializing or deforming resemblance for the complex
human reality of what is being described.

7   Tabooed male descriptives, when they are not openly denigrating to
women, often serve to divorce a male organ or function from any significant
interaction with the female. Take the word "testes," for example, suggesting
"witnesses" (from the Latin *testis*) to the sexual and procreative strengths of the
male organ; and the obscene counterpart of this word, which suggests little
more than a mechanical shape. Or compare almost any of the "rich," "liberating'
sexual verbs, so fashionable today among male writers, with that much-derided
Latin word "copulate" ("to bind or join together") or even that Anglo-Saxon
phrase (which seems to have had no trouble surviving the Norman Conquest)
"make love."

8   How arrogantly self-involved the tabooed words seem in comparison to
either of the other terms, and how contemptuous of the female partner.

Understandably so, of course, if she is only a "skirt," a "broad," or a "chick," a "pussycat" or a "piece." If she is, in other words, no more than her skirt, or what her skirt conceals; no more than a breeder, or the broadest part of her; no more than a piece of a human being or a "piece of tail."

9   The most severely tabooed of all the female descriptives, incidentally, are those like a "piece of tail," which suggest (either explicitly or through antecedents) that there is no significant difference between the female channel through which we are all conceived and born and the anal outlet common to both sexes—a distinction that pornographers have always enjoyed obscuring.

10   This effort to deny women their biological identity, their individuality, their humanness, is such an important aspect of obscene language that one can only marvel at how seldom, in an era preoccupied with definitions of obscenity, this fact is brought to our attention. One problem, of course, is that many of the people in the best position to do this (critics, teachers, writers) are so reluctant today to admit that they are angered or shocked by obscenity. Bored, maybe, unimpressed, aesthetically displeased, but—no matter how brutal or denigrating the material—never angered, never shocked.

11   And yet how eloquently angered, how piously shocked many of these same people become if denigrating language is used about any minority group other than women; if the obscenities are racial or ethnic, that is, rather than sexual. Words like "coon," "kike," "spic," "wop," after all, deform identity, deny individuality and humanness in almost exactly the same way that sexual vulgarisms and obscenities do.

12   No one that I know, least of all my students, would fail to question the values of a society whose literature and entertainment rested heavily on racial or ethnic pejoratives. Are the values of a society whose literature and entertainment rest as heavily as ours on sexual pejoratives any less questionable?

Topic for Discussion or Writing

In addition to giving evidence to support her view, what persuasive devices (for example, irony, analogy) does Lawrence use?

Chapter 13

Persuading

There are several ways to persuade. A threat may persuade you to hand over money; an emotional appeal may also persuade you to hand over money. But in this chapter we are also concerned with persuading by means of *evidence* and *reasonable arguments*.

Making Reasonable Arguments

Persuasive writing that, in addition to offering other evidence, relies chiefly on reasoning (rather than on appeals to the emotions) is usually called *argument*. An argument here is not a wrangle but a reasoned analysis. What distinguishes argument from explanation (for instance, the explanation of a process) is this: whereas both consist of statements, in argument some statements are offered as *reasons* for other statements. Another way of characterizing argument is that argument assumes there is or may be substantial disagreement between informed readers. To overcome this disagreement, the writer tries to offer reasons that convince by their validity. Here, for example, is C. S. Lewis arguing against vivisection (experimentation on live animals for scientific research):

> A rational discussion of this subject begins by inquiring whether pain is, or is not, an evil. If it is not, then the case against vivisection falls. But then so does the case for vivisection. If it is not defended on the ground that it reduces human suffering, on what ground can it be defended? And if pain is not an evil, why should human suffering be

reduced? We must therefore assume as a basis for the whole discussion that pain is an evil, otherwise there is nothing to be discussed.

Now if pain is an evil then the infliction of pain, considered in itself, must clearly be an evil act. But there are such things as necessary evils. Some acts which would be bad, simply in themselves, may be excusable and even laudable when they are necessary means to a greater good. In saying that the infliction of pain, simply in itself, is bad, we are not saying that pain ought never to be inflicted. Most of us think that it can rightly be inflicted for a good purpose—as in dentistry or just and reformatory punishment. The point is that it always requires justification. On the man whom we find inflicting pain rests the burden of showing why an act which in itself would be simply bad is, in those particular circumstances, good. If we find a man giving pleasure it is for us to prove (if we criticize him) that his action is wrong. But if we find a man inflicting pain it is for him to prove that his action is right. If he cannot, he is a wicked man.

And here is Supreme Court Justice Louis Brandeis, concluding his justly famous argument that government may not use evidence illegally obtained by wiretapping:

Decency, security and liberty alike demand that government officials shall be subjected to the same rules of conduct that are commands to the citizen. In a government of laws, existence of the government will be imperilled if it fails to observe the law scrupulously. Our Government is the potent, the omnipresent teacher. For good or for ill, it teaches the whole people by its example. Crime is contagious. If the Government becomes a lawbreaker, it breeds contempt for law; it invites every man to become a law unto himself; it invites anarchy. To declare that in the administration of the criminal law the end justifies the means—to declare that the Government may commit crimes in order to secure the conviction of a private criminal—would bring terrible retribution. Against that pernicious doctrine this Court should resolutely set its face.

Notice here that Brandeis's reasoning is highlighted by his forceful style. Note the resonant use of parallel constructions ("Decency, security and liberty," "For good or for ill," "it breeds . . . it invites," "To declare . . . to declare") and the variation between long and short sentences. Note too the wit in his comparisons: government is a teacher, crime is like a disease.

Making Reasonable Claims

You have only a little time—perhaps a few days, and even for a term paper at most a few weeks—to think about and to support your claim. You probably cannot come up with a comprehensive health-care program within that time, and you may not even be able to evaluate the evidence on whether our planet has or has not been undergoing a greenhouse effect, or whether or not elephants are so endangered that a ban on the sale of ivory is needed in order to preserve the species.

On the other hand, maybe you can. You may encounter a good collection of essays, pro and con, on a topic, and you will find that in the course of a day's reading you can become quite an expert. For instance, you may find, after reading a couple of dozen essays on abortion (or gun control, or the death penalty) that a few arguments on each side keep recurring, and you may rightly feel that you are in a position to offer your own point of view—that is, you may be in a position to make a reasonable and perhaps a novel claim.

Finally, we want to mention that what may at first seem to be an unreasonable claim may, after some reflection, become reasonable. Not much more than a century ago it seemed unreasonable to many intelligent people to argue that slavery was immoral. Issues such as those regarding women as priests, women in the armed forces going into combat, gays in the military, and animal experimentation are still matters on which you can take a stand that your opponents regard as utterly unreasonable. It happens that on the day we are writing these pages, the newspaper includes an account of Andrew Martinez, "the Naked Guy," a junior at the University of California, Berkeley, who strolls the campus naked except for his peace-sign, shoes and socks (and on cool days a sweatshirt), eats naked in the dining hall, and attends class naked. Campus police arrested The Naked Guy, but the state of California refused to prosecute him because nudity without "lewd behavior" is not illegal. The university then passed a ban on campus nudity, addressed specifically at Martinez, and suspended him. He hopes to take the matter to the courts. The university's arguments include the charge that his behavior constitutes sexual harassment of women and creates intolerable conditions for students in the "workplace." On the other hand, Martinez says that clothing is part of a middle-class, body-hating, repressive, consumerist society. Can one make a reasonable case for nudism? Can one make a reasonable case against nudism?

Claims of Fact

We can usually distinguish between two kinds of claims, claims of fact and claims of value, and we can sometimes distinguish these from a third kind of claim, claims of policy. *Claims of fact* assert that something is or was or will be. They include, for instance, arguments about cause and effect, correlation, probability and states of affairs. The following examples can be considered claims of fact:

Vanilla is the most popular flavor of ice cream in the United States.

Pornography stimulates violence against women.

Pornography has the potential of leading to violence.

Capital punishment reduces crime.

Capital punishment does not reduce crime.

Racial integration of the armed forces was achieved with very little conflict during the Korean War.

To support a claim of this sort, you must provide (probably after defining any terms that may be in doubt) information. Such information might, for instance, be testimony (for instance, your own experience, or statements by men who have said that pornography stimulated them to violence), or it might be statistics (gathered from a report in a scholarly journal). Even if the claim has to do with the future—let's say the claim that gun control will not reduce crime—you try to offer information. For example, you might gather information about the experiences of other countries, or even of certain states, that have adopted strict regulations concerning the sale of guns.

Claims of Value

Claims of value concern what is right or wrong, good or bad, better or worse than something else:

> Country music deserves to be taken seriously.
>
> Rock is better than country music.
>
> Capital punishment is barbaric.
>
> Euthanasia is immoral.

Some claims of value may be mere expressions of taste: "Vanilla is better than chocolate." It is hard to imagine how one could go about supporting such a claim—or refuting it. One probably can do no better than reply with the Latin proverb, "De gustibus non est disputandum" (There is no disputing about tastes). Notice, however, that the claim that vanilla is better than chocolate is quite different from the claim that most Americans prefer vanilla to chocolate. The last statement is a claim of fact, not of value, and it can be proved or disproved with information—for example, with information provided by the makers of ice cream.

Claims of value that go beyond the mere expression of taste—for instance, claims of morality or claims of artistic value—are usually supported by appeals to standards ("Such-and-such a proposal is bad *because* governments should not restrict the rights of individuals," or "Such-and-such music is good *because* it is complex"—or because it is popular or because it is sincere or whatever). In supporting claims of value, writers usually appeal to standards that they believe are acceptable to their readers. Examples:

> Sex-education programs in schools are inappropriate *because* aspects of moral education should properly be given only by parents.
>
> Sex-education programs in schools are appropriate *because* society has a duty to provide what most parents obviously are reluctant to provide.
>
> Doctors should be permitted to end a patient's life if the patient makes such a request, *because* each of us should be free to make the decisions that most concern us.
>
> Euthanasia is unacceptable *because* only God can give or take life.

In arguing a claim of value, be sure you have clearly in your mind the standards that you believe support the claim. You may find it appropriate to explain *why* you hold these standards, and *how* adherence to these standards will be of benefit.

Claims of Policy

Claims of policy assert that a policy, law, or custom should be initiated or altered or dropped. Such claims usually are characterized by words like "should," "must," and "ought."

> Children should be allowed to vote, if they wish to.
>
> A course in minority cultures ought to be required.
>
> The federal tax on gasoline must be raised.

In defending an unfamiliar claim of policy, you may want to begin by pointing out that there is a problem that is usually overlooked. For instance, if you urgently believe that children should have the right to vote—a view almost never expressed—you'll probably first have to convince your audience that there really is an arguable issue here, an issue concerning children's rights, an issue that deserves serious thought.

In defending a claim of policy you will probably find yourself providing information, just as you would do in support of a claim of fact. For instance, if your topic is children and the vote, you might point out that until 1920 women could not vote in the United States, the usual arguments being that they were mentally unfit and that they would vote the way their men told them to vote. Experience has proven that these low estimates of the capabilities of the disenfranchised were absurd.

But in defending a claim of policy you will probably have to consider values as well as facts. Thus, in arguing for an increase in the gasoline tax, you might want not only to provide factual information about how much money a five-cents-per-gallon tax would raise, but also to argue that such an increase is *fairer* than an alternative such as reducing social security benefits.

Three Kinds of Evidence: Examples, Testimony, Statistics

Writers of arguments seek to persuade by offering evidence. There are three chief forms of evidence used in argument:

- Examples
- Testimony the citation of authorities
- Statistics

We'll briefly consider each of these.

Examples

"Example" is from the Latin *exemplum,* which means "something taken out." An example is the sort of thing, taken from among many similar things, that one selects and holds up for view, perhaps after saying "For example," or "For instance."

Three categories of examples are especially common in written arguments:

- Real examples
- Invented instances
- Analogies

Real examples are just what they sound like, instances that have occurred. If, for example, we are arguing that gun control won't work, we point to those states that have adopted gun control laws and that nevertheless have had no reduction in crimes using guns. Or, if we want to support the assertion that a woman can be a capable head of state, we may find ourselves pointing to women who actually served as heads of state, such a Golda Meir and Indira Ghandi (prime ministers of Israel and India) and to Margaret Thatcher (prime minister of England).

The advantage of using real example is, clearly, that they are real. Of course an opponent might stubbornly respond that Golda Meir, Indira Gandhi, and Margaret Thatcher for some reason or other could not function as the head of state in *our* country. Someone might argue, for instance, that the case of Golda Meir proves nothing, since the role of women in Israeli society is different from the role of women in the United States (a country in which a majority of the citizens are Christians). And another person might argue that much of Mrs. Gandhi's power came from the fact that she was the daughter of Nehru, an immensely popular Indian statesman. Even the most compelling real example inevitably will in some ways be special or particular, and in the eyes of some readers may not seem to be a fair example.

Consider, for instance, a student who is arguing that peer review should be part of the writing course. The student points out that he or she found it of great help in high school. An opponent argues that things in college are different— college students should be able to help themselves, even highly gifted college students are not competent to offer college-level instruction, and so on. Still, as the feebleness of these objections (and the objections against Meir and Gandhi indicate), real examples can be very compelling.

Invented instances are exempt from the charge that, because of some detail or other, they are not relevant as evidence. Suppose, for example, you are arguing against capital punishment, on the grounds that if an innocent person is executed, there is no way of even attempting to rectify the injustice. If you point to the case of *X,* you may be met with the reply that *X* was not in fact innocent.

Rather than get tangled up in the guilt or innocence of a particular person, it may be better to argue that we can suppose—we can imagine—an innocent person convicted and executed, and we can imagine that evidence later proves the person's innocence.

Invented instances have the advantage of presenting an issue clearly, free from all of the distracting particularities (and irrelevancies) that are bound up with any real instance. But invented instances have the disadvantage of being invented, and they may seem remote from the real issues being argued.

Analogies are comparisons pointing out several resemblances between two rather different things. For instance, one might assert that a government is like a ship, and in times of stress—if the ship is to weather the storm—the authority of the captain must not be questioned.

But don't confuse an analogy with proof. An analogy is an extended comparison between two things: it can be useful in exposition, for it explains the unfamiliar by means of the familiar: "A government is like a ship, and just as a ship has a captain and a crew, so a government has . . . "; "Writing an essay is like building a house; just as an architect must begin with a plan, so the writer must . . . " Such comparisons can be useful, helping to clarify what otherwise might be obscure, but their usefulness goes only so far. Everything is what it is, and not another thing. A government is not a ship, and what is true of a captain's power need not be true of a president's power; and a writer is not an architect. Some of what is true about ships may be roughly true of governments, and some of what is true about architects may be (again, roughly) true of writers, but there are differences too. Consider the following analogy between a lighthouse and the death penalty:

> The death penalty is a warning, just like a lighthouse throwing its
> beams out to sea. We hear about shipwrecks, but we do not hear about
> the ships the lighthouse guides safely on their way. We do not have
> proof of the number of ships it saves, but we do not tear the lighthouse
> down.

> —J. Edgar Hoover

How convincing is Hoover's analogy as an argument, that is, as a reason for retaining the death penalty?

Testimony

Testimony, or the citation of authorities, is rooted in our awareness that some people are recognized as experts. In our daily lives we constantly turn to experts for guidance: we look up the spelling of a word in the dictionary, we listen to weather forecasts on the radio, we take an ailing cat to the vet for a checkup. Similarly, when we wish to become informed about controversial matters, we often turn to experts, first to help educate ourselves, and then to help convince others.

Don't forget that *you* are an authority on many things. For example, today's newspaper includes an article about the cutback in funding for the teaching of the arts in elementary and secondary schools. Art educators are responding that the arts are not a frill, and that in fact the arts provide the analytical thinking, teamwork, motivation, and self-discipline that most people agree are needed to reinvigorate American schools. If you have been involved in the arts in school— for instance, if you studied painting or learned to play a musical instrument— you are in a position to evaluate these claims. Similarly, if you have studied in a bilingual educational program, your own testimony will be invaluable.

There are at least two reasons for offering testimony in an argument. The obvious one is that expert opinion does (and should) carry some weight with any audience; the less obvious one is that a change of voice (if the testimony is not your own) in an essay may afford the reader a bit of pleasure. No matter how engaging your own voice may be, a fresh voice—whether that of Thomas Jefferson, Albert Einstein, or Barbara Jordan—may provide a refreshing change of tone.

But, of course, there are dangers: the chief one is that the words of authorities may be taken out of context or otherwise distorted, and the second is that the authorities may not be authorities on the present topic. Quite rightly we are concerned with what Jefferson said, but it is not entirely clear that his words can be fairly applied, on one side or the other, to such an issue as abortion. Quite rightly we are concerned with what Einstein said, but it is not entirely clear that his eminence as a physicist constitutes him an authority on, say, world peace. In a moment, when we discuss errors in reasoning, we'll have more to say about the proper and improper use of authorities.

Statistics

Statistics, another important form of evidence, are especially useful in arguments concerning social issues. If we want to argue for (or against) raising the driving age, we will probably do some research in the library, and will offer statistics about the number of accidents caused by people in certain age groups.

But a word of caution: the significance of statistics may be difficult to assess. For instance, opponents of gun control legislation have pointed out, in support of the argument that such laws are ineffectual, that homicides in Florida *increased* after Florida adopted gun control laws. Supporters of gun control laws cried "Foul," arguing that in the years after adopting these laws Miami became (for reasons having nothing to do with the laws) the cocaine capital of the United States, and the rise in homicide was chiefly a reflection of murders involved in the drug trade. That is, a significant change in the population has made a comparison of the figures meaningless. This objection seems plausible, and probably the statistics therefore should carry little weight.

How Much Evidence Is Enough?

If you allow yourself ample time to write your essay, you probably will turn up plenty of evidence to illustrate your arguments, such as examples drawn from your own experience and imagination, from your reading, and from your talks with others. Examples will not only help to clarify and to support your assertions, but they will also provide a concreteness that will be welcome in a paper that might be on the whole fairly abstract. Your sense of your audience will have to guide you in making your selection of examples. Generally speaking, a single example may not fully illuminate a difficult point, and so a second example, a clincher, may be desirable. If you offer a third or fourth example you probably are succumbing to a temptation to include something that tickles your fancy. If it is as good as you think it is, the reader probably will accept the unnecessary example and may even be grateful. But before you heap up examples, try to imagine yourself in your reader's place, and ask if the example is needed. If it is not needed, ask yourself if the reader will be glad to receive the overload.

One other point. On most questions, say on the value of bilingual education or on the need for rehabilitation programs in prisons, it's not possible to make a strictly logical case, in the sense of an absolutely airtight proof. Don't assume that it is your job to make an absolute proof. What you are expected to do is to offer a reasonable argument. Virginia Woolf put it this way: "When a subject is highly controversial . . . one cannot hope to tell the truth. One can only show how one came to hold whatever opinion one does hold."

Avoiding Fallacies

Let's further examine writing reasonable arguments by considering some obvious errors in reasoning. In logic these errors are called *fallacies* (from a Latin verb meaning "to deceive". As Tweedledee says in *Through the Looking-Glass,* "If it were so, it would be; but as it isn't, it ain't. That's logic."

To persuade readers to accept your opinions you must persuade them that you are reliable; if your argument includes fallacies, thoughtful readers will not take you seriously. More important, if your argument includes fallacies, you are misleading yourself. When you search your draft for fallacies, you are searching for ways to improve the quality of your thinking.

1. False authority. Don't try to borrow the prestige of authorities who are not authorities on the topic in question—for example, a heart surgeon speaking on politics. Similarly, some former authorities are no longer authorities, because the problems have changed or because later knowledge has superseded their views. Adam Smith, Jefferson, Eleanor Roosevelt, and Einstein remain persons of genius, but an attempt to use their opinions when you are examining modern issues—even in their fields—may be questioned. Remember the last words of

John B. Sedgwick, a Union Army general at the Battle of Spotsylvania in 1864: "They couldn't hit an elephant at this dist—." In short, before you rely on an authority, ask yourself if the person in question *is* an authority on the topic. And don't let stereotypes influence your idea of who is an authority. Remember the Yiddish proverb: "A goat has a beard, but that doesn't make him a rabbi."

2. False quotation. If you do quote from an authority, don't misquote. For example, you may find someone who grants that "there are strong arguments in favor of abolishing the death penalty"; but if she goes on to argue that, on balance, the arguments in favor of retaining it seem stronger to her, it is dishonest to quote her words so as to imply that she favors abolishing it.

3. Suppression of evidence. Don't neglect evidence that is contrary to your own argument. You owe it to yourself and your reader to present all the relevant evidence. Be especially careful not to assume that every question is simply a matter of *either/or*. There may be some truth on both sides. Take the following thesis: "Grades encourage unwholesome competition, and should therefore be abolished." Even if the statement about the evil effect of grading is true, it may not be the whole truth, and therefore it may not follow that grades should be abolished. One might point out that grades do other things too: they may stimulate learning, and they may assist students by telling them how far they have progressed. One might nevertheless conclude, on balance, that the fault outweighs the benefits. But the argument will be more persuasive now that the benefits of grades have been considered.

Concede to the opposition what is due it, and then outscore the opposition. Failure to confront the opposing evidence will be noticed; your readers will keep wondering why you do not consider this point or that, and may consequently dismiss your argument. However, if you confront the opposition you will almost surely strengthen your own argument. As Edmund Burke said 200 years ago, "He that wrestles with us strengthens our nerves, and sharpens our skill. Our antagonist is our helper."

4. Generalization from insufficient evidence. In rereading a draft of an argument that you have written, try to spot your own generalizations. Ask yourself if a reasonable reader is likely to agree that the generalization is based on an adequate sample.

A visitor to a college may sit in on three classes, each taught by a different instructor, and may find all three stimulating. That's a good sign, but can we generalize and say that the teaching at this college is excellent? Are three classes a sufficient sample? If all three are offered by the Biology Department, and if the Biology Department includes only five instructors, perhaps we can tentatively say that the teaching of biology at this institution is good. If the Biology Department contains twenty instructors, perhaps we can still say, though more tentatively, that this sample indicates that the teaching of biology is good. But what does the sample say about the teaching of other subjects at the college? It probably does say something—the institution may be much concerned with teaching across the board—but then again it may not say a great deal, since the Biology Department may be exceptionally concerned with good teaching.

5. The genetic fallacy. Don't assume that something can necessarily be explained in terms of its birth or origin. "He wrote the novel to make money, so it can't be any good" is not a valid inference. The value of a novel does not depend on the author's motivations in writing it. Indeed, the value or worth of a novel needs to be established by reference to other criteria. Neither the highest nor the lowest motivations guarantee the quality of the product. Another example: "Capital punishment arose in days when men sought revenge, so now it ought to be abolished." Again an unconvincing argument: capital punishment may have some current value; for example, it may serve as a deterrent to crime. But that's another argument, and it needs evidence if it is to be believed. Be on guard, too, against the thoughtless tendency to judge people by their origins: Mr. X has a foreign accent, so he is probably untrustworthy or stupid or industrious.

6. Begging the question and **circular reasoning.** Don't assume the truth of the point that you should prove. The term "begging the question" is a trifle odd. It means, in effect, "You, like a beggar, are asking me to grant you something at the outset."

Examples: "The barbaric death penalty should be abolished"; "This senseless language requirement should be dropped." Both of these statements assume what they should prove—that the death penalty is barbaric, and that the language requirement is senseless. You can of course make assertions such as these, but you must go on to prove them.

Circular reasoning is usually an extended form of begging the question. What ought to be proved is covertly assumed. Example: "*X* is the best-qualified candidate for the office, because the most informed people say so." Who are the most informed people? Those who recognize *X's* superiority. Circular reasoning,

"Look, maybe you're right, but for the sake of argument let's assume you're wrong and drop it."

Drawing by Mankoff; © 1983 The New Yorker Magazine, Inc.

then, normally includes intermediate steps absent from begging the question, but the two fallacies are so closely related that they can be considered one. Another example: "I feel sympathy for her because I identify with her." Despite the "because," no reason is really offered. What follows "because" is merely a restatement, in slightly different words, of what precedes; the shift of words, from "feel sympathy" to "identify with" has misled the writer into thinking she is giving a reason. Other examples: "Students are interested in courses when the subject matter and the method of presentation are interesting"; "There cannot be peace in the Middle East because the Jews and the Arabs will always fight." In each case, an assertion that ought to be proved is reasserted as a reason in support of the assertion.

7. Post hoc ergo propter hoc (Latin for "after this, therefore because of this"). Don't assume that because *X* precedes *Y*, *X* must cause *Y*. For example: "He went to college and came back a boozer; college corrupted him." He might have taken up liquor even if he had not gone to college. Another example: "When a fifty-five-mile-per-hour limit was imposed in 1974, after the Arab embargo on oil, the number of auto fatalities decreased sharply, from 55,000 deaths in 1973 to 46,000 in 1974, so it is evident that a fifty-five-mile-per-hour limit—still adhered to in some states—saves lives." Not quite. Because gasoline was expensive after the embargo, the number of miles traveled decreased. The number of fatalities *per mile* remained constant. The price of gas, not the speed limit, seems responsible for the decreased number of fatalities. Moreover, the national death rate has continued to fall. Why? Several factors are at work: seat-belt and child-restraint laws, campaigns against drunk driving, improved auto design, and improved roads. Medicine, too, may have improved so that today doctors can save accident victims who in 1974 would have died. In short, it probably is impossible to isolate the correlation between speed and safety.

8. Argumentum ad hominem (Latin for "argument toward the man"). Here the argument is directed toward the person rather than toward the issue. Don't shift from your topic to your opponent. A speaker argues against legalizing abortions and her opponent, instead of facing the merits of the argument, attacks the character or the associations of the opponent: "You're a Catholic, aren't you?"

9. False assumption. Consider the Scot who argued that Shakespeare must have been a Scot. Asked for his evidence, he replied, "The ability of the man warrants the assumption." Or take a statement such as "She goes to Yale, so she must be rich." Possibly the statement is based on faulty induction (the writer knows four Yale students, and all four are rich) but more likely he is just passing on a cliché. The Yale student in question may be on a scholarship, may be struggling to earn the money, or may be backed by parents of modest means who for eighteen years have saved money for her college education. Other examples: "I haven't heard him complain about French 10, so he must be satisfied"; "She's a writer, so she must be well read." A little thought will show how weak such assertions are; they *may* be true, but they may not.

The errors we have discussed are common. In revising, try to spot them and eliminate or correct them. You have a point to make, and you should make it fairly. If it can be made only unfairly, you do an injustice not only to your reader but to yourself; you should try to change your view of the topic. You don't want to be like the politician whose speech had a marginal note: "Argument weak; shout here."

Wit

In addition to using sound argument and other evidence, writers often use wit, especially irony, to persuade. In irony, the words convey a meaning somewhat different from what they explicitly say. Wry understatement is typical. Here, for instance, is Thoreau explaining why in *Walden*, his book about his two years in relative isolation at Walden Pond, he will talk chiefly about himself:

> In most books, the *I*, or first person, is omitted; in this it will be re-
> tained; that, in respect to egotism, is the main difference. We com-
> monly do not remember that it is, after all, always the first person that
> is speaking. I should not talk so much about myself if there were any-
> body else whom I knew as well. Unfortunately, I am confined to this
> theme by the narrowness of my experience.

Notice the wry apology in his justification for talking about himself: he does not know anyone else as well as he knows himself. Similarly, in "unfortunately" ("Unfortunately, I am confined to this theme by the narrowness of my

"Please forgive Edgar. He has no verbal skills."

Drawing by Lorenz; © 1980 The New Yorker Magazine, Inc.

experience") we again hear a wry voice. After all, Thoreau knows, as we know, that *no one* has experience so deep or broad that he or she knows others better than himself or herself. Thoreau's presentation of himself as someone who happens not to have had the luck of knowing others better than himself is engagingly clever.

Avoiding Sarcasm

Because writers must, among other things, persuade readers that they are humane, sarcasm has little place in persuasive writing. Although desk dictionaries usually define sarcasm as "bitter, caustic irony" or "a kind of satiric wit," if you think of a sarcastic comment that you have heard you will probably agree that "a crude, sneering remark" is a better definition. Lacking the wit of good satire and the carefully controlled mockery of irony, sarcasm usually relies on gross overstatement and intends simply to humiliate. *Sarcasm* is derived from a Greek word meaning "to tear flesh" or "to bite the lips in rage," altogether an unattractive business. Sarcasm is unfair, for it dismisses an opponent's arguments with ridicule rather than with reason; it is also unwise, for it turns the reader against you. Readers hesitate to ally themselves with a writer who apparently enjoys humiliating the opposition. A sarcastic remark can turn the hearers against the speaker and arouse sympathy for the victim. In short, sarcasm usually doesn't work.

Organizing an Argument

As we have said earlier, writers find out what they think partly by means of the act of putting words on paper. But in presenting arguments for their readers, writers rarely duplicate their own acts of discovery. To put it another way, the process of setting forth ideas, and supporting them, does not follow the productive but untidy, repetitive, often haphazard process of preliminary thinking. For instance, a point that did not strike us until the middle of the third draft may, in the final version, appear in the opening paragraph. Or an example that seemed useful early in our thinking may, in the process of revision, be omitted in favor of a stronger example. Through a series of revisions, large and small, we try to work out the best strategy for persuading our readers to accept our reasoning as sound, our conclusion as valid. Unfortunately, we find, an argument cannot be presented either as it occurs to us or all at once.

Nor is there a simple formula that governs the organization of all effective argumentative essays. An essay may begin by announcing its thesis and then set forth the reasons that support the thesis. Or it may begin more casually, calling attention to specific cases, and then generalize from these cases. Probably it will then go on to reveal an underlying unity which brings the thesis into view, and from here it will offer detailed reasoning that supports the thesis.

As the writer of a persuasive essay, you almost always have to handle, in some sequence or other, the following matters:

- The background (for instance, the need to consider the issue)
- The thesis (claim)
- The evidence that supports the thesis
- The counterevidence
- The response to counterclaims and counterevidence (either a refutation or a concession that there *is* merit to the counterclaims but not as much as to the writer's thesis)
- Some sort of reaffirmation, perhaps that the topic needs attention or that the thesis advanced is the most plausible or the most workable or the most moral, or that the ball is now in the reader's court

Three methods of organizing arguments are fairly common, and one or another may suit an essay you're working on.

1. **Begin with the background, then set forth the thesis statement and work from the simplest argument up to the most complex**. Such an arrangement will keep your reader with you, step by step.

2. **After setting forth the background and your thesis, arrange the arguments in order of increasing strength.** The danger in following this plan is that you may lose the reader from the start, because you begin with a weak argument. Avoid this problem by telling your reader that indeed the first argument is relatively weak (if it is terribly weak, it isn't an argument at all, so scrap it), but that you offer it for the sake of completeness or because it is often given, and that you will soon give the reader far stronger arguments. Face the opposition to this initial argument, grant that opposition as much as it deserves, and salvage what is left of the argument. Then proceed to the increasingly strong arguments, devoting at least one paragraph to each. Introduce each argument with an appropriate transition ("another reason," "even more important," "most convincing of all"). State it briefly, summarize the opposing view, and then demolish this opposition. With this organization, your discussion of each of your own arguments ends affirmatively.

3. **After sketching the background and stating your thesis in an introductory paragraph, mass all of the opposing arguments, and then respond to them one by one.**

In short, when you (1) think you have done your initial thinking and your rethinking, (2) have, if appropriate, consulted some published sources, (3) have talked with friends and perhaps with experts, and (4) have moved from random notes and lists to fairly full drafts, you are not quite done.

You still must check what you hope is your last draft to see if you have found the best possible order for the arguments, have given effective examples, and have furnished transitions. In short, you must check to see that you have produced an argument that will strike a reasonable reader as courteous, clear, and concrete.

A Checklist for Revising Drafts of Persuasive Essays

1. Are the terms clearly defined?

2. Is the thesis stated promptly and clearly?

3. Are the assumptions likely to be shared by your readers? If not, are they reasonably argued rather than merely stated?

4. Are the facts verifiable? Is the evidence reliable? (No out-of-date statistics, no generalizations from insufficient evidence?)

5. Is the reasoning sound?

6. Are the authorities really authorities on this matter?

7. Are all of the substantial counterarguments recognized and effectively responded to?

8. Does the essay make use, where appropriate, of concrete examples?

9. Is the organization effective? Does the essay begin interestingly, keep the thesis in view, and end interestingly?

10. Is the tone appropriate? (Avoid sarcasm. Present yourself as fair-minded, and assume that those who hold a view opposed to yours are also fair-minded.)

Topics for Discussion and Writing

1. Analyze and evaluate each of the following arguments. If any of the arguments contain fallacies, name the fallacies.

   a. To the Editor:

   The recent senseless murder of a 15-year-old seminary student again emphasizes the insanity of our gun laws. No matter how guilty the 13-year-old boy who shot into the head of the victim, it seems that our congressional leaders are even more guilty by not enacting stricter gun-control laws. They are supposedly sane, rational individuals; and the kindest thing that can be said about them is that they are merely motivated by greed.

   b. To the Editor:

   Your editorial last Wednesday arguing against censorship as an infringement on freedom is full of clever arguments but it overlooks an obvious fact. We have Pure Food and Drug laws to protect us against poison, and no one believes that such laws interfere with the freedom of those who produce food and drugs. The public is entitled, then, to laws that will similarly protect us from the poison that some movie-makers produce.

c. To the Editor:

On Dec. 5 *The Times* published a story saying that colleges have come under pressure to improve the "quality of their teaching." Unfortunately, nobody knows what good teaching is, let alone how to evaluate it.

Unlike scholarship, which has a visible product, namely published reports, the results of teaching are locked in the heads of students and are usually not apparent, even to the students themselves, for a very long period.

One device which is frequently used is a poll of students, the so-called "student evaluation of teachers." This type of measurement has been studied by Rodin and Rodin, who correlated it with how much the students learned, as demonstrated on tests. The correlation was highly negative (−.75). As the Rodins put it, "Students rate most highly instructors from whom they learn least."

What invariably happens is that attempts to reward "good teaching" turn out to reward good public relations.

d. The following paragraph was written by Walter Lippmann shortly after the United States entered World War II:

The Pacific Coast is in imminent danger of a combined attack from within and from without. . . . It is [true] . . . that since the outbreak of the Japanese war there has been no important sabotage on the Pacific Coast. From what we know about the fifth column in Europe, this is not, as some have liked to think, a sign that there is nothing to be feared. It is a sign that the blow is well-organized and that it is held back until it can be struck with maximum effect. . . . I am sure I understand fully and appreciate thoroughly the unwillingness of Washington to adopt a policy of mass evacuation and internment of all those who are technically enemy aliens. But I submit that Washington is not defining the problem on the coast correctly. . . . The Pacific Coast is officially a combat zone: some part of it may at any moment be a battlefield. Nobody's constitutional rights include the right to reside and do business on a battlefield. And nobody ought to be on a battlefield who has no good reason for being there.

2. In July 1984 President Reagan signed a bill that exerted pressure on the states to enact legislation setting the drinking age at twenty-one. The bill allows the government to withhold 5 percent of federal highway construction funds from states that do not set the drinking age at twenty-one by October 1986. If the age is not set at twenty-one by October 1987, 10 percent of the funds can be withheld.

Read the following letter to a newspaper, written in 1986, and then list and evaluate the persuasive devices that it uses.

To the Editor:

Congress and the President are bullying the states into raising the drinking age.

The law is discriminatory because it withholds a right from certain people merely because of their age.

The law is unreasonable, because it seems to say that people who are old enough to vote and to fight for their country are not old enough to drink alcohol.

The law is illogical, because it takes as proof of its value that fact that those states that already have raised the drinking age to twenty-one have had a reduction in the number of nighttime driving accidents by persons under twenty-one. Of course they have—and if the age were raised to thirty-five there would be a similar reduction in the number of driving accidents by persons under thirty-five. Why not set the age at fifty? Or at sixty-five? Or a hundred?

In any case, the statistics prove nothing. The lower percent of accidents may be due to other factors, such as heightened public awareness, or stricter enforcement of speeding laws.

The real problem is not that people between eighteen and twenty-one drink, but that they do not receive adequate driver education—an education that would of course emphasize that one must never drive while intoxicated. Further, the police do not strictly enforce laws against speeding, and thus they in effect contribute to the accident rate.

YOURS,

STEPHEN OHMANN

3. A writer arguing against gun control made the following three points:

> More criminals are shot by private citizens each year than by the police.
>
> There are twice as many people killed by drunken drivers each year as by handguns (and ten times as many severely injured).
>
> In about half of the handgun murders the people know each other—so they would probably use other weapons if guns were not available.

Trying to put aside your own views about the possession of handguns, make explicit the assumptions that lie beneath the three statements, and then evaluate each of the statements as an argument against outlawing handguns.

4. Read the following passage, from George Will's *The Morning After:*

> When a society becomes, like ours, uneasy about calling prisons penitentiaries or penal institutions, and instead calls them "correctional institutions," the society has lost its bearings. If prisoners are "corrected," that is nice but it is an ancillary outcome. The point of imprisonment is punishment. The idea of punishment is unintelligible if severed from the idea of retribution, which is inseparable from the concept of vengeance, which is an expression of anger. No anger, no justice.

Evaluate this selection as a piece of persuasive writing with attention to the aspects of good—or faulty—argumentation reviewed in this chapter.

Persuasion at Work

Edward Koch

Death and Justice: How Capital Punishment Affirms Life

Edward Koch, born in New York City, was mayor of New York from 1978 to 1989. This essay first appeared in The New Republic.

1   Last December a man named Robert Lee Willie, who had been convicted of raping and murdering an 18-year-old woman, was executed in the Louisiana state prison. In a statement issued several minutes before his death, Mr. Willie said: "Killing people is wrong. . . . It makes no difference whether it's citizens, countries, or governments. Killing is wrong." Two weeks later in South Carolina, an admitted killer named Joseph Carl Shaw was put to death for murdering two teenagers. In an appeal to the governor for clemency, Mr. Shaw wrote: "Killing is wrong when I did it. Killing is wrong when you do it. I hope you have the courage and moral strength to stop the killing."

2   It is a curiosity of modern life that we find ourselves being lectured on morality by cold-blooded killers. Mr. Willie previously had been convicted of aggravated rape, aggravated kidnapping, and the murders of a Louisiana deputy and a man from Missouri. Mr. Shaw committed another murder a week before the two for which he was executed, and admitted mutilating the body of the 14-year-old girl he killed. I can't help wondering what prompted these murderers to speak out against killing as they entered the death-house door. Did their newfound reverence for life stem from the realization that they were about to lose their own?

3   Life is indeed precious, and I believe the death penalty helps to affirm this fact. Had the death penalty been a real possibility in the minds of these murderers, they might well have stayed their hand. They might have shown moral awareness before their victims died, and not after. Consider the tragic death of Rosa Velez, who happened to be home when a man named Luis Vera burglarized her apartment in Brooklyn. "Yeah, I shot her," Vera admitted. "She knew me, and I knew I wouldn't go to the chair."

4   During my twenty-two years in public service, I have heard the pros and cons of capital punishment expressed with special intensity. As a district leader, councilman, congressman, and mayor, I have represented constituencies generally thought of as liberal. Because I support the death penalty for heinous crimes of murder, I have sometimes been the subject of emotional and outraged attacks by voters who find my position reprehensible or worse. I have listened to

their ideas. I have weighed their objections carefully. I still support the death penalty. The reasons I maintain my position can be best understood by examining the arguments most frequently heard in opposition.

5   1. *The death penalty is "barbaric."* Sometimes opponents of capital punishment horrify with tales of lingering death on the gallows, of faulty electric chairs, or of agony in the gas chamber. Partly in response to such protests, several states such as North Carolina and Texas switched to execution by lethal injection. The condemned person is put to death painlessly, without ropes, voltage, bullets, or gas. Did this answer the objections of death penalty opponents? Of course not. On June 22, 1984, *The New York Times* published an editorial that sarcastically attacked the new "hygienic" method of death by injection, and stated that "execution can never be made humane through science." So it's not the method that really troubles opponents. It's the death itself they consider barbaric.

6   Admittedly, capital punishment is not a pleasant topic. However, one does not have to like the death penalty in order to support it any more than one must like radical surgery, radiation, or chemotherapy in order to find necessary these attempts at curing cancer. Ultimately we may learn how to cure cancer with a simple pill. Unfortunately, that day has not yet arrived. Today we are faced with the choice of letting the cancer spread or trying to cure it with the methods available, methods that one day will almost certainly be considered barbaric. But to give up and do nothing would be far more barbaric and would certainly delay the discovery of an eventual cure. The analogy between cancer and murder is imperfect, because murder is not the "disease" we are trying to cure. The disease is injustice. We may not like the death penalty, but it must be available to punish crimes of cold-blooded murder, cases in which any other form of punishment would be inadequate and, therefore, unjust. If we create a society in which injustice is not tolerated, incidents of murder—the most flagrant form of injustice—will diminish.

7   2. *No other major democracy uses the death penalty.* No other major democracy—in fact, few other countries of any description—are plagued by a murder rate such as that in the United States. Fewer and fewer Americans can remember the days when unlocked doors were the norm and murder was a rare and terrible offense. In America the murder rate climbed 122 percent between 1963 and 1980. During that same period, the murder rate in New York City increased by almost 400 percent, and the statistics are even worse in many other cities. A study at M.I.T. showed that based on 1970 homicide rates a person who lived in a large American city ran a greater risk of being murdered than an American soldier in World War II ran of being killed in combat. It is not surprising that the laws of each country differ according to differing conditions and traditions. If other countries had our murder problem, the cry for capital punishment would be just as loud as it is here. And I daresay that any other

major democracy where 75 percent of the people supported the death penalty would soon enact it into law.

8   3. *An innocent person might be executed by mistake.* Consider the work of Hugo Adam Bedau, one of the most implacable foes of capital punishment in this country. According to Mr. Bedau, it is "false sentimentality to argue that the death penalty should be abolished because of the abstract possibility that an innocent person might be executed." He cites a study of the 7,000 executions in this country from 1893 to 1971, and concludes that the record fails to show that such cases occur. The main point, however, is this. If government functioned only when the possibility of error didn't exist, government wouldn't function at all. Human life deserves special protection, and one of the best ways to guarantee that protection is to assure that convicted murderers do not kill again. Only the death penalty can accomplish this end. In a recent case in New Jersey, a man named Richard Biegenwald was freed from prison after serving 18 years for murder; since his release he has been convicted of committing four murders. A prisoner named Lemuel Smith, who, while serving four life sentences for murder (plus two life sentences for kidnapping and robbery) in New York's Green Haven Prison, lured a woman corrections officer into the chaplain's office and strangled her. He then mutilated and dismembered her body. An additional life sentence for Smith is meaningless. Because New York has no death penalty statute, Smith has effectively been given a license to kill.

9   But the problem of multiple murder is not confined to the nation's penitentiaries. In 1981, 91 police officers were killed in the line of duty in this country. Seven percent of those arrested in the cases that have been solved had a previous arrest for murder. In New York City in 1976 and 1977, 85 persons arrested for homicide had a previous arrest for murder. Six of these individuals had two previous arrests for murder, and one had four previous murder arrests. During those two years the New York police were arresting for murder persons with a previous arrest for murder on the average of one every 8.5 days. This is not surprising when we learn that in 1975, for example, the median time served in Massachusetts for homicide was less than two and a half years. In 1976 a study sponsored by the Twentieth Century Fund found that the average time served in the United States for first-degree murder is ten years. The median time served may be considerably lower.

10   4. *Capital punishment cheapens the value of human life.* On the contrary, it can be easily demonstrated that the death penalty strengthens the value of human life. If the penalty for rape were lowered, clearly it would signal a lessened regard for the victims' suffering, humiliation, and personal integrity. It would cheapen their horrible experience, and expose them to an increased danger of recurrence. When we lower the penalty for murder, it signals a lessened regard for the value of the victim's life. Some critics of capital punishment, such as columnist Jimmy Breslin, have suggested that a life sentence is actually a harsher penalty for murder than death. This is sophistic

nonsense. A few killers may decide not to appeal a death sentence, but the overwhelming majority make every effort to stay alive. It is by exacting the highest penalty for the taking of human life that we affirm the highest value of human life.

11   5. *The death penalty is applied in a discriminatory manner.* This factor no longer seems to be the problem it once was. The appeals process for a condemned prisoner is lengthy and painstaking. Every effort is made to see that the verdict and sentence were fairly arrived at. However, assertions of discrimination are not an argument for ending the death penalty but for extending it. It is not justice to exclude everyone from the penalty of the law if a few are found to be so favored. Justice requires that the law be applied equally to all.

12   6. *Thou shalt not kill.* The Bible is our greatest source of moral inspiration. Opponents of the death penalty frequently cite the sixth of the Ten Commandments in an attempt to prove that capital punishment is divinely proscribed. In the original Hebrew, however, the Sixth Commandment reads "Thou shalt not commit murder," and the Torah specifies capital punishment for a variety of offenses. The biblical viewpoint has been upheld by philosophers throughout history. The greatest thinkers of the nineteenth century—Kant, Locke, Hobbes, Rousseau, Montesquieu, and Mill—agreed that natural law properly authorizes the sovereign to take life in order to vindicate justice. Only Jeremy Bentham was ambivalent. Washington, Jefferson, and Franklin endorsed it. Abraham Lincoln authorized executions for deserters in wartime. Alexis de Tocqueville, who expressed profound respect for American institutions, believed that the death penalty was indispensable to the support of social order. The United States Constitution, widely admired as one of the seminal achievements in the history of humanity, condemns cruel and inhuman punishment, but does not condemn capital punishment.

13   7. *The death penalty is state-sanctioned murder.* This is the defense with which Messrs. Willie and Shaw hoped to soften the resolve of those who sentenced them to death. By saying in effect, "You're no better than I am," the murderer seeks to bring his accusers down to his own level. It is also a popular argument among opponents of capital punishment, but a transparently false one. Simply put, the state has rights that the private individual does not. In a democracy, those rights are given to the state by the electorate. The execution of a lawfully condemned killer is no more an act of murder than is legal imprisonment an act of kidnapping. If an individual forces a neighbor to pay him money under threat of punishment, it's called extortion. If the state does it, it's called taxation. Rights and responsibilities surrendered by the individual are what give the state its power to govern. This contract is the foundation of civilization itself.

14   Everyone wants his or her rights, and will defend them jealously. Not everyone, however, wants responsibilities, especially the painful responsibilities

that come with law enforcement. Twenty-one years ago a woman named Kitty Genovese was assaulted and murdered on a street in New York. Dozens of neighbors heard her cries for help but did nothing to assist her. They didn't even call the police. In such a climate the criminal understandably grows bolder. In the presence of moral cowardice, he lectures us on our supposed failings and tries to equate his crimes with our quest for justice.

15   The death of anyone—even a convicted killer—diminishes us all. But we are diminished even more by a justice system that fails to function. It is an illusion to let ourselves believe that doing away with capital punishment removes the murderer's deed from our conscience. The rights of society are paramount. When we protect guilty lives, we give up innocent lives in exchange. When opponents of capital punishment say to the state: "I will not let you kill in my name," they are also saying to murderers: "You can kill in your *own* name as long as I have an excuse for not getting involved."

16   It is hard to imagine anything worse than being murdered while neighbors do nothing. But something worse exists. When those same neighbors shrink back from justly punishing the murderer, the victim dies twice.

Topics for Discussion and Writing

1. Koch is, of course, writing an argument. He wants to persuade his readers. Beginning with paragraph 5 (Koch's first numbered point), he states the opposition's arguments and tries to refute them. But why did he include his first four paragraphs? What, as persuasion, does each contribute?

2. In paragraph 6 Koch compares our use of capital punishment to our use of "radical surgery, radiation, or chemotherapy." Do you find this analogy impressive—or not—and why? (Note that in this paragraph Koch goes on to say that "the analogy between cancer and murder is imperfect." Should he, then, not have used it?)

3. At the end of paragraph 6 Koch says, "If we create a society in which injustice is not tolerated, incidents of murder—the most flagrant form of injustice—will diminish." Has the earlier part of the paragraph prepared us for this statement?

4. Explain why you are or are not persuaded by Koch's second argument, about the likelihood that other countries would enact the death penalty if they too had high rates of murder.

5. In paragraph 9 Koch speaks of "murder" and then of "homicide." Are these two the same? If not, *why* is Koch bringing in statistics about homicide?

6. In paragraph 12, Koch lists authorities who supported the death penalty. Some of them—for instance, Washington and Jefferson—also supported slavery. What can be said in behalf of, and what can be said against, Koch's use of these authorities?

7. In paragraph 15, Koch puts a sentence into the mouths of his opponents. *Is* this what his opponents are in effect saying or thinking? (For the views of at least one of his opponents, see David Bruck's response to Koch, immediately below.)

David Bruck

The Death Penalty

David Bruck, born in 1949, holds a law degree from the University of South Carolina. After serving four years as a public defender in South Carolina he entered private practice in order to devote all of his efforts to defending inmates on death row.

    This essay was written as a direct response to the essay by Edward Koch, beginning on page 282.

1   Mayor Ed Koch contends that the death penalty "affirms life." By failing to execute murderers, he says, we "signal a lessened regard for the value of the victim's life." Koch suggests that people who oppose the death penalty are like Kitty Genovese's neighbors, who heard her cries for help but did nothing while an attacker stabbed her to death.

2   This is the standard "moral" defense of death as punishment: even if executions don't deter violent crime any more effectively than imprisonment, they are still required as the only means we have of doing justice in response to the worst of crimes.

3   Until recently, this "moral" argument had to be considered in the abstract, since no one was being executed in the United States. But the death penalty is back now, at least in the southern states, where every one of the more than 30 executions carried out over the last two years has taken place. Those of us who live in those states are getting to see the difference the death penalty in theory, and what happens when you actually try to use it.

4   South Carolina resumed executing prisoners in January with the electrocution of Joseph Carl Shaw. Shaw was condemned to death for helping to murder two teenagers while he was serving as a military policeman at Fort Jackson, South Carolina. His crime, propelled by mental illness and PCP, was one of terrible brutality. It is Shaw's last words ("Killing was wrong when I did it. It is wrong you do it. . . .") that so outraged Mayor Koch: he finds it "a curiosity of modern life that we are being lectured on morality by cold-blooded killers." And so it is.

5   But it was not "modern life" that brought this curiosity into being. It was capital punishment. The electric chair was J. C. Shaw's platform. (The mayor

mistakenly writes that Shaw's statement came in the form of a plea to the governor for clemency: actually Shaw made it only seconds before his death, as he waited, shaved and strapped into the chair, for the switch to be thrown.) It was the chair that provided Shaw with celebrity and an opportunity to lecture us on right and wrong. What made this weird moral reversal even worse is that J. C. Shaw faced his own death with undeniable dignity and courage. And while Shaw died, the TV crews recorded another "curiosity" of the death penalty—the crowd gathered outside the death-house to cheer on the executioner. Whoops of elation greeted the announcement of Shaw's death. Waiting at the penitentiary gates for the appearance of the hearse bearing Shaw's remains, one demonstrator started yelling, "Where's the beef?"

6　　For those who had to see the execution of J. C. Shaw, it wasn't easy to keep in mind that the purpose of the whole spectacle was to affirm life. It will be harder still when Florida executes a cop-killer named Alvin Ford. Ford has lost his mind during his years of death-row confinement, and now spends his days trembling, rocking back and forth, and muttering unintelligible prayers. This has led to litigation over whether Ford meets a centuries-old legal standard for mental competency. Since the Middle Ages, the Anglo-American legal system has generally prohibited the execution of anyone who is too mentally ill to understand what is about to be done to him and why. If Florida wins its case, it will have earned the right to electrocute Ford in his present condition. If it loses, he will not be executed until the state has nursed him back to some semblance of mental health.

7　　We can at least be thankful that this demoralizing spectacle involves a prisoner who is actually guilty of murder. But this may not always be so. The ordeal of Lenell Jeter—the young black engineer who recently served more than a year of a life sentence for a Texas armed robbery that he didn't commit—should remind us that the system is quite capable of making the very worst sort of mistake. That Jeter was eventually cleared is a fluke. If the robbery had occurred at 7 P.M. rather than 3 P.M., he'd have had no alibi, and would still be in prison today. And if someone had been killed in that robbery, Jeter probably would have been sentenced to death. We'd have seen the usual execution-day interviews with state officials and the victim's relatives, all complaining that Jeter's appeals took too long. And Jeter's last words from the gurney would have taken their place among the growing literature of death-house oration that so irritates the mayor.

8　　Koch quoted Hugo Adam Bedau, a prominent abolitionist, to the effect that the record fails to establish that innocent defendants have been executed in the past. But this doesn't mean, as Koch implies, that it hasn't happened. All Bedau was saying was that doubts concerning executed prisoners' guilt are almost never resolved. Bedau is at work now on an effort to determine how many wrongful death sentences may have been imposed: his list of murder convictions since 1900 in which the state eventually *admitted* error is some 400 cases long. Of course, very few of these cases involved actual executions: the mistakes that Bedau documents were uncovered precisely because the prisoner was alive and able to fight for his vindication. The cases where someone is executed are the very cases in which we're least likely to learn that we got the wrong man.

9   I don't claim that executions of entirely innocent people will occur very often. But they will occur. And other sorts of mistakes already have. Roosevelt Green was executed in Georgia two days before J. C. Shaw. Green and an accomplice kidnapped a young woman. Green swore that his companion shot her to death after Green had left, and that he knew nothing about the murder. Green's claim was supported by a statement that his accomplice made to a witness after the crime. The jury never resolved whether Green was telling the truth, and when he tried to take a polygraph examination a few days before his scheduled execution, the state of Georgia refused to allow the examiner into the prison. As the pressure for symbolic retribution mounts, the courts, like the public, are losing patience with such details. Green was electrocuted on January 9, while members of the Ku Klux Klan rallied outside the prison.

10   Then there is another sort of arbitrariness that happens all the time. Last October, Louisiana executed a man named Ernest Knighton. Knighton had killed a gas station owner during a robbery. Like any murder, this was a terrible crime. But it was not premeditated, and is the sort of crime that very rarely results in a death sentence. Why was Knighton electrocuted when almost everyone else who committed the same offense was not? Was it because he was black? Was it because his victim and all 12 members of the jury that sentenced him were white? Was it because Knighton's court-appointed lawyer presented no evidence on his behalf at his sentence hearing? Or maybe there's no reason except bad luck. One thing is clear: Ernest Knighton was picked out to die the way a fisherman takes a cricket out of a bait jar. No one cares which cricket gets impaled on the hook.

11   Not every prisoner executed recently was chosen that randomly. But many were. And having selected these men so casually, so blindly, the death penalty system asks us to accept that the purpose of killing each of them is to affirm the sanctity of human life.

12   The death penalty states are also learning that the death penalty is easier to advocate than it is to administer. In Florida, where executions have become almost routine, the governor reports that nearly a third of his time is spent reviewing the clemency requests of condemned prisoners. The Florida Supreme Court is hopelessly backlogged with death cases. Some have taken five years to decide, and the rest of the Court's work waits in line behind the death appeals. Florida's death row currently holds more than 230 prisoners. State officials are reportedly considering building a special "death prison" devoted entirely to the isolation and electrocution of the condemned. The state is also considering the

creation of a special public defender unit that will do nothing else but handle death penalty appeals. The death penalty, in short, is spawning death agencies.

13   And what is Florida getting for all of this? The state went through almost all of 1983 without executing anyone: its rate of intentional homicide declined by 17 percent. Last year [1984] Florida executed eight people—the most of any state, and the sixth highest total for any year since Florida started electrocuting people back in 1924. Elsewhere in the U.S. last year, the homicide rate continued to decline. But in Florida, it actually rose by 5.1 percent.

14   But these are just the tiresome facts. The electric chair has been a centerpiece of each of Koch's recent political campaigns, and he knows better than anyone how little the facts have to do with the public's support for capital punishment. What really fuels the death penalty is the justifiable frustration and rage of people who see that the government is not coping with violent crime. So what if the death penalty doesn't work? At least it gives us the satisfaction of knowing that we got one or two of the sons of bitches.

15   Perhaps we want retribution on the flesh and bone of a handful of convicted murderers so badly that we're willing to close our eyes to all of the demoralization and danger that come with it. A lot of politicians think so, and they may be right. But if they are, then let's at least look honestly at what we're doing. This lottery of death both comes from and encourages an attitude toward human life that is not reverent, but reckless.

16   And that is why the mayor is dead wrong when he confuses such fury with justice. He suggests that we trivialize murder unless we kill murderers. By that logic, we also trivialize rape unless we sodomize rapists. The sin of Kitty Genovese's neighbors wasn't that they failed to stab her attacker to death. Justice does demand that murderers be punished. And common sense demands that society be protected from them. But neither justice nor self-preservation demands that we kill men whom we have already imprisoned.

17'   The electric chair in which J. C. Shaw died earlier this year was built in 1912 at the suggestion of South Carolina's governor at the time, Cole Blease. Governor Blease's other criminal justice initiative was an impassioned crusade in favor of lynch law. Any lesser response, the governor insisted, trivialized the loathsome crimes of interracial rape and murder. In 1912 a lot of people agreed with Governor Blease that a proper regard for justice required both lynching and the electric chair. Eventually we are going to learn that justice requires neither.

Topics for Discussion and Writing

1. In paragraph 7 Bruck cites the case of Lenell Jeter in order to show that "the system is quite capable of making the very worst sort of mistake." How relevant, and how convincing, do you find this example?

2. In paragraph 8 Bruck says that of the murder cases in which the state admitted error, "very few . . . involved actual executions." How many do you suppose is "very few?" Why do you think Bruck does not cite the exact number?

3. What precautions, if any, does Bruck take, in the essay, to indicate that he is not soft on crime? Do you regard him as soft on crime? Why, or why not?

4. Bruck argues in paragraphs 10 and 11 that some of the people executed are, in effect, randomly selected from the group of murderers. Do you find paragraph 10 in itself convincing? And, if so, do you take it as a strong argument against the death penalty? If not, why not?

5. Evaluate Bruck's final paragraph as an argument and as a final paragraph.

6. Bruck's article is intended as a refutation of Koch's. Which of Koch's arguments, if any, does Bruck not face?

Tipper Gore
Curbing the Sexploitation Industry

Tipper Gore, cofounder of the Parents' Music Resource Center, is the author of a book about violence and obscenity in the arts. Her husband is the vice president of the United States.

1   I can't even count the times in the last three years, since I began to express my concern about violence and sexuality in rock music, that I have been called a prude, a censor, a music hater, even a book burner. So let me be perfectly clear: I detest censorship. I'm not advocating censorship but rather a candid and vigorous debate about the dangers posed for our children by what I call the "sexploitation industry."

2   We don't need to put a childproof cap on the world, but we do need to remind the nation that children live in it, too, and deserve respect and sensitive treatment.

3   When I launched this campaign in 1985 . . . I went to the source of the problem, sharing my concerns and proposals with the entertainment industry. Many producers were sympathetic. Some cooperated with my efforts. But others have been overtly hostile, accusing me of censorship and suggesting, unfairly, that my motives are political. This resistance and hostility has convinced me of the need for a two-pronged campaign, with equal effort from the entertainment industry and concerned parents. Entertainment producers must take the first step, by labeling sexually explicit material.

4   But the industry cannot be expected to solve the problem on its own. Parents should encourage producers to cooperate and praise them when they do. Producers need to know that parents are aware of the issue and are reading their advisory labels. Above all, they need to know that somebody out there cares, that the community at large is not apathetic about the deep and lasting damage being done to our children.

5   What's at issue is not the occasional sexy rock lyric. What troubles—indeed, outrages—me is far more vicious: a celebration of the most gruesome violence, coupled with the explicit message that sado-masochism is the essence of sex. We're surrounded by examples—in rock lyrics, on television, at the movies and in rental videos. One major TV network recently aired a preview of a soap opera rape scene during a morning game show.

6   The newest craze in horror movies is something called the "teen slasher" film, and it typically depicts the killing, torture and sexual mutilation of women in sickening detail. Several rock groups now simulate sexual torture and murder during live performances. Others titillate youthful audiences with strippers confined in cages on stage and with half-naked dancers, who often act out sex with band members. Sexual brutality has become the common currency of America's youth culture and with it the pervasive degradation of women.

7   Why is this graphic violence dangerous? It's especially damaging for young children because they lack the moral judgment of adults. Many children are only dimly aware of the consequences of their actions, and, as parents know, they are excellent mimics. They often imitate violence they see on TV, without necessarily understanding what they are doing or what the consequences might be. One 5-year-old boy from Boston recently got up from watching a teen-slasher film and stabbed a 2-year-old girl with a butcher knife. He didn't mean to kill her (and luckily he did not). He was just imitating the man in the video.

8   Nor does the danger end as children grow older. National health officials tell us that children younger than teen-agers are apt to react to excessive violence with suicide, satanism, drug and alcohol abuse. Even grown-ups are not immune. One series of studies by researchers at the University of Wisconsin found that men exposed to films in which women are beaten, butchered, maimed and raped were significantly desensitized to the violence. Not only did they express less sympathy for the victims, they even approved of lesser penalties in hypothetical rape trials.

9   Sado-masochistic pornography is a kind of poison. Like most poisons, it probably cannot be totally eliminated, but it certainly could be labeled for what it is and be kept away from those who are most vulnerable. The largest record companies have agreed to this—in principle at least. In November 1985, the Recording Industry Association of America adopted my proposal to alert parents by having producers either put warning labels on records with explicitly sexual lyrics or display the lyrics on the outside of the record jackets. Since then, some

companies have complied in good faith, although others have not complied at all.

10   This is where we parents must step in. We must let the industry know we're angry. We must press for uniform voluntary compliance with labeling guidelines. And we must take an active interest at home in what our children are watching and listening to. After all, we can hardly expect that the labels or printed lyrics alone will discourage young consumers.

11   Some parents may want to write to the record companies. Others can give their support to groups like the Parent Teacher Association, which have endorsed the labeling idea. All of us can use our purchasing power. We have more power than we think, and we must use it. For the sake of our children, we simply can't afford to slip back into apathy.

12   My concern for the health and welfare of children has nothing to do with politics: It is addressed to conservatives and liberals alike. Some civil libertarians believe it is wrong even to raise these questions—just as some conservatives believe that the Government should police popular American culture. I reject both these views. I have no desire to restrain artists or cast a "chill" over popular culture. But I believe parents have First Amendment rights, too.

13   The fate of the family, the dignity of women, the mental health of children— these concerns belong to everyone. We must protect our children with choice, not censorship. Let's start working in our communities to forge a moral consensus for the 1990s. Children need our help, and we must summon the courage to examine the culture that shapes their lives.

Topics for Discussion and Writing

1. Analyze and evaluate Gore's opening paragraph.

2. Gore says she is not advocating censorship. In a sentence or two state what she *is* advocating. If you agree with her position, what can you add to it? If you disagree, what are the grounds for your disagreement?

3. Consider one or two songs of a singer you admire. Do you find the song offensive in any way? If so, explain. If not, explain why parents should not be distressed by the music of the person you have selected.

4. Gore concentrates on rock lyrics, movies, and soap operas. Where else in our society are we given images of violence and of the degradation of women? Do you think that parents can protect their children from such images? If so, how?

Derek Bok

Protecting Freedom of Expression on the Campus

Derek Bok was born in 1930 in Bryn Mawr, Pennsylvania, and was educated at Stanford and Harvard, where he received a law degree. He taught law at Harvard, then served as dean of the law school. From 1971 to 1991 he held the office of president of Harvard. This essay, published in The Boston Globe, *was prompted by the display of Confederate flags hung from the window of a dormitory room.*

1   For several years, universities have been struggling with the problem of trying to reconcile the rights of free speech with the desire to avoid racial tension. In recent weeks, such a controversy has sprung up at Harvard. Two students hung Confederate flags in public view, upsetting students who equate the Confederacy with slavery. A third student tried to protest the flags by displaying a swastika.

2   These incidents have provoked much discussion and disagreement. Some students have urged that Harvard require the removal of symbols that offend many members of the community. Others reply that such symbols are a form of free speech and should be protected.

3   Different universities have resolved similar conflicts in different ways. Some have enacted codes to protect their communities from forms of speech that are deemed to be insensitive to the feelings of other groups. Some have refused to impose such restrictions.

4   It is important to distinguish between the appropriateness of such communications and their status under the First Amendment. The fact that speech is protected by the First Amendment does not necessarily mean that it is right, proper, or civil. I am sure that the vast majority of Harvard students believe that hanging a Confederate flag in public view—or displaying a swastika in response—is insensitive and unwise because any satisfaction it gives to the students who display these symbols is far outweighed by the discomfort it causes to many others.

5   I share this view and regret that the students involved saw fit to behave in this fashion. Whether or not they merely wished to manifest their pride in the South—or to demonstrate the insensitivity of hanging Confederate flags by mounting another offensive symbol in return—they must have known that they would upset many fellow students and ignore the decent regard for the feelings of others so essential to building and preserving a strong and harmonious community.

6   To disapprove of a particular form of communication, however, is not enough to justify prohibiting it. We are faced with a clear example of the conflict

between our commitment to free speech and our desire to foster a community founded on mutual respect. Our society has wrestled with this problem for many years. Interpreting the First Amendment, the Supreme Court has clearly struck the balance in favor of free speech.

7   While communities do have the right to regulate speech in order to uphold aesthetic standards (avoiding defacement of buildings) or to protect the public from disturbing noise, rules of this kind must be applied across the board and cannot be enforced selectively to prohibit certain kinds of messages but not others.

8   Under the Supreme Court's rulings, as I read them, the display of swastikas or Confederate flags clearly falls within the protection of the free-speech clause of the First Amendment and cannot be forbidden simply because it offends the feelings of many members of the community. These rulings apply to all agencies of government, including public universities.

9   Although it is unclear to what extent the First Amendment is enforceable against private institutions, I have difficulty understanding why a university such as Harvard should have less free speech than the surrounding society—or than a public university.

10   One reason why the power of censorship is so dangerous is that it is extremely difficult to decide when a particular communication is offensive enough to warrant prohibition or to weigh the degree of offensiveness against the potential value of the communication. If we begin to forbid flags, it is only a short step to prohibiting offensive speakers.

11   I suspect that no community will become humane and caring by restricting what its members can say. The worst offenders will simply find other ways to irritate and insult.

12   In addition, once we start to declare certain things "offensive," with all the excitement and attention that will follow, I fear that much ingenuity will be exerted trying to test the limits, much time will be expanded trying to draw tenuous distinctions, and the resulting publicity will eventually attract more attention to the offensive material than would ever have occurred otherwise.

13   Rather than prohibit such communications, with all the resulting risks, it would be better to ignore them, since students would then have little reason to create such displays and would soon abandon them. If this response is not possible—and one can understand why—the wisest course is to speak with those who perform insensitive acts and try to help them understand the effects of their actions on others.

14   Appropriate officials and faculty members should take the lead, as the Harvard House Masters have already done in this case. In talking with students, they should seek to educate and persuade, rather than resort to ridicule or intimidation, recognizing that only persuasion is likely to produce a lasting, beneficial effect. Through such effects, I believe that we act in the manner most

consistent with our ideals as an educational institution and most calculated to help us create a truly understanding, supportive community.

Topics for Discussion and Writing

1. In paragraph 8 Bok argues that "the display of swastikas or Confederate flags clearly falls within the free-speech clause of the First Amendment and cannot be forbidden simply because it offends the feelings of many members of the community." Suppose someone replied thus: "The display of swastikas or of Confederate flags—symbols loaded with meaning—is, to a Jew or an African-American, at least equivalent to a slap in the face. Such a display is, in short, an act of violence." What would you reply, and how would your support your response?

2. Do you find Bok persuasive? Support your answer with evidence about the points of his argument and his techniques of argument.

3. What rules, if any, does your school have concerning limitations of speech? What rules, if any, would you propose?

Part Three

Special Assignments, Special Forms

Chapter 14

Outlining and Summarizing

Outlining

When you write an outline, you do pretty much what artists do whey they draw an outline: you give, without detail and shading, the general shape of your subject.

An outline is a kind of blueprint, a diagram showing the arrangement of the parts. It is, then, essentially an analysis of your essay, a classification of its parts. Not all writers use outlines, but those who use them report that an outline helps to make clear to them, before or while they labor through a first draft, what their thesis is, what the main points are, and what the subordinate points are. When the outline is drawn, they have a guide that will help them subordinate what is subordinate, and they can easily see if development from part to part is clear, consistent, and reasonable.

An outline drafted before you write, however, is necessarily tentative. Don't assume that once you have constructed an outline your plan is fixed. If, as you begin to write, previously neglected points come to mind, or if you see that in any way the outline is unsatisfactory, revise or scrap the outline. One other caution: an outline does not indicate connections. In your essay be sure to use transitions like "equally important," "less important but still worth mentioning," and "on the other hand" to make clear the relationships between your points.

Scratch Outline

The simplest outline is a *scratch outline,* half a dozen phrases jotted down, revised, rearranged, listing the topics to be covered in the most effective and logical order. In the example shown here phrases serve as milestones rather than as a road map. Most writers do at least this much.

> travel common in blues--
> disappointed lover
> travel to a job
> from the South
> fantasy travel
> ~~back to the South~~
> life is a trip
> ~~my first trip out of the state~~
> jail

Paragraph Outline

A *paragraph outline* is more developed. It begins with a sentence or a phrase, stating the thesis—this will ensure that you know where you are going—and then it gives the topic sentence (or a phrase summarizing the topic idea) of each paragraph. Thus a paragraph outline of Jeff Greenfield's "Columbo Knows the Butler Didn't Do It" (page 193) might begin like this:

Thesis: *Columbo* is popular because it shows a privileged, undeserving elite brought down by a fellow like us.

i. *Columbo* is popular.

ii. Its popularity is largely due to its hostility toward a social and economic elite.

iii. The killers are all rich and white.

iv. Their lives are privileged.

And so on, one roman numeral for each remaining paragraph. A paragraph outline has its uses, especially for papers under, say, a thousand words; it can help you to write unified paragraphs, and it can help you to write a reasonably organized essay. But after you write your essay, check to see if your paragraphs really are developments of what you assert to be the topic sentences, and check to see if you have made the organization clear to the reader, chiefly by means of transitional words and phrases (see pages 62–64). If your essay departs from your outline, the departures should be improvements.

As this last point suggests, your first paragraph outline, worked out after some preliminary thinking, should be a guide, not a straitjacket. As you jot down what you think may be your topic sentences, you will probably find that the jottings help you to get further ideas, but once you draft your essay you may find that the outline has served its initial purpose and has been superseded by a better organization than you had originally imagined. Of course, you should then sketch a new outline, one that corresponds to your draft, to make sure that the pattern of the essay as it now stands really is more effective than the earlier pattern.

Formal Outline

For longer papers, such as a research paper (usually at least eight pages of double-spaced typing), a more complicated outline is usually needed. The *formal outline* shows relationships, distinguishing between major parts of the essay and subordinate parts. Major parts are indicated by capital roman numerals. The parts should clearly bear on the thesis. Chief divisions within a major part are indicated by indented capital letters. Subdivisions within these divisions are indicated by arabic numerals, further indented. Smaller subdivisions are indicated by lowercase letters, indented still further. Still smaller subdivisions—although they are rarely needed, because they are apt to provide too much detail for an outline—are indicated by small roman numerals, again indented.

The point of indenting is to make the relationship among the parts visibly clear to a reader. If you use I, II, and III, you are identifying three major points that are at least roughly equal. Under point I, A and B are parts roughly equal to each other, and so on. The outline is a sort of table of contents.

Note that you cannot have a single subdivision. In the example that follows, part I is divided into parts A and B; it cannot have only a part A. Similarly, part B cannot be "divided" into 1 without there being a 2. In effect, you can't say, as a naturalist did say, "The snakes in this district may be divided into one species—the venomous." If you have a single subdivision, eliminate it and work the material into the previous heading.

Here is a formal outline of Greenfield's "Columbo." Other versions are, of course, possible. In fact, in order to illustrate the form of divisions and subdivisions, we have written a much fuller outline than is usual for such a short essay. We have also not hesitated to mix sentences and phrases, though some authorities require that an outline use only one form or the other.

Thesis: *Columbo* is popular because it shows the undeserving rich brought low by a member of the working class.

   I. Popularity of *Columbo*
       A. What it is *not* due to

    1. Acting

    2. Clever detection of surprising criminal plot

  B. What it is due to

    1. Hostility to privileged elite

    2. Columbo is poor and shoddy.

    3. The high are brought low.

      a. No black (minority) villains

      b. The villains live far above us.

II. The hero

  A. Physical appearance

    1. Dress

    2. Hair, beard

  B. Manner

  C. Success as an investigator

    1. Adversaries mistakenly treat him as negligible.

      a. They assume his lack of wealth indicates lack of intelligence.

      b. They learn too late.

    2. Columbo understands the elite.

      a. They are not superior mentally or in diligence.

      b. They are in a shaky position.

III. Our satisfaction with the program

  A. The villains do not deserve their privileges.

  B. Villains are undone by a man in the street.

  C. We look forward to an episode when Columbo visits the most privileged house.

There is, of course, no evidence that Greenfield wrote an outline before he wrote his essay. But he may have roughed out something along these lines, thereby providing himself with a ground plan or a road map. And while he looked at it he may have readjusted a few parts to give more emphasis here (changing a subdivision into a major division) or to establish a more reasonable connection there (say, reversing A and B in one of the parts).

Even if you don't write from an outline, when you complete your final draft you ought to be able to outline it—you ought to be able to sketch its parts. If you have trouble outlining the draft, your reader will certainly have trouble following your ideas. Even a paragraph outline made from what you hope is your final draft may help to reveal disproportion or faulty organization (for example, an anticlimactic arrangement of the material) that you can remedy before you write your final copy.

Summarizing

The ability to write an accurate summary (abridgment, condensation) is central to much academic work: for taking notes on reading, and for writing essay examinations, laboratory reports, book reviews, and other informative and analytical essays.

The need to write summaries continues in professional life. Scientists usually begin a scientific paper with an abstract, lawyers write briefs (which are, as the name implies, documents that briefly set forth all the facts and points of law pertinent to a case), and business executives must constantly reduce long memoranda and reports to their essential points. In short, the ability to write summaries is an essential skill to acquire and to practice.

What a Summary Is

Writing a summary requires that you analyze the text you are summarizing, separating out the main points from the examples and details that support these points.

Here are a few principles that govern summaries.

1. A summary is much briefer than the original. It is not a paraphrase—a word-by-word translation of someone's words into your own. A summary is rarely longer than one-fourth the original, and often is much briefer. An entire essay may be summarized in a sentence or two.

2. A summary usually omits almost all the concrete details of the original, presenting only the main points of the original.

3. A summary is accurate; it has no value if it misrepresents the point of the original.

4. The writer of a summary need not state the points in the same order as that of the original. If the writer of an essay has delayed revealing the main point until the end of the essay, the summary usually rearranges the order, stating the main point first. Occasionally, when the original author presents an argument in a disorderly or confusing sequence, a summary clarifies the argument by changing the order of statements.

5. A summary normally is written in the present tense because whether the author wrote the piece last year or a hundred years ago, we assume that the piece speaks to us today.

Here is a summary of Barnet and Stubbs on "summary":

A summary is a condensation or abridgment. Its chief characteristics are: (1) it is rarely more than one-fourth as long as the original; (2) its brevity is achieved by leaving out most of the details of the original; (3) it is accurate; (4) it may rearrange the organization of the original, especially if rearrangement makes things clearer; (5) it is normally phrased in the present tense.

How to Write a Summary

With the text you intend to summarize before you—let's say a chapter of a book, or an essay—get ready to take notes, on your computer or on a pad of lined paper. Read the text quickly to get the gist of it, then begin rereading, slowly and thoughtfully.

On rereading, jot down, after reading each paragraph, a sentence giving the main point the paragraph makes, leaving out the details and examples that support the point. A very long paragraph may require two sentences; a series of short paragraphs, each illustrating the same point, may require only one sentence. One sentence per paragraph is a rule of thumb.

Here is a student's paragraph-by-paragraph summary of Philip Roth's "The Newark Public Library" (page 10):

1. If the City Council shuts down the Newark public library will there be looting, sniping, etc.?

2. I hope not; I hope there is respect for Law and Order, even if there is none for thoughtfulness and pleasure.

3. When I was a child in Newark, the knowledge that the books belonged to the public was comforting to me, and it also civilized me by developing in me a sense of my responsibility as a citizen.

4. The library, quiet and tidy, provided a lesson in order, fostering self-restraint and also self-confidence.

5. The City Council thinks it is solving a fiscal problem, but its solution—an insult to the community—may be very costly in frustration, cynicism, and rage.

When you have written your sentence summarizing the last paragraph, you may have done enough if the summary is intended for your own private use—for example, if it is to help you review for an examination. But if you are going to use it as the basis of a summary within an essay you are writing, you will probably want to reshape it. In an essay of your own, you will seldom want to include a summary longer than three or four sentences, so your job will be to reduce and combine the sentences you have jotted down. Indeed, you may even want to reduce the summary to a single sentence. One student summarized Roth's essay thus:

Philip Roth, in his article, "Reflections on the Death of a Library," argues that the closing of the libraries will be a costly mistake, and that the action will be an insult to the citizens of Newark.

Notice that, since the summary is intended for a reader, the student has introduced the summary with Roth's name and the title of the article.

A writer who wants to devote a little more space to summarizing Roth's essay might come up with this summary:

> Roth, in his article, "Reflections on the Death of a Library," explains in some detail how, when he was a child, the public library gave him confidence and a sense of responsibility. In its orderliness, and in its demand for quiet, it exerted a civilizing effect. The City Council may think that by shutting down the library it is solving a fiscal problem, but it is unaware of the rage that this insult will generate in the citizens (now, mostly black) in Newark.

If you think that your reader needs a summary, you'll also have to think about how long—that is, how detailed—the summary should be. Your awareness of your reader's needs as well as your own purpose will then guide you as you draw upon your summaries of the paragraphs.

Topics for Writing

1. Summarize the following paragraph in one or two sentences:

No society, whether human or animal, can exist without communication. Thoughts, desires, appetites, orders—these have to be conveyed from one brain to another, and they can rarely be conveyed directly. Only with telepathy do we find mind speaking straight to mind, without the intermediacy of signs, and this technique is still strange enough to seem a music-hall trick or a property of science fiction. The vast majority of sentient beings—men, women, cats, dogs, bees, horses—have to rely on signals, symbols of what we think and feel and want, and these signals can assume a vast variety of forms. There is, indeed, hardly any limit to the material devices we can use to express what is in our minds: we can wave our hands, screw up our faces, shrug our shoulders, write poems, write on walls, carve signs out of stone or wood, mould signs with clay or butter, scrawl sky-signs with an aircraft, semaphore, heliograph, telephone, run a pirate radio transmitter, stick pins in dolls. A dog will scratch at a door if it wants to be let in; a cat will mew for milk; a hostess will ring a bell for the course to be changed; a pub-customer will rap with a coin for service; a wolf will whistle; the people in the flat upstairs will bang with a stick if our party is too noisy. One can fill pages with such examples, bringing in the language of flowers and the signaling devices of honey-bees, but one will always end up with human speech as the most subtle, comprehensive, and exact system of communication we possess.

—ANTHONY BURGESS

2. Choose a current editorial and summarize it in about one-fourth its number of words. Include a copy of the editorial with your summary.

3. Using the outline of "Columbo Knows the Butler Didn't Do It" (pages 300–01) and the essay itself (pages 300–01), write a summary of the essay, in about 250 words.

Chapter 15

The Research Essay

Knowledge is of two kinds. We know a subject ourselves, or we know where we can find information upon it.

—SAMUEL JOHNSON, IN A CONVERSATION IN 1775

What Research Is

Research consists of collecting evidence to develop and support ideas. The evidence usually includes the opinions of others, reported in such sources as books, articles, lectures, and interviews. A research paper is an essay based in part on such evidence. It is the kind of paper that you will write in most of your college courses.

In this chapter we explain how to find and evaluate evidence, take useful notes, and acknowledge the work of others. It is in the careful acknowledgment of sources, explained on pages 323–26, that scholarly writing, for which writing research papers prepares you, may differ from other kinds of writing. When you acknowledge sources, giving credit where credit is due for your use of the ideas and words of others, you do two things:

1. You provide a kind of road map for the researcher who comes after you and who may want to retrace some of your steps.
2. You publicly thank those who have helped you on your way.

There are some conventions to learn about the form of acknowledgments, and we'll offer some rules to guide you. But the rules make sense only when you bear in mind the reasons for acknowledgment: courtesy to your readers on the one hand and to your sources on the other.

Primary and Secondary Materials

The materials of most research can be conveniently divided into two categories, primary and secondary. The primary materials or sources are the real subject of study; the secondary materials are critical and historical accounts already written about these primary materials. For example, if you want to know whether Shakespeare's attitude toward Julius Caesar was highly traditional or highly original, or a little of each, you would read *Julius Caesar,* other Elizabethan writings about Caesar, and Roman writings known to the Elizabethans; and in addition to these primary materials you would also read secondary material such as modern books on Shakespeare and on Elizabethan attitudes toward Rome and toward monarchs.

Similarly, the primary material for a paper on a novel by Kate Chopin, *The Awakening* (1899), is of course the novel itself; the secondary material consists of such things as biographies of Chopin and critical essays on the novel. But the line between these two kinds of sources is not always sharp. For example, if you are concerned with the degree to which *The Awakening* is autobiographical, primary materials include not only the novel and also Chopin's comments on her writing but perhaps also the comments of people who knew her. Thus the essays—based on interviews with Chopin—that two of her friends published in newspapers probably can be regarded as primary material because they were contemporary with the novel and because they give direct access to Chopin's views, although, again, the writings of later commentators constitute secondary material.

From Subject to Thesis

First, a subject. No subject is unsuitable—from sports, war, art, and dreams to foods and books. As G. K. Chesterton said, "There is no such thing on earth as an uninteresting subject; the only thing that can exist is an uninterested person." Let's say that you've read Maxine Hong Kingston's *The Woman Warrior* (1976), and you have become interested in Confucian or Buddhist ideas that inform the narrative (your potential topic). Or you have read Chopin's *The Awakening*. One topic, suggested perhaps by your instructor or by an introduction to the book, concerns the critical reception of the novel: How did the first reviewers of *The Awakening* regard it? Or you might be interested in what some recent critics say about it, especially about the significance of the ending.

Let's assume that you arrive at the library with a topic (or two or three possible topics) in mind. We have already mentioned topics based on books by Kingston and Chopin, but other kinds of topics are possible. In a course in American government you may have heard something about the internment, during World War II, of Japanese-Americans who lived in the Pacific states, and you think you would like to know more about it. What were the legal grounds for the action? How did the Japanese-Americans react? How did other Americans react? (For instance, did the press denounce the government's action?) What sort of compensation, if any, has been made to those who were imprisoned?

You want to do some reading on a topic, but exactly what you will focus on, and exactly what your *thesis* or point of view will be, you may not know until you do some investigating. To take the issue of the Japanese-Americans: You may find, as you study the event, that you will focus on the matter of compensation, and your thesis (again, something that develops as you study the material) may be that although the compensation was unduly delayed, it was in other respects reasonable. But how do you find the relevant material?

Finding the Material

Although most research papers that students write are largely based on materials they find in libraries, research can draw also on other sources. Don't neglect the expertise that friends can provide in conversation, or the material that you can garner from lectures and interviews. Field trips, too, may be invaluable for some topics, for example a visit to a day-care center or to a political convention. If you are writing about the confinement of the Japanese-Americans, it may well be that you can interview some of the people who were sent to the camps—they may be your grandparents, or neighbors, or you may find that some of your classmates are descended from such people and can tell you what their parents and grandparents told them. Interviews and field trips are the equivalent of primary sources found in the library.

We will, however, concentrate on ways of getting familiar with material in the library. You may happen already to know of some titles that are relevant to your topic. For instance, the textbook for your government course may cite a study of the relocation of the Japanese-Americans, or the edition you are using of Chopin's *The Awakening* may recommend some critical essays on the book.

Getting Started

If you know very little about the topic—let's say you know nothing or almost nothing about Confucianism, but Maxine Hong Kingston's *The Woman Warrior* has made you want to know something about it—it's not a bad idea to begin with an encyclopedia:

Encyclopedia Americana, or

Encyclopaedia Britannica

The *Americana* uses an alphabetic arrangement: *aardvark* is in the first volume, *zoo* is in the next-to-last (the last volume is an index). If you don't find an entry in the appropriate place, check the index, where you probably *will* find the word, with a reference to see some related entry. But the organization of the thirty volumes of the *Britannica* requires a brief explanation. The set is divided into three parts: (1) *Micropaedia: Ready Reference,* comprising twelve volumes and containing some eighty-two thousand short entries (few are longer than 750 words); (2) *Macropaedia: Knowledge in Depth,* seventeen volumes containing 681 long articles, many of which are equivalent in length to short books; (3) *Propaedia: Outline of Knowledge,* an outline or table of contents for the other volumes. If, for instance, you want to get a very quick introduction to Confucianism, begin with the "ready reference" entry, and then follow the suggested references.

The *Americana* and the *Britannica* are probably the best-known general encyclopedias, but there are others, and there are also hundreds of invaluable specialized encyclopedias, such as *Encyclopedia of Anthropology, Encyclopedia of Crime and Justice, Encyclopedia of Psychology, Encyclopedia of Religion* (a good place to go for an introduction to Confucianism), and *Kodansha Encyclopedia of Japan.* Most articles in encyclopedias include cross-references to other articles within the encyclopedia, and often they also include suggestions for further reading. Thus, if in *Kodansha Encyclopedia of Japan* you look up "Japanese-Americans," you will find not only an entry entitled "Japanese-Americans, wartime relocation of," but also a cross-reference to another article, "War Relocation Authority," and you will also find recommended readings.

How can you find the appropriate encyclopedia or other reference work that may give you the background that you need for a start? Once you are in the library, consider making your first stop at the catalog to find the call number for

First Stop: The Master Index to Subject Encyclopedias (1989).

This hefty volume will introduce you to some 40,000 topics contained in 430 specialized encyclopedias, handbooks, and other reference works. Just look for your topic—Confucianism, or Japanese-Americans, or whatever—in the alphabetic list of thousands of topics at the front of the volume (material on AA [Alcoholics Anonymous], aardvarks, Aaron [the Hebrew priest], and so on, down through zebra, zoos, zoology, and zygote), and follow up the references. For instance, among the seventy-five or so entries under "Japanese," you will find three references that sound relevant to the internment, and under "Japanese-American" you will find two more. Your library may well have one or more of the reference works cited, and it may even have most or all of them.

A second useful reference work is

ARBA Guide to Subject Encyclopedias and Dictionaries (1986).

ARBA stands for American Reference Books Annual. This book, with forty-three chapters arranged alphabetically ("Agricultural Sciences," "Anthropology," and so on), reviews hundreds of reference works. The *Guide* is annually updated by *American Reference Books Annual* (1970–), a review of the year's reference books. Each volume reviews dictionaries, encyclopedias, bibliographies, atlases, and comparable reference works. It will almost surely put you on to some short, up-to-date, authoritative discussions of your topic, and these in turn will probably recommend some books.

A third guide to reference books is

Guide to Reference Books. 10th ed., ed. Eugene P. Sheehy (1986)

and a fourth is an updated supplement of the third,

Guide to Reference Books . . . 1985–1990, ed. Robert Balay (1992).

There are also guides to these guides: reference librarians. If you don't know where to turn to find something, turn to the librarian.

The Catalog: On Cards or Computerized

The card catalog has cards arranged alphabetically not only by author and by title but also by subject. If your library has an on-line catalog, which you access by computer terminals (you use a keyboard and a monitor), the catalog will contain the same material but alphabetization won't matter.

Let's say you are interested in food additives, that is, substances added to preserve desirable properties—color, flavor, freshness—or to suppress undesirable properties. You want to do some reading, and you must now find the articles and books. Of course, as you do the reading, your focus may narrow, for instance to the potentially dangerous effects, in various foods, of sodium nitrate, or to the controversy over the effects of saccharin (an artificial sweetener), or you may concentrate on so-called enriched bread, which is first robbed of many nutrients by refining and bleaching the four and is then enriched by the addition of some of the nutrients in synthetic form. Exactly what you will focus on, and exactly what your *thesis* or point of view will be, you may not know until you do some more reading. But how do you find the relevant material?

The catalog has entries arranged alphabetically not only by author and by title but also by subject. It probably won't have a subject heading for "frankfurter," but it will have one for "food," followed by entries listing books on this topic. And on the "food" card or entry on the monitor will be a note telling you of relevant subjects to consult. In fact, even before you look at the catalog you can know what subject headings it contains by checking one of two books: *Sears List of Subject Headings* (for libraries that use the Dewey decimal system of arranging books) and *Library of Congress Subject Headings,* 15th edition (1992). (Because most academic libraries use the Library of Congress system, the second of these is probably the book you'll use.) If you look for "food" in *Subject Headings,* you will find two pages of listings, including cross references such as "SA [= see also] Animal Food." Among the subject headings that sound relevant are Bacteriology, Food Contamination, and Preservation. Notice also the abbreviations UF (used for), BT (broader topic), RT (related topic), and NT (narrower topic), referring to other headings you may want to look at. If you make use of some of these subject headings, you will probably find that the library has a fair amount of material on your topic.

```
FOOD

    See also

COOKERY
DIET
DIETARIES
FARM PRODUCE
FRUIT
GASTRONOMY
GRAIN
MARKETS
MEAT
NUTRITION
POULTRY                      see next card
```

Whether you went to *Subject Headings* or to the "food" card (or entry on the monitor), you have now gathered a number of subject headings that seem relevant. With this information you can locate useful books—even though you began without knowing the author or title of even one book—simply by turning to the subject heading in the card file or monitor, and writing down the information on the books filed under that subject. For example, if you look up "Diet," "Nutrition," and "Proteins in Human Nutrition" you will find entries for whatever books the library has on each of these topics. A card for a book listed under the subject is called a *subject card*. Notice, in the illustrated example, the following points:

1. The subject is given at the top of the card.

2. The classification number at the left enables you to find the book in the library.

3. The card gives the author's name, title, and other information, such as the fact that this book includes a bibliography.

4. Below this information there is a list of other subject headings under which this card is filed. By checking these other subject headings (called *tracings* by librarians), you will be able to find additional books that probably are relevant to your research.

An *author card,* that is, a card filed alphabetically under the author's last name, is identical with a subject card except that the subject is not given at the

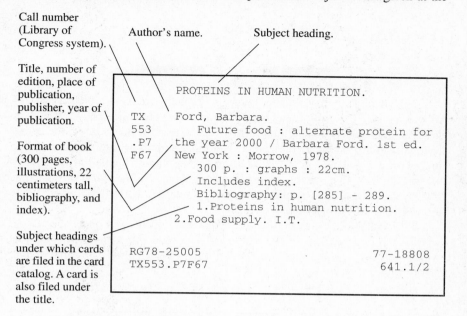

Call number
(Library of
Congress system).

Author's name.   Subject heading.

Title, number of
edition, place of
publication,
publisher, year of
publication.

Format of book
(300 pages,
illustrations, 22
centimeters tall,
bibliography, and
index).

Subject headings
under which cards
are filed in the card
catalog. A card is
also filed under
the title.

```
                    PROTEINS IN HUMAN NUTRITION.

     TX      Ford, Barbara.
     553          Future food : alternate protein for
     .P7     the year 2000 / Barbara Ford. 1st ed.
     F67     New York : Morrow, 1978.
                 300 p. : graphs : 22cm.
                 Includes index.
                 Bibliography: p. [285] - 289.
                 1.Proteins in human nutrition.
             2.Food supply. I.T.

     RG78-25005                           77-18808
     TX553.P7F67                          641.1/2
```

top of the card. If you know the author's name, just look for it in the catalog.

Finally, a *title card* is identical with an author card, except that the title is added to the top of the card and the card is indexed under the first word of the title, or the second word if the first is *A, An,* or *The,* or a foreign equivalent.

A Reminder About On-Line Catalogs

If you are using an on-line catalog, the computer will look up books for you when you command it to search for an author, title, or subject. The monitor will display a record, for each book, that looks similar to the illustrated card in the example shown here and contains the same information about the book.

Three Notes on the Alphabetic Arrangement of the Card Catalog

1. The card catalog is arranged alphabetically from A to Z, of course, but the arrangement is word by word, not letter by letter. This means, for example, that "ion implantation" *precedes* "ionic crystals," because "i-o-n" precedes "i-o-n-i-c." (If the catalog were letter by letter instead of word by word, of course "i-o-n-i-c" would precede "i-o-n-i-m. . . .") Similarly, in the card catalog "folk tales" precedes "folklorists." Here is a short list of cards in the order they are in

the catalog:

Good, Emanual

Good Men and True

Good Old Days

Goodall, Ann

Goodman, Paul

2. Under the author's name, books are usually arranged alphabetically by title, but for highly prolific authors the cards listing the collected works may be grouped before those listing individual works. Cards for books *about* the author follow cards for books *by* the author. Note that authors whose surnames begin *Mc* or *Mac* are all listed—in most libraries—as though spelled *Mac;* authors whose surnames begin with a prefix (for example, *De, Le, Van*) are listed as though the prefixes and surname formed a single word: De Lisle would come after Delano and before Delos.

3. Under the title, remember that books are alphabetized under the *second* word if the first word is *A, An,* or *The,* or a foreign equivalent. Note, too, that words normally abbreviated are spelled out in the catalog: *Doctor Zhivago, Mister Roberts, Saint Joan.*

Scanning Books and Book Reviews

Having checked the card catalog and written down the relevant data (author, title, call number), you can begin to scan the books, or you can postpone looking at the books until you have found some relevant articles in periodicals. For the moment, let's postpone the periodicals.

Put a bunch of books in front of you, and choose one as an introduction. How do you choose one from half a dozen? Partly by its size—choose a thin one—and partly by its quality. Roughly speaking, it should be among the more recent publications, and it should strike you as fair. A pamphlet published by a meat-packers association is desirably thin but you have a hunch that it may be biased. Roger John Williams' *Nutrition in a Nutshell* is published by a well-known commercial press (Doubleday), and it is only 171 pages, but because it was published in 1962 it may not reflect current food chemistry. Though it is rather big (260 pages), Michael Jacobson's *Eater's Digest: The Consumer's Factbook of Food Additives* (Washington: Center for Science in the Public Interest, 1987) probably is about right.

When you have found the book that you think may serve as your introductory study, do the following:

- **Read the preface** in order to get an idea of the author's purpose and outlook.
- **Scan the table of contents** in order to get an idea of the organization and the coverage.

- **Scan the final chapter or the last few pages,** where you may be lucky enough to find a summary.

The index, too, may let you know if the book will suit your purpose, by showing you what topics are covered and how much coverage they get. If the book still seems suitable, scan it.

At this stage it is acceptable to trust your hunches—you are only going to scan the book, not buy it or even read it—but you may want to look up some book reviews to assure yourself that the book has merit. There are two especially useful general indexes to book reviews:

Book Review Digest (published from 1905 onward)

Book Review Index (1965–)

There are also indexes to specialized fields. Given the topic of food additives, you might want to consult, in order to locate reviews in journals,

Business Periodicals Index (1958–)

General Science Index (1978–)

For a list of specialized indexes, see page 18.

Most reviews of books will come out in the same year as the book, or within the next two years. If, for example, a book was published in 1989, look in the 1989 volume of the appropriate index and see what is there. If you want some more reviews, look in 1990 and 1991. Begin with *Book Review Digest,* because it includes excerpts from and synopses of the reviews; if it has your book, the excerpts and synopses may be enough, and you won't have to dig out the reviews themselves. But *Book Review Digest* does not have as broad coverage as the other indexes, and you may have to turn to them for citations, and then to the journals to which they refer you. (*Book Review Digest* covers about 200 periodicals; *Book Review Index* covers about 450.) Read the synopses in *Book Review Digest,* or some reviews in journals, and draw some conclusions about the merit of the book in question. Of course, you cannot assume that every review is fair, but a book that on the whole gets good reviews is probably at least good enough for a start.

By quickly reading such a book (take few or no notes at this stage) you will probably get an overview of your topic, and you will see exactly what part of the topic you wish to pursue.

Finding Bibliographies

Many researchers have published bibliographies, that is, lists of the works they have consulted. Sometimes the bibliographies appear as articles in scholarly journals or as appendices to books, or even as entire books. All of these kinds of bibliographies are listed in *Bibliographic Index,* which is issued three times a year and cumulates in an annual volume. Begin, of course, with the most recent issue, check it for your subject, and then work back for a few years. A recent bibliography will probably offer you as many sources as you will have time to consult.

Finding Periodicals

On some topics, especially recent happenings, there may be few or even no books, but there may well be many articles published in magazines and scholarly journals; you can start thumbing through them at random, but such a procedure is monstrously inefficient. Fortunately, there are indexes to periodicals, so you can quickly find the latest writing (which may be the only writing) on your topic.

These indexes are usually issued several times a year, and then are offered in an annual cumulative volume that supersedes the earlier issues of the year. Some are issued not only in print but are also available on CD-ROM (Compact Disc–Read Only Memory), that is, on compact discs that you insert in a computer drive or select from a menu displayed on computers set up as a network, usually in the reference room. Some libraries have added CD-ROM indexers to their on-line catalogs—again, you select the one you want from the menu list. If you are using CD-ROM, you read the information on a monitor, and you can probably print out the information that you want. Among the most widely used indexes are

Readers' Guide to Periodical Literature (1900–)

InfoTrac (1985–)

Readers' Guide indexes about 200 of the more familiar magazines—such as *Atlantic, Ebony, Nation, Scientific American, Sports Illustrated,* and *Time. InfoTrac* (a CD-ROM system) indexes about a thousand periodicals, including not only the familiar magazines such as those just mentioned, but also some specialized journals.

If you are looking for a piece by, say, the short story writer and novelist Amy Tan, look for it under her name. And when you look under *Tan* you will also find a listing of pieces written *about* her. Similarly, if you want to know something about Confucianism but don't know the names of the authors of any articles, look under *Confucianism* and you will find a listing of current articles. Here is an example; it comes from what at the moment is the current issue of the *Readers' Guide,* November 1993, but of course your library now has more recent issues.

CONFUCIANISM AND CULTURE
Civilization grafting: no culture is an island. Liu Binyan.
Foreign Affairs v72 p19-21 S/O '93
The Islamic-Confucian connection [interview with S. P.
Huntington] N. Gardels. *New Perspectives Quarterly*
v10 p19-23 Summ '93

The first of these citations is to the September/October 1993 issue of a journal called *Foreign Affairs*. The article occupies pages 19–21, and the volume number of the journal is 72.

InfoTrac, a CD-ROM system that searches publications of the last four years, has supplanted *Readers' Guide* on many campuses. The disc is preinstalled in a microcomputer that can be accessed from a computer terminal with a printer, and the instructions are easy to follow. *InfoTrac,* an index to authors and subjects in popular and scholarly magazines and in newspapers, provides access to several database indexes, including the following:

1. *The General Periodical Index,* available in The Academic Library Edition (about 1,100 general and scholarly periodicals) and in The Public Library Edition (about 1,100 popular magazines)

2. *The Academic Index* (400 general-interest publications, all of which are also available in the Academic Library Edition of The General Periodicals Index)

3. *The Magazine Index Plus* (the four most recent years of *The New York Times,* the two most recent months of *The Wall Street Journal,* and 400 popular magazines, all of which are included in The Public Library Edition of The General Periodicals Index)

4. *The National Newspaper Index* (the four most recent years of *The New York Times, The Christian Science Monitor, The Washington Post,* and *The Los Angeles Times*)

5. *LegalTrac* (800 legal publications)

6. *The Government Publications Index* (an index to *Monthly Catalog* of the Government Printing Office)

Another index that you are likely to use is *The New York Times Index* (covering from 1851 to the present). This index, enabling you to locate articles that were published in *The New York Times* newspaper, is especially useful if you are working on a recent public event.

The National Newspaper Index (1979 to the present) indexes articles from five newspapers:

The Christian Science Monitor
The Los Angeles Times
The New York Times

The Wall Street Journal
The Washington Post

Even if your library does not have a file of these newspapers, once you have learned from these indexes the date of an event, you can locate material about it in other newspapers or in weekly magazines such as *Time* or *Newsweek.*

NEXIS, available in larger libraries, is an online database containing the full text of major newspapers as well as many popular and business magazines.

The indexes just mentioned (along with the indexes to book reviews mentioned on page 315) are the ones you are most likely to use, but here are some others that may be valuable, depending on what your topic is:

Accountant's Index (1944–)

America: History and Life (1964–)

Applied Science and Technology Index (1964–)

Art Index (1929–)

Bibliographic Index (1937–)

Biography Index (1947–)

Biological and Agricultural Index (1964–); before 1964 it was known as *Agricultural Index* (1942–64)

Business Periodicals Index (1958–)

Chemical Abstracts (1907–)

Congressional Digest (1921–)

Congressional Quarterly Weekly Reports (1955–); for material on congressional affairs see also PAIS (Public Affairs Information Service)

Dramatic Index (1909–49)

Education Index (1929–); for material on education, see also ERIC

Engineering Index Monthly and Author Index (1906–)

Film Literature Index (1973–)

Historical Abstracts (1955–)

Index to Legal Periodicals (1908–)

International Index to Film Periodicals (1972–)

MLA International Bibliography (1921–); an annual listing of books and scholarly articles on linguistics and on literature in modern languages

Music Index (1949–)

Poole's Index for Periodical Literature (1802–1907)

Psychology Abstracts (1927–)

Public Affairs Information Service Bulletin (1915–)

Whichever indexes you use, begin with the most recent years and work your way back. If you collect the titles of articles published in the last five years you will probably have as much as you can read. These articles will probably incorporate the significant points of earlier writings. But of course it depends on the topic; for instance, if you are writing about the Lindbergh kidnapping, you may have to—and want to—go back fifty or more years before you find a useful body of material.

Caution: Indexes drastically abbreviate the titles of periodicals. Before you put the indexes back on the shelf, be sure to check the key to the abbreviations, usually printed on the inside of the front cover and on the facing page, so that you know the full titles of the periodicals you are looking for.

Taking Bibliographic Notes

Practice and theory differ. In theory, you should write down each citation (whether a book or an article) on a separate three-by-five index card, giving complete information. Our own practice at the start of any research is more shoddy. Instead of carefully recording all of this information from the card catalog (for a book that may be lost) or from an index to periodicals (for a periodical that may not be in the library) we usually jot down the citations of books on one sheet of paper, and of articles on another sheet. Then we see how much of this material is available. When we actually get hold of the material, we make out a card, as illustrated, with the library call number in the upper right-hand corner. True, we sometimes regret our attempted shortcut if we later find that on the sheet we forgot to write the year of the periodical and we must now hunt through indexes again to locate it. We recall the wisdom of the Chinese proverb, "It is foolish to go to bed early to save the candle if the result is twins," but we have never been able to resist economizing at the start.

Caution: Because it is easy to misspell names, turning unfamiliar forms into familiar ones (Barnet into Barnett, Stubbs into Stubbes), it is advisable to *print* the name in block letters, and, having done so, to check your version against the original. Check also to see that the other information—title (and subtitle, if any), place of publication, and date are correctly written on your card.

Reading and Taking Notes

Preliminaries: Index Cards or Word Processor?

Almost all researchers—professionals as well as beginners—find that they end up with some notes that are irrelevant, and, on the other hand, find that when drafting the paper they vaguely remember certain material that they now wish they had taken notes on. Especially in the early stages of one's research, when

TX
553.83
J23

Jacobson, Michael F.
Eater's Digest Washington:
Center for Science in the
Public Interest , 1982

Bibliographic card for a book

Zwerdling, Daniel . "Death for
Dinner," The New York Review,"
21, no. 1 (21 Feb. 1974), 22-24.

Bibliographic card for an article in a periodical

the topic and thesis may still be relatively unfocused, it's hard to know what is noteworthy and what is not. You simply have to flounder a bit.

We cannot overemphasize two points: (1) a certain amount of inefficiency is inevitable (and therefore plenty of time should be allowed), and (2) different people work differently.

Still, we recommend our own practice in reading an article or a chapter of a book. Read it through, without taking notes. By the time you reach the end, you may find it isn't noteworthy. Or you may find a useful summary near the end that will contain most of what you can get from the piece. Or you will find that, having a sense of the whole, you can now quickly reread the piece and take notes on the chief points.

When you take notes, if you are not using a computer, use four-by-six-inch cards, and write on one side only; material on the back of a card is usually neglected when you come to write the paper. Use four-by-six cards because the smaller cards, suitable for bibliographic notes, do not provide enough space for your summaries of useful material.

Instead of taking notes on index cards, some writers use a computer. They then print all of the notes and later scissor them apart, so they can arrange the notes into an appropriate sequence while thinking about the organization of the draft. The trouble, however, is that the notes will not be of uniform size, and so they are cumbersome to handle. Some especially talented (or foolhardy?) writers don't bother to print and scissor the notes, but simply rely on their memory of the notes, and while typing the draft occasionally dip down into the file to retrieve a note. We have never been able to use this system—we have to *see* all of our notes, spread out in front of us, and then arranged into a sequence—but if taking notes on a computer works for you, well, that's the system for you to use.

A Guide to Note Taking

1. **In the upper left corner of the card specify the source in an abbreviated form.** The author's last name, or the name and the first word of the title are usually enough (unless the first word is *A, An,* or *The*).

2. **Write summaries, not paraphrases** (that is, write abridgments rather than restatements, which in fact may be as long as or longer than the original). There is rarely any point to paraphrasing. Generally speaking, either quote exactly (and put the passage in quotation marks, with a notation of the source, including the page number or numbers) or summarize, reducing a page or even an entire article or chapter of a book to a single four-by-six card. Even when you summarize, indicate your source (including the page numbers) on the card, so that you can give appropriate credit in your paper.

3. **Quote sparingly.** Of course in your summary you will sometimes quote a phrase or a sentence—putting it in quotation marks—but quote sparingly. You are not doing stenography; rather you are assimilating knowledge and you are thinking, and so for the most part your source should be digested rather than engorged whole. Thinking now, while taking notes, will also help you later to avoid plagiarism. If, on the other hand, when you take notes you mindlessly copy material at length, later when you are writing the paper you may be tempted to copy it yet again, perhaps without giving credit. Similarly, if you photocopy pages from articles or books, and then merely underline some passages, you probably will not be thinking; you will just be underlining. But if you make a terse summary on a note card you will be forced to think and to find your own words for the idea. Quote directly only those passages that are particularly effective, or crucial, or memorable. In your finished paper these quotations will provide authority and emphasis.

4. **Quote accurately.** After copying a quotation, check your card against the original, correct any misquotation, and then put a checkmark after your quotation to indicate that it is accurate. Verify the page number also, and then put a check on your card, after the page number. If a quotation runs from the

bottom of, say, page 306 to the top of 307, on your card put a distinguishing mark (for instance two parallel vertical lines after the last word of the first page), so that if you later use only part of the quotation, you will know the page on which it appeared.

Use ellipses (three spaced periods) to indicate the omission of any words within a sentence. If the omitted words are at the end of the quoted sentence, put a period immediately at the point where you end the sentence, and then add three spaced periods to indicate the omission. Example:

If the . . . words were at the end of the quoted

sentence, put a period immediately at the end. . . .

Use square brackets to indicate your additions to the quotation. Here is an example.

Here is an [uninteresting] example.

5. *Never* **copy a passage by changing an occasional word,** under the impression that you are thereby putting it into your own words. Notes of this sort may find their way into your paper, your reader will sense a style other than your own, and suspicions of plagiarism may follow. (For a detailed discussion of plagiarism, see pages 323–26).

6. **Write on one side of the card only.** Because when you set out to draft your paper you will probably want to spread out your notes so that you can see all of the material simultaneously, notes on the rear of a card are of little use and they will probably get overlooked. If a note won't fit on one side of a card, continue the note on a second card (and a third, if necessary), and put the appropriate number on each card.

7. **Comment on your notes.** Feel free to jot down your responses to the note. Indeed, consider it your obligation to *think* about the material, evaluating it and using it as a stimulus to further thought. For example, you may want to say "Gold seems to be generalizing from insufficient evidence," or "Corsa made the same point five years earlier"; but make certain that later you will be able to distinguish between these comments and the notes summarizing or quoting your source. A suggestion: surround all comments recording your responses with double parentheses, thus: ((. . .)).

8. **Write a keyword on each card.** In the upper corner of each note card, write a brief key—for example "effect on infants' blood"—so that later you can tell at a glance what is on the card. The sample card shown here summarizes a few pages; notice that it includes a short quotation and records the source. The source is not given in full bibliographic form because the full form is recorded on a bibliography card.

As you work, especially if you are working on a literary or historical topic, you'll of course find yourself returning again and again to the primary materials—and you'll probably find to your surprise that a good deal of the secondary material is unconvincing or even wrong, despite the fact that it is printed in a handsome book. One of the things we learn from research is that not everything in print is true; one of the pleasures we get from research results from this discovery.

> Verrett, pp. 152-154 ✓   botulism argument
>   search for substitute
> p.152 Industry and gov't approved nitrite as color
> fixer. Now shifting ground, saying it prevents
> botulism. Verrett points out "legal snag." New
> approval needed for new use.
> (Thus public hearing and unwanted attention)
>
> p.154 "... the industry--USDA-FDA coalition seems
> firm in its position that there is no substitute for
> nitrate, now or ever. Their posture is misdirected
> at defending nitrites devising ways to keep it
> in food rather than ways to get it out. ✓
>   Verrett and Carper, <u>Eating May Be Hazardous</u>

Acknowledging Sources

Borrowing Without Plagiarizing

As we suggested earlier, respect for your readers and for your sources requires
that you acknowledge your indebtedness for material when

1. you quote directly from a work, or

2. you paraphrase or summarize someone's words (the words of your
   paraphrase or summary are your own, but the points are not), or

3. you appropriate an idea that is not common knowledge.

Let's suppose you are going to make use of William Bascom's comment on
the earliest responses of Europeans to African art:

> The first examples of African art to gain public attention were the
> bronzes and ivories which were brought back to Europe after the sack
> of Benin by a British military expedition in 1897. The superb technol-
> ogy of the Benin bronzes won the praise of experts like Felix von
> Luschan who wrote in 1899, "Cellini himself could not have made bet-
> ter casts, nor anyone else before or since to the present day." Moreover,
> their relatively realistic treatment of human features conformed to the
> prevailing European aesthetic standards. Because of their naturalism
> and technical excellence, it was at first maintained that they had been
> produced by Europeans—a view that was still current when the even
> more realistic bronze heads were discovered at Ife in 1912. The subse-
> quent discovery of new evidence has caused the complete abandonment
> of this theory of European origins of the bronzes of Benin and Ife, both
> of which are cities in Nigeria.

—WILLIAM BASCOM, *AFRICAN ART IN CULTURAL PERSPECTIVE* (NEW
YORK: NORTON, 1973), P. 4

1. Acknowledging a direct quotation. You may want to use some or all of Bascom's words, in which case you will write something like this:

> As William Bascom says, when Europeans first
> encountered Benin and Ife works of art in the late
> nineteenth century, they thought that Europeans had
> produced them, but the discovery of new evidence
> "caused the complete abandonment of this theory of
> European origins of the bronzes of Benin and Ife, both
> of which are cities in Nigeria" (4).

Normally, at the end of a paper a page headed Works Cited will give bibliographic information (author, title, place of publication, name of the publisher, and date of publication) for each work cited within the paper, but of course in a relatively informal paper it may be enough merely to mention, in the body of the paper, the author, title, and page number, without later specifying place of publication, publisher, and date. The point here is not that you must use detailed footnotes but that you must give credit. Not to give credit is to plagiarize, which is a serious breach of the rules governing academic work.

2. Acknowledging a paraphrase or summary. Summaries (abridgments) are usually superior to paraphrases (rewordings, of approximately the same length as the original) because summaries are briefer, but occasionally you may find that you cannot abridge a passage in your source and yet you don't want to quote it word for word—perhaps because it is too technical or because it is poorly written. Even though you are changing some or all of the words, you must give credit to the source because the idea is not yours, nor, probably, is the sequence of the presentation.

Here is an example of a summary:

> William Bascom, in *African Art,* points out that
> the first examples of African art--Benin bronzes and
> ivories--brought to Europe were thought by Europeans
> to be of European origin, because of their naturalism
> and their technical excellence, but evidence was later
> discovered that caused this theory to be abandoned.

Not to give Bascom credit is to plagiarize, even though the words are yours. The offense is just as serious as not acknowledging a direct quotation. And, of course, if you say something like this and do not give credit, you are also plagiarizing, even though almost all of the words are your own:

> The earliest examples of African art to become widely known in Europe were bronzes and ivories that were brought to Europe in 1897. These works were thought to be of European origin, and one expert said that Cellini could not have done better work. Their technical excellence, as well as their realism, fulfilled the European standards of the day. The later discovery of new evidence at Benin and Ife, both in Nigeria, refuted this belief.

It is pointless to offer this sort of rewording: If there is a point, it is to conceal the source and to take credit for thinking that is not your own.

3. Acknowledging an idea. Let us say that you have read an essay in which Irving Kristol argues that journalists who pride themselves on being tireless critics of national policy are in fact irresponsible critics because they have no policy they prefer. If this strikes you as a new idea and you adopt it in an essay—even though you set it forth entirely in your own words and with examples not offered by Kristol—you should acknowledge your debt to Kristol. Not to acknowledge such borrowing is plagiarism. Your readers will not think the less of you for naming your source; rather, they will be grateful to you for telling them about an interesting writer.

Fair Use of Common Knowledge

If in doubt as to whether or not to give credit (either with formal documentation or merely in a phrase such as "Ralph Linton says . . ."), give credit. But as you begin to read widely in your field or subject, you will develop a sense of what is considered common knowledge.

Unsurprising definitions in a dictionary can be considered common knowledge, and so there is no need to say "According to Webster, a novel is a long narrative in prose." (That's weak in three ways: it's unnecessary, it's uninteresting, and it's inexact since "Webster" appears in the titles of several dictionaries, some good and some bad.)

Similarly, the date of Freud's death can be considered common knowledge. Few can give it when asked, but it can be found out from innumerable sources, and no one need get the credit for providing you with the date. Again, if you simply *know,* from your reading of Freud, that Freud was interested in literature, you need not cite a specific source for an assertion to that effect, but if you know only because some commentator on Freud said so, and you have no idea whether the fact is well known or not, you should give credit to the source that gave you the information. Not to give credit—for ideas as well as for quoted words—is to plagiarize.

"But How Else Can I Put It?"

If you have just learned—say from an encyclopedia—something that you sense is common knowledge, you may wonder, How can I change into my own words the simple, clear words that this source uses in setting forth this simple fact? For example, if before writing about the photograph of Buffalo Bill and Sitting Bull (page 188), you look up these names in the *Encyclopaedia Britannica,* you will find this statement about Buffalo Bill (William F. Cody): "In 1883 Cody organized his first Wild West exhibition." You cannot use this statement as your own, word for word, without feeling uneasy. But to put in quotation marks such a routine statement of what can be considered common knowledge, and to cite a source for it, seems pretentious. After all, the *Encyclopedia Americana* says much the same thing in the same routine way: "In 1883, . . . Cody organized Buffalo Bill's Wild West." It may be that the word "organized" is simply the most obvious and the best word, and perhaps you will end up using it. Certainly to change "Cody organized" into "Cody presided over the organization of" or "Cody assembled" or some such thing, in an effort to avoid plagiarizing, would be to make a change for the worse and still to be guilty of plagiarism. But you won't get yourself into this mess of wondering whether to change clear, simple wording into awkward wording if in the first place, when you take notes, you *summarize* your sources, thus: "1883: organized Wild West," or "first Wild West: 1883." Later (even if only thirty minutes later), when drafting your paper, if you turn this nugget—probably combined with others—into the best sentence you can, you will not be in danger of plagiarizing, even if the word "organized" turns up in your sentence.

Of course, even when dealing with material that can be considered common knowledge—and even when you have put it into your own words—you probably *will* cite your source if you are drawing more than just an occasional fact from a source. If, for instance, your paragraph on Buffalo Bill uses half a dozen facts from a source, cite the source. You do this both to avoid charges of plagiarism and to protect yourself in case your source contains errors of fact.

Writing the Paper

There remains the difficult job of writing up your findings. Beyond referring you to the rest of this book, we can offer only seven pieces of advice.

1. **With a tentative thesis in mind, begin by rereading your note cards** and sorting them into packets by topic. Put together what belongs together. Don't hesitate to reject material that—however interesting—now seems

irrelevant or redundant. In doing your research you quite properly took lots of notes (as William Blake said, "You never know what is enough unless you know what is more than enough"), but now, in looking over your material, you see that some of it is unnecessary, and so you reject it. Your finished paper should not sandbag the reader. After sorting, resorting, and rejecting, you will have a kind of first draft without writing a draft.

2. **From your packets of cards you can make a first outline.** In arranging the packets into a sequence, and then in sketching an outline, of course you will be guided by your *thesis*. As you worked, you probably modified your tentative ideas in the light of what your further research produced, but by now you ought to have a firm idea of what you think the evidence adds up to. Without a thesis you will have only a lot of note cards, not a potential essay.

Do not, however, confuse this tentative outline with a paragraph outline; when you come to write your essay, a single heading may require two or three or even more paragraphs. Although you can't yet make a paragraph outline, you may find it useful to make a fairly full outline, indicating, for example, not only the sequence of points but also the quotations that you will use.

3. **When you write your first draft, leave lots of space at the top and bottom of each page** so that you can add material, which will be circled and connected by arrows to the proper place. For example, as you are drafting page 6, from perhaps your tenth packet, you may find a note card that now seems more appropriate to a point you made back on page 2. Write it on page 2, and put the card in the appropriate earlier packet so that if for some reason you later have to check your notes you can find it easily.

A word processor makes all this shifting of material from one place to another easy. You can try out and store several versions of page 6; you can print out whatever versions you want to see on a typed page; you can revise on the screen, or on the page. The possibilities are endless.

4. **Write or type your quotations, even in the first draft, exactly as you want them to appear in the final version.** Of course this takes some time, and the time will be wasted if, as may well turn out, you later see that the quotation is not really useful. (On the other hand, the time has not really been wasted, since it helped you ultimately to delete the unnecessary material.)

If at this early stage you just write a summary of the quotation—something like "here quote Jackson on undecided voters"—when you re-read the draft you won't really know how the page sounds. You won't, for instance, know how much help your reader needs by way of a lead-in to the quotation, or how much discussion should follow. Only if you actually see the quotation are you in the position of your readers—and all good writers try to imagine their readers.

Short quotations (fewer than three lines of poetry or fewer than five lines of prose) are enclosed within quotation marks but are not otherwise set off; longer quotations, however, are set off: they begin a new line, are indented ten spaces, and are *not* within quotation marks. For the form of embedded quotations and of set-off quotations, see pages 329–31.

5. Include, right in the body of the draft, all of the relevant citations so that when you come to revise you don't have to start hunting through your notes to

find who said what, and where. You can, for the moment, enclose these citations within diagonal lines, or within double parentheses—anything at all to remind you that they will be your documentation.

6. Beware of the compulsion to include every note card in your essay. You have taken all these notes, and there is a strong temptation to use them all. But, truth to tell, in hindsight many are useless. By now you will probably have a clearer sense of your thesis. You may have modified it in the light of your research. Consequently, you will probably find, as you write your draft, that some of what you have accumulated is irrelevant, and, on the other hand, here and there you need to do more research, to check a quotation or to collect additional examples. Probably it is best to continue writing your draft if possible, and to incorporate new material in a later draft.

7. As you revise your draft, make sure that you do not merely tell the reader "A says ... B says ... C says. ..." Rather, by such expressions as "A claims," "B provides evidence that," "C gives the usual view," "D concedes that," you help the reader to see the role of the quotation in your paper. When you use sources, you are not merely dumping on the table the contents of a shopping-cart filled at the scholar's supermarket, the library. You are cooking a meal. You must have a point, an opinion, a thesis; you are working toward a conclusion, and your readers should always feel they are moving toward that conclusion (by means of your thoughtful argument and use of sources) rather than reading an anthology of commentary on the topic. Let your reader know why you are quoting, or how the quotation fits into your organization.

A Checklist for Reading Drafts

1. Is the tentative title informative and focused?

2. Does the paper make a point, or does it just accumulate other people's ideas?

3. Does it reveal the thesis early?

4. Are generalizations supported by evidence?

5. Are quotations introduced adequately?

6. Are all of the long quotations necessary, or can some of them be effectively summarized?

7. Are quotations discussed adequately?

8. Are all sources given?

9. Does the paper advance in orderly stages? Can your imagined reader easily follow your thinking?

10. Is the documentation in the correct form?

Documentation

Until recently, sources were regularly acknowledged in footnotes or endnotes, but in 1984 the Modern Language Association, which had established the footnote form used in hundreds of journals, university presses, and classrooms, substituted a new form. It is this new form—parenthetical citations *within* the text (rather than at the foot of the page or the end of the essay)—that we explain here.

MLA Format

Citations Within the Text

Brief parenthetic citations within the body of the essay are made clear by a list of your sources, entitled Works Cited, appended to the essay. This list usually cites books and articles, and films, television programs, interviews, and the like. Thus, an item in your list of Works Cited will clarify such a sentence in your essay as

> The Food and Drug Administration depends heavily
> for research, and advice on the food committees of the
> National Academy of Sciences, which Daniel Zwerdling
> claims are a "Who's Who of the food industry" (34).

This citation means that Zwerdling wrote the quoted words on page 34 of a source listed in Works Cited. More often than not the parenthetic citation appears at the end of a sentence, as in the example just given, but it can appear elsewhere in the sentence; its position will depend chiefly on your ear. You might, for instance, write the sentence thus:

> Daniel Zwerdling says that the food committees of
> the National Academy of Sciences are a "Who's Who of
> the food industry" (34), and it is on these committees
> that the Food and Drug Administration depends.

Six points must be made about these examples:

 1. **Quotation marks.** The closing quotation mark appears after the last word of the quotation, *not* after the parenthetic citation. Since the citation is not part of the quotation, the citation is not included within the quotation marks.

 2. **Omission of words (ellipsis).** If the quoted words are merely a phrase, as

in the example above, you do not need to indicate (by three spaced periods) that you are omitting material before or after the quotation, but if the quotation is longer than a phrase, and is not a complete sentence, you must indicate that you are omitting material. If you are omitting material from the beginning of the sentence, after the opening quotation mark put three spaced periods, and then give the quotation; if you are omitting material from the end of the sentence, put three spaced periods after the quoted words, or four periods if you are ending your sentence, and then close the quotation with a quotation mark, and add a final period.

3. **Punctuation with parenthetic citations.** Look again at the two examples given a moment ago, both referring to Zwerdling's book. Notice that if you follow a quotation with a parenthetic citation, any necessary period, semicolon, or comma *follows* the parenthetic citation. In the first example, a period follows the citation; in the second, a comma. In the next example, notice that the comma follows the citation.

```
Jackson insists that "the figures can be

interpreted in different ways" (72), but he offers no

further discussion.
```

If, however, the quotation itself uses a question mark or an exclamation mark, this mark of punctuation appears *within* the closing quotation mark; even so, a period follows the parenthetic citation.

```
Jackson is the only one to suggest doubt: "How

can we accept such inadequate data?" (78). He

therefore rejects the entire argument.
```

4. **Two or more titles by one author.** If your list of Works Cited includes more than one work by an author, you will have to give additional information (either in your sentence or within the parentheses) in order to indicate *which* of the titles you are referring to. We will go further into this in a moment (on page 339).

5. **Long (set off) quotations.** We have been talking about short quotations, which are not set off but are embedded within your own sentences. Long quotations, usually defined as more than four typed lines, are set off, as in the example below.

```
Michael Jacobson explains the preservative action

of nitrite:

    Nitrite makes botulinum spores sensitive to heat.

    When foods are treated with nitrite and then

    heated, any botulinum spores that may be present
```

are killed. In the absence of nitrite, spores can
be inactivated only at temperatures that ruin the
meat products. . . . Nitrite's preservative action
is particularly important in foods that are not
cooked after they leave the factory, such as ham,
because these offer an oxygen-free environment,
the kind in which *botulinum* can grow. (165)

It seems unlikely that sodium nitrite is
really necessary as a preservative. After
extensive hearings in 1971, a congressional
subcommittee . . .

In introducing a long quotation, keep in mind that a reader will have trouble reading a sentence that consists of a lead-in, a long quotation, and then a continuation of your own sentence. It's better to have a short lead-in ("Michael Jacobson explains the preservative action of nitrite"), and then set off a long quotation that is a complete sentence or group of sentences and therefore ends with a period. The quotation that is set off begins on a new line, is indented ten spaces from the left margin, and is *not* enclosed within quotation marks. Put a period at the end of the quotation (since the quotation is a complete sentence or group of sentences and is not embedded within a longer sentence of your own), hit the space bar three times, and then, on the same line, give the citation in parentheses. Do *not* put a period after the parenthetic citation that follows a long quotation. Next, doublespace, and offer your comment flush with the left margin, or indent the first line of your comment if you are beginning a new paragraph. (Look back at the preceding example.)

6. **Citing a summary or a paraphrase.** Even if you don't quote a source directly, but use its point in a paraphrase or a summary, you will give a citation:

Daniel Zwerdling points out (34) that the Food
and Drug Administration relies for advice on
committees which consist of the most eminent people in
the food business.

The basic point, then, is that the system of in-text citation gives the documentation parenthetically. Notice that in all of the previous examples the author's name is given in the text (rather than within the parenthetic citation). But there are several other ways of giving the citation, and we shall now look at them.

Author and Page Number in Parenthetic Citation

As early as 1899, scientists discovered that
nitrate breaks down into nitrite and that it is the
nitrite which actually preserves the red color in
meats (Jacobson 164-65).

It doesn't matter whether you summarize (as in this example) or quote directly; the parenthetic citation means that your source is pages 164–65 of a work by Jacobson, listed in Works Cited, at the end of your essay.

Title and Page Number in Parentheses

If, as we mentioned earlier, your list of Works Cited includes two or more titles by an author, you cannot in the text simply give a name and a page reference; the reader would not know to which of the titles you are referring. Let's assume that Works Cited includes two items by William Robbins. If in a sentence in your essay you don't specify one title—that is, if you don't say something like, "Robbins, in *The American Food Scandal,* says . . . "—you will have to give the title (in a shortened form) in the parenthetic citation:

William Robbins (*American* 2) characterizes as a
"big lie" the assertion that Americans have better
food than the people of any other nation.

Notice in this example that *American* is a short title for Robbins's book *The American Food Scandal.* The full title is given in Works Cited, as is the title of another work by Robbins, but the short title in the parenthetic citation is enough to direct the reader to page 2 of the correct source in Works Cited.

Notice also that when a short title and a page reference are given in parentheses, a comma is *not* used after the title.

Author, Title, and Page Number in Parentheses

We have just seen that if Works Cited includes two or more works by an author, and if in your lead-in you do not specify which work you are at the moment making use of, you will have to give the title as well as the page number in parentheses. Similarly, if for some reason you do not in your lead-in mention the name of the author, you will have to add this bit of information to the parenthetic citation, thus:

That Americans are the best fed people is a "big
lie" (Robbins, *American* 2).

Notice that, as in the previous example, a comma does *not* separate the title from the page reference; but notice, too, that a comma *does* separate the author's name from the title. (Don't ask us why; ask the Modern Language Association, or, on the other hand, just obey orders.)

A Government Document or a Work of Corporate Authorship

Treat the issuing body as the author. Thus, you will probably write something like this:

> The Commission on Food Control, in *Food Resources Today*, concludes that there is no danger (36–37).

A Work by Two or More Authors

If a work is by *two authors,* give the names of both, either in the parenthetic citation (the first example below) or in a lead-in (the second example):

> The Food and Drug Administration found nitrosamines in salmon "at levels up to twenty-six parts per billion" (Verrett and Carper 146–47).

or

> Verrett and Carper point out that the Food and Drug Administration found nitrosamines in salmon "at levels up to twenty-six parts per billion" (146–47).

If there are more than *three authors,* give the last name of the first author, followed by "et al." (an abbreviation for *et alii,* Latin for "and others"), thus:

> Gardner et al. found that . . .

or

> Sometimes even higher levels are found (Gardner et al. 83).

Parenthetic Citation of an Indirect Source (Citation of Material That Itself Was Quoted or Summarized in Your Source)

Suppose you are reading a book by Jones, and she quotes Smith, and you wish to use Smith's material. Your citation will be to Jones—the source you are using—but of course you cannot attribute the words to Jones. You will have to make it clear that you are quoting not Jones but Smith, and so your parenthetic citation will look like this:

> (qtd. in Jones 84–85)

Parenthetic Citation of Two or More Works

```
    In microorganisms, nitrite enters the blood
(Hervey 72; Lederer 195).
```

Note that a semicolon, followed by a space, separates the two sources.

A Work in More than One Volume

This is a bit tricky.

1. If you have used only one volume, in Works Cited you will specify the volume, and so in your parenthetic in-text citation you will need to give only a page number—the very sort of thing illustrated by most of the examples that we have been giving.

2. If you have used more than one volume, your parenthetic citation will have to specify the volume as well as the page, thus:

```
    Landsdale points out that nitrite combines with
hemoglobin to form a pigment which cannot carry oxygen
(2: 370).
```

The reference is to page 370 of volume 2 of a work by Landsdale.

3. If, however, you are citing not a page but an entire volume—let's say volume 2—your parenthetic citation would be

```
    (vol. 2)
```

Or, if you did not name the author in your lead-in, it would be

```
    (Landsdale, vol. 2)
```

Notice that

- In citing a volume and page, the volume number, like the page number, is given in arabic (not roman) numerals;
- The volume number is followed by a colon, then a space, then the page number;
- Abbreviations such as "vol." and "p." and "pg." are *not* used, except when citing a volume number without a page number, as illustrated in the last two examples.

An Anonymous Work

For an anonymous work, give the title in your lead-in, or give it in a shortened form in your parenthetic citation:

Official Guide to Food Standards includes a
statistical table on nitrates (362).

or

A statistical table on nitrites is available
(*Official Guide* 362).

But double-check to make sure that the work is truly anonymous. Some
encyclopedias, for example, give the authors' names quietly. If initials follow
the article, these are the initials of the author's name. Check the alphabetic list of
authors given at the front of the encyclopedia.

A Literary Work

You will specify the edition in Works Cited—let's say Alvin Kernan's edition of
Othello, or an edition of Conrad's *Heart of Darkness* with a preface by Albert
Guerard–but because classic works of literature are widely available, and your
reader may have at hand an edition different from the one that you have read, it
is customary to use the following forms.

   1. **A novel.** In parentheses give the page number of the edition you specify
in Works Cited, followed by a semicolon, a space, and helpful additional
information, thus:

(181; ch. 6)

or

(272; part 1, ch. 7).

   2. **A play.** Most instructors want the act, scene, and (if the lines are
numbered) the line numbers, rather than a page reference. Until recently, the act
was given in capital roman numerals, the scene in lowercase roman numerals,
and the line(s) in arabic numerals, without spaces between them. Thus,

(II.iv.18–23)

would refer to lines 18–23 of the fourth scene of the second act. Recently,
however, at the urging of the Modern Language Association, there has been a
tendency to use arabic numerals throughout:

(2.4.18–23)

If you are quoting a few words within a sentence of your own, immediately after
closing the brief quotation give the citation (enclosed within parentheses), and,
if your sentence ends with the quotation, put the period after the closing
parenthesis.

```
    That Macbeth fully understands that killing
Duncan is not a manly act but a villainous one is
clear from his words to Lady Macbeth: "I dare do all
that may become a man" (1.7.46). Moreover, even though
he goes on to kill Duncan, he does not go on to
deceive himself into thinking that his act was noble.
```

If, however, your sentence continues beyond the citation, after the parenthetic citation put whatever punctuation may be necessary (for instance, a comma may be needed), complete your sentence, and end it with a period.

```
    This is clear from his words, "I dare do all that
does become a man" (1.7.46), and he never loses his
awareness of true manliness.
```

3. **A poem.** Preferences vary, and you can't go wrong in citing the page, but for a poem longer than say, a sonnet (fourteen lines), most instructors find it useful if students cite the line numbers, in parentheses, after the quotations. In your first use, preface the numerals with "line" or "lines" (not in quotation marks, of course); in subsequent citations simply give the numerals. For very long poems that are divided into books, such as Homer's *Odyssey,* give the page, a semicolon, a space, the book number, and the line number(s). The following example refers to page 327 of a title listed in Works Cited; it goes on to indicate that the passage occurs in the ninth book of the poem, lines 130–35.

```
(327; 9.130-35)
```

Long quotations (more than three lines of poetry) are indented ten spaces. As we explained on page 331, if you give a long quotation, try to give one that can correctly be concluded with a period. After the period, hit the space bar three times, and then, on the same line, give the citation in parentheses.

4. **An interview.** Probably you won't need a parenthetic citation, because you'll say something like

```
    Cyril Jackson, in an interview, said . . .
```

or

```
    According to Cyril Jackson,. . .
```

and when your reader turns to Works Cited, he or she will see that Jackson is listed, along with the date of the interview. But if you do not mention the source's name in the lead-in, you will have to give it in the parentheses, thus:

It has been estimated that chemical additives
earn the drug companies well over five hundred million
dollars annually (Jackson).

A Note on Footnotes in an Essay Using Parenthetic Citations

There are two reasons for using footnotes in an essay that chiefly uses
parenthetic citations.

1. In a research paper you will of course draw on many sources, but in other
kinds of papers you may be using only one source, and yet within the paper you
may often want to specify a reference to a page or (for poetry) a line number, or
(for a play) to an act, scene, and line number. In such a case, to append a page
headed Work Cited, with a single title, is silly; it is better to use a single
footnote when you first allude to the source. Such a note can run something like
this:

[1]All references are to Mary Shelley,
Frankenstein, afterword by Harold Bloom (New York:
Signet, 1965).

Here's another example of this sort of footnote:

[2]All experiments described in this paper were
performed in January 1992 in the laboratory of Dr. Jan
Pechenik, of Tufts University.

2. Footnotes can also be used in another way in a paper that documents
sources by giving parenthetic citations. If you want to include some material that
might seem intrusive in the body of the essay, you may relegate it to a footnote.
For example, in a footnote you might translate a quotation given in a foreign
language, or in a footnote you might write a paragraph—a sort of mini-essay—
in which you offer an amplification of some point. By putting the amplification
in a footnote you are signaling to the reader that it is dispensable; it is, so to
speak, thrown in as something extra, something relevant but not essential to your
argument. On the whole, it's a bad habit to write this sort of note, but there are
times when it is appropriate.

To indicate in the body of your text that you are adding a footnote at this
point, place a raised arabic numeral (without a period, and not enclosed in
parentheses) by raising the typewriter carriage half a line. (If you use a word
processor, your software program probably will automatically elevate the
numeral.)

Joachim Jeremias's *The Parables of Jesus* is
probably the best example of this sort of book.[1]

Usually the number is put at the end of a sentence, immediately after the period, but put it earlier if clarity requires you to do so.

```
Helen Cam¹ as well as many lesser historians held
this view.
```

After you have typed the last line of text on the page, double-space twice, then indent five spaces, elevate the carriage half a line, type the digit (without a period and without parentheses), lower the carriage to the regular position, hit the space bar once, and type the note. If the note runs more than one line, type it single-spaced (unless your instructor tells you to the contrary), flush with the left margin. Double-space between notes, and begin each note with an indented raised numeral and then a capital letter. End each note with a period or, if the sentence calls for one, a question mark.

The List of Works Cited

Your parenthetic documentation consists of references that become meaningful when the reader consults a list entitled Works Cited, given at the end of your essay. We give sample entries below, but see also the list of Works Cited at the end of a student's documented paper, on page 374.

The list of Works Cited continues the pagination of the essay; if the last page of text is 10, then the list begins on page 11. Type your last name and the page number in the upper right corner, half an inch from the top of the sheet. Next, type "Works Cited," centered, one inch from the top, then double-space and type the first entry. Here are the governing conventions.

Alphabetic Order

1. Arrange the list alphabetically by author, with the author's last name first.

2. List an anonymous work alphabetically under the first word of the title, or under the second word if the first word is *A, An,* or *The,* or a foreign equivalent.

3. If your list includes two or more works by one author, the work whose title comes earlier in the alphabet precedes the work whose title comes later in the alphabet.

Form on the Page

1. Begin each entry flush with the left margin, but if an entry runs to more than one line, indent five spaces for each succeeding line of the entry.

2. Double-space each entry, and double-space between entries.

From here on, things get complicated. We will begin with

books, then

films, television and radio programs (page 347), and finally

articles in journals and newspapers and database sources (pages 347–48).

The forms for books are as follows.

The Author's Name

Note that the last name is given first, but otherwise the name is given as on the title page. Do not substitute initials for names written out on the title page.

If your list includes two or more works by an author, the author's name is not repeated for the second title, but is represented by three hyphens followed by a period and two spaces. When you give two or more works by the same author, the sequence is determined by the alphabetic order of the titles, as in the example below, listing two books by Blassingame, where *Black* precedes *Slave*.

```
Bishop, Robert. American Folk Sculpture. New York:
     Dutton, 1974.
Blassingame, John W. Black New Orleans, 1860-1880.
     Chicago: U of Chicago P, 1973.
---. The Slave Community: Plantation Life in the
     Antebellum South. Rev. ed. New York: Oxford UP,
     1979.
Cardinal, Roger. Outsider Art. New York: Praeger,
     1972.
```

We have already discussed the treatment of an anonymous work; in a few moments we will discuss books by more than one author, government documents, and works of corporate authorship.

The Title

Take the title from the title page, not from the cover or the spine, but disregard any unusual typography—for instance, the use of only capital letters, or the use of & for *and*. If your word processor allows you to italicize, do so for the title and subtitle (separate them with a colon). Otherwise, use one continuous underline, to indicate italics, but do not underline the period that concludes this part of the entry. Example:

```
Frankenstein: Or, The Modern Prometheus.
```

A peculiarity: italicizing or underlining is used to indicate the title of a book, but if a title of a book itself includes the title of a book (for instance, a book about

Mary Shelley's *Frankenstein* might include the title of her novel in its own title), the title-within-title is neither italicized nor underlined. Thus the title would be given as

> *The Endurance of* Frankenstein.

Place of Publication, Publisher, and Date

For the place of publication, give the name of the city (you can usually find it either on the title page or on the copyright page, which is the reverse of the title page). If several cities are listed, give only the first. For Canadian cities, list the province abbreviation, and for all other countries, list the abbreviated country name.

The name of the publisher is abbreviated. Usually the first word is enough (Random House becomes Random; Little, Brown and Co. becomes Little), but if the first word is a first name, such as in Alfred A. Knopf, the surname (Knopf) is used instead. University presses are abbreviated thus: Yale UP, U of Chicago P, State U of New York P.

The date of publication of a book is given when known; if no date appears on the book, write n.d. to indicate "no date."

Here are sample entries, illustrating the points we have covered thus far:

Douglas, Ann. *The Feminization of American*

   Culture. New York: Knopf, 1977.

Frye, Northrop. *Fables of Identity: Studies in*

   Poetic Mythology. New York: Harcourt, 1963.

---. *Fools of Time: Studies in Shakespearian*

   Tragedy. Toronto: U of Toronto P. 1967.

Hartman, Chester. *The Transformation of San*

   Francisco. Totowa: Rowman, 1984.

Kellerman, Barbara. *The Political Presidency:*

   Practice of Leadership from Kennedy through

   Reagan. New York: Oxford UP, 1984.

Kennedy, Paul. *Preparing for the Twenty-First*

   Century. New York: Random, 1993.

Notice that a period follows the author's name, and another period follows the title. If a subtitle is given, as it is for Kellerman's book, it is separated from the title by a colon and a space. A colon follows the place of publication, a comma follows the publisher, and a period follows the date.

A Book by More than One Author

The book is alphabetized under the last name of the first author named on the title page. If there are *two or three authors*, the names of these are given (after the first author's name) in the normal order, *first name first*.

Majors, Richard, and Janet Mancini Billson. *Cool*

    Pose: The Dilemmas of Black Manhood in

    America. Lexington: Lexington, 1992.

Notice, again, that although the first author's name is given *last name first*, the second author's name is given in the normal order. Notice, too, that a comma is put after the first name of the first author, separating the authors.

    If there are *more than three authors*, you may name them all or give the name of only the first, and then add (but *not* enclosed within quotation marks) "et al." (Latin for "and others").

Belenky, Mary Field, et al. *Women's Ways of Knowing:*

    The Development of the Self, Voice, and Mind.

    New York: Basic Books, 1986.

Government Documents

If the writer is not known, treat the government and the agency as the author. Most federal national documents are issued by the Government Printing Office (abbreviated to GPO) in Washington.

United States Congress. Office of Technology

    Assessment. *Computerized Manufacturing*

    Automation Employment, Education and the

    Workplace. Washington: GPO. 1984.

Works of Corporate Authorship

Begin the citation with the corporate author, even if the same body is also the publisher, as in the first example:

American Psychiatric Association. *Psychiatric*

    Glossary. Washington: American Psychiatric

    Association, 1984.

Carnegie Council on Policy Studies in Higher

    Education. *Giving Youth a Better Chance:*

    Options for Education, Work, and Service. San

    Francisco: Jossey, 1980.

A Reprint, for Instance a Paperback Version of an Older Hardback

After the title, give the date of original publication (it can usually be found on the copyright page of the reprint you are using), then a period, and then the place, publisher, and date of the edition you are using. The example indicates that Rourke's book was originally published in 1931 and that the student is using the Doubleday reprint of 1953.

Rourke, Constance. *American Humor*. 1931. New York:

Doubleday, 1953.

A Book in Several Volumes

Friedel, Frank. *Franklin D. Roosevelt*. Vol. 3. Boston:

Little, 1973. 4 vols.

If you have used more than one volume, in your essay you will (as has been explained on page 334) indicate a reference to, say, page 250 of volume 3 thus: (3:250).

If, however, you have used only one volume of the set—let's say volume 3—in your entry in Works Cited write, after the period following the date, "Vol. 3," as in the next entry:

Friedel, Frank. *Franklin D. Roosevelt*. 4 vols Boston:

Little, 1973. Vol. 3.

In this case, the parenthetic citation would be to the page only, not to the volume and page, since a reader will understand that the page reference must be to this volume. But notice that in Works Cited, even though you say you used only volume 3, you also give the total number of volumes.

One Book with a Separate Title in a Set of Volumes

Sometimes a set with a title makes use also of a separate title for each book in the set. If you are listing such a book, use the following form (although the supplementary information on the four volumes is optional):

Churchill, Winston. *The Age of Revolution*. New York:

Dodd, 1957. Vol. 3 of *A History of the English-*

Speaking Peoples. 4 vols. 1956-58.

A Book with an Author and an Editor

Shakespeare, William. *The Sonnets*. Ed. William Burto.

New York: NAL, 1965.

Churchill, Winston, and Franklin D. Roosevelt. *The*

Complete Correspondence. 3 vols. Ed. Warren F.

Kimball. Princeton: Princeton UP, 1985.

If a book has one editor, the abbreviation is "ed."; if two or more editors, "eds."

If you are making use of the editor's introduction or other editorial material, rather than of the author's work, list the book under the name of the editor, rather than of the author, following the form below for "An Introduction, Foreword, or Afterword."

A Revised Edition of a Book

Hall, James. *Dictionary of Subjects and Symbols in*
    Art. 2nd ed. New York: Harper, 1979.

A Translated Book

Franqui, Carlos. *Family Portrait with Fidel: A*
    Memoir. Trans. Alfred MacAdam. New York:
    Random, 1984.

But if you are discussing the translation itself, as opposed to the book, list the work under the translator's name. Thus

MacAdam, Alfred, trans. *Family Portrait with Fidel: A*
    Memoir. By Carlos Franqui. New York: Random,
    1984.

An Introduction, Foreword, or Afterword

Wolff, Cynthia Griffin. Introduction. *The House of*
    Mirth. By Edith Warton. New York: Penguin, 1985.
    vii–xxvi.

Usually a book with an introduction or some such comparable material is listed under the name of the author of the book (here Wharton), rather than under the name of the writer of the introduction (here Wolff), but if you are referring to the apparatus rather than to the book itself, use the form just given. The words Introduction, Preface, Foreword, and Afterword are neither enclosd within quotation marks not underlined.

A Book with an Editor but No Author

Anthologies of literature fit this description, but here we have in mind a book of essays written by various people but collected by an editor (or editors), whose name appears on the collection.

Denevan, William M., ed. *The Native Population of the Americas in 1492*. Madison: U of Wisconsin P, 1992.

A Work in a Volume of Works by One Author

The following entry indicates that a short work by Susan Sontag—an essay called "The Aesthetics of Science"—appears in a book by Sontag entitled *Styles of Radical Will*. Notice that the inclusive page numbers of the short work are cited—not merely page numbers that you may happen to refer to, but the page numbers of the entire piece.

Sontag, Susan. "The Aesthetics of Science." In *Styles of Radical Will*. New York: Farrar, 1969. 3-34.

A Work in an Anthology—That Is, in a Collection of Works by Several Authors

There are several possibilities here. Let's assume, for a start, that you have made use of one work in an anthology. In Works Cited, begin with the author (last name first) and title of the work you are citing, not with the name of the anthologist or the title of the anthology. Here is an entry for Coleridge's poem "Kubla Khan," found on pages 353–55 in the second volume of a two-volume anthology edited by M. H. Abrams and several others.

Coleridge, Samuel Taylor. "Kubla Khan." *Norton Anthology of English Literature*. Ed. M. H. Abrams et al. 4th ed. 2 vols. New York: Norton, 1979. 2:353-55.

Now let's assume that during the course of your essay you refer to several, rather than to only one work in this anthology. You can, of course, list each work in the form just given. Or you can have an entry in Works Cited for Abrams's anthology, under Abrams's name, and then in each entry for a work in the anthology you can eliminate some of the data by simply referring to Abrams, thus:

Coleridge, Samuel Taylor. "Kubla Khan." Abrams 2:353-55.

Again, this requires that you also list Abrams's volume, thus:

```
Abrams, M. H. et al., eds.  The Norton Anthology of

      English Literature. 4th ed. 2 vols. New York:

   Norton, 1979.
```

The advantage of listing the anthology separately is that if you are using a dozen works from the anthology, you can shorten the dozen entries in Works Cited merely by adding one entry, that of the anthology itself. Notice, of course, that in the body of the essay you would still refer to Coleridge and to your other eleven authors, not to the editor of the anthology—but the entries in Works Cited will guide the reader to the book you have used.

A Book Review

```
Vendler, Helen.  Rev. of Essays on Style. Ed. Roger

      Fowler. Essays in Criticism 16 (1966): 457-63.
```

If the review has a title, give it between the period following the reviewer's name and "Rev."

If a review is anonymous, list it under the first word of the title, or under the second word if the first word is *A, An,* or *The.* If an anonymous review has no title, begin the entry with "Rev. of " and then give the title of the work reviewed; alphabetize the entry under the title of the work reviewed.

An Article or Essay—Not a Reprint—in a Collection

A book may consist of a collection (edited by one or more persons) of new essays by several authors. Here is a reference to one essay in such a book. (The essay, by Balmforth, occupies pages 19–35 in a collection edited by Bevan.)

```
Balmforth, Henry.  "Science and Religion." Steps to

      Christian Understanding. Ed. R. J. W. Bevan.

   London: Oxford UP, 1958. 19-35.
```

An Article or Essay Reprinted in a Collection

The previous example (Balmforth's essay in Bevan's collection) was for an essay written for a collection. But some collections reprint earlier material, for example essays from journals, or chapters from books. The following example cites an essay that was originally printed in a book called *The Cinema of Alfred Hitchcock.* This essay has been reprinted in a later collection of essays on Hitchcock, edited by Arthur J. LaValley, and it was LaValley's collection that the student used.

```
Bogdanovich, Peter.  "Interviews with Alfred

      Hitchcock." The Cinema of Alfred Hitchcock.
```

New York: Museum of Modern Art, 1963. 15-18. Rpt.

in *Focus on Hitchcock.* Ed. Albert J. LaValley.

Englewood Cliffs: Prentice, 1972. 28-31.

The student has read Bogdanovich's essay or chapter, but not in Bogdanovich's book, where it occupied pages 15–18. The material was actually read on pages 28–31 in a collection of writings on Hitchcock, edited by LaValley. Details of the original publication—title, date, page numbers, and so forth—were found in LaValley's collection. Almost all editors will include this information, either on the copyright page or at the foot of the reprinted essay, but sometimes they do not give the original page numbers. In such a case, the original numbers need not be included in the entry.

Notice that the entry begins with the author and the title of the work you are citing (here, Bogdanovich's interviews), not with the name of the editor of the collection or the title of the collection. In the following example, the student used an essay by Arthur Sewell; the essay was originally on pages 53–56 in a book by Sewell entitled *Character and Society in Shakespeare,* but the student encountered the piece on pages 36–38 in a collection of essays, edited by Leonard Dean, on Shakespeare's *Julius Caesar.* Here is how the entry should run:

Sewell, Arthur. "The Moral Dilemma in Tragedy:

Brutus." *Character and Society in Shakespeare.*

Oxford: Clarendon, 1951. 53-56. Rpt. in *Twentieth

Century Interpretations of* Julius Caesar. Ed.

Leonard F. Dean. Englewood Cliffs: Prentice,

1968. 36-38.

An Encyclopedia or Other Alphabetically Arranged Reference Work
The publisher, place of publication, volume number, and page number do *not* have to be given. For such works, list only the edition (if it is given) and the date.

For a *signed* article, begin with the author's last name. (If the article is signed with initials, check the volume for a list of abbreviations—it is usually near the front, but it may be at the rear—which will say what the initials stand for, and use the following form.)

Messer, Thomas. "Picasso." *Encyclopaedia Americana.*

1980 ed.

For an unsigned article, *begin with the title of the article.*

"Picasso, Pablo (Ruiz y)." *Encyclopaedia Britannica:*

Macropaedia. 1985 ed.

"Automation." *The Business Reference Book*. 1977 ed.

A Film

Begin with the title of the film (unless you are referring to a specific contributor's work, in that case, cite them first) followed by the writer, director, adapter, or performers, if relevant.

Tootsie. Screenplay by Don McGuire and Larry Gelbart.
   Dir. Sydney Pollack. Perf. Dustin Hoffman,
   Jessica Lange, and Teri Garr. Mirage/Punch
   Production. Columbia, 1982.

A Television or Radio Program

As in a film citation, the title is listed first unless you wish to refer to a particular person in the program. Put the episode in quotation marks and underline the program name. A series name (if any) is neither put in quotation marks or underlined. List the narrators, directors, adapters, or performers if relevant.

"Inspector Morse: Cherubim and Seraphim." 2 episodes.
   Mystery. Perf. John Thaw, Kevin Whateley. PBS.
   WNET, New York. 2 March 1995.

An Article in a Scholarly Journal

The title of the article is enclosed within quotation marks, and the title of the journal is underlined to indicate italics.

Some journals are paginated consecutively—the pagination of the second issue begins where the first issue leaves off; but other journals begin each issue with page 1. The forms of the citations differ slightly. First, an article in a *journal that is paginated consecutively:*

Jacobus, Mary. "Tess's Purity." *Essays in Criticism* 26
   (1976): 318-38.

Jacobus's article occupies pages 318–38 of volume 26, which was published in 1976. (Note that the volume number is followed by a space, and then by the year, in parentheses, and then by a colon, a space, and the page numbers of the entire article. Because the journal is paginated consecutively, the issue number does *not* need to be specified.)

For a *journal that begins each issue with page 1* (there will be four page 1's each year if such a journal is a quarterly), the issue number must be given. After the volume number, type a period and (without hitting the space bar) the issue number, as in the next example.

Spillers, Hortense J. "Martin Luther King and the
   Style of the Black Sermon." *The Black Scholar* 3.1
   (1971): 14-27.

Spillers's article on King appeared in the first issue of volume 3 of *The Black Scholar.*

An Article in a Weekly, Biweekly, or Monthly Publication

The date and page numbers are given, but volume numbers and issue numbers are usually omitted for these publications. The first example is for an article in a weekly publication:

```
McCabe, Bernard. "Taking Dickens Seriously."

     Commonwealth 14 May 1965: 245-46.
```

An Article in a Newspaper

Because a newspaper usually consists of several sections, a section number or a capital letter may precede the page number. The example indicates that an article begins on page 1 of section A and is continued on a later page. Always include an edition if there is one, e.g., late ed., natl ed.

```
Dao, James. "New York Senate Approves Revival of

     Death Penalty." New York Times 7 March 1995,

     late ed.: A1+.
```

A Database Source

Treat material obtained from a computer service like other printed material, but at the end of the entry add the name of the service and the date of access.

```
Wilford, John Noble. "Corn in the New World: A

     Relative Latecomer." New York Times 7 Mar. 1995,

     late ed.: C1+. New York Times Online. Online.

     America Online. 7 Mar. 1995.
```

Caution: although we have covered the most usual kinds of sources, for more information see Joseph Gibaldi, *MLA Handbook for Writers of Research Papers,* 4th ed. (New York: Modern Language Association of America, 1995).

APA Format

The MLA style is used chiefly by writers in the humanities. Writers in the social sciences and in business, education, and psychology commonly use a style developed by the American Psychological Association. In the following pages we give the chief principles of the APA style, but for full details the reader should consult the third edition (1983) of *Publication Manual of the American Psychological Association.*

An Overview of References

A paper that uses the format prescribed by the American Psychological Association will end with a page headed "References," which lists all of the author's sources. This list of sources begins on a separate page, continuing the pagination of the last page of the essay itself. Thus, if the text of the essay ends on page 10, the first page of references is page 11.

Here are some general guidelines, followed by examples.

Form on the Page

1. Begin each entry flush with the left margin, but if an entry runs to more than one line, indent three spaces for each succeeding line of the entry.
2. Double-space each entry, and double-space between entries.

Alphabetic Order

1. Arrange the list **alphabetically by author.**
2. Give the **author's last name first,** then the initial of the first and of the middle name (if any).
3. **If there is more than one author,** name all of the authors, again inverting the name (last name first) and giving only initials for first and middle names. (But do not invert the editor's name when the entry begins with the name of an author who has written an article in an edited book. See the example below, page 351, illustrating "A Work in a Collection of Essays.") When there are two or more authors, use an ampersand (&) before the name of the last author. Example (here, of an article in the seventh volume of a journal called *Journal of Experimental Social Psychology*):

```
Berscheid, E., Hatfield, E., & Bohrnstett, G. (1971).
   Physical attractiveness and dating choice: A test
   of the matching hypothesis. Journal of Experimental
   Social Psychology, 7, 173-89.
```

4. If you list more than one work by an author, list the works in the order of publication, the earliest first.

   If two works by an author were published in the same year, give them in alphabetic order by the first letter of the title, disregarding *A, An,* or *The,* and their foreign equivalents. Designate the first work as "a," the second as "b." Repeat the author's name at the start of each entry.

   If the author of a work or works is also the coauthor of other works listed, list the single-author entries first, arranged by date. Following these, list the multiple-author entries, in a sequence determined alphabetically by the second author's name. Thus, in the example below, notice that the works by Bem wrote unassisted are listed first, arranged by date, and when two works appear in the same year they are arranged alphabetically by title. These single-author works are followed by the multiple-author works, with the work written with Lenney preceding the work written with Martyna and Watson.

Bem, S. L. (1974). The measurement of psychological androgyny. *Journal of Consulting and Clinical Psychology, 42,* 155-62.

Bem, S. L. (1981a). The BSRI and gender schema theory: A reply to Spence and Helmreich. *Psychological Review, 88,* 369-71.

Bem, S. L. (1981b). Gender schema theory: A cognitive account of sex typing. *Psychological Review, 88,* 354-64.

Bem, S. L., & Lenney, E. (1976). Sex-typing and the avoidance of cross-sex behavior. *Journal of Personality and Social Psychology, 33,* 48-54.

Bem, S. L., Martyna, W., & Watson, C. (1976). Sex-typing and androgyny: Further exploration of the expressive domain. *Journal of Personality and Social Psychology, 34,* 1016-23.

Form of Title

1. In references to books, capitalize only the first letter of the first word of the title (and of the subtitle, if any) and capitalize proper nouns. Underline the complete title and type a period after it.
2. In references to articles in periodicals or in edited books, capitalize only the first letter of the first word of the article's title (and subtitle, if any), and all proper nouns. Do not put the title within quotation marks. Type a period after the title of the article. For the title of the journal, and the volume and page numbers, see the next instruction.
3. In references to periodicals, give the volume number in arabic numerals, and underline it. Do *not* use *vol.* before the number, and do not use *p.* or *pg.* before the page numbers.

Sample References

A Book by One Author

Money, J. (1980). *Love and love sickness: The science of sex, gender difference and pair-bonding.* Baltimore: Johns Hopkins Press.

A Book by More Than One Author

Spence, J. T., & Helmreich, R. L. (1978). *Masculinity and femininity.* Austin: University of Texas Press.

A Collection of Essays

Bundy, W. P. (Ed.). (1985). *The nuclear controversy.* New York: New American Library.

A Work in a Collection of Essays

Rogers, B. (1985). The Atlantic alliance. In W. P. Bundy (Ed.). *The nuclear controversy* (pp. 41–52). New York: New American Library.

Government Documents

If the writer is not known, treat the government and the agency as the author. Most federal documents are issued by the Government Printing Office in Washington.

United States Congress. Office of Technology Assessment (1984). *Computerized manufacturing automation: Employment, education, and the workplace.* Washington, DC: U.S. Government Printing Office.

An Article in a Journal That Paginates Each Issue Separately

Swinton, E. (1993, Winter). New wine in old casks: Sino-Japanese and Russo-Japanese war prints. *Asian Art,* 27–49.

The publication is issued four times a year, each issue containing a page 27. It is necessary, therefore, to tell the reader that this article appears in the winter issue.

An Article in a Journal with Continuous Pagination

Herdt, G. (1991). Representations of homosexuality.

Journal of the History of Sexuality, 1, 481–504.

An Article from a Monthly or Weekly Magazine

Corliss, R. (1993, March 8). Bill Murray in the

driver's seat. Time, p. 67.

An Article in a Newspaper

Perry, T. (1993, 16 February). Election to give

Latinos new political clout in San Diego. Los

Angeles Times, sec. A, p. 3.

(*Note:* If no author is given, simply begin with the date, in parentheses.)

A Book Review

Bayme, S. (1993). Tradition or modernity? [Review of

Neil Gillman, Sacred fragments: Recovering

theology for the modern Jew.] Judaism, 42,

106–13.

Bayme is the reviewer, not the author of the book. The book under review is called *Sacred Fragments: Recovering Theology for the Modern Jew,* but the review, published in volume 42 of a journal called *Judaism,* had its own title, "Tradition of Modernity?"

If the review does not have a title, after the date (given in parentheses) of the review type a period, two spaces, and then a square bracket, and proceed as in the example just given.

Reminder: For a full account of the APA method of dealing with all sorts of unusual citations, see the third edition (1983) of the *Publication Manual of the American Psychological Association.*

Citations Within the Text

The APA style emphasizes the date of publication; the date appears not only in the list of references at the end of the paper but also in the paper itself, when you give a brief parenthetic citation of a source that you have quoted or summarized or in any other way used. Here is an example:

Statistics for church attendance are highly unreliable
       (Catherton, 1990, p. 17).

The title of Catherton's book or article will be given in your list entitled References. By turning to the list, the reader will learn in what publication Catherton made this point.

A Summary of an Entire Work

Catherton (1991) concluded the opposite.

Or

Similar views are easily found (Catherton, 1991;
       Brinnin and Abse, 1992).

A Reference to a Page or Pages

Catherton (1991, p. 107) argues that "church
       attendance is increasing but religious faith is
       decreasing."

A Reference to an Author Represented by More Than One Work in the References

As we explained in discussing the form of the material in References, if you list two or more works that an author published in the same year, the works are listed in alphabetic order, by the first letter of the title. The first work is labeled *a*, the second *b*, and so on. Here is a reference to the second work that Catherton published in 1991:

Boston is "a typical large Northern city" so far as
       church attendance goes (Catherton, 1991b).

A Note on Other Systems of Documentation

The MLA style is commonly used in the humanities, and the APA style is commonly used in the social sciences, but many other disciplines use their own styles. What follows is a list of handbooks that give the systems used in some other disciplines.

Biology

Council of Biology Editors, Style Manual Committee. *CBE Style Manual.* 6th ed. Bethesda: Council of Biology Editors, 1992.

Chemistry

> American Chemical Society. *Handbook for Authors of Papers in American Chemical Society Publications.* Washington: American Chemical Society, 1978.

Engineering

> Engineers Joint Council, Committee of Engineering Society Editors. *Recommended Practice for Style of References in Engineering Publications.* New York: Engineers Joint Council, 1966.

Geology

> U.S. Geological Survey. *Suggestions to Authors of the Reports of the United States Geological Survey.* 6th ed. Washington: GPO, Department of the Interior, 1978.

Law

> *A Uniform System of Citation.* 15th ed. Cambridge: Harvard Law Review Association.

Mathematics

> American Mathematical Society. *A Manual for Authors of Mathematical Papers.* 9th ed. Providence, R.I.: American Mathematical Society, 1989.

Medicine

> American Medical Association, Scientific Publications Division. *Stylebook.* 6th ed. Acton, Mass.: Publishing Sciences Group, 1976.

Physics

> American Institute of Physics, Publications Board. *Style Manual.* 4th ed. New York: American Institute of Physics, 1990.

Two Sample Research Essays by Students

Here are two essays in which students have drawn on the writing of others in developing their ideas. The first, "Politics and Psychology in *The Awakening*," by Beatrice Cody, uses the MLA form of in-text citations, which are clarified by a list headed "Works Cited."

Beatrice Cody

Writing 125

Ms. Bellanca

May 7, 1994

Politics and Psychology in *The Awakening*

At first glance, Kate Chopin's *The Awakening* (1899) poses no problem to the feminist reader. It is the story of Edna Pontellier, a woman living at the turn of the century who, partly through a half-realized summer romance, discovers that sensual love, art and individuality mean more to her than marriage or motherhood. When she concludes that there can be no compromise between her awakened inner self and the stifling shell of her outer life as a wife and mother, she drowns herself. In such a summary, Edna appears to be yet another victim of the "Feminine Mystique" described by Betty Friedan in the 1950's, a mind-numbing malaise afflicting the typical American housewife whose husband and society expected her to care for family at the expense of personal freedom and fulfillment. However, it is possible that the events leading to Edna's tragic death were not caused solely by the expectations of a sexist society pre-dating Friedan's model, in which a wife was not only dutiful to but also the "property" of her husband (Culley 117), and a mother not only stayed home but also sacrificed even the "essential" for her children

(Chopin *Awakening* 48). Perhaps Edna's suicide resulted from the torments of her individual psyche, her inability to cope with the patriarchal expectations which most women in fact were able to tolerate.

It is difficult to say how Chopin wished *The Awakening* to be interpreted. Heroines who explore their own individuality (with varying degrees of success and failure) abound in her work (Shinn 358); Chopin herself, though married, was a rather nontraditional wife who smoked cigarettes, and, like Edna Pontellier, took walks by herself (Nissenbaum 333-34). One might think therefore that Chopin was making a political statement in *The Awakening* about the position of women in society based on her own rejection of that position. But aside from slim biographical evidence and the assertions of some critics such as Larzer Ziff and Daniel S. Rankin that Chopin sympathized with Edna, we have no way of knowing whether she regarded this protagonist as a victim of sexist oppression or simply, to quote her family doctor in the novel itself, as "a sensitive and highly organized woman,. . . [who] is especially peculiar" (66). It is therefore necessary to explore the two possibilities, using evidence from the novel to determine whether Edna Pontellier's awakening is political or peculiarly personal in nature.

It does not take a deeply feminist awareness to detect the dominant, controlling stance Edna's husband, Leonce, assumes in their marriage. Throughout the novel Chopin documents the resulting injustices, both great and small, which Edna endures. In one

instance Leonce comes home late at night after Edna
has fallen asleep, and, upon visiting their sleeping
children, concludes that both of them are feverish. He
wakes Edna so that she may check on them, despite her
assertion that the children are perfectly well. He
chides her for her "inattention" and "habitual neglect
of the children" (7)—rather than respecting her
ability as their mother to judge the state of their
health or attending to them himself—and reduces her to
tears. She defers to his judgment, looking at the boys
as he had asked, and, finding them entirely healthy,
goes out to the porch where "an indescribable
oppression . . . filled her whole being with a vague
anguish" (8). Though in some ways inconsequential,
actions such as these epitomize Leonce Pontellier's
attitude toward women and particularly toward his
wife. It is his belief that she has a certain role and
specific duties (those of a woman) which must be done
well—according to his (a man's) standards. Although he
would probably claim to love Edna, he does not seem to
regard her as an autonomous individual; she is the
mother of his children, the hostess of such "callers"
as he deems appropriate (i.e., the ones who will bring
him influence and esteem) (51) and essentially another
decoration in his impeccably furnished house (50).
When Edna's awakening leads her to abandon household
chores in favor of painting, Chopin exposes Leonce's
sexism: "Mr. Pontellier had been a rather courteous
husband so long as he met a certain tacit
submissiveness in his wife. But her new and unexpected
line of conduct completely bewildered him . . . her

absolute disregard for her duties as a wife angered him" (57).

It would seem from such evidence that Chopin intended *The Awakening* to depict the wrongs that women suffered at the hands of men in her society. Taking this cue from Chopin, many twentieth-century critics choose to view it in a political light. Larzer Ziff, for example, claims that the novel "rejected the family as the automatic equivalent of feminine self-fulfillment, and on the very eve of the twentieth century it raised the question of what woman was to do with the freedom she struggled toward" (175). Marie Fletcher states that "[Edna's] suicide is the last in a series of rebellions which structure her life, give it pathos, and make of the novel . . . an interpretation of the 'new woman'" (172)—"the emerging suffragist/woman professional of the late nineteenth century" (Culley 118). Even in 1899 an anonymous reviewer in the *New Orleans Times-Democrat* noticed the political implications of the novel, declaring in his own conservative was that

> a woman of twenty-eight, a wife and twice a
> mother who is pondering upon her relations to
> the world about her, fails to perceive that the
> relation of a mother to her children is far more
> important than the gratification of a passion
> which experience has taught her is . . . evanes-
> cent, can hardly be said to be fully awake. (150)

These critics lead us to focus on the socio-political implications of the novel, and on the questions it raises about woman's role and responsibility: when if ever does a woman's personal life become more important than her children? or, how does Edna embody the emanicipated woman? But I believe that more than just the social pressure and politics of the late nineteenth century were acting on Edna. It was the inherent instability of her own psyche, exacerbated by the oppression she suffered as a woman, that drove her to swim out to her death at the end of *The Awakening*.

Despite the feminist undertones discernible in Chopin's work, a strong sense prevails that Edna's tragedy is unique, a result of her own psychology, not only of societal oppression. Throughout the novel Chopin describes Edna's agitated state of mind and drops hints about her upbringing and family life before marriage. Upon piecing all the clues to her personality together one gets a troubling, stereotypical picture. Edna's widowed father is a stern colonel from Kentucky who "was perhaps unaware that he had coerced his own wife into her grave" (71). From the scenes in which he appears one deduces that he is harsh and authoritative with his family; the narrator's comment about his wife implies that perhaps he was abusive (no doubt psychologically, possibly physically) as well. He gambles compulsively on horse-racing (69), which denotes an addictive personality. He also makes his own very strong cocktails—"toddies"—which he drinks almost all day long (71). He retains the appearance of sobriety, however, which indicates a high tolerance built up over much time. From this evidence one may assume that he suffers from alcoholism.

The rest of Edna's family—two sisters—fit the mold of the dysfunctional family that a violent, alcoholic parent tends to create. Her oldest sister seems to be the hyper-responsible, over-functioning "perfect" daughter. She served as a surrogate mother to Edna and her younger sister, and is described by Edna's husband as the only daughter who "has all the Presbyterianism undiluted" (66). Edna's younger sister is, predictably, exactly the opposite: Leonce Pontellier describes her as a "vixen" (66). She has rebelled against all of the rules and expectations that the eldest daughter obeys and fulfills. Edna, the middle child, is hence a curious case. Chopin tells us that "even as a child she had lived her own small life all within herself" (15). In such family situations the middle child is usually rather introverted. Where the two other siblings strive compulsively either to correct or create problems, the sibling in the middle passively escapes from her painful family situation by withdrawing into herself (Seixas and Youcha 48–49).

So far this simplistic but relatively reliable delineation of personalities works for Edna's character. Later in life she perpetuates the patterns of her dysfunctional family by marrying a man who almost mirrors her father in personality; he is simply a workaholic rather than an alcoholic. Edna gives birth to two children, "a responsibility which she had blindly assumed" (20) in her typically passive way. The first time she truly examines her role in this marriage and indeed in the world at large occurs on Grand Isle, a resort island where she and her family

are vacationing for the summer. There she begins to
spend a great deal of time with a young man named
Robert Lebrun, and a mutual desire gradually arises
between them. This desire, and the general sensuality
and openness of the Creole community to which she is
exposed, bring about Edna's sexual, artistic, and
individual awakening. Although the reader is excited
and inspired by this awakening in Edna—a woman
learning to shed the fetters of both her oppressive
marriage and society in general—the way it takes
control of her life is disturbingly reminiscent of
mental illness. She becomes infatuated with Robert,
devotes an inordinate amount of time to painting, and
seeks out classical music, which wracks her soul in a
torturous ecstasy. Throughout her awakening, she
experiences myriad moods and feelings that she had
never felt before in her docile, passive state. Many
of these moods manifest themselves in the form of
mysterious, troubling voices: "the voices were not
soothing that came to her from the darkness and the
sky above and the stars" (53); "she felt like one who
has entered and lingered within the portals of some
forbidden temple in which a thousand muffled voices
bade her begone" (84). Behind the veil of metaphor
here one can detect hints of an almost schizoid
character. Chopin even describes Edna as two selves,
which naturally befits a woman undergoing an emotional
transformation, but which also denotes a distinctly
schizophrenic state of mind: "she was becoming herself
and daily casting aside that fictitious self which we
assume like a garment with which to appear before the

world" (57); "she could only realize that she herself—her present self—was in some way different from the other self" (41). Chopin phrases her descriptions of Edna in such a way that they could in fact describe either a woman gaining her emotional autonomy or a woman losing her mind.

As compelling as I find the suggestion of Edna's insanity, I must admit that her struggle between self-hood and motherhood is one too common to all women to be passed off as the ravings of a madwoman. As to which interpretation she preferred, Chopin offered few clues. For example, in February 1898 Chopin responded to a question, posed by the society page of the *St. Louis Post-Dispatch*, about the possible motives for a recent rash of suicides among young high-society women. Rather than the pressure of society as a likely motive, she suggests a "highly nervous" disposition (qtd. in Toth 120). Indeed, she asserts that "leadership in society is a business . . . there is nothing about it that I can see that would tend to produce an unhealthy condition of mind. On the contrary, it prevents women from becoming morbid, as they might, had they nothing to occupy their attention when at leisure" (qtd. in Toth 120). Perhaps, then, we are to suppose that a combination of psychic instability and extensive leisure, rather than the oppression of her society, caused Edna to take her own life. And yet this same response in the *Post-Dispatch* includes a counter-question to the editor: "Business men commit suicide every day, yet we do not say that suicide is epidemic in the business world. Why should we say the feeling is rife among society women, because half a dozen unfortunates, widely separated, take their own lives?" (qtd. in Toth 120). Her implicit criticism of the double-standard suggests that Chopin was aware of the politics of gender relations in her own society in addition to the existence of an "hysterical tendency" in some women (qtd. in Toth 120). One cannot therefore discount the possibility that Chopin meant Edna's suicide to be in part a reaction to her society's rigid and limiting expectations of women.

Chopin received such harsh criticism of Edna Pontellier's sexual freedom and attitude toward family that, when *The Awakening* was published, if not before, she must have had some idea of how controversial the issue of her protagonist's personal freedom really was. Her critics tend to believe that she sympathized unreservedly with her headstrong heroine; but even the retraction she published soon after her novel does not reveal whether she viewed Edna as oppressed or mentally ill. Apparently written for the benefit of her scandalized reviewers, the retraction ironically relieves Chopin of all responsibility for Edna's "making such a mess of things and working out her own damnation" (159). Again, as in her ambiguous response to the *Post-Dispatch*, Chopin leaves curious readers unsatisfied, and the motive of Edna's suicide unclear.

It is left to the reader therefore to decide whether Edna is a martyr to a feminist cause—the liberation of the American housewife—or the victim of a psychological disturbance that drives her to suicide. I believe that it is best not to dismiss either possibility. To begin with, one cannot deny that in the nineteenth century few options other than marriage and child-rearing were open to women. These narrow options were the result of a societal structure in which men socially, economically, and sexually dominated women. In the late twentieth century we can look back at Chopin's time and feel confident in condemning this state of affairs, but from contemporary criticism of *The Awakening* alone, it is clear that this political view was not so widely accepted at the turn of the century. Perhaps Chopin had an unusually clear and untimely insight into what we now consider the sexism of her society, but she chose to condemn it only implicitly by portraying it as a fact of life against which her unbalanced heroine must struggle and perish. As Larzer Ziff puts it, "Edna Pontellier is trapped between her illusions and the condition which society arbitrarily establishes to maintain itself, and she is made to pay" (175). Chopin fused the political and the personal in Edna Pontellier, who, like most women in the world, suffers not only from the pressures of a society run by and for men, but also from her own individual afflictions.

Works Citied

Chopin, Kate. *The Awakening*. 1899. Ed. Margo Culley.
    New York: Norton, 1976.

---.   "Retraction." In "Aims and Autographs of
    Author." *Book News* 17 (July 1899): 612. Rpt. in
    Chopin. *Awakening* 159.

Culley, Margo. "The Context of The Awakening." Chopin.
    Awakening 119-22.

Fletcher, Marie. "The Southern Woman in the Fiction of
    Kate Chopin." *Louisiana History* 7 (Spring 1966):
    117-32. Rpt. in Chopin. *Awakening* 170-73.

"New Publications." *New Orleans Times-Democrat*. 18
    June 1899: 15. Rpt. in Chopin. *Awakening* 150.

Nissembaum, Stephen. "Chopin, Kate O'Flaherty."
    Notable American Women. 1971 ed.

Rankin, Daniel S. "Influences Upon the Novel." In
    Kate Chopin and Her Creole Stories. Philadelphia.
    U of Penn P, 1932. 173-75. Rpt. in Chopin.
    Awakening 163-65.

Seixas, Judith S. and Geraldine Youcha. *Children of
    Alcoholism: A Survivor's Manual*. New York:
    Harper, 1985.

Shinn, Thelma J. "Kate O'Flaherty Chopin." *American
    Women Writers*. 1979 ed.

Toth, Emily. "Kate Chopin on Divine Love and Suicide:
    Two Rediscovered Articles." *American Literature*
    63 (1991): 115-21.

Ziff, Larzer. *The American 1890's: Life and Times of a
    Lost Generation*. New York: Viking, 1966. 279-305.
    Rpt. in Chopin. *Awakening* 173-75.

This second research paper, Lisa Temple's "Beyond the Institution: The Effects of Labeling on Ex-Mental Patients," uses the APA (American Psychological Association) form of in-text citations, which are clarified by a list headed "References."

```
Lisa Temple
Writing 125 S
May 10, 1994
```

Beyond the Institution: The Effects of Labeling on
Ex-Mental Patients

When mental health professionals decide that an individual is mentally ill and should be hospitalized, the public usually agrees with this judgment. However, when the same professionals determine that a person is no longer mentally ill and has the competence and the right to return to normal society, the public does not generally defer to their decision. Instead, they continue to view the individual under the constraints of his previous label. Thus, they see the ex-mental patient through the bias of a label which is no longer professionally accurate and which places the former patient at a disadvantage in most, if not all, aspects of social integration into the community.

Those social psychologists and others who subscribe to "Labeling Theory" hold that a label does not merely describe a condition; rather, a label helps to produce behavior appropriate to the label. That is, persons who are labeled deviants may, *because of* the label, behave in the expected way. If we accept this theory, there is reason to doubt the widely accepted assumption that social control is a preventative response to deviance. Rather, it can be maintained, this cause-and-effect relationship is in reality reversed; social control causes deviance. According to labeling theorists, when rule breakers are labeled and forced to adopt society's view of themselves as deviant, they begin to act in a manner that conforms to the stereotype commonly associated with this label. Scheff makes this point when he states that ". . . among residual rule breakers, labeling is the single most important cause of careers of residual deviance" (Scheff, 1966, pp. 92–93). In short, supporters of labeling theory claim that societal efforts to control deviance not only fail to effectively reduce deviance but actually increase it.

The potential effects of labeling can be placed into three distinct categories: 1) the creation of deviance, 2) the stabilization of deviant behavior, and 3) the consequences of a label in relation to other areas of an individual's life, such as employment, friendships, family relations, and mate selection (Link, 1982). It is the third category which most affects ex-mental patients as they attempt to reenter conventional society while confronting the effects of their past label on their immediate community, family, and employer.

An important consideration for ex-mental patients is how they are viewed by the community in which they live. Jones and Cochrane of the University of Birmingham found in an experiment (1981) that a stereotype of mental illness exists and that the stereotype is a reasonably accurate impression of the behavior of the mentally ill. Most people believe that mental patients are excessively introverted and are given to rapid, unprovoked mood swings from one emotional extreme to the other. This stereotype closely resembles the behavior of psychiatric patients described in objective studies.

According to labeling theory, this close relationship between stereotype and reality occurs because the cultural stereotype of mental illness acts as a "self-fulfilling prophecy." That is, others react toward the potential patient in a way that leads him or her to fulfill the expected role, which in turn reinforces the original label. This reaction and counterreaction become a cycle which can lead to the point where alternative roles are no longer available to the prospective patient; adopting the role of a mentally ill person may become the only possible way the person can cope with the label. As Jones's and Cochrane's study shows, the general population has a negative attitude toward the mentally ill, and mental patients' attitudes concerning themselves reflect those of the public.

Another experiment, done by Phillips (1966), demonstrates the effect a label can have on "attitudinal social distance," which is a measure of rejection. In this study, several short descriptions of various individuals were given to subjects, and psychiatric hospitalization was mentioned in some of the descriptions to measure the amount of rejection provoked by the label psychiatric hospitalization suggested. Various questions were asked about the individuals described in each vignette, ranging from questions about the desirability of having the person as a neighbor, of working with him, and of the degree to which one should discourage one's children from marrying him. The results showed that a person with a label is very likely to have more difficulty finding a job, friends, a marriage partner, and a place to live than would a person without a label, even if both have exactly the same mental characteristics. Thus it seems that a label has a substantial effect upon the individual it concerns.

It follows, then, that many of us also hold a certain stereotypical attitude toward mental patients after they have left the institution and that this public attitude has an effect on the self-concept and behavior of the ex-mental patient. The relationship between label and self-concept is demonstrated quite effectively in an experiment by Farina et al. (1968). The purpose of this experiment was to show that a label can have a great effect, even when the label in question has no factual basis. In this study, unacquainted male college students were paired randomly. Each member of the pair was led to believe that the other was told that the former was in some way deviant. The results showed that merely believing that one is viewed as stigmatized can influence a person's behavior; the labeled individual is likely to become less confident and thus less capable of adequately fulfilling normal expectations. This failure in turn leads to rejection by the other individuals and to increased feeling of stigmatization.

Another study (Stensrud and Stensrud, 1980) was performed specifically to determine whether the stigma attached to a person who once received psychiatric hospitalization persists over time, even after the individual has shown that he has successfully reintegrated into the society and that the stigma is inappropriate. In this experiment subjects were asked to rate several unknown persons on amount of internal control versus tendency to be controlled by chance and "powerful others." In the study a successful individual who was described as having once experienced depression, and as having sought treatment as a psychiatric inpatient was evaluated by subjects as possessing less internal control than an equally successful person who had experienced depression, but who hadn't sought treatment, even though both had current personal histories that were considered very successful. In other words, a person who had been a psychiatric patient but who had since then stabilized his disability and successfully integrated himself into the culture was still perceived as mentally ill by others. This finding supports the hypothesis that once the label of mental illness is attached to an individual, all future interactions with others are influenced by this label. Regardless of the person's current status, a previous label continues to influence how others perceive the person.

Family is another sphere of the ex-mental patient's life that is affected by a previous label.

Although relatives are closer to the former patient, they do not necessarily place less stigma on the patient's label than does the rest of society. This was shown in a study by Vannicelli et al. (1980), in which the relatives of schizophrenic patients fostered attitudes that were more similar to those prevalent in their own social class than to those held by mental health professionals. Like other members of society, relatives of ex-mental patients tend to associate this label with strong negative connotations. Although one study (Hollingshead and Redlich, 1958) showed a technical difference in the attitudes of family members in differing social classes—higher class relatives were more likely to experience shame and guilt while lower class relatives felt more resentment and fear toward the former patient—all of these attitudes are very clearly negative ones.

Similarly, several other experiments have shown that "...the stigma of mental illness is reflected in the shame and rejection experienced by patients [as well as] ...the sensitivity and embarrassment experienced by close friends and family" (Nuehring, 1979, p. 626; Freeman and Simmons 1963, Siassi et al., 1973, Yarrow et al., 1955). One experiment in particular (Nuehring, 1979) concentrated on feelings of stigma among discharged state mental hospital patients as well as the stigmatizing attitudes held by family and close friends toward these ex-patients. Nuehring discovered that a stigma is not, to any great degree, a result of patients' social characteristics, environment, or functioning. Instead, there are two specific dependent variables which affect feelings of stigma and stigmatizing attitudes: the patient's degree of depression and the degree to which he is seen as a burden to his "significant others."

This study suggests that ex-patients who feel relatively more depressed are more likely to experience stigma, perhaps because feeling depressed and feeling stigmatized are negatively reinforcing. The study also suggests that former patients who receive aftercare are thought of as a burden, especially if they are depressed, or show a lack of anxiety, or are male. It seems possible that these cases are considered more stigmatizing because they are individuals who failed in fulfilling society's norms to an even greater extent than did other ex-mental patients. All mental patients are usually considered deviant, but former mental patients who receive treatment may be more stigmatized than other ex-patients because, although living in the outside community, they are still receiving treatment. Male ex-patients may be more stigmatized than female ex-patients simply because, in our society, males are typically thought of as the stronger and less emotional of the two sexes; thus, male ex-patients seem to stray more from the norm and are more likely to be stigmatized. In addition, the ex-patients most likely to be seen as burdens by family and friends are those who seek high degrees of social interaction. This seems to imply that the more integrated into a community a former patient tries to become, the more unfavorably he is looked upon by the community.

The ex-mental patient's previous label also affects his chances of finding and keeping a job. According to Link (1982), there are two major ways in which former mental patients are harmed in the world of work. One of these is through direct discrimination by employers. As documented in a study done by Olshansky et al. (1958), employers openly admit that they would prefer not to hire former mental patients. Furthermore, it has been shown that ". . . employers are less friendly in an interview situation and rate the applicant's chance of getting the job significantly lower when he reveals a history of mental illness" (Farina and Felner, 1973, p. 270). In fact, individuals with a history of mental hospitalization are automatically prohibited in many states from pursuing certain careers such as firefighter, teacher, or police officer (Ennis and Siegal, 1973). In addition, former mental patients can be refused privileges to which others have access, such as a driver's license, which de facto excludes them from certain jobs. Thus a label, as well as being a source of direct discrimination, can indirectly affect a person's ability to find a job. In other words, a label such as that of the ex-mental patient increases one's chances of being unemployed and decreases one's chances of obtaining a well-paying job.

In addition to increasing discrimination, the label of the former mental patient in another way negatively affects chances of employment. This concerns the ". . . mechanisms which operate through the individual's expectations of rejection" (Link, 1982, p. 204). Even before treatment, most patients fear rejection because of their own beliefs about mental illness and their knowledge of the public's attitude. During treatment, the "mortification process" (Goffman, 1961) strengthens the fears of patient, who come to believe that they need certain restrictions and thus deserve to be regarded negatively. This fear of rejection then becomes a self-fulfilling prophecy. Ex-patients act more defensively, less confidently, or totally avoid threatening contact because they fear and expect rejection. The ex-patient internalizes this negative view and begins to think of himself as "...totally ineffective ... [or as a hopeless case]" (Link, 1982, p. 204). As a result, these former mental patients appear to prospective employers as unconfident and incompetent.

In summary, the previous label of the ex-mental patient negatively affects the former patient's life. Specifically, this label increases environmental stresses such as unemployment and rejection by family and friends, reduces the individual's access to social supports, and produces a tentativeness and lack of confidence which greatly weaken the person's usual means of coping. Moreover, these effects are exactly those which have been found by environmentally oriented researchers to be of most importance in the origins of mental illness. It is entirely possible then, that a previous psychiatric label plays a significant role in the maintenance of mental disorder

(Link, 1982). Any attempt to improve the plight of the ex-mental patient, therefore, must include educational programs not only for ex-patients, but also for the community in which they live. Before former mental patients can be expected to integrate successfully into society, there must first be a significant and necessary change in society's view of these individuals.

References

Bord, R. (1971). Rejection of the Mentally Ill: Continuities and Further Developments. *Social Problems, 18,* 496–509.

Cumming, E., & Cumming, J. (1957). *Closed Ranks: An Experiment in Mental Health.* Cambridge: Harvard.

Ennis, B., & Siegal, L. (1973). *The Rights of Mental Patients.* New York: Avon.

Farina, A., Allen, J., & Saul, B. (1968). The Role of the Stigmatized in Affecting Social Relationships. *Journal of Personality, 36,* 169–82.

Farina, A., & Felner, J. (1973). Reactions of Workers to Male and Female Mental Patient Job Applications. *Journal of Consulting and Clinical Psychology, 41,* 268–81.

Freeman, H., & Simmons, O. (1963). *The Mental Patient Comes Home.* New York: Wiley.

Goffman; E. (1961). *Asylums.* Garden City, New York: Doubleday.

Hollingshead, H., & Redlich, F. (1958). *Social Change and Mental Illness.* New York: Wiley.

Jones, L., & Cochrane, R. (1981). Stereotypes of
    Mental Illness: A Test of the Labeling
    Hypothesis. *International Journal of Social
    Psychiatry, 27,* 99–107.

Link, B. (1982). Mental Patient Status, Work, and
    Income: An Examination of the Effects of a
    Psychiatric Label. *American Sociological Review,
    47,* 202–15.

Nuehring, E. M. (1979). Stigma and State Hospital
    Patients. *American Journal of Orthopsychiatry,
    49,* 626–33.

Nunnally, J. (1961). *Popular Conceptions of Mental
    Health: Their Development and Change.* New York:
    Holt.

Olshansky, S., Grob, S., & Malmud, I. T. (1958).
    Employers' Attitudes and Practices in the Hiring
    of Ex-Mental Patients. *Mental Hygiene, 42,*
    391–401.

Phillips, D. (1966). Public Identification and
    Acceptance of the Mentally Ill. *American Journal
    of Public Health, 56,* 755–63.

Scheff, T. (1966). *Being Mentally Ill: A Sociological
    Theory.* Chicago: Aldine.

Siassi, I., Spiro, H., & Crocetti, G. (1973). The
    Social Acceptance of the Ex-Mental Patient.
    Community Mental Health Journal, 233–43.

Star, S. (1955). *The Public's Ideas About Mental
    Illness.* Chicago: National Opinion Research
    Center.

Stensrud, R., & Stensrud, K. (1980). Attitudes Toward
    Successful Individuals with and without Histories

of Psychiatric Hospitalization. *Psychological Reports, 47,* 495–498.

Vannicelli, M., Washburn, S. L., & Scheff, B. J. (1980). Family Attitudes Toward Mental Illness: Immutable with Respect to Time, Treatment Setting, and Outcome. *American Journal of Orthopsychiatry, 50,* 151–55.

Yarrow, M., Clausen, J., & Robbins, P. (1955). The Social Meaning of Mental Illness. *Journal of Social Issues, 11,* 33–48.

Exercises

1. If you have trouble finding material in the library, don't hesitate to ask a librarian for assistance. But you will soon learn, to solve many of the most common problems yourself. Here are a few.

    You want to do some research for a paper on Mexican immigrants in the United States. You look in the catalog and find only one citation, reprinted below. How can you find other books on the subject?

    ```
           The Mexican immigrant.

    JV     Gamio, Manuel, 1883-1960, comp.
    6798      The Mexican immigrant. New York,
    .M6    Arno Press, 1969.
    G28       xiii, 288 p. map. 22 cm. (The
    1969   American immigration collection)
              Reprint of the 1931 ed.
              1.United States-Emigration and
           immigration. 2.Mexico-Emigration and
           immigration. 3.Mexicans in the United
           States. I.T.


    RG77-115225 r                 69-18778
    JV6798.M6G28 1969               301.453/72/
    ```

2. You want to do a paper on Richard Wright's short stories, and the catalog lists several relevant books, but when you check the stacks you find none of these books is on the shelf. What do you do, short of abandoning the topic or going to another library?

You need reviews of a film released a few months ago. There are no books on this film, and the *Readers' Guide* lists nothing under the film's title. What do you do?

You find references to *CQ Weekly Report,* the *Department of State Bulletin,* and the *Journal of the American Oriental Society,* but these journals don't seem to be listed in the periodical file. Still, you have heard that the library does have them. How can that be?

You are looking for an issue of a journal published a few months ago. It is not on the shelf with the current issues, and it is not on the shelf with the bound volumes. Where is it?

You want to write a paper on bilingual education, or, more exactly, on bilingual education of Mexican Americans. What do you look for in the catalog? And what periodical indexes do you consult?

3. Using the MLA form, list the following items in Works Cited.

A book entitled *Areas of Challenge for Soviet Foreign Policy,* with an introduction by Adam B. Ulam. The book, published in 1985 by the Indiana University Press, in Bloomington, is written by three authors: Gerrit W. Gong, Angela E. Stent, and Rebecca V. Strode. Write *two* entries for Works Cited, the first entry indicating that you referred only to Ulam's introduction, the second entry indicating that you referred to material written by the three authors of the book.

Journal of Political and Military Strategy paginates its issues continuously; the second issue takes up where the first issue leaves off. The issues of 1984 constitute volume 12. Issue number 2 (the fall issue) contains an article that runs from page 229 to page 241. The article, written by James Burke, is entitled "Patriotism and the All-Volunteer Force."

International Security begins the pagination of each issue with page 1. The issues of 1985 constitute volume 9. Issue number 4 (the spring issue) contains an article that runs from page 79 to page 98. The article, written by Klaus Knorr, is entitled "Controlling Nuclear War."

On page 221 of the book you are now holding in your hand you will find an essay by Laura Cunningham. How would you list the essay in Works Cited?

4. Go to your library and prepare entries for Works Cited for each of the following:

A signed article in a recent issue of a journal devoted to some aspect of psychology.

A signed article in a newspaper.

A signed article in a recent issue of *Time.*

An unsigned article in a recent issue of *Newsweek.*

An unsigned article from the Macropaedia portion of *Encyclopaedia Britannica.*

A signed article from the Micropaedia portion of *Encyclopaedia Britannica.*

A catalog from your college.

A book (one of your textbooks will do) written by one author.

5. First, read the following paragraph, by Ernest van den Haag, from a book by van den Haag and John Conrad, *The Death Penalty Pro and Con: A Debate* (1983).

Crime is going to be with us as long as there is any social order articulated by laws. There is no point making laws that prohibit some action or other (e.g., murder or theft) unless there is some temptation to commit it. And however harsh the threats of the law, they will not restrain some people, whether because they discount the risk of punishment or because they are exposed to extraordinary temptation. They may hope for an immense profit; or be passionately angry or vindictive; or be in such misery that they feel they have nothing to lose. Thus, I repeat, the problem every society must attempt to solve (in part by means of punishment) is not eliminating crime but controlling it.

Now write a slightly disguised paragraph, in effect imitating someone who is plagiarizing from van den Haag and Conrad.

Next, write a second paragraph that acknowledges the authors but nevertheless illustrates plagiarism.

Finally, write a third version in which you make honest use of some or all of van den Haag's material.

Chapter 16

Writing About Literature

Why Write?

Much of the writing that you do in your various courses will be in response to written texts—perhaps a sociologist's article on the rise (or decline) of religious faith in the United States, a psychologist's article on the effects of televised violence, a philosopher's argument in favor of (or in opposition to) abortion. *Why* are you writing? Because an instructor has given you a writing assignment, of course. But you will probably agree that instructors give writing assignments largely in order to help you to read closely and to think deeply and clearly about what you have read. Writing requires you to get not only the author's text but also your best responses to it into your mind, into your bones—and perhaps out of your system.

Responding to Literary Texts

In literature courses the texts that you read are especially compact, partly because writers of fiction and poetry are especially skilled in handling words, in packing the most into them and in getting the most out of them. When we read *non*-literary writings, it may be enough to get the gist of the argument; in fact, we may have to prune away a good deal of wordiness before we get to the heart of the matter—say, the three reasons offered on behalf of capital punishment. But when we read a literary work, we must pay extremely close attention to what might be called the feel of the words. For instance, the word *woods* in Robert Frost's "Stopping by Woods on a Snowy Evening" has a rural, folksy quality that *forest* doesn't have, and it is by means of such small distinctions that the poem's effect accumulates.

A chief difference between literary and nonliterary texts, though again the difference is one of degree, is the literary author's concern with presenting human experience concretely, with *showing* rather than with *telling*. Let's consider the briefest literary form, the proverb. Take this example: "A rolling stone gathers no moss." Of course the statement tells us something—it offers an assertion—but what makes it memorable is its concreteness.

Compare the original, for instance, with this unmemorable **paraphrase** or restatement, "If a stone is always moving around, vegetation won't have a chance to grow on it." The original version seems more real, more present, more convincing; it offers a small but complete world, hard (stone) and soft (moss), inorganic and organic, at rest and in motion.

We can go a little further, too, and say that the shapeliness of the proverb makes it memorable. This shapeliness is *felt* rather than consciously recognized, but if we analyze it we see that each of the nouns in the sentence (*stone* and *moss*) has one syllable, and each of the two words of motion (*rolling, gathers*) has two syllables, with the accent on the first of the two. The world of the proverb is complex but it is also unified into a whole by such relationships as these. The result is that the proverb, but not the paraphrase, pleases us and stays in our mind.

And this is the way most poets, storytellers, and dramatists work. They present scenes (for instance, a lover eagerly anticipating a meeting with the beloved) that are memorable for their vividness, their shapeliness, and their rich implications. "John loves Mary," written on a wall, is mere information—mere *telling* rather than *showing*—and there is no reason to value it. Literature is something else; it is, as Robert Frost said, "a performance in words." The Johns and Marys in poems, plays, and stories usually are fairly ordinary people, but they somehow become important to us; writers present them in so interesting and so memorable a way that we care about them, and their doings stay in our mind.

Although literary texts are especially compact or rich and dense, and are especially shapely (interestingly patterned or organized), when you respond to a literary text you are not doing something utterly different from what you do when you respond to *any* written text—for instance, an editorial in the newspaper or a chapter in a psychology textbook. You experience a variety of responses; you mentally agree or disagree, feel pleasure or irritation or puzzlement or boredom. And since your writing will be in large measure a report of your responses, your first reading of a work (which starts the responses) is the beginning of the writing process.

Your responses, or, rather, your thoughtful examination of your responses, will ultimately take shape in essays that you will hand in to the instructor.

Reading Fiction

Fiction usually ranges from the short story of a page or two (but usually more like ten or so pages) to the thousand-page novel. Let's begin with a very short story, an anonymous tale from nineteenth-century Japan. It is said to be literally true, but whether it really occurred or not is unimportant. It is the story, not the history, that counts.

Muddy Road

Two monks, Tanzan and Ekido, were once travelling together down a muddy road. A heavy rain was still falling.

Coming around a bend, they met a lovely girl in a silk kimono and sash, unable to cross the intersection.

"Come on, girl," said Tanzan at once Lifting her in his arms, he carried her over the mud.

Ekido did not speak again until that night when they reached a lodging temple. Then he no longer could restrain himself. "We monks don't go near females," he told Tanzan, "especially not young and lovely ones. It is dangerous. Why did you do that?"

"I left the girl there," said Tanzan. "Are you still carrying her?"

A superb story. The opening paragraph, though simple and matter-of-fact, holds our attention: we sense that something interesting is going to happen during this journey along a muddy road on a rainy day. Perhaps we even sense, somehow, by virtue of the references to the mud and the rain, that the journey itself rather than the travelers' destination will be the heart of the story: getting there will be more than half the fun. And then, after the introduction of the two **characters** (Tanzan and Ekido) and the **setting** (a muddy road), the **plot** (the happenings) introduces a **complication** (the encounter with the girl). Still there is apparently no **conflict,** though in "Ekido did not speak again until that night" we sense an unspoken conflict, an action (or, in this case, an inaction) that must be explained, an imbalance that must be righted before we are finished. At last Ekido, no longer able to contain his thoughts, lets his indignation burst out: "We monks don't go near females, . . . especially not young and lovely ones. It is dangerous. Why did you do that?" His statement and his question reveal not only his moral principles but also his insecurity and the anger that grows from it. And now, when the conflict is out in the open, comes the brief reply that reveals Tanzan's very different character as clearly as the outburst revealed Ekido's. This reply—though we could not have predicted it—strikes us as exactly right, bringing the story to a perfect end, to a point at which there is no more to be said. It provides the **denouement** (literally, the "unknotting"), or resolution. In a longer story we perhaps would find foreshadowing—hints of what is to come, or early details that later gain in significance, but "Muddy Road" is so brief that there is hardly space or need for such significant anticipations. (If you read Shirley Jackson's "The Lottery," on pages 385–92, you probably will be surprised by the ending, but if you then reread it you will notice that early references to the stones and to the general nervousness of the townspeople serve as foreshadowing.)

What does the story add up to, what is its **theme?** We do not want to reduce a story to a neat moral—surely we enjoy the situation, the dialogue, the contrasting characters—but we can say that some idea holds the story together.

There is plenty of room for a difference of opinion about what the idea is; probably no two people will use exactly the same words in talking about a theme. But perhaps we can say the story is about the difference between living according to the spirit of the monastic law (free from attachment to things of this world), and, on the other hand, living by the letter rather than the spirit of the law (complying only outwardly with the law). More briefly, we might say that the theme is about spirituality. Or maybe the theme is understanding, understanding others and oneself.

Of course, different readers may respond differently. The view that the meaning of a work is not something that an author embeds in a work, but that it is something that a reader creates in responding to a work, is called **reader-response theory.** There are several versions of this theory, but essentially it regards meaning as a **transaction** between a text and a reader.

Consider the view that men, by and large, see things somewhat differently from the way women see things. (Whether the differences in responses—if there are differences—are due to biology or to socialization or to both is a topic much discussed.) The idea that our gender shapes our reading (and our writing) is at the heart of **feminist** criticism, which is especially interested in three things: (1) writings by women; (2) the representations of women in literature (whether written by men or by women); and (3) the ways in which women respond to works of art. A feminist critic—a man as well as a woman can adopt a feminist stance, or at least so say the male feminists—might have a very different response from a reader who does not see things from this point of view. The feminist might argue that what is *really* interesting about "Muddy Road" is that it gives women no meaningful place in the world. The woman in the story, one might say, exists only to allow one of the monks to show his superiority to her charms. It is not a story, the feminist might argue, that has anything of interest to say either about women or to women. (Objections along these lines have in fact been made to traditional fairy tales such as Sleeping Beauty, stories in which most women are either utterly passive—sleeping beauties—or, if active, are wicked—evil witches.) As is usual in literature written by men, the woman is regarded as the Other, "The inessential as opposed to the essential." (The words are Simone de Beauvoir's, in *The Second Sex* [1949], page xix.) "Muddy Road" encodes or inscribes (to use the vocabulary of modern criticism) male structures of power.

Does reader-response theory mean that all responses are equally valid, and that no discussion of a work is any better than any other discussion? No. Most advocates of the theory recognize that responses must be grounded in the details of the literary work. A reader who said that Tanzan is a homosexual whose interest is in Ekido rather than in the girl must point to details in the story that support this response. If support cannot be produced—if the reader cannot produce evidence and thus argue the case responsibly—the response cannot be taken very seriously.

Having made the point that who we are will in some measure shape what we see in the work, let's return, so far as we can, to the work as an object "out there." Who tells this story? This is not the same question as, Who wrote the story? The author and the teller (the narrator) of a story are usually quite different. J. D. Salinger is the author of *Catcher in the Rye* but the narrator is Holden Caulfield, a prep school boy who has had a mental breakdown. Salinger's book begins, "If you really want to hear about it, the first thing you'll probably want to know is where I was born. . . ." *Catcher in the Rye* thus is narrated by a **first-person narrator;** that is, the narrator (the teller of the tale) speaks in the first person ("I") and is a character in the story. It happens that the narrator of *Catcher* is the chief character, but you can imagine the story being narrated by a minor figure, perhaps a friend of Holden's, or by Holden's psychiatrist.

Let's turn "Muddy Road" into a first-person narrative. It might begin with an abbot addressing novices:

> As chief abbot of Todaiji, I want to tell you young monks about two of your predecessors, Tanzan and Ekido.

Or (still as a first person narrative, this time narrated by Tanzan) it might begin thus:

> Once I was traveling with a fellow-monk, an extremely conscientious fellow named Ekido. The road was muddy. . . .

Or it might be told by Ekido. Even though the plot (the happenings) of these three stories would be identical, the stories would be significantly different. Let's think of what the story would be like if Ekido were to tell it. He might tell it in such a way that we would see he had learned a profound lesson—or, on the other hand, he might tell it in such a way that we would see he had completely missed the point. In such a version, after the final line of the present version we might get something like this:

> Nice words, but he couldn't fool me; after all, I know that a man's a man.

The reader presumably would perceive that Ekido does not understand the significance of the story that he himself tells. The emphasis of the story would thus be on the **irony**—the wry contrast—that a man who is confident that he understands something may in fact have completely misunderstood it. Or in a version somewhat along the line we have just invented, the reader might sense that the speaker, Ekido, although apparently scornful of Tanzan, is really angry with himself and is trying to conceal from himself his awareness of his weakness by attributing his own feelings to Tanzan.

In contrast to a first-person (or participant) narrator, who is a character in the story, a **third-person narrator** is outside of the story, a nonparticipant. Even here we are talking about a range. A third-person narrator may be a sort of fly on the wall, reporting only what is visible to any outsider, or a third-person narrator may be able to look into the minds of the characters. Again, the stories will be rather different. In the original version, part of the power, we think, comes from the fact that the narrator does *not* get into the minds of the two figures. Thus, we read, "Ekido did not speak again until that night. . . ." An omniscient narrator (a narrator who knows everything) might have said, "Ekido inwardly fumed," thereby telling us more but depriving us of the chance (and the pleasure) of doing our own interpreting.

Asking yourself questions about matters of narrative point of view, plot, and character is a way of seeing what is distinctive about a story. On pages 402–03 we give some additional questions that may help you to get into a story and that therefore may stimulate ideas for essays. But first let's look at a story.

A Story, and Notes and Two Essays by Students

Shirley Jackson

The Lottery

Shirley Jackson (1919–1965) achieved national attention in 1948 when The New Yorker *published the following story.*

The morning of June 27th was clear and sunny, with the fresh warmth of a full-summer day; the flowers were blossoming profusely and the grass was richly green. The people of the village began to gather in the square, between the post office and the bank, around ten o'clock; in some towns there were so many people that the lottery took two days and had to be started on June 26th, but in this village, where there were only about three hundred people, the whole lottery took less than two hours, so it could begin at ten o'clock in the morning and still be through in time to allow the villagers to get home for noon dinner.

The children assembled first, of course. School was recently over for the summer, and the feeling of liberty sat uneasily on most of them; they tended to gather together quietly for a while before they broke into boisterous play, and their talk was still of the classroom and the teacher, of books and reprimands. Bobby Martin had already stuffed his pocket full of stones, and the other boys soon followed his example, selecting the smoothest and roundest stones; Bobby and Harry Jones and Dickie Delacroix—the villagers pronounced this name "Dellacroy"—eventually made a great pile of stones in one corner of the square and guarded it against the raids of the other boys. The girls stood aside, talking among themselves, looking over their shoulders at the boys, and the very small children rolled in the dust or clung to the hands of their older brothers or sisters.

Soon the men began to gather, surveying their own children, speaking of planting and rain, tractors and taxes. They stood together, away from the pile of stones in the corner, and their jokes were quiet and they smiled rather than laughed. The women, wearing faded house dresses and sweaters, came shortly after their menfolk. They greeted one another and exchanged bits of gossip as they went to join their husbands. Soon the women, standing by their husbands, began to call to their children, and the children came reluctantly, having to be called four or five times. Bobby Martin ducked under his mother's grasping hand and ran, laughing, back to the pile of stones. His father spoke up sharply, and Bobby came quickly and took his place between his father and his oldest brother.

The lottery was conducted—as were the square dances, the teenage club, the Halloween program—by Mr. Summers, who had time and energy to devote to civic activities. He was a round-faced, jovial man and he ran the coal business, and people were sorry for him, because he had no children and his wife was a scold. When he arrived in the square, carrying the black wooden box, there was a murmur of conversation among the villagers and he waved and called, "Little late today, folks." The postmaster, Mr. Graves, followed him, carrying a three-legged stool, and the stool was put in the center of the square and Mr. Summers set the black box down on it. The villagers kept their distance, leaving a space between themselves and the stool, and when Mr. Summers said, "Some of you fellows want to give me a hand?" there was a hesitation before two men, Mr. Martin and his oldest son, Baxter, came forward to hold the box steady on the stool while Mr. Summers stirred up the papers inside it.

The original paraphernalia for the lottery had been lost long ago, and the black box now resting on the stool had been put into use even before Old Man Warner, the oldest man in town, was born. Mr. Summers spoke frequently to the villagers about making a new box, but no one liked to upset even as much tradition as was represented by the black box. There was a story that the present box had been made with some pieces of the box that had preceded it, the one that had been constructed when the first people settled down to make a village here. Every year, after the lottery, Mr. Summers began talking again about a new box, but every year the subject was allowed to fade off without anything's being done. The black box grew shabbier each year; by now it was no longer completely black but splintered badly along one side to show the original wood color, and in some places faded or stained.

Mr. Martin and his oldest son, Baxter, held the black box securely on the stool until Mr. Summers had stirred the papers thoroughly with his hand. Because so much of the ritual had been forgotten or discarded, Mr. Summers had been successful in having slips of paper substituted for the chips of wood that had been used for generations. Chips of wood, Mr. Summers had argued, had been all very well when the village was tiny, but now that the population was more than three hundred and likely to keep on growing, it was necessary to use something that would fit more easily into the black box. The night before the lottery, Mr. Summers and Mr. Graves made up the slips of paper and put them in the box, and it was then taken to the safe of Mr. Summers's coal company and locked up until Mr. Summers was ready to take it to the square next morning. The rest of the year, the box was put away, sometimes one place, sometimes another; it had spent one year in Mr. Grave's barn and another year underfoot in the post office, and sometimes it was set on a shelf in the Martin grocery and left there.

There was a great deal of fussing to be done before Mr. Summers declared the lottery open. There were lists to make up—of heads of families, heads of households in each family, members of each household in each family. There was the proper swearing-in of Mr. Summers by the postmaster, as the official of the lottery; at one time, some people remembered, there had been a recital of some sort, performed by the official of the lottery, a perfunctory, tuneless chant that had been rattled off duly each year; some people believed that the official of the lottery used to stand just so when he said or sang it, others believed that he was supposed to walk among the people, but years and years ago this part of the ritual had been allowed to lapse. There had been, also, a ritual salute, which the official of the lottery had had to use in addressing each person who came up to draw from the box, but this also had changed with time, until now it was felt necessary only for the official to speak to each person approaching. Mr. Summers was very good at all this; in his clean white shirt and blue jeans, with one hand resting carelessly on the black box, he seemed very proper and important as he talked interminably to Mr. Graves and the Martins.

Just as Mr. Summers finally left off talking and turned to the assembled villagers, Mrs. Hutchinson came hurriedly along the path to the square, her sweater thrown over her shoulders, and slid into place in the back of the crowd. "Clean forgot what day it was," she said to Mrs. Delacroix, who stood next to her, and they both laughed softly. "Thought my old man was out back stacking wood," Mrs. Hutchinson went on, "and then I looked out the window and the kids were gone, and then I remembered it was the twenty-seventh and came a-running." She dried her hands on her apron, and Mrs. Delacroix said, "You're in time, though. They're still talking away up there."

Mrs. Hutchinson craned her neck to see through the crowd and found her husband and children standing near the front. She tapped Mrs. Delacroix on the arm as a farewell and began to make her way through the crowd. The people separated good humoredly to let her through; two or three people said, in voices just loud enough to be heard across the crowd, "Here comes your Missus, Hutchinson," and "Bill, she made it after all." Mrs. Hutchinson reached her husband, and Mr. Summers, who had been waiting, said cheerfully, "Thought we were going to have to get on without you, Tessie." Mrs. Hutchinson said, grinning, "Wouldn't have me leave m'dishes in the sink, now would you, Joe?," and soft laughter ran through the crowd as the people stirred back into position after Mrs. Hutchinson's arrival.

"Well, now," Mr. Summers said soberly, "guess we better get started, get this over with, so's we can go back to work. Anybody ain't here?"

"Dunbar," several people said. "Dunbar, Dunbar."

Mr. Summers consulted his list. "Clyde Dunbar," he said. "That's right. He's broke his leg, hasn't he? Who's drawing for him?"

"Me, I guess," a woman said, and Mr. Summers turned to look at her. "Wife draws for her husband," Mr. Summers said. "Don't you have a grown boy to do it for you, Janey?" Although Mr. Summers and everyone else in the village knew the answer perfectly well, it was the business of the official of the lottery to ask such questions formally. Mr. Summers waited with an expression of polite interest while Mrs. Dunbar answered.

"Horace's not but sixteen yet," Mrs. Dunbar said regretfully. "Guess I gotta fill in for the old man this year."

"Right," Mr. Summers said. He made a note on the list he was holding. Then he asked, "Watson boy drawing this year?"

A tall boy in the crowd raised his hand. "Here," he said. "I'm drawing for m'mother and me." He blinked his eyes nervously and ducked his head as several voices in the crowd said things like "Good fellow, Jack," and "Glad to see your mother's got a man to do it."

"Well," Mr. Summers said, "guess that's everyone. Old Man Warner make it?"

"Here," a voice said, and Mr. Summers nodded.

A sudden hush fell on the crowd as Mr. Summers cleared his throat and looked at the list. "All ready?" he called. "Now, I'll read the names—heads of families first—and the men come up and take a paper out of the box. Keep the paper folded in your hand without looking at it until everyone has had a turn. Everything clear?"

The people had done it so many times that they only half listened to the directions; most of them were quiet, wetting their lips, not looking around. Then Mr. Summers raised one hand high and said, "Adams." A man disengaged himself from the crowd and came forward. "Hi, Steve," Mr. Summers said, and Mr. Adams said, "Hi, Joe." They grinned at one another humorlessly and nervously. Then Mr. Adams reached into the black box and took out a folded paper. He held it firmly by one corner as he turned and went hastily back to his place in the crowd, where he stood a little apart from his family, not looking down at his hand.

"Allen," Mr. Summers said. "Anderson. . . . Bentham."

"Seems like there's no time at all between lotteries any more," Mrs. Delacroix said to Mrs. Graves in the back row. "Seems like we got through with the last one only last week."

"Time sure goes fast," Mrs. Graves said.

"Clark. . . . Delacroix."

"There goes my old man," Mrs. Delacroix said. She held her breath while her husband went forward.

"Dunbar," Mr. Summers said, and Mrs. Dunbar went steadily to the box while one of the women said, "Go on, Janey," and another said, "There she goes."

"We're next," Mrs. Graves said. She watched while Mr. Graves came around from the side of the box, greeted Mr. Summers gravely, and selected a slip of paper from the box. By now, all through the crowd there were men holding the small folded papers in their large hands, turning them over and over nervously. Mrs. Dunbar and her two sons stood together, Mrs. Dunbar holding the slip of paper.

"Harburt. . . . Hutchinson."

"Get up there, Bill," Mrs. Hutchinson said, and the people near her laughed. "Jones."

"They do say," Mr. Adams said to Old Man Warner, who stood next to him, "that over in the north village they're talking of giving up the lottery."

Old Man Warner snorted. "Pack of crazy fools," he said. "Listening to the young folks, nothing's good enough for *them.* Next thing you know, they'll be wanting to go back to living in caves, nobody work any more, live *that* way for a while. Used to be a saying about 'Lottery in June, corn be heavy soon.' First thing you know, we'd all be eating stewed chickweed and acorns. There's *always* been a lottery," he added petulantly. "Bad enough to see young Joe Summers up there joking with everybody."

"Some places have already quit lotteries," Mrs. Adams said.

"Nothing but trouble in *that,*" Old Man Warner said stoutly. "Pack of young fools."

"Martin." And Bobby Martin watched his father go forward. "Overdyke. . . . Percy."

"I wish they'd hurry," Mrs. Dunbar said to her older son. "I wish they'd hurry."

"They're almost through," her son said.

"You get ready to run tell Dad," Mrs. Dunbar said.

Mr. Summers called his own name and then stepped forward precisely and selected a slip from the box. Then he called, "Warner."

"Seventy-seventh year I been in the lottery," Old Man Warner said as he went through the crowd. "Seventy-seventh time."

"Watson." The tall boy came awkwardly through the crowd. Someone said, "Don't be nervous, Jack," and Mr. Summers said, "Take your time, son."

"Zanini."

After that, there was a long pause, a breathless pause, until Mr. Summers, holding his slip of paper in the air, said, "All right, fellows." For a minute, no one moved, and then all the slips of paper were opened. Suddenly, all women began to speak at once, saying, "Who is it?" "Who's got it?" "Is it the Dunbars?" "Is it the Watsons?" Then the voices began to say, "It's Hutchinson. It's Bill." "Bill Hutchinson's got it."

"Go tell your father," Mrs. Dunbar said to her older son.

People began to look around to see the Hutchinsons. Bill Hutchinson was standing quiet, staring down at the paper in his hand. Suddenly, Tessie Hutchinson shouted to Mr. Summers, "You didn't give him time enough to take any paper he wanted. I saw you. It wasn't fair!"

"Be a good sport, Tessie," Mrs. Delacroix called, and Mrs. Graves said, "All of us took the same chance."

"Shut up, Tessie," Bill Hutchinson said.

"Well, everyone," Mr. Summers said, "that was done pretty fast, and now we've got to be hurrying a little more to get done in time." He consulted his next list. "Bill," he said, "you draw for the Hutchinson family. You got any other households in the Hutchinsons?"

"There's Don and Eva," Mrs. Hutchinson yelled. "Make *them* take their chance!"

"Daughters draw with their husbands' families, Tessie," Mr. Summers said gently. "You know that as well as anyone else."

"It wasn't fair," Tessie said.

"I guess not, Joe," Bill Hutchinson said regretfully. "My daughter draws with her husband's family, that's only fair. And I've got no other family except the kids."

"Then, as far as drawing for families is concerned, it's you," Mr. Summers said in explanation, "and as far as drawing for households is concerned, that's you, too. Right?"

"Right," Bill Hutchinson said.

"How many kids, Bill?" Mr. Summers asked formally.

"Three," Bill Hutchinson said. "There's Bill, Jr., and Nancy, and little Dave. And Tessie and me."

"All right, then," Mr. Summers said. "Harry, you got their tickets back?"

Mr. Graves nodded and held up the slips of paper. "Put them in the box, then," Mr. Summers directed. "Take Bill's and put it in."

"I think we ought to start over," Mrs. Hutchinson said, as quietly as she could. "I tell you it wasn't *fair.* You didn't give him time enough to choose. *Every*body saw that."

Mr. Graves had selected the five slips and put them in the box, and he dropped all the papers but those onto the ground, where the breeze caught them and lifted them off.

"Listen, everybody," Mrs. Hutchinson was saying to the people around her.

"Ready, Bill?" Mr. Summers asked, and Bill Hutchinson, with one quick glance around at his wife and children, nodded.

"Remember," Mr. Summers said, "take the slips and keep them folded until each person has taken one. Harry, you help little Dave." Mr. Graves took the hand of the little boy, who came willingly with him up to the box. "Take a paper out of the box, Davy," Mr. Summers said. Davy put his hand into the box and laughed. "Take just *one* paper," Mr. Summers said. "Harry, you hold it for him." Mr. Graves took the child's hand and removed the folded paper from the tight fist and held it while little Dave stood next to him and looked up at him wonderingly.

"Nancy next," Mr. Summers said. Nancy was twelve, and her school friends breathed heavily as she went forward, switching her skirt, and took a slip daintily from the box. "Bill, Jr.," Mr. Summers said, and Billy, his face red and his feet over-large, nearly knocked the box over as he got a paper out. "Tessie," Mr. Summers said. She hesitated for a minute, looking around defiantly, and then set her lips and went up to the box. She snatched a paper out and held it behind her.

"Bill," Mr. Summers said, and Bill Hutchinson reached into the box and felt around, bringing his hand out at last with the slip of paper in it.

The crowd was quiet. A girl whispered, "I hope it's not Nancy," and the sound of the whisper reached the edges of the crowd.

"It's not the way it used to be," Old Man Warner said clearly. "People ain't the way they used to be."

"All right," Mr. Summers said. "Open the papers. Harry, you open little Dave's."

Mr. Graves opened the slip of paper and there was a general sigh through the crowd as he held it up and everyone could see that it was blank. Nancy and Bill, Jr., opened theirs at the same time, and both beamed and laughed, turning around to the crowd and holding their slips of paper above their heads.

"Tessie," Mr. Summers said. There was a pause, and then Mr. Summers looked at Bill Hutchinson, and Bill unfolded his paper and showed it. It was blank.

"It's Tessie," Mr. Summers said, and his voice was hushed. "Show us her paper, Bill."

Bill Hutchinson went over to his wife and forced the slip of paper out of her hand. It had a black spot on it, the black spot Mr. Summers had made the night before with the heavy pencil in the coal-company office. Bill Hutchinson held it up, and there was a stir in the crowd.

"All right, folks," Mr. Summers said, "let's finish quickly."

Although the villagers had forgotten the ritual and lost the original black box, they still remembered to use stones. The pile of stones the boys had made earlier was ready; there were stones on the ground with the blowing scraps of paper that had come out of the box. Mrs. Delacroix selected a stone so large she had to pick it up with both hands and turned to Mrs. Dunbar. "Come on," she said. "Hurry up."

Mrs. Dunbar had small stones in both hands, and she said, gasping for breath. "I can't run at all. You'll have to go ahead and I'll catch up with you."

The children had stones already, and someone gave little Davy Hutchinson a few pebbles.

Tessie Hutchinson was in the center of a cleared space by now, and she held her hands out desperately as the villagers moved in on her. "It isn't fair," she said. A stone hit her on the side of the head.

Old Man Warner was saying, "Come on, come on, everyone." Steve Adams was in the front of the crowd of villagers, with Mrs. Graves beside him.

"It isn't fair, it isn't right," Mrs. Hutchinson screamed, and then they were upon her.

Student Responses

We give some of the notes and the final drafts of two students, both of whom chose to write about the theme of Jackson's story.

Justin MacNeice's Notes and Final Draft

Justin MacNeice, after reading the story, jotted down the following notes as a sort of preliminary outline. Some of the notes were based on passages he had underlined. Notice that the jottings include some material specifically on the story and other material—references to the outside world—that is relevant to what the student takes to be the theme of the story. When MacNeice reviewed his notes before starting on a first draft, he deleted some of them, having decided that they were not especially useful for his essay. Still, they were worth jotting down; only in retrospect can a writer clearly see which notes are useful.

```
Is Jackson saying that human nature is evil? Prob. no; here,
     people just follow a tradition, and don't examine it. Mr.
     Warner defends lottery, saying "There's always been a
     lottery." No real argument in defense of it.
We are least conscious of the things we take for granted; I
     recall someone's saying "a fish is not aware of water
     until it is out of it."
examples of blindly following society's customs
     compulsory schooling (how many people ever even remotely
          think of schooling their children at home?)
     school is 5 days a week, why not 4 or 6? Bachelor's de-
     gree is 4 years, why not 3 or 5?
     segregation (until 1960s; still in S. Africa)
     women not permitted to drive in Saudi Arabia
     women must wear veil in Saudi Arabia
     eating of meat; might a vegetarian society not look with
          horror at our habit of eating meat?
     slavery (thought to be "natural" by almost all societies
          until nineteenth century)
```

thoughtless following of custom in "The Lottery"
~~exact words of ritual lost, but still necessary to ad-~~
   ~~dress "each person approaching"~~
~~original box gone, but present box said to be made of~~
   ~~parts of previous box~~
lottery an established ritual: "The lottery was conducted
   -as were the square dances, the teenage club, the
   Halloween program-by Mr. Summers, who had time and
   energy to devote to civic activities." <u>Important</u>: the
   lottery is a civic activity, a social action, a <u>sum</u>-
   mer (<u>pun</u>?) ritual.
Evil? Certainly yes, since killing an innocent, but no one
   in the story says it's evil.
   BUT Adams does say that in the north village "they're
      talking of giving up the lottery," and his wife says
      "Some places have already quit lotteries."
   Also: a girl whispers, "I hope it's not Nancy," so at
      least one person feels uneasy about the whole thing
Are these people evil? No, they seem pretty decent. They
   just don't much question what they are doing, and they
   do something terrible
~~the box~~
   ~~black = death?~~
   ~~made out of pieces of old box~~
   ~~"faded," "splintered badly": does this symbolize a need~~
      ~~for a new tradition?~~
~~the papers~~
   ~~earlier, wood chips. At end, wind blows away slips of~~
      ~~papers? Symbolic of life fluttering away? (Prob. not)~~
~~the three-legged stool~~
   ~~symbolic? If so, of what?~~
possible title
   The Violent Lottery
   The Irrational Lottery
   We All Participate in "The Lottery"
   The Meaning of the Lottery

   A lot of the material here is good, though some of it would be more suited
for an essay on symbolism, and it is chiefly this material that the writer wisely
deleted in preparing to draft an essay on the theme of Jackson's story. After
writing a draft and then revising it, MacNeice submitted the revision to a group
for peer review. Ultimately, he turned in the following essay.

   We All Participate in "The Lottery"

   The townsfolk in Shirley Jackson's "The Lottery"
engage in a horrible ritual. They stone an innocent

person to death. It would be horrible enough if the person they stoned were guilty of some crime, and stoning was a form of capital punishment that the society practiced, but in the case of "The Lottery" the person is not guilty of any crime. Tessie Hutchinson simply had the bad luck to pick the wrong slip of paper from a box, a paper marked with a black spot.

The people in this unnamed town every year hold a lottery, to find a victim. On the whole, they seem to believe that the lottery is necessary, or is natural; at least they hardly question it. True, Mr. Adams says that in the north village "they're talking of giving up the lottery," and his wife says that "Some places have already quit lotteries," but that's about as much as one hears of anybody questioning this institution of society. Probably most of the people in the village would agree with Old Man Warner, who says that people who talk about giving up the lottery are a "pack of crazy fools." He adds, "There's *always* been a lottery," and that seems to be about the best answer that anyone can give. Of course the people don't take any special pleasure in the lottery, and there is at least one expression of sympathy, when a girl says, "I hope it's not Nancy." On the whole, however, the people seem to believe that the lottery must be held, and someone has to die.

It's important to notice that the lottery is one of the "civic activities," that is, it is part of the regular life of these people, part (so to speak) of the air they breathe. For the most part they don't question the lottery any more than we question compulsory education, the length of the school year, or the eating of meat. When one thinks about it, one might ask why the government should have the power to compel parents to send children to school, or, for that matter, why a child shouldn't have the right to leave school whenever he or she feels like it. Why should children have almost no rights? People simply don't bother to think about this issue, or about many others. For instance, I can imagine that the member of a vegetarian society—say a Hindu Brahmin society—must be horrified by the way almost all Americans think nothing of raising animals (bringing life into the world) for the sole purpose of eating them. Was just accept these things, without thinking, but from the view of another culture they may be horrible customs.

What Jackson seems to be saying to her readers is this: "Unthinkingly you follow certain conventions. These conventions seem to you to be natural, and for the most part they are harmless, but some of them are barbaric and destructive." That is, Jackson is telling us to examine our lives, and to stop assuming that all of our customs are right. Some of the beliefs we share today may, in time, come to be seen to be as evil as slavery or murder.

Zoë Sullivan's Notes and Final Draft

Now for the notes and the essay by a second student, Zoe Sullivan. This writer came to a very different conclusion about the theme of "The Lottery." After reading this student's notes and her essay, you may want to compare the two essays. Do you find one essay more interesting than the other? More persuasive? If so, why? You may feel that even though the essays come to different conclusions, the two essays are equally interesting and equally valid.

surprise <u>and</u> shock

shock

    violence (at end)

    <u>esp. shocking</u> because violence comes from people who
       seem normal and decent

    (only a few expressions of hesitation; Mr. and Mrs.
       Adams)

    Jackson claimed violence was normal *(quote passage)*

(talk of giving up lotteries)

    surprise

    we don't know, until late, what's going on;
    on rereading, we see lots of clues about what will
      happen

      Example: references to stones

Meanings?

    lottery = the draft in wartime?

    lottery = community violence? Example: War (??)

    lottery = violent U.S. society??

    "   " <u>any</u> violent custom; bad tradition?

    human nature corrupt? sinful? (Note name of Adams, also
      Graves) (other significant names: Summers, Warner);
      human tendency to look for a scapegoat. Is it true?

Jackson quoted on her meaning: "violence and general inhumanity"
      but do we have to believe her?   *Example of such*
                                   a story!
Maybe just a horror story, without "meaning"
Are normal people willing to kill without great provocation?

Possible titles

    Shirley Jackson on Human Nature

    Do We All Participate in "The Lottery"?

    How Fair is Shirley Jackson's Lottery?

    Is "The Lottery" Fair?

When you read the essay, you'll notice that for a title Sullivan settled on the last of her four tentative titles. The first title, "Shirley Jackson on Human Nature," is too broad since the essay is not on all of Jackson's work but on only one story. The second tentative title, "Do We All Participate in 'The Lottery'?", is acceptable, but it sounds a bit clumsy, so the choice apparently came down to the last two titles or to some entirely new title that the writer might discover during the process of revising her drafts.

Notice also that some points mentioned in the preliminary notes—for instance, the reference to Mr. Summers and to Mr. Warner—are omitted from the essay. And some points scarcely mentioned in the outlines are emphasized in the essay. In drafting and revising the essay, the writer found that certain things weren't relevant to her point, and so she dropped them and found that others required considerable amplification.

Is "The Lottery" Fair?

Probably all readers are surprised by the ending
of Shirley Jackson's "The Lottery." But the story does
more than offer a surprise. It shocks, because it
seems to say that people who are perfectly ordinary,
just like ourselves, are capable of killing an
innocent neighbor for apparently no reason at all. On
rereading the story, we can see that Jackson has
carefully prepared for the ending, and we can admire
her skill. For instance, the second paragraph tells us
that "Bobby Martin had already stuffed his pockets
full of stones, and the other boys soon followed his
example, selecting the smoothest and roundest stones"
(863). We almost feel, when we reread the story, that
we should not have been surprised. But even after we
see that the ending had been foreshadowed, we remain
shocked by the violence, and by what the story says
about human beings. But exactly what *does* it say about
them? And does it say anything that strikes us as
true?

If we assume that the story *does* say something
about life, and is not simply a meaningless shocker,
we may come up with several possible interpretations.
Is Jackson saying that Americans seem peaceful and
neighborly but really are quite willing to engage in
violence? (Although she does not clearly set the story
in an identifiable region, she clearly sets it in a
small town in the United States.) Certainly newspapers
every day tell us of violent acts, but the violent
acts are usually of an individual (a mad killer, or a
rapist) or are of nature (an earthquake, a tornado).

Of course someone might conceivably argue that this story, which is about a community, is a sort of allegory about the United States as a whole. It was written in 1948, only three years after the end of World War II, and someone might claim that it is about American willingness to use violence, that is, to go to war. Or one might even say that it is about the wartime draft, which was a sort of lottery that chose certain people whose lives were risked.

4   But to see the story as a reference to World War II seems very strained. Nothing in the story suggests a conscious conflict between groups, as, for instance, Jackson could have suggested if members of this town were allied against another town. And though the story certainly is set in the United States, nothing in the story calls attention to a particularly *American violence*.

Another way of thinking about "The Lottery" is to see it as a story about all human beings—not just Americans—who unthinkingly submit to destructive traditions. This interpretation can be better supported than the first interpretation. For instance, at least two people in the story briefly question the tradition of the lottery. Steve Adams says, "Over in the north village they're talking of giving up the lottery," and a moment later his wife adds, "Some places have already quit lotteries" (866). But of course the story tells us that this community does not give up the lottery; in fact, we are particularly shocked to learn, near the end, that Steve Adams is "in the front of the crowd of villagers" (868) when they attack Tessie Hutchinson.

It's obvious that the story is about a terrible tradition that is accepted with relatively little objection, but we can still ask what connection the story has with our own lives. What traditions do we engage in that are so deadly? The wartime draft has already been mentioned, but even pacifists probably would grant that most of the people who engage in war are aware that war is terrible, and thus they are unlike Jackson's villagers. The story may be about the deadliness of certain traditions, but a reader is left wondering which of our traditions are represented in Jackson's lottery. Racism and sexism have had terrible effects, but it is hard to relate the lottery, which picks a victim at random, to discrimination against people of a certain color or a certain sex.

A third view, and one that I think is somewhat sounder than the first two views, is that the story is about human nature. Although most people are decent, they are also capable of terrible irrational violence. In Christian terms this is explained by Original Sin, a sinfulness that we have inherited from Adam. Jackson certainly allows for the possibility of some sort of Biblical interpretation, since, as we have seen, Mr. Adams is one of the leaders of the assault, and he is accompanied by Mr. Graves. The original sin of the first Adam led to death, and thus to the grave.

8   Shirley Jackson herself from time to time offered comments on the story. According to Judy

Oppenheimer, in Private Demons: The Life of Shirley
Jackson, when the fiction editor of The New Yorker
asked her if "there was anything special she was
trying to convey," she said, "Not really." When the
editor pressed her, and asked if the story "made its
point by an ironic juxtaposition of ancient
superstition and modern setting," Jackson said "Sure,
that would be fine," since she didn't like to discuss
her work (128). Her fullest comment, according to
Oppenheimer, was given to a columnist who was writing
for the San Francisco Chronicle:

I suppose I hoped, by setting a particularly
brutal rite in the present and in my own village, to
shock the readers with a graphic demonstration of the
pointless violence and general inhumanity of their own
lives. (qtd. in Oppenheimer 131)

There are obvious problems with accepting this
comment. First of all, as has been mentioned, Jackson
offered contradictory comments on the meaning of the
story. She seems not to have worried about being
consistent. Second, the words she used by way of
introducing her intention—"I suppose I hoped"—indicate
that she herself was not entirely clear about what she
had intended. Third, even if she did correctly state
her intention, she may not have fulfilled it
adequately.

Certainly the story shows people who seem quite
decent but who with only a little hesitation
participate in a barbaric ritual. Perhaps Jackson did
intend to say in her story that this is what we are
also like. And since the story is related to ancient
rituals in which societies purify themselves by

finding a scapegoat, Jackson seems to be saying that all people, no matter how normal or decent they seem, engage in violence that they think purifies them or is at least in some way necessary for their own wellbeing. But just because Jackson's *said* something like this, and said it in a gripping story, it isn't necessarily true. Despite all of the realistic detail—for instance Mrs. Hutchinson's desperate charge that "It isn't fair"—the final picture of life that "The Lottery" gives does not seem to me to be at all realistic, and therefore I don't think the story says anything about life. The story surprises and it shocks, for instance like Poe's "The Fall of the House of Usher." Maybe it even shows "The pointless violence and general inhumanity" in the lives of Jackson's neighbors, but does it reflect the lives of her readers? Do apparently normal, decent people routinely engage in barbaric behavior? I'm not like these people, and I doubt that Jackson and her neighbors were like them either. "The Lottery" is a cleverly plotted story, but the more you look at it, and the more you admire the skillful foreshadowing, the more it seems to be a clever trick, and the less it seems to be related to life.

Works Cited

Jackson, Shirley. "The Lottery." *The Harper Anthology of Fiction*. Ed. Sylvan Barnet. New York: Harper, 1991. 862–68.

Oppenheimer, Judy. *Private Demons: The Life of Shirley Jackson*. New York: Putnam's, 1988.

Getting Ideas for Writing About Fiction

Here are some questions that may help to stimulate responses and therefore ideas about stories. Not every question is, of course, relevant to every story, but if after reading a story and thinking about it, you then run your eye over these pages, you will probably find some questions that will help you to think further about the story—in short, that will help you to get ideas.

It's best to do your thinking with a pen or pencil in hand. If some of the following questions seem to you to be especially relevant to the story you will be writing about, jot down—freely, without worrying about spelling—your initial responses, interrupting your writing only to glance again at the story when you feel the need to check the evidence.

Checklist: Asking Questions About Fiction

1. What happens in the story? Summarize the **plot.** (Think about what your summary *leaves out.*)

2. Is the story told in chronological order or are there flashbacks, or flashforwards? On rereading, what **foreshadowing** of events do you detect?

3. What **conflicts** does the story include?

4. With which **character** or characters do you sympathize? How does the writer reveal character? How does the author create sympathy for some characters but not for others? Are the characters and their actions plausible? What motivates them? Do their names suggest anything about their characters or functions in the story? What do minor characters contribute to the story?

5. Who tells the story? Is the **narrator** a character in the story? If not, does the narrator represent the action primarily through the thoughts and actions of one of the characters? Or does the narrator seem to stand entirely outside of the characters, to be neutral? If the narrator is a character in the story, how reliable does he or she appear to be? Try to assess your response to or the effect on you of the **point of view.**

6. Where and when does the story take place? What is the relation of the **setting** to the **plot** and **characters?**

7. Do certain characters seem to you to stand for something in addition to themselves; that is, are they **symbolic?** Does the setting—a house, a farm, a landscape, a town, a period—have an extra dimension? (Trust your responses to a story. If you don't sense a symbolic overtone in a character or action, move on. Don't let a hunt for symbols distract you from enjoying and thinking about the story.)

8. What does the story add up to? What **theme** or meanings does it suggest?

Does the theme of the story reinforce values you hold, or does it challenge them?

9. Is the **title** informative? Did the meaning seem to change after you read the story?

10. What do you especially like or dislike about the story? Do you think your responses are in large degree unique, or do you think that most readers share them? Why?

Reading Poetry

Let's begin with an example. The following short poem is by Langston Hughes (1902–1967), an African-American writer. The poem, first published in 1951, provided Lorraine Hansberry with the title of her well-known play, *A Raisin in the Sun.*

Harlem

What happens to a dream deferred?
Does it dry up
like a raisin in the sun?
or fester like a sore—
And then run?
Does it stink like rotten meat?
Or crust and sugar over—
like a syrupy sweet?

Maybe it just sags
like a heavy load.

or does it explode?

Reread the poem, this time thinking about its effect on you. Are there words or ideas that puzzle you, please you, displease you, or what?

Of course, different readers will respond at least somewhat differently to any work. On the other hand, since poets and storytellers, like psychologists, historians, and all other writers, want to communicate, they try to control their readers' responses, and they count on their readers to understand the meanings of words as the writers themselves understand them. Thus Hughes assumed that his readers knew that Harlem was the site of a large African-American community in New York City. A reader who confuses the title of the poem with Haarlem in the Netherlands will wonder what this poem is saying about the tulip-growing center in northern Holland.

Let's assume that the reader understands that Hughes is talking about Harlem, New York, and, further, that the reader understands the "dream deferred" to refer to the unfulfilled hopes of African-Americans who live in a predominantly white society. But Hughes does not say (as we have just said) "hopes"; rather, he says "dream." And he does not say "unfulfilled"; rather, he says "deferred." You might ask yourself exactly what differences there are between these words. Next, when you reread the poem, you might think about which expression is better in the context, "unfulfilled hopes" or "dream deferred," and why? This sort of questioning of the words of the text, or, rather, questioning your responses to the words of the text, is at the heart of writing about literature—just as it is at the heart of writing about any sort of serious text. If after a second reading of a literary text you still feel short of responses—but don't forget that being puzzled is itself a good response to study—you will almost surely be able to generate responses by using the invention devices that we mention in our first chapter: free writing, listing, clustering, keeping a journal, and asking questions. (In the following pages we suggest some specific questions that you can ask yourself when reading fiction or poetry.)

A Student Thinks About "Harlem": Richard Taub's Annotations, Journal Entries, Notes, and Final Draft

Let's turn to an analysis of the poem, an examination of how the parts fit. As you look at the poem, thinks about the parts, and jot down whatever notes come to mind. After you have written you own notes, consider the annotations of one student, Richard Taub.

These annotations chiefly get at the **structure** of the poem, the relationship of the parts. Taub notices that the poem begins with a line set off by itself and ends with a line set off by itself, and he also notices that each of these lines is a question. Further, he indicates that each of these two lines is emphasized in other ways: The first begins further to the left than any of the other lines—as though the other lines are subheadings or are in some way subordinate—and the last is italicized.

Taub later wrote an entry in his journal:

Feb. 18. Since the title is "Harlem," it's obvious that the "dream" is by African-American people. Also, obvious that Hughes thinks that if the "dream" doesn't become real there may be riots ("explode"). I like "raisin in the sun" (maybe because I like the play), and I like the business about "a syrupy sweet"—much more pleasant than the festering sore and the rotten meat. But if the dream becomes "sweet," what's wrong with that? Why should something "sweet" explode?

Feb. 21. Prof. McCabe said to think of structure or form of a poem as a sort of architecture, a build-ing with a foundation, floors, etc. topped by a roof—but since we read a poem from top to bottom, it's like a building upside down. Title or first line is founda-tion (even though it's at top); last line is roof, capping the whole. As you read, you add layers. Foun-dation of "Harlem" is a question (first line). Then, set back a bit from foundation, or built on it by white space, a tall room (7 lines high, with 4 ques-tions); then, on top of this room, another room (two lines, one statement, not a question). Funny; I thought that in poems all stanzas are the same number of lines. Then—more white space, so another unit—the roof. Man this roof is going to fall in—"explode." Not just the roof, may be the whole house.

Feb. 21, pm. I get it; one line at start, one line at end; both are questions, but the last sort of says (because it is in italics) that it is the *most likely* answer to the question of the first line. The last line is also a question, but it's still an answer. The big stanza (7 lines) has 4 questions: 2 lines, 2 lines, 1 line, 2 lines. Maybe the switch to 1 line is to give some variety, so as not to be dull? It's exactly in the middle of the poem. I get the progress from raisin in the sun (dried, but not so terrible), to festering sore and to stinking meat, but I still don't see what's so bad about "a syrupy sweet." Is Hughes saying that after things are very bad they will get better? But why, then, the explosion at the end?

Feb. 23. "Heavy load" and "sags" in next-to-last stanza seems to me to suggest slaves with bales of cotton, or maybe poor cotton pickers dragging big sacks of cotton. Or maybe people doing heavy labor in Harlem. Anyway, very tired. Different from running sore and stinking meat earlier; not disgusting, but pressing down, deadening. Maybe *worse* than a sore or rotten meat—a hard, hopeless life. And then the last line. Just one line, no fancy (and disgusting) simile. Boom! Not just pressed down and tired, like maybe some racist whites think (hope?) blacks will be? Bang! Will there be survivors?

Drawing chiefly on these notes, Taub jotted down some key ideas to guide him through a draft of an analysis of the poem. In organizing his draft, Taub followed the organization of the poem. On the following pages we give his notes and final draft.

11 lines; short, but powerful; explosive
Question (first line)
Answers (set off by space, & also indented)
"raisin in the sun": shrinking
"sore" } *disgusting*
"rotten meat"
"syrupy sweet": relief from disgusting comparisons
Final question (last line): explosion?
  explosive (powerful) because:
    short, condensed, packed
    in italics
    stands by self — like first line
    no fancy comparison; very direct

Langston Hughes's "Harlem"

   "Harlem" is a poem that is only eleven lines
long, but it is charged with power. It explodes.
Hughes sets the stage, so to speak, by telling us in
the title that he is talking about Harlem, and then he
begins by asking "What happens to a dream deferred?"
The rest of the poem is set off by being indented, as
though it is the answer to his question. This answer
is in three parts (three stanzas, of different
lengths).

   In a way, it's wrong to speak of the answer,
since the rest of the poem consists of questions, but
I think Hughes means that each question (for instance,
does a "deferred" hope "dry up / like a raisin in the
sun?") really is an answer, something that really has
happened and that will happen again. The first
question, "Does it dry up / like a raisin in the sun?"
is a famous line. To compare hope to a raisin dried in

the sun is to suggest a terrible shrinking. The next two comparisons are to a "sore" and to "rotten meat." These comparisons are less clever, but they are very effective because they are disgusting. Then, maybe because of the disgusting comparisons, he gives a comparison that is not at all disgusting. In this comparison he says that maybe the "dream deferred" will "crust over— / like a syrupy sweet."

The seven lines with four comparisons are followed by a stanza of two lines with just one comparison:

> Maybe it just sags
> like a heavy load.

So if we thought that this postponed dream might finally turn into something "sweet," we were kidding ourselves. Hughes comes down to earth, in a short stanza, with an image of a heavy load, which probably also calls to mind images of people bent under heavy loads, maybe of cotton, or maybe just any sort of heavy load carried by African-Americans in Harlem and elsewhere.

The opening question ("What happens to a dream deferred?") was followed by four questions in seven lines, but now, with "Maybe it just sags / like a heavy load" we get a statement, as though the poet at last has found an answer. But at the end we get one more question, set off by itself and in italics: "Or does it explode?" This line itself is explosive for three reasons: it is short, it is italicized, and it

```
is a stanza in itself. It's also interesting that this
line, unlike the earlier lines, does not use a simile.
It's almost as though Hughes is saying, "O.K., we've
had enough fancy ways of talking about this terrible
situation; here it is, straight."
```

A Second Poem: Adrienne Rich's "Aunt Jennifer's Tigers"

Let's look at a second poem, and a student's response to it.

Aunt Jennifer's Tigers
Aunt Jennifer's tigers prance across a screen,
Bright topaz denizens of a world of green.
They do not fear the men beneath the tree;
They pace in sleek chivalric certainty.

Aunt Jennifer's fingers fluttering through her wool
Find even the ivory needle hard to pull.
The massive weight of Uncle's wedding band
Sits heavily upon Aunt Jennifer's hand.

When Aunt is dead, her terrified hands will lie
Still ringed with ordeals she was mastered by.
The tigers in the panel that she made
Will go on prancing, proud and unafraid.

[1951]

A Second Student's Essay on a Poem

Like Taub's essay on "Harlem," Maria Fuente's essay is concerned with the reader's perception of the meaning, but unlike Taub, Fuentes does not hesitate to go beyond the text and into "the real world." Her essay is not so personal that the poem disappears (as it might in an essay that says something like "This reminds me of the time that I . . . "), but it does not claim merely to unfold meanings that Rich embodied or entangled in her words on the page.

Maria Fuentes's Annotations and Final Draft

Here are the annotations that an undergraduate, Maria Fuentes, produced in the course of thinking about the poem.

odd—arouses interest

Aunt Jennifer's Tigers

? Aunt Jennifer's tigers prance across a <u>screen</u>,
Bright topaz (denizens) of a world of green.   *her work embroidery?*
They do not fear the men beneath the tree;
They pace in sleek <u>chivalric certainty</u>. **??**

Aunt Jennifer's fingers fluttering through her wool
Find even the ivory needle hard to pull.
The massive weight of <u>Uncle's wedding band</u> — *he tyrannized over her*
<u>Sits heavily</u> upon Aunt Jennifer's hand.

When <u>Aunt is dead</u>, her <u>terrified</u> hands will lie   *contrast to the prancing tigers she created*
Still ringed with ordeals she was (mastered) by.
The tigers in the panel that she made
Will go on prancing, proud and unafraid.

We are told only that she was oppressed & that she created a lively work of art. That's about all we know of her.

Uncle?

in contrast to "terrified" Aunt J. BUT <u>she</u> created these "proud and unafraid" tigers. Her vision of a better life?

Ultimately Fuentes produced the following essay.

Maria Fuentes

Aunt Jennifer's Screen and Adrienne Rich's Poem
     What especially pleases me in Adrienne Rich's
"Aunt Jennifer's Tigers" is the combination of neat,
tight, highly disciplined stanzas of four rhyming
lines (like marching squadrons) with the explosive
rebellious content of the poem. Somehow the message

seems especially powerful *because* it is so tightly
packed, because the form is so restrained.

The poem is, on the surface at least, about what
the title says it is about, "Aunt Jennifer's Tigers."
Aunt Jennifer has made a screen, in embroidery or
needlepoint, showing tigers that "prance." Presumably
Aunt Jennifer was a sweet old lady but she has created
a picture of enormous energy, expressing, through her
work of art, her own repressed energy.

We learn in the second stanza that she was
repressed by the man she was married to:

The massive weight of Uncle's wedding band

Sits heavily upon Aunt Jennifer's hand.

The wedding band for her, as for many women in the
present as well as in the past, is like a heavy chain.
Rich tells us that Aunt Jennifer was "terrified" and
was "mastered," obviously by Uncle. Rich makes a pun
on the word "ringed," but the joke is very bitter:

When Aunt is dead, her terrified hands will lie

Still ringed with ordeals she was mastered by.

And yet, Rich points out, this "terrified" woman
created something beautiful, a picture of tigers who
"go on prancing, proud and unafraid." Apparently Aunt
Jennifer was able, despite being oppressed by Uncle,
to make something that gives pleasure to a later
generation—just as the poet, however unhappy she may
be, produces a work of art that gives pleasure to
those who later read it.

4   Aunt Jennifer's work of art shows, in the
prancing tigers, an energy that she apparently felt
and understood but, because of her husband and perhaps

because of the period in which she lived, she could express herself only in a "lady—like" activity such as embroidering. Aunt Jennifer was "mastered" (line 10), but she has nevertheless "made" (line 11) something depicting creatures who are "proud and unafraid." She was "terrified" (line 9), as many women were terrified by the patriarchal society in which they lived (and still live), but in her art she created an image of energy. Adrienne Rich, too, makes a work of art—a highly patterned poem consisting of three rhymed quatrains—that is as elegantly crafted as a work of embroidery. Rich speaks matter-of-factly and in a disciplined way in her quatrains about Aunt Jennifer and her tigers, but in this elegant poem she conveys energy and outrage on behalf of her terrified aunt who could not openly protest against the role that society had assigned to her.

Getting Ideas for Writing About Poetry

If you are going to write about a fairly short poem (say, under thirty lines), copy out the poem, writing or typing it double spaced. By writing it out you will be forced to notice details, down to the punctuation. After you have copied the poem, proofread it carefully against the original. Catching an error—even the addition or omission of a comma—may help you to notice a detail in the original that you might otherwise have overlooked. And of course, now that you have the poem with ample space between the lines, you have a worksheet with room for jottings.

A good essay is based on a genuine response to a poem; a response may be stimulated in part by first reading the poem aloud and then considering the following questions.

Checklist: Asking Questions About Poems

1. What was your first response? On rereading, what parts interest or puzzle you? What words seem especially striking or unusual? (Consult a dictionary for the several meanings of words you're unsure of.)

2. How would you describe the **speaker** of the poem? What persona or voice is suggested? What **tone** or emotion do you detect—for example, remorse, regret, affection, irony, sorrow?

3. What is the **structure** of the poem? Are there stanzas? Are there rhymes or repeated sounds? Do the lines vary in length or echo each other? Are there unexpected stresses or pauses? How do they affect you?

4. What is the poem about? Is the **theme** stated or implied? How might you state it in a sentence?

5. What **images** do you find? (An image recalls a sensation of sight, sound, taste, touch, or smell.) What does the poem suggest **symbolically** as well as literally?

6. What do you especially like or dislike about the poem? Do you think your responses are in large degree unique, or do you think that most readers share them? Why?

Three Short Works of Fiction

Ernest Hemingway

Cat in the Rain

Ernest Hemingway (1899–1961) was born in Oak Park, Illinois. After graduating from high school in 1917 he worked on the Kansas City Star, but left to serve as a volunteer ambulance driver in Italy, where he was wounded in action. In 1922 he settled in Paris, where he moved in a circle of American expatriates that included Ezra Pound, Gertrude Stein, and F. Scott Fitzgerald. It was in Paris that he wrote stories and novels about what Gertrude Stein called a "lost generation" of rootless Americans in Europe.

There were only two Americans stopping at the hotel. They did not know any of the people they passed on the stairs on their way to and from their room. Their room was on the second floor facing the sea. It also faced the public garden and the war monument. There were big palms and green benches in the public garden. In the good weather there was always an artist with his easel.

Artists liked the way the palms grew and the bright colors of the hotels facing the gardens and the sea. Italians came from a long way off to look up at the war monument. It was made of bronze and glistened in the rain. It was raining. The rain dripped from the palm trees. Water stood in pools on the gravel paths. The sea broke in a long line in the rain and slipped back down the beach to come up and break again in a long line in the rain. The motor cars were gone from the square by the war monument. Across the square in the doorway of the café a waiter stood looking out at the empty square.

The American wife stood at the window looking out. Outside right under their window a cat was crouched under one of the dripping green tables. The cat was trying to make herself so compact that she would not be dripped on.

"I'm going down and get that kitty," the American wife said.

"I'll do it," her husband offered from the bed.

"No, I'll get it. The poor kitty out trying to keep dry under a table."

The husband went on reading, lying propped up with the two pillows at the foot of the bed.

"Don't get wet," he said.

The wife went downstairs and the hotel owner stood up and bowed to her as she passed the office. His desk was at the far end of the office. He was an old man and very tall.

"Il piove,"[1] the wife said. She liked the hotel-keeper.

"Si, si, Signora, brutto tempo. It is very bad weather."

He stood behind his desk in the far end of the dim room. The wife liked him. She liked the deadly serious way he received any complaints. She liked his dignity. She like the way he wanted to serve her. She liked the way he felt about being a hotel-keeper. She liked his old, heavy face and big hands.

Liking him she opened the door and looked out. It was raining harder. A man in a rubber cape was crossing the empty square to the café. The cat would be around to the right. Perhaps she could go along under the eaves. As she stood in the doorway an umbrella opened behind her. It was the maid who looked after their room.

"You must not get wet," she smiled, speaking Italian. Of course, the hotel-keeper had sent her.

With the maid holding the umbrella over her, she walked along the gravel path until she was under their window. The table was there, washed bright green in the rain, but the cat was gone. She was suddenly disappointed. The maid looked up at her.

"Ha perduto qualque cosa, Signora?"[2]

"There was a cat," said the American girl.

---

[1] It's raining (Italian).
[2] Have you lost something, Madam?

"A cat?"

"Si, il gatto."

"A cat?" the maid laughed. "A cat in the rain?"

"Yes," she said, "under the table." Then, "Oh, I wanted it so much. I wanted a kitty."

When she talked English the maid's face tightened.

"Come Signora," she said. "We must get back inside. You will be wet."

"I suppose so," said the American girl.

They went back along the gravel path and passed in the door. The maid stayed outside to close the umbrella. As the American girl passed the office, the padrone bowed from his desk. Something felt very small and tight inside the girl. The padrone made her feel very small and at the same time really important. She had a momentary feeling of being of supreme importance. She went on up the stairs. She opened the door of the room. George was on the bed, reading.

"Did you get the cat?" he asked, putting the book down.

"It was gone."

"Wonder where it went to," he said, resting his eyes from reading.

She sat down on the bed.

"I wanted it so much," she said. "I don't know why I wanted it so much. I wanted that poor kitty. It isn't any fun to be a poor kitty out in the rain."

George was reading again.

She went over and sat in front of the mirror of the dressing table looking at herself with the hand glass. She studied her profile, first one side and then the other. Then she studied the back of her head and her neck.

"Don't you think it would be a good idea if I let my hair grow out?" she asked, looking at her profile again.

George looked up and saw the back of her neck, clipped close like a boy's.

"I like it the way it is."

"I get so tired of it," she said. "I get so tired of looking like a boy."

George shifted his position in the bed. He hadn't looked away from her since she started to speak.

"You look pretty darn nice," he said.

She laid the mirror down on the dresser and went over to the window and looked out. It was getting dark.

"I want to pull my hair back tight and smooth and make a big knot at the back that I can feel," she said. "I want to have a kitty to sit on my lap and purr when I stroke her."

"Yeah?" George said from the bed.

"And I want to eat at a table with my own silver and I want candles. And I want it to be spring and I want to brush my hair out in front of a mirror and I want a kitty and I want some new clothes."

"Oh, shut up and get something to read," George said. He was reading again.

His wife was looking out of the window. It was quite dark now and still raining in the palm trees.

"Anyway, I want a cat," she said, "I want a cat. I want a cat now. If I can't have long hair or any fun, I can have a cat."

George was not listening. He was reading his book. His wife looked out of the window where the light had come on in the square.

Someone knocked at the door.

"Avanti,"[1] George said. He looked up from his book.

In the doorway stood the maid. She held a big tortoise-shell cat pressed tight against her and swung down against her body.

"Excuse me," she said, "the padrone asked me to bring this for the Signora."

Topics for Discussion and Writing

1. One student argued that the cat represents the child that the girl wants to have. Do you think there is something to this idea? How might you support or refute it?

2. Would it make any difference if the animal were a dog instead of a cat?

3. Can we be certain that the cat at the end of the story is the cat that the woman saw in the rain? (When we first hear about the cat in the rain we are not told anything about its color, and at the end of the story we are not told that the tortoise-shell cat is wet.) Does it matter if there are two cats?

4. What do you suppose Hemingway's attitude was toward each of the three chief characters? How might you support your hunch?

5. Hemingway wrote the story in Italy, when his wife Hadley was pregnant. In a letter to F. Scott Fitzgerald he said,

   Cat in the Rain wasn't about Hadley. . . . When I wrote that we were at Rapallo but Hadley was 4 months pregnant with Bumby. The Inn Keeper was the one at Cortina D'Ampezzo. . . . Hadley never made a speech in her life about wanting a baby because she had been told various things by her doctor and I'd—no use going into all that. (*Letters*, p. 180)

   According to some biographers, the story shows that Hemingway knew his marriage was going on the rocks (Hemingway and Hadley divorced). Does knowing that Hemingway's marriage turned out unhappily help you to understand the story? Does it make the story more interesting? And do you think that the story tells a biographer something about Hemingway's life?

[1] Come in.

6. It is sometimes said that a good short story does two things at once: It provides a believable picture of the surface of life, and it also illuminates some moral or psychological complexity that we feel is part of the essence of human life. This dual claim may not be true, but for the moment accept it. Do you think that Hemingway's story fulfills either or both of these specifications? Support your view.

Grace Paley

Samuel

Born in New York City, Grace Paley attended Hunter College and New York University, but left without a degree. (She now teaches at Sarah Lawrence College.) While raising two children she wrote poetry and then, in the 1950s, turned to writing fiction.

Paley's chief subject is the life of little people struggling in the Big City. Of life she has said, "How daily life is lived is a mystery to me. You write about what's mysterious to you. What is it like? Why do people do this?" Of the short story she has said, "It can be just telling a little tale, or writing a complicated philosophical story. It can be a song, almost."

Some boys are very tough. They're afraid of nothing. They are the ones who climb a wall and take a bow at the top. Not only are they brave on the roof, but they make a lot of noise in the darkest part of the cellar where even the super hates to go. They also jiggle and hop on the platform between the locked doors of the subway cars.

Four boys are jiggling on the swaying platform. Their names are Alfred, Calvin, Samuel, and Tom. The men and the women in the cars on either side watch them. They don't like them to jiggle or jump but don't want to interfere. Of course some of the men in the cars were once brave boys like these. One of them had ridden the tail of a speeding truck from New York to Rockaway Beach without getting off, without his sore fingers losing hold. Nothing happened to him then or later. He had made a compact with other boys who preferred to watch: Starting at Eighth Avenue and Fifteenth Street, he would get to some specified place, maybe Twenty-third and the river, by hopping the tops of the moving trucks. This was hard to do when one truck turned a corner in the wrong direction and the nearest truck was a couple of feet too high. He made three or four starts before succeeding. He had gotten his idea from a film at school called *The Romance of Logging.* He had finished high school, married a good friend, was in a responsible job and going to night school.

These two men and others looked at the four boys jumping and jiggling on the platform and thought, It must be fun to ride that way, especially now the weather is nice and we're out of the tunnel and way high over the Bronx. Then they thought, These kids do seem to be acting sort of stupid. They *are* little. Then they thought of some of the brave things they had done when they were boys and jiggling didn't seem so risky.

The ladies in the car became very angry when they looked at the four boys. Most of them brought their brows together and hoped the boys could see their extreme disapproval. One of the ladies wanted to get up and say, Be careful you dumb kids, get off that platform or I'll call a cop. But three of the boys were Negroes and the fourth was something else she couldn't tell for sure. She was afraid they'd be fresh and laugh at her and embarrass her. She wasn't afraid they'd hit her, but she was afraid of embarrassment. Another lady thought, Their mothers never know where they are. It wasn't true in this particular case. Their mothers all knew that they had gone to see the missile exhibit on Fourteenth Street.

Out on the platform, whenever the train accelerated, the boys would raise their hands and point them up to the sky to act like rockets going off, then they rat-tat-tatted the shatterproof glass pane like machine guns, although no machine guns had been exhibited.

For some reason known only to the motorman, the train began a sudden slowdown. The lady who was afraid of embarrassment saw the boys jerk forward and backward and grab the swinging guard chains. She had her own boy at home. She stood up with determination and went to the door. She slid it open and said, "You boys will be hurt. You'll be killed. I'm going to call the conductor if you don't just go into the next car and sit down and be quiet."

Two of the boys said, "Yes'm," and acted as though they were about to go. Two of them blinked their eyes a couple of times and pressed their lips together. The train resumed its speed. The door slid shut, parting the lady and the boys. She leaned against the side door because she had to get off at the next stop.

The boys opened their eyes wide at each other and laughed. The lady blushed. The boys looked at her and laughed harder. They began to pound each other's back. Samuel laughed the hardest and pounded Alfred's back until Alfred coughed and the tears came. Alfred held tight to the chain hook. Samuel pounded him even harder when he saw the tears. He said, "Why you bawling? You a baby, huh?" and laughed. One of the men whose boyhood had been more watchful than brave became angry. He stood up straight and looked at the boys for a couple of seconds. Then he walked in a citizenly way to the end of the car, where he pulled the emergency cord. Almost at once, with a terrible hiss, the pressure of air abandoned the brakes and the wheels were caught and held.

People standing in the most secure places fell forward, then backward. Samuel had let go of his hold on the chain so he could pound Tom as well as Alfred. All the passengers in the cars whipped back and forth, but he pitched only forward and fell head first to be crushed and killed between the cars.

The train had stopped hard, halfway into the station, and the conductor called at once for the trainmen who knew about this kind of death and how to take the body from the wheels and brakes. There was silence except for passengers from other cars who asked, What happened! What happened! The ladies waited around wondering if he might be an only child. The men recalled other afternoons with very bad endings. The little boys stayed close to each other, leaning and touching shoulders and arms and legs.

When the policeman knocked at the door and told her about it, Samuel's mother began to scream. She screamed all day and moaned all night, though the doctors tried to quiet her with pills.

Oh, oh, she hopelessly cried. She did not know how she could ever find another boy like that one. However, she was a young woman and she became pregnant. Then for a few months she was hopeful. The child born to her was a boy. They brought him to be seen and nursed. She smiled. But immediately she saw that this baby wasn't Samuel. She and her husband together have had other children, but never again will a boy exactly like Samuel be known.

Topics for Discussion and Writing

1. Paley wrote the story, but an unspecified person *tells* it. Describe the voice of this narrator in the first paragraph. Is the voice neutral and objective, or do you hear some sort of attitude, a point of view? If you do hear an attitude, what words or phrases in the story indicate it?

2. What do you know about the setting of "Samuel"? What can you infer about the neighborhood?

3. In the fourth paragraph we are told that "three of the boys were Negroes and the fourth was something else." Is race important in this story? Is Samuel "Negro" or "something else"? Does it matter?

4. Exactly *why* did a man walk "in a citizenly way to the end of the car, where he pulled the emergency cord"? Do you think the author blames him? What evidence can you offer to support your view? Do *you* blame him? Or do you blame the boys? Or anyone? Explain.

5. The story is called "Samuel," and it is, surely, about him. But what happens after Samuel dies? (You might want to list the events.) What else is the story about? (You might want to comment on why you believe the items in your list are important.)

6. Can you generalize about what the men think of the jigglers and about what the women think? Is Paley saying something about the sexes? About the attitudes of onlookers in a big city?

Jamaica Kincaid

Girl

---

*Jamaica Kincaid was born in 1949 in Saint John's, Antigua, in the West Indies.
She was educated at the Princess Margaret School in Antigua, and briefly, at
Westchester Community College and Franconia College. Since 1974 she has been
a contributor to* The New Yorker.

Kincaid is the author of four books: At the Bottom of the River *(1983, a
collection of short pieces, including "Girl"),* Annie John *(1985, a second book
recording a girl's growth, including "Columbus in Chains"),* A Small Place *(1988,
a passionate essay about the destructive effects of colonialism), and* Lucy *(1990,
a short novel about a young black woman who comes to the United States from the
West Indies).*

1   Wash the white clothes on Monday and put them on the stone heap; wash
the color clothes on Tuesday and put them on the clothesline to dry; don't walk
barehead in the hot sun; cook pumpkin fritters in very hot sweet oil; soak your
little clothes right after you take them off; when buying cotton to make yourself
a nice blouse, be sure that it doesn't have gum on it, because that way it won't
hold up well after a wash; soak salt fish overnight before you cook it; is it true
that you sing benna[1] in Sunday School?; always eat your food in such a way that
it won't turn someone else's stomach; on Sundays try to walk like a lady and not
like the slut you are so bent on becoming; don't sing benna in Sunday School;
you mustn't speak to wharf-rat boys, not even to give directions; don't eat fruits
on the street—flies will follow you; *but I don't sing benna on Sundays at all and
never in Sunday school;* this is how to sew on a button; this is how to make a
buttonhole for the button you have just sewed on; this is how to hem a dress
when you see the hem coming down and so to prevent yourself from looking
like the slut I know you are so bent on becoming; this is how you iron your
father's khaki shirt so that it doesn't have a crease; this is how you iron your
father's khaki pants so that they don't have a crease; this is how you grow okra—
far from the house, because okra tree harbors red ants; when you are growing
dasheen, make sure it gets plenty of water or else it makes your throat itch when
you are eating it; this is how you sweep a corner; this is how you sweep a whole
house; this is how you sweep a yard; this is how you smile to someone you
don't like too much; this is how you set a table for dinner with an important
guest; this is how you smile to someone you don't like at all; this is how you
smile to someone you like completely; this is how you set a table for tea; this is
how you set a table for dinner; this is how you set a table for lunch; this is how
you set a table for breakfast; this is how to behave in the presence of men who

[1]Calypso music.

don't know you very well, and this way they won't recognize immediately the slut I have warned you against becoming; be sure to wash every day, even if it is with your own spit; don't squat down to play marbles—you are not a boy, you know; don't pick people's flowers—you might catch something; don't throw stones at blackbirds, because it might not be a blackbird at all; this is how to make a bread pudding; this is how to make doukona;[2] this is how to make pepper pot; this is how to make a good medicine for a cold; this is how to make a good medicine to throw away a child before it even becomes a child; this is how to catch a fish; this is how to throw back a fish you don't like, and that way something bad won't fall on you; this is how to bully a man; this is how a man bullies you; this is how to love a man, and if this doesn't work there are other ways, and if they don't work don't feel to bad about giving up; this how to spit up in the air if you feel like it, and this is how to move quick so that it doesn't fall on you; this how to make ends meet; always squeeze bread to make sure it's fresh; *but what if the baker won't let me feel the bread?;* you mean to say that after all you are really going to be the kind of woman who the baker won't let near the bread?

Topics for Discussion and Writing

1. Identify the two characters whose voices we hear in this story. Explain what we know about them (their circumstances and their relationship). How old, approximately, is "girl"? Cite specific evidence from the text.

2. What do we learn about the relationship from frequent repetition of "this is how"? Are there other words or phrases frequently repeated? If so, what are they?

3. Imitating the structure of "Girl," compose a comparable piece, based on some repeated conversation in your family.

THREE POEMS

William Shakespeare (1564–1616) is widely regarded as the world's greatest dramatist, but he also wrote nondramatic poetry, including 154 sonnets. The sonnets were published in 1609 but probably were written from about 1598 to 1605 or so. The fourteen lines of Shakespeare's sonnets can be divided into three quatrains (units of four lines each) and a couplet (a pair of rhyming lines). In each quatrain, the first and third lines rhyme with each other, and the second and fourth lines rhyme. The rhyme scheme thus may be formulated as ababcdcdefefgg.

[2]Spicy pudding made of plantains.

Sonnet 73

That time of year thou mayst in me behold
When yellow leaves, or none, or few, do hang
Upon those boughs which shake against the cold,
Bare ruined choirs[1] where late the sweet birds sang.   4
In me thou see'st the twilight of such day
As after sunset fadeth in the west,
Which by-and-by black night doth take away,
Death's second self that seals up all in rest,   8
In me thou see'st the glowing of such fire
That on the ashes of his youth doth lie,
As the deathbed whereon it must expire,
Consumed with that which it was nourished by.   12
    This thou perceiv'st, which makes thy love more strong,
    To love that well which thou must leave ere long.

Topics for Discussion and Writing

1. Paraphrase—that is, put into your own words—the entire poem.

2. To what does the poet compare himself in the first quatrain? In the second? In the third?

3. What would be gained or lost if the sequence of quatrains were reversed, that is, if the poem began with the last quatrain and ended with the first?

Robert Frost

Robert Frost (1874–1963) in his early years farmed in New Hampshire, published a few poems in local newspapers, left the farm and taught school, and in 1912 left for England, where he hoped to achieve more popular success as a writer. By 1915 he had won a considerable reputation, and he returned to the United States, settling on a farm in New Hampshire and cultivating the image of the country-wise farmer-poet. In fact he was well read in the classics, the Bible, and in English and American literature.

*   Among Frost's many comments about literature, here are three: "Writing is unboring to the extent that it is dramatic"; "Every poem is . . . a figure of the will*

---

[1]The part of the church where services were sung.

braving alien entanglements"; and, finally, a poem "begins in delight and ends in wisdom. . . . It runs a course of lucky events, and ends in a clarification of life—not necessarily a great clarification, such as sects and cults are founded on, but in a momentary stay against confusion."

Stopping by Woods on a Snowy Evening

Whose woods these are I think I know.
His house is in the village though;
He will not see me stopping here   4
To watch his woods fill up with snow.
My little horse must think it queer
To stop without a farmhouse near
Between the woods and frozen lake   8
The darkest evening of the year.
He gives his harness bells a shake
To ask if there is some mistake.
The only other sound's the sweep   12
Of easy wind and downy flake.
The woods are lovely, dark and deep.
But I have promises to keep,
And miles to go before I sleep,   16
And miles to go before I sleep.

Topics For Discussion and Writing

1. Line 5 originally read: "The steaming horses think it queer." Line 7 read: "Between a forest and a lake." Evaluate the changes.

2. How would you describe the pattern of rhymes in the first stanza? In the second and third stanzas? The pattern changes in the fourth. Describe this pattern too, and then offer at least one suggestion as to why Frost may have departed from the earlier pattern.

3. Hearing that the poem had been interpreted as a "death poem," Frost said. "I never intended that, but I did have the feeling it was loaded with ulteriority." What do you understand "ulteriority" to mean in regards to this

poem? For example, what significance do you attach to the time of day and
year?

4. How does the horse's attitude contrast with the man's?

Pat Mora

*Pat Mora did her undergraduate work at Texas Western College, and then earned
a master's degree at the University of Texas at El Paso, where she then served as
Assistant to the Vice President for Academic Affairs, Director of the University
Museum, and then from 1981 to 1989 as Assistant to the President. She has
published essays on Hispanic culture as well as a children's book,* Tomás and the
Library Lady, *but she is best known for her books of poems. Mora has received
several awards, including one from the Southwest Council of Latin American
Studies.*

Immigrants

wrap their babies in the American flag,
feed them mashed hot dogs and apple pie,
name them Bill and Daisy,
buy them blonde dolls that blink blue   5
eyes or a football and tiny cleats
before the baby can even walk,
speak to them in thick English,
 hallo, babee, hallo.
whisper in Spanish or Polish   10
when the babies sleep, whisper
in a dark parent bed, that dark
parent fear, "Will they like
our boy, our girl, our fine american
boy, our fine american girl?"

Topics For Discussion and Writing

1. To say that someone—for example, a politician—"wraps himself in the
American flag" is to suggest disapproval or even anger or contempt. What

behavior does the phrase usually describe? What does Mora mean when she says that immigrants "wrap their babies in the American flag"?

2. What do you suppose is Mora's attitude toward the immigrants? Do you think the poet fully approves of their hopes? On what do you base your answer? Speaking generally, do they seek to assimilate to an Anglo-American culture?

3. Does Mora's description of the behavior of immigrants ring true of the immigrant group you are part of or know best? Speaking generally, do they seek to assimilate to an Anglo-American culture? What is your attitude toward their efforts or their efforts to retain their culture? Explain in an essay of 750 to 1000 words.

Chapter 17

Reviewing

Writing a Book Review

Because book reviews in newspapers or magazines are usually about a newly published work, reviewers normally assume that their readers will be unfamiliar with the book. Reviewers take it as their job to acquaint readers with the book, its contents and its value, and to help them decide whether or not they wish to read it. Since most reviews are brief (500 to 1500 words) they cannot, like explications, comment on everything. On the other hand they cannot, like analyses, focus on one aspect of the writing; they usually attempt in some way to cover the book. Reviews, then, usually contain more summary and more evaluation than explications or analyses. Nevertheless, reviewers must approach the task analytically if they are to accomplish it in the relatively small space allotted. And if they are to be convincing, they must support their opinion by quotations (usually indispensable), examples, and specific references to the text so that readers may think and feel the way the reviewer thinks and feels.

A review commonly has a structure something like this:

1. An opening paragraph that names the author and the title, gives the reader some idea of the nature and scope of the work (a children's book; a book for the general reader; a book for specialists), and establishes the tone of the review (more about tone in a moment).

2. A paragraph or two of plot summary if the book is a novel; some summary of the contents if it is not.

3. A paragraph on the theme, purpose, idea, or vision embodied in the book, perhaps within the context of related works.

4. A paragraph or two on the strengths, if any (for instance, the book fulfills its purpose).

5. A paragraph or two on the weaknesses, if any.

6. A concluding paragraph in which the reviewer delivers his or her point— but the point in some degree has probably been implied from the beginning, because the concluding paragraph is a culmination rather than a surprise.

Tone, as we suggest elsewhere in this book (see page 148), usually refers to the writer's attitude toward the subject, the readers, and the writer's self. The tone of a review is therefore somewhat dependent on the publication in which it will appear. A review in *Scientific American* will have a different tone from one in Ms. Since you have not been commissioned to write your review and are essentially playing a game, you must *imagine* your reader. It's a reasonable idea to imagine that your classmates are your readers, forgetting of course that they may be reviewing the same book you are. (It's a very bad idea to imagine that your teacher is your reader.) And it's always productive to treat both your reader and your subject with respect. This does not mean you need to be solemn or boring; on the contrary, the best way to show your respect for your reader is to write something you would be interested in reading yourself.

Here is a book review from *The New York Times*. Although some reviews are untitled, this one has a title "The Tough Got Going"; unless your instructor tells you otherwise, give your review a title. (Finding your title will help you to see if you have focused your essay.)

Carole Klein
Significant Sisters

The Grassroots of Active Feminism: 1839–1939

   By Margaret Forster

A poem by Marge Piercy, called "Rough Times," begins:

1 We are trying to live
   as if we were an experiment
   conducted by the future.

2   The eight women whose lives form *Significant Sisters* were selected for the ways in which their separately courageous breaks with tradition set the future of feminism in motion. Having decided that feminist history can be divided into eight areas of changed experience, Margaret Forster provides narrative biographies of the women responsible for starting each change that has taken place.

3   Some of these British and American pioneers are familiar to us, such as Margaret Sanger, who made birth control a feminist issue, and Emma Goldman, who served as a bridge between feminist ideologies of the 19th and late 20th centuries. Some other sisters are relatively unknown, and I for one am indebted to Miss Forster for bringing them to my attention. I confess to having scarcely heard, for example, of Caroline Norton. A bitterly unhappy marriage gave her, a well-connected woman and popular writer, the impetus to fight for the reform of English marriage and divorce laws—laws which had made married women powerless chattels, completely at their husbands' mercy. In another sphere of

experience, education, we find Emily Davies, who challenged the entrenched belief that education for British girls should be shorter and softer than for boys, and eventually established Girton College for women at Cambridge University in 1873.

4　　What is particularly provocative in this history is how different these women were from each other in temperament and ideology. By no means were all even purposefully advancing a feminist cause as they fought their separate battles. Indeed, Elizabeth Blackwell, the first woman doctor, born in Britain, educated there and in the United States, was decidedly unsympathetic to organized feminism. She saw her own ambitions as atypical, her success due to special gifts. Other women, she thought, should devote themselves to life's highest calling—being good wives and mothers. Of course, as Miss Forster points out, by establishing the principle that gender doesn't rule out professional achievement, Elizabeth Blackwell was in fact a feminist, indeed one who made immense contributions to feminist history.

5　　I must note here that Miss Forster appears to be a bit insensitive to the feminist commitments of many contemporary women physicians. After discussing Blackwell's hope that future female doctors would devote themselves to humanizing medicine, paying particular attention to the medical problems of women, Miss Forster writes: "There are no measurable signs that the entry of women into the medical profession has significantly humanized it. No broad changes exist for the better which are the result of female medical action." Such categorical dismissal seems to ignore the various and well-organized advances female doctors continue to make by, for example, demystifying the physician's role, helping women to participate in their own health care, and in making childbirth a far less clinical and isolating affair. For the most part, However, Miss Forster seems to be quite clear eyed about her subjects and their legacies, neither romanticizing motives nor being unduly critical of what, from a modern perspective, might seem contradictory or naive behavior.

6　　Margaret Forster has written two biographies, one a highly acclaimed study of Thackeray. She is also the author of 12 novels, among them the sprightly "Georgy Girl." Her substantial research for *Significant Sisters* draws on diaries, private and published papers and autobiographies. But in constructing her profiles from these historical sources, she employs the novelist's tools of evocative language and skillful rendering of character, story and theme.

7　　Perhaps the most persistent theme in these pages is the conflict between being feminine and feminist. Marriage and motherhood, even love and sex, more often than not eroded a woman's strength. Miss Forster does not believe this conflict is over. Many women still fear that a separate self will be submerged in the roles of wife and mother. But she suggests that in the arc of feminist history we are headed towards a time when such integration really will be possible. As a result of reading this engaging book, we shall certainly know which ancestral sisters to thank when that time arrives.

Topics for Discussion and Writing

1. Characterize or describe the tone of Klein's review.

2. Write a one-sentence summary of each paragraph. Your list of sentences should resemble an outline.

3. How well does your outline correspond with the structure we say reviews commonly have? (See page 427.)

4. If there are discrepancies between what we have said about reviews and the review by Klein, can you offer a reasonable explanation for these discrepancies? Or would you argue that we revise our discussion, or that we choose a different review as an example?

5. Write a brief argument (one or two paragraphs) defending your answer to question 4.

Writing Other Reviews

Our suggestions for writing a book review, with obvious modifications, can serve as guidelines for other reviews you may be assigned or choose to write: of a play, a movie, a concert, or other performance. Again, it is the reviewer's job to acquaint readers, real or imagined, with a performance they are assumed to be unfamiliar with (although in fact reviews are often read by readers who want to see their own judgments confirmed, or their small talk improved). And again, you must adopt an appropriate tone, suggesting both your own expert knowledge of your topic and your respect for your readers' intelligence and taste.

Your best preparation for writing a review is to read reviews in publications you trust, consciously noting what you find informative, interesting, and persuasive. Then, if you are covering a live event, you'll find it useful to ask to see in advance the promotional material usually in the hands of the organization sponsoring the event. You'll want to be skeptical of some of the rave reviews you'll find quoted (and of course you mustn't use them in your own review without acknowledging their sources), but you may well find biographical and other background information that will prepare you for the performance and make notetaking easier. And you must go prepared to take notes—often in the dark—and allow yourself sufficient time immediately after the event to type or rewrite your notes legibly.

Reviewing a record or tape obviously has some advantages. You can listen to it many times, you may have access to the score or lyrics and previous recordings, and you can choose your own time and place for listening. Or perhaps the relaxed and witty style of the review we print below just makes it seem easier. The review was written by a student for a college newspaper.

Pat Bellanca

Jimmy Buffett Is Going Coconuts?!

1   This is what Jimmy Buffett used to do: sail around the Caribbean with his friends, smoke a lot of pot, drink a lot of tequila, write some songs—and every year or so return (rather unwillingly, he would have had us believe) to the mainland to record an album, tour the country and make some money so that he could afford to keep his sailboat running and himself pleasantly numbed to the realities of humdrum, everyday American existence.

2   Romantically melancholy escapism is the theme that Buffett has consistently examined, espoused and re-examined in all of the albums he has released since he first achieved a kind of pop stardom with "Margaritaville," the single from his 1977 album *Changes in Latitudes, Changes in Attitudes.* In that album he developed a formula that worked commercially.

3   In his most recent effort, *Coconut Telegraph,* released several weeks ago, he reworks an extremely watered-down version of the formula into yet another of his silly celebrations of sailing, smoking and drinking with fellow "expatriated Americans." But now, in keeping with his absorption into the mainstream of pop music, he writes noticeably less about smoking, drinking and wandering than he did before. It sounds like he's raising a family.

4   *Coconut Telegraph* is a cleanly produced country-rock-pop album which, despite Buffett's latest change in attitude, almost entirely consists of musical and thematic clones of songs he has previously recorded.

5   There is the song about the escapades of the businessman in the islands: "The Weather Is Here, Wish You Were Beautiful," which was recycled from "American Friend," a track from *Son of a Son of a Sailor,* Buffett's seventh album. There's the gee-I-kinda-wish-I-could-go-home song, "Incommunicado," this year's model of "Miss You So Badly" from *Changes.* And there's the campy crooner song, "Stars Fell on Alabama" (a 1934 Parish/Perkins song, actually one of the brighter moments on the album), reminiscent of "Pencil Thin Moustache" which Buffett wrote for his 1974 album, *Living and Dying in 3/4 Time.*

6   With *Coconut Telegraph*, Buffett has completed his transformation from a cult songwriter of nutty hippie anthems (check out "God's Own Drunk" and "The Great Filling Station Hold-up" on two of his earlier albums) to an unambitious, unfunny middle of the middle of the road pop craftsman. In the year in which Christopher Cross walked away with multiple Grammy Awards, it's hardly surprising.

7   In "Growing Older But Not Up" Buffett tells us, "My metabolic rate is pleasantly stuck / So let the winds of change blow over my head. . . ." And that's

probably the best summation of the attitude behind the album. It's entirely pleasant.

8   The combined effect of the ever-present congas, steel drums, acoustic guitars, unobtrusive strings and effortlessly wailing harmonica is pleasantly mellow. The song about Buffett's daughter, "Little Miss Magic," is pleasantly sentimental without being overly gooey. The hooks are pleasantly "catchy," particularly in "The Weather Is Here, Wish You Were Beautiful," a single from the album which seems to be getting a fair amount of airplay on WEEI-FM. Even the photo of the star on the cover of the album is pleasantly unassuming—he is wearing topsiders, chinos and an off-white crew-neck.

9   Of course, all of this is about as relevant and meaningful as sitting in a wad of bubblegum, but if one could prevent oneself from becoming bored and irritated by the unrelieved "pleasantness" of *Coconut Telegraph,* one might find it—a-hem—enjoyable.

Topics for Discussion and Writing

1. Characterize the writer's tone. Is it appropriate to her material and her audience? Explain.

2. On the basis of this review, would you buy *Coconut Telegraph?* If you didn't have to pay for the record, would you be interested, because of the review, in listening to it? Explain why, or why not.

3. If you saw this writer's byline in your newspaper would you read the article? Explain.

4. Write a review of a current album. Or, attend a concert and review it. In a note appended to your review, define your intended audience.

Chapter 18

Interviewing

Writing an Essay Based on an Interview

We have all been treated to the television interview with (and perhaps by) a celebrity: Question: "Which fight was the toughest that you have ever lost?" Answer: "Uh, well, Howard, that's a tough question." Question: "When did you have your first sexual experience?" Answer: "Oh, Barbara, I knew you'd ask me that!" And we've read similarly inspiring transcriptions in popular magazines (while standing in the checkout line at a supermarket). But the interview is also an important tool of social science research and serious journalism. Sociologists and psychologists regularly use interviews, and biographers and historians often rely heavily on interviews when they write about recent events. Interviews with poets and fiction writers in literary magazines help us to learn not only about the writers and their work but also about the craft of poetry or fiction. For the apprentice writer, interviews provide excellent sources for interesting essays about the person being interviewed or about issues and ideas.

A college campus is an ideal place to practice interviewing. Faculties are composed of experts in a variety of fields and distinguished visitors are a regular part of extracurricular life. In the next few pages, we'll offer some advice on conducting interviews and writing essays based on them. If you take our advice, you'll acquire a skill you may well put to further, more specialized use in social science courses; at the same time you'll be developing skill in asking questions and shaping materials relevant to all research and writing.

Before we list the steps for you to follow, we offer two examples, essays based largely on interviews. First read "The Einstein of Happiness." Then answer the questions that follow it.

By Patricia Freeman

The Einstein of Happiness

1   If the truth be known, being a professor of happiness is no picnic. People deride your research, trivialize your interests—then badger you for the secret of

eternal bliss. Nevertheless, Allen Parducci, fifty-seven-year-old professor of psychology at UCLA, has been exploring the fabric of human felicity for over forty years.

2   Parducci became a happiness scholar because of his father, a stern architectural sculptor in Grosse Pointe, Michigan, who voiced a vexing conviction that "things balance out" between happiness and woe—or, as Mark Twain put it, "Every man is a suffering machine and a happiness machine combined, and for every happiness turned out in one department, the other stands ready to modify it with a sorrow or pain." Young Parducci, wondering why he ought to bother getting out of bed in the morning if that were true, set out to debunk the theory.

3   He conducted his research everywhere. He quizzed his college roommates as to the completeness of their contentment. He grilled his fellow sailors during World War II: "As the ship rolled back and forth and they retched, I'd ask them, 'How happy are you now? Are you really unhappy?'"

4   Eventually he received a graduate degree in psychology from Berkeley, where he could finally study the phenomenon scientifically. Today, he is known around the world for his work in "the relativism of absolute judgments"—a fancy phrase meaning that how we evaluate a thing depends on what we compare it to. (Though his work was an outgrowth of his search for the answers to human happiness, hardly anybody in academia has applied it that way.) To back up his ideas, he devised several studies to show that judgments of all kinds depend on the context in which they are made.

5   For one study, he gave a "test" of moral judgments to college students, who were asked to assign each item in a list of behaviors a ranking of from "1— not particularly bad or wrong" to "5—extremely evil." Half of the students were given a list of comparatively mild acts of wrongdoing, including such items as "cheating at solitaire," "wearing shorts on the street where it is illegal" and "stealing towels from a hotel room." The other half were given a much nastier list, including such acts as "selling to a hospital milk from diseased cattle." Both lists contained six of the same items. The crucial feature of the test was that the students were to judge the items according to their own personal values and not to judge them in comparison to one another. Nonetheless, the experiment showed that students' moral judgments depended on how the list was "skewed"—the six acts appearing on both lists were rated more leniently by students who judged them in the context of the nasty list than by those who encountered them on the mild list. "Poisoning a neighbor's barking dog," for example, got a rather harsh score of 4.19 when it appeared along with "playing poker on a Sunday" and a less disapproving 3.65 when it came just after "murdering your mother without justification or provocation."

6   According to the same principle, which Parducci calls a "negatively skewed distribution," our judgments of personal satisfaction depend on how often we experience the things we deem most satisfying. To demonstrate this, he devised a study in which two groups of students selected cards from two different decks

and won money based on the value assigned to each card. One group played with cards marked from 1 cent to 21 cents, with the higher values predominating, and the other groups with cards marked from 7 cents to 27 cents, with low sums predominating. Every player won the same total of money for the series, but group one, which garnered its winnings primarily from the higher end of the scale, reported themselves happier with their winnings.

7   What does all of this mean for us? It means, Parducci says, that just as the cardplayers were happiest when most of their winnings were close to the maximum that could be earned, we will likely be most satisfied if our lives are arranged so that the best of what we experience happens more frequently. The happy person, who finds "zest, fun and joy in life," says Parducci, is one for whom "the things he's experiencing are high relative to his standards." And conversely, the unhappy person—whose life is marked by "terror, anxiety and misery"—sets inappropriate standards for himself often comparing his life to an impossible ideal.

8   Parducci will venture a few tips on living the happy life, but only with prodding. If we want to be happy, he says, we ought not to live in the future, thinking that we'd be happy if only we could double our income, marry this person or get that job; instead we should learn to delight in what we have and look forward to things that happen every day. Above all, we should let go of what's impossible.

9   "We all know people who have had a great love affair break up and their friends say, 'Get it out of your head,' but they can't. But if they could, in effect, drop that relationship out of their context altogether, then the best of their experience with someone new would seem good and wonderful. They could experience the same high even with a lesser person."

10   The happiest person Parducci has ever known (though he doesn't think he's particularly good at telling whether people are happy or not) was a woman who died of cancer in her mid-thirties. "The six months before she died was like a party every night," he recalls. "Her friends would come over, her ex-husbands would visit, and everybody would have a great time. I asked her, 'Joanne, how do you feel about death?' and she said. 'I know I could die any time, but I'm very happy.'" Joanne was married approximately five times if you count both legal and informal spouses. "She'd meet these men anybody would say she shouldn't marry," Parducci says, "and it would be disastrous. She'd see virtues in people that no one else could see. It seemed that she was living in a dream world. I would have said, looking at her life, that she should see things the way they are. But sometimes I think some people are just born to be happy."

11   Most Americans, in fact, say that they are happy. According to national polls the average citizen gives himself a happiness rating of seven on a scale of one to ten. Parducci gives himself a six, a rating he believes actually makes him significantly more sanguine than most Americans. "People's reports of their own happiness show an astonishing positive bias," he says. He thinks people make themselves out to be happier than they really are because "there's the

implication that there's something wrong with you if you can't somehow arrange your life to be satisfying."

12   In fact, unhappiness seems to be a national personality trait. "The success credo of American business is that you're supposed to always be setting higher standards," Parducci says. "And in setting inappropriately high standards, we can't help but doom ourselves to unhappiness. Society is pyramidal. There's only one position at the top, and if everyone is pushing toward that one position, the great majority must inevitably fall by the wayside." But still we push our children to aim for medical school or sports superstardom.

13   Does Parducci hope, in some small way, to make the world a happier place to live? "I'm very skeptical about the possibility of doing that," he says. Still, there are those who would make him into a guru of good cheer. But, unlike Leo Buscaglia, psychologist to the masses and a fixture on the best-seller lists, Parducci is uninterested in providing road maps to felicity and pointers to pleasure. "I've been approached by several literary agents," he says. "There's always a pressure toward self-help. You know. 'The Ten Rules for Happiness.' But if it were that simple, it would have been discovered by now."

14   People tell him that he could make a fortune if only he would become at least a bit of a happiness hawker. "I ask myself, if lightning struck in that way, if I made a million dollars, would I be happier? But friends of mine who have made that kind of money say that it hasn't made them happy," he says.

15   Even though Parducci says he'd like to be "more happy," in the end there's something he considers more important—and that is, "being good." He will readily declares that religion—particularly Christianity—has fostered unhappiness by holding up an ideal of goodness that is impossible to live up to. Still, he says, "I think there are rules that people ought to follow, rules that may be difficult. Suppose Mephistopheles came and said, 'If you kill a few people I'll make you very happy.' I hope I would be strong enough to turn him down. I don't want to be identified with the 'me first' psychology that says we're all out for ourselves."

16   If he can't make people happier and he doesn't consider happiness the most important thing in the world anyway, why does Parducci press on with his work? "There's a satisfaction," he submits, "in just understanding things. We can understand how the planets move around the sun, though we can't affect them. We get satisfaction out of understanding happiness, even though we can't do much about it."

Topics for Discussion and Writing

1. What homework do you think Patricia Freeman did in preparation for the interview?

2. List the questions Freeman might have posed to elicit the information in each paragraph or group of paragraphs. Were there any paragraphs for

which you had difficulty imagining questions? Can you explain why? (Or, what information do you suppose did not come from Professor Parducci's own words? Who or what do you imagine to be the source of this information?)

3. Through much of the article we hear Parducci's voice, either paraphrased or directly quoted. Where do we hear the interviewer's voice as well?

4. Suppose you had begun with only the information that Allen Parducci is a professor of psychology at an American university. What library sources might tell you his age, education, major field of interest, publications, and current academic post? (See if you can find this information in your own library.)

Now read the second article and answer the questions following it.

Eileen Garred

Ethnobotanists Race Against Time to Save Useful Plants

1   Although a white lab coat hangs a bookshelf in his cramped office and an IBM personal computer sits on a nearby table, these are not the tools Mark Plotkin prefers to use. As an ethnobotanist, Plotkin has spent months in the tropical forests of South America, bringing along newspapers and moth balls to press and preserve plant specimens he then hauls back to the Botanical Museum at Harvard.

2   In annual visits over the past eight years, Plotkin has been patiently cultivating the trust of tribal medicine men in the Suriname jungle in order to learn how the native people use forest plants in their cultures. It is a race against time and the steadily increasing influences of civilization.

3   Tropical forests the world over are shrinking as deforestation escalates and development spurred by rapid population growth reaches further into the jungle. The Amazon region alone contains approximately 80,000 species of plants, a vast resource of living organisms, many of which are yet unknown to science. Plants of great potential value of medical, agricultural, and industrial uses are vanishing even before they are identified.

4   Perhaps more important, knowledge about plants long used by native Indians for beneficial purposes is dying out with the witch doctors. "Within one generation after civilization arrives, aboriginal peoples will forget most of their plant lore," predicts Richard Schultes, Director of the Botanical Museum.

5   The Westerners who arrive to build roads or preach the Gospel also bring with them Western medicines. "Our medicines are effective, cheap, and easy to get," Schultes adds. "The natives are not going to run through the forest to look for a leaf their ancestors used to alleviate sickness if they don't have to."

6   Few of the witch doctors today have young apprentices from the tribe because visiting missionaries have strongly discouraged shamanism. The last of the medicine men in the tribes must be coaxed to reveal their secrets to a new breed of botanist like Plotkin.

7   Last year, for example, Plotkin returned from Suriname with a small tree limb called doubredwa. The South American Indians scrape the bark into rum and claim the resulting drink is a powerful male aphrodisiac. "The world doesn't need more people," explains Plotkin. "What it needs is a treatment for impotence—and there it is in a woody vine from the Amazon."

8   Curare, a native arrow poison, has been used for a number of years in hospitals as an anesthetic and muscle relaxant during surgery. Another plant poison that stupefies fish and forces them to the water's surface where they are easy targets for spearfishers is the basis for the pesticide rotenone. Because it is biodegradable, rotenone is widely used in the United States.

9   Fruit from a common Amazonian palm produces oil that is very similar to olive oil, and the fruit from still another species is extremely rich in vitamins C and A.

10   "The so-called 'wonder drugs,' including penicillin, cortisone, and reserpine, that have revolutionized the practice of medicine came from plants that had some use in primitive societies that called the attention of a chemist to the plant," says Schultes.

11   According to Schultes, tribes of the northwest Amazon utilize just under 2000 different plant species for "medicinal" purposes. "In these plants there is a tremendous storehouse of new chemicals," he explains. "In the hands of a chemist, a naturally occurring chemical can be changed to form the basis of many new semi-synthetic chemicals. So if you find in a plant one useful chemical, you are finding literally hundreds that chemists can make using that natural structure as a base. How can chemists hope to procure and analyze 80,000 species of plants?

12   "One shortcut for the chemist is to concentrate on the plants that native peoples by trial and error over thousands of years have found to have some biological activity," he says.

13   Although it often takes two decades or more of research from discovery of a plant to a packaged drug, ethnobotanists who provide chemists with the material must work quickly since the varieties of jungle plants and the numbers of medicine men who know how to identify and use them are disappearing at an alarming rate.

14   As a defined field of study, ethnobotany is more than a century old, but it has received greater attention only in recent years. Schultes, a pioneer in the field, lived and worked in Columbia and Peru from 1941 to 1954. During that time, he collected 24,000 plants and filled dozens of field notebooks, which he is still trying to put into publishable form.

15   "We call this work an 'ethnobotanical salvage operation,'" says Plotkin, "which just means that we are documenting the plants the Indians use and the ways in which they use them." The U.S. Division of the World Wildlife Fund is sponsoring Plotkin's work at the Harvard Botanical Museum. As part of the Tropical South American Conservation and Ethnobotany Project, Plotkin has compiled a catalog of more than 1000 useful plant species, which includes Latin and vernacular names, data on distribution, aboriginal use, chemical composition and economic potential. Previously, much of this information was widely scattered and not available to botanists, conservationists and development planners.

16   Plotkin, whose initial interest in the beneficial uses of plants was cultivated by Schultes, is now primarily concerned with trying ethnobotany to conservation. Money, he says, is the bottom line. In fighting for preservation of the Amazon's tropical forest with its large reserve of natural resources, Plotkin aims to put conservation in economic terms.

17   "The ill-planned development in the tropics by local governments and transnational corporations is causing serious damage," he says. "But you can't tell Brazil, a country with the largest foreign debt in the world, 'Don't cut down the forest because you've got the cutest little monkey living there.' You have to explain that plant A is worth 'x' number of dollars and plant B, if you manage it right, will be worth 'y' number of dollars."

18   "You have to convince the government that it is worth more as a forest than as an agricultural area, which is probably going to fail anyway over the long term. Until you can put it in concrete economic terms, it's just talk."

19   As an example, Plotkin points to the irony that Brazil imports $20 million worth of olive oil a year, although there are millions of the palm trees that produce a similar edible oil within its borders.

20   One of the most common trees in the Amazon, the buriti palm, has a multitude of uses discovered by the Indians. Its fruit is rich in vitamins, an extract from the stem can be used to make bread, the fibers can be used to make twine, houses are built from its wood, and it grows only in swampy areas that could not otherwise be used for agriculture. However, says Plotkin, the Brazilian government has yet to step in to look for high yielding strains of the buriti, or "tap into what is a potential gold mine" by putting it into plantations.

21   "Conservation works best if it's in that country's self-interest." says Plotkin. "Ethnobotany"—the study of the use of plants by native peoples who have intimate knowledge of forests and the useful products they contain—"is really in the forefront of international conservation efforts."

22   "For thousands of years, aboriginal peoples have been living with and depending on the native vegetation. Now civilization is destroying that knowledge," says Schultes. "Much more endangered than any species is the knowledge about plant lore. If we don't pick it up now, we'll never get it."

Topics for Discussion and Writing

1. Is the article primarily about Plotkin or about Schultes? If neither, what is it about?

2. What is ethnobotany? Where in the article is it defined? Should Garred have defined it earlier? Why or why not?

3. Garred is on the editorial staff of the *Harvard Gazette,* a weekly devoted to news of the Harvard community. How do you suppose Garred came upon her story? Reconstruct the steps she probably took to research her article.

4. From what office or offices at your institution might you learn of an activity of more than usual interest engaged in by a faculty member, an administrator, a student, an alumnus, or a trustee? (Check your college catalog and directory for possible leads.)

Guidelines for Conducting the Interview and Writing the Essay

As these two essays illustrate, writers use interviews in writing about people, and they also use interviews in writing about issues. For either purpose, an interview produces, and the writer reproduces, more than information. By skillful selection of the most interesting remarks for quotation and by reporting gestures and settings, the writer allows us to experience both the writer's and the speaker's interest in the topic under discussion.

Here are some steps to follow in conducting an interview and writing an essay based on it.

1. Finding a subject for an interview. As with all writing projects, the best place to start is with your own interest. If you are taking a course from a particularly interesting professor, you might end your search, and begin your research, there. Or, you might use an interview as a way of investigating a department you're thinking of majoring in. Your college catalog lists the names of all faculty members, by department.

Scan the list in the department that interests you and begin to ask questions of upperclassmen. Then, with a name or two in mind, check your library for appropriate biographical reference works. *Directory of American Scholars* contains the most names of academicians, but also check various Who's Who volumes. In addition to *Who's Who in America,* you'll also find such works as *Who's Who in the West,* (and similar titles for the East, South, Southwest, and Midwest), *Who's Who Among Black Americans, Who's Who in Religion, Who's Who of American Women.* In addition, the circulation desk or the research librarian may have a list of current publications by faculty members. In some libraries, current publications by faculty and alumni are on display. Department secretaries are good sources of information not only about the special interests of the faculty but also about guest speakers scheduled by the department in the near future. Investigate the athletic department if you're interested in sports; or the departments of music, art, and drama, for the names of resident or visiting performing artists. Other sources of newsworthy personalities or events: the publicity office, the president's office, the college newspaper. All are potential sources for information about recent awards, or achievements, or upcoming events that may lead you to a subject for an interview, and a good story.

2. Preliminary homework. Find out as much as you can about your potential interviewee's work, from the sources we mentioned above. If the subject of your interview is a faculty member, ask the department secretary if you may see a copy of that person's vita (Latin for "life," and pronounced vee-ta). Many departments have these brief biographical sketches on file for publicity purposes. The vita will list, among other things, publications and current research interests.

3. Requesting the interview. In making your request, don't hesitate to mention that you are fulfilling an assignment, but also make evident your own interest in the person's work or area of expertise. (Showing that you already know something about the work, that you've done some preliminary homework, is persuasive evidence of your interest.) Request the interview, preferably in writing, at least a week in advance, and ask for ample time (probably an hour to an hour and a half) for a thorough interview.

4. Preparing thoroughly. If your subject is a writer, read and take notes on the publications that most interest you. Read book reviews, if available; read reviews of performances if your subject is a performing artist. As you read, write out the questions that occur to you. As you work on them, try to phrase your questions so that they require more than a yes or no answer. A "why" or "how" question is likely to be productive, but don't be afraid of a general question such as "Tell me something about. . . ."

Revise your questions and put them in a reasonable order. Work on an opening question that you think your subject will find both easy and interesting to answer. "How did you get interested in . . . " is often a good start. Type your questions or write them boldly so that you will find them easy to refer to.

Think about how you will record the interview. Although a tape recorder may seem like a good idea, there are good reasons not to rely on one. First of all, your subject may be made uneasy by its presence and freeze up. Second, the recorder (or the operator) may malfunction, leaving you with a partial record, or nothing at all. Third, even if all goes well, when you prepare to write you will face a mass of material, some of it inaudible, and all of it daunting to transcribe.

If, despite these warnings, you decide (with your subject's permission) to tape, expect to take notes anyway. It's the only way you can be sure you will have a record of what was important to you out of all that was said. Think beforehand, then, of how you will take notes, and if you can manage to, practice by interviewing a friend. You'll probably find that you'll want to devise some system of shorthand, perhaps no more than using initials for names that frequently recur, dropping the vowels in words that you transcribe—whatever assists you to write quickly but legibly. But don't think you must transcribe every word. Be prepared to do a lot more listening than writing.

5. Presenting yourself for the interview. Dress appropriately, bring your prepared questions and a notebook or pad for your notes, and appear on time.

6. Conducting the interview. At the start of the interview, try to engage briefly in conversation, without taking notes, to put your subject at ease. Even important people can be shy. Remembering that will help keep you at ease, too. If you want to use a tape recorder, ask your subject's permission, and if it is granted, ask where the microphone may be conveniently placed.

As the interview proceeds, keep your purpose in mind. Are you trying to gain information about an issue or topic, or are you trying to get a portrait of a personality? Listen attentively to your subject's answers and be prepared to follow up with your own responses and spontaneous questions. Here is where your thorough preparation will pay off.

A good interview develops like a conversation. Keep in mind that your prepared questions, however essential, are not sacred. At the same time don't hesitate to steer your subject, courteously, from apparent irrelevancies (what one reporter calls "sawdust") to something that interests you more. "I'd like to hear a little more about . . . " you can say. Or, "Would you mind telling me about how you . . . " It's also perfectly acceptable to ask your subject to repeat a remark so that you can record it accurately, and if you don't understand something, don't be afraid to admit it. Experts are accustomed to knowing more than others do and are particularly happy to explain even the most elementary parts of their lore to an interested listener.

7. Concluding the interview. Near the end of the time you have agreed upon, ask your subject if he or she wishes to add any material, or to clarify something said earlier. Express your thanks and, at the appointed time, leave promptly.

8. Preparing to write. As soon as possible after the interview, review your notes, amplify them with details you wish to remember but might have failed to record, and type them up. You might have discovered during the interview, or you might see now, that there is something more that you want to read by or about your subject. Track it down and take further notes.

9. Writing the essay. In writing your first draft, think about your audience. Unless a better idea occurs to you, consider your college newspaper or magazine, or a local newspaper, as the place you hope to publish your story. Write with the readers of that publication in mind. Thinking of your readers will help you to be clear—for instance to identify names that have come up in the interview but which may be unfamiliar to your readers.

As with other writing, begin your draft with any idea that strikes you, and write at a fast clip until you have exhausted your material (or yourself).

When you revise, remember to keep your audience in mind; your material should, as it unfolds, tell a coherent and interesting story. Interviews, like conversations, tend to be delightfully circular or disorderly. But an essay, like a story, should reveal its contents in a sequence that captures and holds attention.

If you've done a thorough job of interviewing you may find that you have more notes than you can reasonably incorporate without disrupting the flow of your story. Don't be tempted to plug them in anyway. If they're really interesting, save them, perhaps by copying them into your journal; if not, chuck them out. (For a wretched example of a story that ends with a detail the writer couldn't bear to let go, see "Fish Eats Brazilian Fisherman," pages 66–67).

In introducing direct quotations from your source, choose those that are particularly characteristic, or vivid, or memorable. Paraphrase or summarize the rest of what is usable. Although the focus of your essay is almost surely the person you interviewed, it is your story, and most of it should be in your own words. Even though you must keep yourself in the background, your writing will gain in interest if your reader hears your voice as well as your subject's.

You might want to use a particularly good quotation for your conclusion. (Notice that both essays we've chosen as examples conclude this way.) Now make sure that you have an attractive opening paragraph. Identifying the subject of your interview and describing the setting is one way to begin. (Again, look at the sample essays.) Give your essay an attractive title. Before you prepare your final draft, read your essay aloud. You're almost certain to catch phrases you can improve, and places where a transition will help your reader to follow you without effort. Check your quotations for accuracy; check with your subject any quotations or other details you're in doubt about. Type your final draft, then edit and proofread carefully.

10. Going public. Make two copies of your finished essay, one for the person you interviewed, one for yourself. The original is for your instructor; hand it in on time.

Topic for Writing

Write an essay based on an interview. You needn't be limited in your choice of subject by the examples we've given. A very old person, a recent immigrant, the owner or manager of an interesting store or business, a veteran of the Vietnam War, a gardener, are only a few of the possibilities. If you can manage to do so, include a few photographs of your subject, with appropriate captions.

Chapter 19

Taking Examinations

What Examinations Are

An examination not only measures learning and thinking but stimulates them. Even so humble an examination as a short-answer quiz—chiefly a device to coerce the student to do the assigned reading—is a sort of push designed to move the student forward. Of course internal motivation is far superior to external, but even such crude external motivation as a quiz can have a beneficial effect. Students know this; indeed they often seek external compulsion, choosing a course "because I want to know something about it, and I know that I won't do the reading on my own." (Teachers often teach a new course for the same reason; we want to become knowledgeable about, say, communism in China, and we know that despite our lofty intentions we may not seriously confront the subject unless we are under the pressure of facing a class.) In short, however ignoble it sounds, examinations force the student to acquire learning and then to convert learning into thinking.

Sometimes it is not until preparing for the final examination that the student—rereading the chief texts and classroom notes—sees what the course was really about; until this late stage, the trees obscured the forest, but now, as the student reviews and sorts things out, a pattern emerges. The experience of reviewing and then of writing an examination, though fretful, can be highly exciting as connections are made and ideas take on life. Such discoveries about the whole subject matter of a course can almost never be made by writing critical essays on topics of one's own construction, for such topics rarely require a view of the whole. Furthermore, most of us are more likely to make imaginative leaps when trying to answer questions that other people pose to us than when we are trying to answer questions we pose to ourselves. And although questions posed by others cause anxiety, when they have been confronted and responded to on an examination students often make yet another discovery—a self-discovery, a sudden and satisfying awareness of powers they didn't know they had.

W r i t i n g   E s s a y   A n s w e r s

We assume that before the examination you have read the assigned material, made notes in the margins of your books, made summaries of the reading and of the classroom comments, reviewed all of this material, and had a decent night's sleep. Now you are facing the examination sheet.

Here are eight obvious but important practical suggestions.

1. Take a moment to jot down, as a kind of outline or source of further inspiration, a few ideas that strike you after you have thought a little about the question. You may at the outset realize there are three points you want to make: unless you jot these down—three key words will do—you may spend all the allotted time on only one.

2. Don't bother to copy the question in the examination booklet, but if you have been given a choice of questions do indicate the question number, or write a word or two that will serve as a cue to the reader.

3. Answer the question. Consider this question: "Fromm and Lorenz try to explain aggression. Compare their theories, and discuss the extent to which they assist us in understanding the Arab-Israeli conflict." Notice that you must compare—not just summarize—two theories, and that you must also evaluate their relevance to a particular conflict. In short, take seriously such words as *compare, define, evaluate,* and *summarize.* And don't waste time generalizing about aggression; again, answer the question.

4. You can often get a good start merely be turning the question into an affirmation, for example by turning "In what ways is the poetry of Allen Ginsberg influenced by Whitman?" into "The poetry of Ginsberg is influenced by Whitman in at least . . . ways."

5. Don't waste time summarizing at length what you have read, unless asked to do so—but of course occasionally you may have to give a brief summary in order to support a point. The instructor wants to see that you can *use* your reading, not merely that you have done the reading.

6. Budget your time. Do not spend more time on a question than the allotted time—at least, not *much* more.

7. Be concrete. Illustrate your arguments with facts—names, dates, and quotations if possible.

8. Leave space for last minute additions. Either skip a page between essays, or write only on the right-hand pages so that on rereading you can add material at the appropriate place on the left-hand pages.

Beyond these general suggestions, we can best talk about essay examinations by looking at specific types of questions.

Questions on Literature

The most common questions encountered in literature examinations can be sorted into five categories:

1. A passage to explicate
2. A historical question, such as "Trace T. S. Eliot's religious development," "Trace the development of Shakespeare's conception of the tragic hero," or "What are Virginia Woolf's contributions to feminist criticism?"
3. A critical quotation to be evaluated
4. A comparison, such as "Compare the dramatic monologues of Browning with those of T. S. Eliot"
5. A wild question, such as "What would Dickens think of Stephen King?" or "What would Juliet do if she were in Ophelia's position?"

A few remarks on each of these types may be helpful:

1. An explication is a commentary describing what is going on in a poem or in a short passage of prose. As a short rule, look carefully at the tone (speaker's attitude toward self, subject, and audience) and at the implications of the words (the connotations or associations), and see if there is a pattern of imagery. For example, religious language ("adore," "saint") in a secular love poem may define the nature of the lover and of the beloved. Remember, *an explication is not a paraphrase* (a putting into other words) but an attempt to show the relations of the parts, especially by calling attention to implications. Organization of such an essay is rarely a problem, since most explications begin with the first line and go on to the last.

2. A good essay on a historical question will offer a nice combination of argument and evidence; the thesis will be supported by concrete details (names, dates, perhaps even brief quotations). A discussion of Eliot's movement toward the Church of England cannot be convincing if it does not specify certain works as representative of Eliot in certain years. If you are asked to relate a writer or a body of work to an earlier writer or period; list the chief characteristics of the earlier writer or the period and then show *specifically* how the material you are discussing is related to these characteristics. And if you can quote some relevant lines from the works, your reader will feel that you know not only titles and stock phrases but also the works themselves.

3. If you are asked to evaluate a critical quotation, read it carefully and in your answer take account of *all* of the quotation. If the critic has said, "Eliot in his plays always . . . but in his poems rarely. . . " you will have to write about both the plays and the poems; it will not be enough to talk only about the plays (unless, of course, the instructions on the examination ask you to take only as much of the quotation as you wish). Watch especially for words like "always," "for the most part," "never"; although the passage may on the whole approach the truth, you may feel that some important qualifications are needed. This is not

being picky; true thinking involves making subtle distinctions, yielding assent only so far and no further. And, again, be sure to give concrete details, supporting your argument with evidence.

4. Comparisons are discussed on pages 170–78. Because comparisons are especially difficult to write, be sure to take a few moments to jot down a sort of outline so that you can know where you will be going. A comparison of Browning's and Eliot's monologues might treat three poems by each, devoting alternate paragraphs to one author; or it might first treat one author's poems and then turn to the other. But if it adopts this second strategy, the essay may break into two parts. You can guard against this weakness by announcing at the outset that you will treat the authors separately, then by reminding your reader during your treatment of the first author that certain points will be picked up when you get to the second author, and again by briefly reminding your reader during the second part of the essay of certain points already made.

5. Curiously, a wild question such as "What would Dickens think of Stephen King?" or "What would Juliet do in Ophelia's position?" usually produces tame answers: a half dozen ideas about Dickens or Juliet are neatly applied to King or Ophelia, and the gross incompatibilities are thus revealed. But, as the previous paragraph suggests, it may be necessary to do more than to set up bold and obvious oppositions. The interest in such a question and in the answer to it may largely be in the degree to which superficially different figures *resemble* each other in some important ways. And remember that the wildness of the question does not mean that all answers are equally acceptable; as usual, a good answer will be supported by concrete details.

Questions on the Social Sciences

First, an obvious statement: courses in the social sciences almost always require lots of reading. Do the reading when it is assigned, rather than try to do it the night before the examination. Second, when confronted with long reading assignments, you probably will read more efficiently if you scan the table of contents of a book to see the layout of the material, and then read the first and last chapters, where the authors usually summarize their theses. Books and articles on history, psychology, and sociology are not whodunits; there is nothing improper about knowing at the start how it will all turn out. Indeed, if at the start you have a clear grasp of the author's thesis, you may have the pleasure of catching the author perpetrating the crime of arguing from insufficient evidence. The beginning and the end of an article in a journal also may offer summaries that will assist you to read the article with relative ease. But only a reading of the entire work (perhaps with a little skimming) will offer you all of the facts and—no less important—the fully developed view or approach that the instructor believes is essential to an understanding of the course.

The techniques students develop in answering questions on literature may be transferred to examinations in the social sciences. A political science student, for example, can describe through explication the implicit tone or attitude in some of the landmark decisions of the Supreme Court. Similarly, the student of history who has learned to write an essay with a good combination of argument and evidence will not simply offer generalizations or present a list of facts unconnected by some central thesis, but will use relevant facts to support a thesis. The student who is able to evaluate a critical quotation or to compare literary works can also evaluate and compare documents in all the social sciences. Answers to wild questions can be as effective or as trite in the social sciences as in literature. "You are the British ambassador in Petrograd in November 1918. Write a report to your government about the Bolshevik revolution of that month" is to some instructors and students an absurd question but to others it is an interesting and effective way of ascertaining whether a student has not only absorbed the facts of an event but has also learned how to interpret them.

Questions on the Physical Sciences and Mathematics

Although the answer to an examination question in the physical sciences usually requires a mathematical computation, a few sentences may be useful in explaining the general plan of the computation, the assumptions involved, and sometimes the results.

It is particularly valuable to set down at the outset in a brief statement, probably a single sentence, your plan for solving the problem posed by the examination question. The statement is equivalent to the topic sentence of a paragraph. For instance, if the examination question is "What is the time required for an object to fall from the orbit of the moon to the earth?" the statement of your plan might be: "The time required for an object to fall from the orbit of the moon to the earth can be obtained by integration from Newton's law of motion, taking account of the increasing gravitational force as the object approaches the earth." Explicitly setting down your plan in words is useful first in clarifying your thought: is the plan a complete one leading to the desired answer? Do I know what I need to know to implement the plan? If your plan doesn't make sense, you can junk it right away before wasting more time on it.

The statement of plan is useful also in communicating with the instructor. Your plan of solution, although valid, may be a surprise to the instructor (who may have expected a solution to the problem posed above starting from Kepler's laws without any integration). When this is so, the instructor will need your explanation to become oriented to your plan, and to properly assess its merits. Then if you botch the subsequent computation or can't remember how the gravitational force varies with the distance, you will still have demonstrated that you have some comprehension of the problem. If on the other hand you present an erroneous computation without any explanation, the instructor will see nothing but chaos in your effort.

Further opportunities to use words will occur when you make assumptions or simplifications: "I assume the body is released with zero velocity and accordingly set b = 0," or "The third term is negligible and I drop it."

Finally, the results of your computation should be summarized or interpreted in words to answer the question asked. "The object will fall to the earth in five days." (The correct answer, for those who are curious.) Or, if you arrive at the end of your computation and of the examination hour and find you have a preposterous result, you can still exit gracefully (and increase your partial credit) with an explanation: "The answer of 53 days is clearly erroneous since the fall time of an object from the moon's orbit must be less than the seven days required for the moon to travel a quarter orbit."

Chapter 20

Writing Résumés and Letters For Jobs

In writing for a job, you need to send not only a letter but also a résumé (French for summary). The letter will be addressed to a specific person and may be an application for a specific job, but the résumé should give as full a picture of you as is possible to give in one page.

The Résumé

Make every effort to keep your résumé down to one page, so that the reader can get the whole picture—education, experience, interests, and so forth—at a single glance. You need not include any statement about race, religion, weight, sex, marital status, or age, but if you think such information may be to your advantage, include it. Several formats are acceptable, but on page 000 we illustrate the most common. Notice that information in each category is given in *reverse chronological order*—the most recent experience first.

Job Objective
After your name, address, and telephone number (if you live at a college, give your home number as well as your local number, with dates of residence, so that you can be reached during vacations), give a "job objective" *if* you know exactly what you are looking for. Examples:

[SAMPLE RÉSUMÉ]

School Address	Home Address
(until 16 May 1995)	(after 17 May 1995)
Buckminster Hall, #202	38 Barker's Road
Redding College	Somerville, MA 02150
Woodmere, MA 02156	(617) 555-6650
(617) 555-2964	

JOB OBJECTIVE	Marketing or advertising trainee
EDUCATION 1991-95	Redding College, Woodmere, MA Degree: BA (expected in June 1995) Major: Business administration Minor: English
(1987-91)	Somerville High School
WORK EXPERIENCE Summer 1994	Acting Assistant Manager, O'Neill's Sports Center, Medford, MA. Responsible for checking inventory, dealing with retail customers, assisting buyers
Summer 1993	Salesclerk, O'Neill's Sports Center
1992-94	Part-time work in shipping office of Blackston's Department Store. Processed orders. Respon- sible for insuring valuable parcels.
EXTRACURRICULAR ACTIVITIES	Undergraduate Senate, Redding College (1992-94) Debating Society, Redding College (1994-95) Vice President, 1995 Drama Club, Somerville High School (1990-91)
PERSONAL INTERESTS	Drama, photography, crossword puzzles
REFERENCES	Academic References: Office of Student Placement Redding College Woodmere, MA 02156 Mr. Bert Williams O'Neill's Sports Center 200 Main Street Medford, MA 02155

```
    Entry-level sales position with a firm that
provides opportunity to meet people who work with
computer systems
```

```
    Editorial work with publisher of social science
textbooks
```

```
    To work in customer relations in a department
store, to continue my education part time, and
eventually to assume a managerial position.
```

You may, of course, want to prepare two or even three résumés, varying the job objective in order to suit different kinds of potential employers.

If you can't state a job objective, begin with either "Education" or with "Work Experience," whichever seems stronger to you. The point, of course, is to begin with your chief credentials.

Work Experience
Under "Work Experience" do not simply list names of employers, or even titles of jobs; specify the kind of work done, the responsibilities fulfilled. Thus, if you worked at a ski shop you might say:

```
    Sales: assisted buyer at spring ski show
```

If you were a sports medicine intern at the Lahey Clinic, you might add

```
    Administered prescribed treatment for physical
therapy outpatients
```

If honesty allows, use such words as *administered, developed, initiated, installed, operated, responsible for, supervised, advanced to,* and *promoted to.*

Education
Similarly, under "Education" you should not only give the reader a sense of the program you studied but should also specify any academic awards, including scholarships, that you received.

Personal Interests
The heading called "Personal Interests" (or "Personal Data") gives you an additional chance to convey what sort of person you are. Don't hesitate to list hobbies; hobbies often suggest important traits. For example, if you are an amateur magician, you probably are at ease with audiences, and if you are a Go player (Go is a sort of Japanese chess) you probably like to solve problems. But

if you have a collection of snakes, keep that information to yourself unless you are applying for a job in a pet store or on a snake farm.

References

The last heading in a résumé usually is "References." Before you list a name (with an address and telephone number, of course), be sure to get permission; if the person seems cool when you ask if you may give his or her name, find someone else. In fact, since you don't want a lukewarm letter, don't simply ask people if you may list their names as references. Rather, ask if they feel that they know you and your work well enough to write a helpful recommendation. If you state the matter this way, someone who otherwise might write a dutiful but unenthusiastic (and therefore unhelpful and perhaps even damaging) letter can gracefully decline, saying that you ought to turn to someone else who knows you better.

Be sure, also, to allow the letter writer ample time to write a thoughtful, unhurried letter. Ten days is a minimum; two weeks is better. And provide what help you can—a transcript, a résumé, a draft of your letter applying for a job, and possibly copies of course papers that you had submitted.

Revising Your Draft

After you have drafted and typed your résumé, show it to a couple of friends and, if possible, to someone who has had experience in reading résumés. Revise it in the light of their suggestions. In typing the final copy, keep an eye on the design: don't crowd your material into the upper two-thirds of the sheet. Make sure that there are no typographical errors (a prospective employer will take a typo as evidence that you are careless) and no spelling errors.

Finally, take the résumé to a photocopy shop or an offset printer and have it reproduced on 8½-by-11-inch paper. Never use carbon, thermofax, or mimeographed copies.

The Cover Letter

Employers, even if they are philanthropic institutions such as churches, schools, and museums, are not engaged in philanthropy when they hire employees. They are looking to get rather than to give; that is, they are looking for people who can be useful to them. Your letter of application, therefore, must indicate what you can contribute.

The Address

Unlike your résumé, your letter should be an original, not a copy. Address it to a specific person, not to "Dear Sir," Dear Sir or Madam," "Director of Personnel," or "To Whom It May Concern." A vague address means that you haven't bothered to make a telephone call to find out the name of the person to whom you are writing. And be sure to spell the name correctly; a misspelling (Bergman for Bergmann) will be taken as a sign of carelessness. Getting the right name, and spelling it right, shows that you have done at least a little homework; it suggests that you are conscientious, and that you know something about the institution that you are seeking to join. If you are aware of an opening in a particular department, it usually is best to send your letter and résumé to the head of the department rather than to the personnel office. Probably the head will routinely route your material to Personnel, but possibly he or she will scan it, notice something of interest, and may at least scrawl "looks good" at the top of the letter before sending it on to Personnel.

The Content

Try to keep the letter down to one page; since your résumé will accompany the letter, there is no need to repeat much of the information given in the résumé. But there is no harm in stating your job objective early in the letter even though it is also in the résumé. Similarly, you can mention your strongest point (possibly your academic major, or possibly some experience on the job) in the letter as well as in the résumé. Encountering this information near the outset, the reader of the letter may feel that you are indeed the person that the company is looking for. If someone already working for the company suggested that you write—and has given you permission to use his or her name—it's not a bad idea to begin by saying, "Jane Doe has suggested that I write to you. . . ." If Doe is respected, your letter will get extra attention, especially because the reader will assume that Doe is endorsing your candidacy.

The gist of the letter should suggest, if possible, that you are especially interested in this job and in this company. For instance, if you are writing to a small company you may indicate that you are especially interested because you will have the opportunity to work in several departments and thus be able to get a sense of the overall activities of the company. On the other hand, if your interests are fairly specialized and you are writing to a large company, you may want to indicate that you prefer such a company because it can use all of your time in a single sort of activity. If you are writing for a particular job—let's say for one that has been advertised—say so. The implication in the letter should be that you believe the company can use you, perhaps because you have the necessary experience, or, if experience is lacking, because you have the necessary brains and interest. Notice the "you believe" in the previous sentence. Your letter should be affirmative, but it should not be arrogant. Statements such a "I am fully qualified to do . . . " and "I am expert at . . . " will probably turn most readers off. It's better to say something like "My experience as an assistant manager at Pizza Hut taught me to be patient with customers and to make demands on myself," or "The manager of Pizza Hut has recommended me for the position of night manager, but I have decided to. . . ."

Revising the Draft

When you read and reread your draft, try to imagine what sort of person it reveals. It ought to reveal someone diligent and competent, but not a braggart and not a clown (unless you are applying for a job as a clown). It's difficult, of course, to avoid bragging and yet at the same time to convey the impression that it's to the employer's self-interest to invite you for an interview, but it can be done. If your letter is clear and direct, and if it suggests that the job and the

[SAMPLE LETTER APPLYING FOR A JOB]

29 Cleveland Street
Waltham, MA 02254
20 May, 1995

Mr. William C. Bliss, Personnel Director
Conway Products, Inc.
17 Main Street
Wrocester, MA 01610

Dear Mr. Bliss:

Dr. Helen Stone, who serves as a writing consultant to Conway Products and who is one of my professors as Hewson College, has suggested that I write to you about the possibility of a position in the junior management training program at Conway. I will graduate from Hewson, with a major in English, in May 1995, and will then be available for full-time work.

In the second term of my junior year I served as an aide in the Writing Program, assisting freshmen whose native language was not English to improve their writing. I am now an assistant supervisor in this program, guiding ten other upperclass students in their work with freshmen. I am also the assistant advertising manager of The Observer, the college's weekly newspaper, with special responsibility for generating new accounts.

I enjoy working with others and meeting challenges, and these activities have given me experience in dealing with people and in responding to minor crises. Certainly the challenge (successfully met) to double our advertising revenue was a stimulant. I believe that my background would enable me, after training in the management program, to work effectively at Conway Products.

I enclose a résumé so that you may have a more detailed idea of my interests and my qualifications. I can be reached at 555-5000, and I can arrange my schedule so that I will be available for an interview at almost any time.

Sincerely yours,

Doris Cursor

Doris Cursor

company are just the sort of thing you are keenly interested in, you will have a chance.

Let's assume the letter is one page long, probably with three or four paragraphs so that it can be read easily. The last paragraph usually includes a polite request for an interview.

The Final Version

Show your draft of the letter to a friend or two, to an instructor, and if possible to an employer, with an eye toward revising it, and then type up your final version on 8½-by-11-inch paper. (Smaller, personal stationery—especially the type with fancy lettering or with a flower in a corner—will not do.) Single-space all of the writing, but double-space between units—for instance, between the date and the name of the recipient—and double-space between paragraphs, as in the example on page 475. Be sure to check the spelling and the typing; it's not a bad idea to ask a friend to do a second check.

If you do get an interview and if after the interview you are still interested in the job, write a follow-up letter immediately. In this letter, reaffirm your interest, include any information that you wish you had mentioned during the interview, and thank the interviewer for having given you the opportunity to present yourself. Proofread it carefully and mail it promptly.

Topic for Writing

Clip out an advertisement for a job that is of some interest to you, and write a letter of application. (For the purposes of this exercise, assume that you are in your last year of schooling; thus, you can invent reasonable accomplishments for yourself.) Hand in a copy of the advertisement with your letter.

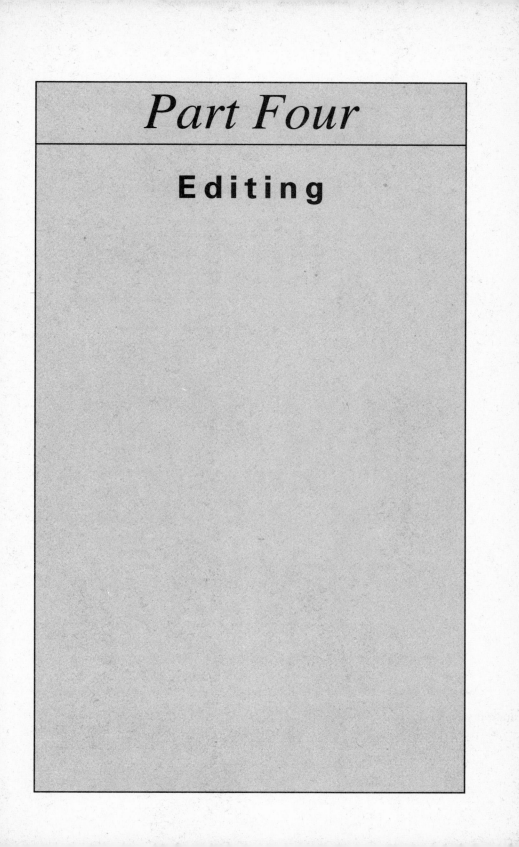

Part Four

Editing

Chapter 21

Punctuation

Speakers can raise or lower the volume or pitch of their voices; they can speak a phrase slowly and distinctly and then (making a parenthetical remark, perhaps) quicken the pace. They can wave their arms, pound a table, or pause, meaningfully. But writers, physically isolated from their audience, have only paper and ink to work with. Nevertheless, they can embody some of the tones and gestures of speech—in the patterns of their written sentences, and in the dots, hooks, and dashes of punctuation that clarify those patterns.

Punctuation clarifies, first of all, by removing or reducing ambiguity. Consider this headline from a story in a newspaper:

SQUAD HELPS DOG BITE VICTIM

Of course, there is no real ambiguity here—only a laugh—because the stated meaning is so clearly absurd, and on second reading we supply the necessary hyphen in *dog-bite*. But other ill-punctuated sentences may be troublesome rather than entertaining. Take the following sentence:

He arrived late for the rehearsal didn't end until midnight.

Almost surely you stumbled in the middle of the sentence, thinking that it was about someone arriving tardily at a rehearsal, and then, since what followed made no sense, you probably went back and mentally added the comma (by pausing) at the necessary place:

> He arrived late, for the rehearsal didn't end until midnight.

Punctuation helps to keep the reader on the right path. And the path is your train of thought. If your punctuation is faulty, you unintentionally point the reader off your path and toward dead end streets and quagmires.

Even when punctuation is not the key to meaning, it usually helps you get your meaning across neatly. Consider the following sentences:

> There are two kinds of feminism—one is the growing struggle of women to understand and change the shape of their lives and the other is a narrow ideology whose adherents are anxious to clear away whatever does not conform to their view.

This is clear enough, but by changing the punctuation it can be sharpened. Because a dash usually indicates an abrupt interruption—it usually precedes a sort of afterthought—a colon would be better. The colon, usually the signal of an amplification of what precedes it, here would suggest that the two classifications are not impromptu thoughts but carefully considered ones. Second, and more important, in the original version the two classifications are run together without any intervening punctuation, but since the point is that the two are utterly different, it is advisable to separate them by inserting a comma or semicolon, indicating a pause. A comma before "and the other" would do, but probably a semi-colon (without the "and") is preferable because it is a heavier pause, thereby making the separation clearer. Here is the sentence, revised:

> There are two kinds of feminism: one is the growing struggle of women to understand and change the shape of their lives; the other is a narrow ideology whose adherents are anxious to clear away whatever does not conform to their view.

The right punctuation enables the reader to move easily through the sentence.

Now, although punctuation helps a reader to move through a sentence, it must be admitted that some of the rules of punctuation do not contribute to meaning or greatly facilitate reading. For example, in American usage a period never comes immediately after quotation marks; it precedes quotation marks, thus:

> She said, "Put the period inside the quotation marks."

If you put the period after the closing quotation mark, the meaning remains the same, but you are also informing your reader that you don't know the relevant convention. Since a misspelled word or a misplaced period often gives the impression of laziness, ignorance, or incompetence, why not generate as little friction as possible by learning the chief conventions?

Three Common Errors: Fragments, Comma Splices, and Run-on Sentences

Fragments and How to Correct Them

A fragment is a part of a sentence set off as if it were a complete sentence: *Because I didn't care. Being an accident. Later in the week. For several reasons. My oldest sister.* Fragments are common in speech, but they are used sparingly in writing, for particular effects (see page 142). A fragment used carelessly in writing often looks like an afterthought—usually because it *was* an afterthought, that is, an explanation or other addition that really belongs to the previous sentence.

With appropriate punctuation (and sometimes with no punctuation at all) a fragment can usually be connected to the previous sentence.

1. *Incorrect*
   Many nineteenth-century horror stories have been made into films. Such as *Dracula* and *Frankenstein.*

   Correct
   Many nineteenth-century horror stories have been made into films, such as *Dracula* and *Frankenstein.*

2. *Incorrect*
   Many schools are putting renewed emphasis on writing. Because SAT scores have declined for ten years.

   Correct
   Many schools are putting renewed emphasis on writing because SAT scores have declined for ten years.

3. *Incorrect*
   He practiced doing card tricks. In order to fool his friends.

   Correct
   He practiced doing card tricks in order to fool his friends.

4. *Incorrect*
   She wore only rope sandals. Being a strict vegetarian.

   Correct
   Being a strict vegetarian, she wore only rope sandals.
   She wore only rope sandals because she was a strict vegetarian.

5. *Incorrect*
   A fragment often looks like an afterthought. Perhaps because it *was* an afterthought.

   Correct
   A fragment often looks like an afterthought—perhaps because it *was* an afterthought.

6. *Incorrect*
   He hoped to get credit for two summer school courses. Batik and Hang-Gliding.

   Correct
   He hoped to get credit for two summer school courses: Batik and Hang-Gliding.

Notice in the examples above that, depending upon the relationship between the two parts, the fragment and the preceding statement can be joined by a comma, a dash, a colon, or by no punctuation at all.

Notice also that unintentional fragments often follow subordinating conjunctions, such as *because* and *although*. Subordinating conjunctions introduce a subordinate (dependent) clause; such a clause cannot stand as a sentence. Here is a list of the most common subordinating conjunctions.

after	though
although	unless
because	until
before	when
if	where
provided	whereas
since	while

Fragments also commonly occur when the writer, as in the fourth example, mistakenly uses *being* as a main verb.

Comma Splices and Run-on Sentences, and How to Correct Them

An error known as a *comma splice* or *comma fault* results when a comma is mistakenly placed between two independent clauses that are not joined by a coordinating conjunction: *and, or, nor, but, for, yet, so*. If the comma is omitted, the error is called a *run-on sentence*.

Examples of the two errors:

- *Comma splice* (or *comma fault*): In the second picture the man leans on the woman's body, he is obviously in pain.
- *Run-on sentence:* In the second picture the man leans on the woman's body he is obviously in pain.

Run-on sentences and comma splices may be corrected in five principal ways:

1. Use a **period** to create two sentences.

   In the second picture the man leans on the woman's body. He is obviously in pain.

2. Use a **semicolon.**

   In the second picture the man leans on the woman's body; he is obviously in pain.

3. Use a **comma and a coordinating conjunction** (*and, or, nor, but, for, yet, so*).

   In the second picture the man leans on the woman's body, and he is obviously in pain.

4. Make one of the clauses dependent (subordinate). **Use a subordinating conjunction** such as *after, although, because, before, if, provided, since, though, unless, until, when, where, whereas, while.*

   In the second picture the man leans on the woman's body because he is in pain.

5. **Reduce one of the independent clauses to a phrase, or even to a single word.**

   In the second picture the man, obviously in pain, leans on the woman's body.

Run-on sentences and comma splices are especially common in sentences containing transitional words or phrases such as the following:

also	however
besides	indeed
consequently	in fact
for example	nevertheless
furthermore	therefore
hence	whereas

When these words join independent clauses, the clauses cannot be linked by a comma.

Incorrect:
She argued from faulty premises, however the conclusions happened to
be correct.

Here are five correct revisions, following the five rules we have just given. (In
the first two revisions we place "however" after, rather than before, "the
conclusions" because we prefer the increase in emphasis, but the grammatical
point is the same.)

1. She argued from faulty premises. The conclusions, however, happened
   to be correct. (Two sentences)
2. She argued from faulty premises; the conclusions, however, happened to
   be correct. (Semicolon)
3. She argued from faulty premises, but the conclusions happened to be
   correct. (Coordinating conjunction)
4. Although she argued from faulty premises, the conclusions happened to
   be correct. (Subordinating conjunction)
5. She argued from faulty premises to correct conclusions. (Reduction of an
   independent clause to a phrase)

The following sentence contains a comma splice:

   The husband is not pleased, in fact, he is embarrassed.

How might it be repaired?

The Period

1. **Periods are used to mark the ends of sentences** (or intentional
   sentence fragments) other than questions and exclamations.

   A sentence normally ends with a period.
   She said, "I'll pass."
   Yes.
   Once more, with feeling.

But a sentence within a sentence is punctuated according to the needs of the
longer sentence. Notice, in the following example, that a period is *not* used after
"pass."

   She said, "I'll pass," but she said it without conviction.

2. **Periods are used with abbreviations of titles and terms of reference.**

Dr., Mr., Mrs., Ms.

p., pp. (for "page" and "pages"), i.e., e.g., etc.

But when the capitalized initial letters of the words naming an organization are used in place of the full name, the periods are commonly omitted:

CBS, CORE, IBM, NBA, UCLA, UNICEF, USAF

3. **Periods are also used to separate chapter from verse in the Bible.**

Genesis 3.2, Mark 6.10

For further details on references to the Bible, see page 159.

The Question Mark

Use a question mark after a direct question:

Did Bacon write Shakespeare's plays?

Do not use a question mark after an indirect question, or after a polite request:

He asked if Bacon wrote Shakespeare's plays.

Would you please explain what the support for Bacon is really all about.

The Colon

The colon has four uses:

- To introduce a list or series of examples
- To introduce an amplification or explanation of what precedes the colon
- To introduce a quotation (though a quotation can be introduced by other means)
- To indicate time.

Now let's look at each of those four uses.

1. **The colon may introduce a list or series.**

Students are required to take one of the following sciences: biology, chemistry, geology, physics.

2. **The colon may introduce an explanation.** It is almost equivalent to *namely,* or *that is.* What is on one side of the colon more or less equals what is on the other side. The material on either side of the colon can stand as a separate sentence.

She explained her fondness for wrestling: she did it to shock her parents.

The forces which in China created a central government were absent in Japan: farming had to be on a small scale, there was no need for extensive canal works, and a standing army was not required to protect the country from foreign invaders.

Many of the best of the Civil War photographs must be read as the fossils of earlier events: The caissons with their mud-encrusted wheels, the dead on the field, the empty landscapes, all speak of deeds already past.

—JOHN SZARKOWSKI

Notice in this last example that the writer uses a capital letter after the colon; the usage is acceptable when a complete sentence follows the colon, as long as that style is followed consistently throughout a paper. But most students find it easier to use lower case letters after colons, the prevalent style in writing today.

3. **The colon, like the comma, may be used to introduce a quotation;** it is more formal than the comma, setting off the quotation to a greater degree.

The black sculptor Ed Wilson tells his students: "Malcolm X is my brother, Martin Luther King is my brother, Eldridge Cleaver is my brother! But Michelangelo is my grandfather!"

—ALBERT E. ELSEN

4. **A colon is used to separate the hour from the minutes** when the time is given in figures.

9:15, 12:00

Colons (like semicolons) go outside of closing quotation marks if they are not part of the quotation.

"There is no such thing as a free lunch": the truth of these words is confirmed every day.

The Semicolon

There are four main uses of the semicolon. Sheridan Baker (in *The Practical Stylist*) summed them up in this admirable formula: "Use a semicolon where you could also use a period, unless desperate." Correctly used, the semicolon can add precision to your writing; it can also help you out of some tight corners.

1. **You may use a semicolon instead of a period between closely related independent clauses not joined by a coordinating conjunction.**

> All happy families resemble one another; every unhappy family is unhappy in its own fashion.
> —LEO TOLSTOY

> The demands that men and women make on marriage will never be fully met; they cannot be.
> —JESSIE BERNARD

> In our fractured culture, we cannot agree on morals; we cannot even agree that moral matters should come before literary ones when there is a conflict between them.
> —FLANNERY O'CONNOR

> When a cat washes its face it does not move its paw; it moves its face.

In each of the above examples the independent clauses might have been written as sentences separated by periods; the semicolon pulls the statements together, emphasizing their relationship. Alternatively, the statements might have been linked by coordinating conjunctions (*and, or, nor, but, for, yet, so*). For example:

> The demands made upon marriage will never be fully met *for* they cannot be.

> When a cat washes its face it does not move its paw *but* it moves its face.

The sentences as originally written, using semicolons, have more bite.

2. **You *must* use a semicolon (rather than a comma) if you use a *conjunctive adverb* to connect independent clauses.** (A conjunctive adverb is a transitional word such as *also, consequently, furthermore, however, moreover, nevertheless, therefore.*)

> His hair was black and wavy; however, it was false.

> We don't like to see our depressed relative cry; nevertheless, tears can provide a healthy emotional outlet.

> She said "I do"; moreover, she repeated the words.

Take note of the following three points:

- A comma goes after the conjunctive adverb.
- Semicolons (like colons) go outside of closing quotation marks if they are not part of the quotation.
- A conjunctive adverb requires a semicolon to join independent clauses. A comma produces a comma splice:

    Incorrect
    His hair was black and wavy, however, it was false.

3. **You may use a semicolon to separate a series of phrases with internal punctuation.**

    He had a car, which he hadn't paid for; a wife, whom he didn't love; and a father, who was unemployed.

4. **Use a semicolon between independent clauses linked by coordinating conjunctions if the sentence would otherwise be difficult to read,** because it is long and complex or because it contains internal punctuation.

    In the greatest age of painting, the nude inspired the greatest works; and even when it ceased to be a compulsive subject it held its position as an academic exercise and a demonstration of mastery.

(Often it is preferable to break such sentences up, or to recast them.)

The Comma

The comma (from a Greek word meaning "to cut") indicates a relatively slight pause within a sentence. If after checking the rules you are still uncertain of whether or not to use a comma in a given sentence, read the sentence aloud and see if it sounds better with or without a pause; you can then add or omit the comma. A women's shoe store in New York has a sign on the door:

NO MEN PLEASE.

If the proprietors would read the sign aloud, they might want to change it to

NO MEN, PLEASE

When you are typing, always follow a comma with a space.

For your reference, here is an outline for the following pages, which summarize the correct uses of the comma.

1. with independent clauses, page 468
2. with introductory subordinate clauses or long phrases, pages 468-69
3. with tacked-on subordinate phrases or long clauses, page 469
4. as parentheses, pages 469-70
5. with nonrestrictive modifiers, pages 470-471
6. with a series, pages 471-72
7. with direct discourse, page 472
8. with "yes" and "no," page 472
9. with words of address, page 472
10. with geographical locations, page 472
11. with dates, page 472
12. with other punctuation, pages 473

1. **Independent clauses (unless short) joined by a coordinating conjunction** *(and, or, nor, but, for, yet, so)* **take a comma before the conjunction.**

> Most students see at least a few football games, and many go to every game of the season.
>
> Most students seem to have an intuitive sense of when to use a comma, but in fact the "intuition" is the result of long training.

If the introductory independent clause is short, the comma is usually omitted:

> She dieted but she continued to gain weight.

2. An **introductory subordinate clause or long phrase** is usually followed by a comma.

> Having revised his manuscript for the third time, he went to bed.
>
> In order to demonstrate her point, the instructor stood on her head.

If the introductory subordinate clause or phrase is short, say four words or fewer, the comma may be omitted, provided no ambiguity results from the omission.

> Having left he soon forgot.

But compare this last example with the following:

> Having left, the instructor soon forgot.

If the comma is omitted, the sentence is misread. Where are commas needed in the following sentences?

> Instead of discussing the book she wrote a summary.
>
> When Shakespeare wrote comedies were already popular.
>
> While he ate his poodle would sit by the table.
>
> As we age small things become killers.

3. **A subordinate clause or long modifying phrase tacked on as an afterthought is usually preceded by a comma.**

> I have decided not to be nostalgic about the 1950s, despite the hoopla over Elvis.
>
> Buster Keaton fell down a flight of stairs without busting, thereby gaining his nickname from Harry Houdini.
>
> By the time he retired, Hank Aaron had 755 home runs, breaking Babe Ruth's record by 41.

With afterthoughts, the comma may be omitted if there is a clear sequence of cause and effect, signaled by such words as *because, for,* and *so.* Compare the following examples:

> In 1601 Shakespeare wrote *Hamlet,* probably his best-known play.
>
> In 1601 Shakespeare wrote *Hamlet* because revenge tragedy was in demand.

4. **A pair of commas can serve as a pair of unobtrusive parentheses.** Be sure not to omit the second comma.

> Doctors, I think, have an insufficient knowledge of acupuncture.
>
> The earliest known paintings of Christ, dating from the third century, are found in the catacombs outside of Rome.
>
> Medicare and Medicaid, the chief sources of federal support for patients in nursing homes, are frequently confused.

Under this heading we can include a conjunctive adverb (a transitional adverb such as *also, besides, consequently, however, likewise, nevertheless, therefore*) inserted within a sentence. These transitional words are set off between a pair of commas.

> Her hair, however, was stringy.

If one of these words begins a sentence, the comma after it is optional. Notice, however, that the presence of such a word as "however" is not always a safeguard against a run-on sentence or comma splice; if the word occurs between two independent clauses and it goes with the second clause, you need a semicolon before it and a comma after it.

> His hair was black and wavy; however, it was false.

(See the discussion of comma splices on pages 461-63.)

5. **Use a comma to set off a nonrestrictive modifier.** A nonrestrictive modifier, as the following examples will make clear, is a sort of parenthetical addition; it gives supplementary information about the subject, but it can be omitted without changing the subject. A restrictive modifier, however, is not supplementary but essential; if a restrictive modifier is omitted, the subject becomes more general. In Dorothy Parker's celebrated poem.

> Men seldom make passes
> At girls who wear glasses,

"who wear glasses" is a restrictive modifier, narrowing or restricting the subject down from "girls" to a particular group of girls, "girls who wear glasses."

Here is a *non*restrictive modifier:

> For the majority of immigrants, who have no knowledge of English, language is the chief problem.

Now a restrictive modifier:

> For the majority of immigrants who have no knowledge of English, language is the chief problem.

The first version says—in addition to its obvious message that language is the chief problem—that the majority of immigrants have no knowledge of English. The second version makes no such assertion; it talks not about the majority of immigrants but only about a more restricted group—those immigrants who have no knowledge of English.

Other examples:

> Shakespeare's shortest tragedy, *Macbeth,* is one of his greatest plays.

In this sentence, *"Macbeth"* is nonrestrictive because the subject is already as restricted as possible; Shakespeare can have written only one "shortest tragedy." That is, *"Macbeth"* is merely an explanatory equivalent of "Shakespeare's shortest tragedy" and it is therefore enclosed in commas. (A noun or noun phrase serving as an explanatory equivalent to another, and in the same syntactical relation to other elements in the sentence, is said to be in apposition.) But compare

> Shakespeare's tragedy *Macbeth* is one of his greatest plays.

with the misleadingly punctuated sentence,

> Shakespeare's tragedy, *Macbeth,* is one of his greatest plays.

The first of these is restrictive, narrowing or restricting the subject "tragedy" down to one particular tragedy, and so it rightly does not separate the modifier from the subject by a comma. The second, punctuated so that it is nonrestrictive, falsely implies that *Macbeth* is Shakespeare's only tragedy. Here is an example of a nonrestrictive modifier correctly punctuated:

> Women, who constitute 51.3 percent of the population and 53 percent of the electorate, constitute only 2.5 percent of the House of Representatives and 1 percent of the Senate.

In the next two examples, the first illustrates the correct use of commas after a nonrestrictive appositive, and the second illustrates the correct omission of commas after a restrictive appositive.

> Hong Yee Chiu, a Chinese-American physicist, abbreviated the compound adjective *quasi-stellar* to *quasar.*
>
> The Chinese-American physicist Hong Yee Chiu abbreviated the compound adjective *quasi-stellar* to *quasar.*

6. **Words, phrases, and clauses in series take a comma after each item except the last.** The comma between the last two items may be omitted if there is no ambiguity.

> Photography is a matter of eyes, intuition, and intellect.
>
> She wrote plays, poems, and stories.
>
> He wrote plays, sang songs, and danced jigs.
>
> She wrote a wise, witty, humane book.

But adjectives in a series may cause difficulty. The next two examples correctly omit the commas.

> a funny silent film
>
> a famous French professor

In each of these last two examples, the adjective immediately before the noun forms with the noun a compound that is modified by the earlier adjective. That is, the adjectives are not a coordinate series (what is funny is not simply a film but a silent film, what is famous is not simply a professor but a French professor) and so commas are not used. Compare:

a famous French professor

a famous, arrogant French professor

In the second example, only "famous" and "arrogant" form a coordinate series. If in doubt, see if you can replace the commas with "and"; if you can, the commas are correct. In the example given, you could insert "and" between "famous" and "arrogant," but not between "arrogant" and "French."

Commas are not needed if all the members of the series are connected by conjunctions.

He ate steak for breakfast and lunch and supper.

7. **Use a comma to set off direct discourse.**

"It's a total failure," she said.

She said, "It's a total failure."

But do not use a comma for indirect discourse.

She said that it is a total failure.

She said it is a total failure.

8. **Use a comma to set off "yes" and "no."**

Yes, he could take Freshman English at ten o'clock.

9. **Use a comma to set off words of address.**

Look, Bill, take Freshman English at ten o'clock.

10. **Use a comma to separate a geographical location within another geographical location.**

She was born in Brooklyn, New York, in 1895.

Another way of putting it is to say that a comma is used after each unit of an address, except that a comma is *not* used between the name of the state and the zip code.

11. **Use a comma to set off the year from the month or day.**

He was born on June 10, 1965.

No comma is needed if you use the form "10 June 1965."

12. Note **the position of the comma when used with other punctuation:** If a comma is required with parenthetic material, it follows the second parenthesis.

> Because Japan was secure from invasion (even the Mongols were beaten back), its history is unusually self-contained.

The only time a comma may precede a parenthesis is when parentheses surround a digit or letter used to enumerate a series.

> Questions usually fall into one of three categories: (1) true-false, (2) multiple choice, (3) essay.

A comma always goes inside closing quotation marks unless the quotation is followed by a parenthesis.

> "Sayonara," he said.
> "Sayonara" (Japanese for "goodbye"), he said.

The Dash

A dash is made by typing two hyphens without hitting the space-bar before, between, or after. It indicates an abrupt break or pause.

1. **The material within dashes may be something like parenthetic material** (material that is not essential), though by setting it within dashes—an emphatic form of punctuation—the writer gives the material more emphasis than it would get within parentheses.

> The bathroom—that private place—has rarely been the subject of scholarly study.
> The Great Wall of China forms a continuous line over 1400 miles long—the distance from New York to Kansas City—running from Peking to the edge of the mountains of Central Asia.

> The old try to survive by cutting corners—eating less, giving up small pleasures like tobacco and movies, doing without warm clothes—and pay the price of ill-health and a shortened life-span.
>
> —SHARON R. CURTIN

Notice that when two dashes are used, if the material within them is deleted the remainder still forms a grammatical sentence.

2. **A dash can serve, somewhat like a colon, as a pause before a series.**
It is more casual than a colon.

> The earliest Shinto holy places were natural objects—trees, boulders,
> mountains, islands.

> Each of the brothers had his distinct comic style—Groucho's
> double-talk, Chico's artfully stupid malapropisms, Harpo's
> horseplay.
>
> —GERALD MAST

A dash is never used next to a comma, and it is used before a period only to
indicate that the sentence is interrupted.

Overuse of the dash—even only a little overuse—gives writing an
unpleasantly agitated—even explosive—quality.

Parentheses

Let's begin with a caution: avoid using parentheses to explain pronouns: "In his
speech he (Hamlet) says . . . " If "he" needs to be explained by "Hamlet," omit
the "he" and just say "Hamlet."

1. **Parentheses subordinate material;** what is in parentheses is almost a
casual aside, less essential than similar material set off in commas, less
vigorously spoken than similar material set off in dashes.

> While guest curator for the Whitney (he has since returned to the
> Denver Art Museum), Feder assembled a magnificent collection of
> masks, totems, paintings, clothing, and beadwork.

Another caution: avoid an abundance of these interruptions, and avoid a long
parenthesis within a sentence (you are now reading a simple example of this
annoying but common habit of writers who have trouble sticking to the point)
because the reader will lose track of the main sentence.

2. **Use parentheses to enclose digits or letters in a list that is given in
running text.**

> The exhibition included: (1) decorative screens, (2) ceramics, (3)
> ink paintings, (4) kimonos.

3. **Do not confuse parentheses with square brackets,** which are used
around material you add to a question. See pages 157-58.

4. **For the use of parentheses in documentation, see Chapter 15, The
Research Essay.**

5. Note **the position of other punctuation with a parenthesis:** The example under rule number 2, of commas preceding parentheses enclosing digits or letters in a list given in running text, is the rare exception to the rule that within a sentence, punctuation other than quotation marks never immediately precedes an opening parenthesis. Notice that in the example under rule number 1, the comma *follows* the closing parenthesis:

> While guest curator for the Whitney (he has since returned to the Denver Art Museum), Feder assembled a magnificent collection of masks, totems, paintings, clothing, and beadwork.

If an entire sentence is in parentheses, put the final punctuation (period, question mark, or exclamation mark) inside the closing parenthesis.

Italics

In typewritten material <u>underlining</u> is the equivalent of *italic* type.

This sentence is printed in italic type.
<u>This sentence is understood to be printed in italic type.</u>

1. **Underline the name of a plane, ship, train, movie, radio or television program, record album, musical work, statue, painting, play, pamphlet, and book.** Do not underline names of sacred works such as the Bible, the Koran, Acts of the Apostles, or political documents such as the Magna Carta and the Declaration of Independence. Notice that when you write of *The New York Times,* you underline *New York* because it is part of the title, but when you write of the London *Times,* you do not underline "London" because "London" is not part of the title, only information added for clarity. Similarly, when you refer to *Time* magazine do not underline "magazine."

2. **Use italics only sparingly for emphasis.** Sometimes, however, this method of indicating your tone of voice is exactly right.

> In 1911 Jacques Henri Lartigue was not merely as unprejudiced as a child; he *was* a child.
> —JOHN SZARKOWSKI

3. Use italics for foreign words that have not become a part of the English language.

> Acupuncture aims to affect the *ch'i,* a sort of vital spirit which circulates through the bodily organs.

But:

> He ate a pizza.
>
> She behaved like a prima donna.
>
> Avoid clichés.

4. **You may use italics in place of quotation marks to identify a word:**

   Honolulu means "safe harbor."

5. **You may also use italics to identify a word or term to which you wish to call special attention.**

   Clause Lévi-Strauss tells us that one of the great purposes of art is that of *miniaturization*. He points out that most works of art are miniatures, being smaller (and therefore more easily understood) than the objects they represent.

Capital Letters

Certain obvious conventions—the use of a capital for the first word in a sentence, for names (of days of the week, holidays, months, people, countries), and for words derived from names (such as pro-French)—need not be discussed here.

1. **Titles of works in English** are usually given according to the following formula. Use a capital for the first letter of the first word, for the first letter of the last word, and for the first letter of all other words that are not articles, conjunctions, or prepositions.

   The Merchant of Venice

   A Midsummer Night's Dream

   Up and Out

   "The Short Happy Life of Francis Macomber"

   The Oakland Bee

2. **Use a capital for a quoted sentence within a sentence,** but not for a quoted phrase (unless it is at the beginning of your sentence) and not for indirect discourse.

   He said, "You can even fool some of the people all of the time."

   He said you can fool some people "all of the time."

   He said that you can even fool some of the people all of the time.

3. **Use a capital for a rank or title preceding a proper name or for a title substituting for a proper name.**

> She said she was Dr. Perez.
>
> He told President Clinton that the Vice President was away.

But:

> Why would anyone wish to be president?
>
> Washington was the first president.

4. **Use a capital when the noun designating a family relationship is used as a substitute for a proper noun.**

> If Mother is busy, ask Tim.

But:

> Because my mother was busy, I asked Tim.

5. **Formal geographical locations (but not mere points on the compass) are capitalized.**

> North America Southeast Asia
>
> In the Southwest, rain sometimes evaporates before touching the ground.
>
> Is Texas part of the South?
>
> The North has its share of racism.

But:

> The wind came from the south.
>
> Texas is bordered on the north by Arkansas, Oklahoma, and New Mexico.

Do *not* capitalize the names of the seasons.

> spring, summer, winter, fall

The Hyphen

The hyphen has five uses, all drawing on the etymology of the word *hyphen,* which comes from the Greek for "in one," "together."

1. Use a hyphen to attach certain prefixes to root words. *All-, pro-, ex-,* and *self-* are the most common of these ("all-powerful," "ex-wife," "pro-labor," "self-made"), but note that even these prefixes are not always followed by a hyphen. If in doubt, check a dictionary. Prefixes before proper names are always followed by a hyphen:

     anti-Semite, pro-NATO un-American

Prefixes ending in *i* are hyphenated before a word beginning with *i:*

     anti-intellectual, semi-intelligible

A hyphen is normally used to break up a triple consonant resulting from the addition of a prefix:

     ill-lit

2. **Use a hyphen to tie compound adjectives into a single visual unit:**

     out-of-date theory, twenty-three books, a no-smoking area

     eighteenth- and nineteenth-century novels

     The sea-tossed raft was a common nineteenth-century symbol of the human tragic condition.

But if a compound modifier follows the modified term, it is usually not hyphenated, thus:

     The theory was out of date.

3. **Use a hyphen to join some compound nouns:**

     Scholar-teacher, philosopher-poet

4. **Use a hyphen to divide a word at the end of a line.** Because words may be divided only as indicated by a dictionary, it is easier to end the line with the last complete word you can type than to keep reaching for a dictionary. But here are some principles governing the division of words at the end of a line:

     a. Never hyphenate words of one syllable, such as *called, doubt, right, through.*

     b. Never hyphenate so that a single letter stands alone: *a-bout, hair-y.*

     c. If a word already has a hyphen, divide it at the hyphen: *anti-intellectual, semi-intelligible.*

     d. Divide prefixes and suffixes from the root: *mis-spell, pro-vide, drunken-ness, walk-ing.*

e. Divide between syllables. If you aren't sure of the proper syllabification, check a dictionary.

5. Use a hyphen to indicate a span of dates or page numbers: 1957-59, pp. 162-68.

The Apostrophe

Use an apostrophe to indicate the possessive, to indicate a contraction, and for certain unusual plurals.

1. **The most common way to indicate the possessive of a singular noun is to add an apostrophe and then an *s*.**

> A dog's life, a week's work
> a mouse's tail, Keats's poems, Marx's doctrines

But some authorities suggest that for a proper noun of more than one syllable that ends in *s* or another sibilant *(-cks, -x, -z)*, it is better to add only an apostrophe:

> Jesus' parables, Sophocles' plays, Chavez' ideas

When in doubt, say the name aloud and notice if you are adding an *s*. If you are adding an *s* when you say it, add an apostrophe and an *s* when you write it. Our own strong preference, however, is to add an apostrophe and an *s* to all proper nouns:

> Jones's book
> Kansas's highways

Possessive pronouns, such as *his, hers, its, theirs, ours,* do not take an apostrophe

> his book, its fur
> The book is hers, not ours.
> The book is theirs.

(*Exception:* indefinite pronouns take an apostrophe, as in "one's hopes" and "others' opinions.")

For plurals ending in *s,* add only an apostrophe to indicate the possessive:

> the boys' father, the Smiths' house, the Joneses' car

If the plural does not end in *s,* add an apostrophe and an *s.*

> women's clothing, mice's eyes

Don't try to form the possessive of the title of a work (for example, of a play, a book, or a film): Write "the imagery in *The Merchant of Venice*" rather than "*The Merchant of Venice*'s imagery." Using an apostrophe gets you into the problem of whether or not to italicize the *s;* similarly, if you use an apostrophe for a work normally enclosed in quotation marks (for instance, a short story), you can't put the apostrophe and the *s* after the quotation marks, but you can't put it inside either.

2. **Use an apostrophe to indicate the omitted letters or numbers in contractions.**

> She won't.
> It's time to go.
> the class of '87

3. **Until recently an apostrophe was used to make plurals of words that do not usually have a plural, and (this is optional) to make the plurals of digits and letters.**

> Her speech was full of if's and and's and but's.
> Ph.D.'s don't know everything.
> Mind your p's and q's. I got two A's and two B's.
> He makes his 4's in two ways.
> the 1920's

This use of the apostrophe is no longer standard, but it remains acceptable.

Abbreviations

In general, avoid abbreviations except in footnotes and except for certain common ones listed below. And don't use an ampersand (&) unless it appears in material you are quoting, or in a title. Abundant use of abbreviations makes an essay sound like a series of newspaper headlines. Usually, *United States* is better than *U.S.* and *the Soviet Union* better than *U.S.S.R.*

1. **Abbreviations, with the first letter capitalized, are used before a name.**

> Dr. Bellini, Ms. Smith, St. Thomas

But:

> The doctor took her temperature and fifty dollars.

2. **Degrees that follow a name are abbreviated:**

> B.A., D.D.S., M.D., Ph.D.

3. **Other acceptable abbreviations include:**

> A.D., B.C., A.M., P.M., e.g., i.e.

(By the way, *e.g.* means *for example; i.e.* means *that is*. The two ought not to be confused. See pages 500 and 503.)

4. **The name of an agency or institution** (for instance, the Congress of Racial Equality; International Business Machines; Southern Methodist University) may be abbreviated by using the initial letters, capitalized and usually without periods (e.g., CORE), but it is advisable to give the name in full when first mentioning it (not everyone knows that AARP means American Association of Retired Persons, for instance), and to use the abbreviation in subsequent references.

Numbers

1. **Write numbers out if you can do so in fewer than three words;** otherwise, use figures.

> sixteen, seventy-two, ten thousand, one sixth
> 10,200; 10,200,000
> There are 336 dimples on a golf ball

But write out round millions and billions, to avoid a string of zeroes.

> a hundred and ten million

For large round numbers you can also use a combination of figures and words.

> The cockroach is about 250 million years old.

Note, however, that because a figure cannot be capitalized, if a number begins a sentence it should always be written out:

> Two hundred and fifty million years ago the cockroach first appeared on earth.

2. **Use figures in dates, addresses, decimals, percentages, page numbers, and hours followed by** A.M. **or** P.M.

> February 29, 1900; .06 percent; 6 percent; 8:16 A.M.

But hours unmodified by minutes are usually written out, and followed by *o'clock*.

> Executions in England regularly took place at eight o'clock.

3. **Use an apostrophe to indicate omitted figures.**

> class of '89
> the '80s (but: the eighties)

4. **Use a hyphen to indicate a span.**

> 1975-79
> 10-20

In giving inclusive numbers, give the second number in full for the numbers up through ninety-nine (2–5, 8–11, 28–34). For larger numbers, give only the last two digits of the second number (101–06; 112–14) unless the full number in necessary (198–202).

5. **Dates** can be given with the month first, followed by numerals, a comma, and the year

> February 10, 1986

or they can be given with the day first, then the month and then the year (without a comma after the day or month)

> 10 February 1986

6. **BC (no periods and no space between the letters) follows the year, but AD precedes it.**

> 10 BC
> AD 200

7. **Roman numerals** are less used than formerly. Capital roman numerals were used to indicate a volume number, but volume numbers are now commonly given in arabic numerals. Capital roman numerals still are used, however, for the names of individuals in a series (Elizabeth II) and

for the primary divisions of an outline; lowercase roman numerals are used for the pages in the front matter (table of contents, foreword, preface, etc.) of a book. The old custom of citing acts and scenes of a play in roman numerals and lines in arabic numerals (II.iv.17–25) is still preferred by many instructors, but the use of arabic numerals throughout (2.4.17–25) is gaining acceptance.

Exercises

1. Correct the following sentence fragments. You may join fragments to independent clauses, or you may recast them as complete sentences.

   a. He left the sentence fragments in the final version of his essay. Instead of trying to fix them.

   b. Her associate left the country. Although their project was unfinished.

   c. Philip Roth argues that closing Newark's libraries will be a costly mistake. That the action will be an insult to Newark's citizens.

   d. He made corrections on the final copy of his essay by hand. Being unwilling to retype the whole paper.

   e. She spent three hours waiting in line in the rain to buy tickets to his concert. Since she was an irrepressibly enthusiastic Springsteen fan.

2. Determine which of the following sentences are run-ons and which contain comma splices. Label them accordingly and correct them appropriately—using any of the five methods shown on pages 461-63.

   a. *CATCH-22* is one of his favorite books, he's reading it now for the fifth time.

   b. Don't write run-on sentences they are not acceptable

   c. The quarterback was intercepted on fourteen consecutive passes, he was traded the following season.

   d. Ambiguously punctuated sentences are usually confusing often they are humorous.

   e. There are those who warn that computers are dehumanizing students, however such people have produced no verifiable evidence.

3. Correct the following sentences, inserting the necessary colons and semicolons.

   a. I signed up for four courses this semester Spanish, geology, calculus, and composition.

   b. "Every dark cloud has a silver lining" I've found that the cliché doesn't always hold true.

   c. The semicolon is tricky it can be effective, but it is often misused.

    d. I finished my final papers three weeks early consequently, I had nothing to do while everyone else was working.

    e. The case for nuclear power has always rested on two claims that reactors were reasonably safe, and that they were indispensable as a source of energy.

    f. Dinner was a disaster he broiled fish, which he burned he steamed broccoli, which came out soggy and he baked a souffle, which fell.

4. In these sentences insert commas where necessary to set off phrases and clauses.

    a. While she was cooking the cat jumped onto the refrigerator.

    b. Geometry is a prerequisite for trigonometry and calculus is a prerequisite for physics.

    c. He wanted to go to Europe in the summer so he had to take a part-time job.

    d. Although she's aware of the dangers of smoking it seems impossible for her to quit.

    e. Final exams they thought were a waste of time.

    f. Turner's painting *The Slave Ship* probably his greatest work was donated to Boston's Museum of Fine Arts.

5. Insert commas to make the restrictive elements in the following sentences nonrestrictive. Be prepared to explain how changing the punctuation changes each sentence's meaning.

    a. My uncle who owns a farm breeds racehorses.

    b. The circus which returns to New York every winter is attended by thousands.

    c. Teachers who are the ones chiefly entrusted with educating people formally should concentrate more heavily on developing their students' analytical skills.

    d. Athletes who ought to know better sometimes play while injured.

6. Punctuate these sentences using the instructions given in items 6–11 on pages 471-72 as guidelines.

    a. A lone masked silent gunman robbed the only bank in Albuquerque New Mexico on March 10, 1885.

    b. Yes it's a sentimental story but I like it.

    c. "You have no taste" he said.

    d. The plot of his detective novel was flimsy weak and unoriginal.

    e. I would prefer not to receive a partridge in a pear tree two French hens three turtle doves and all that other stuff again this Christmas.

7. Place commas correctly in the following sentences.

    a. "Don't write sentence fragments" the instructor said "they are unacceptable."

b. Arguing with him was useless (he was most stubborn when he was wrong) so she decided to drop the subject.

c. To revise Mrs. Beeton's famous recipe: you must (1) find your hare (2) catch it (3) cook it.

d. "A Good Man Is Hard to Find" "Petrified Man" and "A Rose for Emily" are three of his favorite short stories.

8. Correct the following sentences, adding apostrophes where needed. Label each word you correct to indicate whether it is a possessive, a contraction, or an unusual plural.

a. Its easy to learn to use apostrophes.

b. The boys books are on their shelves, under their beds, and in their closets.

c. There are three copies of Barnet and Stubbs *Practical Guide to Writing* in the professors office.

d. My copys falling apart

e. In the 1940s ones dollars went farther.

9. In the following sentences, decide what punctuation is needed, and then add it. If the sentence is correctly punctuated, place a check mark to the left of it.

a. Around his neck is a scarf knotted in front and covering his head is a wide brimmed hat.

b. Buffalo Bill radiates confidence in his bold stance and looks self assured with his head held high.

c. The demands that men and women make on marriage will never be fully met they cannot be.

d. The Polish painter Oskar Kokoschka once said to a man who had posed for a portrait those who know you wont recognize you but those who dont will.

e. Boys on the whole do not keep diaries.

f. Children are unwelcome in most New York restaurants that are not Chinese.

g. Shlomo a giraffe in the Tel Aviv zoo succumbed to the effects of falling down after efforts to raise him with ropes and pulleys were unsuccessful.

h. Character like a photograph develops in darkness.

i. In a grief reaction especially when the person has suffered a loss crying comes easily and produces a healthy release from pent up emotion.

10. We reprint below the fourth paragraph of Jeff Greenfield's essay, "Columbo Knows the Butler Didn't Do It," but without punctuation. Go through the paragraph, adding the punctuation you find necessary. Check your work against the original paragraph on page 194. If you find differences between your punctuation and Greenfield's, try to explain why Greenfield made the choices he did.

columbos villains are not simply rich they are privileged they live the lives that are for most of us hopeless daydreams houses on top of mountains with pools servants and sliding doors parties with women in slinky dresses and endless food and drink plush enclosed box seats at professional sports events the envy and admiration of the crowd while we choose between johnny carson and *invasion of the body snatchers* they are at screenings of movies the rest of us wait in line for on third avenue three months later.

11. Here are the first two paragraphs—but without punctuation—of Raymond A. Sokolov's review of a book by Sarah Stage, *Female Complaints: Lydia Pinkham and the Business of Women's Medicine.* Add the necessary punctuation.

home at the range victorian women in america suffered in shame from all manner of female complaints too intimate to name many of them were the fault of men gonorrhea or men doctors prolapsed uterus and women shrewdly kept shy of the ineffectual and often positively harmful doctors of their day instead they doctored themselves with so called patent medicines the most famous of these was lydia pinkhams vegetable compound mrs pinkham actually existed in lynn mass a center of the progressive spirit hotbed of abolition and feminism sarah stage who has taught american history at williams college had the acuity to see that lydia pinkham was more than a quaint picture on a label that she was a paradigm of the independent woman of her day building a big business with a home remedy to save her family from bankruptcy caused by a neer do well husband she saw furthermore that many of the important themes and forces of american society before world war I clustered around the medicine itself which was largely alcoholic but respectably bitter

Chapter 22

Spelling

Life would be easier if a sound were always represented by the same letter. Some modern European languages come close to this principle, but English is not among them. "You" and "ewe" are pronounced identically, but they do not have even a single letter in common. George Bernard Shaw once called attention to some of the oddities of English spelling by saying that *fish* might be spelled *ghoti*. How? *Gh* is *f,* as in *enough; o* is *i,* as in *women; ti* is *sh,* as in *notion.* So, *ghoti* spells *fish.*

This is not the place to explain why English spelling is so erratic, but it may be consoling to know that the trouble goes back at least to the Norman French Conquest of England in 1066; after the Conquest, French scribes spelled English words more or less as though the words were French. Moreover, though pronunciation kept changing, spelling became relatively fixed, so that even in Shakespeare's time spelling often reflected a pronunciation that had long been abandoned. And today the spelling of many words still reflects the long-lost medieval pronunciation. The silent *e* in *life,* and the silent consonants in *knight* and *through,* for example, were pronounced in Chaucer's day.

Most rules for spelling, then, must immediately be modified with lists of exceptions. Even the most famous,

I before *e* except after *c*
Or when sounded as *a*
In *neighbor* and *sleigh,*

No, no it's *before* *except after* *!*

has more exceptions than cheery handbooks admit. Always *ei* after *c?* What about *ancient, efficient,* and *sufficient?* Oh, but in these words the *c* is pronounced *sh,* an easy enough exception to keep in mind. But how can we explain *financier?* And of words where a *c* does not precede the letters in question, does the rule *ie* really govern all those not "sounded as *a* / In *neighbor* and *sleigh*"? How about *counterfeit, deity, either, foreign, forfeit, heifer, height, neither, leisure, protein, seize, their, weird?*

Instead of offering rules with menacing lists of exceptions, we offer a single list of words commonly misspelled in college writing. And here are four suggestions:

1. Read the list, mark any words whose spelling surprises you, and make a conscientious effort to memorize them.

2. Keep a dictionary at hand, and consult it while you are editing your final draft. If you have not formed a habit of consulting the dictionary, you may have to work at it. Begin by noticing what words or groups of words you have trouble with. Then cultivate the habit of doubting your own spellings of these words. When in doubt, don't guess; look the word up.

3. In a notebook, keep a list of words you misspell and try to classify your errors. Most spelling errors occur in characteristic and even predictable patterns. Some errors originate in mispronunciation, or the dropping or slurring of sounds in speech. (Notice, for example, gove*r*nment, Feb*r*uary, prejudic*ed*.) On the other hand, words with a vowel in an unaccented syllable are troublesome because those vowels all sound alike. You'll have to learn to visualize the correct vowel in such words as: dist*a*nt, it*e*m, ed*i*ble, gall*o*p, circ*u*s. Still other errors stem from confusing pairs of words such as: *accept/except, conscience/conscious, past/passed, capital/capitol.* But you don't have to be aware of all possible errors any more than you need to know all the rules. You need only to classify the errors you *do* make and work at reducing those. The task is really not hopeless.

4. For words that you persistently misspell, invent some device to assist your memory. For example, if you erroneously put an *a* in *cemetery* in place of an *e,* say to yourself "people r*e*st in a cemetery." When you next have to write the word *cemetery* you will remember the associative device *(rest),* and you will spell *cemetery* with an *e.* Another example: if you repeatedly leave out an *l* from *balloon,* say to yourself—really say it—"a ba*ll*oon is a ba*ll*." The next time you have to write *balloon* you will remember *ball.* Similarly, tell yourself there's *a rat* in *sepa*r*ate.* A last example, for people who mistakenly put an *n* in *dilemma:* "*Emma* is in a dilemma." Generally speaking, the sillier the phrase, the more memorable it will be.

Words Commonly Misspelled

abridgment	aging
absence	alcohol
accessible	allege
accidentally	all right (*not* alright
accommodate	a lot (*not* alot)
achievement	already (*not* all ready
acknowledgment	alter (to change)
acquire	altogether
across	analysis
actually	analyze
address	apparent
adjacent	appearance
adolescence	appreciate
adolescent	arctic
advice (noun)	argument
advise (verb)	assassin
aggravate	assistance
aggressive	assistant

athlete

attendance

balloon

beggar

beginner

believe

benefit

bourgeois

bourgeoisie

Britain

bureau

bureaucracy

burglar

business

calendar

capital (noun: seat of government, money; adjective: chief)

capitol (building)

category

ceiling

cemetery

changeable

chief

choose (present tense)

chose (past tense)

chosen (participle)

commit

committee

comparative

competent

complement (noun: that which completes; verb: to complete)

compliment (praise)

conferred

congratulate

conscience

conscious

consistent

controlled

controversy

coolly

corollary

counterfeit

criticism

criticize

curiosity

deceive

decision

defendant

definite

deity

dependent

description

desirable

despair

desperate

develop, develops

development

dilemma

disappear

disappoint

disastrous

divide

divine

dormitory

eighth

embarrass

envelop (verb)

envelope (noun)

environment

equipped

equivalent

especially

essence

exaggerate

exceed

excellence

excellent

exhilarate

existence

experience

explanation

familiar

fascinate

fiend

fiery

foreign

foreword (in a book)

forty

fourth

friend

gauge

genealogy

goddess

government

grammar

grievance

guarantee

height

heroes

hoping

humorous

hypocrisy

imagery

imagination

immediately

impel

incidentally

incredible

independence

independent

indispensable

insistence

insistent

intelligent

interest

interpretation

interrupt

irrelevant

irresistible

judgment

led (past tense of *to lead*)

leisure

license

loneliness

loose (adjective)

lose (verb)

losing

maneuver

marriage

mathematics

medicine

mischievous

misspell

naive

necessary

necessity

niece

ninety

noncommittal

noticeable

occasion

occasionally

occur

occurred

occurrence

omit

omitted

original

parallel

pastime

peaceable

performance

permanent

persistent

playwright

possession

practically

precede

predominant

preferred

prejudice

prevalent

principal (adjective: foremost: noun: chief)

principle (noun: rule)

privilege

probably

procedure

proceed

prominent

prophecy (noun)

prophesy (verb)

pursue

quantity

realize

really

receipt

receiving

recommend

reference

referring

relevance

relevant

relieve

remembrance

repentance

repetition

resistance

rhyme

rhythm

sacrifice

secretary

seize

sense

separate

shining

shriek

siege

significance

similar

solely

specimen

sponsor

stationary (still)

stationery (paper)

strength

subtlety

subtly

succeed

supersede

surprise

syllable

temperament

tendency

theories

therefore

thorough

tragedy

transferred

tried

truly

unforgettable	weird
unnecessary	wholly
useful	who's (contraction: who is)
usually	whose (possessive pronoun:
various	belonging to whom)
vengeance	withhold
villain	writing

Finally, a few words about **spelling programs** designed for use with computers. Programs such as Word Plus or Easy Speller flag any word you use that is not in the program's dictionary. A misspelled word is of course not in the dictionary and thus flagged. But a word flagged is not necessarily misspelled; it may simply not be in the program's dictionary. Proper names, for example, regularly get flagged. Keep in mind also that most programs cannot distinguish between homophones *(to, too, two; there, their, alter, altar)*, nor can they tell you that you should have written *accept* instead of *except*. Since all of these words appear in the program's dictionary, they arouse no response—even when you may use them incorrectly.

Although the limitations in spelling programs will probably be overcome soon, we nevertheless think it reasonable to suggest that (if you are a poor speller) you learn to spell correctly. After all, even if you regularly use a word processor, you can't assume that you will have one available for every writing task. There are, for instance, quizzes and final examinations. Study our list of words, then, and make yourself independent (*not* independent*a*nt) of spelling programs.

Chapter 23

Usage

Some things are said or written and some are not. More precisely, anything can be said or written, but only some things are acceptable to the ears and minds of many readers. "I don't know nothing about it" has been said and will be said again, but many readers who encounter this expression might judge the speaker as a person with nothing of interest to say—and immediately tune out.

Although such a double negative today is not acceptable, it used to be: Chaucer's courteous Knight never spoke no baseness, and Shakespeare's courtly Mercutio, in *Romeo and Juliet,* "will not budge for no man." But things have changed; what was acceptable in the Middle Ages and the Renaissance (for example, emptying chamber pots into the gutter) is not always acceptable now. And some of what was once unacceptable has become acceptable. At the beginning of the twentieth century, grammarians suggested that one cannot use *drive* in speaking of a car; one drives (forces into motion) an ox, or even a person ("He drove her to distraction"), but not a machine. Some eighty years of usage, however, have erased all objections.

This chapter presents a list of expressions that, although commonly used, set many teeth on edge. Seventy years from now some of these expressions may be as acceptable as "drive a car"; but we are writing for today, and we might as well try to hold today's readers by following today's taste in language.

A Note on Idioms

An idiom (from a Greek word meaning "peculiar") is a fixed group of words, peculiar to a given language. Thus in English we say, "I took a walk," but Germans "make a walk," Spaniards "give a walk," and Japanese "do a walk." (If we think the German, Spanish, and Japanese expressions are odd, we might well ask ourselves where it is that we take a walk to.) If a visitor from Argentina says, in English, that she "gave a walk," she is using *un*idiomatic English, just as anyone who says he knows a poem "at heart" instead of "by heart" is using unidiomatic English.

Probably most unidiomatic expressions use the wrong preposition. Examples:

Unidiomatic	*Idiomatic*
comply to	comply with
superior with	superior to

Sometimes while we write, or even while we speak, we are unsure of the idiom and we pause to try an alternative—"parallel with?" "parallel to?"—and we don't know which sounds more natural, more idiomatic. At such moments, more often than not, either is acceptable, but if you are in doubt, check a dictionary when you are editing your work. (The *American Heritage Dictionary* has notes on usage following the definitions of hundreds of its words.)

In any case, if you are a native speaker of English, when you read your draft you will probably detect unidiomatic expressions such as *superior with;* that is, you will hear something that sounds odd, and so you will change it to something that sounds familiar, idiomatic—here, *superior to.* If any unidiomatic expressions remain in your essay, the trouble may be that an effort to write impressively has led you to use unfamiliar language. A reader who sees such unidiomatic language may sense that you are straining for an effect. Try rewriting the passage in your own voice.

If you are a non–native speaker of English, plan to spend extra time revising and editing your work. Check prepositional phrases with special care. In addition to using a college edition of an English language dictionary, consult reference works designed with the foreign or bilingual student in mind. One compact book our students find particularly useful is Michael Swan's *Practical English Usage,* published by Oxford University Press. But don't neglect another invaluable resource: students who are native speakers. They will usually be able to tell you whether or not a phrase "sounds right," though they may not know why.

Glossary

a, an Use *a* before words beginning with a consonant ("a book") or with a vowel sounded as a consonant ("a one-way ticket," "a university"). Use *an* before words beginning with a vowel or a vowel sound, including those beginning with a silent *h* ("an egg," "an hour"). If an initial *h* is pronounced but the accent is not on the first syllable, *an* is acceptable, as in "*an* historian" (but "*a* history course").

above Try to avoid writing *for the above reasons, in view of the above,* or *as above.* These expressions sound unpleasantly legalistic. Substitute *for these reasons,* or *therefore,* or some such expression or word.

academics Only two meanings of this noun are widely accepted: (1) "members of an institution of higher learning," and (2) "persons who are academic in background or outlook." Avoid using it to mean "academic subjects," as in "A student should pay attention not only to academics but also to recreation."

accept, except *Accept* means "to receive with consent." *Except* means "to exclude" or "excluding."

affect, effect *Affect* is usually a verb, meaning (1) "to influence, to produce an effect, to impress," or (2) "to pretend, to put on," as in "He affected an English accent." Psychologists use it as a noun for "feeling," e.g., "The patient experienced no affect." *Effect,* as a verb, means "to bring about" ("The workers effected the rescue in less than an hour"). As a noun, *effect* means "result" ("The effect was negligible").

African American, African-American Both forms are acceptable to denote an American of African ancestry. In recent years these words have been preferred to *black.*

aggravate "To worsen, to increase for the worse," as in "Smoking aggravated the irritation." Although it is widely used to mean "annoy" ("He aggravated me"), many readers are annoyed by such a use.

all ready, already *All ready* means "everything is ready." *Already* means "by this time."

all right, alright The first of these is the preferable spelling; for some readers it is the only acceptable spelling.

all together, altogether *All together* means that members of a group act or are gathered together ("They voted all together"); *altogether* is an adverb meaning "entirely," "wholly" ("This is altogether unnecessary").

allusion, reference, illusion An *allusion* is an implied or indirect reference." As Lincoln says" is a *reference* to Lincoln, but "As a great man has said," along with a phrase quoted from the Gettysburg Address, constitutes an *allusion* to Lincoln. The student who, in a demonstration at Berkeley, carried a placard saying "I am a human being—please do not fold, spindle, or mutilate" *referred* to himself and *alluded* to a computer card. *Allusion* has nothing to do with *illusion* (a deception). Note the spelling (especially the second *i*) in "disillusioned" (left without illusions, disenchanted).

almost See *most.*

a lot Two words (not *alot*).

among, between See *between.*

amount, number *Amount* refers to bulk or quantity: "A small amount of gas was still in the tank." Use *number,* not *amount,* to refer to separate (countable) units: "A large number of people heard the lecture" (not "a large amount of people"). Similarly, "an amount of money," but "a number of dollars."

analyzation Unacceptable; use *analysis.*

and/or Acceptable, but a legalism and unpleasant-sounding. Often *or* by itself will do, as in "students who know Latin or Italian." When *or* is not enough ("The script was written by Groucho and/or Harpo") it is better to recast ("The script was written by Groucho or Harpo, or both").

and etc. Because *etc.* is an abbreviation for *et cetera* ("and others"), the *and* in *and etc.* is redundant. (See also the entry on *et cetera.*)

ante, anti *Ante* means "before" (*antebellum,* "before the Civil War"); *anti* means "against" *(antivivisectionist).* Hyphenate *anti* before capitals *(anti-Semitism)* and before *i (anti-intellectual).*

anxious Best reserved for uses that suggest anxiety ("He was anxious before the examination"), though some authorities now accept it in the sense of "eager" ("He was anxious to serve the community").

anybody One word ("Do you know anybody here?"). If two words (*any body*), you mean any corpse ("Several people died in the fire, but the police cannot identify any body").

any more, anymore *Any more* is used as an adjective: "I don't want any more meat" (here *any more* says something about meat). *Anymore* (one word) is used as an adverb: "I don't eat meat anymore" (here *anymore* says something about eating).

anyone One word ("Why would anyone think that?"), unless you mean "any one thing," as in "Here are three books; you may take any one." *Anyone* is an indefinite singular pronoun meaning *any person:* "If anyone has a clue, he or she should call the police." In an astounding advertisement, the writer moved from *anyone* (singular) to *their* (third person plural) to *your* (second person): "Anyone who thinks a Yonex racquet has improved their game, please raise your hand."

area of Like *field of* and *topic of* ("the field of literature," "the topic of politics"), *area of* can usually be deleted. "The area of marketing" equals "marketing."

around Avoid using *around* in place of *about:* "He wrote it in about three hours." See also *centers on.*

as, like *As* is a conjunction; use it in forming comparisons, to introduce clauses. (A clause has a subject and a verb.)

You can learn to write, as you can learn to swim.

Huck speaks the truth as he sees it.

Like is a preposition; use it to introduce prepositional phrases:

He looks like me.

Like Hamlet, Laertes has lost a father.

She thinks like a lawyer.

A short rule: use *like* when it introduces a noun *not* followed by a verb: "Nothing grabs people like *People*."

Writers who are fearful of incorrectly using *like* resort to cumbersome evasions: "He eats in the same manner that a pig eats." But there's nothing wrong with "He eats like a pig."

as of now Best deleted, or replaced by *now*. Not "As of now I don't smoke" but "Now I don't smoke" or "I don't smoke now" or "I don't smoke."

Asian, Oriental *Asian* as a noun and as an adjective is the preferred word. *Oriental* (from *oriens,* "rising sun," "east") is in disfavor because it implies a Eurocentric view—that is, that things "oriental" are east of the European colonial powers who invented the term. Similarly, **Near East, Middle East,** and **Far East,** are terms that are based on a Eurocentric view. No brief substitute has been agreed on for *Near East* and *Middle East,* but *East Asia* is now regarded as preferable to *Far East.*

aspect Literally, "a view from a particular point," but it has come to mean *topic,* as in "There are several aspects to be considered." Try to get a sharper word; for example, "There are several problems to be considered," or "There are several consequences to be considered."

as such Often meaningless, as in "Tragedy as such evokes pity."

as to Usually *about* is preferable. Not "I know nothing as to the charges," but "I know nothing about the charges."

bad, badly *Bad* used to be only an adjective ("a bad movie"), and *badly* was an adverb ("she sings badly"). In "I felt bad," *bad* describes the subject, not the verb. (Compare "I felt happy," or "I felt good about getting a raise." After verbs of appearing, such as "feel," "look," "seem," "taste," an adjective, not an adverb is used. If you are in doubt, substitute a word for *bad,* for instance *sad,* and see what you say. Since you would say "I feel sad about his failure," you can say "I feel bad. . . .") But "badly" is acceptable and even preferred by many. Note, however, this distinction: "This meat smells bad" (an adjective describing the meat), and "Because I have a stuffed nose I smell badly" (an adverb describing my ability to smell something).

being Do not use *being* as a main verb, as in "The trouble being that his reflexes were too slow." The result is a sentence fragment. See pages 460–62.

being that, being as A sentence such as "Being that she was a stranger . . . " sounds like an awkward translation from the Latin. Use *because.*

beside, besides *Beside* means "at the side of." Because *besides* can mean either "in addition to" or "other than," it is ambiguous, as in "Something besides TB caused his death." It is best, then, to use *in addition to* or *other than,* depending on what you mean.

between Only English teachers who have had a course in Middle English are likely to know that between comes from *by twain.* And only English teachers and editors are likely to object to its use (and to call for *among*) when more than two are concerned, as in "among the three of us." Note, too, that even conservative usage accepts *between* in reference to more than two when the items are at the moment paired: "Negotiations *between* Israel and Egypt, Syria, and Lebanon seem stalled." *Between,* a preposition, takes an object ("between you and me"): not "between you and I".

biannually, bimonthly, biweekly Every two years, every two months, every two weeks (*not* twice a year, etc.). Twice a year is *semiannually.* Because *biannually, bimonthly,* and *biweekly* are commonly misunderstood, it is best to avoid them and to say "every two . . . "

Black, black Although one sometimes sees the word capitalized when it refers to race, most publishers use a lowercase letter, making it consistent with *white,* which is never capitalized. See also *African American.*

can, may When schoolchildren asked "Can I leave the room?" their teachers used to correct them thus: "You *can* leave the room if you have legs, but you *may not* leave the room until you receive permission." In short, *can* indicates physical possibility, *may* indicates permission. But because "you may not" and "why mayn't I?" sound not merely polite but stiff, *can* is usually preferred except in formal contexts.

capital, capitol A *capital* is a city that is a center of government. *Capital* can also mean wealth ("It takes capital to start a business"). A *capitol* is a building in which legislators meet. Notice the distinction in the following sentence: "Washington, D.C., is the nation's capital; the capitol ought to have a gold dome."

centers on, centers around Use *centers on,* because *center* refers to a point, not to a movement around.

Chicana, Chicano A Mexican-American (female or male, respectively; the male plural, *Chicanos,* is used for a group consisting of males and females). Although the term sometimes was felt to be derogatory, today it usually implies ethnic pride.

collective nouns A collective noun, singular in form, names a collection of individuals. Examples: *audience, band, committee, crowd, jury, majority, minority, team.* When you are thinking chiefly of the whole as a unit, use a singular verb (and a singular pronoun, if any): "The majority rules"; "The jury is announcing its verdict." But when you are thinking of the individuals, use a plural verb (and pronoun, if any): "The majority are lawyers"; "The jury are divided and they probably cannot agree." If the plural sounds odd, you can usually rewrite: "The jurors are divided and they probably cannot agree."

compare, contrast To *compare* is to note likenesses or differences: "Compare a motorcycle with a bicycle." To *contrast* is to emphasize differences.

complement, compliment *Complement* as a noun means "that which completes"; as a verb, "to fill out, to complete." *Compliment* as a noun is an expression of praise; as a verb it means "to offer praise."

comprise "To include, contain, consist of": "The university comprises two colleges and a medical school" (not "is comprised of"). Conservative authorities hold that "to be comprised of" is always incorrect, and they reject the form one often hears: "Two colleges and a medical school comprise the university." Here the word should be *compose,* not *comprise.*

concept Should often be deleted. For "The concept of the sales tax is regressive" write "The sales tax is regressive."

contact   Because it is vague, avoid using *contact* as a verb. *Not* "I contacted him" but "I spoke with him" or "I wrote to him," or whatever.

continual, continuous   Conservative authorities hold that *continuous* means "uninterrupted," as in "It rained continuously for six hours"; *continually* means "repeated often, recurring at short intervals," as in "For a year he continually wrote letters to her."

contrast, compare   See *compare*.

could have, could of   See *of*.

criteria   Plural of *criterion,* hence it is always incorrect to speak of "a criteria," or to say "The criteria is . . . "

data   Plural of *datum*. Although some social scientists speak of "this data," "these data" is preferable: "These data are puzzling." Because the singular, *datum,* is rare and sounds odd, it is best to substitute *fact* or *figure* for *datum*.

different from   Prefer it to *different than,* unless you are convinced that in a specific sentence *different from* sounds terribly wrong, as in "These two books are more different than I had expected." (In this example, "more," not "different," governs "than." But this sentence, though correct, is awkward and therefore it should be revised: "These two books differ more than I had expected.")

dilemma   A situation requiring a choice between equally undesirable alternatives; not every difficulty or plight or predicament is a *dilemma*. Not "Her dilemma was that she had nowhere to go," but "Her dilemma was whether to go out or to stay home: one was frightening, the other was embarrassing." And note the spelling (two *m's,* no *n*).

disinterested   Though the word is often used to mean "indifferent," "unconcerned," "uninterested," reserve it to mean "impartial": "A judge should be disinterested."

due to   Some people, holding that *due to* cannot modify a verb (as in "He failed due to illness"), tolerate it only when it modifies a noun or pronoun ("His failure was due to illness"). They also insist that it cannot begin a sentence ("Due to illness, he failed"). In fact, however, daily usage accepts both. But because it almost always sounds stiff, try to substitute *because of,* or *through*.

due to the fact that   Wordy for *because*.

each   Although many authorities hold that *each,* as a subject, is singular, even when followed by "them" ("Each of them is satisfactory"), some authorities accept and even favor the plural ("Each of them are satisfactory"). But it is usually better to avoid the awkwardness by substituting *all* for *each:* "All of them are satisfactory." When *each* refers to a plural subject, the verb must be plural: "They each have a book"; "We each are trying." *Each* cannot be made into a possessive; you cannot say "Each's opinion is acceptable."

effect   See *affect*.

e.g.   Abbreviation for *exempli gratia,* meaning "for example." It is thus different from *i.e.* (an abbreviation for *id est,* meaning "that is"). E.g. (not italicized) introduces an example: i.e. (also not italicized) introduces a definition. Because these two abbreviations of Latin words are often confused, it may be preferable to avoid them and use their English equivalents.

either . . . or, neither . . . nor If the subjects are singular, use a singular verb: "Either the boy or the girl is lying." If one of the subjects joined by *or* or *nor* is plural, most grammarians say that the verb agrees with the nearer subject, thus: "A tree or two shrubs are enough," or "Two shrubs or a tree is enough." But because the singular verb in the second of these sentences may sound odd, follow the first construction; that is, put the plural subject nearer to the verb and use a plural verb. Another point about *either . . . or.* In this construction, "either" serves as advance notice that two equal possibilities are in the offing. Beware of putting "either" too soon, as in "Either he is a genius or a lunatic." Better: "He is either a genius or a lunatic."

enthuse Objectionable to many readers. For "He enthused," say "He was enthusiastic." Use *enthuse* only in the sense of "to be excessively enthusiastic," "to gush."

et cetera, etc. Latin for "and other things"; if you mean "and other people," you need *et al.,* short for *et alii.* Because *etc.* is vague, its use is usually inadvisable. Not "He studied mathematics, etc." but "He studied mathematics, history, economics, and French." Or, if the list is long, cut it by saying something a little more informative than *etc.*—for example, "He studied mathematics, history, and other liberal arts subjects." Even *and so forth* or *and so on* is preferable to *etc.* Confine etc. (and most other abbreviations, including *et al.*) to footnotes, and even in footnotes try to avoid it.

Eurocentric language Language focused on Europe—for instance, the word *Hispanic* when used to refer not to persons from Spain but persons from Mexico and Central and South America, who may in fact have little or no Spanish heritage. (The Latin name for Spain was Hispania.) Similarly, the terms *Near East* and *Far East* represent a European point of view (near to, and far from Europe), objectionable to many persons not of European heritage. See *Asian* and *Hispanic.*

everybody, everyone These take a singular verb ("Everybody is here"), and a pronoun referring to them is usually singular ("Everybody thinks his problems are suitable topics of conversation"), but use a plural pronoun if the singular would seem unnatural ("Everybody was there, weren't they?"). To avoid the sexism of "Everybody thinks his problems . . . " revise to "All people think their problems . . . "

examples, instances See *instances.*

except See *accept.*

exists Often unnecessary and a sign of wordiness. Not "The problem that *exists* here is" but "The problem here is."

expound Usually pretentious for *explain* or *say.* To *expound* is to give a methodical explanation of theological matters.

facet Literally "little face," especially one of the surfaces of a gem. Don't use it (and don't use *aspect* or *factor* either) to mean "part" or "topic." It is most acceptable when, close to its literal meaning, it suggests a new appearance, as when a gem is turned: "Another *facet* appears when we see this law from the taxpayer's point of view."

the fact that Usually wordy. "Because of the fact that boys played female roles in Elizabethan drama" can be reduced to "Because boys played female roles in Elizabethan drama."

factor Strictly speaking, a *factor* helps to produce a result. Although *factor* is often used in the sense of "point" ("Another factor to be studied is . . .), such use is often wordy. "The possibility of plagiarism is a factor that must be considered" simply adds up to "The possibility of plagiarism must be considered." *Factor* is almost never the precise word: "the factors behind Gatsby's actions" are, more precisely, "Gatsby's motives."

famous, notorious See *notorious*.

Far East See *Asian*.

farther, further Some purists claim that *farther* always refers to distance and *further* to time ("The gymnasium is farther than the library"; "Let us think further about this").

fatalistic, pessimistic *Fatalistic* means "characterized by the belief that all events are predetermined and therefore inevitable"; *pessimistic*, "characterized by the belief that the world is evil," or, less gloomily, "expecting the worst."

fewer, less See *less*.

field of See *area of*.

firstly, secondly Acceptable, but it is better to use *first, second*.

former, latter These words are acceptable, but they are often annoying because they force the reader to reread earlier material in order to locate what *the former* and *the latter* refer to. The expressions are legitimately used in order to avoid repeating lengthy terms, but if you are talking about an easily repeated subject—say, Lincoln and Grant—don't hesitate to replace *the former* and *the latter* with their names. The repetition will clarify rather than bore.

good, well *Good* is an adjective ("a good book"). *Well* is usually an adverb ("She writes well"). Standard English does not accept "She writes good." But Standard English requires *good* after verbs of appearing, such as "seems," "looks," "sounds," "tastes": "it looks good," "it sounds good." *Well* can also be an adjective meaning "healthy": "I am well."

graduate, graduate from Use *from* if you name the institution or if you use a substitute word as in "She graduated from high school"; if the institution (or substitute) is not named, *from* is omitted: "She graduated in 1983." The use of the passive ("She was graduated from high school") is acceptable but sounds fussy to many.

he or she, his or her These expressions are awkward, but the implicit male chauvinism in the generic use of the male pronoun ("A citizen should exercise his right to vote") may be more offensive than the awkwardness of *he or she* and *his or her*. Moreover, sometimes the male pronoun, when used for males and females, is ludicrous, as in "The more violence a youngster sees on television, regardless of his age or sex, the more aggressive he is likely to be." Do what you can to avoid the dilemma. Sometimes you can use the plural *their:* "Students are expected to hand in their papers on Monday" (instead of "The student is expected to hand in his or her paper on Monday"). Or eliminate the possessive: "The student must hand in a paper on Monday." See also *man, mankind*.

Hispanic, Latina, Latino A person who traces his or her origin to a Spanish-speaking country is a *Hispanic.* (Hispania was the Latin name for Spain.) But some people object to the term when applied to persons in the western hemisphere, arguing that it overemphasizes the European influence on ethnic identity and neglects the indigenous and black heritages. Many who object to *Hispanic* prefer to call a person of Latin-American descent a *Latina* (the feminine form) or a *Latino* (the masculine form), partly because these words are themselves Latin-American words. (The male plural, *Latinos,* commonly is used for a group consisting of males and females.) But many people object that these words too obscure the unique cultural heritages of, say, Mexican-Americans, Cuban-Americans, and Puerto Ricans.

hopefully Commonly used to mean "I hope" or "It is hoped" ("*Hopefully,* the rain will stop soon"), but it is best to avoid what some consider a dangling modifier. After all, the rain itself is not hopeful. If you mean "I hope the rain will stop soon," say exactly that. Notice, too, that *hopefully* is often evasive; if the president of the college says, "Hopefully tuition will not rise next year," don't think that you have heard a promise to fight against an increase; you only have heard someone evade making a promise. In short, confine *hopefully* to its adverbial use, meaning "in a hopeful manner": "Hopefully he uttered a prayer."

however Independent clauses (for instance, "He tried" and "He failed") should not be linked with a *however* preceded by a comma. *In*correct: "He tried, however he failed." What is required is a period ("He tried. However, he failed") or a semicolon before *however* ("He tried; however, he failed).

the idea that Usually dull and wordy. Not "The idea that we grow old is frightening," but "That we grow old is frightening," or (probably better) "Growing old is frightening."

identify When used in the psychological sense, "to associate oneself closely with a person or an institution," it is preferable to include a reflexive pronoun, thus: "He identified himself with Hamlet," *not* "He identified with Hamlet."

i.e. Latin for *id est,* "that is." The English words are preferable to the Latin abbreviation. On the distinction between *i.e.* and *e.g.,* see *e.g.*

immanent, imminent *Immanent,* "remaining within, intrinsic"; *imminent,* "likely to occur soon, impending."

imply, infer The writer or speaker *implies* (suggests); the perceiver *infers* (draws a conclusion): "Karl Marx implied that . . . but his modern disciples infer from his writings that . . . " Although *infer* is widely used for *imply,* preserve the distinction.

incidence, incident The *incidence* is the extent or frequency of an occurrence: "The incidence of violent crime in Tokyo is very low." The plural, *incidences,* is rarely used: "The incidences of crime and of fire in Tokyo. . . ." An *incident* is one occurrence: "The incident happened yesterday." The plural is *incidents:* "The two incidents happened simultaneously."

individual Avoid using the word to mean only "person": "He was a generous individual." But it is precise when it implicitly makes a contrast with a group: "In a money-mad society, he was a generous individual"; "Although the faculty did not take a stand on this issue, faculty members as individuals spoke out."

instances Instead of *in many instances* use *often.* Strictly speaking an *instance* is not an object or incident in itself but one offered as an example. Thus "another instance of his failure to do his duty" (not "In three instances he failed to do his duty").

irregardless Unacceptable; use *regardless.*

it is Usually this expression needlessly delays the subject: "It is unlikely that many students will attend the lecture" could just as well be "Few students are likely to attend the lecture."

its, it's The first is a possessive pronoun ("The flock lost its leader"); the second is a contraction of *it is* ("It's a wise father that knows his child."). You'll have no trouble if you remember that the possessive pronoun *its,* like other possessive pronouns such as *our, his, their,* does *not* use an apostrophe.

kind of Singular, as in "That kind of movie bothers me." (*Not:* "Those kind of movies bother me.") If, however, you are really talking about more than one kind, use *kinds* and be sure that the demonstrative pronoun and the verb are plural: "Those kinds of movies bother me." Notice also that the phrase is *kind of,* not *kind of a.* Not "What *kind of a* car does she drive?" but "What *kind of* car does she drive?"

Latina, Latino See *Hispanic.*

latter See *former.*

lay, lie *To lay* means "to put, to set, to cause to rest." It takes an object: "May I lay the coats on the table?" The past tense and the participle are *laid:* "I laid the coats on the table"; "I have laid the coats on the table." *To lie* means "to recline," and it does not take an object: "When I am tired I lie down." The past tense is *lay,* the participle is *lain:* "Yesterday I lay down"; "I have lain down hundreds of times without wishing to get up."

lend, loan The usual verb is *lend:* "Lend me a pen." The past tense and the participle are both *lent. Loan* is a noun: "This isn't a gift, it's a loan." But, curiously, *loan* as a verb is acceptable in past forms: "I loaned him my bicycle." In its present form ("I often loan money") it is used chiefly by bankers.

less, fewer *Less* (as an adjective) refers to bulk amounts (also called mass nouns): less milk, less money, less time. *Fewer* refers to separate (countable) items: fewer glasses of milk, fewer dollars, fewer hours.

lifestyle, life-style, life style All three forms are acceptable, but because many readers regard the expression as imprecise, try to find a substitute such as *values.*

like, as See *as.*

literally It means "strictly in accord with the primary meaning; not metaphorically." It is not a mere intensive. "He was literally dead" means that he was a corpse; if he was merely exhausted, *literally* won't do. You cannot be "literally stewed" (except by cannibals), "literally tickled pink," or "literally head over heels in love."

loose, lose *Loose* is an adjective ("The nail is loose"); *lose* is a verb ("Don't lose the nail").

the majority of Usually a wordy way of saying *most.* Of course if you mean "a bare majority," say so; otherwise *most* will usually do. Certainly "The majority of the basement is used for a cafeteria" should be changed to "Most of the basement is used for a cafeteria." *Majority* can take either a singular verb or a plural verb. When *majority* refers to a collection—for example, a group acting as a body—the verb is singular, as in "The majority has withdrawn its support from the mayor." But when *majority* refers to members of a group acting as individuals, as in "The majority of voters in this district vote Republican," a plural verb (here, "vote") is usually preferred. If either construction sounds odd, use "most," with a plural verb: "Most voters in this district vote Republican."

man, mankind The use of these words in reference to males and females sometimes is ludicrous, as in "Man, being a mammal, breastfeeds his young." But even when not ludicrous the practice is sexist, as in "man's brain" and "the greatness of mankind." Consider using such words as *human being, person, humanity, people.* Similarly, for "manmade," *artificial* or *synthetic* may do.

may, can See *can.*

me The right word in such expressions as "between you and me" and "They gave it to John and me." It is the object of verbs and of prepositions. In fact, *me* rather than *I* is the usual form after any verb, including the verb *to be;* "It is me" is nothing to be ashamed of. See the entry on *myself.*

medium, media *Medium* is singular, *media* is plural: "TV is the medium to which most children are most exposed. Other media include film, radio, and publishing." It follows, then, that *mass media* takes a plural verb: "The mass media exert an enormous influence."

Middle East See *Asian.*

might of, might have; must of, must have *Might of* and *must of* are colloquial for *might have* and *must have.* In writing, use the *have* form: "He might have cheated; in fact, he must have cheated."

more Avoid writing a false (incomplete) comparison such as: "His essay includes several anecdotes, making it more enjoyable." Delete "more" unless there really is a comparison with another essay. On false comparisons see also the entry on *other.*

most, almost Although it is acceptable in speech to say "most everyone" and "most anybody," it is preferable in writing to use "almost everyone," "almost anybody." But of course: "Most students passed."

myself *Myself* is often mistakenly used for *I* or *me,* as in "They praised Tony and myself," or "Prof. Chen and myself examined the dead rat." In the first example, *me* is the word to use; after all, if Tony hadn't been there the sentence would say, "They praised me." (No one would say, "They praised myself.") Similarly, in the second example if Prof. Chen were not involved, the sentence would run, "I examined the dead rat," so what is needed here is simply "Prof. Chen and I examined. . . ."

In general, use *myself* only when (1) it refers to the subject of the sentence ("I look out for myself"; "I washed myself") or (2) when it is an intensive: ("I myself saw the break-in"; "I myself have not experienced racism").

nature You can usually delete *the nature of,* as in "The nature of my contribution is not political but psychological."

Near East See *Asian.*

needless to say The reader may well wonder why you go on to say it. Of course this expression is used to let readers know that they are probably familiar with what comes next, but usually *of course* will better serve as this sign.

Negro Capitalized, whether a noun or an adjective, though *white* is not. In recent years *Negro* has been replaced by *black* or African-American.

neither . . . nor See *either . . . or.*

nobody, no one, none *Nobody* and *no one* are singular, requiring a singular verb ("Nobody believes this," "No one knows"); but they can be referred to by a plural pronoun: "Nobody believes this, do they?" "No one knows, do they?" *None,* though it comes from *no one,* almost always requires a plural verb when it refers to people ("Of the ten people present, none are students") and a singular verb when it refers to things ("Of the five assigned books, none is worth reading").

not only . . . but also Keep in mind these two points: (1) many readers object to the omission of "also" in such a sentence as "She not only brought up two children but practiced law," and (2) all readers dislike a faulty parallel, as in "She not only is bringing up two children but practices law." ("Is bringing up" needs to be paralleled with "is also practicing.")

not . . . un- Such an expression as "not unfamiliar" is useful only if it conveys something different from the affirmative. Compare the frostiness of "I am not unfamiliar with your methods" with "I am familiar with your methods." If the negative has no evident advantage, use the affirmative.

notorious Widely and unfavorably known; not merely famous, but famous for some discreditable trait or deed.

number, amount See *amount.*

a number of requires a plural verb: "A number of women are presidents of corporations." But when *number* is preceded by *the* it requires a singular verb: "The number of women who are presidents is small." (The plural noun after *number* of course may require a plural verb, as in "women are," but *the number* itself remains singular; hence its verb is singular, as in "is small.")

of Be careful not to use *of* when *have* is required. Not "He might of died in the woods," but "He might have died in the woods." Note that what we often hear as "would've" or "should've" or "must've" or "could've" is "would have" or "should have" or "must have" or "could have," *not* "would of," etc.

off of Use *off* or *from:* "Take if off the table"; "He jumped from the bridge."

often-times Use *often* instead.

old-fashioned, old-fashion Only the first is acceptable.

one British usage accepts the shift from *one* to *he* in "One begins to die the moment he is born," but American usage prefers "One begins to die the moment one is born." A shift from *one* to *you* ("One begins to die the moment you are born") is unacceptable. As a pronoun, *one* can be useful in impersonal statements such as the sentence about dying, at the beginning of this entry, where it means "a person," but don't use it as a disguise for yourself ("One objects to Smith's argument"). Try to avoid *one;* one *one* usually leads to another, resulting in a sentence that, in James Thurber's words, "sounds like a trombone solo" ("If one takes oneself too seriously, one begins to . . . "). See also *you.*

one of Takes a plural noun, and if this is followed by a clause, the preferred verb is plural: "one of those students who are," "one of those who feel." Thus, in such a sentence as "One of the coaches who have resigned is now seeking reinstatement," notice that "have" is correct; the antecedent of "who" (the subject of the verb) is "coaches," which is plural. Coaches have resigned, though "one . . . is seeking reinstatement." But in such an expression as "one out of a hundred," the following verb may be singular or plural ("One out of a hundred is," "One out of a hundred are").

only Be careful where you put it. The classic textbook example points out that in the sentence "I hit him in the eye," *only* can be inserted in seven places (beginning in front of "I" and ending after "eye") with at least six different meanings. Try to put it just before the expression it qualifies. Thus, not "Presidential aides are only responsible to one man," but "Presidential aides are responsible to only one man" (or "to one man only").

oral, verbal See *verbal.*

Oriental see *Asian.*

other Often necessary in comparisons. "No American president served as many terms as Franklin Roosevelt" falsely implies that Roosevelt was not an American president. The sentence should be revised to "No other American president served as many terms as Franklin Roosevelt."

per Usually it sounds needlessly technical ("twice per hour") or disturbingly impersonal ("as per your request"). Preferable: "twice an hour," "according to your request," or "as you requested."

per cent, percent, percentage The first two of these are interchangeable; both mean "per hundred," "out of a hundred," as in "Ninety per cent (or percent) of the students were white." *Per cent* and *percent* are always accompanied by a number (written out, or in figures). It is usually better to write out *per cent* or *percent* than to use a per cent sign (12%), except in technical or statistical papers. *Percentage* means "a proportion or share in relation to the whole," as in "A very large percentage of the student body is white." Many authorities insist that *percentage* is never preceded by a number. Do not use percentage to mean "a few," as in "Only a percentage of students attended the lecture"; a percentage can be as large as 99.99. It is usually said that with *per cent, percent,* and *percentage,* whether the verb is singular or plural depends on the number of the noun that follows the word, thus: "Ninety percent of his books are paperbacks"; "Fifty percent of his library is worthless"; "A large percentage of his books are worthless." But some readers (including the authors of this book) prefer a singular verb after *percentage* unless the resulting sentence is as grotesque as this one: "A large percentage of the students is unmarried." Still, rather than say a "percentage . . . are," we would recast the sentence: "A large percentage of the student body is unmarried," or "Many (or "Most," or whatever) of the students are unmarried."

per se Latin for "by itself." Usually sounds legalistic or pedantic, as in "Meter per se has an effect."

pessimistic See *fatalistic.*

phenomenon, phenomena The plural is *phenomena;* thus, "these phenomena" but "this phenomenon."

plus Unattractive and imprecise as a noun meaning "asset" or "advantage" ("When he applied for the job, his appearance was a plus"), and equally unattractive as a substitute for *moreover* ("The examination was easy, plus I had studied") or as a substitute for *and* ("I studied the introduction plus the first chapter").

politics Preferably singular ("Ethnic politics has been a strong force for a century") but a plural verb is acceptable.

precede, proceed To *precede* is to go before or ahead ("X precedes Y"). To *proceed* is to go forward ("The spelling lesson proceeded smoothly").

prejudice, prejudiced *Prejudice* is a noun: "It is impossible to live entirely without prejudice." But use the past participle *prejudiced* as an adjective: "He was prejudiced against me from the start."

preventative, preventive Both are acceptable but the second form is the form now used by writers on medicine ("preventive medicine"); *preventative* therefore has come to seem amateurish.

principal, principle *Principal* is (1) an adjective meaning "main," "chief," "most important" ("The principal arguments against IQ testing are three"), and (2) a noun meaning "the chief person" ("Ms. Murphy was the principal of Jefferson High") or "the chief thing" ("She had so much money she could live on the interest and not touch the principal"). *Principle* is always a noun meaning "rule" or "fundamental truth" ("It was against his principles to eat meat").

prior to Pretentious for *before.*

protagonist Literally, the first actor, and, by extension, the chief actor. It is odd, therefore, to speak of "the protagonists" in a single literary work or occurrence. Note also that the prefix is *proto,* "first," not *pro,* "for"; it does *not* mean one who strives for something.

quite Usually a word to delete, along with *definitely, pretty, rather,* and *very. Quite* used to mean "completely" ("I quite understand") but it has come also to mean "to a considerable degree," and so it is ambiguous as well as vague.

quotation, quote Quotation is a noun, quote is a verb. "I will quote Churchill" is fine, but not "these quotes from Churchill." And remember, you may *quote* one of Hamlet's speeches, but Hamlet does not *quote* them; he says them.

rather Avoid use with strong adjectives. "Rather intelligent" makes sense, but "rather tremendous" does not. "Rather brilliant" probably means "bright"; "rather terrifying" probably means "frightening," "rather unique" probably means "unusual." Get the right adjective, not *rather* and the wrong adjective.

the reason . . . is because Usually *because* is enough (not "The reason they fail is because they don't study," but simply "They fail because they don't study"). Similarly, *the reason why* can usually be reduced to *why.* Notice, too, that because *reason* is a noun, it cannot neatly govern a *because* clause: not "The reason for his absence is because he was sick," but "The reason for his absence was illness."

rebut, refute To rebut is to argue against, but not necessarily successfully. If you mean "to disprove," use *disprove* or *refute.*

in regard to, with regard to Often wordy for *about, concerning,* or *on,* and sometimes even these words are unnecessary. Compare: "He knew a great deal in regard to jazz"; "He knew a great deal about jazz." Compare: "Hemingway's story is often misunderstood with regard to Robert Wilson's treatment of Margot Macomber"; "In Hemingway's story, Robert Wilson's treatment of Margot Macomber is often misunderstood."

relate to Usually a vague expression, best avoided, as in "I can relate to Hedda Gabler." Does it mean "respond favorably to," "identify myself with," 'interact with" (and how can a reader "interact with" a character in a play?). Use *relate to* only in the sense of "have connection with" (as in "How does your answer relate to my question?"); even in such a sentence a more exact expression is preferable.

repel, repulse Both verbs mean "to drive back," but only *repel* can mean "to cause distaste," "to disgust," as in "His obscenities repelled the audience."

respectfully, respectively *Respectfully* means "with respect, showing respect" ("Japanese students and teachers bow respectfully to each other"). *Respectively* means "each in turn" ("Professors Arnott, Bahktian, and Cisneros teach, respectively, chemistry, business, and biology").

sarcasm Heavy, malicious sneering ("Oh you're really a great friend, aren't you?" addressed to someone who won't lend the speaker ten dollars). If the apparent praise, which really communicates dispraise, is at all clever, conveying, say, a delicate mockery or wryness, it is irony, not sarcasm.

seem Properly it suggests a suspicion that appearances may be deceptive: "He seems honest (but . . .)." Don't say "The book seems to lack focus" if you believe it does lack focus.

semiannually, semimonthly, semiweekly See *biannually.*

sexist language Language that takes males as the norm. For example, the use of *he* with reference to females as well as to males ("When a legislator votes, he takes account of his constituency"), like the use of *man* for all human beings ("Man is a rational animal"), is now widely perceived as subtly (or not so subtly) favoring males. See the entries on *he or she, man, mankind,* and *s/he.*

shall, will, should would The old principle held that in the first person *shall* is the future indicative of *to be* and *should* the conditional ("I shall go," "We should like to be asked"); and that *will* and *would* are the forms for the second and third persons. When the forms are reversed ("I will go," "Government of the people . . . shall not perish from the earth"), determination is expressed. But today almost nobody adheres to these principles. Indeed, *shall* (except in questions) sounds stilted to many ears.

s/he This new gender-free pronoun ("As soon as the student receives the forms, s/he should fill them out") is sometimes used in place of *he, or she* or *she or he,* which are used to avoid the sexism implied when the male pronoun "he" is used to stand for women as well as men ("As soon as the student receives the forms, he should fill them out"). Other, less noticeable ways of avoiding sexist writing are suggested under *he or she.*

simplistic Means "falsely simplified by ignoring complications." Do not confuse it with *simplified,* whose meanings include "reduced to essentials" and "clarified."

since, because Traditional objections to *since,* in the sense of "because," have all but vanished. Note, however, that when *since* is ambiguous and may also refer to time ("Since he joined the navy, she found another boyfriend") it is better to say *because* or *after,* depending on which you mean.

situation Overused, vague, and often unnecessary. "His situation was that he was unemployed" adds up to "He was unemployed." And "an emergency situation" is probably an emergency.

split infinitives The infinitive is the verb form that merely names the action, without indicating when or by whom performed ("walk," rather than "walked" or "I walk"). Grammarians, however, developed the idea that the infinitive was "to walk," and they held that one cannot separate or split the two words: "to quickly walk." But James Thurber says this idea is "of a piece with the sentimental and outworn notion that it is always wrong to strike a lady." Notice, however, that often the inserted word can be deleted ("to really understand" is "to understand"), and that if many words are inserted between *to* and the verb, the reader may get lost ("to quickly and in the remaining few pages before examining the next question conclude").

stanza See *verse.*

subjunctive For the use of the subjunctive with conditions contrary to fact (for instance, "If I were you"), see the entry on *was/were.* The subjunctive is also used in *that* clauses followed by verbs demanding, requesting, or recommending: "He asked that the students be prepared to take a test." But because this last sort of sentence sounds stiff, it is better to use an alternate construction, such as "He asked the students to prepare for a test."

than, then *Than* is used chiefly in making comparisons ("German is harder than French"), but also after "rather," "other," and "else" ("I'd rather take French than German"; "He thinks of nothing other than sex"). *Then* commonly indicates time ("She took German then, but now she takes French"; "Until then, I'll save you a seat"), but it may also mean "in that case" ("It's agreed, then, that we'll all go"), or "on the other hand" ("Then again, she may find German easy"). The simplest guide: use *than* after comparisons and after "rather," "other," "else"; otherwise use *then.*

that, which, who Many pages have been written on these words; opinions differ, but you will offend no one if you observe the following principles. (1) Use *that* in restrictive (that is, limiting) clauses: "The rocking chair that creaks is on the porch." (2) Use *which* in nonrestrictive (in effect, parenthetic) clauses: "The rocking chair, which creaks, is on the porch." (See pages 490-91.) The difference between these two sentences is this: in the first, one rocking chair is singled out from several—the one that creaks; in the second, the fact that the rocking chair creaks is simply tossed in, and is not added for the purpose of identifying the one chair out of several. (3) Use *who* for people, in restrictive and in nonrestrictive clauses: "The men who were playing poker ignored the women"; "The men, who were playing poker, ignored the women." But note that often *that, which,* and *who* can be omitted: "The creaky rocking chair is on the porch"; "The men, playing poker, ignored the women." In general, omit these words if the sentence remains clear. See page 96.

their, there, they're The first is possessive pronoun: "Chaplin and Keaton made their first films before sound tracks were developed." The second, *there,* sometimes refers to a place ("Go there," "Do you live there?"), and sometimes is what is known in grammar as an introductory expletive ("There are no solutions to this problem"). The third, *they're,* is a contraction of "they are" ("They're going to stay for dinner").

this Often refers vaguely to "what I have been saying." Does it refer to the previous sentence, the previous paragraph, the previous page? Try to modify it by being specific: "This last point"; "This clue gave the police all they needed."

thusly Unacceptable; *thus* is an adverb and needs no adverbial ending.

till, until Both are acceptable, but *until* is preferable because *till*—though common in speech—looks literary in print. The following are *not* acceptable: *til, 'til, 'till.*

to, too, two *To* is toward; *too* is either "also" ("She's a lawyer, too") or "excessively" ("It's too hot"); *two* is one more than one ("Two is company").

topic of See *area of.*

toward, towards Both are standard English; *toward* is more common in the United States, *towards* in Great Britain.

type Often colloquial (and unacceptable in most writing) for *type of,* as in "this type teacher." But *type of* is not especially pleasing either. Better to write "this kind of teacher." And avoid using *type* as a suffix: "essay-type examinations" are essay examinations; "natural-type ice cream" is natural ice cream. Sneaky manufacturers make "Italian-type cheese," implying that their domestic cheese is imported and at the same time protecting themselves against charges of misrepresentation.

unique The only one of its kind. Someone or something cannot be "rather unique" or "very unique" or "somewhat unique," any more than a woman can be somewhat pregnant. Instead of saying "rather unique," then, say *rare,* or *unusual,* or *extraordinary,* or whatever seems to be the best word.

U.S., United States Generally, *United States* is preferable to *U.S.;* similarly, *the Soviet Union* is preferable to *the U.S.S.R.*

usage Don't use *usage* where *use* will do, as in "Here Vonnegut completes his usage of dark images." *Usage* properly implies a customary practice that has created a standard: "Usage has eroded the difference between 'shall' and 'will.'"

use of The use of *use of* is usually unnecessary. "Through the use of setting he conveys a sense of foreboding" may be reduced to "The setting conveys . . . " or "His setting conveys . . . "

utilize, utilization Often inflated for *use* and *using,* as in "The infirmary has noted that it is sophomores who have most utilized the counseling service." But when one means "find an effective use for," *utilize* may be the best word, as in (here we borrow from *The American Heritage Dictionary*), "The teachers were unable to utilize the new computers," where *use* might wrongly suggest that the teachers could not operate the computers.

verbal Often used where *oral* would be more exact. *Verbal* simply means "expressed in words," and thus a *verbal agreement* may be either written or spoken. If you mean spoken, call it an *oral agreement.*

verse, stanza A *verse* is a single line of a poem; a *stanza* is a group of lines, commonly bound by a rhyme scheme. But in speaking or writing about songs, usage sanctions *verse* for *stanza,* as in "Second verse, same as the first."

viable A term from physiology, meaning "capable of living" (for example, referring to a fetus at a stage of its development). Now pretentiously used and overused, especially by politicians and journalists, to mean "workable," as in "a viable presidency." Avoid it.

was, were Use the subjunctive form—*were* (rather than *was*)—in expressing a wish ("I wish I were younger") and in "if-clauses" that are contrary to fact ("If I were rich," "If I were you . . . ").

we If you mean *I,* say *I.* Not "The first fairy tale we heard" but "the first fairy tale I heard." (But of course *we* is appropriate in some statements: "We have all heard fairy tales"; "If we look closely at the evidence, we can agree that. . . .") The rule: don't use *we* as a disguise for *I.* See pages 116-17.

well See *good.*

well known, widely known Athletes, performers, politicians, and such folk are not really *well known* except perhaps by a few of their friends and their relatives; use *widely known* if you mean they are known (however slightly) to many people.

which Often can be deleted. "Students are required to fill out scholarship applications which are lengthy" can be written "Students are required to fill out lengthy scholarship applications." Another example: "*The Tempest,* which is Shakespeare's last play, was written in 1611"; "*The Tempest,* Shakespeare's last play, was written in 1611," or "Shakespeare wrote his last play, *The Tempest,* in 1611." For the distinction between *which* and *that,* see also the entry on *that.*

while Best used in a temporal sense, meaning "during the time": "While I was speaking, I suddenly realized that I didn't know what I was talking about." While it is not wrong to use *while* in a nontemporal sense, meaning "although" (as at the beginning of this sentence), it is better to use *although* in order to avoid any ambiguity. Note the ambiguity in: "While he was fond of movies he chiefly saw westerns." Does it mean "Although he was fond of movies," or does it mean "During the time when he was fond of movies"? Another point: do not use *while* if you mean *and;* "Freshmen take English 1–2, while sophomores take English 10–11" (substitute *and* for *while*).

who, whom Strictly speaking, *who* must be used for subjects, even when they look like objects: "He guessed who would be chosen." (Here *who* is the subject of the clause "who would be chosen.") *Whom* must be used for the objects of a verb, verbal (gerund, participle), or preposition: "Whom did he choose?"; "Whom do you want me to choose?"; "To whom did he show it?" We may feel stuffy in writing "Whom did he choose?" or "Whom are you talking about?" but to use *who* is certain to annoy some reader. Often you can avoid the dilemma by rewriting: "Who was chosen?"; "Who is the topic of conversation?" See also the entry on *that.*

whoever, whomever The second of these is the objective form. It is often incorrectly used as the subject of a clause. "Open the class to whomever wants to take it" is incorrect. The object of "to" is not "whomever" but is the entire clause—"whoever wants to take it"—and of course "whoever" is the subject of "wants."

who's, whose The first is a contraction of *who is* ("I'm everybody who's nobody"). The second is a possessive pronoun: "Whose book is it?" "I know whose it is."

will, would See *shall* and also *would.*

would "I would think that" is a wordy version of "I think that." (On the mistaken use of *would of* for *would have,* see also the entry on *of.*

you In relatively informal writing, *you* is ordinarily preferable to the somewhat stiff *one:* "If you are addicted to cigarettes, you may find it helpful to join Smokenders." (Compare: "If one is addicted to cigarettes, one may . . . ") But because the direct address of *you* may sometimes descend into nagging, it is usually better to write: "Cigarette addicts may find it helpful . . . " Certainly a writer (you?) should not assume that the reader is guilty of vices ("You should not molest children") unless the essay is clearly aimed at an audience that admits to these vices, say a pamphlet directed to child molesters who are seeking help. Thus, it is acceptable to say, "If you are a poor speller," but it is not acceptable to say, to the general reader, "You should improve your spelling"; the reader's spelling may not need improvement. And avoid *you* when the word cannot possibly apply to the reader: "A hundred years ago you were faced with many diseases that now have been eradicated." Something like "A hundred years ago people were faced . . . " is preferable.

your, you're The first is a possessive pronoun ("your book"); the second is a contraction of *you are* ("You're mistaken").

Part Five

Additional Readings

Chapter 24

Maya Angelou

Maya Angelou, born in Saint Louis, Missouri, in 1938, grew up in Arkansas and California. She studied music, dance, and drama (she had a role in the televised version of Alex Haley's Roots*), and she is now a professor of American studies at Wake Forest University. She has also worked as a cook, streetcar conductor, and waitress. In addition to writing books of poetry, she has written five autobiographical volumes.*

"Graduation" (editors' title) comes from her first autobiography, I Know Why the Caged Bird Sings *(1969).*

Graduation

The children in Stamps trembled visibly with anticipation. Some adults were excited too, but to be certain the whole young population had come down with graduation epidemic. Large classes were graduating from both the grammar school and the high school. Even those who were years removed from their own day of glorious release were anxious to help with preparations as a kind of dry run. The junior students who were moving into the vacating classes' chairs were tradition-bound to show their talents for leadership and management. They strutted through the school and around the campus exerting pressure on the lower grades. Their authority was so new that occasionally if they pressed a little too hard it had to be overlooked. After all, next term was coming, and it never hurt a sixth grader to have a play sister in the eighth grade, or a tenth-year student to be able to call a twelfth grader Bubba. So all was endured in a spirit of shared understanding. But the graduating classes themselves were the nobility. Like travelers with exotic destinations on their minds, the graduates were remarkably forgetful. They came to school without their books, or tablets or even pencils. Volunteers fell over themselves to secure replacements for the missing equipment. When accepted, the willing workers might or might not be thanked, and it was of no importance to the pregraduation rites. Even teachers were respectful of the now quiet and aging seniors, and tended to speak to them, if not as equals, as beings only slightly lower than themselves. After tests were returned and grades given, the student body, which acted like an extended family, knew who did well, who excelled, and what piteous ones had failed.

Unlike the white high school, Lafayette County Training School distinguished itself by having neither lawn, nor hedges, nor tennis court, nor climbing ivy. Its two buildings (main classrooms, the grade school and home economics) were set on a dirt hill with no fence to limit either its boundaries or those of bordering farms. There was a large expanse to the left of the school which was used alternately as a baseball diamond or a basketball court. Rusty hoops on the swaying poles represented the permanent recreational equipment, although bats and balls could be borrowed from the P.E. teacher if the borrower was qualified and if the diamond wasn't occupied.

Over this rocky area relieved by a few shady tall persimmon trees the graduating class walked. The girls often held hands and no longer bothered to speak to the lower students. There was a sadness about them, as if this old world was not their home and they were bound for higher ground. The boys, on the other hand, had become more friendly, more outgoing. A decided change from the closed attitude they projected while studying for finals. Now they seemed not ready to give up the old school, the familiar paths and classrooms. Only a small percentage would be continuing on to college—one of the South's A & M (agricultural and mechanical) schools, which trained Negro youths to be carpenters, farmers, handymen, masons, maids, cooks and baby nurses. Their future rode heavily on their shoulders, and blinded them to the collective joy that had pervaded the lives of the boys and girls in the grammar school graduating class.

4   Parents who could afford it had ordered new shoes and ready-made clothes for themselves from Sears and Roebuck or Montgomery Ward. They also engaged the best seamstresses to make the floating graduating dresses and to cut down secondhand pants which would be pressed to a military slickness for the important event.

Oh, it was important, all right. Whitefolks would attend the ceremony, and two or three would speak of God and home, and the Southern way of life, and Mrs. Parsons, the principal's wife, would play the graduation march while the lower-grade graduates paraded down the aisles and took their seats below the platform. The high school seniors would wait in empty classrooms to make their dramatic entrance.

In the Store I was the person of the moment. The birthday girl. The center. Bailey had graduated the year before, although to do so he had had to forfeit all pleasures to make up for his time lost in Baton Rouge.

My class was wearing butter-yellow piqué dresses, and Momma launched out on mine. She smocked the yoke into tiny crisscrossing puckers, then shirred the rest of the bodice. Her dark fingers ducked in and out of the lemony cloth as she embroidered raised daisies around the hem. Before she considered herself finished she had added a crocheted cuff on the puff sleeves, and a pointy crocheted collar.

8   I was going to be lovely. A walking model of all the various styles of fine hand sewing and it didn't worry me that I was only twelve years old and merely graduating from the eighth grade. Besides, many teachers in Arkansas Negro schools had only that diploma and were licensed to impart wisdom.

    The days had become longer and more noticeable. The faded beige of former times had been replaced with strong and sure colors. I began to see my classmates' clothes, their skin tones, and the dust that waved off pussy willows. Clouds that lazed across the sky were objects of great concern to me. Their shiftier shapes might have held a message that in my new happiness and with a little bit of time I'd soon decipher. During that period I looked at the arch of heaven so religiously my neck kept a steady ache. I had taken to smiling more often, and my jaws hurt from the unaccustomed activity. Between the two physical sore spots, I suppose I could have been uncomfortable, but that was not the case. As a member of the winning team (the graduating class of 1940) I had outdistanced unpleasant sensations by miles. I was headed for the freedom of open fields.

    Youth and social approval allied themselves with me and we trammeled memories of slights and insults. The wind of our swift passage remodeled my features. Lost tears were pounded to mud and then to dust. Years of withdrawal were brushed aside and left behind, as hanging ropes of parasitic moss.

    My work alone had awarded me a top place and I was going to be one of the first called in the graduating ceremonies. On the classroom blackboard, as well as on the bulletin board in the auditorium, there were blue stars and white stars and red stars. No absences, no tardinesses, and my academic work was among the best of the year. I could say the preamble to the Constitution even faster than Bailey. We timed ourselves often: "WethepeopleoftheUnited-Statesinordertoformamoreperfect union. . . " I had memorized the Presidents of the United States from Washington to Roosevelt in chronological as well as alphabetical order.

12   My hair pleased me too. Gradually the black mass had lengthened and thickened, so that it kept at last to its braided pattern, and I didn't have to yank my scalp off when I tried to comb it.

    Louise and I had rehearsed the exercises until we tired out ourselves. Henry Reed was class valedictorian. He was a small, very black boy with hooded eyes, a long, broad nose and an oddly shaped head. I had admired him for years because each term he and I vied for the best grades in our class. Most often he bested me, but instead of being disappointed I was pleased that we shared top places between us. Like many Southern Black children, he lived with his grandmother, who was as strict as Momma and as kind as she knew how to be. He was courteous, respectful and soft-spoken to elders, but on the playground he chose to play the roughest games. I admired him. Anyone, I reckoned, sufficiently afraid or sufficiently dull could be polite. But to be able to operate at a top level with both adults and children was admirable.

His valedictory speech was entitled "To Be or Not To Be." The rigid tenth-grade teacher had helped him to write it. He'd been working on the dramatic stresses for months.

The weeks until graduation were filled with heady activities. A group of small children were to be presented in a play about buttercups and daisies and bunny rabbits. They could be heard throughout the building practicing their hops and their little songs that sounded like silver bells. The older girls (non-graduates, of course) were assigned the task of making refreshments for the night's festivities. A tangy scent of ginger, cinnamon, nutmeg and chocolate wafted around the home economics building as the budding cooks made samples for themselves and their teachers.

16   In every corner of the workshop, axes and saws split fresh timber as the woodshop boys made sets and stage scenery. Only the graduates were left out of the general bustle. We were free to sit in the library at the back of the building or look in quite detachedly, naturally, on the measures being taken for our event.

Even the minister preached on graduation the Sunday before. His subject was, "Let your light so shine that men will see your good works and praise your Father, Who is in Heaven." Although the sermon was purported to be addressed to us, he used the occasion to speak to backsliders, gamblers, and general ne'er-do-wells. But since he had called our names at the beginning of the service we were mollified.

Among Negroes the tradition was to give presents to children going only from one grade to another. How much more important this was when the person was graduating at the top of the class. Uncle Willie and Momma had sent away for a Mickey Mouse watch like Bailey's. Louise gave me four embroidered handkerchiefs. (I gave her three crocheted doilies.) Mrs. Sneed, the minister's wife, made me an underskirt to wear for graduation, and nearly every customer gave me a nickel or maybe even a dime with the instruction "Keep on moving to higher ground," or some such encouragement.

Amazingly the great day finally dawned and I was out of bed before I knew it. I threw open the back door to see it more clearly, but Momma said, "Sister, come away from that door and put your robe on."

20   I hoped the memory of that morning would never leave me. Sunlight was itself still young, and the day had none of the insistence maturity would bring it in a few hours. In my robe and barefoot in the backyard, under cover of going to see about my new beans, I gave myself up to the gentle warmth and thanked God that no matter what evil I had done in my life He had allowed me to live to see this day. Somewhere in my fatalism I had expected to die, accidentally, and never have the chance to walk up the stairs in the auditorium and gracefully

receive my hard-earned diploma. Out of God's merciful bosom I had won reprieve.

Bailey came out in his robe and gave me a box wrapped in Christmas paper. He said he had saved his money for months to pay for it. It felt like a box of chocolates, but I knew Bailey wouldn't save money to buy candy when we had all we could want under our noses.

He was as proud of the gift as I. It was a soft-leather-bound copy of a collection of poems by Edgar Allan Poe, or, as Bailey and I called him, "Eap." I turned to "Annabel Lee" and we walked up and down the garden rows, the cool dirt between our toes, reciting the beautifully sad lines.

Momma made a Sunday breakfast although it was only Friday. After we finished the blessing, I opened my eyes to find the watch on my plate. It was a dream of a day. Everything went smoothly and to my credit. I didn't have to be reminded or scolded for anything. Near evening I was too jittery to attend to chores, so Bailey volunteered to do all before his bath.

24   Days before, we had made a sign for the Store and as we turned out the lights Momma hung the cardboard over the doorknob. It read clearly: CLOSED. GRADUATION.

My dress fitted perfectly and everyone said that I looked like a sunbeam in it. On the hill, going toward the school, Bailey walked behind with Uncle Willie, who muttered, "Go on, Ju." He wanted him to walk ahead with us because it embarrassed him to have to walk so slowly. Bailey said he'd let the ladies walk together, and the men would bring up the rear. We all laughed, nicely.

Little children dashed by out of the dark like fireflies. Their crepe-paper dresses and butterfly wings were not made for running and we heard more than one rip, dryly, and the regretful "uh uh" that followed.

The school blazed without gaiety. The windows seemed cold and unfriendly from the lower hill. A sense of ill-fated timing crept over me, and if Momma hadn't reached for my hand I would have drifted back to Bailey and Uncle Willie, and possibly beyond. She made a few slow jokes about my feet getting cold, and tugged me along to the now-strange building.

28   Around the front steps, assurance came back. There were my fellow "greats," the graduating class. Hair brushed back, legs oiled, new dresses and pressed pleats, fresh pocket handkerchiefs and little handbags, all homesewn. Oh, we were up to snuff, all right. I joined my comrades and didn't even see my family go in to find seats in the crowded auditorium.

The school band struck up a march and all classes filed in as had been rehearsed. We stood in front of our seats, as assigned, and on a signal from the choir director, we sat. No sooner had this been accomplished than the band started to play the national anthem. We rose again and sang the song, after which we recited the pledge of allegiance. We remained standing for a brief minute before the choir director and the principal signaled to us, rather desperately I thought, to take our seats. The command was so unusual that our carefully rehearsed and smooth-running machine was thrown off. For a full minute we fumbled for our chairs and bumped into each other awkwardly. Habits change or solidify under pressure, so in our state of nervous tension we had been ready to follow our usual assembly pattern: the American National Anthem, then the pledge of allegiance, then the song every Black person I knew called the Negro National Anthem. All done in the same key, with the same passion and most often standing on the same foot.

Finding my seat at last, I was overcome with a presentiment of worse things to come. Something unrehearsed, unplanned, was going to happen, and we were going to be made to look bad. I distinctly remember being explicit in the choice of pronoun. It was "we," the graduating class, the unit, that concerned me then.

The principal welcomed "parents and friends" and asked the Baptist minister to lead us in prayer. His invocation was brief and punchy, and for a second I thought we were getting back on the high road to right action. When the principal came back to the dais, however, his voice had changed. Sounds always affected me profoundly and the principal's voice was one of my favorites. During assembly it melted and lowed weakly into the audience. It had not been in my plan to listen to him, but my curiosity was piqued and I straightened up to give him my attention.

32   He was talking about Booker T. Washington, our "late great leader," who said we can be as close as the fingers on the hand, etc. . . . Then he said a few vague things about friendship and the friendship of kindly people to those less fortunate than themselves. With that his voice nearly faded, thin, away. Like a river diminishing to a stream and then to a trickle. But he cleared his throat and said, "Our speaker tonight, who is also our friend, came from Texarkana to deliver the commencement address, but due to the irregularity of the train schedule, he's going to, as they say, 'speak and run.' " He said that we understood and wanted the man to know that we were most grateful for the time he was able to give us and then something about how we were willing always to adjust to another's program, and without more ado—"I give you Mr. Edward Donleavy."

Not one but two white men came through the door offstage. The shorter one walked to the speaker's platform, and the tall one moved over to the center seat and sat down. But that was our principal's seat, and already occupied. The dislodged gentleman bounced around for a long breath or two before the Baptist minister gave him his chair, then with more dignity than the situation deserved, the minister walked off the stage.

Donleavy looked at the audience once (on reflection, I'm sure that he wanted only to reassure himself that we were really there), adjusted his glasses and began to read from a sheaf of papers.

He was glad "to be here and to see the work going on just as it was in the other schools."

36   At the first "Amen" from the audience I willed the offender to immediate death by choking on the word. But Amen's and Yes, sir's began to fall around the room like rain through a ragged umbrella.

He told us of the wonderful changes we children in Stamps had in store. The Central School (naturally, the white school was Central) had already been granted improvements that would be in use in the fall. A well-known artist was coming from Little Rock to teach art to them. They were going to have the newest microscopes and chemistry equipment for their laboratory. Mr. Donleavy didn't leave us long in the dark over who made these improvements available to Central High. Nor were we to be ignored in the general betterment scheme he had in mind.

He said that he had pointed out to people at a very high level that one of the first-line football tacklers at Arkansas Agricultural and Mechanical College had graduated from good old Lafayette County Training School. Here fewer Amen's were heard. Those few that did break through lay dully in the air with the heaviness of habit.

He went on to praise us. He went on to say how he had bragged that "one of the best basketball players at Fisk sank his first ball right here at Lafayette County Training School."

40   The white kids were going to have a chance to become Galileos and Madame Curies and Edisons and Gauguins, and our boys (the girls weren't even in on it) would try to be Jesse Owenses and Joe Louises.

Owens and the Brown Bomber were great heroes in our world, but what school official in the white-goddom of Little Rock had the right to decide that those two men must be our only heroes? Who decided that for Henry Reed to become a scientist he had to work like George Washington Carver, as a bootblack, to buy a lousy microscope? Bailey was obviously always going to be too small to be an athlete, so which concrete angel glued to what country seat had decided that if my brother wanted to become a lawyer he had to first pay penance for his skin by picking cotton and hoeing corn and studying correspondence books at night for twenty years?

The man's dead words fell like bricks around the auditorium and too many settled in my belly. Constrained by hard-learned manners I couldn't look behind me, but to my left and right the proud graduating class of 1940 had dropped their heads. Every girl in my row had found something new to do with her handkerchief. Some folded the tiny squares into love knots, some into triangles, but most were wadding them, then pressing them flat on their yellow laps.

On the dais, the ancient tragedy was being replayed. Professor Parsons sat, a sculptor's reject, rigid. His large, heavy body seemed devoid of will or willingness, and his eyes said he was no longer with us. The other teachers examined the flag (which was draped stage right) or their notes, or the windows which opened on our now-famous playing diamond.

44   Graduation, the hush-hush magic time of frills and gifts and congratulations and diplomas, was finished for me before my name was called. The accomplishment was nothing. The meticulous maps, drawn in three colors of ink, learning and spelling decasyllabic words, memorizing the whole of *The Rape of Lucrece*—it was nothing. Donleavy had exposed us.

We were maids and farmers, handymen and washerwomen, and anything higher that we aspired to was farcical and presumptuous. Then I wished that Gabriel Prosser and Nat Turner had killed all whitefolks in their beds and that Abraham Lincoln had been assassinated before the signing of the Emancipation Proclamation, and that Harriet Tubman had been killed by that blow on her head and Christopher Columbus had drowned in the *Santa Maria.*

It was awful to be Negro and have no control over my life. It was brutal to be young and already trained to sit quietly and listen to charges brought against my color and no chance of defense. We should all be dead. I thought I should like to see us all dead, one on top of the other. A pyramid of flesh with the whitefolks on the bottom, as the broad base, then the Indians with their silly tomahawks and teepees and wigwams and treaties, the Negroes with their mops and recipes and cotton sacks and spirituals sticking out of their mouths. The Dutch children should all stumble in their wooden shoes and break their necks. The French should choke to death on the Louisiana Purchase (1803) while silkworms ate all the Chinese with their stupid pigtails. As a species, we were an abomination. All of us.

Donleavy was running for election, and assured our parents that if he won we could count on having the only colored paved playing field in that part of Arkansas. Also—he never looked up to acknowledge the grunts of acceptance— also, we were bound to get some new equipment for the home economics building and the workshop.

48   He finished, and since there was no need to give any more than the most perfunctory thank-you's, he nodded to the men on the stage, and the tall white man who was never introduced joined him at the door. They left with the attitude that now they were off to something really important. (The graduation ceremonies at Lafayette County Training School had been a mere preliminary.)

The ugliness they left was palpable. An uninvited guest who wouldn't leave. The choir was summoned and sang a modern arrangement of "Onward, Christian Soldiers," with new words pertaining to graduates seeking their place in the world. But it didn't work. Elouise, the daughter of the Baptist minister, recited "Invictus," and I could have cried at the impertinence of "I am the master of my fate, I am the captain of my soul."

My name had lost its ring of familiarity and I had to be nudged to go and receive my diploma. All my preparations had fled. I neither marched up to the stage like a conquering Amazon, nor did I look in the audience for Bailey's nod of approval. Marguerite Johnson, I heard the name again, my honors were read, there were noises in the audience of appreciation, and I took my place on the stage as rehearsed.

I thought about colors I hated: ecru, puce, lavender, beige and black.

52   There was shuffling and rustling around me, then Henry Reed was giving his valedictory address, "To Be or Not to Be." Hadn't he heard the whitefolks? We couldn't *be,* so the question was a waste of time. Henry's voice came out clear and strong. I feared to look at him. Hadn't he got the message? There was no "nobler in the mind" for Negroes because the world didn't think we had minds, and they let us know it. "Outrageous fortune"? Now, that was a joke. When the ceremony was over I had to tell Henry Reed some things. That is, if I still cared. Not "rub," Henry, "erase." "Ah, there's the erase." Us.

Henry had been a good student in elocution. His voice rose on tides of promise and fell on waves of warnings. The English teacher had helped him to create a sermon winging through Hamlet's soliloquy. To be a man, a doer, a builder, a leader, or to be a tool, an unfunny joke, a crusher of funky toadstools. I marveled that Henry could go through with the speech as if we had a choice.

I had been listening and silently rebutting each sentence with my eyes closed; then there was a hush, which in an audience warns that something unplanned is happening. I looked up and saw Henry Reed, the conservative, the proper, the A student, turn his back to the audience and turn to us (the proud graduating class of 1940) and sing, nearly speaking,

Lift ev'ry voice and sing
Till earth and heaven ring
Ring with the harmonies of Liberty . . .

It was the poem written by James Weldon Johnson. It was the music composed by J. Rosamond Johnson. It was the Negro National Anthem. Out of habit we were singing it.

Our mothers and fathers stood in the dark hall and joined the hymn of encouragement. A kindergarten teacher led the small children onto the stage and the buttercups and daisies and bunny rabbits marked time and tried to follow:

Stony the road we trod
Bitter the chastening rod
Felt in the days when hope, unborn, had died.
Yet with a steady beat
Have not our weary feet
Come to the place for which our fathers sighed?

56   Every child I knew had learned that song with his ABC's and along with "Jesus Loves Me This I Know." But I personally had never heard it before. Never

heard the words, despite the thousands of times I had sung them. Never thought they had anything to do with me.

On the other hand, the words of Patrick Henry had made such an impression on me that I had been able to stretch myself tall and trembling and say, "I know not what course others may take, but as for me, give me liberty or give me death."

And now I heard, really for the first time:

We have come over a way that with tears has been watered,
We have come, treading our path through the blood of the slaughtered.

While echoes of the song shivered in the air, Henry Reed bowed his head, said "Thank you," and returned to his place in the line. The tears that slipped down many faces were not wiped away in shame.

60   We were on top again. As always, again. We survived. The depths had been icy and dark, but now a bright sun spoke to our souls. I was no longer simply a member of the proud graduating class of 1940; I was a proud member of the wonderful, beautiful Negro race.

Oh, Black known and unknown poets, how often have your auctioned pains sustained us? Who will compute the lonely nights made less lonely by your songs, or the empty pots made less tragic by your tales?

If we were a people much given to revealing secrets, we might raise monuments and sacrifice to the memories of our poets, but slavery cured us of that weakness. It may be enough, however, to have it said that we survive in exact relationship to the dedication of our poets (include preachers, musicians and blues singers).

Topics for Discussion and Writing

1. In paragraph 1 notice such overstatements as "glorious release," "the graduating classes themselves were the nobility," and "exotic destinations." Find further examples in the next few pages. What do you think is the function of this diction?

2. Characterize the writer as you perceive her through paragraph 28. Support your characterization with references to specific passages. Next, characterize her in paragraph 46, which begins "It was awful to be Negro." Next, characterize her on the basis of the entire essay. Finally, in a sentence, try to describe the change, telling the main attitudes or moods that she goes through.

3. How would you define "poets" as Angelou uses the word in the last sentence?

Margaret Atwood

*Margaret Atwood, born in 1939 in Ottawa, Ontario, Canada, did her
undergraduate work at Victoria College and graduate work at Radcliffe College.
She has worked as a cashier, waitress, film writer, and teacher, but she began
writing as a child and established herself as a writer before she was thirty. In
addition to writing films, stories, novels, poetry, and criticism, she has edited
anthologies of Canadian literature.*

The essay that we reprint comes from the second volume of a collection entitled
The Writer on Her Work, *edited by Janet Sternberg, in which writers give their
responses to questions about writing.*

Nine Beginnings

---

1   1. *Why do you write?*

2   I've begun this piece nine times. I've junked each beginning.

3   I hate writing about my writing. I almost never do it. Why am I doing it now?
Because I said I would. I got a letter. I wrote back *no.* Then I was at a party and
the same person was there. It's harder to refuse in person. Saying *yes* had
something to do with being nice, as women are taught to be, and something to
do with being helpful, which we are also taught. Being helpful to women, giving
a pint of blood. With not claiming the sacred prerogatives, the touch-me-not self-
protectiveness of the artist, with not being selfish. With conciliation, with doing
your bit, with appeasement. I was well brought up. I have trouble ignoring social
obligations. Saying you'll write about your writing is a social obligation. It's not
an obligation to the writing.

4   2. *Why do you write?*

5   I've junked each of nine beginnings. They seemed beside the point. Too
assertive, too pedagogical, too frivolous or belligerent, too falsely wise. As if I
had some special self-revelation that would encourage others, or some special
knowledge to impart, some pithy saying that would act like a talisman for the
driven, the obsessed. But I have no such talismans. If I did, I would not continue,
myself, to be so driven and obsessed.

6   3. *Why do you write?*

7   I hate writing about my writing because I have nothing to say about it. I have
nothing to say about it because I can't remember what goes on when I'm doing

it. That time is like small pieces cut out of my brain. It's not time I myself have lived. I can remember the details of the rooms and places where I've written, the circumstances, the other things I did before and after, but not the process itself. Writing about writing requires self-consciousness; writing itself requires the abdication of it.

8   4. *Why do you write?*

9   There are a lot of things that can be said about what goes on around the edges of writing. Certain ideas you may have, certain motivations, grand designs that don't get carried out. I can talk about bad reviews, about sexist reactions to my writing, about making an idiot of myself on television shows. I can talk about books that failed, that never got finished, and about why they failed. The one that had too many characters, the one that had too many layers of time, red herrings that diverted me when what I really wanted to get at was something else, a certain corner of the visual world, a certain voice, an inarticulate landscape.

10   I can talk about the difficulties that women encounter as writers. For instance, if you're a woman writer, sometime, somewhere, you will be asked: *Do you think of yourself as a writer first, or as a woman first?* Look out. Whoever asks this hates and fears both writing and women.

11   Many of us, in my generation at least, ran into teachers or male writers or other defensive jerks who told us women could not really write because they couldn't be truck drivers or Marines and therefore didn't understand the seamier side of life, which included sex with women. We were told we wrote like housewives, or else we were treated like honorary men, as if to be a good writer was to suppress the female.

12   Such pronouncements used to be made as if they were the simple truth. Now they're questioned. Some things have changed for the better, but not all. There's a lack of self-confidence that gets instilled very early in many young girls, before writing is even seen as a possibility. You need a certain amount of nerve to be a writer, an almost physical nerve, the kind you need to walk a log across a river. The horse throws you and you get back on the horse. I learned to swim by being dropped into the water. You need to know you can sink, and survive it. Girls should be allowed to play in the mud. They should be released from the obligations of perfection. Some of your writing, at least, should be as evanescent as play.

13   A ratio of failures is built into the process of writing. The wastebasket has evolved for a reason. Think of it as the altar of the Muse Oblivion, to whom you sacrifice your botched first drafts, the tokens of your human imperfection. She is the tenth Muse, the one without whom none of the others can function. The gift she offers you is the freedom of the second chance. Or as many chances as you'll take.

14 5. *Why do you write?*

15 In the mid-eighties I began a sporadic journal. Today I went back through it, looking for something I could dig out and fob off as pertinent, instead of writing this piece about writing. but it was useless. There was nothing in it about the actual composition of anything I've written over the past six years. Instead there are exhortations to myself—to get up earlier, to walk more, to resist lures and distractions. *Drink more water,* I find. *Go to bed earlier.* There were lists of how many pages I'd written per day, how many I'd retyped, how many yet to go. Other than that, there was nothing but descriptions of rooms, accounts of what we'd cooked and/or eaten and with whom, letters written and received, notable sayings of children, birds and animals seen, the weather. What came up in the garden. Illnesses, my own and those of others. Deaths, births. Nothing about writing.

16 *January 1, 1984. Blakeny, England. As of today, I have about 130 pp. of the novel done and it's just beginning to take shape & reach the point at which I feel that it exists and can be finished and may be worth it. I work in the bedroom of the big house, and here, in the sitting room, with the wood fire in the fireplace and the coke fire in the dilapidated Roeburn in the kitchen. As usual I'm too cold, which is better than being too hot—today is grey, warm for the time of year, damp. If I got up earlier maybe I would work more, but I might just spend more time procrastinating—as now.*

17 And so on.

18 6. *Why do you write?*

19 You learn to write by reading and writing, writing and reading. As a craft it's acquired through the apprentice system, but you choose your own teachers. Sometimes they're alive, sometimes dead.

20 As a vocation, it involves the laying on of hands. You receive your vocation and in your turn you must pass it on. Perhaps you will do this only through your work, perhaps in other ways. Either way, you're part of a community, the community of writers, the community of storytellers that stretches back through time to the beginning of human society.

21 As for the particular human society to which you yourself belong—sometimes you'll feel you're speaking for it, sometimes—when it's taken an unjust form— against it, or for that other community, the community of the oppressed, the exploited, the voiceless. Either way, the pressures on you will be intense; in other countries, perhaps fatal. But even here—speak "for women," or for any other group which is feeling the boot, and there will be many at hand, both for and against, to tell you to shut up, or to say what they want you to say, or to say it a different way. Or to save them. The billboard awaits you, but if you succumb to its temptations you'll end up two-dimensional.

22 Tell what is yours to tell. Let others tell what is theirs.

23 7. *Why do you write?*

24 Why are we so addicted to causality? *Why do you write?* (Treatise by child psychologist, mapping your formative traumas. Conversely: palm-reading, astrology and genetic studies, pointing to the stars, fate, heredity.) *Why do you write?* (That is, why not do something useful instead?) If you were a doctor, you could tell some acceptable moral tale about how you put Band-Aids on your cats as a child, how you've always longed to cure suffering. No one can argue with that. But writing? What is it *for?*

25 Some possible answers: *Why does the sun shine? In the face of the absurdity of modern society, why do anything else? Because I'm a writer. Because I want to discover the patterns in the chaos of time. Because I must. Because someone has to bear witness. Why do you read?* (This last is tricky: maybe they don't.) *Because I wish to forge in the smithy of my soul the uncreated conscience of my race. Because I wish to make an axe to break the frozen sea within.*[1] (These have been used, but they're good.)

26 If at a loss, perfect the shrug. Or say: *It's better than working in a bank.* Or say: *For fun.* If you say this, you won't be believed, or else you'll be dismissed as trivial. Either way, you'll have avoided the question.

27 8. *Why do you write?*

28 Not long ago, in the course of clearing some of the excess paper out of my workroom, I opened a filing cabinet drawer I hadn't looked into for years. In it was a bundle of loose sheets, folded, creased, and grubby, tied up with leftover string. It consisted of things I'd written in the late fifties, in high school and the early years of university. There were scrawled, inky poems, about snow, despair, and the Hungarian Revolution. There were short stories dealing with girls who'd had to get married, and dispirited, mousy-haired high-school English teachers— to end up as either was at that time my vision of Hell—typed finger-by-finger on an ancient machine that made all the letters half-red.

29 There I am, then, back in grade twelve, going through the writers' magazines after I'd finished my French Composition homework, typing out my lugubrious poems and my grit-filled stories. (I was big on grit. I had an eye for lawn-litter and dog turds on sidewalks. In these stories it was usually snowing damply, or raining; at the very least there was slush. If it was summer, the heat and humidity were always wiltingly high and my characters had sweat marks under their arms; if it was spring, wet clay stuck to their feet. Though some would say all this was just normal Toronto weather.)

[1] The passage about the smithy is from the end of James Joyce's novel, *A Portrait of the Artist as a Young Man* (1916). The next sentence, about an axe to break the frozen sea wiithin us, is from a letter (1904) by Franz Kafka. Each passage is offered by the author as an explanation of why he writes. [Editor's note]

30 In the top right-hand corners of some of these, my hopeful seventeen-year-old self had typed, "First North American Rights Only." I was not sure what "First North American Rights" were; I put it in because the writing magazines said you should. I was at that time an aficionado of writing magazines, having no one else to turn to for professional advice.

31 If I were an archeologist, digging through the layers of old paper that mark the eras in my life as a writer, I'd have found, at the lowest or Stone Age level—say around ages five to seven—a few poems and stories, unremarkable precursors of all my frenetic later scribbling. (Many children write at that age, just as many children draw. The strange thing is that so few of them go on to become writers or painters.) After that there's a great blank. For eight years, I simply didn't write. Then, suddenly, and with no missing links in between, there's a wad of manuscripts. One week I wasn't a writer, the next I was.

32 Who did I think I was, to be able to get away with this? What did I think I was doing? How did I get that way? To these questions I still have no answers.

33 *9. Why do you write?*

34 There's the blank page, and the thing that obsesses you. There's the story that wants to take you over and there's your resistance to it. There's your longing to get out of this, this servitude, to play hooky, to do anything else: wash the laundry, see a movie. There are words and their inertias, their biases, their insufficiencies, their glories. There are the risks you take and your loss of nerve, and the help that comes when you're least expecting it. There's the laborious revision, the scrawled-over, crumpled-up pages that drift across the floor like spilled litter. There's the one sentence you know you will save.

35 Next day there's the blank page. You give yourself up to it like a sleepwalker. Something goes on that you can't remember afterwards. You look at what you've done. It's hopeless.

36 You begin again. It never gets any easier.

Topics for Discussion and Writing

1. In her first try, Atwood doesn't answer the question "Why do you write?" What question does she answer and how does she answer it?

2. The beginning of her second try, like the beginning of her first, tells us that she began nine times and "junked each of nine beginnings." But we can see that there are nine beginnings here. What is going on? Why has she not "junked" these?

3. Atwood says in her third try, "Writing about writing requires self-consciousness; writing itself requires the abdication of it." What does it mean to abdicate self-consciousness? How do you think abdicating self-consciousness affects or would affect your writing?

4. In her sixth try, Atwood says, "You learn to write by reading and writing, writing and reading." To what extent do you agree? What have you learned about writing by reading or by writing? What have you learned about writing—and writers—from reading "Nine Beginnings?"

5. Why does Atwood write?

Black Elk

Black Elk, a wichasha wakon *(holy man) of the Oglala Sioux, as a small boy witnessed the Battle of Little Bighorn (1876). He lived to see his people all but annihilated and his hopes for them extinguished. In 1931, toward the end of his life, he told his life story to the poet and scholar John G. Neihardt in order to preserve a sacred vision given him. "High Horse's Courting" provides a comic interlude in a predominantly tragic memoir.*

High Horse's Courting

You know, in the old days, it was not so very easy to get a girl when you wanted to be married. Sometimes it was hard work for a young man and he had to stand a great deal. Say I am a young man and I have seen a young girl who looks so beautiful to me that I feel all sick when I think about her. I can not just go and tell her about it and then get married if she is willing. I have to be a very sneaky fellow to talk to her at all, and after I have managed to talk to her, that is only the beginning.

Probably for a long time I have been feeling sick about a certain girl because I love her so much, but she will not even look at me, and her parents keep a good watch over her. But I keep feeling worse and worse all the time; so maybe I sneak up to her tepee in the dark and wait until she comes out. Maybe I just wait there all night and don't get any sleep at all and she does not come out. Then I feel sicker than ever about her.

Maybe I hide in the brush by a spring where she sometimes goes to get water, and when she comes by, if nobody is looking, then I jump out and hold her and just make her listen to me. If she likes me too, I can tell that from the way she acts, for she is very bashful and maybe will not say a word or even look at me the first time. So I let her go, and then maybe I sneak around until I can see her father alone, and I tell him how many horses I can give him for his beautiful girl, and by now I am feeling so sick that maybe I would give him all the horses in the world if I had them.

4 Well, this young man I am telling about was called High Horse, and there was a girl in the village who looked so beautiful to him that he was just sick all over from thinking about her so much and he was getting sicker all the time. The girl was very shy, and her parents thought a great deal of her because they were not young any more and this was the only child they had. So they watched her all day long, and they fixed it so that she would be safe at night too when they were asleep. They thought so much of her that they had made a rawhide bed for her to sleep in, and after they knew that High Horse was sneaking around after her, they took rawhide thongs and tied the girl in bed at night so that nobody could steal her when they were asleep, for they were not sure but that their girl might really want to be stolen.

Well, after High Horse had been sneaking around a good while and hiding and waiting for the girl and getting sicker all the time, he finally caught her alone and made her talk to him. Then he found out that she liked him maybe a little. Of course this did not make him feel well. It made him sicker than ever, but now he felt as brave as a bison bull, and so he went right to her father and said he loved the girl so much that he would give two good horses for her—one of them young and the other one not so very old.

But the old man just waved his hand, meaning for High Horse to go away and quit talking foolishness like that.

High Horse was feeling sicker than ever about it; but there was another young fellow who said he would loan High Horse two ponies and when he got some more horses, why, he could just give them back for the ones he had borrowed.

8 Then High Horse went back to the old man and said he would give four horses for the girl—two of them young and the other two not hardly old at all. But the old man just waved his hand and would not say anything.

So High Horse sneaked around until he could talk to the girl again, and he asked her to run away with him. He told her he thought he would just fall over and die if she did not. But she said she would not do that; she wanted to be bought like a fine woman. You see she thought a great deal of herself too.

That made High Horse feel so very sick that he could not eat a bite, and he went around with his head hanging down as though he might just fall down and die any time.

Red Deer was another young fellow, and he and High Horse were great comrades, always doing things together. Red Deer saw how High Horse was acting, and he said: "Cousin, what is the matter? Are you sick in the belly? You look as though you were going to die."

12 Then High Horse told Red Deer how it was, and said he thought he could not stay alive much longer if he could not marry the girl pretty quick.

Red Deer thought awhile about it, and then he said: "Cousin, I have a plan, and if you are man enough to do as I tell you, then everything will be all right.

She will not run away with you; her old man will not take four horses; and four horses are all you can get. You must steal her and run away with her. Then afterwhile you can come back and the old man cannot do anything because she will be your woman. Probably she wants you to steal her anyway."

So they planned what High Horse had to do, and he said he loved the girl so much that he was man enough to do anything Red Deer or anybody else could think up.

So this is what they did.

16   That night late they sneaked up to the girl's tepee and waited until it sounded inside as though the old man and the old woman and the girl were sound asleep. Then High Horse crawled under the tepee with a knife. He had to cut the rawhide thongs first, and then Red Deer, who was pulling up the stakes around that side of the tepee, was going to help drag the girl outside and gag her. After that, High Horse could put her across his pony in front of him and hurry out of there and be happy all the rest of his life.

When High Horse had crawled inside, he felt so nervous that he could hear his heart drumming, and it seemed so loud he felt sure it would 'waken the old folks. But it did not, and afterwhile he began cutting the thongs. Every time he cut one it made a pop and nearly scared him to death. But he was getting along all right and all the thongs were cut down as far as the girl's thighs, when he became so nervous that his knife slipped and stuck the girl. She gave a big, loud yell. Then the old folks jumped up and yelled too. By this time High Horse was outside, and he and Red Deer were running away like antelope. The old man and some other people chased the young men but they got away in the dark and nobody knew who it was.

Well, if you ever wanted a beautiful girl you will know how sick High Horse was now. It was very bad the way he felt, and it looked as though he would starve even if he did not drop over dead sometime.

Red Deer kept thinking about this, and after a few days he went to High Horse and said: "Cousin, take courage! I have another plan, and I am sure, if you are man enough, we can steal her this time." And High Horse said: "I am man enough to do anything anybody can think up, if I can only get that girl."

20   So this is what they did.

They went away from the village alone, and Red Deer made High Horse strip naked. Then he painted High Horse solid white all over, and after that he painted black stripes all over the white and put black rings around High Horse's eyes. High Horse looked terrible. He looked so terrible that when Red Deer was through painting and took a good look at what he had done, he said it scared even him a little.

"Now," Red Deer said, "if you get caught again, everybody will be so scared they will think you are a bad spirit and will be afraid to chase you."

So when the night was getting old and everybody was sound asleep, they sneaked back to the girl's tepee. High Horse crawled in with his knife, as before, and Red Deer waited outside, ready to drag the girl out and gag her when High Horse had all the thongs cut.

24   High Horse crept up by the girl's bed and began cutting at the thongs. But he kept thinking, "If they see me they will shoot me because I look so terrible." The girl was restless and kept squirming around in bed, and when a thong was cut, it popped. So High Horse worked very slowly and carefully.

But he must have made some noise, for suddenly the old woman awoke and said to her old man: "Old Man, wake up! There is somebody in this tepee!" But the old man was sleepy and didn't want to be bothered. He said: "Of course there is somebody in this tepee. Go to sleep and don't bother me." Then he snored some more.

But High Horse was so scared by now that he lay very still and as flat to the ground as he could. Now, you see, he had not been sleeping very well for a long time because he was so sick about the girl. And while he was lying there waiting for the old woman to snore, he just forgot everything, even how beautiful the girl was. Red Deer who was lying outside ready to do his part, wondered and wondered what had happened in there, but he did not dare call out to High Horse.

Afterwhile the day began to break and Red Deer had to leave with the two ponies he had staked there for his comrade and girl, or somebody would see him.

28   So he left.

Now when it was getting light in the tepee, the girl awoke and the first thing she saw was a terrible animal, all white with black stripes on it, lying asleep beside her bed. So she screamed, and then the old woman screamed and the old man yelled. High Horse jumped up, scared almost to death, and he nearly knocked the tepee down getting out of there.

People were coming running from all over the village with guns and bows and axes, and everybody was yelling.

By now High Horse was running so fast that he hardly touched the ground at all, and he looked so terrible that the people fled from him and let him run. Some braves wanted to shoot at him, but the others said he might be some sacred being and it would bring bad trouble to kill him.

32   High Horse made for the river that was near, and in among the brush he found a hollow tree and dived into it. Afterwhile some braves came there and he could hear them saying that it was some bad spirit that had come out of the water and gone back in again.

That morning the people were ordered to break camp and move away from there. So they did, while High Horse was hiding in his hollow tree.

Now Red Deer had been watching all this from his own tepee and trying to look as though he were as much surprised and scared as all the others. So when the camp moved, he sneaked back to where he had seen his comrade disappear. When he was down there in the brush, he called, and High Horse answered, because he knew his friend's voice. They washed off the paint from High Horse and sat down on the river bank to talk about their troubles.

High Horse said he never would go back to the village as long as he lived and he did not care what happened to him now. He said he was going to go on the war-path all by himself. Red Deer said: "No, cousin, you are not going on the war-path alone, because I am going with you."

36   So Red Deer got everything ready, and at night they started out on the war-path all alone. After several days they came to a Crow camp just about sundown, and when it was dark they sneaked up to where the Crow horses were grazing, killed the horse guard, who was not thinking about enemies because he thought all the Lakotas were far away, and drove off about a hundred horses.

They got a big start because all the Crow horses stampeded and it was probably morning before the Crow warriors could catch any horses to ride. Red Deer and High Horse fled with their herd three days and nights before they reached the village of their people. Then they drove the whole herd right into the village and up in front of the girl's tepee. The old man was there, and High Horse called out to him and asked if he thought maybe that would be enough horses for his girl. The old man did not wave him away this time. It was not the horses that he wanted. What he wanted was a son who was a real man and good for something.

So High Horse got his girl after all, and I think he deserved her.

Topics for Discussion and Writing

1. The story "High Horse's Courting" is told by Black Elk, an Oglala Sioux holy man. Though High Horse's behavior is amusing and at times ridiculous, how does Black Elk make it clear that he is not ridiculing the young man, but is instead sympathetic with him? Consider the following questions:

   a. What is the effect of the first three paragraphs? Consider the first two sentences, and then the passage beginning "Say I am a young man . . . " and ending ". . . I would give him all the horses in the world if I had them."

   b. Describe the behavior of the young girl, and of her father and mother. How do they contribute to the comedy? How does their behavior affect your understanding of Black Elk's attitude toward High Horse?

   c. What is the function of Red Deer?

   d. The narrative consists of several episodes. List them in the order in which they occur, and then describe the narrative's structure. How does the structure of the narrative affect the tone?

   e. What is the effect of the last two sentences?

2. What similarities, if any, are there between the courting customs and attitudes toward courting that Black Elk describes and those you are familiar with? Consider the behavior and attitudes not only of High Horse, the girl, her parents, and his friend, but also of the old man who tells the story.

Sissela Bok

Sissela Bok teaches courses in medical ethics and in decision-making at the Harvard Medical School. She is the author of Lying, *a book concerned with such problems as whether or not to lie to people for their own good.*

To Lie or Not to Lie?—The Doctor's Dilemma

Should doctors ever lie to benefit their patients—to speed recovery or to conceal the approach of death? In medicine as in law, government, and other lines of work, the requirements of honesty often seem dwarfed by greater needs: the need to shelter from brutal news or to uphold a promise of secrecy; to expose corruption or to promote the public interest.

What should doctors say, for example, to a forty-six-year-old man coming in for a routine physical checkup just before going on vacation with his family who, though he feels in perfect health, is found to have a form of cancer that will cause him to die within six months? Is it best to tell him the truth? If he asks, should the doctors deny that he is ill, or minimize the gravity of the prognosis? Should they at least conceal the truth until after the family vacation?

Doctors confront such choices often and urgently. At times, they see important reasons to lie for the patient's own sake; in their eyes, such lies differ sharply from self-serving ones.

4   Studies show that most doctors sincerely believe that the seriously ill do not want to know the truth about their condition, and that informing them risks destroying their hope, so that they may recover more slowly, or deteriorate faster, perhaps even commit suicide. As one physician wrote: "Ours is a profession which traditionally has been guided by a precept that transcends the virtue of uttering the truth for truth's sake, and that is 'as far as possible do no harm.'"

Armed with such a precept, a number of doctors may slip into deceptive practices that they assume will "do no harm" and may well help their patients. They may prescribe innumerable placebos, sound more encouraging than the facts warrant, and distort grave news, especially to the incurably ill and the dying.

But the illusory nature of the benefits such deception is meant to bestow is now coming to be documented. Studies show that, contrary to the belief of many physicians, an overwhelming majority of patients do want to be told the truth, even about grave illness, and feel betrayed when they learn that they have been misled. We are also learning that truthful information, humanely conveyed, helps patients cope with illness: helps them tolerate pain better, need less medication, and even recover faster after surgery.

Not only do lies not provide the "help" hoped for by advocates of benevolent deception; they invade the autonomy of patients and render them unable to make informed choices concerning their own health, including the choice of whether to *be* a patient in the first place. We are becoming increasingly aware of all that can be fall patients in the course of their illness when information is denied or distorted.

8   Dying patients especially—who are easiest to mislead and most often kept in the dark—can then not make decisions about the end of life: about whether or not to enter a hospital, or to have surgery; about where and with whom to spend their remaining time; about how to bring their affairs to a close and take leave.

Lies also do harm to those who tell them: harm to their integrity and, in the long run, to their credibility. Lies hurt their colleagues as well. The suspicion of deceit undercuts the work of the many doctors who are scrupulously honest with their patients; it contributes to the spiral of litigation and of "defensive medicine," and thus it injures, in turn, the entire medical profession.

Sharp conflicts are now arising. Patients are learning to press for answers. Patients' bills of rights require that they be informed about their condition and about alternatives for treatment. Many doctors go to great lengths to provide such information. Yet even in hospitals with the most eloquent bill of rights, believers in benevolent deception continue their age-old practices. Colleagues may disapprove but refrain from remonstrating. Nurses may bitterly resent having to take part, day after day, in deceiving patients, but feel powerless to take a stand.

There is urgent need to debate this issue openly. Not only in medicine, but in other professions as well, practitioners may find themselves repeatedly in straits where serious consequences seem avoidable only through deception. Yet the public has every reason to be wary of professional deception, for such practices are peculiarly likely to become ingrained, to spread, and to erode trust. Neither in medicine, nor in law, government, or the social sciences can there be comfort in the old saw, "What you don't know can't hurt you."

Topics for Discussion and Writing

1. Is there anything in Bok's opening paragraph that prepares the reader for Bok's own position on whether or not lying is ever justifiable?

2. List the reasons Bok offers on behalf of telling the truth to patients. Are some of these reasons presented more convincingly than others? If any are unconvincing, rewrite them to make them more convincing.

3. Suppose Bok's last sentence was revised to read thus: "In medicine, law, government, and the social sciences, what you don't know *can* hurt you." Which version do you prefer, and why?

4. "What you don't know can't hurt you." Weigh the truth of this assertion in your own life. Were there instances of a truth being withheld from you that did hurt you? Were there occasions when you were told a truth that you now judge would have been better withheld? On the whole, do you come out in favor of the assertion, against it, or somewhere in between?

5. How much should adopted children be told about their biological parents? Consider reasons both for and against telling all. Use not only your own experiences and opinions but those of others, such as friends and class-mates.

Jorge Luis Borges

Jorge Luis Borges (1899–1986), one of the first writers of Spanish to achieve an international reputation, was born in Buenos Aires. In the early 1920s he began to establish himself as a writer, and in 1938 he accepted a post as municipal librarian in Buenos Aires, but in 1946—by which time Borges's fiction had won him an international reputation—the dictator Juan Perón removed him from the post. In 1955, after Perón was deposed, Borges was made director of the National Library of Buenos Aires, and in 1956 he was appointed Professor of English Literature at the University of Buenos Aires. For Borges, narratives were not representations of the surface of life but were re-creations of the cultural myths that human beings have devised.

The Gaucho and the City: Stories of Horsemen

They are many and they may be countless. My first story is quite modest; those that follow will lend it greater depth.

A rancher from Uruguay had bought a country establishment (I am sure this is the word he used) in the province of Buenos Aires. From Paso de los Toros, in the middle of Uruguay, he brought a horse breaker, a man who had his complete trust but was extremely shy. The rancher put the man up in an inn near the Once markets. Three days later, on going to see him, the rancher found his horseman brewing maté in his room on the upper floor. When asked what he thought of Buenos Aires, the man admitted that he had not once stuck his head out in the street.

The second story is not much different. In 1903, Aparicio Saravia staged an uprising in the Uruguayan provinces; at a certain point of the campaign, it was feared that his men might break into Montevideo. My father, who happened to be there at the time, went to ask advice of a relative of his, the historian Luis Melián Lafinur, only to be told that there was no danger "because the gaucho stands in fear of cities." In fact, Saravia's troops did change their route, and somewhat to his amazement my father found out that the study of history could be useful as well as pleasurable.

4 My third story also belongs to the oral tradition of my family. Toward the end of 1870, forces of the Entre Ríos caudillo, López Jordán, commanded by a gaucho who was called (because he had a bullet embedded in him) "El Chumbiao," surrounded the city of Parana. One night, catching the garrison off guard, the rebels broke through the defenses and rode right around the central square, whooping like Indians and hurling insults. Then, still shouting and whistling, they galloped off. To them war was not a systematic plan of action but a manly sport.

The fourth of these stories, and my last, comes from the pages of an excellent book, *L'Empire des Steppes* (1939), by the Orientalist René Grousset. Two passages from the second chapter are particularly relevant. Here is the first:

> Genghis Khan's war against the Chin, begun in 1211, was the last—with brief periods of truce—until his death (1227), only to be finished by his successor (1234). With their mobile cavalry, the Mongols could devastate the countryside and open settlements, but for a long time they knew nothing of the art of taking towns fortified by Chinese engineers. Besides, they fought in China as on the steppe, in a series of raids, after which they withdrew with their booty, leaving the Chinese behind them to reoccupy their towns, rebuild the ruins, repair the breaches in the walls, and reconstruct the fortifications, so that in the course of that war the Mongol generals found themselves obliged to reconquer the same places two or three times.

Here is the second passage:

> The Mongols took Peking, massacred the whole population, looted the houses, and then set fire to them. The devastation lasted a month. Clearly, the nomads had no idea what to do with a great city or how to use it for the consolidation and expansion of their power. We have here a highly interesting case for specialists in human geography: the predicament of the peoples of the steppe when, without a period of transition, chance hands them old countries with an urban civilization.

They burn and kill not out of sadism but because they find themselves out of their element and simply know no better.

I now give a story that all the authorities agree upon. During Genghis Khan's last campaign, one of his generals remarked that his new Chinese subjects were of no use to him, since they were inept in war, and that, consequently, the wisest course was to exterminate them all, raze the cities, and turn the almost boundless Middle Kingdom into one enormous pasture for the Mongol horses. In this way, at least, use could be made of the land, since nothing else was of any value. The Khan was about to follow this counsel when another adviser pointed out to him that it would be more advantageous to levy taxes on the land and on goods. Civilization was saved, the Mongols grew old in the cities that they had once longed to destroy, and doubtless they ended up, in symmetrical gardens, appreciating the despised and peaceable arts of prosody and pottery.

Distant in time and space, the stories I have assembled are really one. The protagonist is eternal, and the wary ranch hand who spends three days behind a door that looks out into a backyard—although he has come down in life—is the same one who, with two bows, a lasso made of horse hair, and a scimitar, was poised to raze and obliterate the world's most ancient kingdom under the hooves of his steppe pony. There is a pleasure in detecting beneath the masks of time the eternal species of horseman and city. This pleasure, in the case of these stories, may leave the Argentine with a melancholy aftertaste, since (through Hernández's gaucho, Martín Fierro, or through the weight of our past) we identify with the horseman, who in the end is the loser. The centaurs defeated by the Lapiths; the death of the shepherd Abel at the hand of Cain, who was a farmer; the defeat of Napoleon's cavalry by British infantry at Waterloo are all emblems and portents of such a destiny.

8   The horseman vanishing into the distance with a hint of defeat is, in our literature, the gaucho. And so we read in *Martín Fierro:*

Cruz y Fierro de una estancia
una tropilla se arriaron;
por delante se la echaron
como criollos entendidos,
y pronto, sin ser sentidos,
por la frontera cruzaron.

Y cuando la habían pasao,
una madrugada clara,
le dijo Cruz que mirara
las últimas poblaciones;
y a Fierro dos lagrimones
le rodaron por la cara.

Y siguiendo el fiel del rumbo
se entraron en el desierto . . .

From a ranch, Cruz and Fierro rounded up a herd of horses and, being practical gauchos, drove it before them. Undetected, they soon crossed over the border.

After this was done, early one morning Cruz told Fierro to look back on the last settlements. Two big tears rolled down Fierro's face.

Then, continuing on their course, the men set off into the wilderness . . .

And in Lugones's *El Payador:*

In the fading twilight, turning brown as a dove's wing, we may have seen him vanish beyond the familiar hillocks, trotting on his horse, slowly, so that no one would think him afraid, under his gloomy hat and the poncho that hung from his shoulders in the limp folds of a flag at half mast.

12   And in *Don Segundo Sombra:*

Still smaller now, my godfather's silhouette appeared on the slope. My eyes concentrated on that tiny movement on the sleepy plain. He was about to reach the crest of the trail and vanish. He grew smaller and smaller, as if he were being whittled away from below. My gaze clung to the black speck of his hat, trying to preserve that last trace of him.

In the texts just quoted, space stands for time and history.

The figure of the man on the horse is, secretly, poignant. Under Attila, the "Scourage of God," under Genghis Khan, and under Tamerlane, the horseman tempestuously destroys and founds extensive empires, but all he destroys and founds is illusory. His work, like him, is ephemeral. From the farmer comes the word "culture" and from cities the word "civilization," but the horseman is a storm that fades away. In his book *Die Germanen der Volkerwanderung* (Stuttgart, 1939), Capelle remarks apropos of this that the Greeks, the Romans, and the Germans were agricultural peoples.

Topics for Discussion and Writings

1. Are you a city person or a country (farm, mountain) person? Explain, in an essay of 250 to 500 words.

2. Briefly set forth a narrative of a kind of person (again, city, farm, mountain, or similar category) and then offer a paragraph of reflection on the kind. (If, like Borges, you can give more than one narrative, do so.)

Judy Brady

Judy Brady was born in San Francisco in 1937. She received a bachelor's degree from the University of Iowa in 1960 and wanted to do the graduate work that would qualify her for teaching in a university, but her male teachers discouraged her. "Why I Want a Wife" originally appeared in 1971, in the first issue of Ms.

Why I Want a Wife

I belong to that classification of people known as wives. I am A Wife. And, not altogether incidentally, I am a mother.

Not too long ago a male friend of mine appeared on the scene fresh from a recent divorce. He had one child, who is, of course, with his ex-wife. He is looking for another wife. As I thought about him while I was ironing one evening, it suddenly occurred to me that I, too, would like to have a wife. Why do I want a wife?

I would like to go back to school so that I can become economically independent, support myself, and, if need be, support those dependent upon me. I want a wife who will work and send me to school. And while I am going to school I want a wife to take care of my children. I want a wife to keep track of the children's doctor and dentist appointments. And to keep track of mine, too. I want a wife to make sure my children eat properly and are kept clean. I want a wife who will wash the children's clothes and keep them mended. I want a wife who is a good nurturant attendant to my children, who arranges for their schooling, makes sure that they have an adequate social life with their peers, takes them to the park, the zoo, etc. I want a wife who takes care of the children when they are sick, a wife who arranges to be around when the children need special care, because, of course, I cannot miss classes at school. My wife must arrange to lose time at work and not lose the job. It may mean a small cut in my wife's income from time to time, but I guess I can tolerate that. Needless to say, my wife will arrange and pay for the care of the children while my wife is working.

4   I want a wife who will take care of *my* physical needs. I want a wife who will keep my house clean. A wife who will pick up after my children, a wife who will pick up after me. I want a wife who will keep my clothes clean, ironed, mended, replaced when need be, and who will see to it that my personal things are kept in their proper place so that I can find what I need the minute I need it. I want a wife who cooks the meals, a wife who is a *good* cook. I want a wife who will plan the menus, do the necessary grocery shopping, prepare the meals, serve them pleasantly, and then do the cleaning up while I do my studying. I want a wife who will care for me when I am sick and sympathize with my pain and loss of

time from school. I want a wife to go along when our family takes a vacation so that someone can continue to care for me and my children when I need a rest and change of scene.

I want a wife who will not bother me with rambling complaints about a wife's duties. But I want a wife who will listen to me when I feel the need to explain a rather difficult point I have come across in my course of studies. And I want a wife who will type my papers for me when I have written them.

I want a wife who will take care of the details of my social life. When my wife and I are invited out by my friends, I want a wife who will take care of the babysitting arrangements. When I meet people at school that I like and want to entertain, I want a wife who will have the house clean, will prepare a special meal, serve it to me and my friends, and not interrupt when I talk about things that interest me and my friends. I want a wife who will have arranged that the children are fed and ready for bed before my guests arrive so that the children do not bother us. I want a wife who takes care of the needs of my guests so that they feel comfortable, who makes sure that they have an ashtray, that they are passed the hors d'oeuvres, that they are offered a second helping of the food, that their wine glasses are replenished when necessary, that their coffee is served to them as they like it. And I want a wife who knows that sometimes I need a night out by myself.

I want a wife who is sensitive to my sexual needs, a wife who makes love passionately and eagerly when I feel like it, a wife who makes sure that I am satisfied. And, of course, I want a wife who will not demand sexual attention when I am not in the mood for it. I want a wife who assumes the complete responsibility for birth control, because I do not want more children. I want a wife who will remain sexually faithful to me so that I do not have to clutter up my intellectual life with jealousies. And I want a wife who understands that *my* sexual needs may entail more than strict adherence to monogamy. I must, after all, be able to relate to people as fully as possible.

8   If, by chance, I find another person more suitable as a wife than the wife I already have, I want the liberty to replace my present wife with another one. Naturally, I will expect a fresh, new life; my wife will take the children and be solely responsible for them so that I am left free.

When I am through with school and have a job, I want my wife to quit working and remain at home so that my wife can more fully and completely take care of a wife's duties.

My God, who *wouldn't* want a wife?

Topics for Discussion and Writing

1. Does the second sentence of the essay mean anything different from the first? If so, what? If not, why is it there?

2. Describing a recently divorced man, Brady says in paragraph 2: "He had one child, who is, of course, with his ex-wife." What information does "of course" convey? What attitude or tone?

3. If the constant repetition of "I want a wife who. . . " is not boring, what keeps it from being boring?

4. Brady is attacking sexual stereotyping. Do you find in her essay any assumptions or details that limit the stereotyping to an economic class or to an ethnic or racial group? Explain.

5. The essay was first published in 1971. Do you think it is now dated? Explain.

Joan Didion

Joan Didion was born in California in 1934 and educated at the University of California, Berkeley. While she was a senior in college she wrote a prize-winning essay for a contest sponsored by Vogue, *and soon she became an associate feature editor for* Vogue. *She has written novels, essays, and screenplays.*

On Keeping a Notebook

"'That woman Estelle,'" the note reads, "'is partly the reason why George Sharp and I are separated today.' *Dirty crepe-de-Chine wrapper, hotel bar, Wilmington RR, 9:45 a.m. August Monday morning.*"

Since the note is in my notebook, it presumably has some meaning to me. I study it for a long while. At first I have only the most general notion of what I was doing on an August Monday morning in the bar of the hotel across from the Pennsylvania Railroad station in Wilmington, Delaware (waiting for a train? missing one? 1960? 1961? why Wilmington?), but I do remember being there. The woman in the dirty crepe-de-Chine wrapper had come down from her room for a beer, and the bartender had heard before the reason why George Sharp and she were separated today. "Sure," he said, and went on mopping the floor. "You told me." At the other end of the bar is a girl. She is talking, pointedly, not to the man beside her but to a cat lying in the triangle of sunlight cast through the open door. She is wearing a plaid silk dress from Peck & Peck, and the hem is coming down.

Here is what it is: the girl has been on the Eastern Shore, and now she is going back to the city, leaving the man beside her, and all she can see ahead are the viscous summer sidewalks and the 3 a.m. long-distance calls that will make her lie awake and then sleep drugged through all the steaming mornings left in August (1960? 1961?). Because she must go directly from the train to lunch in New York, she wishes that she had a safety pin for the hem of the plaid silk, dress, and she also wishes that she could forget about the hem and the lunch and stay in the cool bar that smells of disinfectant and malt and make friends with the woman in the crepe-de-Chine wrapper. She is afflicted by a little self-pity, and she wants to compare Estelles. That is what that was all about.

4   In fact I have abandoned altogether that kind of pointless entry; instead I tell what some would call lies. "That's simply not true," the members of my family frequently tell me when they come up against my memory of a shared event. "The party was *not* for you, the spider was *not* a black widow, *it wasn't that way at all.*" Very likely they are right, for not only have I always had trouble distinguishing between what happened and what merely might have happened, but I remain unconvinced that the distinction, for my purposes, matters. The cracked crab that I recall having for lunch the day my father came home from Detroit in 1945 must certainly be embroidery, worked into the day's pattern to lend verisimilitude; I was ten years old and would not now remember the cracked crab. The day's events did not turn on cracked crab. And yet it is precisely that fictitious crab that makes me see the afternoon all over again, a home movie run all too often, the father bearing gifts, the child weeping, an exercise in family love and guilt. Or that is what it was to me. Similarly, perhaps it never did snow that August in Vermont; perhaps there never were flurries in the night wind, and maybe no one else felt the ground hardening and summer already dead even as we pretended to bask in it, but that was how it felt to me, and it might as well have snowed, could have snowed, did snow.

How it felt to me: that is getting closer to the truth about a notebook. I sometimes delude myself about why I keep a notebook, imagine that some thrifty virtue derives from preserving everything observed. See enough and write it down, I tell myself, and then some morning when the world seems drained of wonder, some day when I am only going through the motions of doing what I am supposed to do, which is write—on that bankrupt morning I will simply open my notebook and there it will all be, a forgotten account with accumulated interest, paid passage back to the world out there: dialogue overheard in hotels and elevators and at the hat-check counter in Pavillon (one middle-aged man shows his hat check to another and says, "That's my old football number"); impressions of Bettina Aptheker and Benjamin Sonnenberg and Teddy ("Mr. Acapulco") Stauffer; careful *aperçus* about tennis bums and failed fashion models and Greek shipping heiresses, one of whom taught me a significant lesson (a lesson I could have learned from F. Scott Fitzgerald, but perhaps we all must meet the very rich for ourselves) by asking, when I arrived to interview her in her orchid-filled sitting room on the second day of a paralyzing New York blizzard, whether it was snowing outside.

Why did I write it down? In order to remember, of course, but exactly what was it I wanted to remember? How much of it actually happened? Did any of it? Why do I keep a notebook at all? It is easy to deceive oneself on all those scores. The impulse to write things down is a peculiarly compulsive one, inexplicable to those who do not share it, useful only accidentally, only secondarily, in the way that any compulsion tries to justify itself. I suppose that it begins or does not begin in the cradle. Although I have felt compelled to write things down since I was five years old, I doubt that my daughter ever will, for she is a singularly blessed and accepting child, delighted with life exactly as life presents itself to her, unafraid to go to sleep and unafraid to wake up. Keepers of private notebooks are a different breed altogether, lonely and resistant rearrangers of things, anxious malcontents, children afflicted apparently at birth with some presentiment of loss.

My first notebook was a Big Five tablet, given to me by my mother with the sensible suggestion that I stop whining and learn to amuse myself by writing down my thoughts. She returned the tablet to me a few years ago; the first entry is an account of a woman who believed herself to be freezing to death in the Arctic night, only to find, when day broke, that she had stumbled onto the Sahara Desert, where she would die of the heat before lunch. I have no idea what turn of a five-year-old's mind could have prompted so insistently "ironic" and exotic a story, but it does reveal a certain predilection for the extreme which has dogged me into adult life; perhaps if I were analytically inclined I would find it a truer story than any I might have told about Donald Johnson's birthday party or the day my cousin Brenda put Kitty Litter in the aquarium.

8   So the point of my keeping a notebook has never been, nor is it now, to have an accurate factual record of what I have been doing or thinking. That would be a different impulse entirely, an instinct for reality which I sometimes envy but do not possess. At no point have I ever been able successfully to keep a diary; my approach to daily life ranges from the grossly negligent to the merely absent, and on those few occasions when I have tried dutifully to record a day's events, boredom has so overcome me that the results are mysterious at best. What is this business about "shopping, typing piece, dinner with E, depressed"? Shopping for what? Typing what piece? Who is E? Was this "E" depressed, or was I depressed? Who cares?

I imagine, in other words, that the notebook is about other people. But of course it is not. I have no real business with what one stranger said to another at the hat-check counter in Pavillon; in fact I suspect that the line. "That's my old football number" touched not my own imagination at all, but merely some memory of something once read, probably "The Eighty-Yard Run." Nor is my concern with a woman in a dirty crepe-de-Chine wrapper in a Wilmington bar. My stake is always, of course, in the unmentioned girl in the plaid silk dress. *Remember what it was to be me:* that is always the point.

It is a difficult point to admit. We are brought up in the ethic that others, any others, all others, are by definition more interesting than ourselves; taught to be diffident, just this side of self-effacing. ("You're the least important person in the room and don't forget it," Jessica Mitford's governess would hiss in her ear on the advent of any social occasion: I copied that into my notebook because it is only recently that I have been able to enter a room without hearing some such phrase in my inner ear.) Only the very young and the very old may recount their dreams at breakfast, dwell upon self, interrupt with memories of beach picnics and favorite Liberty lawn dresses and the rainbow trout in a creek near Colorado Springs. The rest of us are expected, rightly, to affect absorption in other people's favorite dresses, other people's trout.

And so we do. But our notebooks give us away, for however dutifully we record what we see around us, the common denominator of all we see is always, transparently, shamelessly, the implacable "I." We are not talking here about the kind of notebook that is patently for public consumption, a structural conceit for binding together a series of graceful *pensées;* we are talking about something private, about bits of the mind's string too short to use, an indiscriminate and erratic assemblage with meaning only for its maker.

12   And sometimes even the maker has difficulty with the meaning. There does not seem to be, for example, any point in my knowing for the rest of my life that, during 1964, 720 tons of soot fell on every square mile of New York City, yet there it is in my notebook, labeled "FACT." Nor do I really need to remember that Ambrose Bierce liked to spell Leland Stanford's name "£eland $tanford" or that "smart women almost always wear black in Cuba," a fashion hint without much potential for practical application. And does not the relevance of these notes seem marginal at best?:

> In the basement museum of the Inyo County Courthouse in Independence, California, sign pinned to a mandarin coat: "This Mandarin Coat was often worn by Mrs. Minnie S. Brooks when giving lectures on her TEAPOT COLLECTION."
> Redhead getting out of car in front of Beverly Wilshire Hotel, chinchilla stole, Vuitton bags and tags reading:
> MRS. LOU FOX
> HOTEL SAHARA
> VEGAS

Well, perhaps not entirely marginal. As a matter of fact, Mrs. Minnie S. Brooks and her MANDARIN COAT pull me back into my own childhood, for although I never knew Mrs. Brooks and did not visit Inyo County until I was thirty, I grew up in just such a world, in houses cluttered with Indian relics and bits of gold ore and ambergris and the souvenirs my Aunt Mercy Farnsworth brought back from the Orient. It is a long way from that world to Mrs. Lou Fox's world, where we all live now, and is it not just as well to remember that? Might not Mrs. Minnie S.

Brooks help me to remember what I am? Might not Mrs. Lou Fox help me to remember what I am not?

But sometimes the point is harder to discern. What exactly did I have in mind when I noted down that it cost the father of someone I know $650 a month to light the place on the Hudson in which he lived before the Crash? What use was I planning to make of this line by Jimmy Hoffa: "I may have my faults, but being wrong ain't one of them"? And although I think it interesting to know where the girls who travel with the Syndicate have their hair done when they find themselves on the West Coast, will I ever make suitable use if it? Might I not be better off just passing it on to John O'Hara? What is a recipe for sauerkraut doing in my notebook? What kind of magpie keeps this notebook? "*He was born the night the Titanic went down.*" That seems a nice enough line, and I even recall who said it, but is it not really a better line in life than it could ever be in fiction?

But of course that is exactly it: not that I should ever use the line, but that I should remember the woman who said it and the afternoon I heard it. We were on her terrace by the sea, and we were finishing the wine left from lunch, trying to get what sun there was, a California winter sun. The woman whose husband was born the night the *Titanic* went down wanted to rent her house, wanted to go back to her children in Paris. I remember wishing that I could afford the house, which cost $1,000 a month. "Someday you will," she said lazily. "Someday it all comes." There in the sun on her terrace it seemed easy to believe in someday, but later I had a low-grade afternoon hangover and ran over a black snake on the way to the supermarket and was flooded with inexplicable fear when I heard the checkout clerk explaining to the man ahead of me why she was finally divorcing her husband. "He left me no choice," she said over and over as she punched the register. "He has a little seven-month-old baby by her, he left me no choice." I would like to believe that my dread then was for the human condition, but of course it was for me, because I wanted a baby and did not then have one and because I wanted to own a house that cost $1,000 a month to rent and because I had a hangover.

16   It all comes back. Perhaps it is difficult to see the value in having one's self back in that kind of mood, but I do see it: I think we are well advised to keep on nodding terms with the people we used to be, whether we find them attractive company or not. Otherwise they turn up unannounced and surprise us, come hammering on the mind's door at 4 a.m. of a bad night and demand to know who deserted them, who betrayed them, who is going to make amends. We forget all too soon the things we thought we could never forget. We forget the loves and the betrayals alike, forget what we whispered and what we screamed, forget who we were. I have already lost touch with a couple of people I used to be: one of them, a seventeen-year-old, presents little threat, although it would be of some interest to me to know again what it feels like to sit on a river levee drinking vodka-and-orange-juice and listening to Les Paul and Mary Ford and

their echoes sing "How High the Moon" on the car radio. You see I still have the scenes, but I no longer perceive myself among those present, no longer could even improvise the dialogue. The other one, a twenty-three-year-old, bothers me more. She was always a good deal of trouble, and I suspect she will reappear when I least want to see her, skirts too long, shy to the point of aggravation, always the injured party, full of recriminations and little hurts and stories I do not want to hear again, at once saddening me and angering me with her vulnerability and ignorance, an apparition all the more insistent for being so long banished.

It is a good idea, then, to keep in touch, and I suppose that keeping in touch is what notebooks are all about. And we are all on our own when it comes to keeping those lines open to ourselves: your notebook will never help me, nor mine you. "*So what's new in the whiskey business?*" What could that possibly mean to you? To me it means a blonde in a Pucci bathing suit sitting with a couple of fat men by the pool at the Beverly Hills Hotel. Another man approaches, and they all regard one another in silence for a while. "So what's new in the whiskey business?" one of the fat men finally says by way of welcome, and the blonde stands up, arches one foot and dips it in the pool, looking all the while at the cabaña where Baby Pignatari is talking on the telephone. That is all there is to that, except that several years later I saw the blonde coming out of Saks Fifth Avenue in New York with her California complexion and a voluminous mink coat. In the harsh wind that day she looked old and irrevocably tired to me, and even the skins in the mink coat were not worked the way they were doing them that year, not the way she would have wanted them done, and there is the point of the story. For a while after that I did not like to look in the mirror, and my eyes would skim the newspapers and pick out only the deaths, the cancer victims, the premature coronaries, the suicides, and I stopped riding the Lexington Avenue IRT because I noticed for the first time that all the strangers I had seen for years—the man with the Seeing Eye dog, the spinster who read the classified pages every day, the fat girl who always got off with me at Grand Central—looked older than they once had.

It all comes back. Even that recipe for sauerkraut: even that brings it back. I was on Fire Island when I first made that sauerkraut, and it was raining, and we drank a lot of bourbon and ate the sauerkraut and went to bed at ten, and I listened to the rain and the Atlantic and felt safe. I made the sauerkraut again last night and it did not make me feel any safer, but that is, as they say, another story.

Topics for Discussion and Writing

1. In the sixth paragraph, beginning "Why did I write it down?" Didion says that "it is easy to deceive oneself" about the reasons for keeping a notebook.

What self-deceptive reasons does she go on to give? What others can be added? And exactly why *does* she keep a notebook? (Didion in her last three paragraphs—and especially in the first two of these—makes explicit her reasons, but try to state her reasons in a paragraph of your own.)

2. In paragraph 5 Didion refers to a lesson she might have learned from F. Scott Fitzgerald and goes on to say, "but perhaps we all must meet the very rich for ourselves." If you have read a book by Fitzgerald, explain (in a paragraph) the point to someone who doesn't get it.

3. In paragraph 13 Didion says, "It is a long way from that world to Mrs. Lou Fox's world, where we all live now." What does she mean?

4. If you keep a notebook (or diary or journal), explain in one to three paragraphs why you keep it. Following Didion's example, use one entry or two to illustrate the notebook's usefulness to you. If you don't keep a notebook, explain in one to three paragraphs why you don't, and explain what effect, if any, Didion's essay had on you. Do you now think it would be a good idea to keep a notebook? Or did the essay reinforce your belief that there's nothing useful in it for you? Explain.

Nora Ephron

Nora Ephron, born in 1941, is the daughter of two Hollywood writers. She has published several volumes of essays and a memoir.

A Few Words About Breasts: Shaping Up Absurd

I have to begin with a few words about androgyny. In grammar school, in the fifth and sixth grades, we were all tyrannized by a rigid set of rules that supposedly determined whether we were boys or girls. The episode in *Huckleberry Finn* where Huck is disguised as a girl and gives himself away by the way he threads a needle and catches a ball—that kind of thing. We learned that the way you sat, crossed your legs, held a cigarette and looked at your nails, your wristwatch, the way you did these things instinctively was absolute proof of your sex. Now obviously most children did not take this literally, but I did. I thought that just one slip, just one incorrect cross of my legs or flick of an imaginary cigarette ash would turn me from whatever I was into the other thing; that would be all it took, really. Even though I was outwardly a girl and had many of the trappings generally associated with the field of girldom—a girl's name, for example, and dresses, my own telephone, an autograph book—I spent the early years of my adolescence absolutely certain that I might at any point gum it up. I did not feel at all like a girl. I was boyish. I was athletic, ambitious, outspoken, competitive, noisy, rambunctious. I had scabs on my knees and my socks slid into my loafers and I could throw a football. I wanted desperately not to be that way, not to be a mixture of both things but instead just one, a girl, a definite indisputable girl. As soft and as pink as a nursery. And nothing would do that for me, I felt, but breasts.

I was about six months younger than everyone in my class, and so for about six months after it began, for six months after my friends had begun to develop—that was the word we used, develop—I was not particularly worried. I would sit in the bathtub and look down at my breasts and know that any day now, any second now, they would start growing like everyone else's. They didn't. "I want to buy a bra," I said to my mother one night. "What for?" she said. My mother was really hateful about bras, and by the time my third sister had gotten to that point where she was ready to want one, my mother had worked the whole business into a comedy routine. "Why not use a Band-Aid instead?" she would say. It was a source of great pride to my mother that she had never even had to wear a brassiere until she had her fourth child, and then only because her gynecologist made her. It was incomprehensible to me that anyone would ever be proud of something like that. It was the 1950's, for God's sake. Jane Russell. Cashmere sweaters. Couldn't my mother see that? "*I am too old to wear an undershirt,*" Screaming. Weeping. Shouting. "Then don't wear an undershirt," said my mother. "But I want to buy a bra." "What for?"

I suppose that for most girls, breasts, brassieres, that entire thing, has more trauma, more to do with the coming of adolescence, of becoming a woman, than anything else. Certainly more than getting your period, although that too was traumatic, symbolic. But you could *see* breasts; they were there; they were visible. Whereas a girl could claim to have her period for months before she actually got it and nobody would ever know the difference. Which is exactly what I did. All you had to do was make a great fuss over having enough nickels for the Kotex machine and walk around clutching your stomach and moaning for three to five days a month about The Curse and you could convince anybody. There is a school of thought somewhere in the women's lib/women's mag/gynecology establishment that claims that menstrual cramps are purely psychological, and I lean toward it. Not that I didn't have them finally. Agonizing cramps, heating-pad cramps, go-down-to-the-school-nurse-and-lie-on-the-cot cramps. But unlike any pain I had ever suffered, I adored the pain of cramps, welcomed it, wallowed in it, bragged about it. "I can't go. I have cramps." "I can't do that. I have cramps." And most of all, gigglingly, blushingly: "I can't swim. I have cramps." Nobody ever used the hard-core word. Menstruation. God, what an awful word. Never that. "I have cramps."

4   The morning I first got my period, I went into my mother's bedroom to tell her. And my mother, my utterly-hateful-about-bras mother, burst into tears. It was really a lovely moment, and I remember it so clearly not just because it was one of the two times I ever saw my mother cry on my account (the other was when I was caught being a six-year-old kleptomaniac), but also because the incident did not mean to me what it meant to her. Her little girl, her firstborn, had finally become a woman. That was what she was crying about. My reaction to the event, however, was that I might well be a woman in some scientific, textbook sense (and could at least stop faking every month and stop wasting all those nickels). But in another sense—in a visible sense—I was as androgynous and as liable to tip over into boyhood as ever.

I started with a 28AA bra. I don't think they made them any smaller in those days, although I gather that now you can buy bras for five year olds that don't have any cups whatsoever in them; trainer bras they are called. My first brassiere came from Robinson's Department Store in Beverly Hills. I went there alone, shaking, positive they would look me over and smile and tell me to come back next year. An actual fitter took me into the dressing room and stood over me while I took off my blouse and tried the first one on. The little puffs stood out on my chest. "Lean over," said the fitter (to this day I am not sure what fitters in bra departments do except to tell you to lean over). I leaned over, with the fleeting hope that my breasts would miraculously fall out of my body and into the puffs. Nothing.

"Don't worry about it," said my friend Libby some months later, when things had not improved. "You'll get them after you're married."

"What are you talking about?" I said.

8   "When you get married," Libby explained, "your husband will touch your breasts and rub them and kiss them and they'll grow."

That was the killer. Necking I could deal with. Intercourse I could deal with. But it had never crossed my mind that a man was going to touch my breasts, that breasts had something to do with all that, petting, my God they never mentioned petting in my little sex manual about the fertilization of the ovum. I became dizzy. For I knew instantly—as naive as I had been only a moment before—that only part of what she was saying was true: the touching, rubbing, kissing part, not the growing part. And I knew that no one would ever want to marry me. I had no breasts. I would never have breasts.

My best friend in school was Diana Raskob. She lived a block from me in a house full of wonders. English muffins, for instance. The Raskobs were the first people in Beverly Hills to have English muffins for breakfast. They also had an apricot tree in the back, and a badminton court, and a subscription to *Seventeen* magazine, and hundreds of games like Sorry and Parcheesi and Treasure Hunt and Anagrams. Diana and I spent three or four afternoons a week in their den reading and playing and eating. Diana's mother's kitchen was full of the most colossal assortment of junk food I have ever been exposed to. My house was full of apples and peaches and milk and homemade chocolate-chip cookies—which were nice, and good for you, but-not-right-before-dinner-or you'll-spoil-your-appetite. Diana's house had nothing in it that was good for you, and what's more, you could stuff it in right up until dinner and nobody cared. Bar-B-Q potato chips (they were the first in them, too), giant bottles of ginger ale, fresh popcorn with melted butter, hot fudge sauce on Baskin-Robbins jamoca ice cream, powdered-sugar doughnuts from Van de Kamps. Diana and I had been best friends since we were seven; we were about equally popular in school (which is to say, not particularly), we had about the same success with boys (extremely intermittent) and we looked much the same. Dark. Tall. Gangly.

It is September, just before school begins. I am eleven years old, about to enter the seventh grade, and Diana and I have not seen each other all summer. I have been to camp and she has been somewhere like Banff with her parents. We are meeting, as we often do, on the street midway between our two houses and we will walk back to Diana's and eat junk and talk about what has happened to each of us that summer. I am walking down Walden Drive in my jeans and my father's shirt hanging out and my old red loafers with the socks falling into them and coming toward me is . . . I take a deep breath . . . a young woman. Diana. Her hair is curled and she has a waist and hips and a bust and she is wearing a straight skirt, an article of clothing I have been repeatedly told I will be unable to wear until I have the hips to hold it up. My jaw drops, and suddenly I am crying, crying hysterically, can't catch my breath sobbing. My best friend has betrayed me. She has gone ahead without me and done it. She has shaped up.

12 Here are some things I did to help:

Bought a Mark Eden Bust Developer.

Slept on my back for four years.

Splashed cold water on them every night because some French actress said in *Life* magazine that that was what *she* did for her perfect bustline.

16 Ultimately, I resigned myself to a bad toss and began to wear padded bras. I think about them now, think about all those years in high school I went around in them, my three padded bras, every single one of them with different sized breasts. Each time I changed bras I changed sizes: one week nice perky but not too obtrusive breasts, the next medium-sized slightly pointed ones, the next week knockers, true knockers; all the time, whatever size I was, carrying around this rubberized appendage on my chest that occasionally crashed into a wall and was poked inward and had to be poked outward—I think about all that and wonder how anyone kept a straight face through it. My parents, who normally had no restraints about needling me—why did they say nothing as they watched my chest go up and down? My friends, who would periodically inspect my breasts for signs of growth and reassure me—why didn't they at least counsel consistency?

And the bathing suits. I die when I think about the bathing suits. That was the era when you could lay an uninhabited bathing suit on the beach and someone would make a pass at it. I would put one on, an absurd swimsuit with its enormous bust built into it, the bones from the suit stabbing me in the rib cage and leaving little red welts on my body, and there I would be, my chest plunging straight downward absolutely vertically from my collarbone to the top of my suit and then suddenly, wham, out came all that padding and material and wiring absolutely horizontally.

Buster Klepper was the first boy who ever touched them. He was my boyfriend my senior year of high school. There is a picture of him in my high-school yearbook that makes him look quite attractive in a Jewish, horn-rimmed glasses sort of way, but the picture does not show the pimples, which were air-brushed out, or the dumbness. Well, that isn't really fair. He wasn't dumb. He just wasn't terribly bright. His mother refused to accept it, refused to accept the relentlessly average report cards, refused to deal with her son's inevitable destiny in some junior college or other. "He was tested," she would say to me, apropos of nothing, "and it came out 145. That's near-genius." Had the word underachiever been coined, she probably would have lobbed that one at me, too. Anyway, Buster was really very sweet—which is, I know, damning with faint praise, but there it is. I was the editor of the front page of the high-school newspaper and he was editor of the back page; we had to work together, side by side, in the print shop, and that was how it started. On our first date, we went to see *April Love* starring Pat Boone. Then we started going together. Buster had a green coupe, a 1950 Ford with an engine he had handchromed until it shone, dazzled, reflected the image of anyone who looked into it, anyone usually being Buster polishing it or the gas-station attendants he constantly asked to check the oil in order for them to be overwhelmed by the sparkle on the valves. The car also had a boot stretched over the back seat for reasons I never understood; hanging from the rear-view mirror, as was the custom, was a pair of angora dice. A previous girl friend named Solange who was famous throughout Beverly Hills High School for having no pigment in her right eyebrow had knitted them for him. Buster and I would ride around town, the two of us seated to the left of the steering wheel. I would shift gears. It was nice.

There was necking. Terrific necking. First in the car, overlooking Los Angeles from what is now the Trousdale Estates. Then on the bed of his parents' cabana at Ocean House. Incredibly wonderful, frustrating necking, I loved it, really, but no further than necking, please don't, please, because there I was absolutely terrified of the general implications of going-a-step-further with a near-dummy and also terrified of his finding out there was next to nothing there (which he knew, of course; he wasn't that dumb).

20   I broke up with him at one point. I think we were apart for about two weeks. At the end of that time I drove down to see a friend at a boarding school in Palos Verdes Estates and a disc jockey played *April Love* on the radio four times during the trip. I took it as a sign. I drove straight back to Griffith Park to a golf tournament Buster was playing in (he was the sixth-seeded teen-age golf player in Southern California) and presented myself back to him on the green of the 18th hole. It was all very dramatic. That night we went to a drive-in and I let him

get his hand under my protuberances and onto my breasts. He really didn't seem to mind at all.

"Do you want to marry my son?" the woman asked me.

"Yes," I said.

I was nineteen years old, a virgin, going with this woman's son, this big strange woman who was married to a Lutheran minister in New Hampshire and pretended she was Gentile and had this son, by her first husband, this total fool of a son who ran the hero-sandwich concession at Harvard Business School and whom for one moment one December in New Hampshire I said—as much out of politeness as anything else—that I wanted to marry.

24   *"Fine," she said. "Now, here's what you do. Always make sure you're on top of him so you won't seem so small. My bust is very large, you see, so I always lie on my back to make it look smaller, but you'll have to be on top most of the time."*

I nodded. "Thank you," I said.

"I have a book for you to read," she went on. "Take it with you when you leave. Keep it." She went to the bookshelf, found it, and gave it to me. It was a book on frigidity.

"Thank you," I said.

28   That is a true story. Everything in this article is a true story, but I feel I have to point out that that story in particular is true. It happened on December 30, 1960. I think about it often. When it first happened, I naturally assumed that the woman's son, my boyfriend, was responsible. I invented a scenario where he had had a little heart-to-heart with his mother and had confessed that his only objection to me was that my breasts were small; his mother then took it upon herself to help out. Now I think I was wrong about the incident. The mother was acting on her own, I think: that was her way of being cruel and competitive under the guise of being helpful and maternal. You have small breasts, she was saying; therefore you will never make him as happy as I have. Or you have small breasts; therefore you will doubtless have sexual problems. Or you have small breasts; therefore you are less woman than I am. She was, as it happens, only the first of what seems to me to be a never-ending string of women who have made competitive remarks to me about breast size. "I would love to wear a dress like that," my friend Emily says to me, "but my bust is too big." Like that. Why do women say these things to me? Do I attract these remarks the way other women attract married men or alcoholics or homosexuals? This summer, for example, I am at a party in East Hampton and I am introduced to a woman from Washington. She is a minor celebrity, very pretty and Southern and blonde and outspoken and I am flattered because she has read something I have written. We are talking animatedly, we have been talking no more than five minutes, when a man comes up to join us. "Look at the two of us," the woman says to the man, indicating me and her. "The two of us together couldn't fill an A cup." Why does she say that? It isn't even true, dammit, so why? Is she even more addled than I am on this subject? Does she honestly believe there is something wrong with

her size breasts, which, it seems to me, now that I look hard at them, are just right. Do I unconsciously bring out competitiveness in women? In that form? What did I do to deserve it?

As for men.

There were men who minded and let me know they minded. There were men who did not mind. In any case, I always minded.

And even now, now that I have been countlessly reassured that my figure is a good one, now that I am grown up enough to understand that most of my feelings have very little to do with the reality of my shape, I am nonetheless obsessed by breasts. I cannot help it. I grew up in the terrible Fifties—with rigid stereotypical sex roles, the insistence that men be men and dress like men and women be women and dress like women, the intolerance of androgyny—and I cannot shake it, cannot shake my feelings of inadequacy. Well, that time is gone, right? All those exaggerated examples of breast worship are gone, right? Those women were freaks, right? I know all that. And yet, here I am, stuck with the psychological remains of it all, stuck with my own peculiar version of breast worship. You probably think I am crazy to go on like this: here I have set out to write a confession that is meant to hit you with the shock of recognition and instead you are sitting there thinking I am thoroughly warped. Well, what can I tell you? If I had had them, I would have been a completely different person. I honestly believe that.

32   After I went into therapy, a process that made it possible for me to tell total strangers at cocktail parties that breasts were the hang-up of my life, I was often told that I was insane to have been bothered by my condition. I was also frequently told, by close friends, that I was extremely boring on the subject. And my girl friends, the ones with nice big breasts, would go on endlessly about how their lives had been far more miserable than mine. Their bra straps were snapped in class. They couldn't sleep on their stomachs. They were started at whenever the word "mountain" cropped up in geography. And *Evangeline,* good God what they went through every time someone had to stand up and recite the Prologue to Longfellow's *Evangeline: "... stand like druids of eld ... With beards that rest on their bosoms."* It was much worse for them, they tell me. They had a terrible time of it, they assure me. I don't know how lucky I was, they say.

I have thought about their remarks, tried to put myself in their place, considered their point of view. I think they are full of shit.

Topics for Discussion and Writing

1. In her first paragraph Ephron says that Huck Finn gives himself away by his manner of threading a needle and catching a ball. In what ways does a boy

supposedly differ from a girl in performing these activities? And how do they supposedly differ in the other activities that Ephron mentions in this paragraph?

2. Toward the end of the second paragraph Ephron writes several sentence fragments. How can you justify them?

3. Is the essay offensive? If so, why, and if not, why not?

4. On the basis of this essay characterize Nora Ephron, quoting a few words or phrases to support your characterization.

E. M. Forster

E[dward] M[organ] Forster (1879–1970) was born in London and was graduated from King's College, Cambridge. He traveled widely and lived for a while in India, but most of his life was spent back at King's College. His best-known novel, A Passage to India *(1926), is alluded to in the first line of the essay that we reprint.*

My Wood

A few years ago I wrote a book which dealt in part with the difficulties of the English in India. Feeling that they would have had no difficulties in India themselves, the Americans read the book freely. The more they read it the better it made them feel, and a cheque to the author was the result. I bought a wood with the cheque. It is not a large wood—it contains scarcely any trees, and it is intersected, blast it, by a public footpath. Still, it is the first property that I have owned, so it is right that other people should participate in my shame, and should ask themselves, in accents that will vary in horror, this very important question: What is the effect of property upon the character? Don't let's touch economics; the effect of private ownership upon the community as a whole is another question—a more important question, perhaps, but another one. Let's keep to psychology. If you own things, what's their effect on you? What's the effect on me of my wood?

In the first place, it makes me feel heavy. Property does have this effect. Property produces men of weight, and it was a man of weight who failed to get into the Kingdom of Heaven. He was not wicked, that unfortunate millionaire in the parable, he was only stout; he stuck out in front, not to mention behind, and as he wedged himself this way and that in the crystalline entrance and bruised his well-fed flanks, he saw beneath him a comparatively slim camel passing through the eye of a needle and being woven into the robe of God. The Gospels all through couple stoutness and slowness. They point out what is perfectly obvious, yet seldom realized: that if you have a lot of things you cannot move about a lot, that furniture requires dusting, dusters require servants, servants require insurance stamps, and the whole tangle of them makes you think twice before you accept an invitation to dinner or go for a bathe in the Jordan. Sometimes the Gospels proceed further and say with Tolstoy that property is sinful; they approach the difficult ground of asceticism here, where I cannot follow them. But as to the immediate effects of property on people, they just show straightforward logic. It produces men of weight. Men of weight cannot, by definition, move like the lightning from the East unto the West, and the ascent of a fourteen-stone[1] bishop into a pulpit is thus the exact antithesis of the coming of the Son of Man. My wood makes me feel heavy.

In the second place, it makes me feel it ought to be larger.

4   The other day I heard a twig snap in it. I was annoyed at first, for I thought that someone was blackberrying, and depreciating the value of the undergrowth. On coming nearer, I saw it was not a man who had trodden on the twig and snapped it, but a bird, and I felt pleased. My bird. The bird was not equally pleased. Ignoring the relation between us, it took fright as soon as it saw the shape of my face, and flew straight over the boundary hedge into a field, the property of Mrs. Henessy, where it sat down with a loud squawk. It had become Mrs. Henessy's bird. Something seemed grossly amiss here, something that would not have occurred had the wood been larger. I could not afford to buy Mrs. Henessy out, I dared not murder her, and limitations of this sort beset me on every side. Ahab[2] did not want that vineyard—he only needed it to round off his property, preparatory to plotting a new curve—and all the land around my wood has become necessary to me in order to round off the wood. A boundary protects. But—poor little thing—the boundary ought in its turn to be protected. Noises on the edge of it. Children throw stones. A little more, and then a little more, until we reach the sea. Happy Canute! Happier Alexander![3] And after all, why should even the world be the limit of possession? A rocket containing a Union Jack, will, it is hoped, be shortly fired at the moon. Mars. Sirius. Beyond which . . . But these immensities ended by saddening me. I could not suppose that my wood was the destined nucleus of universal dominion—it is so very small and contains no mineral wealth beyond the blackberries. Nor was I comforted when Mrs. Henessy's bird took alarm for the second time and flew clean away from us all, under the belief that it belonged to itself.

---

1. Fourteen stones is equivalent 196 pounds. [All notes are the editors']
2. In the Hebrew Bible (1 Kings 20–21), Ahab coveted his neighbor's vineyard.
3. Canute (995?–1035), king of England, Norway, and Denmark, thought he could command even the sea; when he failed, he removed his crown. Alexander the Great (356–323 BC), king of Macedon, conquered Persia, Syria, and Egypt and part of India. He died in Babylon while planning further conquests.

In the third place, property makes its owner feel that he ought to do something to it. Yet he isn't sure what. A restlessness comes over him, a vague sense that he has a personality to express—the same sense which, without any vagueness, leads the artist to an act of creation. Sometimes I think I will cut down such trees as remain in the wood, at other times I want to fill up the gaps between them with new trees. Both impulses are pretentious and empty. They are not honest movements towards money-making or beauty. They spring from a foolish desire to express myself and from an inability to enjoy what I have got. Creation, property, enjoyment form a sinister trinity in the human mind. Creation and enjoyment are both very very good, yet they are often unattainable without a material basis, and at such moments property pushes itself in as a substitute, saying, "Accept me instead—I'm good enough for all three." It is not enough. It is, as Shakespeare said of lust, "The expense of spirit in a waste of shame": it is "Before, a joy proposed; behind, a dream." Yet we don't know how to shun it. It is forced on us by our economic system as the alternative to starvation. It is also forced on us by an internal defect in the soul, by the feeling that in property may lie the germs of self-development and of exquisite or heroic deeds. Our life on earth is, and ought to be, material and carnal. But we have not yet learned to manage our materialism and carnality properly; they are still entangled with the desire for ownership, where (in the words of Dante) "Possession is one with loss."

And this brings us to our fourth and final point: the blackberries.

Blackberries are not plentiful in this meagre grove, but they are easily seen from the public footpath which traverses it, and all too easily gathered. Foxgloves, too—people will pull up the foxgloves, and ladies of an educational tendency even grub for toadstools to show them on the Monday in class. Other ladies, less educated, roll down the bracken in the arms of their gentlemen friends. There is paper, there are tins. Pray, does my wood belong to me or doesn't it? And, if it does, should I not own it best by allowing no one else to walk there? There is a wood near Lyme Regis, also cursed by a public footpath, where the owner has not hesitated on this point. He has built high stone walls each side of the path, and has spanned it by bridges, so that the public circulate like termites while he gorges on the blackberries unseen. He really does own his wood, this able chap. Dives in Hell did pretty well, but the gulf dividing him from Lazarus could be traversed by vision, and nothing traverses it here[4] And perhaps I shall come to this in time. I shall wall in and fence out until I really taste the sweets of property. Enormously stout, endlessly avaricious, pseudo-creative, intensely selfish, I shall weave upon my forehead the quadruple crown of possession until those nasty Bolshies come and take it off again and thrust me aside into the outer darkness.

4. According to Christ's parable in Luke 16:19–26, the rich man (unnamed, but traditionally known as Dives) at whose gate the poor man Lazarus had begged was sent to hell, from where he could see Lazarus in heaven.

Topic for Discussion and Writing

Much of the strength of the essay lies in its concrete presentation of generalities. Note, for example, that the essay is called "My Wood," but we might say that the general idea of the essay is "The Effect of Property on Owners." Forster gives four effects, chiefly through concrete statements. Put these four effects into four general statements.

Stephen Jay Gould

Stephen Jay Gould, born in 1941, is a professor of geology at Harvard University, where he teaches paleontology, biology, and the history of science. The essays he has written for the magazine Natural History *have been collected in a series of highly readable books.*

Women's Brains

In the Prelude to *Middlemarch,* George Eliot lamented the unfulfilled lives of talented women:

> Some have felt that these blundering lives are due to the inconvenient indefiniteness with which the Supreme Power has fashioned the natures of women: if there were one level of feminine incompetence as strict as the ability to count three and no more, the social lot of women might be treated with scientific certitude.

Eliot goes on to discount the idea of innate limitation, but while she wrote in 1872, the leaders of European anthropometry were trying to measure "with scientific certitude" the inferiority of women. Anthropometry, or measurement of the human body, is not so fashionable a field these days, but it dominated the human sciences for much of the nineteenth century and remained popular until intelligence testing replaced skull measurement as a favored device for making invidious comparisons among races, classes, and sexes. Craniometry, or measurement of the skull, commanded the most attention and respect. Its unquestioned leader, Paul Broca (1824–80), professor of clinical surgery at the Faculty of Medicine in Paris, gathered a school of disciples and imitators around himself. Their work, so meticulous and apparently irrefutable, exerted great influence and won high esteem as a jewel of nineteenth-century science.

Broca's work seemed particularly invulnerable to refutation. Had he not measured with the most scrupulous care and accuracy? (Indeed, he had. I have the greatest respect for Broca's meticulous procedure. His numbers are sound. But science is an inferential exercise, not a catalog of facts. Numbers, by themselves, specify nothing. All depends upon what you do with them.) Broca depicted himself as an apostle of objectivity, a man who bowed before facts and cast aside superstition and sentimentality. He declared that "there is no faith, however respectable, no interest, however legitimate, which must not accommodate itself to the progress of human knowledge and bend before truth." Women, like it or not, had smaller brains than men and, therefore, could not equal them in intelligence. This fact, Broca argued, may reinforce a common prejudice in male society, but it is also a scientific truth. L. Manouvrier, a black sheep in Broca's fold, rejected the inferiority of women and wrote with feeling about the burden imposed upon them by Broca's numbers:

> Women displayed their talents and their diplomas. They also invoked philosophical authorities. But they were opposed by *numbers* unknown to Condorcet or to John Stuart Mill. These numbers fell upon poor women like a sledge hammer, and they were accompanied by commentaries and sarcasms more ferocious than the most misogynist imprecations of certain church fathers. The theologians had asked if women had a soul. Several centuries later, some scientists were ready to refuse them a human intelligence.

4   Broca's argument rested upon two sets of data: the larger brains of men in modern societies, and a supposed increase in male superiority through time. His most extensive data came from autopsies performed personally in four Parisian hospitals. For 292 male brains, he calculated an average weight of 1,325 grams; 140 female brains averaged, 1,144 grams for a difference of 181 grams, or 14 percent of the male weight. Broca understood, of course, that part of this difference could be attributed to the greater height of males. Yet he made no attempt to measure the effect of size alone and actually stated that it cannot account for the entire difference because we know, a priori, that women are not as intelligent as men (a premise that the data were supposed to test, not rest upon):

> We might ask if the small size of the female brain depends exclusively upon the small size of her body. Tiedemann has proposed this explanation. But we must not forget that women are, on the average, a little less intelligent than men, a difference which we should not exaggerate but which is, nonetheless, real. We are therefore permitted to suppose that the relatively small size of the female brain depends in part upon her physical inferiority and in part upon her intellectual inferiority.

In 1873, the year after Eliot published *Middlemarch*, Broca measured the cranial capacities of prehistoric skulls from L'Homme Mort cave. Here he found a difference of only 99.5 cubic centimeters between males and females, while modern populations range from 129.5 to 220.7. Topinard, Broca's chief disciple, explained the increasing discrepancy through time as a result of differing evolutionary pressures upon dominant men and passive women:

> The man who fights for two or more in the struggle for existence, who has all the responsibility and the cares of tomorrow, who is constantly active in combating the environment and human rivals, needs more brain than the woman whom he must protect and nourish, the

sedentary woman, lacking any interior occupations, whose role is to raise children, love, and be passive.

In 1879, Gustave Le Bon, chief misogynist of Broca's school, used these data to publish what must be the most vicious attack upon women in modern scientific literature (no one can top Aristotle). I do not claim his views were representative of Broca's school, but they were published in France's most respected anthropological journal. Le Bon concluded:

> In the most intelligent races, as among the Parisians, there are a large number of women whose brains are closer in size to those of gorillas than to the most developed male brains. This inferiority is so obvious that no one can contest it for a moment; only its degree is worth discussion. All pyschologists who have studied the intelligence of women, as well as poets and novelists, recognize today that they represent the most inferior forms of human evolution and that they are closer to children and savages than to an adult, civilized man. They excel in fickleness, inconstancy, absence of thought and logic, and incapacity to reason. Without doubt there exist some distinguished women, very superior to the average man, but they are as exceptional as the birth of any monstrosity, as, for example, of a gorilla with two heads; consequently, we may neglect them entirely.

Nor did Le Bon shrink from the social implications of his views. He was horrified by the proposal of some American reformers to grant women higher education on the same basis as men:

> A desire to give them the same education, and, as a consequence, to propose the same goals for them, is a dangerous chimera. . . . The day when, misunderstanding the inferior occupations which nature has given her, women leave the home and take part in our battles; on this day a social revolution will begin, and everything that maintains the sacred ties of the family will disappear.

Sound familiar?*

8   I have reexamined Broca's data, the basis for all this derivative pronouncement, and I find his numbers sound but his interpretation ill-founded, to say the least. The data supporting his claim for increased difference through time can be easily dismissed. Broca based his contention on the samples from L'Homme Mort alone—only seven male and six female skulls in all. Never have so little data yielded such far ranging conclusions.

In 1888, Topinard published Broca's more extensive data on the Parisian hospitals. Since Broca recorded height and age as well as brain size, we may use modern statistics to remove their effect. Brain weight decreases with age, and Broca's women were, on average, considerably older than his men. Brain weight increases with height, and his average man was almost half a foot taller than his

---

* When I wrote this essay, I assumed that Le Bon was a marginal, if colorful, figure. I have since learned that he was a leading scientist, one of the founders of social pyschology, and best known for a seminal study on crowd behavior, still cited today (*La psychologie des foules*, 1895), and for his work on unconscious motivation.

average woman. I used multiple regression, a technique that allowed me to assess simultaneously the influence of height and age upon brain size. In an analysis of the data for women, I found that, at average male height and age, a woman's brain would weigh 1,212 grams. Correction for height and age reduces Broca's measured difference of 181 grams by more than a third, to 113 grams.

I don't know what to make of this remaining difference because I cannot assess other factors known to influence brain size in a major way. Cause of death has an important effect: degenerative disease often entails a substantial diminution of brain size. (This effect is separate from the decrease attributed to age alone.) Eugene Schreider, also working with Broca's data, found that men killed in accidents had brains weighing, on average, 60 grams more than men dying of infectious diseases. The best modern data I can find (from American hospitals) records a full 100-gram difference between death by degenerative arteriosclerosis and by violence or accident. Since so many of Broca's subjects were very elderly women, we may assume that lengthy degenerative disease was more common among them than among the men.

More importantly, modern students of brain size still have not agreed on a proper measure for eliminating the powerful effect of body size. Height is partly adequate, but men and women of the same height do not share the same body build. Weight is even worse than height, because most of its variation reflects nutrition rather than intrinsic size—fat versus skinny exerts little influence upon the brain. Manouvrier took up this subject in the 1880s and argued that muscular mass and force should be used. He tried to measure this elusive property in various ways and found a marked difference in favor of men, even in men and women of the same height. When he corrected for what he called "sexual mass," women actually came out slightly ahead in brain size.

12   Thus, the corrected 113-gram difference is surely too large; the true figure is probably close to zero and may as well favor women as men. And 113 grams, by the way, is exactly the average difference between a 5 foot 4 inch and a 6 foot 4 inch male in Broca's data. We would not (especially us short folks) want to ascribe greater intelligence to tall men. In short, who knows what to do with Broca's data? They certainly don't permit any confident claim that men have bigger brains than women.

To appreciate the social role of Broca and his school, we must recognize that his statements about the brains of women do not reflect an isolated prejudice toward a single disadvantaged group. They must be weighed in the context of a general theory that supported contemporary social distinctions as biologically ordained. Women, blacks, and poor people suffered the same disparagement, but women bore the brunt of Broca's argument because he had easier access to data on women's brains. Women were singularly denigrated but they also stood as surrogates for other disenfranchised groups. As one of Broca's disciples wrote in 1881: "Men of the black races have a brain scarcely heavier than that of white women." This juxtaposition extended into many other realms of anthropological argument, particularly to claims that, anatomically and emotionally, both women and blacks were like white children—and that white children, by the theory of recapitulation, represented an ancestral (primitive) adult stage of human evolution. I do not regard as empty rhetoric the claim that women's battles are for all of us.

Maria Montessori did not confine her activities to educational reform for young children. She lectured on anthropology for several years at the University of Rome, and wrote an influential book entitled *Pedagogical Anthropology* (English edition, 1913). Montessori was no egalitarian. She supported most of Broca's work and the theory of innate criminality proposed by her compatriot Cesare Lombroso. She measured the circumference of children's heads in her schools and inferred that the best prospects had bigger brains. But she had no use for Broca's conclusions about women. She discussed Manouvrier's work at length and made much of his tentative claim that women, after proper correction of the data, had slightly larger brains than men. Women, she concluded, were intellectually superior, but men had prevailed heretofore by dint of physical force. Since technology has abolished force as an instrument of power, the era of women may soon be upon us: "In such an epoch there will really be superior human beings, there will really be men strong in morality and in sentiment. Perhaps in this way the reign of women is approaching, when the enigma of her anthropological superiority will be deciphered. Woman was always the custodian of human sentiment, morality and honor."

This represents one possible antidote to "scientific" claims for the constitutional inferiority of certain groups. One may affirm the validity of biological distinctions but argue that the data have been misinterpreted by prejudiced men with a stake in the outcome, and that disadvantaged groups are truly superior. In recent years, Elaine Morgan has followed this strategy in her *Descent of Woman,* a speculative reconstruction of human prehistory from the woman's point of view—and as farcical as more famous tall tales by and for men.

16   I prefer another strategy. Montessori and Morgan followed Broca's philosophy to reach a more congenial conclusion. I would rather label the whole enterprise of setting a biological value upon groups for what it is: irrelevant and highly injurious. George Eliot well appreciated the special tragedy that biological labeling imposed upon members of disadvantaged groups. She expressed it for people like herself—women of extraordinary talent. I would apply it more widely—not only to those whose dreams are flouted but also to those who never realize that they may dream—but I cannot match her prose. In conclusion, then, the rest of Eliot's prelude to *Middlemarch:*

> The limits of variation are really much wider than anyone would imag-
> ine from the sameness of women's coiffure and the favorite love sto-
> ries in prose and verse. Here and there a cygnet is reared uneasily
> among the ducklings in the brown pond, and never finds the living
> stream in fellowship with its own oary-footed kind. Here and there is
> born a Saint Theresa, foundress of nothing, whose loving heartbeats

and sobs after an unattained goodness tremble off and are dispersed among hindrances instead of centering in some long-recognizable deed.

Topics for Discussion and Writing

1. In paragraph 3, what does Gould mean when he says, "But science is an inferential exercise, not a catalog of facts"?

2. Gould quotes (paragraph 5) Topinard's explanation for the increasing discrepancy in the size of brains. Given your own understanding of evolution, what do you think of Topinard's explanation?

3. In paragraph 9 Gould says, "Brain weight decreases with age." Do you believe this? Why? How would one establish the truth or falsity of the assertion?

4. In paragraph 12 Gould says, "Thus, the corrected 113-gram difference is surely too large; the true figure is probably close to zero and may as well favor women as men." Why "thus"? What evidence or what assumptions prompt Gould to say that the figure is surely too large?

5. In paragraph 13 Gould says, "I do not regard as empty rhetoric the claim that women's battles are for all of us." What does this mean?

6. Also in paragraph 13 Gould refers to the "social role of Broca and his school." What does he mean by that? On the basis of this essay (and other essays of Gould's you may have read) try to formulate in a sentence or two the social role of Gould.

bell hooks

bell hooks (Gloria Watkins) teaches English and Women's Studies at Oberlin College. She is the author of Feminist Theory: From Margin to Center *(1984),* Talking Back *(1989), and* Yearning: Race, Gender and Culture *(1990).*

Talking Back

In the world of the southern black community I grew up in "back talk" and "talking back" meant speaking as an equal to an authority figure. It meant daring to disagree and sometimes it just meant having an opinion. In the "old school" children were meant to be seen and not heard. My great-grandparents, grandparents, and parents were all from the old school. To make yourself heard, if you were a child, was to invite punishment, the backhand lick, the slap across the face that would catch you unaware, or the feel of switches stinging your arms and legs.

To speak then when one was not spoken to was a courageous act—an act of risking and daring. And yet it was hard not to speak in warm rooms where heated discussions began at the crack of dawn, women's voices filling the air, giving orders, making threats, fussing. Black men may have excelled in the art of poetic preaching in the male dominated church but in the church of the home where the everyday rules of how to live and how to act were established it was black women who preached. There, black women spoke in a language so rich, so poetic, that it felt to me like being shut off from life, smothered to death if one was not allowed to participate.

It was in that world of woman talk (the men were often silent, often absent) that was born in me the craving to speak, to have a voice, and not just any voice but one that could be identified as belonging to me. To make my voice I had to speak, to hear myself talk—and talk I did—darting in and out of grown folk's conversations and dialogues, answering questions that were not directed at me, endlessly asking questions, making speeches. Needless to say, the punishments for these acts of speech seemed endless. They were intended to silence me—the child—and more particularly the girl child. Had I been a boy they might have encouraged me to speak believing that I might someday be called to preach. There was no "calling" for talking girls, no legitimized rewarded speech. The punishments I received for "talking back" were intended to suppress all possibility that I would create my own speech. That speech was to be suppressed so the "right speech of womanhood" would emerge.

4   Within feminist circles silence is often seen as the sexist defined "right speech of womanhood"—the sign of woman's submission to patriarchal authority. This emphasis on woman's silence may be an accurate remembering of what has taken place in the households of women from WASP backgrounds in the United States but in black communities (and in other diverse ethnic communities) women have not been silent. Their voices can be heard. Certainly for black women our struggle has not been to emerge from silence into speech but to change the nature and direction of our speech. To make a speech that compels listeners, one that is heard.

Our speech, "the right speech of womanhood," was often the soliloquy, the talking into thin air, the talking to ears that do not hear you—the talk that is simply not listened to. Unlike the black male preacher whose speech was to be heard, who was to be listened to, whose words were to be remembered, the voices of black women—giving orders, making threats, fussing—could be tuned out, could become a kind of background music, audible but not acknowledged as significant speech. Dialogue, the sharing of speech and recognition, took place not between mother and child or mother and male authority figure but with other black women. I can remember watching, fascinated, as our mother talked with her mother, sisters, and women friends. The intimacy and intensity of their speech—the satisfaction they received from talking to one another, the pleasure, the joy. It was in this world of woman speech, loud talk, angry words, women with tongues quick and sharp, tender sweet tongues, touching our world with their words, that I made speech my birthright—and the right to voice, to authorship, a privilege I would not be denied. It was in that world and because of it that I came to dream of writing, to write.

Writing was a way to capture speech, to hold onto it, to keep it close. And so I wrote down bits and pieces of conversations, confessing in cheap diaries that soon fell apart from too much handling, expressing the intensity of my sorrow, the anguish of speech—for I was always saying the wrong thing, asking the wrong questions. I could not confine my speech to the necessary corners and concerns of life. These writings I hid under my bed, in pillow stuffings, among faded underwear. When my sisters found and read them, they ridiculed and mocked me—poking fun. I felt violated, ashamed, as if the secret parts of my self had been exposed, brought into the open, and hung like newly clean laundry, out in the air for everyone to see. The fear of exposure, the fear that one's deepest emotions and innermost thoughts would be dismissed as mere nonsense, felt by so many young girls keeping diaries, keeping and hiding speech, seems to me now one of the barriers that women have needed and need to destroy so that we are no longer pushed into secrecy or silence.

Despite my feelings of violation, of exposure, I continued to speak and write, choosing my hiding places well, learning to destroy work when no safe place could be found. Rather than teaching me absolute silence. I was taught that it was important to speak but to talk a talk that was in itself a silence. Taught to speak and yet to beware of the betrayal of too much heard speech, I experienced intense confusion and deep anxiety in my efforts to speak and write. Reciting poems at Sunday afternoon church service might be rewarded speech. Writing a poem (when one's time could be "better" spent sweeping, ironing, learning to cook) was luxurious activity, indulged in at the expense of others. Questioning authority, raising issues that were not deemed appropriate subjects, brought pain, punishments—like telling mama I wanted to die before her because I could not live without her—that was crazy talk, crazy speech, the kind that would lead you to end up in a mental institution. "Little girl," I would be told, "if you don't stop all this crazy talk and crazy acting you are going to end up right out there at Western State."

8   Madness too then, not just physical abuse, was the punishment for too much talk if you were female. Yet even as this fear of madness haunted me, hung over my writing like a monstrous shadow, I could not stop the words,

making thought, writing speech. For this terrible madness which I feared, which I was sure was the destiny of daring women born to intense speech (after all the authorities emphasized this point daily), was not as threatening as imposed silence, as suppressed speech.

Safety and sanity were to be sacrificed if I was to experience defiant speech. Though I risked the two, deep-seated fears and anxieties characterized my childhood days. I would speak, but I would not ride a bike, play hard ball, or hold the gray kitten. Writing about the ways we are hurt by negative traumas in our growing-up years, psychoanalyst Alice Miller makes the point in *For Her Own Good* that it is not clear why wounding in childhood becomes for some folk an opportunity to grow, to move forward in the process of self-realization rather than a retardation of that process. Certainly, when I reflect on the trials of my growing-up years, the many punishments, I can see now that in resistance I learned then to be vigilant in the nourishment of my spirit, to be tough, to courageously protect that spirit from forces that would break it.

While punishing me, my parents often spoke about the necessity of breaking my spirit. Now when I ponder the silences, the voices that are not heard, the voices of those wounded and/or oppressed individuals who do not speak or write, I contemplate the acts of persecution, torture—the terrorism that breaks spirits, that makes creativity impossible. I write these words to bear witness to the primacy of struggle in any situation of domination (even within family life), to the strength and power that emerges from sustained resistance, and the profound conviction that these forces can be healing, can protect us from dehumanization and despair.

These early trials, wherein I learned to stand my ground, to keep my spirit intact, came vividly to mind after I published *Ain't I a Woman* and the work was sharply and harshly criticized. While I had expected a climate of critical dialogue, I was not expecting a critical avalanche that had the power in its intensity to crush spirit, to push one into silence. Since that time I have heard stories about black women, about women of color, who write and publish, having nervous breakdowns (even when the work is quite successful), being made mad because they cannot bear the harsh responses of family, friends, and unknown critics, or becoming silent, unproductive. Surely, the absence of a humane critical response has tremendous impact on the writer from any group, but especially for those writers from oppressed, colonized groups who endeavor to speak. For us, true speaking is not solely an expression of creative power, it is an act of resistance, a political gesture that challenges the politics of domination that would render us nameless and voiceless. As such it is a courageous act; as such it represents a threat. To those who wield oppressive power that which is threatening must necessarily be wiped out, annihilated, silenced.

12   Recent efforts by black women writers to call attention to our work serve to highlight both our presence and absence. Whenever I peruse women's

bookstores I am struck not by the rapidly growing body of feminist writing by black women but by the paucity of available published material. Those of us who write and are published remain few in number. The context of silence is varied and multi-dimensional. Most obvious are the ways racism, sexism, and class exploitation act as agents to suppress and silence. Less obvious are the inner struggles, the effort made to gain necessary confidence to write, to rewrite, to fully develop craft and skill, the extent to which such efforts fail.

Although I have wanted writing to be a life work for me since childhood, it has been difficult for me to claim "writer" as part of that which identifies and shapes my everyday reality. Even after publishing books I would often speak of wanting to be a writer as though these works did not exist. And though I would be told, "you are a writer," I was not ready yet to affirm fully this truth. Part of myself was still held captive by domineering forces of history, of familial life that had charted a map of silence, of right speech. I had not completely let go the fear of saying the wrong thing, of being punished. Somewhere in the deep recesses of my mind I believed I could avoid both responsibility and punishment if I did not declare myself a writer.

One of the many reasons I chose to write using the pseudonym bell hooks, a family name (mother to Sarah Oldham, grandmother to Rosa Bell Oldham, great-grandmother to me) was to construct a writer identity that would challenge and subdue all impulses that would lead me away from speech into silence. I was a young girl buying bubble gum at the corner store when I first "really" heard the full name Bell Hooks: I had just "talked back" to a grown person. Even now I can recall the surprised look, the mocking tones that informed me I must be kin to Bell Hooks—a sharp-tongued woman, a woman who spoke her mind, a woman who was not afraid to talk back. I claimed this legacy of defiance, of will, of courage, affirming my link to female ancestors who were bold and daring in their speech. Unlike my bold and daring mother and grandmother, who were not supportive of talking back, even though they were assertive and powerful in their speech, Bell Hooks, as I discovered, claimed, and invented her, was my ally, my support.

The initial act of talking back outside the home was an empowering moment. It was the first of many acts of defiant speech that would make it possible for me to emerge as independent thinker and writer. Seen in retrospect, "talking back" became for me a rite of initiation, testing my courage, strengthening my commitment, preparing me for the days ahead—the days when writing seems impossible but necessary, rejection notices, periods of silence, publication, ongoing development.

16   Moving from silence into speech is for the oppressed, the colonized, the exploited, and those who stand and struggle side by side, a gesture of defiance that heals, that makes new life, and new growth possible. It is that act of speech, of "talking back" that is no mere gesture of empty words, that is the expression of moving from object to subject, that is the liberated voice.

Topics for Discussion and Writing

1. hooks makes it clear, in her first paragraph, that in her family children were not expected to speak to adults unless they were spoken to. Nevertheless, and despite frequent punishment, she insisted on speaking. Where and how does hooks suggest why she so needed to speak?

2. How did the speech of men and women differ in hooks's family and community? When you were a child, what differences between the speech of men and women were you aware of?

3. What was the connection for hooks between her desire to speak and her beginnings as a writer?

4. In paragraph 6, writing about her diaries, hooks describes her "fear of exposure," a feeling shared by many young girls. She assumes here that only girls, not boys, keep diaries. Do you think that is true, and if so, why is it true? Under what circumstances might boys as well as girls experience "the fear of exposure" from their writing, and how do you account for it?

5. In paragraph 11 hooks speaks of writers of "oppressed, colonized groups" and characterizes their writing as "an act of resistance, a political gesture." What connects her observations here and in the next paragraph with what she has told us of her experience as a child?

6. If you have sometimes "talked back" in bell hooks's sense, describe a particular occasion, and indicate whether it empowered you (paragraph 15) or not.

Jane Jacobs

Jane Jacobs was born in Scranton, Pennsylvania, in 1916. From 1952 until 1962 she served as an associate editor of Architectural Forum. *In addition to writing* The Death and Life of Great American Cities, *from which our selection comes, she has written* The Economy of Cities.

The Use of Sidewalks

Under the seeming disorder of the old city, wherever the old city is working successfully, is a marvelous order for maintaining the safety of the streets and the freedom of the city. It is a complex order. Its essence is intricacy of sidewalk use, bringing with it a constant succession of eyes. This order is all composed of movement and change, and although it is life, not art, we may fancifully call it the art form of the city and liken it to the dance—not to a simple-minded precision dance with everyone kicking up at the same time, twirling in unison and bowing off en masse, but to an intricate ballet in which the individual dancers and ensembles all have distinctive parts which miraculously reinforce each other and compose an orderly whole. The ballet of the good city sidewalk never repeats itself from place to place, and in any one place is always replete with new improvisations.

The stretch of Hudson Street where I live is each day the scene of an intricate sidewalk ballet. I make my own first entrance into it a little after eight when I put out the garbage can, surely a prosaic occupation, but I enjoy my part, my little clang, as the droves of junior high school students walk by the center of the stage dropping candy wrappers. (How do they eat so much candy so early in the morning?)

While I sweep up the wrappers I watch the other rituals of morning: Mr. Halpert unlocking the laundry's handcart from its mooring to a cellar door, Joe Cornacchia's son-in-law stacking out the empty crates from the delicatessen, the barber bringing out his sidewalk folding chair, Mr. Goldstein arranging the coils of wire which proclaim the hardware store is open, the wife of the tenement's superintendent depositing her chunky three-year-old with a toy mandolin on the stoop, the vantage point from which he is learning the English his mother cannot speak. Now the primary children, heading for St. Luke's, dribble through to the south; the children for St. Veronica's cross, heading to the west, and the children for P.S. 41, heading toward the east. Two new entrances are being made from the wings: well-dressed and even elegant women and men with brief cases emerge from doorways and side streets. Most of these are heading for the bus and subways, but some hover on the curbs, stopping taxis which have miraculously appeared at the right moment, for the taxis are part of a wider morning ritual: having dropped passengers from midtown in the downtown financial district, they are now bringing downtowners up to midtown. Simultaneously, numbers of women in housedresses have emerged and as they crisscross with one another they pause for quick conversations that sound with either laughter or joint indignation, never, it seems, anything between. It is time for me to hurry to work too, and I exchange my ritual farewell with Mr. Lofaro, the short, thick-bodied, white-aproned fruit man who stands outside his doorway a little up the street, his arms folded, his feet planted, looking solid as earth itself. We nod; we each glance quickly up and down the street, then look back to each other and smile. We have done this many a morning for more than ten years, and we both know what it means: All is well.

4   The heart-of-the-day ballet I seldom see, because part of the nature of it is that working people who live there, like me, are mostly gone, filling the roles of strangers on other sidewalks. But from days off, I know enough of it to know that it becomes more and more intricate. Longshoremen who are not working that day gather at the White Horse or the Ideal or the International for beer and conversation. The executives and business lunchers from the industries just to

the west throng the Dorgene restaurant and the Lion's Head coffee house; meat-market workers and communications scientists fill the bakery lunchroom. Character dancers come on, a strange old man with strings of old shoes over his shoulder, motor-scooter riders with big beards and girl friends who bounce on the back of the scooters and wear their hair long in front of their faces as well as behind, drunks who follow the advice of the Hat Council and are always turned out in hats, but not hats the Council would approve. Mr. Lacey, the locksmith, shuts up his shop for a while and goes to exchange the time of day with Mr. Slube at the cigar store. Mr. Koochagian, the tailor, waters the luxuriant jungle of plants in his window, gives them a critical look from the outside, accepts a compliment on them from two passers-by, fingers the leaves on the plane tree in front of our house with a thoughtful gardener's appraisal, and crosses the street for a bite at the Ideal where he can keep an eye on customers and wigwag across the message that he is coming. The baby carriages come out, and clusters of everyone from toddlers with dolls to teen-agers with homework gather at the stoops.

When I get home after work, the ballet is reaching its crescendo. This is the time of roller skates and stilts and tricycles, and games in the lee of the stoop with bottletops and plastic cowboys; this is the time of bundles and packages, zigzagging from the drug store to the fruit stand and back over to the butcher's; this is the time when teen-agers, all dressed up, are pausing to ask if their slips show or their collars look right; this is the time when beautiful girls get out of MG's; this is the time when the fire engines go through; this is the time when anybody you know around Hudson Street will go by.

As darkness thickens and Mr. Halpert moors the laundry cart to the cellar door again, the ballet goes on under lights, eddying back and forth but intensifying at the bright spotlight pools of Joe's sidewalk pizza dispensary, the bars, the delicatessen, the restaurant and the drug store. The night workers stop now at the delicatessen, to pick up salami and a container of milk. Things have settled down for the evening but the street and its ballet have not come to a stop.

I know the deep night ballet and its seasons best from waking long after midnight to tend a baby and, sitting in the dark, seeing the shadows and hearing the sounds of the sidewalk. Mostly it is a sound like infinitely pattering snatches of party conversation and, about three in the morning, singing, very good singing. Sometimes there is sharpness and anger or sad, sad weeping, or a flurry of search for a string of beads broken. One night a young man came roaring along, bellowing terrible language at two girls whom he had apparently picked up and who were disappointing him. Doors opened, a wary semicircle formed around him, not too close, until the police came. Out came the heads, too, along Hudson Street, offering opinion. "Drunk . . . Crazy . . . A wild kid from the suburbs."*

* He turned out to be a wild kid from the suburbs. Sometimes, on Hudson Street, we are tempted to believe the suburbs must be a difficult place to bring up children.

8   Deep in the night, I am almost unaware how many people are on the street unless something calls them together, like the bagpipe. Who the piper was and why he favored our street I have no idea. The bagpipe just skirled out in the February night, and as if it were a signal the random, dwindled movements of the sidewalk took on direction. Swiftly, quietly, almost magically a little crowd was there, a crowd that evolved into a circle with a Highland fling inside it. The crowd could be seen on the shadowy sidewalk, the dancers could be seen, but the bagpiper himself was almost invisible because his bravura was all in his music. He was a very little man in a plain brown overcoat. When he finished and vanished, the dancers and watchers applauded, and applause came from the galleries too, half a dozen of the hundred windows on Hudson Street. Then the windows closed, and the little crowd dissolved into the random movements of the night street.

The strangers on Hudson Street, the allies whose eyes help us natives keep the peace of the street, are so many that they always seem to be different people from one day to the next. That does not matter. Whether they are so many always-different people as they seem to be. I do not know. Likely they are. When Jimmy Rogan fell through a plate-glass window (he was separating some scuffling friends) and almost lost his arm, a stranger in an old T shirt emerged from the Ideal bar, swiftly applied an expert tourniquet and, according to the hospital's emergency staff, saved Jimmy's life. Nobody remembered seeing the man before and no one has seen him since. The hospital was called in this way: a woman sitting on the steps next to the accident ran over to the bus stop, wordlessly snatched the dime from the hand of a stranger who was waiting with his fifteen-cent fare ready, and raced into the Ideal's phone booth. The stranger raced after her to offer the nickel too. Nobody remembered seeing him before, and no one has seen him since. When you see the same stranger three or four times on Hudson Street, you begin to nod. This is almost getting to be an acquaintance, a public acquaintance, of course.

I have made the daily ballet of Hudson Street sound more frenetic than it is, because writing it telescopes it. In real life, it is not that way. In real life, to be sure, something is always going on, the ballet is never at a halt, but the general effect is peaceful and the general tenor even leisurely. People who know well such animated city streets will know how it is. I am afraid people who do not will always have it a little wrong in their heads—like the old prints of rhinoceroses made from travelers' descriptions of rhinoceroses.

On Hudson Street, the same as in the North End of Boston or in any other animated neighborhoods of great cities, we are not innately more competent at keeping the sidewalks safe than are the people who try to live off the hostile truce of Turf in a blind-eyed city. We are the lucky possessors of a city order that makes it relatively simple to keep the peace because there are plenty of eyes on the street. But there is nothing simple about that order itself, or the bewildering number of components that go into it. Most of those components are specialized in one way or another. They unite in their joint effect upon the sidewalk which is not specialized in the least. That is its strength.

Topics for Discussion and Writing

1. Evaluate the effectiveness of the extended metaphor Jacobs uses, the comparison of the activity on her street with a ballet. Did the comparison help you to share her point of view, or did you find it obtrusive and distracting? If you found the device useful or pleasing, explain why ballet is a better metaphor than, say, a concert or circus. Or, can you think of a metaphor that is better than ballet?

2. What is Jacobs's thesis? Locate the thesis sentence, or summarize the thesis in your own words.

3. Would you agree that the inherent superiority of cities over suburbs is a secondary argument or theme of the essay? If so, try to locate the passages in which this argument is stated or implied.

4. In her next-to-last paragraph, Jacobs briefly apologizes for the inadequacy of her description of life on the sidewalk. Does your experience allow you to detect inadequacies in her description? If so, what are they?

5. Explain Jacobs's next-to-last sentence.

Martin Luther King, Jr.

Martin Luther King, Jr. (1929–1968), clergyman and civil rights leader, achieved national fame in mid-1950s when he led the boycott against segregated bus lines in Montgomery, Alabama. In 1964 he was awarded the Nobel Peace Prize, but he continued to encounter strong opposition. On April 4, 1968, while in Memphis to support striking sanitation workers, he was shot and killed.

Nonviolent Resistance

Oppressed people deal with their oppression in three characteristic ways. One way is acquiescence: the oppressed resign themselves to their doom. They tacitly adjust themselves to oppression, and thereby become conditioned to it. In every movement toward freedom some of the oppressed prefer to remain oppressed. Almost 2800 years ago Moses set out to lead the children of Israel from the slavery of Egypt to the freedom of the promised land. He soon discovered that slaves do not always welcome their deliverers. They become accustomed to being slaves. They would rather bear those ills they have, as Shakespeare pointed out, than flee to others that they know not of. They prefer the "fleshpots of Egypt" to the ordeals of emancipation.

There is such a thing as the freedom of exhaustion. Some people are so worn down by the yoke of oppression that they give up. A few years ago in the slum areas of Atlanta, a Negro guitarist used to sing almost daily: "Ben down so long that down don't bother me." This is the type of negative freedom and resignation that often engulfs the life of the oppressed.

But this is not the way out. To accept passively an unjust system is to cooperate with that system; thereby the oppressed become as evil as the oppressor. Noncooperation with evil is as much a moral obligation as is cooperation with good. The oppressed must never allow the conscience of the oppressor to slumber. Religion reminds every man that he is his brother's keeper. To accept injustice or segregation passively is to say to the oppressor that his actions are morally right. It is a way of allowing his conscience to fall asleep. At this moment the oppressed fails to be his brother's keeper. So acquiescence—while often the easier way—is not the moral way. It is the way of the coward. The Negro cannot win the respect of his oppressor by acquiescing; he merely increases the oppressor's arrogance and contempt. Acquiescence is interpreted as proof of the Negro's inferiority. The Negro cannot win the respect of the white people of the South or the peoples of the world if he is willing to sell the future of his children for his personal and immediate comfort and safety.

4   A second way that oppressed people sometimes deal with oppression is to resort to physical violence and corroding hatred. Violence often brings about momentary results. Nations have frequently won their independence in battle. But in spite of temporary victories, violence never brings permanent peace. It solves no social problem; it merely creates new and more complicated ones.

Violence as a way of achieving racial justice is both impractical and immoral. It is impractical because it is a descending spiral ending in destruction for all. The old law of an eye for an eye leaves everybody blind. It is immoral because it seeks to humiliate the opponent rather than win his understanding; it seeks to annihilate rather than to convert. Violence is immoral because it thrives on hatred rather than love. It destroys community and makes brotherhood impossible. It leaves society in monologue rather than dialogue. Violence ends by defeating itself. It creates bitterness in the survivors and brutality in the destroyers. A voice echoes through time saying to every potential Peter, "Put up your sword." History is cluttered with the wreckage of nations that failed to follow this command.

If the American Negro and other victims of oppression succumb to the temptation of using violence in the struggle for freedom, future generations will be the recipients of a desolate night of bitterness, and our chief legacy to them will be an endless reign of meaningless chaos. Violence is not the way.

The third way open to oppressed people in their quest for freedom is the way of nonviolent resistance. Like the synthesis in Hegelian philosophy, the principle of nonviolent resistance seeks to reconcile the truths of two opposites—acquiescence and violence—while avoiding the extremes and immoralities of both. The nonviolent resister agrees with the person who acquiesces that one should not be physically aggressive toward his opponent; but he balances the equation by agreeing with the person of violence that evil must be resisted. He avoids the nonresistance of the former and the violent resistance of the latter. With nonviolent resistance, no individual or group need submit to any wrong, nor need anyone resort to violence in order to right a wrong.

8   It seems to me that this is the method that must guide the actions of the Negro in the present crisis in race relations. Through nonviolent resistance the Negro will be able to rise to the noble height of opposing the unjust system while loving the perpetrators of the system. The Negro must work passionately and unrelentingly for full stature as a citizen, but he must not use inferior methods to gain it. He must never come to terms with falsehood, malice, hate, or destruction.

Nonviolent resistance makes it possible for the Negro to remain in the South and struggle for his rights. The Negro's problem will not be solved by running away. He cannot listen to the glib suggestion of those who would urge him to migrate en masse to other sections of the country. By grasping his great opportunity in the South he can make a lasting contribution to the moral strength of the nation and set a sublime example of courage for generations yet unborn.

By nonviolent resistance, the Negro can also enlist all men of good will in his struggle for equality. The problem is not a purely racial one, with Negroes set against whites. In the end, it is not a struggle between people at all, but a tension between justice and injustice. Nonviolent resistance is not aimed against oppressors but against oppression. Under its banner consciences, not racial groups, are enlisted.

If the Negro is to achieve the goal of integration, he must organize himself into a militant and nonviolent mass movement. All three elements are indispensable. The movement for equality and justice can only be a success if it has both a mass and militant character; the barriers to be overcome require both. Nonviolence is an imperative in order to bring about ultimate community.

12   A mass movement of militant quality that is not at the same time committed to nonviolence tends to generate conflict, which in turn breeds anarchy. The support of the participants and the sympathy of the uncommitted are both inhibited by the threat that bloodshed will engulf the community. This reaction in turn encourages the opposition to threaten and resort to force. When, however, the mass movement repudiates violence while moving resolutely toward its goal, its opponents are revealed as the instigators and practitioners of

violence if it occurs. Then public support is magnetically attracted to the advocates of nonviolence, while those who employ violence are literally disarmed by overwhelming sentiment against their stand.

Topics for Discussion and Writing

1. Analysis is a term from science, and to some people it suggests coldness, a dispassionate clinical examination. Point to passages in this essay where King communicates his warmth, or sympathy, or passion.

2. In the first paragraph the passage about Moses and the children of Israel is not strictly necessary; the essential idea of the paragraph is stated in the previous sentence. Why, then, does King add this material? And why the quotation from Shakespeare?

3. Pick out two or three sentences that seem to you to be especially effective, and analyze the sources of their power. You can choose either isolated sentences or (because King often effectively links sentences with repetition of words or of constructions) consecutive ones.

4. In a paragraph, set forth your understanding of what nonviolent resistance is. Use whatever examples from your own experience or reading you find useful. In a second paragraph, explain how Maya Angelou's "Graduation" (page 516) offers an example of nonviolent resistance.

Stephen King

Stephen King, with 50 million copies of his books in print, is one of America's most popular authors. King was born in Portland, Maine, in 1947. After graduating from the University of Maine he taught high school English until he was able to devote himself full-time to writing. In addition to writing stories and novels—some of which have been made into films—he has written Danse Macabre, *a book that, like the essay we reprint here, discusses the appeal of horror.*

Why We Crave Horror Movies

I think that we're all mentally ill; those of us outside the asylums only hide it a little better—and maybe not all that much better, after all. We've all known people who talk to themselves, people who sometimes squinch their faces into horrible grimaces when they believe no one is watching, people who have some hysterical fear—of snakes, the dark, the tight place, the long drop . . . and, of course, those final worms and grubs that are waiting so patiently underground.

When we pay our four or five bucks and seat ourselves at tenth-row center in a theater showing a horror movie, we are daring the nightmare.

Why? Some of the reasons are simple and obvious. To show that we can, that we are not afraid, that we can ride this roller coaster. Which is not to say that a really good horror movie may not surprise a scream out of us at some point, the way we may scream when the roller coaster twists through a complete 360 or plows through a lake at the bottom of the drop. And horror movies, like roller coasters, have always been the special province of the young; by the time one turns 40 or 50, one's appetite for double twists or 360-degree loops may be considerably depleted.

4   We also go to re-establish our feelings of essential normality; the horror movie is innately conservative, even reactionary. Freda Jackson as the horrible melting woman in *Die, Monster, Die!* confirms for us that no matter how far we may be removed from the beauty of a Robert Redford or a Diana Ross, we are still light-years from true ugliness.

And we go to have fun.

Ah, but this is where the ground starts to slope away, isn't it? Because this is a very peculiar sort of fun, indeed. The fun comes from seeing others menaced—sometimes killed. One critic has suggested that if pro football has become the voyeur's version of combat, then the horror film has become the modern version of the public lynching.

It is true that the mythic, "fairy-tale" horror film intends to take away the shades of gray. . . . It urges us to put away our more civilized and adult penchant for analysis and to become children again, seeing things in pure blacks and whites. It may be that horror movies provide psychic relief on this level because this invitation to lapse into simplicity, irrationality and even outright madness is extended so rarely. We are told we may allow our emotions a free rein . . . or no rein at all.

8   If we are all insane, then sanity becomes a matter of degree. If your insanity leads you to carve up women like Jack the Ripper or the Cleveland Torso Murderer, we clap you away in the funny farm (but neither of those two amateur-night surgeons was ever caught, heh-heh-heh); if, on the other hand, your insanity leads you only to talk to yourself when you're under stress or to pick your nose on your morning bus, then you are left alone to go about your business . . . though it is doubtful that you will ever be invited to the best parties.

The potential lyncher is in almost all of us (excluding saints, past and present; but then, most saints have been crazy in their own ways), and every now and then, he has to be let loose to scream and roll around in the grass. Our emotions and our fears form their own body, and we recognize that it demands its own exercise to maintain proper muscle tone. Certain of these emotional muscles are accepted—even exalted—in civilized society; they are, of course, the emotions that tend to maintain the status quo of civilization itself. Love, friendship, loyalty, kindness—these are all the emotions that we applaud, emotions that have been immortalized in the couplets of Hallmark cards and in the verses (I don't dare call it poetry) of Leonard Nimoy.

When we exhibit these emotions, society showers us with positive reinforcement; we learn this even before we get out of diapers. When, as children, we hug our rotten little puke of a sister and give her a kiss, all the aunts and uncles smile and twit and cry, "Isn't he the sweetest little thing?" Such coveted treats as chocolate-covered graham crackers often follow. But if we deliberately slam the rotten little puke of a sister's fingers in the door, sanctions follow—angry remonstrance from parents, aunts and uncles; instead of a chocolate-covered graham cracker, a spanking.

But anticivilization emotions don't go away, and they demand periodic exercise. We have such "sick" jokes as, "What's the difference between a truckload of bowling balls and a truckload of dead babies?" (You can't unload a truckload of bowling balls with a pitchfork . . . a joke, by the way, that I heard originally from a ten-year-old). Such a joke may surprise a laugh or a grin out of us even as we recoil, a possibility that confirms the thesis: If we share a brotherhood of man, then we also share an insanity of man. None of which is intended as a defense of either the sick joke or insanity but merely as an explanation of why the best horror films, like the best fairy tales, manage to be reactionary, anarchistic, and revolutionary all at the same time.

12   The mythic horror movie, like the sick joke, has a dirty job to do. It deliberately appeals to all that is worst in us. It is morbidity unchained, our most base instincts let free, our nastiest fantasies realized . . . and it all happens, fittingly enough, in the dark. For those reasons, good liberals often shy away from horror films. For myself, I like to see the most aggressive of them—*Dawn of the Dead,* for instance—as lifting a trap door in the civilized forebrain and throwing a basket of raw meat to the hungry alligators swimming around in that subterranean river beneath.

Why bother? Because it keeps them from getting out, man. It keeps them down there and me up here. It was Lennon and McCartney who said that all you need is love, and I would agree with that.

As long as you keep the gators fed.

Topics for Discussion and Writing

1. In paragraph 6 King, paraphrasing an unnamed critic, suggests that "the horror film has become the modern version of the public lynching." In your opinion, why did some people find excitement in a lynching? Does the horror film offer somewhat similar excitement(s)?

2. King suggests in paragraph 11 that we have within us a stock of "anticivilization emotions [that] don't go away, and they demand

periodic exercise." What, if any, evidence are you aware of that supports this view?

3. In paragraph 11 King tells a joke about dead babies. He suggests that jokes of this sort "may surprise a laugh or a grin out of us even as we recoil." Analyze your own response to the joke, or to similar jokes. Did you laugh, or grin? Or was your response utterly different? If so, what was it?

4. In paragraphs 12 and 13 King says that horror movies serve a valuable social purpose. Do you think he has proved this point? What are the strengths (if any) and the weaknesses (if any) of his argument?

C. S. Lewis

C[live] S[taples] Lewis (1898–1963) taught medieval and Renaissance literature at Oxford and later at Cambridge. In addition to writing about literature, he wrote fiction (including The Chronicles of Narnia)*, poetry, and numerous essays and books on moral and religious topics.*

Vivisection

It is the rarest thing in the world to hear a rational discussion of vivisection. These who disapprove of it are commonly accused of "sentimentality," and very often their arguments justify the accusation. They paint pictures of pretty little dogs on dissecting tables. But the other side lies open to exactly the same charge. They also often defend the practice by drawing pictures of suffering women and children whose pain can be relieved we are assured only by the fruits of vivisection. The one appeal, quite as clearly as the other, is addressed to emotion, to the particular emotion we call pity. And neither appeal proves anything. If the thing is right—and if right at all, it is a duty—then pity for the animal is one of the temptations we must resist in order to perform that duty. It the thing is wrong, then pity for human suffering is precisely the temptation which will most probably lure us into doing that wrong thing. But the real question—*whether* it is right or wrong—remains meanwhile just where it was.

A rational discussion of this subject begins by inquiring whether pain is, or is not, an evil. If it is not, then the case against vivisection falls. But then so does the case for vivisection. If it is not defended on the ground that it reduces human suffering, on what ground can it be defended? And if pain is not an evil, why should human suffering be reduced? We must therefore assume as a basis for the whole discussion that pain is an evil, otherwise there is nothing to be discussed.

Now if pain is an evil then the infliction of pain, considered in itself, must clearly be an evil act. But there are such things as necessary evils. Some acts which would be bad, simply in themselves, may be excusable and even laudable when they are necessary means to a greater good. In saying that the infliction of pain, simply in itself, is bad, we are not saying that pain ought never to be inflicted. Most of us think that it can rightly be inflicted for a good purpose—as in dentistry or just and reformatory punishment. The point is that it always requires justification. On the man whom we find inflicting pain rests the burden of showing why an act which in itself would be simply bad is, in those particular circumstances, good. If we find a man giving pleasure it is for us to prove (if we criticize him) that his action is wrong. But if we find a man inflicting pain it is for him to prove that his action is right. If he cannot, he is a wicked man.

4   Now vivisection can only be defended by showing it to be right that one species should suffer in order that another species should be happier. And here we come to the parting of the ways. The Christian defender and the ordinary "scientific" (i.e., naturalistic) defender of vivisection, have to take quite different lines.

The Christian defender, especially in the Latin countries, is very apt to say that we are entitled to do anything we please to animals because they "have no souls." But what does this mean? If it means that animals have no consciousness, then how is this known? They certainly behave as if they had, or at least the higher animals do. I myself am inclined to think that far fewer animals than is supposed have what we should recognize as consciousness. But that is only an opinion. Unless we know on other grounds that vivisection is right we must not take the moral risk of tormenting them on a mere opinion. On the other hand, the statement that they "have no souls" may mean that they have no moral responsibilities and are not immortal. But the absence of "soul" in that sense makes the infliction of pain upon them not easier but harder to justify. For it means that animals cannot deserve pain, nor profit morally by the discipline of pain, nor be recompensed by happiness in another life for suffering in this. Thus all the factors which render pain more tolerable or make it less totally evil in the case of human beings will be lacking in the beasts. "Soullessness," in so far as it is relevant to the question at all, is an argument against vivisection.

The only rational line for the Christian vivisectionist to take is to say that the superiority of man over beast is a real objective fact, guaranteed by Revelation, and that the propriety of sacrificing beast to man is a logical consequence. We are "worth more than many sparrows,"[1] and in saying this we are not merely expressing a natural preference for our own species simply because it is our own but conforming to a hierarchical order created by God and really present in the universe whether any one acknowledges it or not. The position may not be satisfactory. We may fail to see how a benevolent Deity could wish us to draw such conclusions from the hierarchical order He has created. We may find it

1. Matthew x.31

difficult to formulate a human right of tormenting beasts in terms which would not equally imply an angelic right of tormenting men. And we may feel that though objective superiority is rightly claimed for men, yet that very superiority ought partly to *consist in* not behaving like a vivisector: that we ought to prove ourselves better than the beasts precisely by the fact of acknowledging duties to them which they do not acknowledge to us. But on all these questions different opinions can be honestly held. If on grounds of our real, divinely ordained, superiority a Christian pathologist thinks it right to vivisect, and does so with scrupulous care to avoid the least dram or scruple of unnecessary pain, in a trembling awe at the responsibility which he assumes, and with a vivid sense of the high mode in which human life must be lived if it is to justify the sacrifices made for it, then (whether we agree with him or not) we can respect his point of view.

But of course the vast majority of vivisectors have no such theological background. They are most of them naturalistic and Darwinian. Now here, surely, we come up against a very alarming fact. The very same people who will most contemptuously brush aside any consideration of animal suffering if it stands in the way of "research" will also, on another context, most vehemently deny that there is any radical difference between man and the other animals. On the naturalistic view the beasts are at bottom just the same *sort* of thing as ourselves. Man is simply the cleverest of the anthropoids. All the grounds on which a Christian might defend vivisection are thus cut from under our feet. We sacrifice other species to our own not because our own has any objective metaphysical privilege over others, but simply because it is ours. It may be very natural to have this loyalty to our own species, but let us hear no more from the naturalists about the "sentimentality" of antivivisectionists. If loyalty to our own species, preference for man simply because we are men, is not a sentiment, then what is? It may be a good sentiment or a bad one. But a sentiment it certainly is. Try to base it on logic and see what happens!

8   But the most sinister thing about modern vivisection is this. If a mere sentiment justifies cruelty, why stop at a sentiment for the whole human race? There is also a sentiment for the white man against the black, for a *Herrenvolk*[2] against the non-Aryans, for "civilized" or "progressive" peoples against "savages" or "backward" peoples. Finally, for our own country, party or class against others. Once the old Christian idea of a total difference in kind between man and beast has been abandoned, then no argument for experiments on animals can be found which is not also an argument for experiments on inferior men. If we cut up beasts simply because they cannot prevent us and because we are backing our own side in the struggle for existence, it is only logical to cut up imbeciles, criminals, enemies or capitalists for the same reasons. Indeed,

___

2. Editors' note: German for "master race."

experiments on men have already begun. We all hear that Nazi scientists have done them. We all suspect that our own scientists may begin to do so, in secret, at any moment.

The alarming thing is that the vivisectors have won the first round. In the nineteenth and eighteenth centuries a man was not stamped as a "crank" for protesting against vivisection. Lewis Carroll protested, if I remember his famous letter correctly, on the very same ground which I have just used.[3] Dr. Johnson—a man whose mind had as much *iron* in it as any man's—protested in a note on *Cymbeline* which is worth quoting in full. In Act I, scene v, the Queen explains to the Doctor that she wants poisons to experiment on "such creatures as We count not worth the hanging,—but none human."[4] The Doctor replies:

Your Highness
Shall from this practice but make hard your heart.[5]

Johnson comments: "The thought would probably have been more amplified, had our author lived to be shocked with such experiments as have been published in later times, by a race of men that have practised tortures without pity, and related them without shame, and are yet suffered to erect their heads among human beings."[6]

The words are his, not mine, and in truth we hardly dare in these days to use such calmly stern language. The reason why we do not dare is that the other side has in fact won. And though cruelty even to beasts is an important matter, their victory is symptomatic of matters more important still. The victory of vivisection marks a great advance in the triumph of ruthless, non-moral, utilitarianism over the old world of ethical law; a triumph in which we, as well as animals, are already the victims, and of which Dachau and Hiroshima mark the more recent achievements. In justifying cruelty to animals we put ourselves also on the animal level. We choose the jungle and must abide by our choice.

You will notice I have spent no time in discussing what actually goes on in the laboratories. We shall be told, of course, that there is surprisingly little cruelty. That is a question with which, at present, I have nothing to do. We must first decide what should be allowed: after that it is for the police to discover what is already being done.

3. "Vivisection as a Sign of the Times," *The Works of Lewis Carroll*, ed. Roger Lancelyn Green (London, 1965), pp. 1089–92. See also "Some Popular Fallacies about Vivisection," ibid., pp. 1092–1100.
4. Shakespeare, *Cymbeline*, I, v, 19–20.
5. Ibid., 23.
6. *Johnson on Shakespeare: Essays and Notes Selected and Set Forth with an Introduction* by Sir Walter Raleigh (London, 1908), p. 181.

Topics for Discussion and Writing

1. What purpose does Lewis's first paragraph serve? Is his implied definition of sentimentality adequate for his purpose?

2. By the end of the second paragraph are you willing to agree, at least for the sake of argument, that pain is an evil?

3. In the third paragraph Lewis gives two examples dentistry and reformatory punishment) to prove that the infliction of pain "always requires justification." Are these two examples adequate and effective?

4. By the end of the fifth paragraph (the paragraph beginning "The Christian defender") are we more or less convinced that Lewis is fully aware of both sides of the argument? Do we feel he is fairly presenting both sides?

5. Characterize the tone (Lewis's attitude) implied in "The position may not be satisfactory" (paragraph 6). Notice also the effect of the repetition (in the same paragraph) of "We may fail to see," "We may find it difficult." "And we may feel. . . ." How tentative do you think Lewis really is?

6. The eighth paragraph begins. "But the most sinister thing about modern vivisection is this." How surprising is the word "sinister"? And why does Lewis bring in (drag in?) racist and religious persecution?

7. Late in his essay (paragraph 9) Lewis quotes Lewis Carroll, Shakespeare, and Dr. Johnson. Except for a phrase from the Bible, these are the first quotations he uses. Should he have introduced these quotations, or others, earlier?

8. Analyze the final paragraph. Is Lewis correct in dismissing the question of how much cruelty there is in laboratories? Characterize the tone of the last sentence.

Flannery O'Connor

Flannery O'Connor (1925–1964) was born in Georgia and spent most of her short life there. The Complete Stories of Flannery O'Connor *received the National Book Award for fiction in 1971; another posthumous volume,* Mystery and Manners, *includes essays on literature and an account of her experiences raising peacocks in Georgia.*

Total Effect and the Eighth Grade

In two recent instances in Georgia, parents have objected to their eighth- and ninth-grade children's reading assignments in modern fiction. This seems to happen with some regularity in cases throughout the country. The unwitting parent picks up his child's book, glances through it, comes upon passages of erotic detail or profanity, and takes off at once to complain to the school board. Sometimes, as in one of the Georgia cases, the teacher is dismissed and hackles rise in liberal circles everywhere.

The two cases in Georgia, which involved Steinbeck's *East of Eden* and John Hersey's *A Bell for Adano,* provoked considerable newspaper comment. One columnist, in commending the enterprise of the teachers, announced that students do not like to read the fusty works of the nineteenth century, that their attention can best be held by novels dealing with the realities of our own time, and that the Bible, too, is full of racy stories.

Mr. Hersey himself addressed a letter to the State School Superintendent in behalf of the teacher who had been dismissed. He pointed out that his book is not scandalous, that it attempts to convey an earnest message about the nature of democracy, and that it falls well within the limits of the principle of "total effect," that principle followed in legal cases by which a book is judged not for isolated parts but by the final effect of the whole book upon the general reader.

4   I do not want to comment on the merits of these particular cases. What concerns me is what novels ought to be assigned in the eighth and ninth grades as a matter of course, for if these cases indicate anything, they indicate the haphazard way in which fiction is approached in our high schools. Presumably there is a state reading list which contains "safe" books for teachers to assign; after that it is up to the teacher.

English teachers come in Good, Bad, and Indifferent, but too frequently in high schools anyone who can speak English is allowed to teach it. Since several novels can't easily be gathered into one textbook, the fiction that students are assigned depends upon their teacher's knowledge, ability, and taste: variable factors at best. More often than not, the teacher assigns what he thinks will hold the attention and interest of the students. Modern fiction will certainly hold it.

Ours is the first age in history which has asked the child what he would tolerate learning, but that is a part of the problem with which I am not equipped to deal. The devil of Educationism that possesses us is the kind that can be "cast out only by prayer and fasting." No one has yet come along strong enough to do it. In other ages the attention of children was held by Homer and Virgil, among others, but, by the reverse evolutionary process, that is no longer possible; our children are too stupid now to enter the past imaginatively. No one asks the student if algebra pleases him or if he finds it satisfactory that some French verbs are irregular, but if he prefers Hersey to Hawthorne, his taste must prevail.

I would like to put forward the proposition, repugnant to most English teachers, that fiction, if it is going to be taught in the high schools, should be taught as a subject and as a subject with a history. The total effect of a novel depends not only on its innate impact, but upon the experience, literary and otherwise, with which it is approached. No child needs to be assigned Hersey or Steinbeck until he is familiar with a certain amount of the best work of Cooper, Hawthorne, Melville, the early James, and Crane, and he does not need to be assigned these until he has been introduced to some of the better English novelists of the eighteenth and nineteenth centuries.

8   The fact that these works do not present him with the realities of his own time is all to the good. He is surrounded by the realities of his own time, and he

has no perspective whatever from which to view them. Like the college student who wrote in her paper on Lincoln that he went to the movies and got shot, many students go to college unaware that the world was not made yesterday; their studies began with the present and dipped backward occasionally when it seemed necessary or unavoidable.

There is much to be enjoyed in the great British novels of the nineteenth century, much that a good teacher can open up in them for the young student. There is no reason why these novels should be either too simple or too difficult for the eighth grade. For the simple, they offer simple pleasures; for the more precocious, they can be made to yield subtler ones if the teacher is up to it. Let the student discover, after reading the nineteenth-century British novel, that the nineteenth-century American novel is quite different as to its literary characteristics, and he will thereby learn something not only about these individual works but about the sea-change which a new historical situation can effect in a literary form. Let him come to modern fiction with this experience behind him, and he will be better able to see and to deal with the more complicated demands of the best twentieth-century fiction.

Modern fiction often looks simpler than the fiction that preceded it, but in reality it is more complex. A natural evolution has taken place. The author has for the most part absented himself from direct participation in the work and has left the reader to make his own way amid experiences dramatically rendered and symbolically ordered. The modern novelist merges the reader in the experience; he tends to raise the passions he touches upon. If he is a good novelist, he raises them to effect by their order and clarity a new experience—the total effect—which is not in itself sensuous or simply of the moment. Unless the child has had some literary experience before, he is not going to be able to resolve the immediate passions the book arouses into any true, total picture.

It is here the moral problem will arise. It is one thing for a child to read about adultery in the Bible or in *Anna Karenina,* and quite another for him to read about it in most modern fiction. This is not only because in both the former instances adultery is considered a sin, and in the latter, at most, an inconvenience, but because modern writing involves the reader in the action with a new degree of intensity, and literary mores permit him to be involved in any action a human being can perform.

12   In our fractured culture, we cannot agree on morals; we cannot even agree that moral matters should come before literary ones when there is a conflict between them. All this is another reason why the high schools would do well to return to their proper business of preparing foundations. Whether in the senior year students should be assigned modern novelists should depend both on their parents' consent and on what they have already read and understood.

The high-school English teacher will be fulfilling his responsibility if he furnishes the student a guided opportunity, through the best writing of the past, to come, in time, to an understanding of the best writing of the present. He will teach literature, not social studies or little lessons in democracy or the customs of many lands.

And if the student finds that this is not to his taste? Well, that is regrettable. Most regrettable. His taste should not be consulted; it is being formed.

Topics for Discussion and Writing

1. What is the function of the first three paragraphs of "Total Effect and the Eighth Grade"? Can you justify O'Connor's abrupt dismissal ("I do not want to comment on the merits of these particular cases") of the opposing argument summarized in the second and third paragraphs? How?

2. "English teachers come in Good, Bad, and Indifferent, but too frequently in high schools anyone who can speak English is allowed to teach it." Can you, from your own experience, support this view?

3. Is the tone of the sixth paragraph, beginning "Ours is the first age," sarcastic? If not, how would you characterize it?

4. Which of O'Connor's arguments might be used to support the rating of movies X, R, PG, and G? Are you for or against these ratings? How would you support your position?

George Orwell

George Orwell (1903–1950), an Englishman, adopted this name; he was born Eric Blair, in India. He was educated at Eton, in England, but in 1921 he returned to the East and served for five years as a police officer in Burma. He then returned to Europe, doing odd jobs while writing novels and stories. In 1936 he fought in the Spanish Civil War on the side of the Republicans, an experience reported in Homage to Catalonia *(1938). His last years were spent writing in England.*

Shooting an Elephant

In Moulmein, in Lower Burma, I was hated by large numbers of people—the only time in my life that I have been important enough for this to happen to me. I was sub-divisional police officer of the town, and in an aimless, petty kind of way anti-European feeling was very bitter. No one had the guts to raise a riot, but if a European woman went through the bazaars alone somebody would probably spit betel juice over her dress. As a police officer I was an obvious target and was baited whenever it seemed safe to do so. When a nimble Burman tripped me up on the football field and the referee (another Burman) looked the other way, the crowd yelled with hideous laughter. This happened more than once. In the end the sneering yellow faces of young men that met me everywhere, the insults hooted after me when I was at a safe distance, got badly on my nerves. The young Buddhist priests were the worst of all. There were several thousands of them in the town and none of them seemed to have anything to do except stand on street corners and jeer at Europeans.

All this was perplexing and upsetting. For at that time I had already made up my mind that imperialism was an evil thing and the sooner I chucked up my job and got out of it the better. Theoretically—and secretly, of course—I was all for the Burmese and all against their oppressors, the British. As for the job I was doing, I hated it more bitterly than I can perhaps make clear. In a job like that you see the dirty work of Empire at close quarters. The wretched prisoners huddling in the stinking cages of the lockups, the grey, cowed faces of the long-term convicts, the scarred buttocks of the men who had been flogged with bamboos—all these oppressed me with an intolerable sense of guilt. But I could get nothing into perspective. I was young and ill-educated and I had had to think out my problems in the utter silence that is imposed on every Englishman in the East. I did not even know that the British Empire is dying, still less did I know that it is a great deal better than the younger empires that are going to supplant it. All I knew was that I was stuck between my hatred of the empire I served and my rage against the evil-spirited little beasts who tried to make my job impossible. With one part of my mind I thought of the British Raj as an unbreakable tyranny, as something clamped down, in *saecula saeculorum,*[1] upon the will of prostrate peoples; with another part I thought that the greatest joy in the world would be to drive a bayonet into a Buddhist priest's guts. Feelings like these are the normal by-products of imperialism; ask any Anglo-Indian official, if you can catch him off duty.

One day something happened which in a roundabout way was enlightening. It was a tiny incident in itself, but it gave me a better glimpse than I had had before of the real nature of imperialism—the real motives for which despotic governments act. Early one morning the sub-inspector at a police station at the other end of the town rang me up on the 'phone and said that an elephant was ravaging the bazaar. Would I please come and do something about it? I did not know what I could do, but I wanted to see what was happening and I got on to a pony and started out. I took my rifle, an old .44 Winchester and much too small to kill an elephant, but I thought the noise might be useful *in terrorem.*[2] Various Burmans stopped me on the way and told me about the elephant's doings. It was not, of course, a wild elephant, but a tame one which had gone

1. For world without end.
2. As a warning.

"must." It had been chained up, as tame elephants always are when their attack of "must" is due, but on the previous night it had broken its chain and escaped. Its mahout, the only person who could manage it when it was in that state, had set out in pursuit, but had taken the wrong direction and was now twelve hours' journey away, and in the morning the elephant had suddenly reappeared in the town. The Burmese population had no weapons and were quite helpless against it. It had already destroyed somebody's bamboo hut, killed a cow and raided some fruit-stalls and devoured the stock; also it had met the municipal rubbish van and, when the driver jumped out and took to his heels, had turned the van over and inflicted violences upon it.

4   The Burmese sub-inspector and some Indian constables were waiting for me in the quarter where the elephant had been seen. It was a very poor quarter, a labyrinth of squalid bamboo huts, thatched with palmleaf, winding all over a steep hillside. I remember that it was a cloudy, stuffy morning at the beginning of the rains. We began questioning the people as to where the elephant had gone and, as usual, failed to get any definite information. That is invariably the case in the East; a story always sounds clear enough at a distance, but the nearer you get to the scene of events the vaguer it becomes. Some of the people said that the elephant had gone in one direction, some said that he had gone in another, some professed not even to have heard of any elephant. I had almost made up my mind that the whole story was a pack of lies, when we heard yells a little distance away. There was a loud, scandalized cry of "Go away, child! Go away this instant!" and an old woman with a switch in her hand came round the corner of a hut, violently shooing away a crowd of naked children. Some more women followed, clicking their tongues and exclaiming; evidently there was something that the children ought not to have seen. I rounded the hut and saw a man's dead body sprawling in the mud. He was an Indian, a black Dravidian coolie, almost naked, and he could not have been dead many minutes. The people said that the elephant had come suddenly upon him round the corner of the hut, caught him with its trunk, put its foot on his back and ground him into the earth. This was the rainy season and the ground was soft, and his face had scored a trench a foot deep and a couple of yards long. He was lying on his belly with arms crucified and head sharply twisted to one side. His face was coated with mud, the eyes wide open, the teeth bared and grinning with an expression of unendurable agony. (Never tell me, by the way, that the dead look peaceful. Most of the corpses I have seen look devilish.) The friction of the great beast's foot had stripped the skin from his back as neatly as one skins a rabbit. As soon as I saw the dead man I sent an orderly to a friend's house nearby to borrow an elephant rifle. I had already sent back the pony, not wanting it to go mad with fright and throw me if it smelt the elephant.

The orderly came back in a few minutes with a rifle and five cartridges, and meanwhile some Burmans had arrived and told us that the elephant was in the paddy fields below, only a few hundred yards away. As I started forward practically the whole population of the quarter flocked out of the houses and followed me. They had seen the rifle and were all shouting excitedly that I was going to shoot the elephant. They had not shown much interest in the elephant when he was merely ravaging their homes, but it was different now that he was going to be shot. It was a bit of fun to them, as it would be to an English crowd; besides they wanted the meat. It made me vaguely uneasy. I had no intention of shooting the elephant—I had merely sent for the rifle to defend myself if necessary—and it is always unnerving to have a crowd following you. I marched down the hill, looking and feeling a fool, with the rifle over my shoulder and an ever-growing army of people jostling at my heels. At the bottom, when you got away from the huts, there was a metalled road and beyond that a miry waste of paddy fields a thousand yards across, not yet ploughed but soggy from the first rains and dotted with coarse grass. The elephant was standing eight yards from the road, his left side towards us. He took not the slightest notice of the crowd's approach. He was tearing up bunches of grass, beating them against his knees to clean them and stuffing them into his mouth.

I had halted on the road. As soon as I saw the elephant I knew with perfect certainty that I ought not to shoot him. It is a serious matter to shoot a working elephant—it is comparable to destroying a huge and costly piece of machinery— and obviously one ought not to do it if it can possibly be avoided. And at that distance, peacefully eating, the elephant looked no more dangerous than a cow. I thought then and I think now that his attack of "must" was already passing off; in which case he would merely wander harmlessly about until the mahout came back and caught him. Moreover, I did not in the least want to shoot him. I decided that I would watch him for a little while to make sure that he did not turn savage again, and then go home.

But at that moment I glanced round at the crowd that had followed me. It was an immense crowd, two thousand at the least and growing every minute. It blocked the road for a long distance on either side. I looked at the sea of yellow faces above the garish clothes—faces all happy and excited over this bit of fun, all certain that the elephant was going to be shot. They were watching me as they would watch a conjurer about to perform a trick. They did not like me, but with the magical rifle in my hands I was momentarily worth watching. And suddenly I realized that I should have to shoot the elephant after all. The people expected it of me and I had got to do it; I could feel their two thousand wills pressing me forward, irresistibly. And it was at this moment, as I stood there with the rifle in my hands, that I first grasped the hollowness, the futility of the white man's dominion in the East. Here was I, the white man with his gun, standing in front of the unarmed native crowd—seemingly the leading actor of the piece; but in reality I was only an absurd puppet pushed to and fro by the will of those yellow faces behind. I perceived in this moment that when the white man turns tyrant it is his own freedom that he destroys. He becomes a sort of hollow, posing dummy, the conventionalized figure of a sahib. For it is the condition of his rule that he shall spend his life in trying to impress the "natives," and so in every crisis he has got to do what the "natives" expect of him. He wears a mask, and his face grows to fit it. I had got to shoot the elephant. I had committed myself to doing it when I sent for the rifle. A sahib has got to act like a sahib; he has got to appear resolute, to know his own mind and do definite things. To come all that way, rifle in hand, with two thousand people marching at my heels, and then to trail feebly away, having done nothing—no, that was impossible. The crowd would laugh at me. And my whole life, every white man's life in the East, was one long struggle not to be laughed at.

8   But I did not want to shoot the elephant. I watched him beating his bunch of grass against his knees, with that preoccupied grandmotherly air that elephants have. It seemed to me that it would be murder to shoot him. At that age I was not squeamish about killing animals, but I had never shot an elephant and never wanted to. (Somehow it always seems worse to kill a *large* animal.) Besides, there was the beast's owner to be considered. Alive, the elephant was worth at least a hundred pounds; dead, he would only be worth the value of his tusks, five pounds, possibly. But I had got to act quickly. I turned to some experienced-looking Burmans who had been there when we arrived, and asked them how the elephant had been behaving. They all said the same thing: he took no notice of you if you left him alone, but he might charge if you went too close to him.

It was perfectly clear to me what I ought to do. I ought to walk up to within, say, twenty-five yards of the elephant and test his behavior. If he charged, I could shoot; if he took no notice of me, it would be safe to leave him until the mahout came back. But also I knew that I was going to do no such thing. I was a poor shot with a rifle and the ground was soft mud into which one would sink at every step. If the elephant charged and I missed him, I should have about as much chance as a toad under a steam-roller. But even then I was not thinking particularly of my own skin, only of the watchful yellow faces behind. For at that moment, with the crowd watching me, I was not afraid in the ordinary sense, as I would have been if I had been alone. A white man mustn't be frightened in front of "natives"; and so, in general, he isn't frightened. The sole thought in my mind was that if anything went wrong those two thousand Burmans would see me pursued, caught, trampled on and reduced to a grinning corpse like that Indian up the hill. And if that happened it was quite probable that some of them would laugh. That would never do. There was only one alternative. I shoved the cartridges into the magazine and lay down on the road to get a better aim.

The crowd grew very still, and a deep, low, happy sigh, as of people who see the theatre curtain go up at last, breathed from innumerable throats. They were going to have their bit of fun after all. The rifle was a beautiful German thing with cross-hair sights. I did not then know that in shooting an elephant one would shoot to cut an imaginary bar running from ear-hole to ear-hole. I ought, therefore, as the elephant was sideways on, to have aimed straight at his ear-hole; actually I aimed several inches in front of this, thinking the brain would be further forward.

When I pulled the trigger I did not hear the bang or feel the kick—one never does when a shot goes home—but I heard the devilish roar of glee that went up from the crowd. In that instant, in too short a time, one would have thought, even for the bullet to get there, a mysterious, terrible change had come over the elephant. He neither stirred nor fell, but every line of his body had altered. He looked suddenly stricken, shrunken, immensely old, as though the frightful impact of the bullet had paralysed him without knocking him down. At last, after what seemed a long time—it might have been five seconds, I dare say—he sagged flabbily to his knees. His mouth slobbered. An enormous senility seemed to have settled upon him. One could have imagined him thousands of years old. I fired again into the same spot. At the second shot he did not collapse but climbed with desperate slowness to his feet and stood weakly upright, with legs sagging and head drooping. I fired a third time. That was the shot that did for him. You could see the agony of it jolt his whole body and knock the last remnant of strength from his legs. But in falling he seemed for a moment to rise, for as his hind legs collapsed beneath him he seemed to tower upward like a huge rock toppling, his trunk reaching skywards like a tree. He trumpeted, for the first and only time. And then down he came, his belly towards me, with a crash that seemed to shake the ground even where I lay.

12   I got up. The Burmans were already racing past me across the mud. It was obvious that the elephant would never rise again, but he was not dead. He was breathing very rhythmically with long rattling gasps, his great mound of a side painfully rising and falling. His mouth was wide open. I could see far down into caverns of pale pink throat. I waited a long time for him to die, but his breathing did not weaken. Finally I fired my two remaining shots into the spot where I thought his heart must be. The thick blood welled out of him like red velvet, but still he did not die. His body did not even jerk when the shots hit him, the tortured breathing continued without a pause. He was dying, very slowly and in great agony, but in some world remote from me where not even a bullet could damage him further. I felt I had got to put an end to that dreadful noise. It seemed dreadful to see the great beast lying there, powerless to move and yet powerless to die, and not even to be able to finish him. I sent back for my small rifle and poured shot after shot into his heart and down his throat. They seemed to make no impression. The tortured gasps continued as steadily as the ticking of a clock.

In the end I could not stand it any longer and went away. I heard later that it took him half an hour to die. Burmans were bringing dahs and baskets even before I left, and I was told they had stripped his body almost to the bones by the afternoon.

Afterwards, of course, there were endless discussions about the shooting of the elephant. The owner was furious, but he was only an Indian and could do nothing. Besides, legally I had done the right thing, for a mad elephant has to be killed, like a mad dog, if its owner fails to control it. Among the Europeans opinion was divided. The older men said I was right, the younger men said it was a damn shame to shoot an elephant for killing a coolie, because an elephant was worth more than any damn Coringhee coolie. And afterwards I was very glad that the coolie had been killed; it put me legally in the right and it gave me a sufficient pretext for shooting the elephant. I often wondered whether any of the others grasped that I had done it solely to avoid looking a fool.

Topics for Discussion and Writing

1. How does Orwell characterize himself at the time of the events he describes? What evidence in the essay suggests that he wrote it some years later?

2. Orwell says the incident was "enlightening." What does he mean? Picking up this clue, state in a sentence or two the thesis or main point of the essay.

3. Compare Orwell's description of the dead coolie (in the fourth paragraph) with his description of the elephant's death (in the eleventh and twelfth paragraphs). Why does Orwell devote more space to the death of the elephant?

4. How would you describe the tone of the last paragraph, particularly of the last two sentences? Do you find the paragraph an effective conclusion to the essay? Explain.

Camille Paglia

Camille Paglia, born in Endicott, New York, in 1947, and educated at the State University of New York at Binghamton and at Yale University, teaches humanities at the University of the Arts, in Philadelphia. Paglia achieved fame in 1990 with the publication of a book entitled Sexual Personae, *a study of pornographic, voyeuristic, and sadistic elements in literature. She considers herself a feminist but she has sharply criticized many other feminists, and in turn she has been sharply criticized. As she said in the preface to* Sexual Personae, *"My stress on the truth in sexual stereotypes and on the biologic basis of sex difference is sure to cause controversy." We reprint an especially controversial essay that was first printed in a popular journal,* New York Newsday, *in 1992, and has been reprinted in a collection of Paglia's essays,* Sex, Art, and American Culture.

Rape and Modern Sex War

Rape is an outrage that cannot be tolerated in civilized society. Yet feminism, which has waged a crusade for rape to be taken more seriously, has put young women in danger by hiding the truth about sex from them.

In dramatizing the pervasiveness of rape, feminists have told young women that before they have sex with a man, they must give consent as explicit as a legal contract's. In this way, young women have been convinced that they have been the victims of rape. On elite campuses in the Northeast and on the West Coast, they have held consciousness-raising sessions, petitioned administrations, demanded inquests. At Brown University, outraged, panicky "victims" have scrawled the names of alleged attackers on the walls of women's rest rooms. What marital rape was to the Seventies, "date rape" is to the Nineties.

The incidence and seriousness of rape do not require this kind of exaggeration. Real acquaintance rape is nothing new. It has been a horrible problem for women for all of recorded history. Once fathers and brothers protected women from rape. Once the penalty for rape was death. I come from a fierce Italian tradition where, not so long ago in the motherland, a rapist would end up knifed, castrated, and hung out to dry.

4   But the old clans and small rural communities have broken down. In our cities, on our campuses far from home, young women are vulnerable and defenseless. Feminism has not prepared them for this. Feminism keeps saying the sexes are the same. It keeps telling women they can do anything, go anywhere, say anything, wear anything. No, they can't. Women will always be in sexual danger.

One of my male students recently slept overnight with a friend in a passageway of the Great Pyramid in Egypt. He described the moon and sand, the ancient silence and eerie echoes. I will never experience that. I am a woman. I am not stupid enough to believe I could ever be safe there. There is a world of solitary adventure I will never have. Women have always known these somber truths. But feminism, with its pie-in-the-sky fantasies about the perfect world, keeps young women from seeing life as it is.

We must remedy social injustice whenever we can. But there are some things we cannot change. There are sexual differences that are based in biology. Academic feminism is lost in a fog of social constructionism. It believes we are totally the product of our environment. This idea was invented by Rousseau. He was wrong. Emboldened by dumb French language theory, academic feminists repeat the same hollow slogans over and over to each other. Their view of sex is naïve and prudish. Leaving sex to the feminists is like letting your dog vacation at the taxidermist's.

The sexes are at war. Men must struggle for identity against the overwhelming power of their mothers. Women have menstruation to tell them they are women. Men must do or risk something to be men. Men become masculine only when other men say they are. Having sex with a woman is one way a boy becomes a man.

8   College men are at their hormonal peak. They have just left their mothers and are questing for their male identity. In groups, they are dangerous. A woman going to a fraternity party is walking into Testosterone Flats, full of prickly cacti and blazing guns. If she goes, she should be armed with resolute alertness. She should arrive with girlfriends and leave with them. A girl who lets herself get dead drunk at a fraternity party is a fool. A girl who goes upstairs

alone with a brother at a fraternity party is an idiot. Feminists call this "blaming the victim." I call it common sense.

For a decade, feminists have drilled their disciples to say, "Rape is a crime of violence but not of sex." This sugar-coated Shirley Temple nonsense has exposed young women to disaster. Misled by feminism, they do not expect rape from the nice boys from good homes who sit next to them in class.

Aggression and eroticism are deeply intertwined. Hunt, pursuit, and capture are biologically programmed into male sexuality. Generation after generation, men must be educated, refined, and ethically persuaded away from their tendency toward anarchy and brutishness. Society is not the enemy, as feminism ignorantly claims. Society is woman's protection against rape. Feminism, with its solemn Carry Nation* repressiveness, does not see what is for men the eroticism or fun element in rape, especially the wild, infectious delirium of gang rape. Women who do not understand rape cannot defend themselves against it.

The date-rape controversy shows feminism hitting the wall of its own broken promises. The women of my Sixties generation were the first respectable girls in history to swear like sailors, get drunk, stay out all night—in short, to act like men. We sought total sexual freedom and equality. But as time passed, we woke up to cold reality. The old double standard protected women. When anything goes, it's women who lose.

12   Today's young women don't know what they want. They see that feminism has not brought sexual happiness. The theatrics of public rage over date rape are their way of restoring the old sexual rules that were shattered by my generation. Because nothing about the sexes has really changed. The comic film *Where the Boys Are* (1960), the ultimate expression of Fifties man-chasing, still speaks directly to our time. It shows smart, lively women skillfully anticipating and fending off the dozens of strategies with which horny men try to get them into bed. The agonizing date-rape subplot and climax are brilliantly done. The victim, Yvette Mimieux, makes mistake after mistake, obvious to the other girls. She allows herself to be lured away from her girlfriends and into isolation with boys whose character and intentions she misreads. *Where the Boys Are* tells the truth. It shows courtship as a dangerous game in which the signals are not verbal but subliminal.

Neither militant feminism, which is obsessed with politically correct language, nor academic feminism, which believes that knowledge and experience are "constituted by" language, can understand preverbal or nonverbal communication. Feminism, focusing on sexual politics, cannot see that sex exists in and through the body. Sexual desire and arousal cannot be fully translated into verbal terms. This is why men and women misunderstand each other.

Trying to remake the future, feminism cut itself off from sexual history. It discarded and suppressed the sexual myths of literature, art, and religion. Those

* Carry Nation, American temperance crusader (1846–1911), known for destroying bottles of liquor and barroom furniture with a hatchet.

myths show us the turbulence, the mysteries and passions of sex. In mythology we see men's sexual anxiety, their fear of woman's dominance. Much sexual violence is rooted in men's sense of psychological weakness toward women. It takes many men to deal with one woman. Woman's voracity is a persistent motif. Clara Bow, it was rumored, took on the USC football team on weekends. Marilyn Monroe, singing "Diamonds Are a Girl's Best Friend," rules a conga line of men in tuxes. Half-clad Cher, in the video for "If I Could Turn Back Time," deranges a battleship of screaming sailors and straddles a pink-lit cannon. Feminism, coveting social power, is blind to woman's cosmic sexual power.

To understand rape, you must study the past. There never was and never will be sexual harmony. Every woman must take personal responsibility for her sexuality, which is nature's red flame. She must be prudent and cautious about where she goes and with whom. When she makes a mistake, she must accept the consequences and, through self-criticism, resolve never to make that mistake again. Running to Mommy and Daddy on the campus grievance committee is unworthy of strong women. Posting lists of guilty men in the toilet is cowardly, infantile stuff.

16   The Italian philosophy of life espouses high-energy confrontation. A male student makes a vulgar remark about your breasts? Don't slink off to whimper and simper with the campus shrinking violets. Deal with it. On the spot. Say, "Shut up, you jerk! And crawl back to the barnyard where you belong!" In general, women who project this take-charge attitude toward life get harassed less often. I see too many dopey, immature, self-pitying women walking around like melting sticks of butter. It's the Yvette Mimieux syndrome: make me happy. And listen to me weep when I'm not.

The date-rape debate is already smothering in propaganda churned out by the expensive Northeastern colleges and universities, with their overconcentration of boring, uptight academic feminists and spoiled, affluent students. Beware of the deep manipulativeness of rich students who were neglected by their parents. They love to turn the campus into hysterical psychodramas of sexual transgression, followed by assertions of parental authority and concern. And don't look for sexual enlightenment from academe, which spews out mountains of books but never looks at life directly.

As a fan of football and rock music, I see in the simple, swaggering masculinity of the jock and in the noisy posturing of the heavy-metal guitarist certain fundamental, unchanging truths about sex. Masculinity is aggressive, unstable, combustible. It is also the most creative cultural force in history. Women must reorient themselves toward the elemental powers of sex, which can strengthen or destroy.

The only solution to date rape is female self-awareness and self-control. A woman's number one line of defense is herself. When a real rape occurs, she should report it to the police. Complaining to college committees because the courts "take too long" is ridiculous. College administrations are not a branch of the judiciary. They are not equipped or trained for legal inquiry. Colleges must alert incoming students to the problems and dangers of adulthood. Then colleges must stand back and get out of the sex game.

Topics for Discussion and Writing

1. In her first paragraph Paglia says that "Feminism has put young women in danger by hiding the truth about sex from them." What evidence does her essay offer to support this assertion?

2. In paragraph 7 Paglia asserts that "the sexes are at war," and she offers a brief explanation here and in paragraph 10 of why men behave as they do (or as she thinks they do). Do you find her explanation adequate? If not, why not?

3. In paragraph 17 Paglia refers to "the date-rape" debate. From this essay, or from your own experience, what issues would you say are being debated and by whom?

4. How would you define date rape? If a friend told you she had been raped on a date by another student, what would you advise her to do? What would Paglia advise her to do, or not do?

5. In her final paragraph Paglia mentions "real rape." What do you think she means by this term? What do you think she would include and what not include?

6. Also in her final paragraph Paglia says "College must alert incoming students to the problems and dangers of adulthood." How can colleges fulfill this responsibility? In your experience, how do they fulfill this responsibility? What do you think they should or should not do?

Nancy Sakamoto

Nancy Masterson Sakamoto, professor of Buddhism at the University of Hawaii, lived for a while in Osaka, where she taught English to Japanese people. This essay is a chapter from a textbook written in English, used by Japanese students taking a course in conversational English.

Conversational Ballgames

After I was married and had lived in Japan for a while, my Japanese gradually improved to the point where I could take part in simple conversations with my husband and his friends and family. And I began to notice that often, when I joined in, the others would look startled, and the conversational topic would come to a halt. After this happened several times, it became clear to me that I was doing something wrong. But for a long time, I didn't know what it was.

Finally, after listening carefully to many Japanese conversations, I discovered what my problem was. Even though I was speaking Japanese, I was handling the conversation in a western way.

Japanese-style conversations develop quite differently from western-style conversations. And the difference isn't only in the languages. I realized that just as I kept trying to hold western-style conversations even when I was speaking Japanese, so my English students kept trying to hold Japanese-style conversations even when they were speaking English. We were unconsciously playing entirely different conversational ballgames.

4   A western-style conversation between two people is like a game of tennis. If I introduce a topic, a conversational ball, I expect you to hit it back. If you agree with me, I don't expect you simply to agree and do nothing more. I expect you to add something—a reason for agreeing, another example, or an elaboration to carry the idea further. But I don't expect you always to agree. I am just as happy if you question me, or challenge me, or completely disagree with me. Whether you agree or disagree, your response will return the ball to me.

And then it is my turn again. I don't serve a new ball from my original starting line. I hit your ball back again from where it has bounced. I carry your idea further, or answer your questions or objections, or challenge or question you. And so the ball goes back and forth, with each of us doing our best to give it a new twist, an original spin, or a powerful smash.

And the more vigorous the action, the more interesting and exciting the game. Of course, if one of us gets angry, it spoils the conversation, just as it spoils a tennis game. But getting excited is not at all the same as getting angry. After all, we are not trying to hit each other. We are trying to hit the ball. So long as we attack only each other's opinions, and do not attack each other personally, we don't expect anyone to get hurt. A good conversation is supposed to be interesting and exciting.

If there are more than two people in the conversation, then it is like doubles in tennis, or like volleyball. There's no waiting in line. Whoever is nearest and quickest hits the ball, and if you step back, someone else will hit it. No one stops the game to give you a turn. You're responsible for taking your own turn.

8   But whether it's two players or a group, everyone does his best to keep the ball going, and no one person has the ball for very long.

A Japanese-style conversation, however, is not at all like tennis or volleyball. It's like bowling. You wait for your turn. And you always know your place in line. It depends on such things as whether you are older or younger, a close friend or a relative stranger to the previous speaker, in a senior or junior position, and so on.

When your turn comes, you step up to the starting line with your bowling ball, and carefully bowl it. Everyone else stands back and watches politely, murmuring encouragement. Everyone waits until the ball has reached the end of the alley, and watches to see if it knocks down all the pins, or only some of them, or none of them. There is a pause, while everyone registers your score.

Then, after everyone is sure that you have completely finished your turn, the next person in line steps up to the same starting line, with a different ball. He doesn't return your ball, and he does not begin from where your ball stopped. There is no back and forth at all. All the balls run parallel. And there is always a suitable pause between turns. There is no rush, no excitement, no scramble for the ball.

12   No wonder everyone looked startled when I took part in Japanese conversations. I paid no attention to whose turn it was, and kept snatching the ball halfway down the alley and throwing it back at the bowler. Of course the conversation died. I was playing the wrong game.

This explains why it is almost impossible to get a western-style conversation or discussion going with English students in Japan. I used to think that the problem was their lack of English language ability. But I finally came to realize that the biggest problem is that they, too, are playing the wrong game.

Whenever I serve a volleyball, everyone just stands back and watches it fall, with occasional murmurs of encouragement. No one hits it back. Everyone waits until I call on someone to take a turn. And when that person speaks, he doesn't hit my ball back. He serves a new ball. Again, everyone just watches it fall.

So I call on someone else. This person does not refer to what the previous speaker has said. He also serves a new ball. Nobody seems to have paid any attention to what anyone else has said. Everyone begins again from same starting line, and all the balls run parallel. There is never any back and forth. Everyone is trying to bowl with a volleyball.

16   And if I try a simpler conversation, with only two of us, then the other person tries to bowl with my tennis ball. No wonder foreign English teachers in Japan get discouraged.

Now that you know about the difference in the conversational ballgames, you may think that all your troubles are over. But if you have been trained all your life to play one game, it is no simple matter to switch to another, even if you know the rules. Knowing the rules is not at all the same thing as playing the game.

Even now, during a conversation in Japanese I will notice a startled reaction, and belatedly realize that once again I have rudely interrupted by instinctively trying to hit back the other person's bowling ball. It is no easier for me to "just listen" during a conversation, than it is for my Japanese students to "just relax" when speaking with foreigners. Now I can truly sympathize with how hard they must find it to try to carry on a western-style conversation.

If I have not yet learned to do conversational bowling in Japanese, at least I have figured out one thing that puzzled me for a long time. After his first trip to America, my husband complained that Americans asked him so many questions and made him talk so much at the dinner table that he never had a chance to eat.

When I asked him why he couldn't talk and eat at the same time, he said that Japanese do not customarily think that dinner, especially on fairly formal occasions, is a suitable time for extended conversation.

20   Since westerners think that conversation is an indispensable part of dining, and indeed would consider it impolite not to converse with one's dinner partner, I found this Japanese custom rather strange. Still, I could accept it as a cultural difference even though I didn't really understand it. But when my husband added, in explanation, that Japanese consider it extremely rude to talk with one's mouth full, I got confused. Talking with one's mouth full is certainly not an American custom. We think it very rude, too. Yet we still manage to talk a lot and eat at the same time. How do we do it?

For a long time, I couldn't explain it, and it bothered me. But after I discovered the conversational ballgames, I finally found the answer. Of course! In a western-style conversation, you hit the ball, and while someone else is hitting it back, you take a bite, chew, and swallow. Then you hit the ball again, and then eat some more. The more people there are in the conversation, the more chances you have to eat. But even with only two of you talking, you still have plenty of chances to eat.

Maybe that's why polite conversation at the dinner table has never been a traditional part of Japanese etiquette. Your turn to talk would last so long without interruption that you'd never get a chance to eat.

Topics for Discussion and Writing

1. This essay, by an American woman married to a Japanese man, comes from a textbook designed to teach Japanese students to read English and to learn about American culture. Strictly speaking, the first two paragraphs are not necessary to the points that follow. Do they serve any function?

2. The writer is chiefly seeking to tell her Japanese students something about Western habits of conversation. Why, then, does she also tell them about Japanese habits?

3. Why does Sakamoto bother to use a metaphor (or figurative comparison), seeing conversations as ballgames?

4. If you are familiar with a culture other than what can be called Anglo-American, what metaphor might you use to clarify differences between some Anglo-American social act—say, eating, or talking, or child care, or courting—and the corresponding act in the other culture?

5. For the next few days eavesdrop and try to take notes on a particularly lively conversation you happen to hear. As soon as possible, try to recon-struct the entire conversation in writing. Then analyze it. Does it follow the "rules" Sakamoto describes for either a Western-style or a Japanese-style

conversation? Or does it resemble something other than a game, perhaps a musical composition? Whatever you find, record your observations in a paragraph. (A suggestion: if you can manage to do so, record a conversation—and the accompanying gestures—between preschool children.)

May Sarton

May Sarton, born in Belgium in 1912, was brought to the United States in 1916; in 1924 she became a citizen. A teacher of writing and a distinguished writer herself, she has received numerous awards for her fiction, poetry, and essays.

The Rewards of Living a Solitary Life

The other day an acquaintance of mine, a gregarious and charming man, told me he had found himself unexpectedly alone in New York for an hour or two between appointments. He went to the Whitney and spent the "empty" time looking at things in solitary bliss. For him it proved to be a shock nearly as great as falling in love to discover that he could enjoy himself so much alone.

What had he been afraid of, I asked myself? That, suddenly alone, he would discover that he bored himself, or that there was, quite simply, no self there to meet? But having taken the plunge, he is now on the brink of adventure; he is about to be launched into his own inner space, space as immense, unexplored, and sometimes frightening as outer space to the astronaut. His every perception will come to him with a new freshness and, for a time, seem startlingly original. For anyone who can see things for himself with a naked eye becomes, for a moment or two, something of a genius. With another human being present vision becomes double vision, inevitably. We are busy wondering, what does my companion see or think of this, and what do I think of it? The original impact gets lost, or diffused.

"Music I heard with you was more than music."[*] Exactly. And therefore music *itself* can only be heard alone. Solitude is the salt of personhood. It brings out the authentic flavor of every experience.

4   "Alone one is never lonely: the spirit adventures, walking / In a quiet garden, in a cool house, abiding single there."

* A line from Conrad Aiken's *Bread and Music* (1914).

Loneliness is most acutely felt with other people, for with others, even with a lover sometimes, we suffer from our differences of taste, temperament, mood. Human intercourse often demands that we soften the edge of perception, or withdraw at the very instant of personal truth for fear of hurting, or of being inappropriately present, which is to say naked, in a social situation. Alone we can afford to be wholly whatever we are, and to feel whatever we feel absolutely. That is a great luxury!

For me the most interesting thing about a solitary life, and mine has been that for the last twenty years, is that it becomes increasingly rewarding. When I can wake up and watch the sun rise over the ocean, as I do most days, and know that I have an entire day ahead, uninterrupted, in which to write a few pages, take a walk with my dog, lie down in the afternoon for a long think (why does one think better in a horizontal position?), read and listen to music, I am flooded with happiness.

I am lonely only when I am overtired, when I have worked too long without a break, when for the time being I feel empty and need filling up. And I am lonely sometimes when I come back home after a lecture trip, when I have seen a lot of people and talked a lot, and am full to the brim with experience that needs to be sorted out.

8   Then for a little while the house feels huge and empty, and I wonder where my self is hiding. It has to be recaptured slowly by watering the plants, perhaps, and looking again at each one as though it were a person, by feeding the two cats, by cooking a meal.

It takes a while, as I watch the surf blowing up in fountains at the end of the field, but the moment comes when the world falls away, and the self emerges again from the deep unconscious, bringing back all I have recently experienced to be explored and slowly understood, when I can converse again with my hidden powers, and so grow, and so be renewed, till death do us part.

Topics for Discussion and Writing

1. The essay opens with an anecdote about an acquaintance of the author's. Why are we told at the outset that he is "a gregarious and charming man"?

2. In paragraph 2 Sarton compares inner space with outer space. And in paragraph 3 she writes, "Solitude is the salt of personhood." How do you interpret these metaphors? How do they enrich her main point, that solitude is rewarding?

3. What does Sarton mean when in her first paragraph she says, "Anyone who can see things for himself with a naked eye becomes, for a moment or two, something of a genius"? Does your own experience confirm her comment? Explain.

4. What phrase in the last paragraph connects the ending with the first paragraph?

5. Drawing on Sarton's essay, in a paragraph explain the distinction between being "alone" and being "lonely."

6. In an essay of about 500 words explain the difference between loving and being in love.

Jonathan Swift

Jonathan Swift (1667–1745) was born in Ireland of an English family. He was ordained in the Church of Ireland in 1694, and in 1714 he became dean of Saint Patrick's Cathedral, Dublin. He wrote abundantly on political and religious topics, often motivated (in his own words) by "savage indignation." It is ironic that Gulliver's Travels, *the masterpiece by this master of irony, is most widely thought of as a book for children.*

From the middle of the sixteenth century the English regulated the Irish economy so that it would enrich England. Heavy taxes and other repressive legislation impoverished Ireland, and in 1728, the year before Swift wrote "A Modest Proposal," Ireland was further weakened by a severe famine. Swift, deeply moved by the injustice, the stupidity, and the suffering that he found in Ireland, adopts the disguise or persona of an economist and offers an ironic suggestion on how Irish families may improve their conditions.

A Modest Proposal

For Preventing the Children of Poor People in Ireland from Being a Burden to Their Parents or Country, and for Making Them Beneficial to the Public

It is melancholy object to those who walk through this great town or travel in the country, when they see the streets, the roads, and cabin doors, crowded with beggars of the female sex, followed by three, four, or six children, all in rags and importuning every passenger for an alms. These mothers, instead of being able to work for their honest livelihood, are forced to employ all their time in strolling to beg sustenance for their helpless infants: who as they grow up either turn thieves for want of work, or leave their dear native country to fight for the pretender in Spain, or sell themselves to the Barbadoes.

I think it is agreed by all parties that this prodigious number of children in the arms, or on the backs, or at the heels of their mothers, and frequently of their fathers, is in the present deplorable state of the kingdom a very great additional grievance; and, therefore, whoever could find out a fair, cheap, and easy method of making these children sound, useful members of the commonwealth, would deserve so well of the public as to have his statue set up for a preserver of the nation.

But my intention is very far from being confined to provide only for the children of professed beggars; it is of a much greater extent, and shall take in the whole number of infants at a certain age who are born of parents in effect as little able to support them as those who demand our charity in the streets.

4   As to my own part, having turned my thoughts for many years upon this important subject, and maturely weighed the several schemes of our projectors, I have always found them grossly mistaken in their computation. It is true, a child just dropped from its dam may be supported by her milk for a solar year, with little other nourishment; at most not above the value of 2s.,* which the mother may certainly get, or the value in scraps, by her lawful occupation of begging; and it is exactly at one year old that I propose to provide for them in such a manner as instead of being a charge upon their parents or the parish, or wanting food and raiment for the rest of their lives, they shall on the contrary contribute to the feeding, and partly to the clothing, of many thousands.

There is likewise another great advantage in my scheme, that it will prevent those voluntary abortions, and that horrid practice of women murdering their bastard children, alas! too frequent among us! sacrificing the poor innocent babes I doubt more to avoid the expense than the shame, which would move tears and pity in the most savage and inhuman breast.

The number of souls in this kingdom being usually reckoned one million and a half, of these I calculate there may be about 200,000 couple whose wives are breeders; from which number I subtract 30,000 couple who are able to maintain their own children (although I apprehend there cannot be so many, under the present distress of the kingdom); but this being granted, there will remain 170,000 breeders. I again subtract 50,000 for those women who miscarry, or whose children die by accident or disease within the year. There only remain 120,000 children of poor parents annually born. The question therefore is, how this number shall be reared and provided for? which, as I have already said, under the present situation of affairs, is utterly impossible by all the methods hitherto proposed. For we can neither employ them in handicraft or agriculture; we neither build houses (I mean in the country) nor cultivate land; they can very seldom pick up a livelihood by stealing, till they arrive at six years old, except where they are of towardly parts; although I confess they learn the rudiments much earlier; during which time they can, however, be properly looked upon only as probationers; as I have been informed by a principal gentleman in the county of Cavan, who protested to me that he never knew above one or two instances under the age of six, even in a part of the kingdom so renowned for the quickest proficiency in that art.

I am assured by our merchants, that a boy or a girl before twelve years old is no saleable commodity; and even when they come to this age they will not yield above 31. or 31.2s.6d. at most on the exchange; which cannot turn to account either to the parents or kingdom, the charge of nutriment and rags having been at least four times that value.

8   I shall now therefore humbly propose my own thoughts, which I hope will not be liable to the least objection.

I have been assured by a very knowing American of my acquaintance in London, that a young healthy child well nursed is at a year old a most delicious, nourishing, and wholesome food, whether stewed, roasted, baked, or broiled; and I make no doubt that it will equally serve in a fricassee or a ragout.

I do therefore humbly offer it to public consideration that of the 120,000 children already computed, 20,000 may be reserved for breed, whereof only one-fourth part to be males; which is more than we allow to sheep, black cattle, or swine; and my reason is, that these children are seldom the fruits of marriage, a circumstance not much regarded by our savages; therefore one male will be sufficient to serve four females. That the remaining 100,000 may, at a year old, be offered in sale to the persons of quality and fortune through the kingdom; always advising the mother to let them suck plentifully in the last month, so as to render them plump and fat for a good table. A child will make two dishes at an entertainment for friends; and when the family dines alone, the fore or hind quarter will make a reasonable dish, and seasoned with a little pepper or salt will be very good boiled on the fourth day, especially in winter.

I have reckoned upon a medium that a child just born will weigh 12 pounds, and in a solar year, if tolerably nursed, will increase to 28 pounds.

12   I grant this food will be somewhat dear, and therefore very proper for landlords, who, as they have already devoured most of the parents, seem to have the best title to the children.

Infant's flesh will be in season throughout the year, but more plentiful in March, and a little before and after: for we are told by a grave author, an eminent French physician, that fish being a prolific diet, there are more children born in Roman Catholic countries about nine months after Lent than at any other season; therefore, reckoning a year after Lent, the markets will be more glutted than usual, because the number of popish infants is at least three to one in this kingdom: and therefore it will have one other collateral advantage, by lessening the number of papists among us.

I have already computed the charge of nursing a beggar's child (in which list I reckon all cottagers, laborers, and four-fifths of the farmers) to be about 2s. per annum, rags included; and I believe no gentleman would repine to give 10s. for the carcass of a good fat child, which, as I have said, will make four dishes of excellent nutritive meat, when he has only some particular friend or his own family to dine with him. Thus the squire will learn to be a good landlord, and grow popular among the tenants; the mother will have 8s. net profit, and be fit for work till she produces another child.

Those who are more thrifty (as I must confess the times require) may flay the carcass; the skin of which artificially dressed will make admirable gloves for ladies, and summer boots for fine gentlemen.

16   As to our city of Dublin, shambles may be appointed for this purpose in the most convenient parts of it, and butchers we may be assured will not be wanting: although I rather recommend buying the children alive, and dressing them hot from the knife as we do roasting pigs.

A very worthy person, a true lover of his country, and whose virtues I highly esteem, was lately pleased in discoursing on this matter to offer a refinement upon my scheme. He said that many gentlemen of this kingdom, having of late destroyed their deer, he conceived that the want of venison might be well supplied by the bodies of young lads and maidens, not exceeding fourteen years of age nor under twelve; so great a number of both sexes in every country being now ready to starve for want of work and service; and these to be disposed of by their parents, if alive, or otherwise by their nearest relations. But with due deference to so excellent a friend and so deserving a patriot, I cannot be altogether in his sentiments; for as to the males, my American acquaintance assured me from frequent experience that their flesh was generally tough and lean, like that of our schoolboys by continual exercise, and their taste disagreeable; and to fatten them would not answer the charge. Then as to the females, it would, I think, with humble submission be a loss to the public, because they soon would become breeders themselves: and besides, it is not improbable that some scrupulous people might be apt to censure such a practice (although indeed very unjustly), as a little bordering upon cruelty; which, I confess, has always been with me the strongest objection against any project, how well soever intended.

But in order to justify my friend, he confessed that this expedient was put into his head by the famous Psalmanazar, a native of the island Formosa, who came from thence to London about twenty years ago: and in conversation told my friend, that in his country when any young person happened to be put to death, the executioner sold the carcass to persons of quality as a prime dainty; and that in his time the body of a plump girl of fifteen, who was crucified for an attempt to poison the emperor, was sold to his imperial majesty's prime minister of state, and other great mandarins of the court, in joints from the gibbet, at 400 crowns. Neither indeed can I deny, that if the same use were made of several plump young girls in this town, who without one single groat to their fortunes cannot stir abroad without a chair, and appear at the playhouse and assemblies in foreign fineries which they never will pay for, the kingdom would not be the worse.

Some persons of a desponding spirit are in great concern about that vast number of poor people, who are aged, diseased, or maimed, and I have been desired to employ my thoughts what course may be taken to ease the nation of so grievous an encumbrance. But I am not in the least pain upon that matter, because it is very well known that they are every day dying and rotting by cold and famine, and filth and vermin, as fast as can be reasonably expected. And as to the young laborers, they are now in as hopeful a condition: they cannot get work, and consequently pine away for want of nourishment, to a degree that if at any time they are accidentally hired to common labor, they have not strength to perform it; and thus the country and themselves are happily delivered from the evils to come.

20   I have too long digressed, and therefore shall return to my subject. I think the advantages by the proposal which I have made are obvious and many, as well as of the highest importance.

For first, as I have already observed, it would greatly lessen the number of papists, with whom we are yearly overrun, being the principal breeders of the nation as well as our most dangerous enemies; and who stay at home on purpose to deliver the kingdom to the Pretender, hoping to take their advantage by the absence of so many good Protestants, who have chosen rather to leave their country than stay at home and pay tithes against their conscience to an Episcopal curate.

Secondly, The poor tenants will have something valuable of their own, which by law may be made liable to distress and help to pay their landlord's rent, their corn and cattle being already seized, and money a thing unknown.

Thirdly, Whereas the maintenance of 100,000 children from two years old and upward, cannot be computed at less than 10s. a-piece per annum, the nation's stock will be thereby increased £50,000 per annum, beside the profit of a new dish introduced to the tables of all gentlemen of fortune in the kingdom who have any refinement in taste. And the money will circulate among ourselves, the goods being entirely of our own growth and manufacture.

24   Fourthly, The constant breeders beside the gain of 8s. sterling per annum by the sale of their children, will be rid of the charge of maintaining them after the first year.

Fifthly, This food would likewise bring great custom to taverns, where the vintners will certainly be so prudent as to procure the best receipts for dressing it to perfection, and consequently have their houses frequented by all the fine gentlemen, who justly value themselves upon their knowledge in good eating; and a skilful cook who understands how to oblige his guests, will contrive to make it as expensive as they please.

Sixthly, This would be a great inducement to marriage, which all wise nations have either encouraged by rewards or enforced by laws and penalties. It would increase the care and tenderness of mothers toward their children, when they were sure of a settlement for life to the poor babes, provided in some sort by the public, to their annual profit instead of expense. We should see an honest emulation among the married women, which of them would bring the fattest child to the market. Men would become as fond of their wives during the time of their pregnancy as they are now of their mares in foal, their cows in calf, their sows when they are ready to farrow; nor offer to beat or kick them (as is too frequent a practice) for fear of a miscarriage.

Many other advantages might be enumerated. For instance, the addition of some thousand carcasses in our exportation of barreled beef, the propagation of swine's flesh, and improvement in the art of making good bacon, so much wanted among us by the great destruction of pigs, too frequent at our table; which are no way comparable in taste or magnificence to a well-grown, fat, yearling child, which roasted whole will make a considerable figure at a lord mayor's feast or any other public entertainment. But this and many others I omit, being studious of brevity.

28   Supposing that 1,000 families in this city would be constant customers for infants' flesh, besides others who might have it at merry-meetings, particularly at weddings and christenings, I compute that Dublin would take off annually about 20,000 carcasses; and the rest of the kingdom (where probably they will be sold somewhat cheaper) the remaining 80,000.

I can think of no one objection that will possibly be raised against this proposal, unless it should be urged that the number of people will be thereby much lessened in the kingdom. This I freely own, and it was indeed one principal design in offering it to the world. I desire the reader will observe, that I calculate my remedy for this one individual kingdom of Ireland and for no other that ever was, is, or I think ever can be upon earth. Therefore let no man talk to me of other expedients: of taxing our absentees at 5s. a pound: of using neither clothes nor household furniture except what is of our own growth and manufacture: of utterly rejecting the materials and instruments that promote foreign luxury: of curing the expensiveness of pride, vanity, idleness,and gaming in our women: of introducing a vein of parsimony, prudence, and temperance: of learning to love our country, in the want of which we differ even from Laplanders and the inhabitants of Topinamboo: of quitting our animosities and factions, nor acting any longer like the Jews, who were murdering one another at the very moment their city was taken: of being a little cautious not to sell our country and conscience for nothing: of teaching landlords to have at least one degree of mercy toward their tenants: lastly, of putting a spirit of honesty, industry, and skill into our shopkeepers; who, if a resolution could now be taken to buy only our native goods, would immediately unite to cheat and exact upon us in the price, the measure, and the goodness, nor could ever yet be brought to make one fair proposal of just dealing, though often and earnestly invited to it.

Therefore, I repeat, let no man talk to me of these and the like expedients, till he has at least some glimpse of hope that there will be ever some hearty and sincere attempt to put them in practice.

But as to myself, having been wearied out for many years with offering vain, idle, visionary thoughts, and at length utterly despairing of success, I fortunately fell upon this proposal; which, as it is wholly new, so it has something solid and real, of no expense and little trouble, full in our own power, and whereby we can incur no danger in disobliging England. For this kind of commodity will not bear exportation, the flesh being of too tender a consistence to admit a long continuance in salt, although perhaps I could name a country which would be glad to eat up our whole nation without it.

32   After all, I am not so violently bent upon my own opinion as to reject any offer proposed by wise men, which shall be found equally innocent, cheap, easy, and effectual. But before something of that kind shall be advanced in contradiction to my scheme, and offering a better, I desire the author or authors will be pleased maturely to consider two points. First, as things now stand, how they will be able to find food and raiment for 100,000 useless mouths and backs. And secondly, there being a round million of creatures in human figure throughout this kingdom, whose subsistence put into a common stock would leave them in debt 200,000,000*l.* sterling, adding those who are beggars by profession to the bulk of farmers, cottagers, and laborers, with the wives and children who are beggars in effect; I desire those politicians who dislike my overture, and may perhaps be so bold as to attempt an answer, that they will first ask the parents of these mortals, whether they would not at this day think it a great happiness to have been sold for food at a year old in the manner, I prescribe, and thereby have avoided such a perpetual scene of misfortunes as they have since gone through by the oppression of landlords, the impossibility of paying rent without money or trade, the want of common sustenance, with neither house nor clothes to cover them from the inclemencies of the weather, and the most inevitable prospect of entailing the like or greater miseries upon their breed for ever.

I profess, in the sincerity of my heart, that I have not the least personal interest in endeavoring to promote this necessary work, having no other motive than the public good of my country, by advancing our trade, providing for infants, relieving the poor, and giving some pleasure to the rich. I have no children by which I can propose to get a single penny; the youngest being nine years old, and my wife past child-bearing.

Topics for Discussion and Writing

1. Characterize the pamphleteer (not Swift but his persona) who offers his "modest proposal." What sort of man does he think he is? What sort of man do we regard him as? Support your assertions with evidence.

2. In the first paragraph the speaker says that the sight of mothers begging is "melancholy." In this paragraph what assumption does the speaker make about women that in part gives rise to this melancholy? Now that you are familiar with the entire essay, explain Swift's strategy in his first paragraph.

3. Explain the function of the "other expedients" (listed in paragraph 29).

4. How might you argue that although this satire is primarily ferocious, it also contains some playful touches? What specific passages might support your argument?

Studs Terkel

Studs Terkel was born Louis Terkel in New York City in 1912. He was brought up in Chicago and graduated from the University of Chicago. Terkel has been an actor, playwright, columnist, and disc jockey, but he is best known as the man who makes books out of tape recordings of people he gets to talk. We print an interview from American Dreams: Lost and Found *(1980).*

Stephen Cruz

He is thirty-nine.

"The family came in stages from Mexico. Your grandparents usually came first, did a little work, found little roots, put together a few bucks, and brought the family in, one at a time. Those were the days when controls at the border didn't exist as they do now."

You just tried very hard to be whatever it is the system wanted of you. I was a good student and, as small as I was, a pretty good athlete. I was well liked, I thought. We were fairly affluent, but we lived down where all the trashy whites were. It was the only housing we could get. As kids, we never understood why. We did everything right. We didn't have those Mexican accents, we were never on welfare. Dad wouldn't be on welfare to save his soul. He woulda died first. He worked during the depression. He carries that pride with him, even today.

4   Of the five children, I'm the only one who really got into the business world. We learned quickly that you have to look for opportunities and add things up very quickly. I was in liberal arts, but as soon as Sputnik went up, well, golly, hell, we knew where the bucks were. I went right over to the registrar's office and signed up for engineering. I got my degree in '62. If you had a master's in business as well, they were just paying all kinds of bucks. So that's what I did.

Sure enough, the market was super. I had fourteen job offers. I could have had a hundred if I wanted to look around.

I never once associated these offers with my being a minority. I was aware of the Civil Rights Act of 1964, but I was still self-confident enough to feel they wanted me because of my abilities. Looking back, the reason I got more offers than the other guys was because of the government edict. And I thought it was because I was so goddamned brilliant. (Laughs.) In 1962, I didn't get as many offers as those who were less qualified. You have a tendency to blame the job market. You just don't want to face the issue of discrimination.

I went to work with Procter & Gamble. After about two years, they told me I was one of the best supervisors they ever had and they were gonna promote me. Okay, I went into personnel. Again, I thought it was because I was such a brilliant guy. Now I started getting wise to the ways of the American Dream. My office was glass-enclosed, while all the other offices were enclosed so you couldn't see into them. I was the visible man.

They made sure I interviewed most of the people that came in. I just didn't really think there was anything wrong until we got a new plant manager, a southerner. I received instructions from him on how I should interview blacks. Just check and see if they smell, okay? That was the beginning of my training program. I started asking: Why weren't we hiring more minorities? I realized I was the only one in a management position.

8   I guess as a Mexican I was more acceptable because I wasn't really black. I was a good compromise. I was visibly good. I hired a black secretary, which was *verboten*. When I came back from my vacation, she was gone. My boss fired her while I was away. I asked why and never got a good reason.

Until then, I never questioned the American Dream. I was convinced if you worked hard, you could make it. I never considered myself different. That was the trouble. We had been discriminated against a lot, but I never associated it with society. I considered it an individual matter. Bad people, my mother used to say. In '68 I began to question.

I was doing fine. My very first year out of college, I was making twelve thousand dollars. I left Procter & Gamble because I really saw no opportunity. They were content to leave me visible, but my thoughts were not really solicited. I may have overreacted a bit, with the plant manager's attitude, but I felt there's no way a Mexican could get ahead here.

I went to work for Blue Cross. It's 1969. The Great Society is in full swing. Those who never thought of being minorities before are being turned on. Consciousness raising is going on. Black programs are popping up in universities. Cultural identity and all that. But what about the one issue in this country: economics? There were very few management jobs for minorities, especially blacks.

12   The stereotypes popped up again. If you're Oriental, you're real good in mathematics. If you're Mexican, you're a happy guy to have around, pleasant

but emotional. Mexicans are either sleeping or laughing all the time. Life is just one big happy kind of event. *Mañana.* Good to have as part of the management team, as long as you weren't allowed to make decisions.

I was thinking there were two possibilities why minorities were not making it in business. One was deep, ingrained racism. But there was still the possibility that they were simply a bunch of bad managers who just couldn't cut it. You see, until now I believed everything I was taught about the dream: the American businessman is omnipotent and fair. If we could show these turkeys there's money to be made in hiring minorities, these businessmen-good managers, good decision makers-would respond. I naïvely thought American businessmen gave a damn about society, that given a choice they would do the right thing. I had that faith.

I was hungry for learning about decision-making criteria. I was still too far away from top management to see exactly how they were working. I needed to learn more. Hey, just learn more and you'll make it. That part of the dream hadn't left me yet. I was still clinging to the notion of work your ass off, learn more than anybody else, and you'll get in that sphere.

During my fifth year at Blue Cross, I discovered another flaw in the American Dream. Minorities are as bad to other minorities as whites are to minorities. The strongest weapon the white manager had is the old divide and conquer routine. My mistake was thinking we were all at the same level of consciousness.

16   I had attempted to bring together some blacks with the other minorities. There weren't too many of them anyway. The Orientals never really got involved. The blacks misunderstood what I was presenting, perhaps I said it badly. They were on the cultural kick: a manager should be crucified for saying "Negro" instead of "black." I said as long as the Negro or the black gets the job, it doesn't mean a damn what he's called. We got into a huge hassle. Management, of course, merely smiled. The whole struggle fell flat on its face. It crumpled from divisiveness. So I learned another lesson. People have their own agenda. It doesn't matter what group you're with, there is a tendency to put the other guy down regardless.

The American Dream began to look so damn complicated, I began to think: Hell, if I wanted, I could just back away and reap the harvest myself. By this time, I'm up to twenty-five thousand dollars a year. It's beginning to look good, and a lot of people are beginning to look good. And they're saying: "Hey, the American Dream, you got it. Why don't you lay off?" I wasn't falling in line.

My bosses were telling me I had all the "ingredients" for top management. All that was required was to "get to know our business." This term comes up all the time. If I could just warn all minorities and women whenever you hear "get to know our business," they're really saying "fall in line." Stay within that fence, and glory can be yours. I left Blue Cross disillusioned. They offered me a director's job at thirty thousand dollars before I quit.

All I had to do was behave myself. I had the "ingredients" of being the good Chicano, the equivalent of the good nigger. I was smart. I could articulate well. People didn't know by my speech patterns that I was of Mexican heritage. Some tell me I don't look Mexican, that I have a certain amount of Italian, Lebanese, or who knows. (Laughs.)

20   One could easily say: "Hey, what's your bitch? The American Dream has treated you beautifully. So just knock it off and quit this crap you're spreading around." It was a real problem. Every time I turned around, America seemed to be treating me very well.

Hell, I even thought of dropping out, the hell with it. Maybe get a job in a factory. But what happened? Offers kept coming in. I just said to myself: God, isn't this silly? You might as well take the bucks and continue looking for the answer. So I did that. But each time I took the money, the conflict in me got more intense, not less.

Wow, I'm up to thirty-five thousand a year. This is a savings and loan business. I have faith in the executive director. He was the kind of guy I was looking for in top management: understanding, humane, also looking for the formula. Until he was up for consideration as executive v.p. of the entire organization. All of a sudden everything changed. It wasn't until I saw this guy flip-flop that I realized how powerful vested interests are. Suddenly he's saying: "Don't rock the boat. Keep a low profile. Get in line." Another disappointment.

Subsequently, I went to work for a consulting firm. I said to myself: Okay, I've got to get close to the executive mind. I need to know how they work. Wow, a consulting firm.

24   Consulting firms are saving a lot of American businessmen. They're doing it in ways that defy the whole notion of capitalism. They're not allowing these businesses to fail. Lockheed was successful in getting U.S. funding guarantees because of the efforts of consulting firms working on their behalf, helping them look better. In this kind of work, you don't find minorities. You've got to be a proven success in business before you get there.

The American Dream, I see now, is governed not by education, opportunity, and hard work, but by power and fear. The higher up in the organization you go, the more you have to lose. The dream is *not* losing. This is the notion pervading America today: Don't lose.

When I left the consulting business, I was making fifty-five thousand dollars a year. My last performance appraisal was: You can go a long way in this business, you can be a partner, but you gotta know our business. It came up again. At this point, I was incapable of being disillusioned any more. How easy it is to be swallowed up by the same set of values that governs the top guy. I was becoming that way. I was becoming concerned about losing that fifty grand or so a year. So I asked other minorities who had it made. I'd go up and ask 'em: "Look, do you owe anything to others?" The answer was: "We owe nothing to anybody." They drew from the civil rights movement but felt no debt. They've quickly forgotten how it happened. It's like I was when I first got out of college. Hey, it's really me, I'm great. I'm as angry with these guys as I am with the top guys.

Right now, it's confused. I've had fifteen years in the business world as "a success." Many Anglos would be envious of my progress. Fifty thousand dollars a year puts you in the one or two top percent of all Americans. Plus my wife making another thirty thousand. We had lots of money. When I gave it up, my cohorts looked at me not just as strange, but as something of a traitor. "You're screwing it up for all of us. You're part of our union, we're the elite, we should govern. What the hell are you doing?" So now I'm looked at suspiciously by my peer groups as well.

28   I'm teaching at the University of Wisconsin at Platteville. It's nice. My colleagues tell me what's on their minds. I got a farm next-door to Platteville. With farm prices being what they are (laughs), it's a losing proposition. But with university work and what money we've saved, we're gonna be all right.

The American Dream is getting more elusive. The dream is being governed by a few people's notion of what the dream is. Sometimes I feel it's a small group of financiers that gets together once a year and decides all the world's issues.

It's getting so big. The small-business venture is not there any more. Business has become too big to influence. It can't be changed internally. A counterpower is needed.

Topics for Discussion and Writing

1. In paragraph 10, Cruz refers to "The Great Society." What is (or was) "The Great Society" and how is it relevant to Cruz's story? If you aren't sure what The Great Society was, what can you learn about it from this pararaph, or others in Cruz's account?

2. In paragraphs 14 and 15 Cruz says he discovered that "Minorities are as bad to other minorities as whites are to minorities." Does this view come as a surprise to you? Or have you had experiences that tend to confirm it? Conversely, have you had experiences that tend to refute it? Explain.

3. In paragraph 17 Cruz says, "If I could just warn all minorities and women whenever you hear 'get to know the business,' they're really saying 'fall in line.' Stay within that fence. . . " If someone were to tell you "get to know the business" how else might you interpret it? Do you agree with Cruz that the message you were being given would depend on whether or not you were a member of a minority culture or a woman?

4. Cruz frequently cites The American Dream. What is Cruz's idea of the American Dream and what has disillusioned him with it? Do you find yourself in sympathy with his complaints? Why or why not?

5. Suppose you were in a position to offer Cruz a job in management, how would you evaluate him as a candidate? You might try to do this by writing a memo to your supervisor, arguing Cruz's strengths and weaknesses and making a recommendation to hire or not. (You can take as much license as you need to invent the company, your position in it, the job opening, and the resumé Cruz has presented.)

Lewis Thomas

Lewis Thomas (1913–1993) was a distinguished medical researcher and administrator. He was also a writer; among his books is Lives of a Cell, *a collection of twenty-nine short essays, which won a National Book Award in 1974, and* The Medusa and the Snail.

On Natural Death

There are so many new books about dying that there are now special shelves set aside for them in bookshops, along with the health-diet and home-repair paperbacks and the sex manuals. Some of them are so packed with detailed information and step-by-step instructions for performing the function that you'd think this was a new sort of skill which all of us are now required to learn. The strongest impression the casual reader gets, leafing through, is that proper dying has become an extraordinary, even an exotic experience, something only the specially trained get to do.

Also, you could be led to believe that we are the only creatures capable of the awareness of death, that when all the rest of nature is being cycled through dying, one generation after another, it is a different kind of process, done automatically and trivially, more "natural," as we say.

An elm in our backyard caught the blight this summer and dropped stone dead, leafless, almost overnight. One weekend it was a normal-looking elm, maybe a little bare in spots but nothing alarming, and the next weekend it was gone, passed over, departed, taken. Taken is right, for the tree surgeon came by yesterday with his crew of young helpers and their cherry picker, and took it down branch by branch and carted it off in the back of a red truck, everyone singing.

4   The dying of a field mouse, at the jaws of an amiable household cat, is a spectacle I have beheld many times. It used to make me wince. Early in life I

gave up throwing sticks at the cat to make him drop the mouse, because the dropped mouse regularly went ahead and died anyway, but I always shouted unaffections at the cat to let him know the sort of animal he had become. Nature, I thought, was an abomination.

Recently I've done some thinking about that mouse, and I wonder if his dying is necessarily all that different from the passing of our elm. The main difference, if there is one, would be in the matter of pain. I do not believe than an elm tree has pain receptors, and even so, the blight seems to me a relatively painless way to go even if there were nerve endings in a tree, which there are not. But the mouse dangling tail-down from the teeth of a gray cat is something else again, with pain beyond bearing, you'd think, all over his small body.

There are now some plausible reasons for thinking it is not like that at all, and you can make up an entirely different story about the mouse and his dying if you like. At the instant of being trapped and penetrated by teeth, peptide hormones are released by cells in the hypothalamus and the pituitary gland; instantly these substances, called endorphins, are attached to the surfaces of other cells responsible for pain perception; the hormones have the pharmacologic properties of opium; there is no pain. Thus it is that the mouse seems always to dangle so languidly from the jaws, lies there so quietly when dropped, dies of his injuries without a struggle. If a mouse could shrug, he'd shrug.

I do not know if this is true or not, nor do I know how to prove it if it is true. Maybe if you could get in there quickly enough and administer naloxone, a specific morphine antagonist, you could turn off the endorphins and observe the restoration of pain, but this is not something I would care to do or see. I think I will leave it there, as a good guess about the dying of a cat-chewed mouse, perhaps about dying in general.

8   Montaigne had a hunch about dying, based on his own close call in a riding accident. He was so badly injured as to be believed dead by his companions, and was carried home with lamentations, "all bloody, stained all over with the blood I had thrown up." He remembers the entire episode, despite having been "dead, for two full hours," with wonderment:

> It seemed to me that my life was hanging only by the tip of my lips. I closed my eyes in order, it seemed to me, to help push it out, and took pleasure in growing languid and letting myself go. It was an idea that was only floating on the surface of my soul, as delicate and feeble as all the rest, but in truth not only free from distress but mingled with that sweet feeling that people have who have let themselves slide into sleep. I believe that this is the same state in which people find themselves whom we see fainting in the agony of death, and I maintain that we pity them without cause. . . . In order to get used to the idea of death, I find there is nothing like coming close to it.

Later, in another essay, Montaigne returns to it:

If you know not how to die, never trouble yourself; Nature will in a moment fully and sufficiently instruct you; she will exactly do that business for you; take you no care for it.

The worst accident I've ever seen was on Okinawa, in the early days of the invasion, when a jeep ran into a troop carrier and was crushed nearly flat. Inside were two young MPs, trapped in bent steel, both mortally hurt, with only their heads and shoulders visible. We had a conversation while people with the right tools were prying them free. Sorry about the accident, they said. No, they said, they felt fine. Is everyone else okay, one of them said. Well, the other one said, no hurry now. And then they died.

Pain is useful for avoidance, for getting away when there's time to get away, but when it is end game, and no way back, pain is likely to be turned off, and the mechanisms for this are wonderfully precise and quick. If I had to design an ecosystem in which creatures had to live off each other and in which dying was an indispensable part of living, I could not think of a better way to manage.

Topics for Discussion and Writing

1. We find the first paragraph witty, in a quiet way. In a paragraph point out the wit to a friend who missed it.

2. Make a rough outline of Thomas's essay—perhaps a sentence for each paragraph or group of closely related paragraphs—and then, on the basis of this outline, explain the organization of the essay. In particular, account for the relation between the first paragraph and the last.

3. Thomas uses "I" fairly often. Does he talk too much about himself? Explain.

Alice Walker

Alice Walker was born in 1944 in Eatonton, Georgia, where her parents eked out a living as sharecroppers and dairy farmers: her mother also worked as a domestic. (In a collection of essays, In Search of Our Mothers' Gardens *[1984], Walker celebrates women who, like her mother, passed on a "respect for the possibilities [of life]—and the will to grasp them.") Walker attended Spelman College in Atlanta, and in 1965 finished her undergraduate work at Sarah Lawrence College near New York City. She then became active in the welfare rights movement in New York and in the voter registration movement in Georgia. Later she taught writing and literature in Mississippi, at Jackson State College and Tougaloo College, and at Wellesley College, the University of Massachusetts, and Yale University.*

Walker has written essays, poetry, and fiction. Her best-known novel, The
Color Purple (1982), won a Pulitzer Prize and the National Book Award. She has
said that her chief concern is "exploring the oppressions, the insanities, the
loyalties, and the triumphs of black women."

In Search of Our Mothers' Gardens

I described her own nature and temperament. Told how they
needed a larger life for their expression. . . . I pointed out that
in lieu of proper channels, her emotions had overflowed into
paths and dissipated them. I talked beautifully I thought, about
an art that would be born, an art that would open the way for
women the likes of her. I asked her to hope, and build up an in-
ner life against the coming of that day. . . . I sang, with a
strange quiver in my voice, a promise song.

—"AVEY," JEAN TOOMER, CANE

The poet speaking to a prostitute who falls asleep while he's talking—

When the poet Jean Toomer walked through the South in the early
twenties, he discovered a curious thing: Black women whose spirituality was so
intense, so deep, so *unconscious,* they were themselves unaware of the richness
they held. They stumbled blindly through their lives: creatures so abused and
mutilated in body, so dimmed and confused by pain, that they considered
themselves unworthy even of hope. In the selfless abstractions their bodies
became to the men who used them, they became more than "sexual objects,"
more even than mere women: they became Saints. Instead of being perceived as
whole persons, their bodies became shrines; what was thought to be their minds
became temples suitable for worship. These crazy "Saints" stared out at the
world, wildly, like lunatics—or quietly, like suicides; and the "God" that was in
their gate was as mute as a great stone.

Who were these "Saints"? These crazy, loony, pitiful women?

4 Some of them without a doubt, were out mothers and grandmothers.

In the still heat of the post-Reconstruction South, this is how they seemed
to Jean Toomer: exquisite butterflies trapped in an evil honey, toiling away their
lives in an era, a century, that did not acknowledge them, except as "the *mule* of
the world." They dreamed dreams that no one knew—not even themselves, in
any coherent fashion—and saw visions no one could understand. They

wandered or sat about the countryside crooning lullabies to ghosts, and drawing the mother of Christ in charcoal on courthouse walls.

They forced their minds to desert their bodies and their striving spirits sought to rise, the frail whirlwinds from the hard red clay. And when those frail whirlwinds, fell, in scattered particles, upon the ground, no one mourned. Instead, men lit candles to celebrate the emptiness that remained, as people do who enter a beautiful but vacant space to resurrect a God.

Our mothers and grandmothers, some of them: moving to music not yet written. And they waited.

8   They waited for a day when the unknown thing that was in them would be made known; but guessed, somehow in their darkness, that on the day of their revelation they would be long dead. Therefore to Toomer they walked, and even ran, in slow motion. For they were going nowhere immediate, and the future was not yet within their grasp. And men took our mothers and grandmothers, "but got no pleasure from it." So complex was their passion and their calm.

To Toomer, they lay vacant and fallow as autumn fields, with harvest time never in sight: and he saw them enter loveless marriages, without joy; and become prostitutes, without resistance; and become mothers of children without fulfillment.

For these grandmothers and mothers of ours were not "Saints," but Artists; driven to a numb and bleeding madness by the springs of creativity in them for which there was no release. They were Creators, who lived lives of spiritual waste, because they were so rich in spirituality—which is the basis of Art—that the strain of enduring their unused and unwanted talent drove them insane. Throwing away this spirituality was their pathetic attempts to lighten the soul to a weight their work-worn, sexually abused bodies could bear.

What did it mean for a Black woman to be an artist in our grandmothers' time? In our great-grandmothers' day? It is a question with an answer cruel enough to stop the blood.

12   Did you have a genius of a great-great-grandmother who died under some ignorant and depraved white overseer's lash? Or was she required to bake biscuits for a lazy backwater tramp, when she cried out in her soul to paint watercolors of sunsets, or the rain falling on the green and peaceful pasturelands? Or was her body broken and forced to bear children (who were more often that not sold away from her)—eight, ten, fifteen, twenty children— when her one joy was the thought of modeling heroic figures of Rebellion, in stone or clay?

How was the creativity of the Black woman kept alive, year after year and century after century, when for most of the years Black people have been in America, it was a punishable crime for a Black person to read or write? And the freedom to paint, to sculpt, to expand the mind with action, did not exist. Consider, if you can bear to imagine it, what might have been the result if singing, too, had been forbidden by law. Listen to the voices of Bessie Smith,

Billie Holiday, Nina Simone, Roberta Flack, and Aretha Franklin, among others, and imagine those voices muzzled for life. Then you may begin to comprehend the lives of our "crazy," "Sainted" mothers and grandmothers. The agony of the lives of women who might have been Poets, Novelists, Essayists, and Short Story Writers (over a period of centuries), who died with their real gifts stifled within them.

And, if this were the end of the story, we would have cause to cry out in my paraphrase of Okot p'Bitek's great poem:

O, My clanswomen
Let us call cry together!
Come,
Let us mourn the death of our mother,
The death of a Queen
The ash that was produced
By a great fire!
O this homestead is utterly dead
Close the gates
With *lacari* thorns,
For our mother
The creator of the Stool is lost!
And all the young women
Have perished in the wilderness.*

But this is not the end of the story, for all the young women—our mothers and grandmothers, *ourselves*—have not perished in the wilderness. And if we ask ourselves why, and search for and find the answer, we will know beyond all efforts to erase it from our minds, just exactly who, and of what, we Black American women are.

16   One example, perhaps the most pathetic, most misunderstood one, can provide a backdrop for our mothers' work: Phillis Wheatley, a slave in the 1700s.

Virginia Woolf, in her book, *A Room of One's Own,* wrote that in order for a woman to write fiction she must have two things, certainly: a room of her own (with a key and lock) and enough money to support herself.

What then are we to make of Phillis Wheatley, a slave, who owned not even herself? This sickly, frail, Black girl who required a servant of her own at times—her health was so precarious—and who, had she been white, would have been easily considered the intellectual superior of all the women and most of the men in the society of her day.

Virginia Woolf wrote further, speaking of course not of our Phillis, that "any woman born with a great gift in the sixteenth century [insert *eighteenth century,*

* Okot p'Bitek, *Song of Lawino: An Africa Lament* (Nairobi: East African Publishing House, 1966).

insert *Black woman,* insert *born or made a slave*] would certainly have gone crazed, shot herself, or ended her days in some lonely cottage outside the village, half witch, half wizard [insert *Saint,*] feared and mocked at. For it needs little skill and psychology to be sure that a highly gifted girl who had tried to use her gift for poetry would have been so thwarted and hindered by contrary instincts [add *chains, guns, the lash, the ownership of one's body by someone else, submission to an alien religion,*] that she must have lost her health and sanity to a certainty."

20   The key words, as they relate to Phillis, are "contrary instincts." For when we read the poetry of Phillis Wheatley—as when we read the novels of Nella Larsen or the oddly false-sounding autobiography of that freest of all Black women writers, Zora Hurston—evidence of "contrary instincts" is everywhere. Her loyalties were completely divided, as was, without question, her mind.

But how could this be otherwise? Captured at seven, a slave of wealthy, doting whites who instilled in her the "savagery" of the Africa they "rescued" her from . . . one wonders if she was even able to remember her homeland as she had known it, or as it really was.

Yet, because she did try to use her gift for poetry in a world that made her a slave, she was "so thwarted and hindered by . . . contrary instincts that she . . . lost her health. . . ." In the last years of her brief life, burdened not only with the need to express her gift but also with a penniless, friendless "freedom" and several small children for whom she was forced to do strenuous work to feed, she lost her health, certainly. Suffering from malnutrition and neglect and who knows what mental agonies, Phillis Wheately died.

So torn by "contrary instincts" was Black, kidnapped, enslaved Phillis that her description of "the Goddess"—as she poetically called the Liberty she did not have—is ironically, cruelly humorous. And, in fact, has held Phillis up to ridicule for more than a century. It is usually read prior to hanging Phillis's memory as that of a fool. She wrote:

The Goddess comes, she moves divinely fair,
Olive and laurel binds her *golden* hair:
Wherever shines this native of the skies,
Unnumber'd charms and recent graces rise.

[EMPHASIS MINE]

24   It is obvious that Phillis, the slave, combed the "Goddess's" hair every morning; prior, perhaps, to bringing in the milk, or fixing her mistress's lunch. She took her imagery from one one thing she saw elevated above all others.

With the benefit of hindsight we ask, "How could she?"

But at last, Phillis, we understand. No more snickering when your stiff, struggling, ambivalent lines are forced on us. We know now that you were not an idiot nor a traitor; only a sickly little Black girl, snatched from your home and country and made a slave; a woman who still struggled to sing the song that was your gift, although in a land of barbarians who praised you for your bewildered tongue. It is not so much what you sang, as that you kept alive, in so many of our ancestors, *the notion of song.*

II

Black women are called, in the folklore that so aptly identifies one's status in society, "the *mule* of the world," because we have been handed the burdens that everyone else—*everyone* else—refused to carry. We have been called "Matriarchs," "Superwomen," and "Mean and Evil Bitches." Not to mention "Castrators" and "Sapphire's Mama." When we have pleaded for under-standing, our character has been distorted; when we have asked for simple caring, we have been handed empty inspirational appellations, then stuck in the farthest corner. When we have asked for love, we have been given children. In short, even our plainer gifts, our labors of fidelity and love, have been knocked down our throats. To be an Artist and a Black woman, even today, lowers our status in many respects, rather than raises it: and yet, Artists we will be.

28   Therefore we must fearlessly pull out of ourselves and look at and identify with our lives the living creativity some of our great-grandmothers were not allowed to know. I stress *some* of them because it is well known that the majority of our great-grandmothers knew, even without "knowing" it, the reality of their spirituality, even if they didn't recognize it beyond what happened in the singing at church—and they never had any intention of giving it up.

How they did it: those millions of Black women who were not Phillis Wheatley, or Lucy Terry or Frances Harper or Zora Hurston or Nella Larsen or Bessie Smith—nor Elizabeth Catlett, nor Katherine Dunham, either—brings me to the title of this essay, "In Search of Our Mothers' Gardens," which is a personal account that is yet shared, in its theme and its meaning, by all of us. I found, while thinking about the far—reaching world of the creative Black woman, that often the truest answer to a question that really matters can be found very close.

In the late 1920s my mother ran away from home to marry my father. Marriage, if not running away, was expected of seventeen-year-old girls. By the time she was twenty, she had two children and was pregnant with a third. Five children later, I was born. And this is how I came to know my mother: she seemed a large, soft, loving-eyed woman who was rarely impatient in our home. Her quick, violent temper was on view only a few times a year, when she battled with the white landlord who had the misfortune to suggest to her that her children did not need to go to school.

She made all the clothes we wore, even my brothers' overalls. She made all the towels and sheets we used. She spent the summers canning vegetables and fruits. She spent the winter evenings making quilts enough to cover all our beds.

32   During the "working" day, she labored beside—not behind—my father in the fields. Her day began before sunup, and did not end until late at night. There was never a moment for her to sit down, undisturbed, to unravel her own private thoughts; never a time free from interruption—by work or the noisy inquiries of her many children. And yet, it is to my mother—and all our mothers who were not famous—that I went in search of the secret of what has fed that muzzled and often mutilated, but vibrant, creative spirit that the Black woman has inherited, and that pops out in wild and unlikely places to this day.

But when, you will ask, did my overworked mother have time to know or care about feeding the creative spirit?

The answer is so simple that many of us have spent years discovering it. We have constantly looked high, when we should have looked high—and low.

For example: in the Smithsonian Institution in Washington, D.C., there hangs a quilt unlike any other in the world. In fanciful, inspired, and yet simple and identifiable figures, it portrays the story of the Crucifixion. It is considered rare, beyond price. Though it follows no known pattern of quiltmaking, and though it is made of bits and pieces of worthless rags, it is obviously the work of a person of powerful imagination and deep spiritual feelings. Below this quilt I saw a note that says it was made by "an anonymous Black woman in Alabama, a hundred years ago."

36   If we could locate this "anonymous" Black woman from Alabama, she would turn out to be one of our grandmothers—an artist who left her mark in the only materials she could afford, and in the only medium her position in society allowed her to use.

As Virginia Woolf wrote further, in *A Room of One's Own:*

"Yet genius of a sort must have existed among women as it must have existed among the working class. [Change this to *slaves* and *the wives and daughters of sharecroppers.*] Now and again an Emily Brontë or a Robert Burns [change this to *a Zora Hurston or a Richard Wright*] blazes out and proves its presence. But certainly it never got itself on to paper. When, however, one reads of a witch being ducked, of a woman possessed by devils [or *Sainthood*], of a wise woman selling herbs [our rootworkers], or even a very remarkable man who had a mother, then I think we are on the track of a suppressed poet, of some mute and inglorious Jane Austen. . . . Indeed, I would venture to guess that Anon, who wrote so many poems without singing them, was often a woman. . . ."

And so our mothers and grandmothers have, more often than not anonymously, handed on the creative spark, the seed of the flower they themselves never hoped to see: or like a sealed letter they could not plainly read.

40   And so it is, certainly, with my own mother. Unlike Ma Rainey's songs, which retained their creator's name even while blasting forth from Bessie Smith's mouth, no song or poem will bear my mother's name. Yet so many of the stories that I write, that we all write, are my mother's stories. Only recently

did I fully realize this: that through years of listening to my mother's stories of her life, I have absorbed not only the stories themselves, but something of the manner in which she spoke, something of the urgency that involves the knowledge that her stories—like her life—must be recorded. It is probably for this reason that so much of what I have written is about characters whose counterparts in real life are so much older than I am.

But the telling of these stories, which came from my mother's lips as naturally as breathing, was not the only way my mother showed herself as an artist. For stories, too, were subject to being distracted, to dying without conclusion. Dinners must be started, and cotton must be gathered before the big rains. The artist that was and is my mother showed itself to me only after many years. This is what I finally noticed:

Like Mem, a character in *The Third Life of Grange Copeland,* my mother adorned with flowers whatever shabby house we were forced to live in. And not just your typical straggly country stand of zinnias, either. She planted ambitious gardens—and still does—with over fifty different varieties of plants that bloom profusely from early March until later November. Before she left home for the fields, she watered her flowers, chopped up the grass, and laid out new beds. When she returned from the fields she might divide clumps of bulbs, dig a cold pit, uproot and replant roses, or prune branches from her taller bushes or trees—until night came and it was too dark to see.

Whatever she planted grew as if by magic, and her fame as a grower of flowers spread over three counties. Because of her creativity with her flowers, even my memories of poverty are seen through a screen of blooms—sunflowers, petunias, roses, dahlias, forsythia, spirea, delphiniums, verbena . . . and on and on.

44   And I remember people coming to my mother's yard to be given cuttings from her flowers; I hear again the praise showered on her because whatever rocky soil she landed on, she turned into a garden. A garden so brilliant with colors, so original in its design, so magnificent with life and creativity, that to this day people drive by our house in Georgia—perfect strangers and imperfect strangers—and ask to stand or walk among my mother's art.

I notice that it is only when my mother is working in her flowers that she is radiant, almost to the point of being invisible—except as Creator: hand and eye. She is involved in work her soul must have. Ordering the universe in the image of her personal conception of Beauty.

Her face, as she prepares the Art that is her gift, is a legacy of respect she leaves to me, for all that illuminates and cherishes life. She had handed down respect for the possibilities—and the will to grasp them.

For her, so hindered and intruded upon in so many ways, being an artist has still been a daily part of her life. This ability to hold on, even in very simple ways, is work Black women have done for a very long time.

48   This poem is not enough, but it is something, for the woman who literally covered the holes in our walls with sunflowers:

They were women then
My mama's generation
Husky of voice—Stout of
Step
With fists as well as
Hands
How they battered down
Doors
And ironed
Starched white
Shirts
How they led
Armies
Headragged Generals
Across mined
Fields
Booby-trapped
Ditches
To discover books
Desks
A place for us
How they knew what we
Must know
Without knowing a page
Of it
Themselves.

Guided by my heritage of love and beauty and a respect for strength—in search of my mother's garden, I found my own.

And perhaps in Africa over two hundred years ago, there was just such a mother; perhaps she painted vivid and daring decorations in oranges and yellows and greens on the walls of her hut; perhaps she sang—in a voice like Roberta Flack's—*sweetly* over the compounds of her village; perhaps she wove the most stunning mats or told the most ingenious stories of all village story-tellers. Perhaps she was herself a poet—though only her daughter's name is signed to the poems that we know.

Perhaps Phillis Wheatley's mother was also an artist.

52   Perhaps in more than Phillis Wheatley's biological life is her mother's signature made clear.

Topics for Discussion and Writing

1. Can you justify the great shift in tone between "their gaze was as mute as a great stone" and "loony" (second and third paragraphs)? If so, how?
2. Explain Walker's assertion (paragraph 10) that "these grandmothers and mothers of ours were not 'Saints,' but Artists." In this view, what are the qualities of an artist?
3. Pick out two or three sentences that strike you as especially interesting, either because of what they say or because of the way they say it (or both), and try to account for their appeal.
4. Explain the last sentence of the essay.
5. Outline the organization of this essay; that is, list in order the main topics and then explain the relationships between these parts. Then, in one or two sentences, summarize Walker's thesis or argument.

Virginia Woolf

Virginia Woolf (1882–1941) was born in London into an upper-middle class literary family. In 1912 she married a writer, and with him she founded The Hogarth Press, whose important publications included not only books by T.S. Eliot but her own novels.

Professions for Women*

When your secretary invited me to come here, she told me that your Society is concerned with the employment of women and she suggested that I might tell you something about my own professional experiences. It is true I am a woman; it is true I am employed; but what professional experiences have I had? It is difficult to say. My profession is literature; and in that profession there are fewer experiences for women than in any other, with the exception of the stage— fewer, I mean, that are peculiar to women. For the road was cut many years ago—by Fanny Burney, by Aphra Behn, by Harriet Martineau, by Jane Austen, by George Eliot—many famous women, and many more unknown and

* This essay was originally a talk delivered in 1931 to the Women's Service League [Editors' note]

forgotten, have been before me, making the path smooth, and regulating my steps. Thus, when I came to write, there were very few material obstacles in my way. Writing was a reputable and harmless occupation. The family peace was not broken by the scratching of a pen. No demand was made upon the family purse. For ten and sixpence one can buy paper enough to write all the plays of Shakespeare—if one has a mind that way. Pianos and models, Paris, Vienna and Berlin, masters and mistresses, are not needed by a writer. The cheapness of writing paper is, of course, the reason why women have succeeded as writers before they have succeeded in the other professions.

But to tell you my story—it is a simple one. You have only got to figure to yourselves a girl in a bedroom with a pen in her hand. She had only to move that pen from left to right—from ten o'clock to one. Then it occurred to her to do what is simple and cheap enough after all—to slip a few of those pages into an envelope, fix a penny stamp in the corner, and drop the envelope into the red box at the corner. It was thus that I became a journalist; and my effort was rewarded on the first day of the following month—a very glorious day it was for me—by a letter from an editor containing a check for one pound ten shillings and sixpence. But to show you how little I deserve to be called a professional woman, how little I know of the struggles and difficulties of such lives, I have to admit that instead of spending that sum upon bread and butter, rent, shoes and stockings, or butcher's bills, I went out and bought a cat—a beautiful cat, a Persian cat, which very soon involved me in bitter disputes with my neighbors.

What could be easier than to write articles and to buy Persian cats with the profits? But wait a moment. Articles have to be about something. Mine, I seem to remember, was about a novel by a famous man. And while I was writing this review, I discovered that if I were going to review books I should need to do battle with a certain phantom. And the phantom was a woman, and when I came to know her better I called her after the heroine of a famous poem, The Angel in the House. It was she who used to come between me and my paper when I was writing reviews. It was she who bothered me and wasted my time and so tormented me that at last I killed her. You who come of a younger and happier generation may not have heard of her—you may not know what I mean by the Angel in the House. I will describe her as shortly as I can. She was intensely sympathetic. She was immensely charming. She was utterly unselfish. She excelled in the difficult arts of family life. She sacrificed herself daily. If there was chicken, she took the leg; if there was a draught she sat in it—in short she was so constituted that she never had a mind or a wish of her own, but preferred to sympathize always with the minds and wishes of others. Above all—I need not say it—she was pure. Her purity was supposed to be her chief beauty—her blushes, her great grace. In those days—the last of Queen Victoria—every house had its Angel. And when I came to write I encountered her with the very first words. The shadow of her wings fell on my page; I heard the rustling of her skirts in the room. Directly, that is to say, I took my pen in hand to review that novel by a famous man, she slipped behind me and whispered: "My dear, you are a young woman. You are writing about a book that has been written by a man. Be sympathetic; be tender; flatter; deceive; use all the arts and wiles of our sex. Never let anybody guess that you have a mind of your own. Above all, be pure." And she made as if to guide my pen. I now record the one act for which I take some credit to myself, though the credit rightly belongs to some excellent ancestors of mine who left me a certain sum of money—shall we say five hundred pounds a year?—so that it was not necessary for me to depend solely on charm for my living. I turned upon her and caught her by the throat. I did my best to kill her. My excuse, if I were to be had up in a court of law, would be that I acted in self-defense. Had I not killed her she would have killed me. She would have plucked the heart out of my writing. For, as I found, directly I put pen to paper, you cannot review even a novel without having a mind of your own, without expressing what you think to be the truth about human relations, morality, sex. And all these questions, according to the Angel in the House, cannot be dealt with freely and openly by women; they must charm, they must conciliate, they must—to put it bluntly—tell lies if they are to succeed. Thus, whenever I felt the shadow of her wing or the radiance of her halo upon my page, I took up the inkpot and flung it at her. She died hard. Her fictitious nature was of great assistance to her. It is far harder to kill a phantom than a reality. She was always creeping back when I thought I had despatched her. Though I flatter myself that I killed her in the end, the struggle was severe; it took much time that had better have been spent upon learning Greek grammar; or in roaming the world in search of adventures. But it was a real experience; it was an experience that was bound to befall all women writers at the time. Killing the Angel in the House was part of the occupation of a woman writer.

4   But to continue my story. The Angel was dead; what then remained? You may say that what remained was a simple and common object—a young woman in a bedroom with an inkpot. In other words, now that she had rid herself of falsehood, that young woman had only to be herself. Ah, but what is "herself"? I mean, what is a woman? I assure you, I do not know. I do not believe that you know. I do not believe that anybody can know until she has expressed herself in all the arts and professions open to human skill. That indeed is one of the reasons why I have come here—out of respect for you, who are in process of showing us by your experiments what a woman is, who are in process of providing us, by your failures and successes, with that extremely important piece of information.

But to continue the story of my professional experiences. I made one pound ten and six by my first review; and I bought a Persian cat with the proceeds. Then I grew ambitious. A Persian cat is all very well, I said; but a Persian cat is not enough. I must have a motor car. And it was thus that I became a novelist—for it is a very strange thing that people will give you a motor car if you will tell them a story. It is a still stranger thing that there is nothing so delightful in the world as telling stories. It is far pleasanter than writing reviews of famous novels. And yet, if I am to obey your secretary and tell you my professional experiences as a novelist, I must tell you about a very strange experience that befell me as a novelist. And to understand it you must try first to imagine a novelist's state of mind. I hope I am not giving away professional secrets if I say that a novelist's chief desire is to be as unconscious as possible. He has to induce in himself a state of perpetual lethargy. He wants life to proceed with the utmost quiet and regularity. He wants to see the same faces, to read the same books, to do the same things day after day, month after month, while he is writing, so that nothing may break the illusion in which he is living—so that nothing may disturb or disquiet the mysterious nosings about, feelings round, darts, dashes and sudden discoveries of that very shy and illusive spirit, the imagination. I suspect that this state is the same both for men and women. Be that as it may, I want you to imagine me writing a novel in a state of trance. I want you to figure to yourselves a girl sitting with a pen in her hand, which for minutes, and indeed for hours, she never dips into the inkpot. The image that comes to my mind when I think of this girl is the image of a fisherman lying sunk in dreams on the verge of a deep lake with a rod held out over the water. She was letting her imagination sweep unchecked round every rock and cranny of the world that lies submerged in the depths of our unconscious being. Now came the experience, the experience that I believe to be far commoner with women writers than with men. The line raced through the girl's fingers. Her imagination had rushed away. It had sought the pools, the depths, the dark places where the largest fish slumber. And then there was a smash. There was an explosion. There was foam and confusion. The imagination had dashed itself against something hard. The girl was roused from her dream. She was indeed in a state of the most acute and difficult distress. To speak without figure she had thought of something, something about the body, about the passions which it was unfitting for her as a woman to say. Men, her reason told her, would be shocked. The consciousness of what men will say of a woman who speaks the truth about her passions had roused her from her artist's state of unconsciousness. She could write no more. This I believe to be a very common experience with women writers—they are impeded by the extreme conventionality of the other sex. For though men sensibly allow themselves great freedom in these respects. I doubt that they realize or can control the extreme severity with which they condemn such freedom in women.

These then were two very genuine experiences of my own. These were two of the adventures of my professional life. The first—killing the Angel in the House—I think I solved. She died. But the second, telling the truth about my own experiences as a body, I do not think I solved. I doubt that any woman has solved it yet. The obstacles against her are still immensely powerful—and yet they are very difficult to define. Outwardly, what is simpler than to write books? Outwardly, what obstacles are there for a woman rather than for a man?

Inwardly, I think, the case is very different; she has still many ghosts to fight, many prejudices to overcome. Indeed it will be a long time still, I think, before a woman can sit down to write a book without finding a phantom to be slain, a rock to be dashed against. And if this is so in literature, the freest of all professions for women, how is it in the new professions which you are now for the first time entering?

Those are the questions that I should like, had I time, to ask you. And indeed, if I have laid stress upon these professional experiences of mine, it is because I believe that they are, though in different forms, yours also. Even when the path is nominally open—when there is nothing to prevent a woman from being a doctor, a lawyer, a civil servant—there are many phantoms and obstacles, as I believe, looming in her way. To discuss and define them is I think of great value and importance; for thus only can the labor be shared, the difficulties be solved. But besides this, it is necessary also to discuss the ends and the aims for which we are fighting, for which we are doing battle with these formidable obstacles. Those aims cannot be taken for granted; they must be perpetually questioned and examined. The whole position, as I see it—here in this hall surrounded by women practising for the first time in history I know not how many different professions—is one of extraordinary interest and importance. You have won rooms of your own in the house hitherto exclusively owned by men. You are able, though not without great labor and effort, to pay the rent. You are earning your five hundred pounds a year. But this freedom is only a beginning; the room is your own, but it is still bare. It has to be furnished; it has to be decorated; it has to be shared. How are you going to furnish it, how are you going to decorate it? With whom are you going to share it, and upon what terms? These, I think, are questions of the utmost importance and interest. For the first time in history you are able to ask them; for the first time you are able to decide for yourselves what the answers should be. Willingly would I stay and discuss those questions and answers—but not tonight. My time is up; and I must cease.

Topics for Discussion and Writing

1. The first two paragraphs seem to describe the ease with which women enter writing as a profession. What difficulties or obstacles for women do these paragraphs imply?
2. Try to characterize Woolf's tone, especially her attitude toward her subject and herself, in the first paragraph.
3. What do you think Woolf means when she says, near the end of paragraph 3, "It is far harder to kill a phantom than a reality"?

4. Woolf conjectures (paragraph 6) that she has not solved the problem of "telling the truth about my own experiences as a body." Is there any reason to believe that today a woman has more difficulty than a man in telling the truth about the experiences of the body?

5. In her final paragraph, Woolf suggests that phantoms as well as obstacles impede women from becoming doctors and lawyers. What might some of these phantoms be?

6. This essay is highly metaphoric. Speaking roughly (or, rather, as precisely as possible), what is the meaning of the metaphor of "rooms" in the final paragraph? What does Woolf mean when she says, "The room is your own, but it is still bare. . . . With whom are you going to share it, and upon what terms?"

7. Explain, to a reader who doesn't understand it, the analogy making use of fishing in paragraph 5.

8. Evaluate the last two sentences. Are they too abrupt and mechanical? Or do they provide a fitting conclusion to the speech?

Last Words

A rich patron once gave money to the painter Chu Ta, asking him to paint a picture of a fish. Three years later, when he still had not received the painting, the patron went to Chu Ta's house to ask why the picture was not done. Chu Ta did not answer, but dipped a brush in ink and with a few strokes drew a splendid fish. "If it is so easy," asked the patron, "why didn't you give me the picture three years ago?" Again Chu Ta did not answer. Instead, he opened the door of a large cabinet. Thousands of pictures of fish tumbled out.

Text Credits

Photo Credits

Index

To the Student

Please help us make *Barnet & Stubbs's Practical Guide to Writing, With Readings,* an even better book. To improve our textbooks, we revise them every few years, taking into account the experiences of both instructors and students with the previous editions. At some time, your instructor will most likely be asked to comment extensively on *Barnet & Stubbs's Practical Guide to Writing, With Readings.* Now we would like to hear from you.

Complete this questionnaire and return it to:
Literature Editor
HarperCollins College Publisher
10 East 53rd St.
New York, NY 10022

School _____

City, State, Zip Code _____

Course title _____

Instructor's full name _____

Other books required _____

_____

1. Did you like the book?
Yes ___ No ___

2. Was it too easy? ___ Too difficult? ___

Did you read it all?
Yes ___ No ___

Which chapters were most useful? Why?

_____

_____

_____

_____

Which chapters were least useful? Why?

_____

_____

_____

_____

3. Were the exercises useful?
Yes ___ No ___

4. Did you like the examples?
Yes ___ No ___

5. Please give us your reactions to the following readings:

	Keep	Drop	Didn't Read
Mary Field Belenky, Blythe McVicker Clinchy, Nancy Rule Goldberger, and Jill Mattuck Tarule, "Toward an Education for Women"	___	___	___
Martin Luther King, Jr., "Nonviolent Resistance"	___	___	___
Paul Goldberger, "The Statue of Liberty: Transcending the Trivial"	___	___	___
Peter H. Lewis, "But can you say it in I's and O's?"	___	___	___
Woody Allen, "The Colorization of Films Insults Artists and Society"	___	___	___

6. Please give us your reactions to the additional readings in Part Four:

	Keep	Drop	Didn't Read
Russell Baker, "The Flag"	___	___	___
Robert Benchley, "How to Get Things Done"	___	___	___
Barbara R. Bergmann, "Pay Equity—How to Argue Back"	___	___	___
Sissela Bok, "To Lie or Not to Lie?—The Doctor's Dilemma"	___	___	___
Jorge Luis Borges, "The Gaucho and the City: Stories of Horsemen"	___	___	___
Laura Cunningham, "The Girl's Room"	___	___	___
Joan Didion, "On Keeping a Notebook"	___	___	___
Nora Ephron, "A Few Words About Breasts: Shaping Up Absurd"	___	___	___
Paul Goodman, "A Proposal to Abolish Grades"	___	___	___
Stephen Jay Gould, "Women's Brains"	___	___	___
Elbert Hubbard, "A Message to Garcia"	___	___	___
Elizabeth Janeway, "Soaps, Cynicism, and Mind Control: Randomness in Everyday Life"	___	___	___
C. S. Lewis, "Vivisection"	___	___	___

Flannery O'Connor, "Total Effect and the Eighth
   Grade"   ___   ___   ___

George Orwell, "Politics and the English Language"   ___   ___   ___

Patricia Meyer Spacks, "What Have 60 Million
   Readers Found in Nancy Drew?"   ___   ___   ___

John Steinbeck, "Mobile Homes"   ___   ___   ___

Studs Terkel, "Fathers and Sons"   ___   ___   ___

Lewis Thomas, "On Natural Death"   ___   ___   ___

Lester C. Thurow, "Why Women are Paid Less Than
   Men"   ___   ___   ___

7. Do you think the professor should continue to assign this book next year?
Yes ___   No ___

Did you tell her or him?
Yes ___   No ___

8. What would you have us change next time?

_____

_____

_____

_____

_____

_____

_____

9. May we quote you in our promotion efforts for this book?
Yes ___   No ___

Date _____   Signature _____

Mailing address

_____

_____

_____

_____

Literature Editor
HarperCollins College Publisher
10 East 53rd St.
New York, NY 10022